# Praise for
# *Confessions of a Jewish Wagnerite*

The author is a major figure in gay history, especially for New York. In various chapters on different topics, we learn his autobiography, and the great struggles he endured with his self-realization of being gay, as well as dealing with some discrimination also for being Jewish. Top it all off with the fact that he was a self-described "opera queen" and had been somewhat of a Wagner specialist until analysis and counseling led him to conclude how this love of Wagner was related to self-loathing for being Jewish and gay. I was surprised at this at first, but gradually became convinced that this occurred with him, and it provided me with some insights which I find interesting. He is an accomplished physician who was the first to publish in mainstream press warnings about the apparently then-new illness later called AIDS. He became the first medical director of the main AIDS organization serving New York. His lover and eventual life partner is Arnie Kantrowitz (*Under the Rainbow*), himself a writer. They indulged in a kinky side of the New York scene in the 1970's and 1980's that I had heard of, but previously not in such interesting narrative. The brutal honesty of Mass's self-disclosure is praise-worthy and certainly makes for interesting reading.

**~ Amazon Reviewer**

# On the Future of Wagnerism

## Art, Intoxication, Addiction, Codependence and Recovery

by

Lawrence D. Mass

Introduction by Adam J. Sacks

Published By
Sentinel Voices

On the Future of Wagnerism: Art, Intoxication, Addiction, Codependence and Recovery

Published by Sentinel Voices



ISBN 978-1629672212 (Paperback)
Library of Congress Control Number: 2021919090



Produced by Brian Schwartz for Wise Media Group
Cover Design by Tatiana Vila

Rev 11.10

# Table of Contents

Figure 1 - *Lisztomania* (1975), Warner Bros, Photo Gallery IMDb

*From Ken Russell's scathingly satirical film, *Lisztomania*, in which Wagner is depicted as a blood-sucking vampire who inspires Hitler and Nazism. "Lisztomania" was a term used by Heinrich Heine in 1844 to describe the hysteria of fandom that attended Hungarian composer Franz Liszt, mentor and future father-in-law of Richard Wagner. Such was the frenzy of Lisztomania that it was sometimes described as a contagious medical condition from which the public needed to be immunized.

For Gottfried Wagner

For Jewish Wagnerites—Past, Present, Future, and "Honorary"

***All truth passes through three stages. First, it is ridiculed. Second, it is violently opposed. Third, it is accepted as being self-evident.***

***–Arthur Schopenhauer.***

# Prologue

In 1997 I traveled to central Europe, visiting Geneva, Prague and Budapest. In the main square in Budapest I chanced upon what turned out to be Hungary's first Gay Pride demonstration. A handful of rainbow-festooned kids, most of them teenagers, held up a Gay Pride banner. I was witness to something historic, personal for me as a gay man who had struggled to come out himself, and very moving.

Then, right before my eyes, these kids were beset upon and beaten bloody by goons. Though Gay Pride gatherings and the Gay Rights movement have advanced in Hungary over the ensuing years, the goons keep returning. Today, gay life is increasingly menaced by populist uprisings, more in reaction to immigrants, especially Muslims, than the more traditionally scapegoated minorities —Jews, gays, gypsies, women, Latinos—but against them as well. Under Hungary's authoritarian leader Viktor Orban, anti-gay initiatives like those in Putin's Russia are increasingly imposed on a people long inured to state-sponsored exploitation and oppression. A run of the musical Billy Elliott in Budapest was cancelled for being "gay propaganda."

Little did I know that Hungary would remain thematic in my life, not only around the edges of my writing on Wagner but as well at a more personal level. In early 2017, I married an undocumented Hungarian immigrant who joined Arnie and me to become family. Attila (whose brother resembles Cosima Wagner) is an itinerant laborer and contractor from Hungary who has struggled long and courageously to achieve his life's greatest dream—to become an American citizen. Hence his favorite symbol—a Native American "dream catcher." On our kitchen wall, he posted a photo of 911 firefighters.

We met on Haulover Beach, in the heart of "Little Moscow," as it's called because of the Hollywood-North Miami Beach area's dense concentration of Russian emigres, coincidentally in the heart of the greatest concentration of Trump properties anywhere. Isolated, afraid and overwhelmed in his efforts to navigate full time work in construction with the hurdles of pursuing immigration status, he seemed like a puppy in the middle of a swamp surrounded by alligators, pythons and bobcats.

Undaunted by the ambient anti-immigrant bigotry and like others who still look to America with hope and faith in its principles and systems, Attila held fast to his love of America. It remained his inspiration, despite years of dispiriting encounters with unscrupulous profiteers promising easy citizenship for up-front cash. The latest of these turned out to be one of Florida's biggest fraudulent immigration schemes, run by self-described Christian ministries. The good news is that the ringleaders are serving time in prison. The bad news for Attila was that they took all his savings and left him listed with an order for deportation. The order was based on his not showing up for a court hearing he was never informed about because of the abrupt shutting down of the scam operation, which in any case never sent notifications, carefully ensuring not to leave any paper trail.

Despite these and other obstacles and the atmosphere of terrorism against immigrants stoked by the Trump administration and copycat autocratic goons worldwide, and with the support and efforts of many good people, we moved forward with the painstaking, often intimidating process of seeking immigration status. After nearly three years Attila's application for immigration was finally approved and he is now on track to become an American citizen.

Attila's experience lingers for another reason. He was duped by unscrupulous manipulators cloaked in religion into believing they could help him in his quest, even though much of what they were saying and doing wasn't making sense and wasn't consistent, and even though the personal costs of proceeding seemed evermore exorbitant, perilous and demeaning.

All of which raises a question for me. In being so taken in and exploited, was Attila's experience with these fraudsters really any different from my own with regard to Wagner and Wagnerism? Had I been comparably deceived by the intoxication of Wagnerism into compromising my own soul?

# Introduction by Adam J. Sacks

## Art, Medical Humanism and Civil Society

The voice of Dr. Lawrence Mass unites the worlds of music, gay history and activism with addiction medicine. He has found a novel and effective means to communicate his expertise and concerns in these areas via the figure of Richard Wagner. The current volume is a successor text to his acclaimed memoir, *Confessions of a Jewish Wagnerite: Being Gay and Jewish in America* (currently available on Amazon Kindle).

A sequel to Confessions, *On the Future of Wagnerism* is a wide-ranging anthology of memoir, personal journalism and essays that elucidate common denominators of recurrent maladies of our world: antisemitism and homophobia, addiction and codependence, health care inadequacy and malfeasance. Mass accomplishes this while maintaining an accessible style filled with valuable accounts of the culture and politics of late 20th Century Europe and America. His role as a co-founder of Gay Men's Health Crisis and gay rights activist who wrote the first press reports on AIDS render him a figure of historical significance.

His engagement with Wagner, however, brings his reflections to a mode of thought and criticism rarely seen in any widely available fashion since the Weimar Republic: that of the doctor of medicine who diagnoses and engages with cultural life. From Albert Schweitzer to Max Nordau, the medical humanist once carried authority throughout civic life. Mass renders this seemingly esoteric objective with clarity and friendliness.

But why the German composer Richard Wagner as a central focus? Richard Wagner and the cult following that emerged in his wake—"Wagnerism"— is unique in the annals of modern culture. Wagner was an artistic and technical genius who used his formidable talents in support of a deeply antimodern, antagonistic and exclusionary worldview. Wagner, who still stands astride concert and opera houses all over the world, challenges the presumptions of any link between genius and goodness, as well as the role of representative arts in a healthy democratic civic sphere.

As Mass attests via his own experience of being acculturated to Wagnerism, the cult of Wagner not only lives on, it provides a lens through which to reconsider many of the greatest challenges of Mass's own life experience, and of the various minorities and subcultures—gay, Jewish, recovery—that experience reflects.

Written against the backdrop of our Post-9/11 era of backlash against globalization and the international turn to authoritarianism, Mass offers an arsenal of cultural perspectives and psychological tools to understand how individuals become seduced by malevolent magicians of politics and art. For it is too often images—whether visual, literary or musical signatures—that at first fascinate, then intoxicate and play their key roles in the indoctrination of paranoia and intolerance. It is sensitive outsiders like Mass who have attennae keenly attuned to these workings, who best shed light on their mechanisms and fallout.

The interrelationships Mass charts of Wagner with antisemtism and homophobia reveal the basic but startling ways in which art, music and visual culture can turn toxic. As Wagner ultimately emerged as a prime incubator of the National Socialist ethos, any effort to stem the tide of the rehabilitation of Nazism must turn back to him. Thus the project of working through the troubled past of Wagner is part of a larger effort of establishing and securing Enlightenment values of human rights and inclusivity.

Notwithstanding considerations of aesthetic and musical greatness, Wagner may always stand for narratives of racial purity and reactionary retrenchment, for a bygone era that existed only in myth, an outbreak of romantic, antimodern idealization which brought great suffering and death to countless millions. Such populist myth-making is nothing less than fake news on a global scale. Mass's effort in bringing the light of humanist reason, by virtue of his own personal struggles and activism, to this iconic historical lesson suggests that there is a path forward to the future of contemporary cultural maladies and conflict.

Above all, the power of this volume lies in the personal intimacy of its narrative. Mass does not illustrate through abstraction but rather through storytelling of his own lived experience. His contact and friendship with many notable figures in recent American cultural life, including leading gay and AIDS activist and writer Larry Kramer, and his relationship with his brother Steve Mass, impresario of the famed

Mudd Club (at the heart of the downtown NYC underground art scene of the late 1970's), all receive fascinating biographical detail and critical scrutiny. Through it all Mass never shies away from the disturbing and often unacknowledged reality that those most engaged with unconvention and creativity, so often heroicized, are often driven by phenomena of narcissism and addiction at the expense of maturity, responsibility and ethics. Underlying his effort throughout is a commitment shared with colleagues such as Dr. Gottfried Wagner, great grandson of the composer, who have long endorsed Mass's work: that art can and must be united with humanism and inclusion, as it directly impacts upon matters of civil society.

It is the interweaving of minority experience, the political impact of music, and perspectives of addiction that distinguishes this book and renders it a unique document of our time. Mass's examination of the wellsprings and mechanisms of scapegoating and paranoia, while delineating processes of recovery, could not be more pertinent for a world suffering deeply from the ills of addiction—to drugs, to escapism and self-indulgence, to arrogance and bigotry, to power. An important contribution to literature on the legacy of Nazism and the Holocaust, *On The Future of Wagnerism* provides a visceral but subtle *cri de coeur*, a call to us to come out of our complacency, to reposition our assumptions, and reckon anew with false idols that retain their ability to intoxicate.

Without pat answers or didacticism, Mass brings hope for a future concerned not merely with uncovering hidden history or finding new ways to reinterpret fallen idols, but which looks beyond, via self-affirmation and personal recovery, to new narratives for an art of the future not held captive by past demons.

Adam J. Sacks*

*Editor and Creative Consultant for *On The Future of Wagnerism*, Adam J Sacks is a PhD in History from Brown University. He is now serving as Lecturer in the Faculty of the Arts at the University of Hong Kong and publishes regularly in specialist and non-specialist venues.

# Introduction by Lawrence D. Mass

Figure 2 - Drawing of Richard Wagner by Lawrence D. Mass, Boston, 1975

In 1994, I published my memoir, *Confessions of a Jewish Wagnerite: Being Gay and Jewish in America*. Here, from that book's dust-jacket, is its description:

> In 1981, Lawrence Mass was a 35-year-old physician, writer and gay activist living in New York City. On his living-room wall, among other opera memorabilia, there were five pictures of Richard Wagner, one of them a drawing by Mass himself. While researching what would become the first feature article on the epidemic that later became known as AIDS, the author had the first confrontation of his adult life with overt anti-Semitism, an incident he was completely unprepared to deal with psychologically. As AIDS spread, and every sexually active gay man was forced to confront his own mortality, the need to understand the even greater depths of fear touched by

> the incident became urgent, and Mass began to face the reality that his life had been dominated by internalized anti-Semitism, even as he came to grips with his gay identity.
>
> A series of self-contained autobiographical essays, *Confessions* examines a vast panorama of events, issues and personalities in the worlds of identity politics, AIDS and the arts. As it probes the interconnectedness of gay, Jewish and musical cultures in post-World War II America against a backdrop of resurgent anti-Semitism, it reveals one human being's quest for personal and spiritual identity. From his adolescent infatuation with Wagner to his friendship with Gottfried Wagner, great-grandson of the composer, and his life-partnership with a fellow gay activist and Jewish-American writer, *Confessions of a Jewish Wagnerite* is the story of that voyage of discovery.

Little did I know that beyond this ten-year odyssey there would be a lot more to recall, observe and ponder. In 2012 I found myself inspired to write again about Wagner, about this most challenging of figures in the history of art and culture, and my own experiential window of Jewish Wagnerite codependence. In 2012, I attended a *New York Times* Festival talk called "The Wagner Vortex" by music writer Alex Ross. The event was in anticipation of Ross's book, *Wagnerism*, portions of which have appeared in his column in the *New Yorker*. That same week coincidentally, there was a news feature on Hitler's private art collection, much of which was previously unknown to the public. The piece I became inspired to write was called "On The Future of Wagnerism: Do The New Revelations about Hitler's Taste in Art Cast New Light on Wagner Appreciation?."

There began an unintended second odyssey of discovery with a series of essays under the heading "On The Future of Wagnerism." There are pieces on Jewish Wagnerites, the Wagner Family, Questions of Forgiveness, Wagner and the *Klinghoffer* Controversies, German Cinema and an autobiographical subseries on how my relationships with my siblings intersected with and cast light on my

Wagnerism around phenomena of addiction, codependence and recovery.

Without my realizing it, this writing had been gestating. It was happening, much like my *Confessions of a Jewish Wagnerite*, as an unplanned pregnancy. Likewise unplanned as such, *On The Future of Wagnerism* was emerging as the sequel to my *Confessions.*

For all of the many Jews who have written eloquently and in depth about Wagner's role in the history of antisemitism and Nazism and about antisemitism in Wagner's life, times and work, I'm not aware of any other *Wagneriana* quite like my own work—a memoir of personal and cultural reflections on what it has meant and what it has felt like to be a Jewish Wagnerite; a memoir of someone who became deeply involved in Wagner's music and milieus of Wagnerism but who, past the standard impersonal, obligatory and perfunctory acknowledgment of Wagner's antisemitism in his life, times and work, emerged from that altered state into the daylight of feeling the psychological and spiritual pain and conflict of being in such troubled thrall.

Most Jews find ways to compartmentalize Wagner's music and art as independent of the character of their creator. So far as I can glean, for a Jewish Wagnerite to admit such great ambivalence and discomfort on this issue is still rare. In fact, I know of no other such testimony. In any case, whatever its assets and deficits, I don't think it's too self-aggrandizing to suggest that *On The Future of Wagnerism*, together with *Confessions of a Jewish Wagnerite*, can make a distinctive contribution to Wagner, Jewish, LGBTQ and musical-cultural literatures.

One friend, a non-Jewish college professor of English who shared my Wagnerism in the late 1960s when I was an undergraduate at the University of California at Berkeley, upon seeing some of my current writing on Wagner, couldn't resist asking, "Will you ever be done?" My answer was right there, from the heart and gut: "Not so long as the writing keeps happening and the future keeps unfolding. In this sense, Wagner has been a gift that keeps on giving."

As for the greater potential of this work, let me conclude this brief introduction with a comparison. *Hitler's Hollywood: From Caligari to Hitler* is a 2017 documentary from Germany, written and directed by Rutiger Suchsland and narrated by Udo Kier. The film is an impressive inventory of filmmaking in the Third Reich. Categories of films, chronologies, actors and directors, and the shaping of them all into the most powerful engine of propaganda in history are all discussed. It's a great overview and resource. Because of work like this, it's now easier to look back and have broader perspective of how the masses were intoxicated and duped by Hitler and Nazism.

It's my hope and purpose that my *Confessions of a Jewish Wagnerite* and *On the Future of Wagnerism* will coalesce with other of this generation's critical reevaluations of Wagner and Wagnerism to result in something comparable to the Kier documentary. That is, as this challenging work of reassessing Wagner and Wagnerism gains momentum, credibility and standing, we'll be able to look back with greater clarity and confidence at a comparably bigger picture of how the worlds of music, art and culture were intoxicated and duped by one of history's most influential and celebrated figures—the only artist acknowledged by Hitler to have been his spiritual godfather: Richard Wagner.

– Lawrence D. Mass, New York City, 2020

# Context, Terminologies and Paradigms

## Context

***On the Future of Wagnerism*** (OTFOW) has two greater parts. The first is the body of OTFOW. The second, **Context**, consists of my other writings from the same time period of 2013-2021. There are pieces on identity politics, culture and health care as well on AIDS, activism and Larry Kramer, most of them subjects that are contemporaneous and contextual to those of OTFOW.

Larry Kramer, the great gay and AIDS activist and writer who co-founded the organizations Gay Men's Health Crisis (GMHC) and ACT UP, is the embodiment of the ACT UP logo SILENCE = DEATH. What this means is exactly what it might seem in the most literal sense. The most salient feature and accomplishment of ACT UP was its ability to make enough noise, clamor and disruption that the grinding business of death, of genocide—of what might be called passive genocide or "genocide by sloth," as I've called it— was not able to proceed apace. In the case of gay people and persons with AIDS, unlike the death trains of Nazism, the overt and covert business of genocide was stopped in its tracks.

One of political philosopher Hannah Arendt's most controversial conclusions about the Holocaust is that, although there were heroic Jewish freedom fighters and protests, and opposition was far more likely to be brutally and totally crushed, Jewish resistance efforts were notably uncommon as Hitler and Nazism swept Germany and Europe. It's no coincidence that Kramer greatly admired Arendt. Though her major writings preceded Kramer's, he is just the kind of activist, apparently, that she gleaned to have been missing from Jewish opposition to Hitler and Nazism. In fact, the logo of ACT UP, "Silence=Death," was inspired by Larry Kramer's deepest conviction that gay silence during the holocaust of AIDS was reflective of Jewish silence during the sweep of Nazism and the Holocaust.

Most of the pieces in this collection were published on *Huffington Post* (Huffpost) and Medium.com. The dates of the original publications are indicated. In some cases there has been minor editing, updating and annotation.

Because these pieces were written and published independent of their being collected for this anthology, there is some repetition of narrative contexting, inspired in part by that which Wagner uses to revisit and summarize developments in the *Ring* cycle.

## Terminologies and Paradigms

### *Wagnerism*

Like "gay sensibility" and "homosexuality," "Wagnerism" is a term in wide and common usage that can't be defined precisely. Even Alex Ross, in his new compendium, *Wagnerism*, makes little effort to do so.

Gay drag humor would seem a good example of gay sensibility. But what about the variations of gender and sexual orientation and behavior that can color, shape and also lay claim to it? Is it more "gay" or more a phenomenon of transvestism, whose practitioners are often heterosexual, and whose traditions date back centuries (e.g., Shakespeare)?

My brother Steve Mass, impresario of the legendary Mudd Club, was a pioneering practitioner of what we call "camp," but he wasn't gay. Nor, at least not officially, was closeted, bisexual Susan Sontag, whose essay, "Notes on Camp," is most famously associated with this term for the special blend of humor and sensibility that upends standard notions of sex and gender. As a former *Village Voice* writer, Jeff Weinstein, famously observed, "No, there's no such thing as a gay sensibility and, yes, it has an enormous impact on our culture."

"Homosexuality" is another category that eludes circumscription, and evermore so as we move into the age of the internet and greater openness about sexuality and sexual variance. On closer scrutiny, how diluted is "homosexuality" by various permutations of bisexuality? As with gay sensibility, efforts at precise definition will inevitably fall short. The only way the subject can be talked about credibly is by pluralizing it, the way Bell and Weinberg did in their second Kinsey Institute study, *Homosexualities: A Study of Diversity Among Men and Women.* Meanwhile, so long as there is oppression of homosexuality by law, the term "homosexuality" will remain political and pertinent, however nonspecific.

Like "gay sensibility" and "homosexuality," "Wagnerism" is used to describe many different things. To such an extent that perhaps the "Wagnerism" of my title should be changed to Wagnerisms. Alex Ross uses the singular of Wagnerism as the title of his impressive study but seems disinclined towards further explanation or circumscription of the term. Meanwhile, with no counterpart in all of musical culture—there is no Mozartism, Bachism, Stravinskyism, Beethovenism or Verdiism—"Wagnerism"suggests a school, belief system, movement or sensibility such as humanism, mannerism, realism, romanticism, modernism, post-modernism, Nazism, Bolshevism, Zionism or anti-Semitism. And indeed there have been impressive movements of followers and admirers of Wagner from varying and sometimes oppositional vantage points—especially around his concepts of opera as drama, but as Ross so exhaustively demonstrates, as well around countless other cultural and sectarian phenomena.

For many, "Wagnerism" presumes the composer's concept of the "*Gesamtkunstwerk*"—the total work of art wherein no element is treated as secondary. Every aspect—whether it be the ballet, libretto, chorus, *mis-en-scene*, or "lesser" roles—is given studied placement and seems critical to the fabric and impact of the greater work. One need only think of the importance and power of Donner's Call in *Das Rheingold*, of the summons of the Herald in *Lohengrin*, of the sailors' laments in *The Flying Dutchman* and *Tristan*, of the Forest Bird in *Siegfried*, of the Landgraf and Shepard boy in *Tannhäuser,* to have an immediate and clear sense of the veracity of this concept for us as well as for Wagner. However small these parts, they are crucial to the greater experience of Wagner's music dramas, even if one can point to some exceptions to this rule with roles that have contrastingly little impact such as Mary in *Dutchman*, Magdalena in *Meistersinger,* Gunther and Gutrune in *Götterdämmerung.* As theater director Peter Sellars observed of his experience mounting a puppet version of the *Ring* cycle, there's very little "fat" in Wagner. For all the great length, sprawl and repetition in Wagner, one is hard pressed to find what could be eliminated without damage to the greater work's integrity. Such has been our reverence for Wagner's commitment and achievement in this regard that, beyond adaptations at Bayreuth geared to children, virtually no musician or director of renown has succeeded in promoting a version of any of Wagner's main works that has been substantially edited down to what might seem more manageable and digestible portions.

Such were the depth and consistency of Wagner's feelings about dramatic integrity that he struggled for most of his career with his early opera *Tannhäuser*, which had its world premiere in Dresden in 1845. In what became known as the Paris version of the opera 16 years later, Wagner acceded to the tradition of providing a ballet, which Wagner initially regarded as a superficial imposition that would demean the artwork as such, and which some critics have felt is notably more advanced musically than the rest of the earlier-composed opera. But Wagner did break tradition by putting the ballet in the first act, as opposed to the second or third; and while the Dresden and Paris versions have both been performed continuously, no one could argue that the ballet is not deeply engaged with the soul, momentum and impact of the greater work in either case.

So Wagnerism is often used to characterize developments in art, musical culture, theater and opera, especially around Wagner's articulation of the importance of making vital and integrating, as opposed to merely ornamental, all elements of an artwork. Between 1849 and 1851 Wagner wrote several major essays spelling out his beliefs: *Art and Revolution* (1849), *The Artwork of the Future* (1849), *Jewishness in Music* (1850), and *Opera as Drama* (1851), the latter a book-length essay with attacks on Rossini and especially Meyerbeer for creating operas more notable for "effects without causes," which Wagner further deconstructs as exemplary of the greater panorama of "Jewishness in music."

Judaism and music is a subject that would malignantly obsess Wagner for the rest of his life, even though Mendelssohn converted to Christianity and Meyerbeer, though he never converted, tried graciously and generously to support Wagner. Whatever the subterranean appeal of Wagner's *Weltanschauung*—his "world view"—his concepts of "opera as drama" have had unparalleled influence on the musical culture and arts of his era and ever since.

Along with Wagnerism came the term Wagnerian. While any composer might lend his name (the paucity of women composers was and remains such that using "his" seems not to require even this qualification) to descriptions like Mozartean, Verdian or Brahmsian,

"Wagnerian" suggests Wagner's trademark "music drama" that continuously flows without the more formal structures and breaks that demarcated more traditional works. In common vernacular, however, "Wagnerian," together with "Mahlerian" and "Straussian," has mostly come to refer to the great scale of resources called for, especially innovations in stagecraft as well as in orchestral and choral forces.

Great scale is in many ways what was most notable about French grand opera, which had reached its apex in the milieu of Wagner—in the works of the world's most famous composer of grand opera and Wagner's most famous patron, Giacomo Meyerbeer. Instead of appreciating and crediting his mentor, however, Wagner appropriated these ideas as his own, antisemitically trashing his rival and benefactor to the extent that what used to be thought of as Meyerbeerian for the magnitude of resources employed henceforth came to be appreciated as Wagnerian. The inheritance of this mantle by Wagner, however, has been a mixed blessing, often implying excessive length, ponderousness, and bellicosity, much as the term "Meyerbeerian" implied, for Wagner, meaningless ornamentalism and "effects without causes."

Wagnerism also developed around cultural phenomena such as those documented by Joseph Horowitz in his book on Wagner in America at the turn of the century, *Wagner Nights*. Here Wagnerism was seen as a stimulant to American-style meliorism–the belief that the world can improve and people can help it do so—as well as the early women's movement.

It's the other use of "Wagnerism" that arouses the most controversy. Wagnerites like Joseph Horowitz and Alex Ross are at pains to promote the viewpoint of Wagner as a cultural titan who transformed all of music and culture to the inestimable benefit of humankind. Yes, there was Hitler and Nazism but that dark chapter of Wagnerism is seen to have been so aberrant, so unreflective of the greater and surpassing humanity and complexity in Wagner, and of his incomparably protean influence on art and Wagner appreciation, as to render suspect and unacceptable lingering discomfort.

While Horowitz does acknowledge Wagner's antisemitism to have been "egregious," and Ross can be unflinching in his acknowledgments of Wagner's antisemitism, their principal investment is in defending Wagner from critics like me who would despoil Wagner appreciation with an outsized preoccupation with Hitler and Nazism.

We've acknowledged Wagner's antisemitism and what happened with Hitler and Nazism, Wagnerites say. And acknowledgement, often qualified and perfunctory, is about all that seems warranted in analysis and discussion of these detours from the greater journey of Wagner appreciation. Time to move on from dwelling on what Ross has called "the Nazi rut." Those who choose to linger are those in whom universal demarcators of humanity like forgiveness can seem to be lacking.

"Wagnerism," then, is really Wagnerisms. Like gay sensibility, we recognize it, know it exists, know it's important and use it in discourse, beyond which we are at a loss to precisely define or otherwise circumscribe it, and thereby neither to countenance nor counteract it.

### *Nazi Art*

If you google "Nazi art," you come up with something like the opposite of what the Nazis termed "Degenerate Art." Many of those so stigmatized by the Nazis were expressionist and otherwise modernist, and though by no means were all of them Jewish, the Nazis saw the Jews as the infectious source of all degeneracy in art and culture.

At the other extreme, "Nazi art" would mostly conjure *kitsch*, the nostalgic, romantic, sentimental work of artists like Hitler, of Biedermeier, but also of Arno Breker, a leading artist of the Third Reich who sculpted busts of Hitler, Speer, Winifred Wagner, Wieland Wagner, Franz Liszt (who was not antisemitic) and, most famously, Wagner. While the Hitler statues are no longer public, the Wagner busts continue to set the tone at Bayreuth, Dusseldorf and elsewhere. Like Wagnerism and gay sensibility, "Nazi art" and "degenerate art" are more similar than different in their vagueness, openness to interpretation and facilitation of disparagement.

Understandably, calling something "Nazi art" will mostly be appreciated as derogatory. Not only does this designation taint the artist and artwork with Nazism, but it seems a denunciation of both as inferior—e.g., Breker. On those rare occasions when it is extended to include Wagner, it is especially controversial because it carries the suggestion that Wagner's art, widely considered supreme, widely regarded as among the greatest ever known, is on some level corrupt and thereby and ultimately, and perhaps to a degree irreparably, damaged.

Say what you like about Wagner the antisemite. Say what you like about Wagner being exploited by Hitler and the Nazis. But to suggest that the art itself is seriously corrupted—compromised by these associations or its own undercurrents —will be understood to be tantamount to saying that not only Wagner but much of the western culture he has so incomparably influenced is thereby tainted. All of this is apart from the fact that Wagner died 40 years before the rise of Nazism. For Wagnerites and arbiters of Western culture, to call Wagner's art "Nazi art," as I've selectively done, will be appreciated as incendiary, slanderous, wrong and unacceptable. Surely, there must be ways, in fact many ways, for Wagner's art to remain surpassingly great, to get out of "the Nazi rut." That is what the arbiters of art and culture are at this point demanding with evermore exasperation, impatience and desperation.

It bears repeating that what Wagnerites—those who love Wagner to the extent of being acolytes as for no other composer, and like most arbiters of Western culture and civilization—want is for us to get past this "Nazi rut," this moment in time; to reach that time when we can once again appreciate the supreme art of the supreme artist Wagner without guilt, remorse or the background noise of resentment of Wagner's acknowledged egomania and antisemitism. With the historical reality of art virtually always eventually triumphing over circumstantial or temporal politics or any characterological or biographical issues attending the artist, they feel confident about the future. In view of which the suggestion that Wagner might now be, like one of his own creations, eternally cursed for this legacy is not going to be accepted passively by Wagnerites, any more than the American South is ever going to accept the wholesale vitiation of its Civil War history and heroes, or Germany its military, cultural and ethnic history. These are the controversies of *On The Future of Wagnerism*.

## Antisemitism vs Anti-Semitism

Though one encounters the term "antisemitism" more commonly now, there continues to be little consistency in its usage versus "anti-Semitism." This is likewise the case in *On The Future of Wagnerism.* Though Marc A Weiner and I now preferentially use "antisemitism," his book retains its title: *Richard Wagner and the Anti-Semitic Imagination.*"

### *Addiction*

Addiction is a primary, chronic disease of brain reward, motivation, memory and related circuitry. Dysfunction in these circuits leads to characteristic biological, psychological, social and spiritual manifestations. This is reflected in an individual pathologically pursuing reward and/or relief by substance use and other behaviors. Addiction is characterized by inability to consistently abstain, impairment in behavioral control, craving, diminished recognition of significant problems with one's behaviors and interpersonal relationships, and a dysfunctional emotional response. Like other chronic diseases, addiction often involves cycles of relapse and remission. Without treatment or engagement in recovery activities, addiction is progressive and can result in disability or premature death.

– Public Policy Statement of the
American Society of Addiction Medicine

∇

The above "short definition" ahead of a "Long Definition" of addiction by the American Society of Addiction Medicine (ASAM) is considered state-of-the-art.

I am a physician and my specialty is addiction medicine. Addiction is a term we all use and can relate to. We all know what alcoholism is; likewise addiction to opiates such as heroin and oxycontin, tranquilizers like barbituates and xanax, and stimulants like cocaine, nicotine and crystal meth.

Often jokingly, we also routinely admit what we call our addictions to everyday pleasures, temptations and habits—to shopping, sweets, the news, gossip, the internet, sex, television, spending, debting etc. Sometimes we get more specific—e.g., "I'm addicted to Wagner." In fact, it's not uncommon for Wagnerites to describe their involvement with Wagner in this way. Meanwhile, that some Wagnerism might have some features and characteristics of clinical compulsivity or addiction, just as being "addicted to sex" (who isn't?, we ask reflexively) might share some features of clinical sexual compulsivity or addiction, is not something that would occur to most of us. But *are* some Wagnerites in some measure(s) never previously analyzed or articulated indeed like drug addicts in their Wagnerism?

In the realm of art, corollary to the perspective of addictive behaviors—of compulsively using and behaving—is that of the addictive processes and pitfalls of creativity. It will neither surprise nor especially challenge anybody to suggest that many if not most artists tend to be compulsive and obsessive in their lives and creative work. So does this mean that artists tend to share traits with addicts? Indeed, it does seem so, in general, and likewise in the case of Wagner. Strikingly like other addicts, and for the same reasons of obsession and compulsion, of addiction, artists can be clinically, sometimes monstrously egomaniacal, and this can be discernible in their lives and work.

*"Political sentiments and professional jealousies fail to explain the fervency of Wagner's hatred...It welled up from deep in his psyche. As he admitted to Liszt: 'This rancor is as necessary to my nature as gall is to the blood.'"*

– from *Wagnerism* by Alex Ross

∇

In the case of Wagner, and very much in sync with his egomania, is the extent to which Wagner became obsessed with and fueled by antisemitism. Not so unlike the way the heroine of the Darren Aronovsky film *Black Swan* is unable to realize her full artistic potential without resorting to her addiction to self-cutting, one might posit that Wagner was unable to conjure his greatest art without resorting to progressive levels of antisemitism. To what extent addiction has been a factor in the creative lives of artists we can only begin to imagine. In the future, when mechanisms of addiction and their relationships to love and creativity are better understood, we may look back with new perspective at a wide range of artists and their creativity—from Robin Williams and Bill Cosby to van Gogh, Nijinsky, Picasso and Richard Wagner.

Two other concepts pertinent to discussions of addiction are intoxication and dependence. Intoxication, as in inebriation with alcohol, refers to the state of being intoxicated, suggesting physical instability and intellectual and emotional irrationality; it denotes disturbances of speech, thought, behavior, balance and coordination.

Dependence is distinguished from addiction in not necessarily being progressive the way addiction tends to be. One can be dependent on opiates for pain but not considered addicted where there is no instability or progression, even if both are risks with opiate usage. Similarly, one can be dependent on alcohol without being addicted—that is, without it being progressive to the extent of loss of control. It's the "-ism" that makes alcoholism an addiction rather than simply habitual. Is this likewise true of Wagnerism? Is one reason we don't speak of Beethovenism or Mozartism because of this never previously analyzed or even specified difference in appreciation of their art?

While a physical state of intoxication with Wagner would be challenging to demonstrate, some features of dependence around Wagnerite preferences, choices, priorities and psychological defenses invite scrutiny in this context. Discussion of intoxication and dependence with regard to Wagnerites and Wagnerism may be fraught with perils of imprecision, but that should not inhibit exploration and open-mindedness. Just as one is free to say openly and casually "I'm addicted to Wagner," one should not shy away from probing what that might mean.

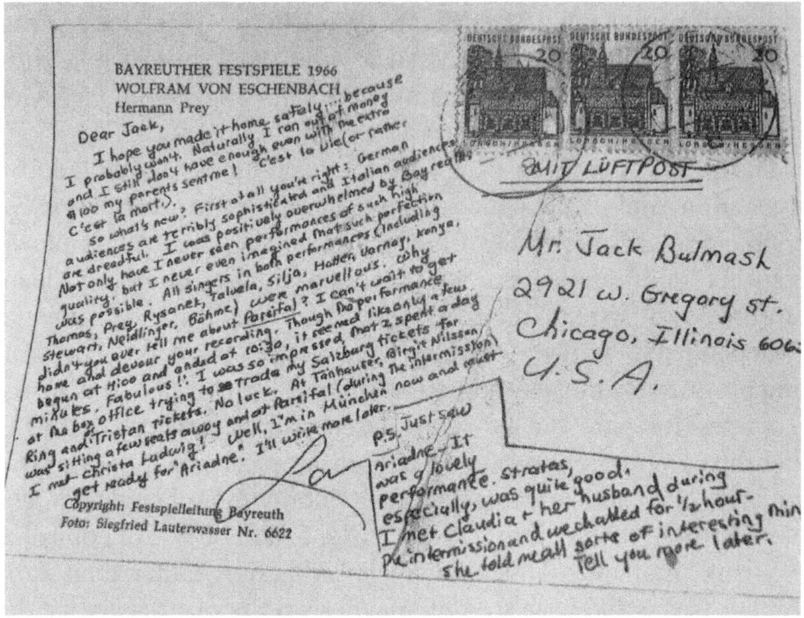
BAYREUTHER FESTSPIELE 1966
WOLFRAM VON ESCHENBACH
Hermann Prey

Dear Jack,
I hope you made it home safely ... because
I probably won't. Naturally I ran out of money
and I still don't have enough even with the extra
$100 my parents sent me! C'est la vie (or rather
C'est la mort.).
So what's new? First of all you're right: German
audiences are terribly sophisticated and Italian audiences
are dreadful. I was positively overwhelmed by Bayreuth.
Not only have I never seen performances of such high
quality, but I never even imagined that such perfection
was possible. All singers in both performances (including
Thomas, Prey, Rysanek, Talvela, Silja, Hotter, Varnay, Konya,
Stewart, Neidlinger, Böhme) were marvellous. Why
didn't you ever tell me about Parsifal? I can't wait to get
home and devour your recording. Though the performance
began at 4:00 and ended at 10:30, it seemed like only a few
minutes. Fabulous!! I was so impressed that I spent a day
at the box office trying to trade my Salzburg tickets for
Ring and Tristan tickets. No luck. At Tannhauser, Birgit Nilsson
was sitting a few seats away and at Parsifal (during the intermission)
I met Christa Ludwig! Well, I'm in München now and must
get ready for "Ariadne." I'll write more later.
Larry

Copyright: Festspielleitung Bayreuth
Foto: Siegfried Lauterwasser Nr. 6622

P.S. Just saw Ariadne—It was a lovely performance. Stratas, especially, was quite good. I met Claudia + her husband during the intermission and we chatted for ½ hour. She told me all sorts of interesting ... Tell you more later.

MIT LUFTPOST

Mr. Jack Bulmash
2921 W. Gregory St.
Chicago, Illinois 606
U.S.A.

Figure 3 - A postcard from my youthful "pilgrimage" to Bayreuth, 1966

## *Codependence*

Broadly and generally speaking, codependence or codependency is a type of dysfunctional helping relationship where one person supports or enables another person's drug addiction, alcoholism, gambling, poor mental health, immaturity, irresponsibility or under-achievement.

Or, one might add, prejudice. One of the most interesting aspects of addiction is what we call codependence or codependency. In the classic circumstance of alcoholism, the person in a codependent relationship with the alcoholic puts up with and inevitably enables the alcoholic and alcoholism. The codependent person is typically in denial and will lie about the extent of harm that has been caused to herself or himself and others, and find all kinds of ways to tolerate and excuse the perpetrator's abusive behavior. In order to keep the father of her children connected with the family and responsibilities and other secondary gain, the wife may suffer extremes of such abuse before she hits bottom and realizes she needs to seek professional help.

In the world of art, as in the world of everyday life and business, this situation can be greatly aggravated by the success of the perpetrator. If the alcoholic, politician or artist is widely revered, then their bad behavior is comparably excused or tolerated. Donald Trump and Wagner are good examples of this. Instead of more realistically appreciating them for the monsters they've tended to be, they become "*monstres sacrés*," and codependent enabling of them, of permitting the impermissible, of accepting the unacceptable, becomes comparably outsized. In my own case with regard to Wagner, my idolatry of a composer who hated my people more consequentially than any other major artist in history, codependence and enabling are gleanable in the five pictures of Wagner on my living room wall, one of them lovingly drawn by me.

This psychological defense mechanism of appeasement of the monster is by no means limited to art or politics. It's what priests have done throughout history in demanding sacrifices. Just as it apparently didn't occur to most of them to question their worship of the god or gods that wrought misfortune upon them, so it doesn't occur to Trumpers to question their pooh-bah's more extreme behaviors and pronouncements. Nor does it occur to most Wagnerites to more seriously question why we do likewise with Wagner. If there are abiding problems of the most vicious and extreme antisemitism with Wagner, rather than question ourselves, we look to evermore resourceful ways to rationalize, deny, dilute and counterbalance our misgivings and sacrifice our values to continue to worship at Wagner's shrine.

### *Recovery*

Recovery is another term in general and widespread usage with regard to addiction. The term is most often used in reference to Alcoholics Anonymous, the program of recovery originated by Bill Wilson and Dr. Bob Smith. Using what are called the 12 Steps of recovery, AA became the template for more than 200 offshoots for everything from "shop-aholism" to Gamblers Anonymous to Sexual Compulsives Anonymous, Narcotics Anonymous, Marijuana Anonymous, Crystal Meth Anonymous, Cocaine Anonymous, Debtors Anonymous, and many others, though not yet for several that might have helped Wagner and Trump: Bullies Anonymous, Bigots Anonymous, Racists Anonymous and Antisemites Anonymous.

The first three of these template 12 steps are about admitting powerlessness over one's addiction or inclination and developing faith in "a power greater than ourselves" ("God, as we understood Him" or "Higher Power") in seeking help. The next six steps are personal inventory steps, of acknowledging what's often referred to as "the wreckage of the past," with an emphasis on "rigorous honesty" about one's role in what happened; and making amends, when possible and appropriate, where harm was done—to oneself as well as to others. The last 3 steps are sometimes referred to as the "maintenance steps." They are guides to the ongoing, daily, continuous work of recovery, of taking inventory and promptly admitting and addressing mistakes, of maintaining emotional sobriety, of being of service to others, and otherwise nurturing spirituality.

If we were to incorporate the word "Wagner" in place of "alcohol" for "Wagnerism Anonymous" or "Wagnerites Anonymous," the first step would read as follows: We admitted we were powerless over Wagner, that our lives had become unmanageable.

Several of the many 12-step fellowships that have emerged are for those who are codependent. The first and best known of these is Alanon, for those who are in co-dependent relationships with alcoholics. Alanon was established by Lois Wilson, AA co-founder Bill Wilson's wife. Since then, other fellowships have emerged—e.g., Codependents Anonymous or CODA and ACOA, Adult Children of Alcoholics.

Other 12-step fellowships that deal with codependence in relationships include those that deal with sexual compulsivity and romantic obsession—e.g. Sexual Compulsives Anonymous (SCA), Sex Addicts Anonymous (SAA) and Sex and Love Addicts Anonymous (SLAA). In addition to its reliance on the 12 steps based on those of AA, SCA utilizes what it calls the 14 "characteristics most of us seem to have in common." Among these is one that seems especially pertinent to my own and more widely to Jewish experience of Wagnerism: "We were drawn to people who were not available to us or who would reject or abuse us."

SLAA incorporates 12 characteristics of romantic obsession. Several of these as well seem pertinent to my own experience of Wagnerism:

- Having few healthy boundaries, we become...emotionally attached to people without knowing them.

- Fearing abandonment and loneliness, we stay in and return to painful, destructive relationships…
- We confuse love with neediness…We use sex or emotional dependence as substitutes for nurturing, care and support.
- We avoid responsibility for ourselves by attaching ourselves to people who are emotionally unavailable.
- We stay enslaved to emotional dependency…
- We assign magical qualities to others. We idealize and pursue them, then blame them for not fulfilling our fantasies and expectations.

In this paradigm of romantic obsession, I can almost imagine myself in a post-modern production of *Tannhäuser*, wherein I am Tannhäuser, Wagner is Venus and his operas are the Venusberg. In the actual opera, Tannhäuser longs to break free of his enslavement to Venus, goddess of sensual pleasure. In my fantasy post-modern version, in order to break free of my enslavement to the emotional dependency and sensual pleasures of Wagnerism, I must embark on a pilgrimage to find my true self and real-life calling.

In codependence recovery, one learns to detach from those with whom one is codependent. In the case of the wife with the alcoholic husband, and specifically in this case Lois Wilson, the relationship is not necessarily severed or destroyed or denounced; rather, it is reconfigured. Lois learned to no longer blame her husband (AA co-founder Bill Wilson) for his alcoholism, for the ways he failed to meet her needs or for the abuse she suffered when he was actively alcoholic. Nor did she keep trying to change him via the classic means of the codependent, the so-called 4 M's: mothering, management, martyrdom and manipulation. Instead, she learned to see and accept the reality of his alcoholism, and later his recovery, and meet her needs more appropriately with greater focus on herself and her own life.

Models of codependence and recovery have been good ones for me vis a vis Wagner and may be helpful for others struggling with the dilemma of how to relate to this most troubling of great artists. While I do believe that we are past due for a more generalized better understanding and more qualified appreciation of Wagner, I do not believe he should perforce be banned, forgotten or even relegated but accepted more realistically and with greater detachment. Just as we accept that alcoholics and compulsive gamblers are who and how they are, we can nurture detachment for the antisemitism that comes with the territory of Wagnerism while remaining vigilant about potential harm.

In my own case, when and where I recognize sensual intoxication with Wagner's music to be too painful and injurious to my self-esteem, I have learned to use the tools of codependence recovery—principally detachment. I've learned to be realistic about the relationship I have been in with Wagner, to not keep trying to make him into someone he wasn't and can never be for me, to not keep trying to distort or dilute history and culture in efforts to make him more acceptable, to accept the reality of who and how Wagner was and remains in art and culture, and to be cognizant of that reality in future interactions. While such an adjustment does not preclude pleasure and appreciation, it does preclude intoxication, a state of sensual distortion that in my case has proven inimical to self-possession and self-respect.

I believe that utilizing emerging concepts and paradigms of addiction, codependence and recovery may sometimes help us to better place Wagner, Wagnerites and Wagnerisms in perspective. What this implies is that the answer to a better understanding and more realistic appreciation of Wagner may lie not with newly or previously undiscovered historical documents of Wagner's character and behavior or intentions, or cultural or national histories like those of Germany, Bayreuth, or of art and artists, so much as with us, with we ourselves. In what ways are *we* addictively and codependently rationalizing and enabling the troubled art of Richard Wagner? In this paradigm, the future of Wagnerism will have less to do with who and how and what Wagner was and is than with who, what and how we ourselves are becoming.

# Do New Revelations of Hitler's Taste in Art Cast New Light on Wagner Appreciation?

– *Huffington Post*, 2/18/2014

Figure 4 - Richard Wagner in Paris, 1867, Wikimedia Commons, public domain

Widely regarded as one of history's greatest composers and artists, Richard Wagner is also widely known as one of history's most virulent antisemites. Like many opera lovers, I fell in love with Wagner. Yet my memoir, *Confessions of a Jewish Wagnerite: Being Gay and Jewish in America*, with an introduction by Gottfried Wagner, great-grandson of the composer, is the story of my own personal journey away from that love, and away from identifying myself as a Wagnerite.

As the AIDS epidemic began to unfold in 1981, I began to confront mortality as never before — as a physican, as a writer, as a gay man, and as a Jew. At that time I had 5 pictures of Wagner on my living room wall, one of them a drawing by me. Not so coincidentally

I began to come to grips with the extent of my own internalization of antisemitism, an odyssey of self-discovery that paralleled the great theme of my life up to that point, of coming out and into my own as a gay man. Slowly and painfully, I came to grips with the depth and seriousness of Wagner's antisemitism and its entanglements with what became Nazism. Past all the rationalizations commonly expounded by Wagnerites, Jewish and non-Jewish alike, I finally began to see that being a "Wagnerite," and especially a Jewish Wagnerite, was psychologically and morally troubled.

What's to be done about someone whose art is or seems to be so great, but whose prejudices unquestionably contributed to great evil? How do you continue to appreciate art once aware of the enormity it was accessory to? This is the ring of fire that continues to surround composer Richard Wagner.

To judge from the way the still smoldering controversies regarding Wagner and Wagner appreciation are playing out in our own time, there are several key strategies. First and foremost is to further extol the composer's art by finding ever new approaches and contexts of interpretation, the way we do with such other great artists as Sophocles and Shakespeare. Within this strategy of exhaustive reinterpretation is that of exploiting the passage of time and the receding of history. Still another apposing strategy is to come clean about the seriousness and reach of the antisemitism, a process that has gained momentum in recent research and publications. Finally, there is the effort to humanize the composer by noting exceptions and contradictions in his biases, complexity in his rendering of villains and heroes alike, and examples of diversity in his circles, including a number of Jews and other non-Aryans. Between the lines of all these approaches is invariably a discernible longing if not impatience to get past...well, the past.

All of these strategies have been working together to further place the composer in perspective, a much larger process that, like all history, will continue to reconfigure over time. Today we can appreciate Egyptian, Greek and Roman antiquities, even the Roman Coliseum or a southern plantation, without having that appreciation entirely vitiated by our knowledge of the oppression and atrocities of slavery that produced them and which they produced. Something comparable is happening with Wagner appreciation. It's anticipated that the controversies will eventually weaken and die, leaving just the art in their wake. The bathwater will finally get thrown out, the baby saved. This is the view that is almost universally shared by our arbiters of culture, whatever the intellectual acrobatics, re the present and future of Richard Wagner.

As we look to the future of Wagner and Wagnerism, the ill-defined cult of the composer that has no counterpart in all of music (there is no Beethovenism, Verdiism, Mozartism), we might consider the commentary of *New Yorker* music critic Alex Ross, author of *Wagnerism*, who feels that pondering the Hitler connection with Wagner has gone too far. As he observed of his experience of the 2013 Wagner bicentennial Bayreuth Festival, "discussion of Wagner is stuck in a Nazi rut. His multifarious influence on artistic, intellectual, and political life has been largely forgotten; in the media, it is practically obligatory to identify him as 'Hitler's favorite composer.'" Ross anticipates the time when can we get past the Wagner/Hitler detour and back onto the greater journey of Wagner appreciation.

Meanwhile, scholarship keeps casting new light on the composer. With the opening of some previously inaccessible archives, there are ever-accumulating revelations of the already heavily documented relationships of the Wagner family and Bayreuth with Hitler and Nazism, and new insights on Hitler's reverence for Wagner. Alex Ross has researched this material in preparation for his book, *Wagnerism: Art and Politics in the Shadow of Music*, which can seem effective in distancing the composer from Hitler. Why should one arch-criminal's appreciation of Wagner, which was—at least as Ross tries so hard to see it — myopic, delimited and superficial, ruin everybody else's appreciation forever?

In July of 2013 Ross published an essay called "Othello's Daughter" in the *New Yorker* about an an interracial singer who studied with Wagner's widow, vehemently antisemitic Cosima Wagner, and who had been slated to be one of the Valkyries in Bayreuth's first fully staged *Ring* cycle. Ross understands the seriousness of Wagner's racism and antisemitism. In an earlier *New Yorker* piece, "Wagner in Israel," he wrote what seemed a sensitive and insightful analysis, reminding us, among other twists and turns in the Wagner-and-the-Jews saga, that Theodore Herzl, founding father of the state of Israel, loved Wagner. Yet even as Ross notes the naivete of exculpating so great a prejudice as racism and Wagner's role in it on the basis of a few exceptions, he appears to be a lot more seduced by "Othello's Daughter" and other such exceptions than he realizes. Much the way I myself, alongside virtually every Jewish and for that matter non-Jewish Wagnerite of my knowledge and acquaintance, have seized on comparable tidbits to redeem Wagner from the curse of Hitler and Nazism.

One of which, luring me presently like the *Blumenmädchen* in *Parsifal* from my Wagnerism apostasy, is the degree to which the composer seemed to foretell of his own fate. In the face of what can appear to be an eternal curse with no way out, Wagner himself can be evermore clearly seen in such Wandering Jewish figures as The Flying Dutchman, The Wanderer and Kundry.

"The endless Nazi fixation is unsettling," Ross writes. "Hitler has won a posthumous victory in seeing his idea of Wagner become the defining one." Ross is so impatient with all this that he neglected to mention in the New Yorker pieces a development that he does cite in his book, *Wagnerism*—the special exhibit mounted at Bayreuth in 2012 and during the 2013 bicentennial (of Wagner's birth) festival and in subsequent seasons called "Silenced Voices" (covered by Zachary Woolfe in the *New York Times*), commemorating the Wagner-and Bayreuth-associated Jewish musicians and singers, most of whom were murdered as a result of Bayreuth's collaborations with Hitler. Apparently more in keeping with the idea of celebrating the composer's bicentennial, Ross explored Wagner's writings on America, where the composer once considered moving, and Wagner landmarks in New York City and environs.

So henceforth we should be thinking of Wagner, like the Jews, as a victim of Hitler? What I came to see is that while there are some-of-his-close-associates-were-Jews, exception-to-the-rule puzzle pieces that don't fit neatly into paradgims of more monolithic and implacable prejudice, the bigger picture is still strong and clear. Whatever the caveats and qualifiers, Hitler's and the Wagner family's shared understanding of Wagner was, at the least, no less legitimate than the countless other interpretations of Wagner so exhaustively documented in *Wagnerism*; an understanding that became the philosophical and spiritual undergirding of what became, under Hitler, Nazism. If Hitler happened to be an aesthetic peasant and vulgarian, his love of Wagner was certainly not regarded as such by most Wagner family members or many other notable Germans—as being superficial, naive, delimited, even if that's what some really thought and a few brave artists and others gave voice to. On the contrary, as the Wagners — especially Winifred (who married into the Wagner family) and with the notable exception of Friedelind (who fled Germany) — and Bayreuth came to see it, Hitler was the culmination, the realization, of Wagner's *Weltanshauung*.

Figure 5 - Adolf Hitler, cropped, restored photo, unknown author, 1937, Wikimedia Commons, Public Domain

Meanwhile, new revelations about Hitler's art collections coincidentally invite a revisiting of Hitler's infatuation with Wagner. As it turns out, Hitler, whose favorite composer and sole acknowledged spiritual mentor was Wagner, was an even bigger fan of kitsch, of sentimentality and vulgarity in art, than anything we had already surmised. (See "Reading The Pictures: Fact is, We Can't Get Enough of Hitler," by Michael Shaw, HuffPost, Politics, 11/8/2013).

All of which suggests a different direction of inquiry than that being pursued by Ross and most other Wagnerites. What if Hitler's appreciation of art and taste in art, including Wagner, is more clue than aberration? In other words, when all is said and done, as the long-silenced criticisms of Wagner's music dramas for being coarse, ponderous, pompous and bombastic begin to be reconsidered, is it possible that Wagner's art is really something closer to grandiloquent kitsch than classical Greek antiquity or Shakespeare? That Wagner might eventually be perceived as less rather than more of an artist seems to be an outcome that pretty much no one since Eduard Hanslick, the Jewish critic of Wagner so retaliatorily caricatured by Wagner in *Die Meistersinger*, has thought much about, much less dared to propose, certainly not in the current era of Wagner and Wagnerism.

As is clear from the work of Alex Ross, Wagner appreciation and with it Wagnerism will almost certainly continue its march forward. Eventually, Wagner's art will seem less and less tainted by antisemitism, its greatness unfettered by temporal and topical political considerations, distractions, detours, ruts. When appreciating Greek tragedy, how much do we now care about the wars and politics that cradled it? The same fate will almost certainly await Wagner, right? The only remaining question, certainly for Wagnerites, would seem to be how quickly can we get there.

Or is another outcome also possible? As time and Wagnerism solider onward, can it be that Wagner's art might seem less like that of the great Greek tragedians or Shakespeare and more like the pictures and statues of *Schwarzwald* moose that are emblematic centerpieces of Hitler's art collections and taste in art?

Figure 6 - Zentralinstitut für Kunstgeschicte, phototek, from Deutsche Welle

And if so, can such a dethroning of Wagner be key to understanding Bayreuth's bicentennial *Ring* cycle production directed by iconoclast and "cultural terrorist" Frank Castorf, whose zeal in confounding preconceptions and expectations, in thwarting meaning and interpretation, seemed to have reached new heights of irreverence? "If the composer's great-granddaughters cannot guard Wagner's physical or artistic legacy, why are they in charge of the festival?" asked Neil Fisher in the *London Times*. Could no less than the heart and soul of Wagner appreciation, Bayreuth itself and the Wagner family, be setting the stage and direction for a more anarchic anti-future of Wagner appreciation?

And if so, finally, is such a "*das Ende*" not what Wagner himself foresaw and in the deepest sense accepted and even longed for?

# Jewish Wagnerites and Wagner Societies

– *Huffington Post*, 4/29/14

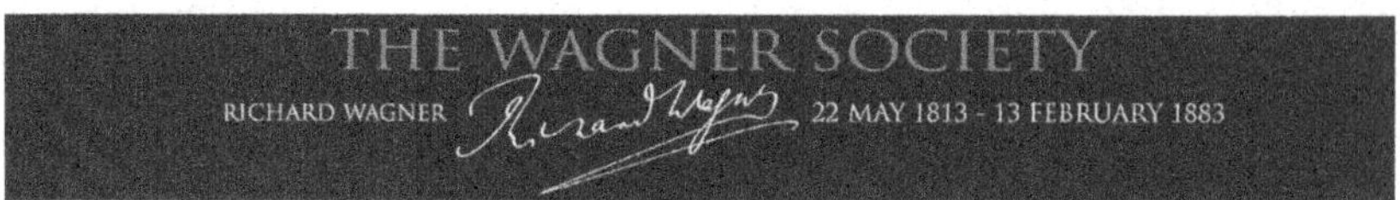


Figure 7 - Wagnersociety.org

*On The Future of Wagnerism* commenced with an exploration of the implications for Wagner appreciation of emerging revelations about Hitler's taste in art. It also considered the related question of whether Wagner is "stuck in a Nazi rut," as *New Yorker* music critic Alex Ross has put it. Ross doubtless speaks for many Wagnerites who have grown impatient with what they feel to be the exhausted and myopic discussion of Wagner's links to Hitler and Nazism at the expense of Wagner appreciation, especially as we mark the bicentennial of the composer's birth (1813).

What will be Wagner's place in the next century? Two trends are forseeable. The first is an inevitable receding of the Hitler-Wagner connection, as time and history move on. Just as we no longer concern ourselves with the wars and politics and biases that cradled the Greek tragedies, presumably we will care less and less about those that nurtured Wagner. The bathwater of Hitler and Nazism will eventually get thrown out, the baby of Wagner's art saved. The countervailing trend suggests that the ongoing fallout from Wagner's epochal antisemitism, Hitler's adoration of Wagner and Bayreuth's enthusiastic collaborations with Hitler and Nazism will continue to lead to a less exalted, more qualified place for the composer in the annals of art.

"Fifty years after the demise of the Third Reich, it is incomprehensible that intelligent people still deny the obvious truth that if the *New Testament* of the Nazi political and religious cult was *Mein Kampf*, the *Old Testament* was the work of Richard Wagner." That's how Gottfried Wagner (the composer's great grandson), playwright William M. Hoffman, composer John Corigliano (co-creators of *The Ghosts of Versailles*), composer Michael Shapiro and I put it in a published letter to the editor of the *New York Times* in 1998, in response to a *New York Times* piece, "The Specter of Hitler in the Music of Wagner," by music critic and historian Joseph Horowitz.

Reviewing Germanic studies professor Marc Weiner's *Wagner and The Anti-Semitic Imagination*, which shows how Wagner's texts and music are riddled with anti-Semitic allusions, Horowitz wrote in what's now a long-established tradition of Wagnerites — many of them, like Horowitz, impressively learned and accomplished, and a striking number of them Jewish — whose willingness and often enough eagerness to rationalize, minimize, obfuscate and deny the presence and toxicity of Wagner's anti-Semitism can strain credulity.

*Wagner and Me* is a recent documentary created by and featuring the wonderful actor and brave gay activist Stephen Fry, a Jewish Wagnerite who claims his Jewish identity while making an admirable but not very in-depth effort to face some of the history and truth about Bayreuth, Wagner and Wagner's operas, as he tours the Wagner Festival's grounds. Like Horowitz, Fry acknowledges Wagner's anti-Semitism and Bayreuth's Nazi history. In his tone and body language in the film, Fry elicits the kind of surpassing forgiveness and trust, a feeling of comfort, of being at home, that the Jews of Wagner's circle who so revered the composer must have felt, notwithstanding the abundance of evidence to the contrary around and about them. It's the same feeling of comfort and trust you sense in the Wagnerism of Joseph Horowitz.

Surely so supreme an artist as Wagner simply must be surpassingly worthy of trust. Therefore, so this logic goes, trust not what Wagner ranted in treatises and journals and letters, or undeniably depicted in his music and texts, but what's otherwise intuitable, however inchoately, in the interstices of his art, especially in what Horowitz and others see as the complexity, empathy and ambiguity of his characterizations of villains and heroes alike. In this view, Wotan, Siegfried, Alberich and Mime, like Amfortas, Parsifal, Klingsor and Kundry, exist in a kind of musico-dramatic ether of human, moral and characterological equipoise. However villainous Alberich, Mime and Kundry may really be, they are more recognizably human and capable of arousing levels of compassion denied the too often insufferably virtuous Siegfried and Parsifal. That this is precisely Wagner's point about the Jews — that they can appeal in ways that mask their reality, and that those who perceive and act on that awareness can seem comparatively smug and self-righteous — seems ever to elude Wagnerites.

I, too, always knew about Wagner's antisemitism and Bayreuth's Nazi history. Notwithstanding that knowledge, I embraced that same deep feeling of trust, that comfort of *Heimat, within* the universe of Wagner's art, which held me bewitched for much of my younger opera-going life. We Wagnerites all, non-Jewish and Jewish alike, became Kundrys under the spell of "the sorcerer of Bayreuth." Wagner, "the master of Bayreuth," was the master of our senses, but at the price of our souls? We had no idea how far we had wandered into the realms of—and how complicit we had become with—racist, nationalist and anti-Semitic ideologies and agendas.

Fast forward to a generation later, when Ned Rorem, never a Wagnerite, tried to bring me to my senses, to get me to see what we Wagnerites never could, no matter what kind of lip service we gave to critical and qualifying views of Wagner, no matter how hard we tried: that greatness of the art does not mean greatness — nobility, humanity, character — of the artist. That greatness of art equals greatness of heart is an equation that turns out to be no more true for composers than for train conductors.

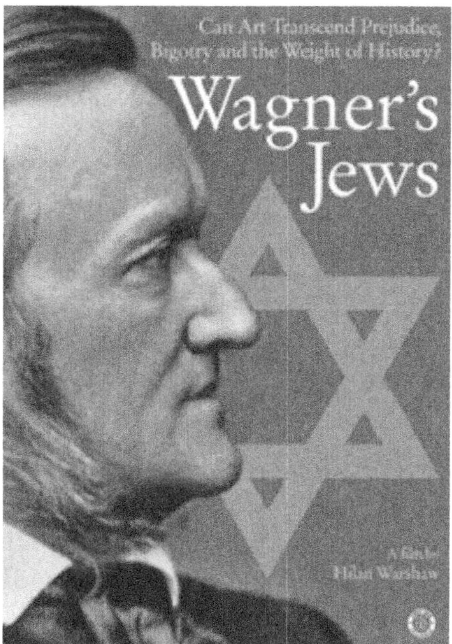

Figure 8 - Wagner's Jews, a film by Hilan Warshaw, overtonefilms.com

Most notable of recent contributions to this discourse is a documentary film, *Wagner's Jews,* created by Hilan Warshaw, a filmmaker, writer and musician, which explores the remarkable extent and complexity of the social and psychological sadomasochism of Wagner's relationships with a number of Jews. In the process, it documents with singular clarity and accessibility the depth, seriousness and progression of Wagner's antisemitism. Warshaw's film features commentary from a number of prominent Jewish musicians and writers, including Leon Botstein, Paul Lawrence Rose and Robert Gutman. So effective is Warshaw's exposure of the psychosocial masochism of Jews in their relations with Wagner that it's impossible not to consider parallels with the most infamous of such behaviors — the Jewish *kapos* and *Judenräte* in their relationships with the Nazis. With great respect for the impossible circumstances and choices forced upon these Jews by the Nazis, and notwithstanding Alex Ross's wishful certainty that most Nazis paid little attention to and didn't care much about Wagner, when the Nazis were looking for tutorials of how to exploit the psychology of the vulnerability and self-effacement of Jews — what we more commonly refer to as the internalization of antisemitism — they would have found no greater or more sophisticated an exemplar than Richard Wagner.

Figure 9 - Daniel Barenboim, opus3artists.com

Not interviewed in Warshaw's film is Daniel Barenboim, a Jewish Wagnerite who fits right into this discussion. (Scheduling conflicts prevented Barenboim's participation in the film.) Barenboim, whose humanitarian efforts to work with Palestinian musicians are widely lauded, is the author of a recent essay, "Wagner and the Jews," in the *New York Review of Books*, which shows that the distinguished Israeli conductor and pianist still clings to the Wagnerite and especially Jewish Wagnerite delusion that Wagner's admittedly extreme antisemitism does not infect his music or operas, their meaning or appreciation. The art, Barenboim keeps trying to believe and insist, is independent of the man. In their public conversation together at Columbia, no matter how hard the eminent Palestinian intellectual and literary theorist Edward Said tried to get his friend Barenboim to acknowledge the obvious taint of antisemitism in Wagner's works, the conductor would not budge.

To my knowledge, no conductor of international renown has refused to conduct Wagner. Some, however, have refused or declined to conduct at Bayreuth, most famously Toscanini during WWII in protest to Bayreuth's embracement of Hitler and Nazism and more ambiguously Leonard Bernstein in the postwar period. Bernstein had been in correspondence with Wolfgang Wagner (Wagner's grandson, Gottfried's father and, together with his brother Wieland, a Hitler youth and confidant) about leading a new production of *Tristan und Isolde* there. *Tristan*, Bernstein felt, was free of the antisemitism that infected a lot of Wagner's other work. Ostensibly these negotiations fell through because of scheduling conflicts, but I was acquainted with

Bernstein during that period and, as I recall and as likewise alluded to by Gottfried Wagner in his memoir, *Twilight of the Wagners*, the main issue for Lenny, as he was universally and affectionately referred to, was the never adequately reconciled Nazi past of the Wagner family and Bayreuth. Although Bernstein, wildly popular in Germany and Austria, often conducted orchestras such as the Vienna Philharmonic and in venues where questions of Nazi collaboration remained comparably reverberant, Bayreuth seemed to represent a higher level of challenge in confronting this history.

Figure 10 - James Levine, public domain

Like Barenboim, James Levine is another leading Jewish conductor who accepted Bayreuth's invitations to conduct there. Unlike Barenboim, however, Levine, who rarely gives interviews, shies away from discussion of social and political issues, concerns, causes. In the heyday of AIDS and gay liberation, Levine worked with prominent artists known to be gay such as John Corigliano and William M. Hoffman, and he co-conducted a gala benefit concert for Gay Men's Health Crisis. But his public silence about gay liberation, gays in music, and gays in Russia is the *doppelganger* of his public silence about anti-Semitism, Jews in music, Wagner, Bayreuth and Wagnerism. After many decades in the spotlight, it's clear that Levine is not an avid or gifted public speaker, and he now struggles with considerable health challenges. Even so, it's disappointing and also sad that so outstanding and important an American musician and cultural figure, whose grandfather was a synagogue cantor, has never found a way to express himself publicly regarding these controversies, especially as they might relate to his own experience, identities and feelings. [In 2018, a number of accusations of sexual misconduct spanning decades and involving many male musicians, were brought against the conductor, who was suspended from his post as principal conductor and artistic director of the Metropolitan Opera.]

Perhaps all Jewish Wagnerites appreciate that at some level they must accede to Wagner since his reign over the worlds of music, art and culture, however clamorous, has never been toppled, not even in the wake of Hitler and Nazism. On the contrary, proving the PR maxim that there is no such thing as bad publicity, Wagnerism seems if anything to feed on these controversies. Rationalizing, mitigating, denying and compromising with Wagner's ever-present antisemitism— whether vehemently explicit in public rants or vehemently implicit in his music dramas (Wagner doesn't explicitly defame the Jews as Jews in his operas) — allows Jews to continue to participate freely and fully in all levels of art and what is still widely regarded, certainly by Wagnerites, as the highest experience of art, Wagner appreciation.

The alternative would be a huge mess. Imagine leading conductors, singers and directors refusing to perform Wagner or audience cohorts refusing to attend Wagner performances. Imagine a larger scale of what happened in Israel with the banning of Wagner, or of the more recent debacle in Los Angeles, where some patrons tried unsuccessfully to prevent a mounting of the *Ring* cycle by the Los Angeles Opera. Such is Wagner's hold that if and when a choice is forced between Wagner and Jewish sensitivities, Wagner invariably will be chosen, often with strong Jewish backing, a reality that is emergent even in Israel. More unconsciously and instinctively than clearly and honestly, probably the majority of Jews in music and art and culture appreciate this reality and continue to do all they can to prevent such confrontations, to defend themselves psychologically as well as socially and professionally. Hence Jewish Wagnerites as we mostly see them today. They're like black or gay Republicans, gay Catholics, gay or female Islamists, or Jewish Marxists, incongruously supporting individuals and institutions that are impressively inimical to them, with a logic and intellectualism that can be breathtakingly circuitous and an enthusiasm that can appear outsized and troubled.

Jews need Wagner in order to be fully integrated into the music and arts communities, much as Mahler needed to convert to Catholicism for the same reasons, and much as Wagner needed Jews to build his career at multiple levels. But parity this is not. It's crucial to distinguish here between Wagner, who genocidally hated Jews, and Jewish Wagnerites, who unwaveringly adored and worshiped Wagner the vanguard artist. An additional perspective about this emerges from the work of Hilan Warshaw, who captures in his paper, "No One Can Serve Our Cause Better Than You: Wagner's Jewish Collaborators After 1869," Wagner's sense of Jews as crucial to the vision and execution of his artistic vision. Avid Jewish participation in the building and execution of that vision is seen as a proof of its rightness and provides a level of satisfaction that is mostly tacit and paraconscious; paraconscious—implying glimmerings of consciousness that never fully develop.

Wagner, in other words, had less than a full awareness of what he was doing and the reasons why. His antisemitism was like an addictive drug that rendered him blind to its reality. That Jewish Wagnerites in Wagner's eyes were a "proof" of the rightness of the "cause" of Wagnerism is like solipsistically concluding that the success of his art is also a "proof" of the rightness of the "cause" of Wagnerism. Inevitably, it's the same satisfaction that the Nazis took in the "enthusiastic" participation of Jewish elders and councils in the processesing of Jews for plunder, slavery and extermination. In this perspective, what Jewish Wagnerites like Joseph Horowitz glean to be the composer's ostensibly transcendent musical-dramatic insight into himself and others, the villains as well as the heroes, the real Wagner that emerges is not Shakespeare, whose anti-Semitic creation Shylock was pointed enough to be exploited by the Nazis, but the Nazi propaganda creations *Ewige Jude* and *Jud Suss*.

In other words, Wagner wasn't the great Shakespeare-like genius Jewish Wagnerites like Horowitz want to believe he is. Though we see antisemitism in Shakespeare, we grant Shakespeare a degree of license because of the genius and complexity of his characterizations of Shylock and his hypocritical, corrupt society, even if it plays off stereotypes. With Wagner, by contrast, the antisemitism feels programmatic, more important, more an end to itself, than the characterizations of such villains as Alberich, Mime, Beckmesser, Klingsor and Kundry.

What Shakespeare achieved with the otherwise dramatic and powerful character of Shylock and the tragicomic ambiguity of *The Merchant of Venice* is what Wagnerites like Horowitz want to believe

Wagner achieved with Alberich, Mime, Beckmesser, Klingsor and Kundry in the *Ring* cycle, *Die Meistersinger*, and *Parsifal*. But so far as we know, Shakespeare was no more personally or dramatically invested in antisemitism in *The Merchant of Venice* than he was in racism in *Othello*. Nothing remotely comparable can be claimed for Wagner, who was in an entirely different universe of racist, nationalist and antisemitic agendas.

Figure 11 - Joseph Horowitz, Wikipedia, public domain

When I was writing my memoir, *Confessions of a Jewish Wagnerite*, I met one-on-one with Horowitz, who tried to make the case for Wagner's antisemitism being of its time and place and therefore to some extent understandable and forgivable. In addition, he seemed to imply that some of Wagner's stereotyping may have had more of a basis than Wagner's critics have allowed, which doubtless explains what Gustav Mahler, perhaps the most famous Jewish Wagnerite, was trying to say in comparing himself to Mime. In other words, as a number of Jewish Wagnerites who should know better have seen it, Wagner's antisemitism should be regarded as to a degree accurate and justified. As we now know, such thinking was all too typical among the German Jews who were transported to the camps in the same train cars as their social inferiors, still secretly priding themselves on not being "one of *those* people."

There is another analogy to the Wagner and the Jews situation, one closer to home here in America and parallel in time to the life of Wagner and the inception of Wagnerism — the slavemasters and slaves of the pre-Civil War American South. In the *New York Times*, music critic Zachary Woolfe pondered the connections between the film "Django" with Wagner and the *Ring* cycle, allusions to which color Quentin Tarantino's highly acclaimed film. There, Woolfe finds as many implications as there are twists and turns in the director's use and mischievously irreverent misuse of Wagner: "What we are required to do is to remain aware, as Mr. Tarantino's film perhaps inadvertently reminds us, that Wagner's operas do not exist outside history or politics."

"Robert Lepage's production of the *Ring* cycle is proudly apolitical," Woolfe observes, "but when it returns to the Metropolitan Opera...audiences will ideally have 'Django' in the back of their minds..." And likewise ideally, they will further consider that whatever *Gone With The Wind* moments of seemingly benign, mutually supportive relationships between Wagner and his Jewish disciples may have existed at Wahnfried, the Wagner equivalent of Tara (e.g., between Wagner and Hermann Levi, who conducted the world premiere of *Parsifal* and was a pall-bearer at Wagner's funeral in Venice), it's not Cap'n Butler and Mammy so much as the slavemasters of "Django" and "12 Years a Slave" that most successfully convey the psychological and philosophical atmosphere of The Master of Bayreuth's relationships to Jews.

Meanwhile, is it unreasonable to probe deeper than we have beneath the rock we call Wagnerism? Is there a Bachism, Beethovenism or Mozartism? Is it like "gay sensibility," a phenomenon we know exists but which eludes precision and certainty of definition? Is it a philosophy, movement, religion? Is it a cult? Apart from the issue of the relationship between Wagner societies, Bayreuth and the Wagner family (lest we forget, Wagner continues to be a family business), and apart from their history, which goes back to the first Bayreuth festivals, Wagnerism is a sociocultural phenomenon that begs for greater critical scrutiny as such. Alex Ross's *Wagnerism*, it may seem, is the answer to that call. Yet even this encyclopedic work is evasive on central these questions of the origins and nature of Wagnerism.

In his book, *Wagner Nights*, about the history of Wagnerism in America at the turn of the century, Joseph Horowitz gives a sense of the scale of this phenomenon but not of its uniqueness in legitimizing, however indirectly or tacitly under the mantle of high art, the contemplation and appreciation of racist and anti-Semitic perspectives. Reading *Wagner Nights*, one would have little awareness that this heyday of early Wagnerism chronicled by Horowitz took place in an America, where racism fostered the greatest industry and excesses of slavery in recorded history, leading to one of history's bloodiest and costliest of civil wars, and where antisemitism, though less entrenched and cultivated than in Europe, was endemic and pervasive. At that time in America, there were quotas for Jews at the leading universities, including Harvard and Yale, and Jews were widely excluded from clubs, apartment buildings, neighborhoods and jobs; segregation was the law of the land.

But that's not what Horowitz finds worthy of observation and analysis. Rather, he mostly writes about what a meliorist social movement Wagnerism was, how it was for a time dominated by women, giving them a place and voice they did not otherwise have. Not surprisingly in Horowitz's account, antisemitism does not seem a notable aspect of Wagnerism, at least not consciously or explicitly in those years in America, in contrast to what happened to Wagnerism over the ensuing decades in Europe.

Ross's *Wagnerism* is the first major study to place Horowitz's work in a greater perspective that is at once verifying and affirming. In the original version of this article I wrote that "in the case of Horowitz, whose Wagnerism is unrelentingly affirming and defensive and notwithstanding Horowitz's indubitable erudition, you wouldn't look for a comprehensive overview of Wagnerism's impact from him any more than you'd look to Donald Trump to give an unbiased assessment of Vladimir Putin." While that observation might seem over-the-top, especially in light of Ross's work, both writers rely heavily on phenomena Ross seems more aware of but not often articulate about—Wagner's nonspecificity and public taciturnity around questions of racism and antisemitism.

On the surface, today's Wagner societies seem fully open to discussion of controversy. Critical inquiry is welcome, including discussion of Wagner's antisemitism. Jews are invited to participate, to play the same prominent roles in promoting Wagner's legacy that we played in Wagner's own life and career, especially when that participation, however critical on this point or that, is discernibly enthusiastic, as it so unwaveringly is. All the world's Wagner societies include Jews, who are sometimes presidents of these organizations. There is even an Israeli Wagner society. But let that participation strike the wrong chord and a different kind of reception may result. When it was published, *Confessions of a Jewish Wagnerite*, with its introduction by Gottfried Wagner, was banned from the literature table of the Wagner Society of New York by its President Forever," (as I call her) Nathalie D. Wagner, apparently by fiat. (Has the Wagner Society of New York ever held an election?) The reaction of Wagner societies to Gottfried Wagner has been comparably frosty. Why do these books inspire such revulsion?

*Confessions of a Jewish Wagnerite* is a personal memoir of my recognition of the psychological and moral troubledness of my own Wagnerism, bound up, as I discovered it to be, with my own internalized antisemitism, within greater concerns about the cult of Wagnerism and its influence on society and politics. Gottfried Wagner's memoir, *Twilight of The Wagners*, shares those concerns as it takes an unflinchingly hard look at the already heavily but still far from fully addressed Nazi history of Bayreuth and his family's, especially his never repentant father Wolfgang Wagner's, collaborations with Nazism. (Some of this family discord is also captured in the Tony Palmer film, *The Wagner Family.*)

Admittedly, these memoirs tell of movement away from the composer. And their threat may be that as such, they are just too undermining of Wagner and inimical to Wagnerism, which is inevitably about the principal mission of Wagner Societies: Wagner appreciation.

Meanwhile, one can't help but wonder to what extent Jewish as well as non-Jewish Wagnerites are experiencing the same satisfaction, albeit a lot more tacitly and preconsciously, that Richard and Cosima Wagner clearly savored in witnessing such enthusiastic Jewish participation in the promotion of Wagnerism. Like Alberich, Mime and the Nibelungs, as Wagner saw us, we never miss an opportunity to exploit and betray one another. In any event, I wouldn't anticipate finding much discussion of such things at Wagner Society gatherings, even those that are hosting screenings of *Wagner's Jews.*

# More on Jews, Wagnerites and The Bigger Picture

**Regina Resnik, Birgit Nilsson, Max Lorenz, Manuela Hoelterhoff, Eva Rieger, Melanie Yolles, Joseph Horowitz, Leon Botstein, and Professor Alberich**

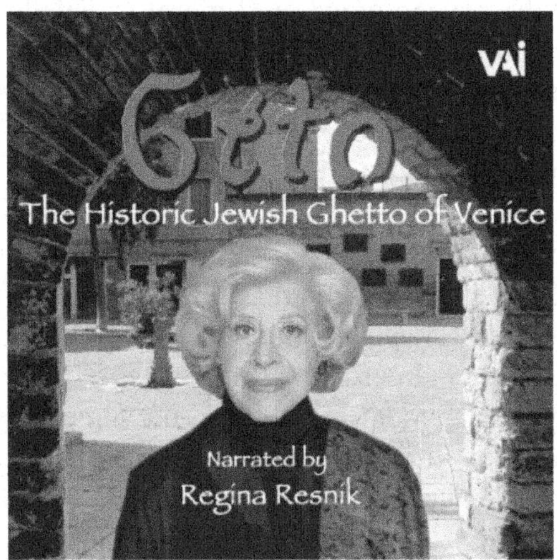


Figure 12 - Regina Resnik, Video Artists International, VAIMUSIC.COM

## Siegfried's Mother Was a Brooklyn Jew

In the heyday of my opera-going, in the late 1960's and 70's, Regina Resnik was a fabled presence. My first experiences at the Metropolitan Opera in New York were of its last season in the old house on Broadway and 39th Street. That year, 1964, saw the debut at the Met of Leonard Bernstein conducting a new production of Verdi's *Falstaff* under the exuberant direction of Franco Zeffirelli and featuring the now legendary Mistress Quickly of Regina Resnik.

In 1953, Resnik became the first Jewish woman to sing a leading role at Bayreuth after the war. I say the first but who knows? As we now appreciate, there are other artists whose lineage may have been more Jewish than has been acknowledged or verified. One keeps uncovering these things. Rise Stevens, for example. And Rudolf Bing!

And there are always rumors/ The latest for me was of Astrid Varnay. Other Jewish-American singers, contemporaries of Resnik, became sources of Jewish pride, among them Robert Merrill, Jan Peerce, Roberta Peters and Richard Tucker. But none of these stars sang Wagner; nor, with the exception of Peters as Zirbinetta, were they known for German repertoire.

Resnik was what might be called a singer's singer. Though not endowed with the most sumptuous voice, she was a serious artist, impressively musical, intelligent, a master of inflection, nuance and presence. Even among those whose criticism could be withering, she was taken seriously and commanded respect. It's not surprising that like Regine Crespin, another singer in the autumn of her career who became better known for her maturity and resourcefulness than tonal beauty, Resnik became a notable, beloved Carmen.

With the assistance of her son, Michael Philip Davis, Resnik wrote entries for a memoir that was never completed, but excerpts of which are with her papers at the New York Public Library and which are referred to in a fascinating, polished and painstakingly detailed documentary on her, *Regina Resnik, New York Original.* Here, in addition to some of the memoir excerpts, there is some surprising and edgy discussion of her experience at Bayreuth.

In those days Resnik, like the rest of us Jewish and non-Jewish Wagnerites, made her peace with the discomfort around Wagner in relationship to Hitler by the distinguishing of the man from his art that was standard at that time and still proclaimed by the majority of Wagnerites and music lovers. The music is sublime and the art is great, even if the man could be a monster. That was the standard understanding and response to the always hovering issue of Wagner's antisemitism.

"Goddamn anti-Semite," Davis recalls his mother once cursing in private. Because of the universality of this conspiracy to separate the art from the artist, Resnik was able to accommodate any misgivings and what her director and mentor at Bayreuth, Wieland Wagner, insisted on: "*Hier wird kein politik gesprochen. Nur Richard Wagner gesungen*" ("Here we won't talk politics. We're only going to sing Wagner"), Resnik remembered him saying at the outset of their collaboration.

At Bayreuth Resnik was housed by a local family. One day she was looking for one of her garments in the bedroom's large closet where she chanced upon some photographs from the war showing the man of the house in full Nazi regalia, saluting Hitler. Resnik recalls finding the pictures so upsetting that she immediately vacated these accommodations, spending the rest of her time in Bayreuth at a local inn.

Despite this incident and Resnik's sense of the background presence of Hitler-loyalist Winifred Wagner (Wieland's mother) and inevitably other Nazi-tainted closet skeletons, she did not try to probe further, to otherwise try to confront or discuss the incident or anything else political, with Wieland or others, including her Jewish colleague there at Bayreuth in 1953, George London (the first openly Jewish male singer at Bayreuth following the war?), or Clemens Krauss, who helped guide her transition into the mezzo repertoire, something Wieland likewise encouraged.

Like the rest of us opera people and Wagnerites, Resnik was content to be moving into the future regarding Wagner, Germans, Germany, music and opera. If there was still much work to be done in acknowledging what happened at Bayreuth and Wagner's role in it all, that's not something that even someone as observant, inquisitive, insightful and self-possessed as Resnik was motivated to break every protocol of priority and propriety to pursue, at least not at that time. It bears repeating that in those years, the details and extent of the Wagner family's collaborations with Hitler and Nazism were a lot less well known. Many years later, Resnik and Davis joined a salon, which the librettist William M. Hoffman spearheaded to try to address issues of resurgent anti-Semitism in the arts and elsewhere. That's where I met them.

Though Resnik's willingness to sing at Bayreuth and for Wieland Wagner may now raise questions, I don't recall any singer of comparable renown who refused to sing Wagner or refused on principle to sing at the new "de-Nazified" Bayreuth or elsewhere in Germany. In the world of opera, I don't recall any important artist ever saying publicly what Isaac Stern told me privately in the mid-1960's when I asked if he had ever played with von Karajan. "I don't play with Germans," he said summarily. In my sophomore year at the University of Wisconsin in Madison in 1966, I had worked with Fan Taylor in putting together and hosting the campus's impressive concert series, which included Janos Starker, Victoria de los Angeles, Isaac Stern and Hermann Prey, who brought the substantially

Wisconsin-German audience to its feet with an encore rendition of "*Heimat*."

Nor, according to Davis, did Resnik ever articulate any qualms about Wagner's antisemitism infecting his music. In those days to my knowledge, and notwithstanding the Israeli ban on Wagner, nor did any other leading musicians (e.g., Toscanini), Jewish or otherwise. I had wondered if it had occurred to Resnik that the character of Kundry, who laughed at Christ's agony, and who she portrayed in Venice, carried any perceived antisemitic weight for her.

But I did ask Davis about the Klytemnestras she did with Wieland, and about Herodias, another reincarnation, like Kundry, of the Wandering Jew. Davis and I did see eye-to-eye on the overt antisemitism of the Wilde-Strauss *Salome*. I also asked him about her work with von Karajan. But I did not ask him a more difficult question, one that might have vexed him as much as readers here: Did it ever occur to her or to him that her Jewishness might be figuring into the casting choices of von Karajan as well as Wieland Wagner?

Just as the casting of Grace Bumbry as "*Die Schwarze Venus*" in his legendary Bayreuth production of *Tannhäuser* whispers the possibilities—and dangers—of miscegenation (of Germans with other races), so does the casting of Jews in these roles—as Sieglinde, as Venus (which Resnik also sang), as Wotan, suggest racial shadings and layerings of possible meaning within character and plot.

People in opera and theater are now used to encountering these circumstances, which are evermore common in our evermore multi-racial world. That such innuendos would matter any more for Wieland Wagner or von Karajan than they would for others might seem myopic. But in glossing over such possible associations, would they be skirting the issue of honesty in the pretense that no one is thinking about or cares about these issues, only the singing and to a lesser extent the acting?

Such was the issue of race at the Met that no person of color ever sang there until Marion Anderson broke that barrier with her Met debut as Ulrica, the gypsy fortune-teller in *Un Ballo in Maschera* (featuring Jewish Roberta Peters in the trouser role of Oscar). In 1961, tenor George Shirley became the first African-American male to perform a major role (Ferrando in *Cosi Fan Tutte*) at the Met. In 2014, President Obama awarded Shirley the National Medal of Arts for his pioneering contributions to breaking racial barriers. Decades later, no one made much fuss when Leontyne Price sang Fiordiligi at the Met, at least not in print. And von Karajan did celebrated appearances and recordings of *Tosca, Carmen, Trovatore* and other operas with her. So why speculate on any negative associations of "Jewishness" in von Karajan's casting of Resnik as Klytemnestra or, more beningnly and affirmingly, as Orlofsky in *Die Fledermaus*? Such thinking can seem ungenerous and outdated as well as fixated, whatever skeletons von Karajan may have kept in the closet of his Nazi past.

Meanwhile, however, to pretend that racial issues no longer matter in Wagner, and that the proof of that is in having a Wotan who is black or Jewish, or a Sigelinde who is Jewish, seems more questionable in Wagner than elsewhere, no matter how simply and how disarming and moot such casting can seem to put to rest the question of Wagner's racism and anti-Semitism. Indeed, however ridiculous Wagner's anti-Semitism may seem to have been rendered by the casting of Jewish Friedrich Schorr, Bayreuth's and perhaps history's greatest Wotan and Hans Sachs, the worst of Wagner's messages on race prevailed, and metastasized.

Though Resnik distinguished herself in several Wagner roles and cast some light on the early post-war history of Bayreuth, calling her a Jewish Wagnerite would be something of a misnomer in that she was not engaged in rationalizing away or otherwise excusing Wagner's antisemitism, even if she recognized issues of conflict by appearing at Bayreuth. Some of the most distinguished figures in operatic history maintained their success with the Wagner repertoire before and during the war in the US and elsewhere, among them Lauritz Melchior, the greatest of all heldentenors, Lotte Lehman, a supreme Sieglinde, and Helen Traubel, a reigning Brunhilde and Isolde, in addition to the aforementioned Schorr who lived out the war years in New York, singing leading Wagner roles at the Met, along with Melchior, Traubel and Lehmann.

# Birgit Nilsson – Past, Present and the Future

Figure 13 - The tombstone of Birgit Nilsson (1918-2005), world-known Swedish opera singer, at the cemetery of Västra Karup, Skåne, Fredrik Tersmeden, Creative Commons

If a friend's listserve hadn't alerted me to it I would have missed something that, in the heyday of my Wagnerism, would have seemed a sentinel event: a documentary about the great *Heldensoprano* Birgit Nilsson. I've written elsewhere about my awareness of the difficulty of finding adequate singers for the Wagner repertoire and the rarity of finding great ones.

Probably the greatest singer of Wagner who ever lived was the *Heldentenor* Lauritz Melchior. There were other acclaimed Wagner *Helden*-singers who were contemporaries of Melchior such as Max Lorenz, Frida Leider, Kirsten Flagstad and Helen Traubel, and before them the legendary Lili Lehmann, Lilian Nordica, Ernestine Schumann-Heink and others; but none of those who were recorded rendered the Wagner repertoire so triumphantly and with such consistency as Melchior.

In the next generation, there were likewise notable singers of Wagner such as Martha Mödl, Astrid Varnay, Jon Vickers and Leonie

Rysanek—all personal favorites; but only one who evinced greatness in the biggest soprano roles of Brünhilde and Isolde as naturally and consistently as Melchior had rendered Siegfried, Tristan, Tannhauser, Walter and Lohengrin. That singer was Birgit Nilsson.

No other singer of our time, of the 1960's and 70's, made Wagnerites feel so at home. No other of her contemporaries exuded such confidence, commanded the stage with such presence and authority, had such clarion top notes or the ability to bestir audiences into such frenzies of enthusiasm. I was fortunate to hear Nilsson not only as Isolde and all 3 Brünhildes, but as Elektra, Lady Macbeth, Aida and Turandot, the latter two with Franco Corelli, whose thrilling dramatic tenor made his pairings with her comparable, for vocal power and brilliance, to those between Melchior and Flagstad.

The documentary on Nilsson that was shown on PBS was of course a lovefest, but it was also informative. There were scenes of her in her greatest roles as well as in some less well-known. Interview segments captured her wit, intelligence and self-possession. Like Joan Sutherland, because her stature was sustained at such peak levels where there really were no rivals, she had no need to play the diva and never did. On the contrary, she often spoke of her pride in being a farm girl. When ego would rear its head, as it did in her relations with conductor Herbert von Karajan, she never lost her cool. The documentary also highlighted her career-crowning association with Wieland Wagner, in whose productions at Bayreuth she gave some of her most acclaimed performances. This is a documentary that I would have kvelled over for weeks or months had I seen it a quarter century earlier.

Now, however, I can't help but note what's missing, at least for me. The thoughts I had while watching it would have been as iconoclastic and dystonic to my old Wagnerite self as I would anticipate them to be for Wagnerites today. In the heyday of the Nilsson-Wieland productions, the discourse on Wagner and antisemitism was in that fixed place of silence, of no-politics-just-art that allowed everyone to practice their Wagnerism with impunity. This taciturnity seemed to work as well for me as for everyone else. But Nilsson was no fool, and even though the discourse on Wagner was stuck resolutely in don't-ask-don't-tell, I now find myself, like Elsa in *Lohengrin*, wanting to know answers to forbidden questions.

Did Nilsson have any feelings about Wagner's antisemitism, Bayreuth's Nazi history and the Wagner family's associations with Hitler and Nazism? What was her family's situation during the war? What I would imagine is that whatever her thoughts or misgivings and whatever the details of her family history, the savvy Nilsson would not want to find herself, as Flagstad did, saying or doing things that might be misinterpreted as indifferent or reflective of her country's episodically controversial "neutrality" during the war; even if, in the silence surrounding her on this subject and however inadvertently, she would be doing precisely that.

Not surprisingly for such a committed Wagnerite, Alex Ross reviewed the Nilsson documentary and weighed in on his regard for Nilsson's gifts and accomplishments, never quite surmounting his preference for Nilsson's colleague Astrid Varnay. Many, including me, would agree with Ross that Varnay could be the more affecting singer and stage presence. But also not surprisingly, there were no probing comments or questions in Ross's column about Nilsson's or Varnay's close association with Wieland and Bayreuth. In those days, as today, such wafting questions were rarely articulated.

Did Nilsson have any feelings about the controversies that swirled around bringing Herbert von Karajan to the Met (in view of his Nazi party membership and collaborations during the war)? Her beefs with the famed and ill-famed conductor seemed primarily about the dark lighting in his productions and minor personality skirmishes. If there was anything else of concern, that's not something she would or was expected to weigh in on in those years, any more than today's Anna Netrebko could be expected to weigh in on her friend Vladimir Putin or gay rights issues in Russia.

Ned Rorem once accused me of being "like Reagan looking for Commies under every fig leaf" in my eagerness, as he saw it, to expose closetedness. Perhaps he was right. Moreover, perhaps this zeal in the heyday of homophobic oppression, as with Nazism and fascism colluders, is not counterbalanced by other considerations. I've pursued Joseph Horowitz for his Wagnerism and criticism of Toscanini, but have I given that criticism its due? However toweringly heroic an anti-fascist Toscanini was and however intoxicated Horowitz's Wagnerism might seem as a motivation for his critique of Toscanini, have I devalued that criticism because of its, for me, political incorrectness? Do we all tend to relegate the sins of those we favor?

A few days after seeing the Nilsson documentary, I chanced upon a community acquaintance who stereotypically—for opera, theater, film and diva queens—can always cite chapter and verse about any singer or actress. "So, speaking of Ethel Merman," I said in trying to greet him on his own turf, "guess what I saw on tv the other day? He couldn't guess. "That PBS documentary on Birgit Nilsson." His face lit up, he launched into a stream of Nilsson anecdotes, all of them familiar and seeming, like our repartee, the "faeries' basketball" (to use William M. Hoffman's phrase), the vernacular of a bygone era. When I finally managed to get a word in edgewise, I said something that wasn't meant to be so challenging, but which did emerge from my current preoccupations: "Nilsson was like Callas in never having said anything about the legions of gay people who were a cornerstone of her fan base." "Who cares?" he shot back, moments after saying something derogatory about the behavior of "opera queens" at the Met, without a hint of self-awareness.

All of which segued into my dinner conversation some nights later with my partner Arnie and Maryann Feola, Arnie's close friend and colleague from his years at the College of Staten Island. We had just seen the Mike Leigh film, *Peterloo*, about what might be called generic fascism, in this case British and historical, and we were talking about our writing. Maryann, a specialist in the works of Christopher Marlowe, has written an eloquent memoir, *The Geography of Shame*, about her Italian family history and its afflictions of sexism, abuse, addiction and codependence.

Maryann asked how my current writing was going. After summary comments, I observed something I've otherwise had trouble articulating, even to myself: that I'm not sure who the audience is or would be for my current writing because what I have to say is not something that most opera and Wagner people would care to read or discuss. So who or what *am* I doing this writing for? I was at once pleased and surprised at how quickly and clearly the answers were there. It's for myself, for Jewish and non-Jewish Wagnerites, and for the future.

# Deconstructing a German Documentary on Max Lorenz—Wagner's Mastersinger and Hitler's Gay, Jewish-Married Siegfried

There is nothing that conveys, however inadvertently, a clearer picture of why and how Jewish Wagnerites were able to be so comfortable in our Wagnerism than *Wagner's Mastersinger-Hitler's Siegfried*, a 2009 film documentary by Eric Schulz and Claus Wischmann about the life and times of the celebrated *Heldentenor* Max Lorenz. Here we are led to believe the narrative promulgated by postwar Germany and Bayreuth apologists that most of the collaboration between Bayreuth and Hitler was circumstantial and had more to do with the operations of the Festival than what otherwise appeared to be enthusiastic support. If you knew nothing else about Winifred Wagner, who ran Bayreuth in the years leading up to and during the war, you would come away from this film with some acceptance, understanding and even compassion for the ordeals she faced in navigating between Nazi *fatwahs* against individuals deemed immoral and/or criminal by virtue of their behavior or genetics—i.e., homosexual Lorenz and his Jewish wife—and the exigencies of casting and running the show. On learning of Lorenz's homosexuality, Hitler wanted Lorenz taken out. Without Lorenz, however, as Winifred put it to her putative lover, Hitler, the Festival would have to shut down. It's true that Winifred helped some Jewish artists to escape persecution, most notably Lorenz's Jewish wife Lotte, but it's these details, rather than the bigger picture, that shape the film's narrative.

The impressions you are left with by the filmmakers and narrators, who include tenors Waldemar Kmentt and Rene Kollo, Jewish-born soprano Hilda Zadek and legendary lieder master, baritone Dietrich Fischer-Dieskau, are a summation of the official German post-Nazi view of the relationships between Hitler and Bayreuth, between Nazism and Wagner, and in the bigger picture between Germany and Nazism. Germans and everybody else loved Max Lorenz, and rightly so, whatever his sexual inclinations and even if his wife were Jewish. He was a dignified, professional and courageous artist, an impressive singer in repertoire where there were few rivals or even understudies, especially after the political emigration of Lauritz Melchior from Bayreuth and Germany.

It's telling, however, that Melchior is not mentioned in the documentary, which tacitly exonerates those who, like Lorenz, showed bravery and somehow retained their humanity and principles in the face of Hitler's madness. The film is very German in seeing as heroic those who stayed and endured, in contrast to those who fled, like Melchior, Arturo Toscanini, Lotte Lehmann and Wagner's granddaughter Friedelind Wagner (most of them likewise unmentioned in the film), to say nothing of those who were forced out because of their being Jewish or married to Jews. *Hitlerjugend* Fischer-Dieskau is the most notable of these voices in the documentary. By what he does and doesn't say, he captures his and the film's ethos and viewpoint: that many or even most of the Germans who stayed were not raving antisemites and not rabidly pro-Hitler. They did what they did in service to their country and countrymen. With such clarity of purpose and commitment in mind, of a sense of security about their having done their best to fulfill their duties as German soldiers and citizens, they feel they have thereby retained their honor and dignity.

## Manuela Hoelterhoff Struggles with The Bigger Picture

Figure 14 - Max Lorenz and Maria Callas, 1955, Pinterest

The Max Lorenz documentary is from 2009. In 2017, the *Wall Street Journal* and Pulitzer-Prize winning music and arts writer Manuela Hoelterhoff gave an insightful and arresting presentation at the American Academy in Berlin on Lorenz and his world based on this documentary (the lecture is available online). Her vignettes were numerous, some of them sterling, and related in a manner at once personal and authoritative. Turns out Lorenz and Melchior were friends and remained in correspondence during and after the war. In her later years, Maria Callas wrote to Lorenz reminiscing warmly about the *Tristan* they had sung together decades earlier and wondering if he might have a tape of it. There was no *Tristan* tape. As Hoelterhoff also noted, Lorenz never wrote a memoir reflecting on his experience.

Figure 15 - Manuela Hoelterhoff, Parterre Box, parterre.com

At the end of the Q&A with Hoelterhoff, an inevitable question arose from the audience: Did Lorenz ever express remorse about having stayed in Germany and thereby, however reluctantly, facilitating Hitler's hostage-taking of German culture? Though Hoelterhoff did not use the analogy to Richard Strauss, the feelings one has for Lorenz can feel similar. Neither Lorenz nor Strauss was ardently or even appreciably pro-Nazi, pro-Hitler or antisemitic (*Salome* notwithstanding), and both were bound to Jews by marriage and close personal and professional relationships (notwithstanding the suicide of Strauss's Jewish librettist, Stefan Zweig).

It's difficult to deeply resent either of these passive, facultative collaborationists. But should they have renounced Germany and Hitler as some of their most illustrious colleagues did—e.g., Melchior, Toscanini, Lotte Lehmann or Friedelind Wagner, even at great personal risk to themselves, those closest to them and their beloved musical institutions, and even if it meant they might suffer the same fate of being thought of as betraying Germany? Hoelterhoff, like the documentary she extols and presents, doesn't have the answer to these difficult questions and hesitates when asked to do so. Rather, she thinks that maybe we need to consider how hard it is for people to give up their lives and responsibilities and leave a homeland. In the case of Max Lorenz and as so eloquently captured and articulated in both the documentary and Hoelterhoff's commentary, it's difficult to disagree.

If we reconfigure the question, however, the bigger picture emerges. How grateful are we that heroic figures like Toscanini, Melchior, Lotte Lehmann and Friedelind Wagner, at considerable risk and cost to their own lives and careers, stood up to Hitler, Nazism and fascism? The answer: Very. Do we wish that Richard Strauss had taken a comparable stand? The answer: Unquestionably. And finally, however sympathetic we might feel to those who chose less heroic alternatives, like Hitler's gay Siegfried Max Lorenz who acted in real measure to protect his Jewish wife, do we wish he had done so as well? While we might agree that judgment is a complicated, difficult and risky business and that hindsight is easier than foresight, the answers to that question would be, nonetheless and likewise surpassingly, Yes. Even if it had meant the shutting down of the Bayreuth Festival for want of adequate casting? All the more so Yes.

The Lorenz documentary concludes with an unsentimental look at the singer in his later years. Though Lorenz's career was long and distinguished, he was plagued by a sadness that seems less than fully explained by the waning of his powers and the supercessions of time. If he had any regrets about decisions made or not made, in letters, interviews or elsewhere, the documentary makes no mention of them.

## Richard Wagner and Women: Eva Rieger and Melanie Yolles

Figure 16 - Wagner's Women by Eva Rieger, amazon.com

Eva Rieger, feminist and musicologist, has done notable work on sex and gender in Wagner's life and works. Like women among the famed composers and musicians of Western culture, her book, *Richard Wagner's Women* (2011), is all too singular a contribution not only to the subject of women in Wagner but to the much bigger subject of women in opera. As Rieger points out, what history there is has been neglected because of sexism. While Rieger's work feels fresh and contemporary, her conclusions about Wagner's women are less than startling: that Wagner gave the men who were heroes the most heroic musical signatures and shadings, while those used for women are less heroic and often used for villains, and that Wagner's love affairs and experience with women in his personal life are reflected in his operas. "In spite of women's inferior status and restricted scope," she concludes in a talk on Wagner and Gender at the Bayreuth Institute that can be seen on YouTube, "they are elevated by their singing which shows greatness and strength."

Rieger is also the author of *Friedelind Wagner: Wagner's Rebellious Grandaughter*. Rieger was helpful to me in trying to understand Friedelind's experience vis a vis Wagner's works. In the course of a series of email exchanges with me she forthrightly acknowledged that she didn't have much to offer that was clarifying regarding Friedelind's thinking or not thinking about Wagner's antisemitism or anti-Semitism in her grandfather's operas. In those days, one might surmise, those of Friedelind's ilk and acquaintance, including close friends like Toscanini, thought as everyone did: that Wagner's anti-Semitism was apart from rather than intrinsic to the operas.

Rieger's respect for the problem of antisemitism in Wagner's life and works is earnest and bound up with her own family background of Nazism. Her father had joined the Nazi party early on but had helped Jews in the later years of the war. As for Bayreuth's remaining a beacon for the old Nazi guard in the early post war years, she sent me an article on the continuation of Nazi colleagues working at Bayreuth after 1945.

Alas, a subsequent exchange with Rieger was more fraught. It was just before Gay Pride 2018 here in New York City. 2019 would be the year of World Pride, celebrating the 50th Anniversary of the Stonewall Inn rebellion that is widely accepted as the demarcator of the modern Gay Liberation Movement, which had antecedents in Germany and America during the preceding decades.

I had been perusing Rieger's book, *Richard Wagner's Women*, as well as a Wagner blog site that seemed somewhat gay-oriented and which made reference to Rieger, when a stream-of-consciousness thought occurred to me. Might Friedelind Wagner, who never married and never had children and whose documented romantic life appears to have been as adrift as her professional ambitions, have been lesbian? For that matter, was Rieger lesbian? I don't remember having had either of those thoughts on reading Rieger's biography of Friedelind. And I had nothing to base these questions on regarding Rieger herself except what we used to call "gaydar." Naively, and with that "gaydar" sense of Rieger as extended family, I emailed my double-headed question to her.

What I did was based on what I assumed to be a level of friendship, though I did qualify my inquiry, allowing that I meant no disrespect and was open to corrective information. However artless my inquiry may have read, I was unprepared for the intensity of Rieger's response. First, she claimed to have no recollection of our having corresponded, even though there had been multiple points of reference and email exchanges. Beyond which her responses seemed unduly defensive:

> Your questions might seem to be "simple and straightforward" to you, but they are not for me. As I wrote, you can read for yourself in my Friedelind biography. She certainly was not a lesbian, but she was very much engaged in an intensive friendship when on the Isle of Man in 1940. This may be due to the fact that the prison was only for women, the men's camp was on the other side of the island.
>
> I know women who are married with men, yet have side-affairs with women, and of young women who sleep with women and sometimes with men, and I know of couples who call themselves "lesbian" but haven't slept with one another for years, what would you call them? These labels are historically explainable but superfluous today.
>
> I do not feel inclined to reply to your question about my sexual life, as I do not know you, besides, I do not deduct my identity from my such labels. Heterosexual people are usually not asked whether they are gay or "normal", so why should I reply? [In my previous email to her I had said that I agreed with her that "uptightness" about sexual preference is "very old fashioned."] You misunderstood me: I did not say that "uptightness about being gay or lesbian is very old-fashioned", I meant that asking people what sex-life they have is absolutely outdated and superfluous in a Western world where everything is allowed.

Eva Rieger is an impressive scholar who has done singular work on gender and music, and who has made notable contributions to Wagner scholarship. I have the utmost respect for her intelligence, seriousness, courage and accomplishments. Everything she says here is, of course, true. And add to all this an article that appeared in the *New York Times* on Gay Pride Day laying out the confusion of today's plethora of acronyms (LGBT, LGBTQ, LGBTQI, etc.), saying in comparable terms exactly what Rieger is saying and what I myself have often said and say about the complexities of gender identity, preference and experience.

But have we really come so far in our progress that the terms gay and lesbian can no longer casually be used, especially when in many locales those identities and associated behaviors are still religiously and legally proscribed? And do they not still apply very broadly, notwithstanding the wide range and scale of behaviors suggested by Kinsey many decades ago, and the individual variance that we now see and accept as extending to everyone?

And does this mean that we can no longer even raise the issue of someone's sexuality in historical context or as a political issue? In gay life there have been so many instances of people staying in the closet not because of this complexity of sexual preference and experience so much as a way of not having to take a stand in defense of a minority whose community resources they are availing themselves of but political responsibility for which they abjure. In the guise of principled intellectual honesty, what emerges can seem more like taking the easy way out and having it both ways.

Did Susan Sontag remain in the closet primarily because of her intellectual commitment to not erroneously categorizing herself, or did she not want to sully and jeopardize her unique status as a cultural icon by being "pigeonholed" as "lesbian"? It's my sense that despite the unassailable truth of the fluidity and complexity of sexual preference and experience, in times that remain fraught with homophobia and with regard to historical figures who may have been navigating these prejudices in their own lives and times, these questions remain legitimate.

With all due respect, I can't retract my questions about Friedelind Wagner and Eva Rieger as misguided or inappropriate. Meanwhile, I don't recall Rieger having such defensiveness about the homosexuality of Friedelind's father (Wagner's son) Siegfried Wagner, who was known to be homosexual nothwithstanding his marriage to Winifred Wagner and siring four children with her.

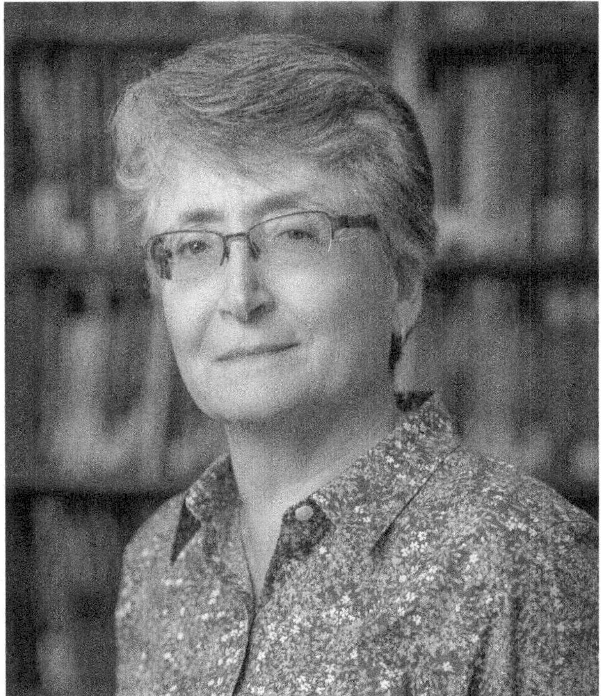

Figure 17 - Melanie Yolles, New York Public Library

Another Jewish Wagnerite of my acquaintance is Melanie Yolles. Melanie has done decades of distinguished organizational and archival work for the New York Public Library and in fact is a curator of our (my and my partner Arnie Kantrowitz's) papers there. Our papers are in the LGBT collections, Resnik's are in the music division.

Almost immediately Melanie and I struck up a friendship based on our shared interest in Wagner. We were both Wagnerites and Jewish Wagnerites at that. There was more commonality. I never met Melanie's father, Dr. Stanley Yolles, a distinguished figure in American Psychiatry and mental health. Although psychiatry was in its psychoanalytically homophobic heyday, Dr. Yolles was ahead of his time in denouncing what he saw as "stupid, punitive laws" on drug use. Eventually he was forced out of his position as head of the National Institute of Mental Health, which he held from 1964-1970, by the Nixon administration.

Melanie has said that Jewishness and Israel were important to her father. As for her Wagnerism, I didn't get the sense that it smarted for her father, though he would not himself venture travel to Germany and would have been appalled, Melanie sensed, if she had visited Bayreuth.

By contrast, Joseph Horowitz's Wagnerism may have seemed more troubled and challenging to his father, Dr. Jacob Horowitz, who I got to know in my work in addiction medicine. While Dr. Yolles wouldn't have been particularly dismayed that his daughter was a Wagnerite, Dr. Horowitz, by contrast, probably was dismayed to learn that his son Joseph was such an ardent Wagnerite. Dr. Horowitz oversaw addiction services for the New York State Department of Health and we would meet and chat annually. Knowing I was Jewish and a more ambivalent Wagnerite than his son, who I would later meet, Dr. Horowitz would regale me with stories of his experience in the armed forces contingent that liberated Bayreuth, of his bringing home some scattered scenery materials from that tour, including what may have been a Siegfried's sword. Our conversations would always end with his urging me to observe the major Jewish holidays and take those days off at work.

Figure 18 - Understanding Toscanini by Joseph Horowitz

I don't recall Dr. Horowitz ever directly addressing his son's Wagnerism. My suggestion that he must be very proud to have a son of such learning and accomplishment was met with a reticence which, at the time, I took for modesty of pride. *Understanding Toscanini* is dedicated to "my parents and my sister." Dr. Horowitz not only fought in the WW2 against the Nazis and was part of the occupying army at Bayreuth, but was, of course, of the generation that so revered Toscanini for his heroism in standing up to Mussolini and fascism, for sustaining a beating from thugs, and for refusing to return to Bayreuth under Hitler.

This is the Toscanini who comes under such intense personal attack for being, as Horowitz tries to depict him, a superficial metacultural icon who bears a lot of responsibility as the template for the crassly commercial cult of personality and celebrity that became increasingly predominant in the worlds of classical music and opera. I may be venturing too far into conjecture here, but it's hard not to read into *Understanding Toscanini* a deeply personal attack on the generation of Horowitz's parents, on those who participated in the "cultism" (as Joe repeatedly stigmatizes it for being) around Toscanini and indirectly on those who were reflexively uncomfortable with Wagnerism in light of their own Judaism and a general sense of Wagner's proto-Nazi role in the Holocaust.

Horowitz is persuasive in showing how reverence for Europe and its culture—epitomized by the "cult" of Toscanini— had some regrettable consequences for concert going and music appreciation in America. With so much adoration of the masters and their celebrity conductors there was arguably a neglect of American arts and artists, even if cause and effect here is neither simple nor clear.

In the case of Wagner, around whom cultism reached a level of fervor and adoration that swept up Horowitz himself and is otherwise without precedent in the history of cultism in music and the arts, Horowitz's *Wagner Nights* wants us to see Wagner primarily as a protean force for progressive social and artistic change. Why not be comparably affirming about Toscanini, whose moral accountability and heroism set a standard for artists that has rarely been matched and whose conducting even Horowitz has to admit was great, whatever the qualifiers? "Yes, but…" we want to proclaim each of the many times on so many of the pages where Horowitz trashes as "cultism" —like Trump indicting "fake news" on CNN— the celebration and promotion of Toscanini that is seen as leading to the selling of personality-cult figures like Herbert von Karajan. Perhaps we'd be more willing to take Horowitz more seriously if he were more honest about his addiction to the cult of Richard Wagner.

My relationship with Melanie Yolles took its own circuitous route. Bright, articulate and attractive, Melanie inspired me to greater awareness of the complexity of transgender identity conflicts and issues, in her own life and beyond. After years of psychoanalysis, she eventually settled into her life-partnership with a woman, photographer RoughAcres.

From the beginning of our association, Melanie and I were drawn to each other. Both of us were strongly opinionated and though we often disagreed, we were both Wagnerites, Jewish and queer. The problem, or what seemed to be the problem, that emerged is that at a personal level of deep conviction Melanie could only go so far with me in my journey away from Wagnerism. My trajectory was not hers, and my failure to appreciate this better led to a painful disappointment for me, especially her decision not to attend the launch of my *Confessions of a Jewish Wagnerite*. However divergent we may have been on Wagner controversies, in my own egotism and codependence I had somehow failed to appreciate the extent of her conflict with and disaffection from growing estrangement from Wagnerism.

Or was it something more subterranean? The problem for me was that I was never sure what was genuine difference of opinion versus some version of "fairies' basketball," that gay jockeying for dominance around issues in opera, more often performance values than issues of greater substance. I remember one occasion of having a strong sense of this. I'd said or written something to Melanie about Christa Ludwig, about the ravishing beauty of her voice and her incredible musicianship in rendering so irresistible Venus's seduction of Tannhauser (in the Solti recording for Decca-London). Melanie shot back that she found Ludwig's voice irritating, didn't care for her. I paused for a moment, then responded. Did she have any idea how eccentric this opinion was? Was there even one other individual anywhere who shared it? Alternatively, was this a more psychological reaction—to me as a man or gay man and/or otherwise veering too close or skirmishing for hegemony in our relationship, with its ultimate prize of credibility about Wagner? Alternatively and psychoanalytically speaking, to what extent was this disharmony transferential?

Another perspective that may be pertinent here is the tension that can exist between factions of the LGBTQ movement and community. While GLBTQ history boasts many impressive examples of coexistence, cooperative endeavor and achievement—e.g., the priceless contributions of lesbians to ACT UP and AIDS—there have also been many moments of disjunction and schism. Was the fault line that can exist between lesbians and gay men, or between mainstream gay men and transgender persons, a factor in the intermittent tensions between us?

More generically, I learned to back away from fairies basketball, so inevitably fraught with extraneous psychology and emotions, and I never got heatedly engaged in challenging lesbian and transgender critiques of gay men, the validity of which I respected. Because Melanie is keenly intelligent and has stores of information and ideas about Wagner and opera, and because she is a custodian of our papers, I learned to try to give her whatever space and freedom she seemed to need to express herself, especially with regard to her love of Wagner. It has been my hope that she would find a way to write about Wagner and women, ideally some paragraphs for this chapter. I think it could help illuminate findings such as those mined by Joseph Horowitz and Ross around the Wagnerism of Willa Cather and other women, and on linkages between Wagnerism and the early women's movement in America.

It's easy to imagine how appealing Brünhilde and the Valkyries must be at the level of acknowledging the courage and strength of women and in their ability to be warriors. All of which would probably supercede other more misogynistic prototypes and stereotypes of women to be found in Wagner as well as everywhere else in opera, which doesn't yet have a single female—or for that matter a black—composer, past or present, of preeminence.

Meanwhile, Melanie can seem selective in her reactions. While she can forgive and recalibrate the sexism of *Cosi Fan Tutte* as a vicissitude of the opera's surpassing humanity, she has made it clear that violence against women is something she has real trouble with in opera—e.g., *Pagliacci* and *Otello*, operas she says she will no longer see for that reason.

Whatever our differences, Melanie and I have maintained our friendship and dialogue over decades about Wagner, opera and our lives. After years of ever-longer periods of non-communication, we were back in touch around my decision to proceed with the current collection, *On The Future of Wagnerism*. Over lunch at Bryant Park Grill, I handed her a first draft of the manuscript (for which this chapter hadn't yet been conceived), and she agreed to be my guest for the last *Parsifal* of the Met's 2018 season. I had never seen this production directed by Francois Girard, now some years old, with its flows of blood and its cosmic images (conjuring the musico-dramatic ether of *Parsifal*, where, as Gurnemanz famously explains to *Der Reine Tor*, Parsifal, "Here does time become space."). The production has been a hit with the critics as well as the public. Melanie had already seen it twice this season alone.

In the heyday of my own Wagnerism, as I recall it, and even now, we Wagnerites were so grateful just to be able to see these extremely taxing operas that tolerance and appreciation tended to prevail, regardless of deficiencies or disappointments, as was invariably the case with lead singers. In fact, it's very rare for leading Wagner singers, always at a premium, to be all-out great. The Birgit Nilssons have been very few and far between. And there have been no other Lauritz Melchiors. The closest after the war was Jon Vickers, who did sing Parsifal, Siegmund and a rare Tristan but who recoiled from Walther, Siegfried and Tannhäuser. Even when the singers have been mediocre, we were always grateful that they were doing these roles at all. While booing not infrequently greets some of the more controversial contemporary stagings at Bayreuth and elsewhere, enthusiasm and gratitude remain the predominant reactions of Wagnerites for singers. In the less than incandescent but honorably rendered *Parsifal* I saw with Melanie, underwhelmingly conducted (as likewise noted by Joseph Horowitz) by the Met's new *Wunderkind*, Yannick Nezet-Seguin, and featuring the now legendary but at this performance somewhat undersung Gurnemanz of Rene Pape, such was the collective reverence and gratitude—rather like that of the knights for the unveiling of the Grail—that I don't think I heard a single cough or candy wrapper crinkle during the entire 6 hours.

Figure 19 - From the Legend of The Wandering Jew by Gustave Dore, public domain.

Before the performance, Melanie and I met for an early light dinner in the Alice Tully foyer. *Parsifal*, one of the longest of operas, began at 6 pm. It felt good to be back at the opera with Melanie, even with the potential for eruption of the differences of opinion between us. Knowing how happy Wagnerites have been with this production and how enthralled they remain with the opera itself, I opted for being polite and affirming. Following the first intermission, Melanie's curiosity got the better of her and she asked, What did I "*really* think"?

I remained friendly and positive about re-experiencing this musically magnificent artwork, but several days later, I sent her a more considered opinion. Likening *Parsifal* to the Passion Play at Oberammergau, in sync with Wagner's own description of it as a *Bühnenweihfestspiel* (play for the consecration of the stage), I conveyed my sense of it as a special festival and religious work that belongs less on the world's stages than, as Wagner originally intended it, primarily under the aegis of Bayreuth:

> In response to your wanting to know what did I "*really* think," I do have stronger impressions and feelings that were inchoate during the performance and over the ensuing days but which are coming into

sharper focus now. Kundry may not be specified as a Jew, or as representing Jews, just as Beckmesser isn't specifically said to be Jewish, nor the Nibelungs, even though their "Jewishness" is obvious at multiple levels, whatever the ambiguities and however enshrouded they are in great art. This is likewise the case in *Parsifal*. Here, however, the ante is upped considerably. In Wagner's portrayal of Kundry is the fiercest and most damaging anti-Semitic slander ever perpetrated and on a scale of culture and exposure, and with a palpable rage (Wagner's), that is without precedent—that of the Jews as having laughed at Christ's torment. The only comparable defamation is the "blood libel" of Jews using Christian babies and blood to prepare the Passover seder matzos.

A less serious and less disastrous but nonetheless comparably anti-Semitic slander in *Parsifal* is in Wagner's portrayal, in Klingsor, of Jewish self-emasculation—of Jewish masochism accompanied by the most bitter envy and resentment (like Alberich, Mime and Beckmesser)—in efforts to be accepted by the worlds of "authentic" mankind and humanity. (That some think Klingsor's self-castration is about circumcision did elicit bemusement in these otherwise all-too-humorless ponderings.) While Jewish masochism is all too real a phenomenon, the *mitleid* that is the ostensible subject and theme of *Parsifal* is completely missing from Wagner's depiction of Klingsor. The exposing of Wagner's sadism and pitilessness in depicting this trope of Jewish character inspired the genius stroke of [Bayreuth Centennial *Ring* cycle director Patrice] Chéreau's having Mime in concentration camp garb.

As a result of no longer being in the old reflexive denial about my real feelings and misgivings—of awakening, like Kundry, to the reality of what I've been party to—I feel vaguely and chronically heartsick as the fallout of seeing *Parsifal* again plays out.

But isn't the *mitleid* Parsifal and Gurnemanz feel for Kundry mitigating? Wagner would certainly have us think so, and perhaps at some level of internal conflict, he really does share that compassion for these *miserables* of his own creation. Meanwhile, however, the damage done by capturing and broadcasting the perceived nature and crimes of the Jews cannot be undone. Love your enemy, have compassion for your enemy, Wagner is saying, perhaps with some, albeit ambivalent, sincerity, but obfuscating the fact that he is at the same time circumscribing and indicting the Jews as enemies of humanity.

The world of Wagner is a deeply troubled place, certainly for Jews, but for everyone else as well. It's not a place I have any inclination to keep returning to beyond what comes with the territory of being an opera lover, observer and critic, and as the vessel of my writing. Not so unlike Kundry, I keep being summoned against my will.

Experiencing the Act 1 transformation scene of *Parsifal* at Bayreuth was the single most intense musical-operatic experience of my life. That experience is indelible. It can never be erased or changed. That said, however, I've journeyed far to have my own sense of *Parsifal* as proto-Nazi art, and of Wagner's art, whatever else it may also be, as Nazi art. Though Nazi art is by no means perforce *kitsch*, closer scrutiny of the relationship between the two is unavoidable.

I'd liken my own coming to awareness to that of Siegfried. Once you've tasted the blood of the dragon and see what you see, you can't go back to not seeing.

The same might be said of Parsifal himself. Once he sees what he sees and develops compassion, he can't go back to being the pure fool. At my clearest and best, I've come to have the kind of compassion for Wagner and Wagnerites that Wagner and Parsifal have for Kundry.

Enjoy *Semiramide*. As you know, Wagner was fond [if also critical] of Rossini. Oh, and if you're traveling in today's storm, be safe.

Ever,
Larry

During the first intermission of that performance of *Parsifal*, Melanie said she wanted to introduce me to her friends, a bevy of Wagnerites. I don't know what she may have told them about me ahead of my meeting them, but I sensed neither friendliness nor curiosity from them. In fact such was their avoidance of interaction that I forewent a second round during the next intermission. Instead, Melanie joined me in the foyer where we chatted with my friend David del Tredici, the neo-romantic composer and as such a Wagnerite of sorts.

In a subsequent exchange, Melanie admitted that her Wagner and opera friends are production-and-performance oriented in their appreciation and aren't much interested in scholarship or social-political-historical controversies. She also indulged some soul-searching around her own Wagnerism, describing it as a drug, a not uncommon description by Wagnerites themselves (Susan Sontag has said that her Wagner friends often speak of it as such). As I told her, I thought Melanie's description of Wagner as "a drug and addiction" was "honest and accurate."

Why do Wagnerites recoil from me? It seems a question worth asking. Although I get and accept that most Wagnerites aren't on the same page as me, I can't help but think that they should be sufficiently interested in Wagner and Wagnerism to consider viewpoints that challenge. Questions of Jews, Jewishness, anti-Semitism and internalized anti-Semitism are everywhere in the worlds of Wagner and Wagnerism. So what is it about my work that so strongly renders me, and for that matter Gottfried Wagner, as *personae non gratae* in these milieus?

Surpassingly, I think it's the sense that we are activists and revisionists trying to communicate with a world that doesn't want to see its status quo messed with. Typically, activists, like prophets, are initially despised and rejected. And when the activists are Jews or partisans of Jewishness, outcries over recurrent anti-Semitism can seem the way Black, Hispanic, feminist or gay activism can seem to mainstream and majority whites, even those who think of themselves liberal and tolerant. If too confrontational, activist voices will be rejected as "shrill," "uppity" "pushy" and "whiney"—as judgmental and demanding. Self-effacing and conforming Jews are tolerated, even welcome, the way assimilationist Blacks, women and gays are, but the discernibly angry and accusatory ones are seen as off-putting, even menacing. Ultimately for Wagnerites, the issue seems less about antisemitism per se than about maintaining their status quo, a picture that comes into sharper focus in the context of addiction.

Put simply, I don't think most Wagnerites care that much how these controversies play out, or that they even exist, so long as they can continue to have their drug of Wagner on a regular and dependable basis. Most addicts, however also in denial, have thought about the problems associated with their addiction and are in some measure open to discussing them, just as most mainstream, middle-class whites, even those who lean conservative politically, are open to discussing problems of antisemitism, racism, sexism and homophobia. Wagnerites by and large have no problem discussing Wagner's antisemitism. On the contrary, they seem to tacitly relish these controversies. They'll admit there are issues, with which many of them seem sincerely to commiserate, but they feel stuck between a rock and a hard place and want to move on.

When push comes to shove, they don't want anything to interfere with their guilty pleasure. But take the additional step of threatening Wagnerites with a withdrawal of their drug—by relegating, deprioritizing and thereby delimiting access to Wagner performances, with their tacit elements of ritual and group bonding, of communion—and you will encounter a sharper level of resistance. They can sense that the fallout would leave them feel bereft, deprived, in withdrawal and craving, like the knights without their Grail; like addicts without their drugs.

Addicts can agree with criticism and speak of reform in principle but have a tougher time of it in reality. In reality, addicts don't take deprivation easily or willingly. As Hermione Gingold put it in her cabaret song, "Cocaine" (from her revue, Live at the Café de Paris), "You can take away my kisses and hugs, but don't take away my dangerous drugs!"

## Joseph Horowitz's "Lifetime Obsession With Wagner"

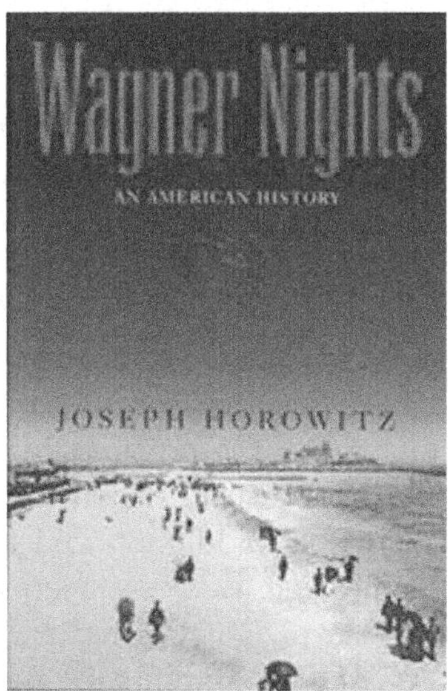


Figure 20 - Wagner Nights by Joseph Horowitz

While some people might take offense at my description of them as ardent Wagnerites, with its implication of a failure of balanced, critical discernment, others might delight in being appreciated as such. Perhaps no one more so than Joseph Horowitz. Like Alex Ross, Horowitz has become a Knight of the Holy Grail of the Legacy of Wagner, fortified with impressive knowledge and critical skills. While this has long been clear, I was nonetheless somewhat amazed to read a recent description of his own Wagnerism—by Horowitz himself—as "my lifetime obsession with Wagner." There it is, spelled out on his blog, The Unanswered Question, in his commentary on a restored version of the Visconti film, *Ludwig*.

Is it plausible to have a lifetime obsession with a composer other than Wagner? George Perle had something like that for Alban Berg, and there are probably many other examples. But only with Wagner does the invocation of "obsession" raise the specter of cultism and questions of sobriety. Just as Wagnerism has no counterpart in all of musical culture—as we've observed, there's no Mahlerism, Verdiism or Mozartism—so the "obsession" with Wagner that Horowitz admits to and that we otherwise know to be common among Wagnerites is likewise unique in musical culture. While devotion to Mahler, Mozart and Verdi can be impressive, and periodically smack of obsession with this musicologist or that conductor or music lover, it gives further testimony to there being no other following of a composer comparable to Wagner for cultism and obsession.

His commentary on *Ludwig* is vintage Horowitz. On the surface, it's informative, accessible, interesting, well documented and open to discussion. None of what Horowitz says is assailable regarding how beautiful the film is and how thoughtful it is in conveying the relationship between Ludwig and Wagner. Horowitz cannot be accused of ignorance of European history and its antisemitism. Nor can he be accused of ignorance of Wagner's essay "Judaism in Music," which he has acknowledged to be "egregiously anti-Semitic." The problem is that Horowitz is otherwise and mostly so busy affirming all the things he finds so wonderful in Wagner's life and art while defending them against criticism of Wagner's excesses and prejudices, as well as against those who want to indict Wagner as "a monster" (as Horowitz tends to perceive a lot of Wagner criticism), that he loses sobriety, propriety, circumspection and perspective.

Like me, Horowitz fell deeply in love with Wagner. But unlike me, he is still battling at the ramparts in defense of Wagner. Like Trump's lawyer Michael Cohen, he's willing to keep taking bullets for the master. Such sweet suffering unto martyrdom is something Horowitz, like Don Quixote, is aiming to do yet again, in yet another book on Wagner, this time on "Wagner the man." Should another tidal wave of antisemitism reach Horowitz's doorstep one day in this new post WW II era where the possibility of exploiting Wagner's antisemitism could serve a new Hitler, one can't help but wonder if Horowitz's altruism for Wagner would be held up, like and with that of Hermann Levi, as a proof of the rightness of Wagner's antisemitism.

In his spirited and endless defense of Wagner, Horowitz is too scrupulous and conscientious a scholar not to consider the greater range of critical inquiry he might face. If confronted as to why he seems to care so little about the composer's antisemitism, he would doubtless affirm that issues of antisemitism aren't given greater scrutiny and emphasis by him because they are not warranted. The Achilles heel of Horowitz's Wagner and Wagnerism is not that his descriptions and affirmations of Wagner and Wagnerism are indefensible, it's that they are excessively and conspicuously removed from the broader context of concerns about Wagner, racism and antisemitism. Pretending there's nothing there or giving minimal lip service to them, as we all did in previous generations and discourses, is no longer a tenable or credible approach.

Visconti's *Ludwig* makes a compelling case for the humanity of the King and the mutual depth and fecundity of his relationship with Wagner. But the growing issues of Jews and antisemitism in the background of the relationship between philo-Semitic Ludwig and increasingly, virulently anti-Semitic Wagner are scarcely broached in Visconti's film and not mentioned at all in Horowitz's commentary, just as racism and antisemitism in America are scarcely mentioned in *Wagner Nights*.

Horowitz, like Visconti, may well be within his rights to relegate this subject as not central to the greater history of the intimate relationship between Ludwig and Wagner. But for someone like Horowitz, who is otherwise asking us to look between the lines for surpassing meaning, not to mention the background issue of antisemitism between Ludwig and Wagner, especially around the premiere of *Parsifal*, seems willfully obfuscatory.

The marginalization of racism and antisemitism in America in *Wagner Nights* and *Understanding Toscanini* seems likewise to serve the cause of obfuscation. Yes, Horowitz is writing primarily as a historian of concert and musical life in America. And, yes, there's some obligatory description of politics in both books. In *Wagner Nights*, Horowitz acknowledges what happened in Europe, and in *Understanding Toscanini,* Toscanini's falling out with Bayreuth and his confrontations with fascists are noted. But it's creepy that despite the significant truth of Horowitz's claims of the commercialization of culture that Toscanini's enshrinement abetted, Horowitz's heart seems to be in defending Wagner while taking down our premiere icon of cultural resistance to fascism in a world that was otherwise notoriously reticent and non-participatory in resisting fascism, nor explicit in any regrets and apologies for this failing.

To put it even more indelicately, what was Horowitz's real motivation in writing *Understanding Toscanini*? Was it really to be this great champion of neglected American music and composers, and to reconfigure a more inclusive and representatively American appreciation and participation in the arts and cultural life?

That Toscanini was exploited for popularization and commercialization, sometimes at the expense of more native creativity, that he was a beacon of European culture and a harbinger of what was to come with Pavarotti and the Three Tenors, is not exactly rocket science. What Horowitz is saying is that Toscanini was exploited by commercial interests and that he, Toscanini, colluded with that exploitation. For this, Horowitz holds everybody— Toscanini, the classical music industry and the public— accountable. Meanwhile, is there a connection between Horowitz's depedestalization of Toscanini for his role in the parochialization of music appreciation and our culture's gathering depedestalization of Wagner for his antisemitism? I suspect that in between the lines of what Horowitz writes the answer to that question can be gleaned in what Horowitz acknowledges as his "lifetime obsession with Wagner."

Figure 21 - Leon Botstein, photo by Matthew Dine for the American Symphony Orchestra, Wikimedia Commons

The Swiss-American Jewish scholar Leon Botstein, President of Bard College and music director and principal conductor of The American Symphony Orchestra, has contributed mightily to contemporary musical culture. It's Botstein who brought the the New York area's first fully staged *Les Hugenots* (at his Bard College Summer Festival in 2009) in nearly a century, rendering ridiculous the excuses of opera companies like the Met for suppressing this thrilling and soulful masterpiece and thereby casting new light on the enduring toxicity of Wagner's epochal antisemitism as the source of that neglect.

More creatively than any other musical figure of our time, Botstein has recreated the social, political and cultural milieus of music and modernity. In doing so, he has charted the complexities, pathologies and pathos of Jewish relations with Wagner and Wagnerism. Discussion of the latter is the subject of his chapter, "German Jews and Wagner," for an edited volume, *Richard Wagner and His World*, edited by Thomas S. Grey for the 2009 Bard Music Festival devoted to the program of Wagner and His World, published by Princeton University Press.

The problem with Botstein for me is the same problem I have with the work of Marc A. Weiner, author of *Richard Wagner and The Anti-Semitic Imagination.* I got to know Marc during the period of the publication of his book, a work of singular importance in resetting the bar for the more traditional separation of Wagner's operas from the composer's antisemitism. Prior to Weiner's book, we could still rationalize that the art is separate from its author. We could always say, like Daniel Barenboim, that the music itself is not necessarily infected by the composer's antisemitism. Like no other work before or since, Weiner's book demonstrates that antisemitism is commonplace in the music, as well as in the texts, of much of Wagner's creative work.

What can seem problematic about Botstein, as with Weiner and Robert Gutman, is an unwillingness to step across that line in the sand of the greatness of Wagner's art. They've opted, as we all have, for acknowledging the seriousness of Wagner's antisemitism but defending as sacrosanct the status of the operas as great art. Especially in light of their own scholarly work, I fail to appreciate why we have to continue to cling so tightly to past defenses and appreciations of Wagner's art as inviolable. In my view, a view shared by Gottfried Wagner, the time has come for Wagner's art to be appreciated with more careful and explicit qualification regarding the composer's antisemitism, the way we've come to appreciate the pathbreaking D.W. Griffin film, *Birth of a Nation* in light of its racism. In the future, we should be enabled to see and to speak of Wagner's *Ring* cycle, *Die Meistersinger* and *Parsifal* as so seriously flawed and distorted by antisemitism that it should no longer be surprising, unacceptable or artistic blasphemy that people accordingly turn away from, qualify or otherwise decline to subject themselves to the toxicity of minority prejudice that attends these works. I've had many declined opportunities to re-view Birth of a Nation. Why must I feel guilty for having comparable reactions to Wagner's operas?

Botstein's essay on German Jews and Wagner is structured around the question of Wagner's status in Israel, where a not very tight ban on Wagner was declared and remains in effect. Botstein comes down on the side of urging a lifting of the ban. His reason? To put it succinctly, as he does in his conclusion to his essay:

> Only an active and critical encounter with Wagner as composer and dramatist can clarify his place in modern European Jewish history, in the history of anti-Semitism, and in the Nazi era. Israel must restore Wagner to the stage for the sake of the survivors, so that the causes of the Holocaust can be better understood and contemporary Israel can flourish in ways that shed any residual internalization of the deceptions and conceits of Wagner and pre-1933 German culture and society.

So we must be supportive of the Passion Play at Oberammergau and *Mein Kampf* and promote their staging and publication in Israel and elsewhere so that people can better understand and defend against antisemitism? While endorsement of any kind of banning or censorship is reflexively dystonic for me as well, I feel a lot more affirmative of the Israeli ban than Botstein, Ross and others. I think it's great that outrage about Wagner reached that level of action. Just as Hitler and Nazi symbolism are banned in Germany, I don't see why a ban on Wagner in Israel should arouse such discomfort among conscientious patrons and critics.

While I would never endorse outright censorship, I would be gratified to encounter more protest and depedestalization of Wagner, including confrontational acts and tactics. For example, I would like to see more—not less—of leading artists and conductors decline to conduct and stage Wagner and perform at Bayreuth. I would like to see more of the kind of protest mounted against a proposed staging of the *Ring* cycle in Los Angeles. I would like to see Wagner deprioritized in the repertoire. I'd like to see Jews selectively and peacefully protest works like *Meistersinger*, *Parsifal* and the *Ring* cycle for their antisemitism, the way they did for *Klinghoffer*. I'd be pleased to see such protests outside the opera house, as opposed to disrupting performances. I would welcome these developments for the same reasons that, if I were black, I wouldn't want to keep seeing the statues of Confederate heroes in public spaces. I don't want to keep having to deal with Wagner in concert halls and opera houses where there aren't adequate qualifiers. Like *Birth of a Nation*, Wagner's art may continue to be appreciated as great by various measures, and for its importance in the history of film and of America, but such is its potential toxicity, especially in the ongoing wake of excesses and extremes of racism in America that its presentation should always be qualified.

Those who decline to affirm Wagner and Wagnerism should be respected and given space. Just as we no longer express surprise or disapproval if someone declines to re-view or even initially view *Birth of a Nation*, we should have the same reaction to stagings of the *Ring* cycle, *Die Meistersinger* and *Parsifal*.

## Professor Alberich

Figure 22 - Community Yard Sale, Painting by Edward Williams

Following the publication of my memoir, *Confessions of a Jewish Wagnerite*, I received a letter from an admirer. A fellow gay Jewish

Wagnerite, he had read my book and strongly related to it. It was wonderful to receive such affirmation of my work, especially from someone who was clearly knowledgeable and intelligent; and also accomplished. As it turns out, he was a nuclear physicist of formidable rank and renown. We became immediate and fast friends.

I'm going to call him Professor Alberich, an appellation that occurred to me early in the course of our friendship. My reasons for calling him that are not what you might think—that he's loathsome or an antisemitic caricature drawn emanating from my own internalized antisemitism. On the contrary, my invocation of Alberich here was respectful and positive, and seemed to shed light on Wagner's psychology and as well that of Nazism.

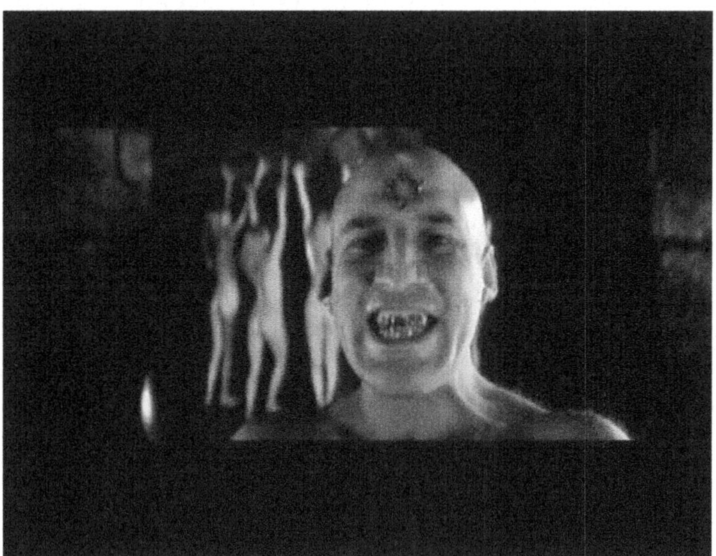

Figure 23 - Alberich in Ken Russell's Lisztomania, Warmer Bros

Yes, it's true that the overall portrait of Alberich by Wagner could not be darker or more antisemitic unless, as in Ken Russell's *Lisztomania*, he were to be a cyclops with a star of David on his forehead. But there are some other things to note of Wagner's and the *Ring* cycle's supreme villain, not only in terms of Wagner's own psychology but of Wagner's rendering of Alberich's.

Alberich may be seen as a loathsome toad by the Rhinemaidens, Wotan and Siegfried, as an arch-enemy of humanity by Wagner and an exemplar of Jewishness by Germans, but as with other Wagnerian villains, his is a remarkably powerful presence. Like Ortrud, Kundry and Klingsor, but in sharp contrast to Beckmesser, Alberich commands our attention, fear and, at times, even our respect. As a stereotype of Jewish character and traits, Alberich epitomizes how the hatred, envy and malevolence of the Nibelungs (the Jews) undermine and endanger all of humanity, especially racially pure Germanic humanity.

As captured by Wagner, however, Alberich is not a villain to be underestimated. Indeed, and though it's not entirely clear what happens at the conclusion of the *Ring* cycle, Wagner has him surviving as the gods and heroes perish in the conflagration. Thus does Alberich become the "eternal Jew" of Nazi propaganda.

"Who knows when another Alberich will come along to set the entire cycle in motion again?," asked Wagner's granddaughter Friedelind Wagner, during the telecast of the Bayreuth Centennial *Ring* cycle production directed by Patrice Chéreau. Certainly, that question must have haunted Wagner in his premonitions of "*Das Ende,*" that singular moment of the *Ring* cycle in Act 2 of *Die Walküre*, when Wotan, in dialogue with his daughter Brünhilde, at once foresees and even longs for an end to it all—the scheming and fighting for power, for his own existence and that of the gods.

In my friend Professor Alberich, what I saw early on was this formidably brilliant, commanding. deep-voiced Jew who may have evinced some of the physical features and character traits Wagner pilloried in his music dramas and essays, and who may also have shared measures of Alberich's resentment, hatred and even his vindictiveness, in equipoise with measures of that character's vanity, gullibility and self-importance, but who otherwise was, like Wagner's Alberich, a figure to be reckoned with. As Wagner foresaw, Alberich had the power to bring about nothing less than the twilight of the gods.

In the course of our friendship, my sense of all this turned out to be perspicacious. You could differ in opinion and even argue with Professor Alberich but not allowing him to prevail in argument was done at your peril. As for all those Jew-haters out there, from leftists to Nazis to Muslim fanatics, Professor Alberich was very far from being a Ghandi or Dr. Martin Luther King Jr. On the contrary, Professor Alberich, in demeanor and intensity, could seem like the medieval Jewish legend of folkloric tales, the Golem, the mythical monster conjured by the Rabbi of Prague to defend against antisemitic onslaughts. I don't recall if Professor Alberich had ever worked on nuclear weapons, and though he never expressed himself on this issue and I was politic enough not to probe, I had the sense that here was an Alberich the likes of whose potential anger could catalyze a Samsonian conflagration of Wagnerian scale.

Figure 24 - Postcard of a painting by M. Califano, "Ignominy of the XXth Century," 1934, with the caption: "Neither hatred nor persecution can stay the progress of science and civilization"; public domain

I recall seeing a contemporary Orthodox Jew, an Israeli, being interviewed about Hitler and the Holocaust. What has stayed with me was his warning to the world in the deep dark voice of an Alberich that "Jewish blood doesn't come cheap." I believe history has borne that out and I believe that people like Professor Alberich and Einstein are why.

Professor Alberich was sympathetic and admirable in so many particulars, mostly having to do with his impressive store of knowledge on a vast array of subjects. Yet with regard to our deep concern we shared about resurgent antisemitism I often felt I was up against the same rigidity that I sensed in religious extremists and which left me grappling with another close gay Jewish friend during that period, the playwright and librettist William M. Hoffman.

Though I could appreciate Jewish political conservatism as a survival strategy in a world where genocidal antisemitism was always lurking, the levels of conservatism being espoused veered easily into tolerance, if not embracement, of values and initiatives that were inimical to me as a gay man and a liberal. Bill Hoffman may not have voted Republican (I don't know for sure), but his idea of a political hero was Rudolph Giuliani. And though Bill seemed in many ways instinctively repelled by Donald Trump, Bill's close buddy, the noted feminist and writer Phyllis Chesler, sacrificed her considerable and estimable legacy of contributions to feminism to become, in all but signature, a Trumper.

Though never very specific about his politics, it was clear that Professor Alberich was Republican and had Bill Hoffman's same contempt for liberals and leftists, largely in light of their often unwitting antisemitism, and especially with regard to related issues of terrorism and the Israeli occupation of Palestinian territories. It's at this front line of politics—of conservative versus liberal, and that of separating Wagner's art from the man—that my disagreements and discomfort with Professor Alberich began to escalate.

Like Bill Hoffman, Phyllis Chesler and me, Professor Alberich was especially concerned about resurgent antisemitism among the intelligentsia, which seemed to have plunged headlong and heedlessly into an appeasement politics of embracing Islam at the expense of Israel. While concerns about the growing apartheid in Israel seemed legitimate to many liberals, including me, many leftists, intellectuals, artists and feminists seemed to be silent about and thereby abetting Islamic extremism. Nowhere was this more apparent than at the United Nations, where hawkish Republicans like John Bolton but likewise the less trigger-happy Nikki Haley, could seem singular and isolated in denouncing the scapegoating of Israel for everything wrong in Islam, Israel and the world while failing to condemn, seek reform, address or even mention the incomparably worse excesses in abuses of human rights and the oppression of women and minorities in Islamic countries and elsewhere.

As a liberal, I've no problem acknowledging real concerns about the oppression of Palestinians in Israel. What I have never able to do however, is to thereby sanction liberal antisemitism in the guise of legitimate criticism of Israel. Late in her long career as a feminist, Phyllis Chesler wrote insightful critiques of the left and the women's movement and what she called "the new anti-Semitism." Then she devalued it all—certainly for me—by aligning herself with elements of the far right—*Breitbart*, the Republicans, Trump, Evangelicals, and retreating to the closet about being lesbian. Just as feminists have aligned themselves with Islamism, Chesler aligned herself with Trump and the Evangelicals.

I might appreciate Trump's denunciations of Iran, but otherwise aligning myself with such a monster of fascism, racism, sexism, ignorance, mendacity and egomania is inconceivable to me. It has also always been clear to me that despite Trump's many pro-Jewish involvements and alliances, the risks of a trigger-happy autocratic igniting nuclear-fallout levels of antisemitism is far worse than any advantages his presidency may seem to be conferring for Israel at the outset of his tenure.

What I ask of those on the right and left is the same: careful qualifications of any endorsements of controversial figures or policies rather than consistency of political allegiance. Yes, Trump's speeches to AIPAC about Jews and Israel and his criticism of the UN and denunciation of Iran as the leading sponsor of terrorism, were valid and way overdue. But Trump is at the same time a psychopathically narcissistic, fascistic maniac who lies constantly and cannot be trusted with anything, even when he sometimes gets things right, as in some of his denunciations of Islamic terrorism and Chinese aggression. He's like that broken clock that gets the time right twice a day. Can I appear to contradict myself? Well, then, I can appear to contradict myself. Better to try to be clear and honest, however challenging to consistency, than to prevaricate, obfuscate, distort and lie; or worse, to make pacts with the devil.

Rightist intransigence is the problem that emerged for me with Professor Alberich. We were in sync and in agreement on leftist antisemitism, and especially that among the intelligentsia and in the arts, but we parted company on similar and even worse extremes of bias on the right. Like Phyllis Chesler, Professor Alberich remained not only silent about them, he was in alliance with them. That he was gay meant little to him, just as it meant little to Chesler. Their Jewishness was seen by both of them as far more important and justifying of politics of oppression, so long as it was wasn't of their own.

In the case of Professor Alberich as well as Chesler, some of this was discernibly about class. They were both well to do and evinced little or no interest in the disenfranchised, except for Jews under the yoke of antisemitism and in Chesler's case, women under the yoke of Islam or other primitive patriarchal setups. Whatever Chesler's previous, well-argued positions on the disenfranchisement of women in relation to class, they carry much less credibility now, certainly for me. Although it can be argued that the temporal twists and turns of one's politics and associations should not vitiate appreciation of one's achievements, I would say that just as these twists and turns were ones that felt necessary to Chesler in time and place, so my devaluations of their work and integrity, in time and place, are likewise twists and turns in my own journey.

Beyond these issues of class and society, my falling out with Professor Alberich, like my falling out with Professor Chesler, was as much about stubbornness and tenacity as anything else. Like me, both of these people are opinionated, strong-willed and overbearing. I've written elsewhere about my fork-in-the road turning away from Chesler. [See "Phyllis Chesler, Sarah Schulman and Me: Strange Bedfellows in the Age of Trump," *Huffington Post*.]

With Professor Alberich, the byways were more complicated. The main conceptual problem between us was much the same as between myself, Marc Weiner, Hilan Warshaw and others who have spent a lot of time and energy pondering Wagner, Jews and antisemitism.

The old bottom line for virtually all Jewish Wagnerites is that of separating the man from his art, a bottom line that they believe exculpates their Wagnerism.

In the case of Professor Alberich, however, and in light of his impressive knowledge of the seriousness and depth of Wagner's antisemitism, the tenacity of his attachment to Wagner simply did not seem to me to jibe with the claim of clean separation of the man from his music. If you confronted Professor Alberich about this, he'd point out that he did not excuse or admire the composer himself. Unlike me, he'd observe, he never had pictures or busts or framed letters of Wagner in his apartment. Wagner was never a kind of "first love," as he had been for me.

In reality, actually and so far as I could glean, Professor Alberich had never had a first love; nor a subsequent one. In fact, the absence of love in his life could seem redolent of the situation of Wagner's

Alberich, who forfeits pursuit of love for pursuit of power. But though he was solidly, often eloquently and sometimes passionately condemnatory of Wagner's antisemitism, Professor Alberich was unable to concede the cognitive dissonance necessary to remaining a Jewish Wagnerite. He couldn't acknowledge that being a Jewish Wagnerite was *so* painful and troubling because he thought he was successfully doing what all the rest of us thought we were successfully doing—separating the art from the artist.

When push came to shove on this issue of the extent, nature, subtext and origins of his Wagnerism and questions of internalized antisemitism, he'd become defensive and overbearing, qualities which would express themselves in other ways and on other issues, resulting in an ever-widening breach between us.

Together we visited Prague and Budapest, stopping in Geneva for a visit to CERN, the European Organization for Nuclear Research, home of what had been the world's largest and most powerful particle accelerator. In Geneva we stayed in relatively Spartan residence quarters at CERN. In Budapest we stayed at the Hotel Gellert, the largest and most luxurious of the pre-war era grand hotels and spas. There we also visited the Budapest Dohany Street synagogue, beautifully restored but notably empty, as well as the Hungarian State Opera, now likewise beautifully restored and empty (at that off-season time). Notwithstanding Trump's total disinterest in culture and art, he was a strong supporter of his populist buddy Hungarian Prime Minister Viktor Orban, but who has promoted Hungarian arts and culture with the same enthusiasm that Vladimir Putin promotes Russian arts and artists at home and abroad. Outside Prague we visited Theresienstadt, the cemetery in the environs of which have been left in shocking disarray. All of these travels went well enough.

A subsequent visit with me in South Florida, however, went less well. Throughout our time together, class and political differences kept intruding. It all erupted, finally, during a drive to see local sights. My second home in Hollywood Florida is a modest apartment in an over-55 cooperative. It has been a blessing in my life. A folksy "Home Sweet Home" plaque is on the front door, a holdover from the previous owners, Venezuelan diplomats who chose to return home to be with their daughter in the years before the devolution of their country into relentless chaos and crisis under the socialist autocracies of Chavez and Maduro.

Class-wise, alas, this simply wasn't Professor Alberich's milieu or one he could hope to be comfortable in, even though South Florida is heavily populated with Jews of every background and affiliation. Though I did finally persuade him to visit me there, his attitude was dominated by expectation, entitlement and disgruntlement. There was no humility. Nor in retrospect had there ever been much, even in what had at first seemed praise for my memoir. As turns out to be the case with many fans, his attachment to me was a lot more about himself than genuine appreciation of what I'd done. Meanwhile, despite the extent to which I had extended myself to treat him as my guest in Florida, to be my best in offering hospitality, no gratitude was forthcoming or discernible. What came across, rather, was that it was me who owed him gratitude for his condescending to visit me in such common environs.

So there we were driving around the area's neighborhoods. I showed him our few landmarks. Hollywood has at least two claims to fame, or rather to infamy. It's where Jeffrey Dahmer came to live briefly after a stint in the army. And it's where Anna Nicole Smith overdosed on opiates and other drugs. My efforts to have a sense of humor about this, about the extent to which Hollywood and South Florida are provincial backwaters, was less than successful. It wasn't met with bemusement, but rather with an irritability that made me feel I needed to apologize for something.

During the drive, I made note of a local custom. In Florida it's a tradition to have yard sales. Often it reflects class; people of lesser means finding ways to manage, but it's also social, a way for people of all classes and milieus to meet, mingle and be friendly. Mostly, the yard sales are of junk but sometimes you can find small treasures. Although these yard sales were clearly not terribly important, neither to me nor anyone else, Professor Alberich became discernibly impatient with something he saw as unworthy of his time and interest, all the while seemingly without an inkling of self-awareness of or humility in how self-centered and intolerant he was revealing himself to be.

This was the proverbial last straw for me. It would be different if it had been an isolated incident, something entirely unexpected and attributable to the odd moment of personal idiosyncrasy, mood or circumstance. And it would be different if I'd had more of a sense of this just being two strong personalities not meshing well together rather than something deeper and less remediable. And it would be different if I could identify my own vanity, anger, competitiveness or envy as the culprits. And, finally, it might be different if we had more successfully bonded at deeper levels of identification and empathy—e.g., around being gay and Jewish. Though definitely gay in terms of his preferences and the limited sex life he'd had, his gay identity was like Roy Cohn's in being more circumstantial rather in any way actually valued or otherwise affirmed. I don't think he was out as gay in his orthodox/conservative Jewish milieu nor in his work. When we returned to the apartment from the drive I asked him to gather his things and leave.

At my request, he left the apartment summarily, and with palpable rage. Antisemitically on my part, it seemed in character for him to reveal the kind of anger and rage Wagner had gleaned and indicted in Alberich (hence the leitmotif of "Nibelungs' hate") as stereotypical, and based on inchoate envy, spite, anger, and resentment. It was a painful moment of realization that I was seeing eye-to-eye on this with Wagner! But just as I understood it to be antisemitic in Wagner, I immediately perceived it to be likewise so in myself.

My cogitations had carried me way too far. Collecting myself in the spirit of my own recovery, I sent Professor Alberich a follow up email acknowledging that although it seemed clear that we had reached that proverbial fork in the road in our relations with each other, I wanted to express my appreciation for the rich and challenging exchanges, however otherwise fraught, that we had had, and to wish him well. He replied in kind.

When it comes to identification and alliances, my own as gay and liberal, alongside those of being Jewish, apparently run a lot deeper than those of Phyllis Chesler and Professor Alberich. When push came to shove, their alliances were more strongly with their ethnicity and class than with their sexual orientation. While I imagine that in another tsunami of antisemitism I could be pushed to the threshold of embracing my Jewish identity over that of being gay (whichever minority identity is more oppressed is that which I suspect I would tend to feel and identify with more strongly in time and place), I'm really not there presently, and it's hard for me to see that I ever will or could be. As I see it and feel it in my marrow, I cannot relegate my being gay any more than I can relegate being a man, a human being or being Jewish.

Meanwhile, in the vehemence of our disagreements, another antisemitic stereotype captured by the Germans could seem discernible—that of contentiousness. However antisemitic they can seem as caricatures, were we not in some real measure like the quarreling Jews of Strauss's *Salome*?

# **Beckmesser, Kissinger and the *Klinghoffer* Controversy**

– *Huffington Post*, 7/18/14

Figure 25 - The Death of Klinghoffer, recording of the opera by John Adams, libretto by Alice Goodman; Discogs, Amazon, public domain

Playing out before us is the Wagner situation redux. In the run up to the Metropolitan Opera's new production of *The Death of Klinghoffer*, a co-creation of composer John Adams, librettist Alice Goodman and director Peter Sellars, Jewish individuals and groups are again expressing concerns about the perceived antisemitic content and the potential to stoke antisemitism by this opera, which has aroused strong reactions from all sides since its world premiere in Brussels in 1991. Defenders of artistic freedom and partisans of *Klinghoffer* are once again indignant about any proposed accommodations of those concerns as well as about the concerns themselves.

From my accounts of the enduring toxicity of Wagner's antisemitism, it might be inferred that I would support the Met's decision not to broadcast *Klinghoffer* on its Live from the Met HD series (screenings in movie theaters worldwide) While I do evermore often question decisions about Wagner's undisputed predominance in music and opera and share Jewish concerns about *Klinghoffer*, and have felt sympathy for the Israeli ban on Wagner, let me be clear that I do not believe any composer or work of art should be censored or banned.

But apart from the singular situation of Israel, just as I neither want nor expect Wagner to be banned or censored—as opposed to reconsidered and qualified—I do not want discussion of the depth and seriousness of Wagner's anti-Semitism to be bullied into submission or silence. Though I support his right to say it, I don't want to be told that Wagner is "stuck in a Nazi rut," as *New Yorker* music critic Alex Ross observed, with the implication that discussion of the Wagner-Hitler connection is exhausted, inappropriate and unwelcome. I do not want to be told implicitly what my life-partner Arnie Kantrowitz was told explicitly by his close boyhood friend when Arnie asked him if Wagner's art was more important than the lives of 6 million Jews: "Yes."

The same holds true for *Klinghoffer* and its creators. Having made the questionable, controversial decision to stage it, the Met should not submit to eleventh-hour misgivings about its broadcast, even though concerns about it playing into escalating antisemitism in Europe and elsewhere seem justified. Consider Graham Vick's production of *Moses in Egypt*, a long-neglected Rossini masterpiece, for the Rossini Festival in Pesaro (Rossini's birthplace) in 2011, the video of which was released in 2013. In a staging that sounds more like a satire of the whole "Eurotrash" era of deconstructing opera rather than revealing abiding truth, Vick, an epigone of Sellars, turned the Jews into the terrorists. The Egyptians became their Palestinian victims and Moses was made to resemble Osama bin Laden. Although such a staging might not be expected to play well in New York, it garnered plenty of attention and praise during its run in Europe, receiving one of Italy's most prestigious critics' awards. In "Using Minds To Poison Opera Against Israel," Myron Kaplan draws the unavoidable conclusion in *The Jewish Voice* that "The production, a huge success in Europe, is meant to indoctrinate people with the idea that Israel is the villain in its conflict with the Palestinian Arabs." Nearly a decade later, of course, this viewpoint is even more widely shared among liberals and leftists, artists and intellectuals.

So what are the issues here? In order to appreciate the problem surrounding *Klinghoffer*, we have to go back to *Nixon in China*, an earlier co-creation of Adams, Sellars and Goodman. It has been a tenet of Goodman's work, as she herself has repeatedly tried to characterize it, to give balance and dimension to the various protagonists and cohorts, to allow them to express themselves, to give voice to their inner thoughts and feelings. Thus Mao, one of history's greatest mass-murderers (some would rank his democide as the greatest in human history), is humanized in her libretto for *Nixon in China*. Likewise Nixon, Pat Nixon, Chou en Lai and even Madame Mao, whose portrait is not flattering but who has the opera's most thrilling music. Goodman's intention to be fair is indeed apparent almost everywhere, at least on the surface, and this is likewise true of *Klinghoffer*, however one might question her claim to a balanced portrayal of the plight of the Palestinians vs. the Jews and Israelis. Of course, the ostensible balance and fairness of Goodman's libretto is apart from questions Richard Taruskin has raised in *The Danger of Music and Other Anti-Utopian Essays* suggesting that Adams' musical characterizations favor the Palestinians.

Goodman's professed balance calls attention to itself at every turn, but with one very big exception: the portrayal of Henry Kissinger in *Nixon in China*. There isn't a moment of his role that is anything less than a vicious and gratuitous caricature. Goodman's—and Sellars's and Adams's—hostility towards this character begs for greater scrutiny than it got from many of our critics, although some did note that Kissinger was singularly pilloried.

Reviewing the opera's premiere at the Metropolitan Opera in 2011, Anthony Tommasini observed in the *New York Times* that "With the exception of Henry Kissinger, all the historic players in the drama are treated seriously and given a dignity that allows for plenty of humor and absurdity...I have never understood why the Kissinger character alone is turned into a caricature." In *Opera and Medicine*, Neil Kurtzman wrote that "The libretto by Alice Goodman treats all of the characters in the piece seriously with the exception of Henry Kissinger, whose X-rated cartoon depiction is so out of keeping with the rest of the action that it can only be considered the result of sophomoric malice." In the *New York Jewish Week*, Eric Herschethal wrote that "'Nixon in China' gives comfort to Kissinger's most vociferous critics...the opera portrays him as cruel, cunning and entirely devoid of human feeling." Tim Page, a Pulitzer Prize-winning music critic, concluded in his original 1988 review that "to treat the president even-handedly and then to transform the secretary of state into a venal, jibbering, opportunistic buffoon is to lower the level of discourse considerably." (If Alex Ross, an ardent admirer of *Nixon in China*, ever commented on the opera's characterization of Kissinger, I could not locate it.)

Why was Kissinger targeted for such singular treatment, so much worse, so much more culpable, so much less human, than Mao, Nixon or even Madame Mao? Is it because he deserved that level of derision? Or is it because of some other aspect of the character or the way the character is perceived by the authors that isn't explicit? That Kissinger, like Goodman's parents, is a Jew and Holocaust survivor might have been an inspiration and basis for humanizing this character in the opera. Instead, he seems only to have aroused the kind of malice that sophomores, or Jewish adolescents who have internalized anti-Semitism and who want to deny and reject the burden of their ethnic heritage, harbor for their parents.

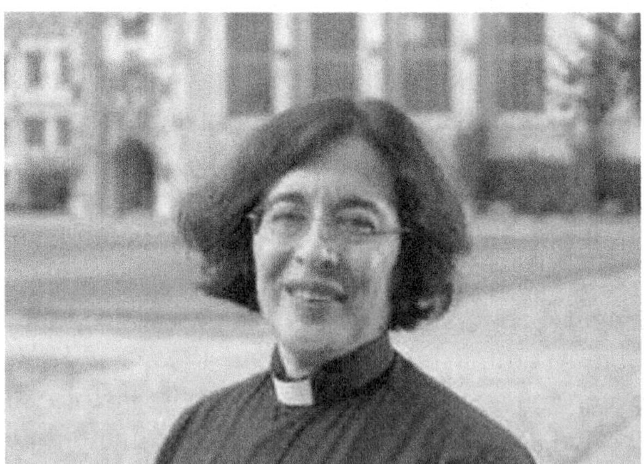

Figure 26 - Alice Goodman, librettist for The Death of Klinghoffer, Discogs.net, public domain

In such troubled hands, Kissinger was destined to become European culture's old standby—the lecherous, treacherous, power-mad Jew, a figure that reemerged after the Holocaust more notably among leftists, intellectuals, and artists than conservatives and rightists. Lest we forget, *Nixon in China* and *Klinghoffer* were written in the heyday of a great international resurgence of antisemitism, fueled by the blame and scapegoating of America, Israel and the Jews for the entire global and historical phenomena we call *jihad*; a blame centered in the circumstances of the Palestinians; a blame that continues. Goodman, whose admitted anti-Zionism can't help but raise conjoined questions of internalized antisemitism, would appear to share these sentiments with no small number of other Jewish and non-Jewish socialists, progressives, intellectuals and artists. In the wake of Jewish indignation and criticism following the premiere of *Klinghoffer*, including from members of the Klinghoffer family who have denounced the opera as antisemitic, and in the context of her marriage to the British poet Geoffrey Hill, Goodman converted to Christianity, becoming an ordained Anglican minister. Somebody needs to explain to her that when the next roundup of Jews happens, her Anglican cloak won't save her. She'll be in the same cattle cars as the rest of us.

Meanwhile, how does the character of Kissinger fit into the greater operatic canon? If you compare the depiction of Kissinger in *Nixon in China* with Beckmesser in *Die Meistersinger*, the similarities are striking. Both are Jewish caricatures whose Jewishness is vehemently implicit rather than explicit. Both are dehumanized, cartoon scapegoats for all the cultural wrong surrounding them. Neither has a moment of self-expression that could invite any level of identification or sympathy. On the contrary, the audience can only have loathing and contempt for both of them.

Figure 27 - From Nixon in China, Canadian Opera Company, 2011, public domain

The most notable efforts to mitigate Wagner's malevolently satirical portrait of Beckmesser have occurred recently, just as scholars like Barry Millington, Marc A. Weiner and Paul Lawrence Rose increasingly identify the antisemitism as intrinsic to *Die Meistersinger*—with the casting of one of Germany's greatest mastersingers, Hermann Prey, as Beckmesser at Bayreuth, the Met and elsewhere. Alas, Beckmesser's music is so relentlessly ugly and unsingable that not even Prey could render more than a modicum of dignity to the role. So stirred-up is the audience's contempt that when Beckmesser is beset by a mob of the*Volk* and beaten to a pulp, you want to join in, but perhaps a little less so when Beckmesser is Hermann Prey. If the Kissinger caricature weren't so poorly drawn, the same moderation of inclination would be true in *Nixon in China*. Would the problem be solved if we cast a great and beloved leading singer, a Bryn Terfel or Rene Pape, as Kissinger?

Goodman has recently said that she looked into herself in her portrayals of all the characters in *Nixon in China*, including Kissinger. But this admission seems disingenuous, after the fact and defensive. Kissinger has also been described by the opera's co-creators as a "buffo" figure, as if the casting of him in this stock operatic role somehow mitigates, justifies and supersedes questions of prejudice any more than such an explanation would mitigate Wagner's treatment of Beckmesser in *Die Meistersinger*.

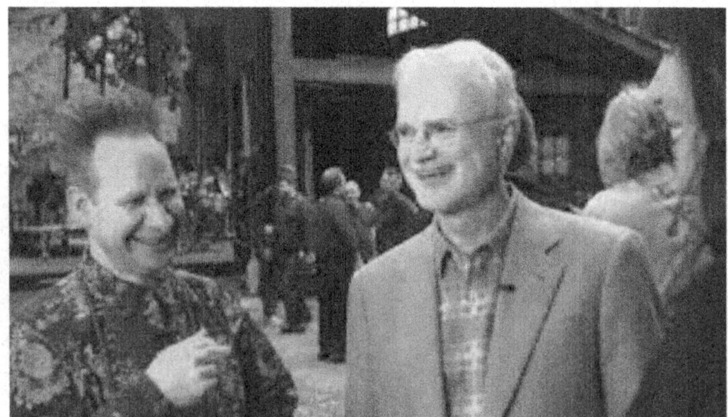

Figure 28 - Peter Sellars (L) and John Adams, Youtube, SFO La Fanciulla del West premiere, 2011, public domain

*Nixon in China* is otherwise an original work that qualifies as one of contemporary opera's notable creations. I was an early admirer of

Peter Sellars' gift for rendering opera and theater more vital for contemporary and younger audiences, from his first production of *Don Giovanni* in a Massachusetts high school gymnasium with the Don as a heroin addict in Spanish Harlem, on through to his signature Mozart productions of *The Marriage of Figaro* set in Trump Tower and *Cosi fan Tutte* set in a Cape Cod diner. So I was curious about his later productions —a televangelical *Tannhauser*, a homoerotic *Tristan, The Merchant of Venice* with a black Shylock, *The Magic Flute, Orlando, Theodora, St Francois D'Assisi*, even his cell-phone *Othello*. Sellars's daring retained its appeal, even as the whole deconstructive approach to opera and theater he had spearheaded began to deflate. Though I liked what Sellars was trying to do in theory, the results seemed in increasingly uneasy alliance with the artworks themselves; and though I did see all the Adams operas he collaborated on, I made little effort to see other Sellarsizations of classics. Peter Sellars deserves a lion's share of credit for the deconstruction and post-modernism that became the predominant modes of theater and opera in our time. But after those early Mozart productions, nothing he himself staged approached the achievement in cultural and historical reverberance of, say, the Patrice Chéreau *Ring* cycle production at Bayreuth.

I've also admired the work of John Adams. I found some of the pieces in *Nixon in China* to be exhilarating, and some of his music for *Klinghoffer* and *Dr. Atomic* to be expressive and beautiful. Sellars and Adams are talents I've wanted to be on board with. But so troubling a figure is Alice Goodman and so troubling is their portrayal of Kissinger that, as with Wagner's work in the aftermath of his epochal hatefest, "Judaism in Music," that the rest of their work feels thereby tainted. Just as I can never again be really comfortable with Wagner, I can likewise never again be really comfortable with Goodman, Adams, and Sellars.

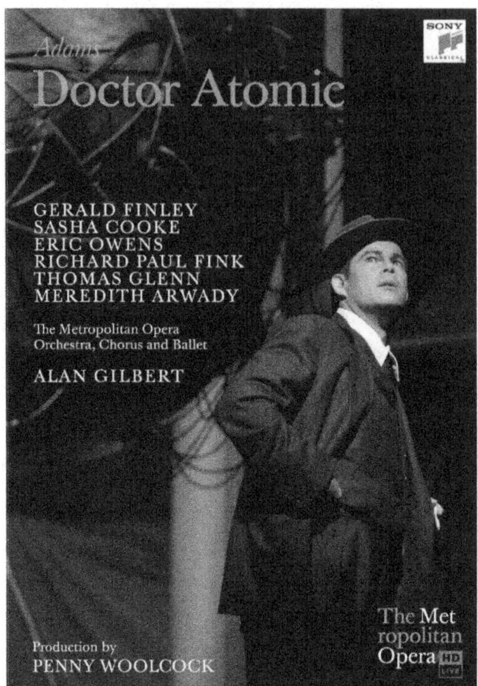


Figure 29 - Dr. Atomic, opera by John Adams, Sony Classical, Amazon.com, public domain

In fact, so on guard did I become regarding their work that I experienced a paranoid illusion during the premiere of *Dr. Atomic* at the Met. Not unlike the way Pat Nixon imagines a rapacious Henry Kissinger dancing in the ballet, "The Red Detachment of Women," in *Nixon in China*, I imagined that the chains covering the big atomic bomb hovering over nearly all of the proceedings were arranged to suggest a star of David covering the globe. (Full disclosure: Neither my partner Arnie, with whom I attended the performance, nor anyone else I know who saw *Dr. Atomic* felt they saw this. Nor was any such pattern discernible in my subsequent perusals of photographs of the production.) *Dr. Atomic* was directed by Penny Woolcock, who also directed a film version of *The Death of Klinghoffer* for British television.

Whatever my own misgivings or apprehensions, everyone should be free to see and admire this or any other art. But it should not be demanded that I do, or that I endorse this art as of such greatness as to transcend and surpass any other concerns. Meanwhile, whatever the team of Adams, Goodman and Sellars have achieved, however ostensibly humanitarian and laudable their intentions, it's difficult for me to get past their rendering of Kissinger, which I can't but see as the ugliest and most hateful Jewish caricature in all of opera, the first real successor to Beckmesser, Alberich and Mime. I can't help but sense the old "Protocols of the Elders of Zion" wafting within and about their *oeuvre*.

Which brings us back to the Klinghoffers who are portrayed as stereotypical Jewish-American materialists. The opera may contain a number of small moments and details that show the humanity of all characters, yet this does not resolve the problem that lies at the heart of this composition: its globalization of circumstances, grievances and evils in its equilibration of the Holocaust with the occupation of Palestinians, and its analogizing of the latter to the Nazi persecutions of Jews or the apartheid in South Africa.

In 2003 Edward Rothstein updated his stage review of *Klinghoffer* to critique Penny Woolcock's filmed version for its affirmation of "two ideas now commonplace among radical critics of Israel: that Jews acted like Nazis, and that refugees from the Holocaust were instrumental in the founding of the state, visiting upon Palestinians the sins of others." "The Judaism I was raised in was strongly Zionist," said Alice Goodman in an interview in *the Guardian* in 2012. "It had two foci almost - the *Shoah* [the Holocaust] and the State of Israel, and they were related in the same way the crucifixion is related to the resurrection in Christianity. Even when I was a child, I didn't totally buy that. I didn't buy the State of Israel being the recompense for the murder of European Jewry, recompense not being quite the right word, of course. The word one wants would be more like apotheosis or elevation."

[Following the presentation to our class of a Holocaust documentary when I was 8 years old], Goodman continued, "our very traumatized junior rabbi quoted the song that begins, 'Cast out your wrath upon the nations that know ye not.' In Hebrew it is, 'Cast out your wrath upon the *goyim* [which can be a disparaging term for non-Jews],' which is what he said. My infantile brain thought, 'No, that's not the right answer.' That thought is the thing that's brought me here. And it has to do with *Klinghoffer* as well." Since Goodman knows that most Israelis, like her parents, are more secular than orthodox, why is she basing her judgments on impressions she admits were made on her when she was preadolescent?

In anticipation of the ENO premiere of *The Death of Klinghoffer* there was a flurry of advance press, including the interview with Goodman. Lisa Klinghoffer, one of Leon and Marilyn Klinghoffer's daughters, is also quoted in *the Guardian* piece. "The opera displays thoughts and feelings about our parents and friends they never had or expressed. Prior to the production, I tried to tell Peter Sellars [the director of the original staging] about our parents, but he said that he did not want or need to hear them. To us he was willing to distort the image of our parents and to show a stereotypical picture of the 'fat cat' American Jew to express his political agenda."

Setting aside the issue of the trio's ideological orientation, a case can always be made for the motivation and psychology of fascists. Why did the Nazis do what they did? What did the Jews do to make the Germans so angry at them? There must have been reasons for it. Fat-cat wealth and arrogance! Bolshevism! Why did Osama bin Laden hate America, Israel and the Jews as much as he did? There must have been reasons for this too. Colonialism! Likewise the Taliban's blowing up of Afghanistan's great Buddha statues. Infidels! In the case of the Palestinians, who live under conditions of occupation by Israel but who have never been willing to recognize Israel's right to exist and who voted to be co-governed by Hamas, an Iran-backed terrorist organization unremittingly committed to Israel's destruction, the issues might appear to be more complicated. Even so, the commission of fascistic and terrorist acts and atrocities is far more a matter of prosecution and prevention than compassion, understanding and forgiveness. That proved to be true of Nazism and it is likewise true of the greater arc of Islamic extremism and terrorism. The challenge is less to explain, understand, mollify and forgive terrorism and extremism than to stop and prevent it. However reasonable and even laudable its intentions and whatever the qualifiers of the Israeli-Palestinian conflict, *The Death of Klinghoffer* does more to obscure, retard and inflame that process of prevention than help it.

As Richard Taruskin concluded in his *New York Times* response to the controversy surrounding the scheduled productions of *The Death of Klinghoffer* in the aftermath of 9/11, "If terrorism — specifically, the commission or advocacy of deliberate acts of deadly violence directed randomly at the innocent — is to be defeated, world public opinion has to be turned decisively against it. The only way to do that is to focus resolutely on the acts rather than their claimed (or conjectured) motivations, and to characterize all such acts, whatever their motivation, as crimes. This means no longer romanticizing terrorists as Robin Hoods and no longer idealizing their deeds as rough poetic justice. If we indulge such notions when we happen to agree or sympathize with the aims, then we have forfeited the moral ground from which any such acts can be convincingly condemned...In the wake of Sept. 11, we might want, finally, to get beyond sentimental complacency about art. Art is not blameless. Art can inflict harm."

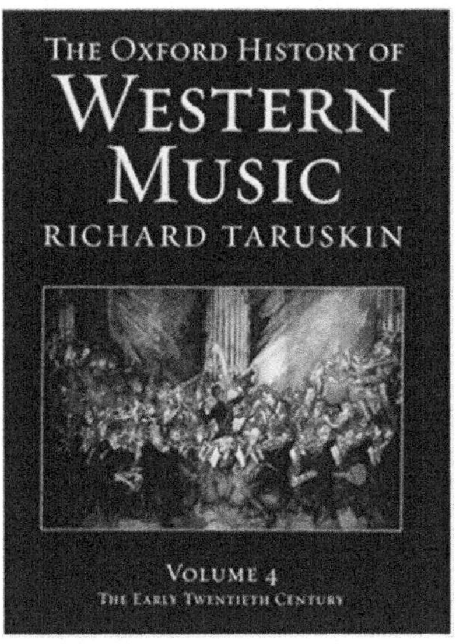


Figure 30 - The Oxford History of Western Music, Richard Taruskin, Amazon.com, public domain

So is there a lesson to be learned by the co-creators of *Nixon and China* and *Klinghoffer* from the experience of Wagner? Yes, there is. It's an addendum to the famous saying attributed to Santayana that those who do not learn the lessons of the past are condemned to repeat it: But even when they do learn those lessons, they are likely to repeat past transgressions if they think they can get away with and benefit from doing so. Wagner not only got away with doing so, it's increasingly clear that his career thereby knowingly and greatly benefited. However tacit the influence of Wagner, the controversies surrounding *Nixon in China* and *The Death of Klinghoffer* are playing out along a comparable trajectory.

Perhaps the Met should consider a new option for its mini-series trio subscriptions: *Die Meistersinger, Nixon in China* and *The Death of Klinghoffer.*

# Comparing the Jewish Protests of *Klinghoffer* with the Gay Protests of *Cruising* and ACT UP

– *Huffington Post*, 11/12/2014

Figure 31 - Former Mayor Rudy Giuliani speaks to demonstrators on the opening night of *The Death Of Klinghoffer* at the Met. (Credit: Marla Diamond/WCBS 880)

On Sept 20, 2014, the opening night of the Metropolitan Opera season, I ventured to Lincoln Center to observe an organized Jewish protest of the Met for its planned presentation of the opera *The Death of Klinghoffer*. The Oct 20 Met premiere drew an even larger demonstration. I saw the US premiere of the opera at BAM in 1991 and had little inclination to experience it again, notwithstanding the subsequent elimination of a scene emphasizing the opera's conceptualization of Leon and Marilyn Klinghoffer as stereotypical Jewish-American materialists.

Apart from controversy about the opera's politics, the bigger problem with *Klinghoffer* is its weakness as music drama. Though it has passages of expressive music and some moments that are insightful, challenging and moving, most of this quasi-oratorio is textually opaque and musically inert. By comparison, and apart from its conspicuously outsized caricature of Henry Kissinger, *Nixon in China* is a more coherent, dramatic and engaging work, though it too, inevitably deflates. Though I was more drawn to attend that opera's revival by the Met in 2011, I finally decided against doing so because of my discomfort with what seemed to me its covertly antisemitic depiction of Kissinger.

In the wake of all the protest, a number of artists, intellectuals and other distinguished persons have responded positively to *Klinghoffer*. As quoted in the *Wall Street Journal*, Supreme Court Justice Ruth Bader Ginsburg found the opera to be "a most sympathetic portrayal of the Klinghoffers...both of [whom] come across as very strong, very brave characters...There was nothing antisemitic about the opera." Justice Ginsburg also disputed claims that the opera glorified terrorism. "The terrorists are not portrayed as people that you would like. Far from it...They are being portrayed as bullies and irrational...There is one very dramatic scene of a Palestinian mother raising this child, his toy is a gun from when he's five years old, and she's raising him so that he will one day do a very brave act that will result in his own death and then he will go to paradise...It was chilling."

Prior to the Met premiere, I already shared my more critical viewpoint on *Huffington Post* in my essay, "Beckmesser, Kissinger and The *Klinghoffer* Controversy." A number of the protesters were calling for the Met to cancel the opera. As an opponent of censorship, I did not feel I could join their ranks. But as a Jew who is concerned about past, current and future resurgences of antisemitism, I was heartened and inspired to see such organized, courageous and spirited Jewish protest.

The *Klinghoffer* clashes bring to mind a comparably sentinel episode in the history of minorities, art and censorship occasioned by the William Friedkin movie, *Cruising*, starring Al Pacino, in 1979/80. Just as *Klinghoffer* was originally seen by many Jews as yet another antisemitic attack, so was *Cruising* seen by gays as yet another homophobic assault. In both cases, the works themselves were far from being the worst of their genre. Nor did their creators explicitly endorse extremist views.

Friedkin was a kind of macho Hollywood liberal who may not have been sure what he thought about gays but didn't think of himself as homophobic; rather, he believed he was making an artistic contribution. Similarly, composer John Adams, librettist Alice Goodman and director Peter Sellars saw themselves primarily as artists and humanitarians; they didn't think of themselves as antisemitic or endorsing terrorism. Fortunately for both communities but unfortunately for the artworks and their creators, both works struck sensitivities that ignited historical protests.

Figure 32 - Gay Protesters of the movie Cruising, from "On Cruising: Why the Village Went Wild" by Richard Goldstein, *Village Voice*, 8/6/79

Just as cohorts of Jews called for the cancellation of *Klinghoffer*, legions of gay people, spearheaded by influential *Village Voice* columnist Arthur Bell, were determined to shut down the filming of *Cruising.* At that time I myself was writing a piece for the gay press that asked "Why is Hollywood Dressing Gays to Kill?" It complemented the work of our extended family member Vito Russo, the closest friend of my life partner Arnie Kantrowitz. Russo was the author of the landmark work of gay consciousness, *The Celluloid Closet*, about the history of homosexuality and film. Like Arthur and many other LGBT people, we — Arnie, Vito and I — were fed up with the "necrology," as Vito called it, of gay people in film, the vast majority of whom ended up dead — murdered or having committed suicide, being imprisoned as criminal, stigmatized as evil, or institutionalized as insane. This was a genre and tradition that Friedkin's film, a dark look at the gay S&M scene and gay murders by gays and of gays, was clearly going to play right into. Thus did *Cruising* become a lightning rod for the pent-up gay anger of decades.

Alas, there was a problem with Bell's call for a shutdown of the film, one Vito and Arnie realized almost immediately. Though they felt deeply in sync with this as with most gay activist protest, they did not feel they could go the full distance of calling for the banning or censorship of this film or any other artwork, no matter how biased, exploitative, smarmy or even dangerous. As with Jewish concerns that *Klinghoffer* would inflame antisemitic violence, especially in Europe, what seemed most urgent in *Cruising* was its potential to incite more hate crimes against gays, who already had sustained the sky-high rates of violent assault, murder, and savagery as well as suicide that continues unabated today in Russia, Iran, in Africa and throughout the Islamic world, and as well in America, especially of transgender people.

It was difficult to keep one's neutrality on this film's potential to incite violence, but the censorship boundary prevailed for Arnie, Vito, other gay observers and me. (I was acquainted with Vito but didn't get to know him until I met Arnie in 1981.) Neither Arnie nor Vito marched with the protesters. Nor, as I recall, did I. In the aftermath, just as *Klinghoffer* was adapted to take out its most offensive references, *Cruising* was adapted to include a new gay-affirmative line or two under pressure from the protesters. Filming was completed and *Cruising* opened to mostly critical reviews. Eventually, of course, the controversy died and the film took its place in the annals of film as an historical curiosity rather than anything more controversial, substantial or enduring. Apart from some favorable reviews, with one critic calling it a "masterpiece," a similar trajectory followed for *Klinghoffer* which is likely to encounter a comparable fate of being an historically significant but artistically minor work in the annals of music and opera.

Although the *Cruising* episode wasn't a shining moment for the history of censorship and art, it was a shining moment for the history of the gay civil rights struggle. And I would propose that whatever the fallout of any tarnishing of the sanctity of art, the *Klinghoffer* protests were likewise a shining moment in the history of minority and Jewish consciousness and activism, in the U.S. and worldwide.

Not surprisingly, critics were secure in their opposition to censorship as well as towards the protesters. From that vantage point they could return to their routines of performance reviewing and being guardians of the sanctity of art rather than as truly independent and in-depth observers.

Figure 33 - Richard Taruskin, Oxford University Faculty of Music

Richard Taruskin had been the only prominent critical voice to defend the Boston Symphony's cancellation of a scheduled concert performance of *Klinghoffer* in the wake of 9/11. No mainstream outlet gave in-depth credibility or respect to Jewish concerns or the Met's decision to cancel a live broadcast of the production, notwithstanding widespread mention of the dignified statement of protest by the Klinghoffer daughters, who consider the opera to be antisemitic and thereby dishonest and dishonoring of their parents. Notably, most critics chose to showcase the more extremist expressions of protest at the expense of weighing more challenging ones.

In the *New Yorker*, Alex Ross noted that both former Governor David Paterson and former Mayor Rudolph Giuliani, an opera lover who otherwise admires Adams' music, weighed in at the rally with concerns about the opera's potential to stoke hostilities. Ross then proceeded to expose the rally as little more than a forum for fanaticism.

> "The most aggressive rhetoric came from Jeffrey Wiesenfeld, a money manager who has also worked as a political operative...A few years ago, Wiesenfeld won notoriety for seeking, unsuccessfully, to deny the playwright Tony Kushner an honorary degree, on account of Kushner's criticisms of Israel. Wiesenfeld led the *Klinghoffer* rally, and he had much to say. 'This is not art," he thundered. This is crap. This is detritus. This is garbage.' He declared, as he did at an anti-*Klinghoffer* event last month, that the set should be burned. He made a cryptic joke to the effect that, if something were to happen to Gelb that night, the board of the Met would be the first suspects. The rally went on in that vein."

Wiesenfeld is a former CUNY trustee who was quoted in the *Forward* as having "once said that his mother would have called playwright Tony Kushner a 'Kapo.'" Alas, Wiesenfeld's remarks recalled the bitter and protracted opposition to the New York City gay civil rights bill by conservative and orthodox Jews. Also of concern, however, were some of the angrier reactions to that opposition, including from some gay Jews. Never underestimate the power of "justification"—whether we're talking about magnets of vilification like Roy Cohn, Henry Kissinger and Bernie Madoff, or the acts of homophobic or Islamophobic Jewish bigots and zealots — to "justify" prejudice and resentments. Meanwhile, if the *Klinghoffer* rallies had any value or invited any deeper level of analysis, that's not something you were going to find in the defensive coverage of our leading music critics.

If the critics did have any misgivings about their stance, they needed only to look to Peter Gelb (who is Jewish) and The *New York Times* editorial board for reassurance; and to a wide range of Jewish artists and intellectuals, most of whom all too easily and quickly embrace the dominant philosophy of "*art uber alles*" at the expense of their own minority consciousness and personal dignity. "For people to call me a self-hating Jew is so ludicrous that it's beyond chilling,"

Gelb told the *Forward*. Translation: I'm Jewish and some of my best friends are Jewish. Thereby and therefore, I cannot be cited for harboring or condoning antisemitism.

In the bigger picture, this splitting of Jewish opinion is reminiscent of Europe under Nazism: educated, assimilated Jewish intellectuals, artists and *kultur* lovers on the one hand and the *Ostjuden*—the "loud," "vulgar" Eastern European and Russian Jewish rabble—on the other. Meanwhile, as pogroms against gays in Russia continue, Gelb has yet to issue any statement of protest, even as the Met continues to showcase an unprecedented array of politically silent Russians, most notably Anna Netrebko and Valery Gergiev, who remain unapologetically and unqualifiedly supportive of their sponsor Vladimir Putin.

Several years ago in Los Angeles, some Jews protested the L.A. Opera's plans for a new *Ring* cycle. They questioned the priority of appropriating large sums of money for the tainted works of one of history's most virulent antisemites. Although aggressively defeated, these protests proved to be a harbinger of the *Klinghoffe*r confrontations. Do they likewise foretell of escalating fractiousness and confrontations around Wagner?

What would have happened if the upper-class Jews of Wagner's time—especially those in Wagner's circles and the music world — had been more forthright, organized and as determined to protest Wagner's antisemitism as the Jews who protested *Klinghoffer*? There were in fact some protests of Wagner around *Die Meistersinger*. But would better organized and more outspoken, disruptive and frequent demonstrations have made a difference in Wagner's choice of subjects or in the expression of his prejudices? Might Wagner have been influenced—the way Dickens was to respond with more sensitivity to Jewish concerns about his Jewish stereotype Fagin, the unscrupulous pickpocket ringleader of *Oliver Twist*—to write a retraction or modification of his infamous diatribe, "Judaism in Music"? Unlikely perhaps, but if a leading antisemite like Henry Ford could be thus influenced, albeit via anti-defamation litigation, why not Wagner?

If Jews had been more outspoken in Nazi Germany, might the course of history have been different? Hannah Arendt seems to have thought so, and, in our time likewise one of her disciples, Larry Kramer, the great gay and AIDS activist and author of *The Normal Heart*. Kramer was inspired by Arendt in the conviction that — for gay people, in their greatest crisis, like the Jews in theirs — silence equals death.

Figure 34 - ACT UP protestors at the NIH, 5/21/90, NIH History Office, public domain

This brings us to another example of (predominantly) gay protest pertinent to our discussion, the aggressive demonstrations of the monumentally heroic and successful AIDS activist organization founded by Kramer: ACT UP (AIDS Coalition to Unleash Power). At its most confrontational, this organization used extremely provocative rhetoric with highly confrontational but technically peaceful tactics to pursue its agenda of influencing AIDS research and health care. Ed Koch and Ronald Reagan were repeatedly denounced by Kramer and ACT UP as "murderers" and "mass-murderers," as "Hitlerian" and as "Nazis" committing "genocide."

As with some of the more extremist statements of those protesting *Klinghoffer* and *Cruising*, I could not go to these same lengths myself. I could not carry banners that accused people like Anthony Fauci, Director of the National Institutes of Health, and others, of being akin to Nazis and Hitler because of their lackluster leadership. I could not join in denunciations of Fauci for committing "genocide." But I did march with ACT UP and did carry a banner that read: "We Need Experts, Not Bigots." The point here is that I marched in solidarity with Larry Kramer and ACT UP, even though I couldn't endorse some of their more extreme rhetoric and tactics. My reaction to the protesters of *Cruising* and *Klinghoffer* was strongly analogous. I couldn't agree with their exaggerations of the intentions or dangers of these works nor with their calls for more extreme responses, but I did feel in solidarity with their anger and concerns.

In the case of *Klinghoffer* and *Cruising*, the bottom line is simple for me. I am concerned about the rhetoric and tactics of some gay radicals, but I am a lot more concerned about homophobia. While I share humanitarian concerns about the Palestinians and Israel's occupation of disputed territories, I'm a lot more concerned about Islamic aggression, antisemitism and homophobia.

As for the value of art weighed against the value of life, I've told the story of my partner Arnie asking his boyhood German-American friend if Wagner's art were more important than the lives of 6 million Jews. The answer of the "friend" was "yes." Needless to add, I do not agree. While I have yet to betray my standard of not endorsing censorship, if I could press a button to eliminate Wagner's art from history and memory as the cost of changing the history of World War 2, my finger would press that button so quickly and so hard it would probably break.

# The Wagner Family and Questions of Forgiveness

– *Huffington Post*, 5/12/15

Figure 35 - Wagner's grandsons, Wieland and Wolfgang Wagner, with Hitler, Jerusalem Post, public domain

*Richard Wagner's grandsons, Wieland and Wolfgang Wagner, who led the postwar Bayreuth Festival, were Hitler youth. Wolfgang fought on the front lines of the war. Wieland was a titular director of the Flossenbürg Concentration Camp near Bayreuth, 30,000 of whose 90,000 inmates were murdered. Neither was criminally prosecuted. Neither ever publicly repented or asked for forgiveness.*

**On the eve of the 100th anniversary of the Armenian genocide, which Pope Francis called "the first genocide of the twentieth century," questions persist of disclosure and forgiveness surrounding the Wagner family's embrace of Hitler and Nazism. "Concealing or denying evil," said Francis, who has said he was inspired by Parsifal's journey from ignorance to knowledge, "is like allowing a wound to keep bleeding without bandaging it." With regard to Wagner and Bayreuth, the wound of concealment will perforce continue its cycles of bleeding and bandaging, as we await greater levels of accountability.**

In 1998 the *New Yorker* published an essay about Wagner and the Jews called "The Unforgiven" by Alex Ross. Ross had met with Wagner's great grandson, the writer and musicologist Gottfried Wagner, whose autobiographical account of the Wagner family, *Twilight of the Wagners: The Unveiling of a Family's Legacy,* Bayreuth's collaborations with Hitler and Nazism, and the aftermath, had been published in 1997.

I read Ross's essay when it came out. At that time, I was so impressed with what seemed to be its scope, insights and caring that I wondered whether the title had been chosen by an editor rather than by Ross himself. Calling it "The Unforgiven" seemed to raise questions of who were the unforgiving and who the unforgiven, and why. Since forgiveness is, after all, widely held to be a virtue, criticism seemed implicit not of the unforgiven but of the unforgiving. As it turns out, the essay does make clarifying reference to "The Unforgiven." Reviewing the situation in Israel, Ross noted that the music of Richard Strauss was being played there following years of banishment and that "it is now only Wagner — The Unforgiven — who has an asterisk next to his name."

What Ross was saying is that among leading cultural figures tainted by antisemitism and/or Nazism, only Wagner has remained *persona non grata*, "unforgiven," and only in Israel. At first, any reservations I might have had about this statement and the essay's title were offset by Ross's notable inventory of Wagner's antisemitism and his acknowledgment of Wagner's having been in this what Ross, quoting Auden, called "an absolute shit." Indeed, Ross's essay concludes with the respectful, sensitive observation that if there's a shrine like Bayreuth where Wagner can still be contemplated with religious singularity and fervor, perhaps it's right that there also be a place (Israel) where his presence is absent, unheard.

But what does it say about Israel and Jews that some among us seem not to have forgiven Wagner? Isn't forgiveness one of the most fundamental of all religious, philosophical and spiritual precepts? Didn't Pope John Paul II make a special point of visiting and forgiving his attempted assassin? Didn't Jesus on the cross ask that his persecutors be forgiven? And wasn't it Shylock's eye-for-an-eye inability to forgive his Christian adversaries that provoked their antisemitic retaliations?

Inevitably, it's difficult not to conclude that such thinking underlies Ross' viewpoint about the ongoing animus of some Jews against Wagner and his music, and the tension still felt by many more. Isn't it, as Ross otherwise has repeatedly suggested, finally time to move on, acknowledging, but also accepting the past and forgiving its sins and sinners? Isn't it time that we accept Ross's challenge to forgive Wagner more thoroughly, with fewer reservations and with greater unanimity than we ever have before?

Let's take a closer look at the issue of forgiveness as it has played out among Jews and Germans in music and culture thus far. How many famous Jews have expressed their admiration and appreciation of Wagner, notwithstanding his genocidal antisemitism, even in the aftermath of the Holocaust? Hundreds? Easily. And what of the countless other Jews, many of whom unselfconsciously identify as Wagnerites, who so ardently admire the *Ring* cycle, *Die Meistersinger* and *Parsifal*, despite their antisemitic stereotypes? In fact, I believe I may be the only self-designated Jewish Wagnerite who has ever rescinded that identity — of being a Wagnerite — in the wake of the ever-worsening revelations of Wagner's antisemitism and its influence on his family, Hitler and Nazism.

Whatever justification that separates the composer from his art they acknowledge when pressed, virtually all leading Jewish figures in music — from Hermann Levi, who conducted the world premiere of *Parsifal* and was a pall bearer at Wagner's funeral, to Gustav Mahler, to Bruno Walter, Leo Blech, Otto Klemperer, Georg Solti, James Levine, Daniel Barenboim and even Leonard Bernstein — have resolutely refused to qualify their love of Wagner's music or their commitment to preserving his legacy. Whatever their discomfort around Wagner's antisemitism, and however inchoate their attendant concerns about maintaining their own integration in music and cultural circles, such was the excitement around the success of Wagner the outsider and champion of new music that they were otherwise swept away in the maelstrom of Wagnermania that continues to this day.

In fact, the question that needs to be asked is exactly the opposite of that posed earlier: except for what is doubtless a very small minority of survivors of concentration camps, amongst anti-Wagner musical activists how rare is it to find a prominent Jewish opera commentator or cultural arbiter who has *not* forgiven Wagner, to the extent of ceasing defense of the *de facto* Wagner ban in Israel ? Can even one such prominent musician or cultural spokesperson be identified?

On the other hand, has any Wagner family member, or for that matter any leading German musical or cultural figure, ever asked for forgiveness? Over a recent dinner a German friend and I shared memories of favorite singers. Elisabeth Schwarzkopf was high up on both our lists. He opined that despite the greatness of her art and career, she was never forgiven for having been a *Hitlerjugend.* I rejoined that while it's true that her reputation was thus tarnished, the problem that persisted for her, Herbert von Karajan and so many others, including Richard Strauss and Wagner himself, isn't simply that she wasn't forgiven. Schwarzkopf was married to Jewish musical culture mogul Walter Legge and was greatly admired by many Jewish music and opera people, including me. The surpassing problem is that neither she nor von Karajan nor virtually any of the other German artists, including Strauss and Wagner, who were Nazis or who in varying degrees contributed to or collaborated with Nazism, ever admitted to any wrongdoing, ever expressed any regrets or asked anyone for forgiveness. Instead of asking for forgiveness, expressing regret for the past, or even honest and clear acknowledgment, what most Nazi-tainted German artists have done at best, might be called gestures of redress — e.g., Schwarzkopf's marrying Walter Legge (a career move that reflected her explicit defense and credo of "Vissi d'arte"), von Karajan's conducting of the "Jewish music" of Mahler, Bayreuth's engagement of Jewish conductors and the Villa Wahnfried's 1985 exhibit on "Wagner and the Jews" that Gottfried Wagner dismissed as a whitewash.

Let's look at Bayreuth. When I was coming of age as a young Jewish Wagnerite, we knew of Wagner's antisemitism and Hitler's adoration of Wagner. We knew that Winifred Wagner, who succeeded Siegfried Wagner (her gay husband, the composer's son) had befriended Hitler to the extent of welcoming him as family at Bayreuth. We knew that she remained unwaveringly loyal to "Wolf" (Hitler) even after the war, as a result of which she was officially interdicted from participating in the postwar administration of the Bayreuth Festival. We knew that her sons Wieland and Wolfgang likewise embraced "*Onkel Wolf.*" But they were young adults at that time, and after the war, with Jews back on Bayreuth's rosters and with

Bayreuth readmitted to the Western world of music, Bayreuth and the Wagner family, ostensibly *sans* Winifred, seemed to have made credible efforts to move beyond the past.

And of course, there was the shining beacon of credibility and trust that was Wagner's granddaughter, Friedelind, an outspoken anti-Nazi who fled Nazi Germany for America during the war. As an exemplar of German resistance to Hitler, she lent unparalleled credibility to our wishful thinking that the whole Nazi and Wagner family embrace of Wagner was pretty much an aberration, a distortion of the composer's art that would have been as disturbing to Wagner himself as it was allegedly to the majority of educated Germans. We Wagnerites so wanted to believe that most Germans were overwhelmed by Hitler and Nazism and that their collaborations were increasingly, if not initially, involuntary and reluctant.

In addition to Friedelind, there were other leading Wagner singers and conductors who denounced Hitler and refused to appear in Nazi Germany, including Arturo Toscanini, Lotte Lehmann, Lauritz Melchior and Erich Kleiber, as well as those who were Jewish, such as Friederich Schorr and Bruno Walter. These exceptions notwithstanding, we simply did not know the extent of Bayreuth's collusions with Hitler and Nazism, just as we underestimated the extent of the enthusiastic collaboration of the vast majority of Germans with Hitler and Nazism. Nor did we have any real sense of the scale of nonexistent remorse and regret by the Wagner family, Bayreuth and Hitler's willing executioners, the German *Volk*.

Beyond our credulity and denial about the silence surrounding the *Nazizeit* at Bayreuth, we Wagnerites accepted what could be interpreted as at least indirectly addressing the past. Ostensibly, we had an all new and de-Nazified Bayreuth Festival under the auspices of Wieland Wagner and Wolfgang Wagner. They seemed to look boldly to the future, with international and multi-racial castings and with modernist, Freudian, minimalist and progressive stagings, which in the case of Wieland's productions held the once again international and multi-racial audiences in a thrall that has yet to be matched.

So innovative were the stagings of Wieland Wagner that they seemed to effortlessly acknowledge and transcend the past and its controversies. Wagner the racist? Then why not toy with that concept by provocatively casting the first black singer to appear at Bayreuth, Grace Bumbry, in the role of Venus in *Tannhäuser*? Thus was the stage set by Wieland Wagner for Wagner's art to subsume every Wagner controversy and challenge and attempt an artistic legacy to even take on antisemitism and the war Wagner enkindled against the Jews.

Following Wieland's death from lung cancer in 1966, Bayreuth staged many such productions by a variety of leading directors, peaking with the Bayreuth centennial production of the *Ring* cycle, set in the Industrial Age by Patrice Chéreau, in which the Nibelungs were overtly depicted as Jews, and a *Meistersinger in 2018* by Wagner's great granddaughter Katherina that evoked the Nurnberg of Adolf Hitler. Clearly, it seemed, whatever happened in the past, Wagner and Bayreuth were greater than that past, than "the Nazi rut" of Hitler and WW2. These biggest of controversies became subsumed in endlessly imaginative, deconstructive stagings. Wagner's art, it seemed, was well on its way to becoming the great art of the future as originally intended by Wagner, and as Wagner declaimed it to be.

# The Wagner Family and Questions of Forgiveness (continued)

– *Huffington Post*, 5/12/2015

**Just as we think of the films of the exceptionally gifted Leni Riefenstahl as Nazi art, so we are in an inexorable process of appreciating much of the art of Richard Wagner as such.**

To recap, we know that with the later exception of Wagner's granddaughter Friedelind, the Wagner family collaborated enthusiastically with Hitler; they never protested or participated in any level of resistance. Wagner's grandsons Wieland and Wolfgang were teens under Hitler, and while their silence about Hitler and Nazism was disappointing, they were officially "de-Nazified," along with their unwaveringly Hitler-loyal mother, Winifred, on the basis of a rather threadbare pretext. Winifred did help a few Jewish artists to emigrate, and she protected a few others who were essential to casting, like Max Lorenz, whose wife was Jewish. In any event, with a mandate from their American conquerors, and the support of many Jews (who had likewise been so supportive of Wagner himself despite his Judeophobia and hatred), Bayreuth and the Wagners appeared eager to move forward, which they seemed to be doing with notable success. Time for all of us to let bygones be bygones, right?

Figure 36 - Winifred Wagner with Hitler and her sons Wieland and Wolfgang Wagner at Bayreuth, Wikimedia Commons, public domain

What we failed to appreciate was the seriousness and depth of the Wagner family's entanglements with Hitler and Nazism. What we already knew was bad enough, but what emerged was worse. And who knows what revelations there are in documents that remain unreleased at Bayreuth. Though it became common to refer to Wolfgang Wagner as an unrepentant old Nazi wounded on the front lines of the war, what came to light about Wieland Wagner years later is a lot more disturbing. At Hitler's alleged insistence, Wieland became a titular head of the Flossenbürg concentration camp in the environs of Bayreuth.

The camp, we were reassured, was more for political prisoners and wasn't a death camp *per se*. And we were likewise reassured that Wieland, whose deep commitment to his artistic calling is hard to doubt, spent most of his time there working on staging concepts for Wagner, albeit with the assistance of slave labor. Flossenbürg may not have had crematoria on the scale of Auschwitz but of the 90,000 prisoners who passed through it, 30,000 were murdered there.

According to Wieland Wagner's mistress, the soprano Anja Silja, this was a source of personal regret and remorse for Wieland, who, however, never found a way — unlike, for example, the recently deceased Gunther Grass — to publicly acknowledge, express remorse or seek forgiveness for this shameful past. Apart from his own silence, the question now is not: why was Wieland Wagner de-Nazified. It's why wasn't Wieland Wagner tried and prosecuted for war crimes and mass murder.

Parallel questions about Wolfgang Wagner and Winifred Wagner are inevitable. Apparently, the reason the Wagners weren't prosecuted is the same as the decision to exploit rather than punish rocket scientist Werner von Braun. Unlike Winifred, however, von Braun didn't continue to publicly proclaim loyalty to Hitler following the war. Several generations later, it's clear that the whole business of the "de-Nazification" of music and cultural figures is past due for reconsideration.

It's widely known that Wolfgang Wagner, whose absence of talent as a stage director was such that he relinquished artistic direction of the Festival to his brother, remained defensive and mum on questions of Bayreuth's collaborations with Nazism. For forty years after Wieland's death Wolfgang prevailed as CEO of the Bayreuth Festival, the securing of whose finances was his greatest achievement. Any questioning of this domineering administrator's Nazism was tacitly offset by his engagement of prominent Jewish conductors and other artists, as well as of Patrice Chéreau for the controversial centennial production, with its sensational clothing of Mime in concentration camp garb. In October 2010, Wolfgang's daughter, Katharina Wagner — awarded co-directorship with her half-sister Eva Wagner-Pasquier — planned to visit Israel to invite the Israel Chamber Orchestra to play a concert in July 2011 at the Bayreuth town hall. Her visit was canceled after hostility from Holocaust survivors.

As for Winifred, her enduring and outspokenly unapologetic loyalty to Hitler was among the reasons she was officially banned from direct participation in the postwar management of the Bayreuth festival. But what did that mild wrist-tap mean? As is clear from Eva Rieger's 2013 *Friedelind Wagner*, Winifred's greater plan for Bayreuth was always that her two sons, Wieland and Wolfgang, would run the festival. Winifred did not take her rebellious daughter Friedelind seriously nor the other Wagner sibling, Verena, who was never under consideration for any role at Bayreuth. Winifred may have been officially proscribed from direct involvement in the administration of the Bayreuth Festival, but it's Winifred—Hitler's devoted partisan and possibly lover, and who provided the paper on which Hitler wrote *Mein Kampf*—whose blueprint for Bayreuth was adopted.

A related bill of goods we were sold about Wagner likewise had to do with Winifred. From the 1960's well into the 1990's music critics were reassuring that to literally read racism and antisemitism into Wagner's works was to distort them. During those years, there wasn't enough information to know better and it seemed right to be affirming. As I discuss in my *Confessions of a Jewish Wagnerite*, for a number of these writers, being in the closet as gay and/or Jewish and not probing Wagner's antisemitism seemed to be conjoined phenomena. Throughout that period of time, in mainstream news about opera, Winifred was presented as this crazy old crone, fanatical in her inability to acknowledge the greater truth about Hitler and Nazism, and otherwise ultraconservative and myopic in her viewpoints about Wagner staging.

Alas, this cartoon image of Winifred doesn't begin to convey the articulate figure captured by Hans-Jürgen Syberberg in his 5-hour, 1975 documentary interview with her. Winifred essentially ran Bayreuth throughout the Nazi era and continued to run it subsequently in the sense that her plans for the direction of the festival were being implemented by her sons. To suggest that she — together with many other prominent Nazi cultural figures — had no real in-depth understanding or appreciation of Wagner is a mythology that was questionable to begin with but which became untenable in the wake of Syberberg's film.

It bears repeating that the bill of goods we've been sold — that Nazis like Hitler and Winifred had no real understanding of Wagner's art — can now be put to rest. Whatever "complexity" denialists and apologists — with Jewish Wagnerites forefront among them — might want to read into the interstices and nether reaches of Wagner's art, there is no longer any credibility to the old rationalizations that Nazi appreciations of Wagner were profoundly ignorant, unsophisticated, artless and wrong. Nor, as further probings are suggesting, were they always so aberrant. Nazi interpretations of Wagner was at least as credible as any other, perhaps more so.

Not coincidentally, the entire business of our belief that Bayreuth was deeply and genuinely committed to refuting and transcending its Nazi past turns out to have been as naive as it was deluded. Where this leaves Wagner's art on the spectrum from grandiloquent kitsch to

*Heilige Kunst* may continue to be debated, but to deny the racist, antisemitic appeal of so much of it now rings loudly hollow and untrue.

However artistically or dramatically impressive they may be, the *Ring* cycle, *Die Meistersinger* and *Parsifal* are racist and antisemitic works that qualify as such for at least conversational designation as Nazi art. Just as we think of the films of the exceptionally gifted Leni Riefenstahl as Nazi art, so we are in an inexorable process of understanding much of the art of Richard Wagner as such. Such has been this transformation of my own awareness that I winced when I learned that German Chancellor Angela Merkel had become a regular opening night attendee of the Bayreuth Festival.

Many of the ostensibly progressive developments of postwar Bayreuth — e.g., Wieland's productions, the Chéreau *Ring*, Wolfgang's featuring of prominent Jewish conductors — could be seen in retrospect to have served antisemitic viewpoints. While Grace Bumbry's "*Schwarze Venus*" in Wieland's *Tannhäuser* may have seemed momentous in breaking race barriers in casting at Bayreuth, Wagner's racism was thereby tacitly exposed, hissing the dangers of miscegenation attendant to erotic adventuring. Just as Tannhauser was being led astray spiritually, the Germans were being led astray racially. Even as the Chéreau *Ring* exposed Wagner's antisemitism, it also sharpened prevailing socialist viewpoints of Jews as miscreants of capitalism and enemies of humanity. Finally, Wagner himself established the precedent of featuring Jewish conductors (even if the choice of Levi for *Parsifal* proved contentious) and exploiting Jewish talent in the greater cause of Wagnerism.

Figure 37 - Friedelind Wagner (right) with Hitler and Verena Wagner at the Bayreuth Festival, public domain

Even Friedelind Wagner is not who we thought she was. Yes, she bravely left her family during the war, denouncing Hitler, and choosing to live in America. The ordeals she endured do indeed qualify her for comparisons to Wotan's beloved and heroic daughter Brünhilde, whose defiance of her father's wishes not to defend Siegmund in battle reverberate in Friedelind's defiance of her family's embrace of Hitler and Nazism. It's also clear that she was systematically excluded from involvement at Bayreuth before, during, and after the war, largely because of her mother's wishes and manipulations. Not only was Friedelind a woman, deemed to be difficult, competitive with her brothers, and comparatively ungifted, she was widely seen and therefore rejected as a traitor to family and country. Her return to Germany, not unlike Marlene Dietrich's, was anything but triumphant.

The picture of Friedelind that emerges from Rieger's biography is a lot more mixed than previous histories, including Friedelind's autobiography, *Heritage of Fire*. It's certain that Friedelind became anti-Nazi following years of regarding Hitler as family, and it's clear she believed grandfather Richard would not have been supportive of Hitler, but it remains unclear what she thought about antisemitism in

Wagner's life, writings and works. Indeed, although Friedelind later befriended a number of Jews, it remains unclear what she thought about Jews.

In an effort to better understand Friedelind's journey I contacted Eva Rieger. According to Rieger, Friedelind claimed in her autobiography that she became anti-Nazi earlier than was apparently the case; as late as 1937, Friedelind was still praising Hitler. It's also clear that however fractured the Wagner family's interrelationships, Friedelind never severed those ties, which she resumed after the war. There was, after all, an estate to be settled and Friedelind still held hopes of greater involvement with Bayreuth.

As for the question of what Friedelind thought about Jews and of the antisemitism in Wagner's life and works, Rieger was neither able to clarify Friedelind's thinking nor to offer reassurance that Friedelind had ever really grappled with these issues. "I think that being a direct relative of Wagner," Rieger evasively concluded, "it is most difficult to admit that he was an antisemite." In view of this, it's difficult not to revisit the old distrust of Friedelind as someone whose grievances were engendered more by lifelong family rivalries and resentments than by her later rejection of antisemitism, Hitler and Nazism.

As the host of the internationally broadcast Chereau centennial *Ring* cycle in 1976, her most visible role since the war, Friedelind's concluding observation now takes on additional resonance. "Who knows when another Alberich will come along to set the entire cycle in motion again?" asked Friedelind from a script prepared for her by music critic John Ardoin. In the Chereau production, as described earlier, the Nibelungs are depicted as Jews. Whatever other villains, complexities and layers of blame there are in the *Ring* cycle, and however otherwise layered questions of blame can seem in Wagner, what Friedelind was reciting what is overt in Wagner's tetraology—that this Jew in the Thornbush, Alberich, is the bottom line of all the trouble that ensues. Despite Friedelind's known resistance to Hitler and her brave acts of anti-Nazi defiance, including against her own family, her failure to question Wagner's antisemitism would seem to warrant further scrutiny and analysis.

This task of full disclosure fell to the only Wagner ever to look squarely at the issue, to publicly and fully articulate the bigger picture of the import of Wagner's antisemitism and Bayreuth's ardent collaborations with Nazism: Friedelind's nephew, Wolfgang's son,

Gottfried Wagner, whose *Twilight of The Wagners* seemed to be the *raison d'etre* of Ross's essay, "The Unforgiven."

In his essay Ross clearly understood and succeeded in capturing Gottfried's belief that Wagner was foundationally and crucially influential to the advent of Hitler and Nazism. He even noted Gottfried's allegation that Hitler copied Wagner in his phraseology. Determined to test this hypothesis, Ross decided to submit Hitler and Wagner phrases to a sophisticated library computer program that can prove complementarity, which indeed it did verify! Having acknowledged this astounding truth, Ross then proceeded to never again mention Gottfried, whose condemnations of Wagner, the Wagner family, Bayreuth, the troubledness of Wagner's Jews and glossing over of Wagner's legacy, are resolute. For Gottfried, there can be no talk of acceptance or forgiveness in the absence of full disclosure. Gottfried is the only Wagner to have taken on this exceedingly difficult and excruciatingly thankless work in his writings while also giving unauthorized Wagner family testimony on panels such as "The Post Holocaust Dialogue Group," in which Richard Wagner, much of his family, and Bayreuth are designated by Gottfried Wagner as "Holocaust perpetrators."

Talk about "the Unforgiven." The price Gottfried Wagner has paid for all this is virtually complete ostracism from his family, Bayreuth, the Wagner Societies and the greater world of Wagner appreciation. (Adding insult to injury in that world, Dr. Wagner also wrote a Foreword, "Redemption from Wagner the Redeemer: some introductory thoughts on Wagner's anti-Semitism," to my memoir, *Confessions of a Jewish Wagnerite*.)

Ross understood and accepted to some degree what Gottfried had demonstrated and concluded. In his quest to save Wagnerism, Ross knows he must fully and unflinchingly acknowledge the past. But having done that to a commendable extent, as he did in "The Unforgiven," he expected that he now would have the credibility and license to move forward again with Wagner appreciation. He is now hopeful that laying everything out on the table will fortify himself and others with the defense that, yes, we do now know and we do now fully acknowledge what happened, and that what happened is deeply troubling and regrettable. NOW can we move on?

Not unlike opera commentator William Berger's easy recipes for appreciating "Wagner Without Fear," Ross wants to do whatever will allow us to appreciate Wagner, the musical and artistic titan, without so much interference, without so much background noise, without so much discomfort, without so much resistance.

Alternatively, that full disclosure on Wagner's antisemitism and the Wagner family's perpetration of Hitler, Nazism and the Holocaust might seriously, and indefinitely into the future, taint or even cripple Wagner appreciation — and much of musical culture with it — is simply too overwhelming to contemplate. It's not surprising that this alternative would seem unacceptable to Ross, other Wagnerites, and musical culture arbiters who are admittedly dismayed that the controversies are not only not diminishing, but growing.

So, is Wagner destined to be perpetually labeled, like Jews with yellow stars, with an asterisk as one of history's most virulent antisemites and an instigator of the Holocaust? And if so, is the failure of more Jews to unconditionally forgive Wagner to blame for that? If Jews were to die out or otherwise be eliminated would that solve the problem? If Israel were to lift the ban on Wagner and sign an affidavit of forgiveness would that do it?

Or is Wagner himself, in company with the accursed of his own creation —the Flying Dutchman, Tannhäuser, Lohengrin, the Nibelungs, the Wanderer, Wotan and the gods, Beckmesser, Amfortas, the Knights of the Grail, Klingsor, Kundry— now doomed to bear the burden of a curse, that asterisk, likewise of his own creation? And is the only hope for redemption the "*das Ende*" that Wagner seemed so profoundly to understand, foretell and invoke?

Which brings us, finally, to the question of where forgiveness rests for me personally. In my experience, bearing resentment, however justifiable, is like taking poison and waiting for the other person to get sick; I cannot be like Larry Kramer, who risks every stereotype of being the vindictive, unforgiving Jew, like Shylock, in his self-righteously insistent "I forgive no one," a quote from Beckett that concludes his list of self-reflecting citations for the opening of his novel, *The American People*.

In my own life's trajectory, by contrast, forgiveness has been crucial to my equanimity, spirituality and serenity. So, yes, I do feel that forgiveness is in order. First, I forgive myself for going against the grain of mainstream musical culture and Wagner appreciation in sharing and affirming the perspective of Gottfried Wagner that Richard Wagner and his family were Holocaust perpetrators.

Beyond this, I also forgive Richard Wagner. And I do so with the mix of tenderness and detachment of Wotan's forgiveness of his beloved errant daughter Brünhilde, and that of another of Wagner's creations, Kundry, as he bestows upon each the sentence, but also the gift and blessing, of rest.

If I wish to retain my humanity and my sobriety, I cannot harbor resentment. Therefore, I conclude these reflections with a prayer for redemption. In this as, in all things, May Thy Will Be Done.

# The Nazi Legacy, Current Cinema and Questions of Judgment

– *Huffington Post*, Dec 6, 2017

Figure 38 - Bust of Wagner by Nazi sculptor Arno Breker, still overlooking the Festival grounds at Bayreuth, Wikimedia Commons

I've recently seen a number of films about the history and legacy of Nazism, most of them German and contemporary, and a book on two legends of German cinema. The juxtaposition of these events seemed coincidental. Or was it?

"Synchronicity" is a concept popularized by Carl Jung to describe concurrent events that may have no apparent or causal relationship, but which seem meaningfully related, even if the meaning is neither intended nor clear. Jung, the pioneering dream-interpretation psychoanalyst and "collective unconscious" spiritualist who broke with Freud, passively collaborated with Nazism, and spearheaded the founding of Alcoholics Anonymous and the addiction recovery movement.

Fascinated and unsettled by the ways Jung has influenced my own life, via my own recovery and work in addiction, I decided to call the memoir I began writing in 1984 "*Synchronicities*." This working title came to me in a dream, beckoning me to tell my story. That story took me ten years to write and is ongoing beyond its publication. Somewhere along the way I decided to change its title to "Confessions of a Jewish Wagnerite." There was something about being a Jewish Wagnerite amidst a global resurgence of anti-Semitism and the unfolding of the AIDS epidemic that seemed synchronicitous.

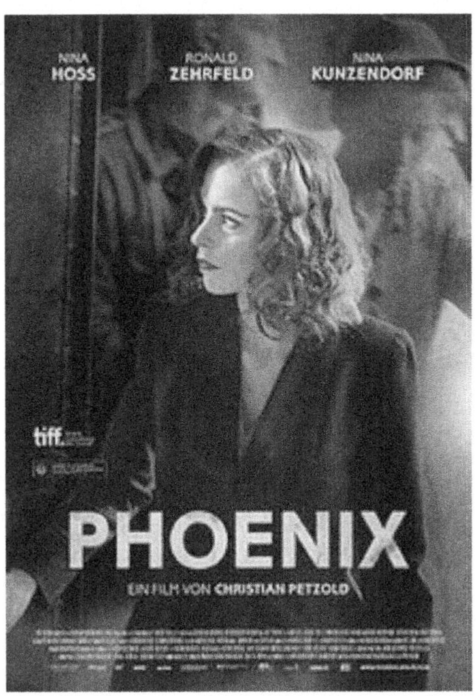


Figure 39 - *Phoenix*, a 2014 film directed by Christian Petzold, theatrical release poster, Wikipedia

The first of the German films, *Phoenix*, was directed by Christian Petzold, It's a suspenseful film *noir* about a Jewish woman, Lene, who returns to Berlin in the earliest days following World War II. The streets were still mostly rubble and no one had any money, goods or food, or anywhere to go, except a night club called Phoenix, a sleazy Mudd Club-like cabaret. (My brother Steve Mass, creator of the original Mudd Club in New York City, legendary home of many underground New Wave artists and musicians of the late 1970's, has been living in Berlin for the last 25 years, running a kind of Mudd Club *Ost*).

Mutilated in a concentration camp, Lene managed to have reparative cosmetic surgery, which so altered her appearance that she is not easily recognizable as her former self, not even to her husband, a bouncer at Phoenix, with whom she longs to be reunited. She is still in denial about her husband's betrayal of her to the Gestapo, just as she is still in denial about Germany's betrayal of its Jews. Even as she must increasingly face the enormity of those betrayals, she is willing to betray every conceivable standard of personal integrity if that will somehow return her to the connubial bliss she felt with her former husband and the Germany she called *Heimat*. Eventually, she sees the truth and viscerally realizes that the husband and homeland she remains so drawn to and in denial about have irreconcilably divorced themselves from her, her people and their fate. What's done cannot be undone. There is and can be no going back.

Notwithstanding some accusations of slickness, *Phoenix* has been widely acclaimed by critics and audiences. For me, it had great resonance because it so remarkably captures my own relationship to German musical culture, with which—I started to say with whom—I had such an intense bond. With much the same codependence with which Lene sustains her love and loyalty to her husband and Germany, I sustained my love of Wagner, Strauss, the Berlin and Vienna Philharmonics and for the many great artists and conductors of this music—e.g., Schwarzkopf, Furtwängler, von Karajan—in the face of ever-gathering and ever-worsening revelations of their contributions to and collaborations with Nazism, absent any expressed regret, remorse or apologies.

At the time I began *Confessions of a Jewish Wagnerite*, there were five pictures of Wagner on my living room wall, one of them a drawing by me. Like Lene, and though it took me decades, I finally recognized the reality that kept slapping me ever harder in the face. Finally, I see it and am resigned to never being able to go back.

Loving Wagner is an impossible situation to reconcile for any Jew of any real awareness and integrity. Whatever the complexity of the complicity of musicians, composers, and artists and however much I might turn to intellectual and emotional acrobatics to minimize and relegate, to forgive and forget, there can be no return to the old unguarded, unequivocal love and adoration of *Heilige Kunst* and *Hochkultur*. These no longer feel like safe places. If at one time they seemed places of spiritual *Heimat*, they no longer do. Never say never, but it is unlikely they will ever seem so again.

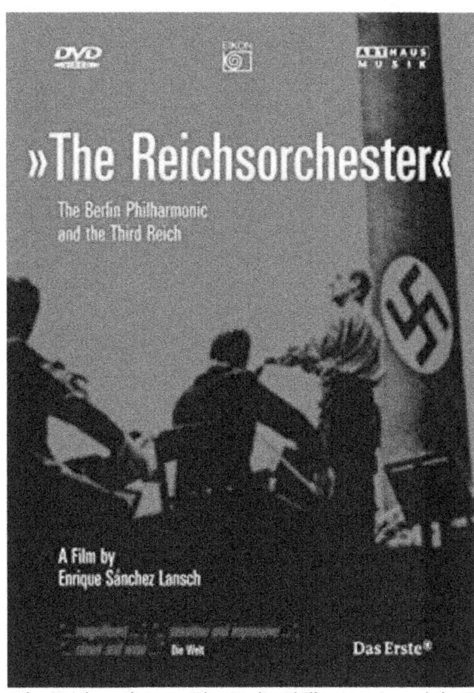


Figure 40 - *The Reichsorchester, The Berlin Philharmonic and the Third Reich*, a film by Enrique Sanchez Lansch, Amazon.com

The second of these films was *Reichsorchester*, made by German documentary filmmaker Enrique Sanchez Lansch, referred to me by my friend of many years, the noted German avant-garde and underground filmmaker Rosa von Praunheim. Lansch was considering doing a film on gay men and opera and wanted to contact me about my memoir.

Incidentally, von Prauheim's latest film, *Tough Love*, a true story of incest and violence against women, is as trenchant as cinema gets. It's a film Rainer Werner Fassbinder or Ingmar Bergman would have been proud to call their own. Though not about Nazism or its legacy per se, its scrupulously nonjudgmental portrait of warped mentalities during the early postwar period says more between the lines about the legacy of Nazism than some documentaries of the *Nazizeit* that prize objectivity.

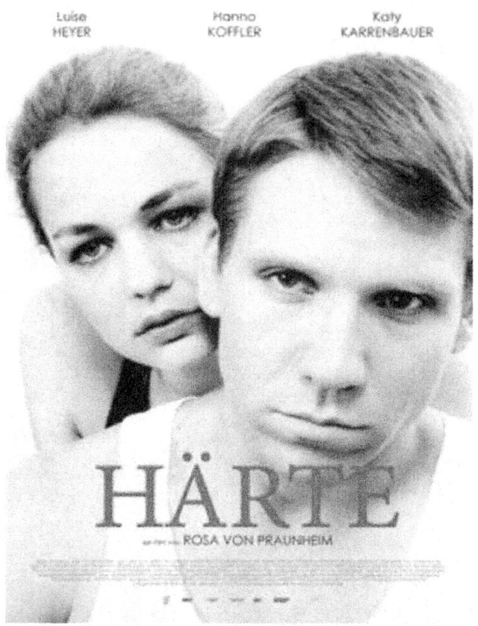


Figure 41 - *Härte (Tough Love)*, a 2015 film by Rosa von Praunheim, theatrical release poster

*Reichsorchester* is the story of the Berlin Philharmonic under Hitler, covering the years 1933-1945, with references to the post-war era. I saw this documentary when it was first released in 2007. Because of my current work, and the referral of Lansch to me by von Praunheim, I re-viewed the film, which meticulously and dispassionately chronicles what happened to the orchestra and its players over those 12 years. It specifies which players became Nazi party members and which Jews were fired, fled or disappeared. It also covers how instruments were confiscated, players were spied upon and spied on each another, and the way programs were presented under the auspices of the Reich. As a document of cultural and political history, it is priceless. And its dispassion can seem remarkable; there is no narrative voice other than the minimally descriptive, the neutrality of which approach seems crucial to eliciting of a lot of information that might not otherwise have been forthcoming.

That said, something troubled me about this film; so much so I found myself writing an emotional impression to Lansch. What so disturbed me is what I sensed to be the film's absence of judgment, remorse or regret—on the part of both the narrator as well as the players. Certainly, judgment can seem implicit and regret can be inferred, and failure to emote cannot be equated with failure to care. And aren't dispassion and the nonjudgmental, as in *Tough Love*, unassailable benchmarks of artistic integrity and quality?

Notwithstanding these caveats, the absence of feelings haunts *Reichsorchester*, much as it haunts Hans-Jürgen Syberberg's exhaustive documentary interview with Winifred Wagner. While no one wishes that the Winifred Wagner documentary was never made and no one wishes questions of morality to have been so aggressively pressed that she would not have revealed her real feelings, one can't help but feel deeply unsettled that the shocking and terrible truths she did tell remain so unattached to emotion; which seems consistent with the fact that few of these figures were ever prosecuted or censured. Does *Reichsorchester* adequately engage those challenges, or is it, beyond its acknowledgment of facts and not unlike *Winifred Wagner*, complicit in evading them?

I don't know Lansch or Syberberg personally, but the latter relinquished any claims to dispassion and objectivity when, many years after completing his 3 big Germany-Wagner-opera films, *Our Hitler*, *Winifred Wagner* and *Parsifal*, he expressed what seemed to a number of observers to be pro-Nazi and antisemitic statements. Lansch does include several understated moments in *Reichsorchester* that seem tantamount to indictment. The first is a photo of Jewish protesters at a postwar visit by the Berlin Philharmonic to New York. Placards explicitly decried the orchestra's complicity in Nazism and mass murder. And it was moving when one of the players interviewed recalled that at the first postwar concert in Berlin, Mendelssohn, who had been banned by the Nazis, was on the program. Still, Lansch's dispassion and reticence suggest distaste for judgment, a reaction often cited by critics as an aggregate and concerning response to the Holocaust by Germans. Like Winifred Wagner, the Berlin Philharmonic players were officially "de-Nazified." As in the case of Winifred, one can't help but ask if the chapter on "de-Nazified" musicians can really be closed solely on the basis of disclosure. Not unlike *Winifred Wagner*, *Reichsorchester* does not make a compelling case for closure.

Closure is something we all seek in German art, an expectation German artists and audiences are well aware of. We are always looking for it, hopeful of finding it and eager to proclaim it. But buyer beware. Remember Syberberg's *Unser Hitler* (*Our Hitler-A Film from Germany*)? Interpreting ambiguity as implicitly accomplishing the work of judgment, remorse, regret, and atonement, Susan Sontag dubbed it "one of the great works of art of the twentieth century." Of course, that was some years before Syberberg revealed himself to be an apologist for Nazism.

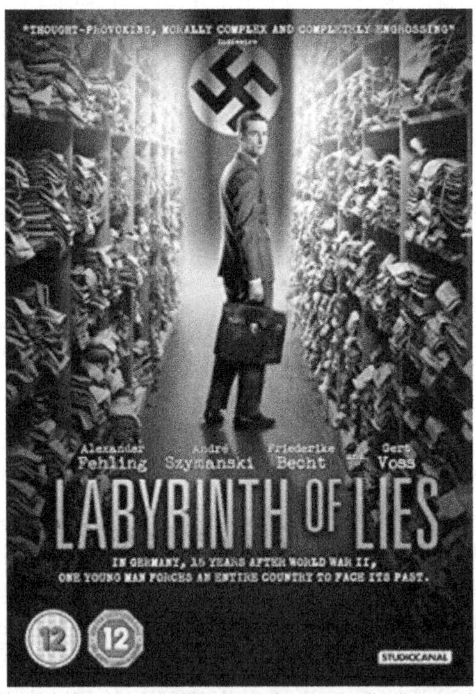


Figure 42 - Labyrinth of Lies, a 2014 film by Giulio Ricciarelli, theatrical release poster

Another recent German film was *Labyrinth of Lies*, directed by Giulio Ricciarelli. The critics were not very kind to this film, criticized for not knowing which genre to belong to, revealing their discomfort with the subject matter. What came to mind in reading *The Guardian*'s harsh take on *Labyrinth* was Pauline Kael's *New Yorker* review of *Shoah*, which she reviewed purely as a film. As such, she found it clunky, repetitive, and not well made. Meanwhile, nowhere in her review did she indicate any real feeling for the enormity and importance of its revelations, among the greatest and most disturbing in the history of documentary film.

Set in 1958, *Labyrinth of Lies* reprises the Auschwitz trials that were held in Frankfurt, the only other major trial in Germany, after Nurnberg, of former Nazis. Though 17 concentration camp attendants were tried and prosecuted, the trial remains a distressingly singular episode in a country that retained collective amnesia but little collective conscience about pervasive, enthusiastic collaborations with Nazism and wartime atrocities. The film imparts valuable and excruciating history. More importantly, however, it manages to convey that sense of regret and remorse, of genuinely endeavoring to truly, emotionally and viscerally come to grips with what happened, that are notably missing from cultural documentary histories of the Nazi period such as *Winifred Wagner* and *Reichsorchester.*

At the conclusion of *Winifred Wagner* and *Reichsorchester*, I felt a deep sense of injustice left unjudged. By contrast, at the end of both *Phoenix* and *Labyrinth of Lies*, I felt a genuine sense of catharsis.

*Reichsorchester* was made in 2007, when the challenge to document what happened still seemed urgent. The acknowledgement of the truth—of the specifics and statistics of what happened during the Holocaust—remains a paramount objective impressively engaged and achieved by *Reichsorchester*. Yet today's challenge, as evidenced by *Phoenix* and *Labyrinth of Lies*—as a younger generation understandably claims distance from the Holocaust—seems more about processing that information, and experiencing and articulating feelings of judgment, remorse and regret. Credible contributions to the vast, unfinished business of atonement remain vital, all the more so as the opportunities to do so become increasingly lost. The younger generation, which can legitimately disclaim responsibility for the Holocaust, is beginning to articulate and affirm a level of spiritual reparation that those who perpetrated this history have notably failed to do.

Figure 43 - Marelene Dietrich, Anna Mae Wong and Leni Riefenstahl (left to right) in Berlin, 1929, Pinterest

In *Dietrich & Riefenstahl: Hollywood, Berlin and a Century in Two Lives,* Karin Wieland compares the two legendary German stars whose lives intersected prophetically before diverging mightily. Dietrich was the outspokenly anti-Nazi actress and chanteuse, while Riefenstahl was a key figure in the success and legacy of Nazism. Beyond fascinating and telling details, Wieland's conclusions and judgments are hardly surprising. Still, there seems abiding value in retelling these stories. There is still resonance in the film *Judgment at Nuremberg,* in which Dietrich conveys an iconic image of handsome, patrician, German respectability. As the wife of a convicted Nazi general who is in denial about what she knew, she is, as Claudia Roth Pierpont observed in the *New Yorker,* "the aggrieved persona of German innocence" who has no response to the guilty verdict of her husband.

"Who am I to judge?" asked Pope Francis in response to questions about homosexuality. "Judge not lest Ye be judged," Jesus said. "JUDGE NOT!" reads a large poster at an AA meeting in Florida. In Christianity and other religions and movements such as those of recovery, suspending judgment and having compassion, mercy, and forgiveness are supreme values. In our times, peak demonstrations of forgiveness include the nonviolent civil rights movements led by Mohandas Gandhi, Dr. Martin Luther King Jr and Nelson Mandela, and the Tutsi reconciliation with the genocide in Rwanda.

For Plato, justice, together with temperance, courage, and wisdom, was one of the four cardinal virtues. However miraculous compassion, mercy and forgiveness can be, they are not meant to supplant basic precepts of morality, law, order and justice. The priest who gives succor to a convicted criminal does not expect that criminal to be spared his sentence. Courts of law are not expected to absolve alcoholics convicted of major crimes while intoxicated. Nor did the nonviolence and forgiveness of Gandhi, King, Mandela and the Tutsi absolve their former enemies of accountability.

Like *Labyrinth of Lies*, *Judgment at Nuremberg* reminds us that even when individuals are revealed to be human in extenuating circumstances, and where compassion, mercy, forgiveness and reconciliation would seem to be admirable, desirable and inevitable, the abiding challenge—with the legacy of Nazism, as with other major violations of society, morality, law and justice—is to articulate judgment and call for accountability, even when it might be tempting, and expedient, to devalue such priority as lacking in "the quality of mercy."

# Macon, Georgia, The Road Leads Back to You

– *Huffington Post*, 7/3/16

Figure 44 - Sidney Lanier, Macon, Georgia poet (1842-1881), Wikimedia Commons, public domain

"O Wagner, westward bring thy heavenly art,
    No trifler thou: Siegfried and Wotan be
Names for big ballads of the modern heart.
    Thine ears hear deeper than thine eyes can see.
Voice of the monstrous mill, the shouting mart,
    Not less of airy cloud and wave and tree,
Thou, thou, if even to thyself unknown,
    Hast power to say the Time in terms of tone."

**—from Street Cries/To Richard Wagner by Sidney Lanier, 1877**

In the years before the High Line emerged as a new epicenter of New York City's high culture, my sister Ellen and I were browsing in an art gallery on West 22nd Street between 10th Avenue and the West Side Highway, steps from the pre-AIDS generation's legendary gay leather bars, The Eagle and The Spike. Though the bars had been closed and shuttered since the mid-1980's, they silently bespoke their place as the soul of the greater area's transfiguration. The meatpacking district, as it was otherwise known, was the heart of the after-hours gay cruising scene, with its leather bars and clubs, and the large open-back trucks that were left there overnight and known in gay lingo as "the trucks."

Following an impressive but uncredited national pattern of gay settlement and transformation of urban slums, West Chelsea was awakening from decades of abandonment and neglect. Among its first sprouts were art installations and galleries that seemed haunted by denizens past. Though designated as environmental touchstones, a series of abstract granite statues accompanying planted trees along the 22nd Street block suggested Michelangelo's unfinished slaves, and the legions of those AIDS casualties, so many of them into what we called "leathersex," who had cruised there.

The gallery's featured artist was someone neither of us had heard of. Ellen, an environmentalist and artist whose progressive politics are more discernible in her probing photography of the ordinary and downtrodden than in her watercolor landscapes with their subtle pastels, was pleased by what she was seeing. What did I think? Yes, I agreed, the paintings were sensual and abstractly appealing. But I felt I had to know more about the artist, subject and context of the art before I could render an opinion.

Dinner with Hilan Warshaw at Café Tallulah, a French bistro on Manhattan's Upper West Side. Warshaw is the creator of several music documentaries, including *Wagner's Jews* and *Lyric Suite*, a work-in-progress which tells the story of Alban Berg's previously unknown affair with a Jewish woman and features a performance of the work with Renee Fleming and the Emerson String Quartet. Hilan and I are mostly on the same page about Wagner, frustrated at how difficult it is to get beyond the controversies that continue to waft within and around Wagner's works and their appreciation. Though we are in agreement against censorship in principle, Hilan wondered if he should expose his baby son to Wagner's music.

Discourse on aesthetics has a long history. Every orientation has been articulated and labored over. The one reflected by me in reaction to my sister's question is not widely endorsed: that initial impressions of art cannot be trusted. People do not want to be told that their spontaneous reactions to music or paintings need vetting. And in truth, I accept and respect their viewpoint as one I myself otherwise might endorse.

Yet because of how much pain love-at-first-hearing and intoxication with art eventually caused me, I have been aversively conditioned to approach art with a lot more caution. Because of the fallout for me personally of my own Wagnerism, all art has become suspect, guilty until proven innocent, and my reactions must be cleared through security and sobriety checkpoints, like screening passengers at airports and museums for weapons, or testing for blood alcohol levels. Like someone who slowly realizes they were raped, abused or otherwise exploited and henceforth will meet all romantic overtures with guardedness, or Holocaust survivors who reflexively distrust everyone, I am now reprogrammed to never again allow myself the freedom to fall head over heels in love with art at first sight or hearing.

When Richard Boch, a doorman at the Mudd Club, was working on his book about his experience there, he wanted to interview me about my brother, Steve Mass, who collaborated with several others in the creation of the club in 1977. With inchoate misgivings, I agreed to speak with Richard, with whom I was otherwise acquainted. Though I've remained friendly with Richard and admire the book he completed, I withdrew when I sensed that this would not be the right venue for me to try to express myself about Steve and our estrangement.

Figure 45 - Steve Mass, an owner of the Mudd Club in TriBeCa, in its Jayne Mansfield Room in 1981. Photo Credit...Kate Simon, caption from "The Mudd Club Comes Back To Life, For One Night," *New York Times*, Nov. 25, 1981

I look at the two best-known photographs of Steve, of him in a plaid suit and another with him looking like the proverbial mad scientist, leering with one eye, as he looks with the other, like a gecko, through an old microscope, perhaps the one my father the pathologist had at home when we were growing up. The plaid suit appears to be a costume or fashion statement of some kind, the mad scientist a fantasized "Dr. Mudd." These are fictional personae, I think to myself, and their creator is someone I never really knew.

The reasons for this are so various and elusive that I've decided to embark on these reflections to help me do what art and writing are best at—recouping people, places, things and times from memory, history and sensibility, in hopes of giving them context and perspective.

Plaids in curtains, upholstery and clothes—like those of the Catholic school uniform skirts that became mandatory in America in the 1940's, and the madras plaid shirts favored by Steve's high school peers—were in style in the 1950's America where Steve came of age...

Steven Arnold Mass, nearly six years my senior, was born in Macon, Georgia, in 1940. Not an optimum time or place for Jews, to say nothing of gays. Steve wasn't gay but, unbeknownst to both of us during a time when even the word "homosexuality" was so taboo that it was virtually never uttered or even written, I was.

A German American family down the road had a sign in their driveway that read "No Dogs or Jews Allowed." Later, I learned that "No Dogs or [substitute any immigrant group] Allowed" was not an uncommon posting in the history of so-called melting pot America. Though I knew we were Jewish, my disconnection with our Jewishness was such that I'd no idea this had anything to do with me. I would play there with the other boys, searching the abandoned and overgrown pool for turtles and snakes. I don't recall ever mentioning the sign to my parents or to Steve or Ellen.

Likewise down the street was my best boyhood friend, Chester, whose American-Gothic lookalike mother ranted endlessly about "niggers," and who later decided to forbid Chester to play with me because I was a Jew, which made me cry. Chester's dad worked at a gas station. I think they were Klan members. The Klan was very active in our area. Crosses were burned and it was said that a black man had been hanged in front of one of the downtown's 2 movie theaters.

This was the Southern heartland—with its pervasive mentality of bigotry and intolerance, of cruelty, meanness and hatred—that Tennessee Williams captured in his play *Orpheus Descending*. It's the South that never really surrendered to the North and which has been key to the rise of the present-day carpetbagger Donald Trump.

Such was the stigma we felt being Jewish that we kids would walk on opposite sides of the streets from the town's two Jewish houses of worship, both of which our family belonged to—the orthodox synagogue ("*Schul*"), Temple Sherah Israel, where Steve had his *bar mitzvah*, and the reformed temple, Beth Israel, where my sister was confirmed, where we went to Sunday school, and where we all got dressed up in costumes for the Jewish holiday *Purim*. Meanwhile, that we needed to "blend in" and not call attention to ourselves as Jewish became as reflexive and "natural" growing up in Macon as many of the Jewish girls getting "nose jobs" seemed in our teenage years in Chicago.

That we were members of orthodox as well as reformed communities, in Macon and later in Chicago, seemed reflective of our uncertain place and marginality as Jews even amongst our own. In the bigger picture, our parents' orthodox backgrounds were making their best if uneasy efforts at intermingling with modernity. Though more comfortable with reform Judaism, our parents, especially my mother, were still conscience-ridden about conforming to the orthodoxy of theirs.

Just as Verdi's *Nabucco* captures key aspects of our conflicts in Iraq with startling prescience, so *Purim* likewise foretells of those with Iran. Haman, the King's confidante who attempts to foment genocide against the Jews, has his precise counterparts in former Prime Minister Ahmadinejad and Supreme Leader Ali Khamenei. And Esther's ascendancy as Queen, with the power to denounce Haman and influence the King favorably with regard to the Jews, has its admittedly troubled reincarnation in Ivanka Trump's marriage to Jared Kushner, a conservative Jew.

I remember choosing to dress as King Ahashueras (coincidentally the name most often used for "the Wandering Jew") after my initial secret, taboo choice of Queen Vashti. In contrast to youthful, naturally beautiful, plainly dressed Esther, middle-aged Vashti got to wear a lot of jewelry and makeup. Early gay longings entangled with Jewish lore and festivity.

Figure 46 - Temple Sherah Israel, Macon, Georgia

Meanwhile, outside those confines of Temple and *Schul,* consciously or unconsciously, we kids would seize every opportunity to minimize our status as Jews. As mandated by our parents, we attended Friday Sabbath and holiday services, Sunday school and

Hebrew school, but with the same enthusiasm we had for going to the dentist. I remember once seeing our *Schul* rabbi crying, frustrated at the difficulty of successfully imparting what he felt we needed to know about being Jewish and Judaism. Sadness. Weakness. Not things we wanted to feel or be around.

However thick the ambient antisemitism, I don't recall any major incidents of antisemitic violence during the years of our upbringing, like the notorious Leo Frank lynching in Atlanta in 1913, and the crimes of racism against African-Americans that we later learned were commonplace. As it turns out, the South has deep Jewish roots, communities that went way back, preceding the Civil War. This was true of Macon and elsewhere in Georgia, especially Atlanta and Savannah, in neighboring states, and including some who figured prominently in the history and heritage of the South, like Confederacy treasurer Judah Benjamin and David Emmanuel, the first Jewish U.S. governor. The University of Georgia Law School is named after Harold Hirsch, a prominent Atlanta attorney.

As during the French Revolution, Jews found themselves on both sides of the American Civil War without being a major scapegoat of either, a situation that seemed to lay the groundwork for a future of relative security. Meanwhile, Jewish history includes episodic, disturbing, regrettable and sometimes tragic collaborations with racists and fascists, such as Southern Confederates and Mussolini. However ostensibly circumstantial, complicated and defensible or sympathetic as being in the greater interest of Jewish survival, this strategy of getting close to power has emboldened Jews and public perceptions of them as elitist. Notwithstanding the considerable risk of those perceptions contributing to recurrent tsunamis of antisemitism, this strategy persists, most strikingly in our own time in the ascendency of Donald Trump and his protectiveness of Jewish extremists in Israel.

Figure 47 - Temple Beth Israel, Macon, Georgia

Growing up in Macon, Steve excelled at ROTC (Reserve Officer Training Corps, which still recruits students in high schools as well as at colleges) at Lanier High, where he became adept at the operation of the M-1 rifle they gave all the young cadets to keep and practice with at home. He had graduated to his rifle expertise from the bb gun he owned and handed down to me, having taught me how to use it to shoot birds and squirrels. Shooting small animals without conscience was as common to small-town Southern life as cornbread and grits.

The school was named after the revered Macon poet, musician and educator Sidney Lanier, whose Wagnerism *New Yorker* music critic Alex Ross has affirmed but whose military service in the Confederacy he has not commented on.

Ross keeps chalking up Wagnerites from a wide range of backgrounds to demonstrate that the composer's influence has been so great, vast and varied as to subsume and transcend his legacy of antisemitism and racism. Notwithstanding Lanier's later distancing himself from his Confederate service and support for slavery, efforts were underway in Houston to change the name of Lanier Middle School because of the name's association with the Confederacy.

At that time before the tidal wave of Black Lives Matter, the move to rename Lanier Middle School was not the only such initiative. A harbinger of what was to come and also in Texas, this time in Austin, the school board voted to change the name of Robert E. Lee Elementary School. According to CNN, "the decision came amid a larger trend of questioning Confederate memorials across the American South, given the Confederacy's legacy of violence, racism and white supremacy."

The dominoes began falling. As reported in the *New York Times*, the Washington National Cathedral, one of the nation's most prominent houses of worship, said it would remove two images of the Confederate battle flag that have been part of its stained-glass windows for more than 60 years. I discussed this story with my close friend, Joel Bradley, a liberal Southern New Yorker and distinguished addiction treatment specialist in employee assistance programs. Joel hails from Elberton, Georgia. His grandfather fought in the Confederacy. Though we both wondered if some efforts to eliminate emblems of historical events weren't going too far, we agreed that great change was in the air, and rightly so.

Though the name of Richard Wagner has not been directly equated with Nazism and the swastika and though Wagner will most likely remain a predominant presence in musical culture, it seems probable that just as Southern institutions and landmarks are being scrutinized and cleansed of Confederate symbols and associations, future generations of Germans, Europeans and Americans will scrutinize and sometimes sideline Wagner for some name designations he might otherwise have claimed—for institutes, schools and landmarks.

At home and with straight faces, Steve, Ellen and I would march around the room singing the Christian hymnals we had to sing at school. (Our parents advised us to just mush-mouth any references to Jesus.) "Onward Christian soldiers, marching off to war, with the cross of Jesus...Jesus loves me, yes I know, Father Bible tells me so..." And of course, "Dixie": "Oh, I wish I were in the land of cotton..." To say that old times there in Dixieland were not forgotten, specifically the glory days of the plantations and Confederate heroes like Robert E. Lee, whose birthday we still celebrated at school, would be as big an understatement as you could make about the post-Reconstructionist South we called home.

We were too young to have a real awareness of our status as outsiders, even as we could vaguely sense the distress it caused our parents. Though my father seemed welcome in all circles, following the period of his medical education when many institutions had quotas for Jews, my mother's encounters with the shut doors of the Junior League—remember Ms Hilly in *The Help*?—were hurtful.

At home, meanwhile, our parents tried to acculturate us. Dutifully, I practiced piano, which I had no real penchant for. For my first and last recital, I effortfully banged out "From the Halls of Montezuma To

The Shores of Tripoli." I guess our involvement in Libya goes way back. Who knew?

I was never to become a musician, but my love for music did evolve from childhood crushes on Elvis Presley, the Everly Brothers, Jerry Lee Lewis, Theresa Brewer and Brenda Lee, whose hairdresser I was to meet and befriend years later at the baths in Fort Lauderdale. His clientele was mostly elderly women in senior residential facilities. At their first session, he would patiently explain: "This is a comb, not a wand." From my first vinyl 45-rpm (revolutions per minute) rock-and-roll records to Broadway show LP (long-playing) albums like *My Fair Lady*, I eventually moved on to what became the first great love of my life, opera, and its Grand Poobah, Richard Wagner.

In those same years I labored over one of my first books, James Michener's *The Bridges at Toko Ri*, which won a Pulitzer Prize and was made into a 1954 Hollywood film starring William Holden, Grace Kelly, Frederic March and Mickey Rooney. It's about the war with North Korea, which, like the Civil War, and for that matter the Crusades, and for that matter again the American Civil War, we are still playing out. Though I never became a voracious reader, my interest in things literary developed in tandem with my love for music and opera.

At school we read *The Jungle Book* and *Lazy, Liza Lizard*, and our teacher would model the costumes she acquired from her around-the-world tour, one of which, a kimono, set the stage for my first opera, *Madama Butterfly*. I can't remember at which of Macon's two historic universities it played—Mercer, named for Jesse Mercer, a prominent Baptist minister, or Weslyan College, one of America's first women's colleges and a birthplace of alumnae associations and sororities. More than a half century later, in "Racism on Campus, Stories from *New York Times* readers," one Weslyan graduate recalled, "The racial diversity at my college was basically all brochure pictures and no substance."

It was otherness that seemed the matrix of brother Steve's inimitable intelligence and wry, often twisted humor. Sensing our difference from the mainstream of Southern society, Steve, my sister and I were drawn to black singers of the times who appeared locally and later became legends, especially Little Richard, who in fact hailed from Macon. Just as these musicians were breaking through racial barriers by sheer talent, appeal and box office success, they gave inspiration to all outsiders, Jews prominent among them. But it wasn't until our move to Chicago that I attended my first concert with one of these legends—Ray Charles, whose "Georgia on My Mind," written by Hoagy Carmichael in 1930, became the state's official song in 1979.

Figure 48 - The Girl Can't Help It, directed by Frank Tashlin, 1956, theatrical release poster, Amazon.com

Enter Jayne Mansfield and her 1956 film, *The Girl Can't Help It.* The title song by Little Richard, and two of his other biggest hits, "Ready Teddy" and "She's Got It," helped make what was otherwise this B-est of B movies into one of the richest assemblages of period pop music on film, featuring other leading artists of the day such as Gene Vincent, Fats Domino, Eddie Cochran, Julie London, The Platters, Ray Anthony, Johnny Olenn, The Bell Boys, Abbey Lincoln, Eddie Fontaine, and Teddy Randazzo and the Three Chuckles. It was outside the theater where the movie played, incidentally, where the Klan was said to have carried out its lynchings.

The year before, Mansfield's co-star Edmund O'Brien was the villain in another film that offered rich hearings of pop era greats, *Pete Kelly's Blues*. Starring Jack Webb, best known for the television cop drama *Dragnet*, and the legendary Peggy Lee, it had cameos with the likes of Ella Fitzgerald, and, as a cigarette girl, Jayne Mansfield. Squeak!

It's hard to imagine more fertile soil for someone with a good ear for music and talent. Even in the heyday of the Mudd Club, however, I don't remember Steve ever singing a refrain or humming a tune in a way that reflected straightforward affection. Rather, in those 1950's years of our childhood and adolescence he would exaggerate and parody singers and songs, the hits we all loved but especially the crooned renditions of standbys like "Fascinating Rhythm" by popular B-list singers like Julius LaRosa, Marguerite Piazza, Perry Como and Dinah Shore.

What Steve seemed to be trying to convey was his "weisenheimer" sense of humor was that the decorum we were seeing and hearing in mainstream entertainment was artificial, insipid, sentimental, ennervated, desexed, hypocritical, and funny as such. In Steve's sensibility, artifice became the basis of what Susan Sontag would later become known for identifying as "camp." Steve was not gay, but he had what we gay people thought of as our special instinct for subverting social pretense with exaggeration, humor, affection and nostalgia. A droll and insightful if never exactly hilarious observer of people, and especially of 1950's culture, Steve was nonetheless an offshoot of the Jewish comedians we first saw on our 12" black-and-white Motorola TV who endeared themselves to mainstream America by using wit and facetiousness to upend provincialism and prejudice—Groucho Marx, Milton Berle, Sid Ceasar, Phil Silvers. Later, there was Lenny Bruce and eventually Woody Allen. At his most imaginative, Steve was the creator, operator-in-chief and behind-the-scenes (mostly) star of a *Cabaret*-style panoply of retro and cutting-edge fashion, design, theater, personalities, politics, happenings, music and arts. At his more sardonic and reclusive, he was a shadowy figure from a performance artwork by Mudd Clubbers Laurie Anderson and Lou Reed.

How else to react to what was expected of Steve—daily ROTC exercises and daily application of the phylacteries our Grandma—my mother's Orthodox Jewish mother—insisted on? Obediently but with that mix of pride and irony, arrogance and defiance that became hallmarks of his personality, Steve did both, meanwhile excelling among his genteel, gentile Southern peers in two key areas. Though he had to endure a lot of hazing, doubtless some of it antisemitic, he became an Eagle Scout, a serious achievement for any young man at that time; and he was so good at golf, the ultimate entree into Southern male society, that his picture was featured with several other state champion team members in the *Macon Telegraph*.

Steve was on his way, to be sure, but from Georgia to where? I don't think Steve ever thought of himself as belonging to the beats or any other movement, school, party, decade or even generational divide. Like people in recovery, and as stated in the preambles of recovery groups like Alcoholics Anonymous, Steve was "not allied with any sect, denomination, politics, organization or institution." Meanwhile, however, it was Jack Kerouac rather than recovery that could have been speaking for Steve when he wrote in 1957, on the eve of our move to Chicago: "Nothing behind me, everything ahead of me, as is ever so on the road."

# Waltzing With The Enemy

– *Huffington Post*, 7/4/2016

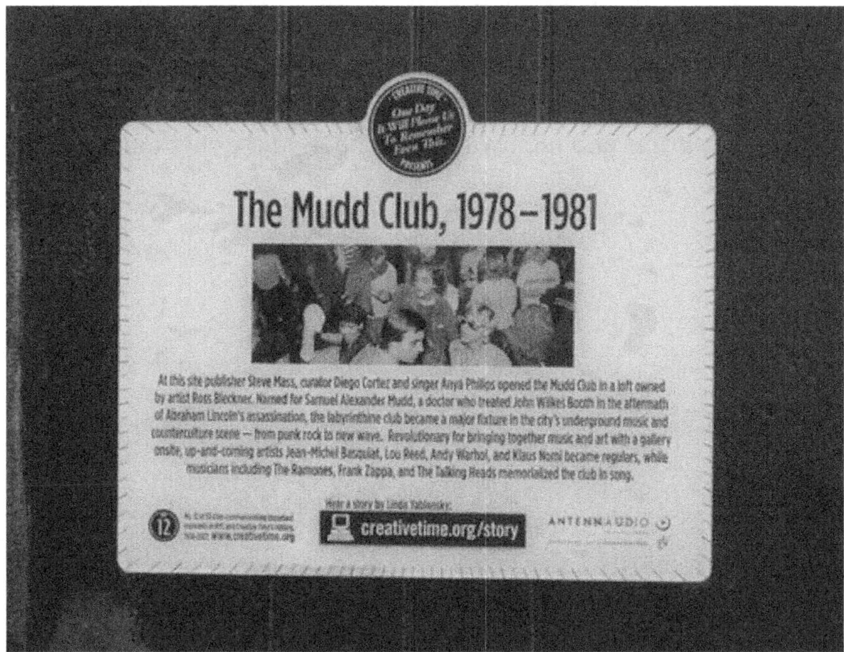


Figure 49 - "77 White Street-Mudd Club," photograph by Peter Comitini, Creative Commons

For those who've wondered about the origins of Steve Mass's embrace of Dr. Samuel Mudd, a distant relative of news anchor Rodger Mudd and a staunch confederate who was convicted of conspiracy in the murder of Lincoln but later pardoned, Steve himself has acknowledged that the name was little more than an affectation without any meaning beyond the name's catchiness.

Even so, one can't help pondering associations. Steve, like Mudd, was born and bred in the South. When he agreed to treat John Wilkes Booth, the wounded assassin of Lincoln, where should Mudd's loyalties have been—as a physician, rebel or law-abiding citizen? Where should Steve's loyalties have been when growing up: as a Southerner, Jew, or his own independent self? Later, when he came of age, should he have chosen to be a responsible wage earner or free-spirit entrepreneur? Having made the choice to become a club impresario, what should Steve's priorities have been as he attempted to cultivate and showcase writers, artists and musicians, many of them unknown and many whose needs could be peculiar, clandestine, demanding and illicit?

As he simultaneously struggled to create and lead a tribe, to fashion an image, to promote and manage his club, to stay afloat financially and wrestle with his own personal demons, what were the standards and values to be? Like Mudd's place in the orbit of Lincoln's assassination, Steve's place in the club scene swirl of arts, culture, sex, drugs and money remains open to speculation.

Figure 50 - "Home of Dr. Samuel Mudd" by crazysanman.history, Creative Commons

Another unintended association with Dr. Mudd may have been an awareness of our Dad's role as a pathologist and medical examiner in a time and place of segregation, where racist crimes of omission as well as commission were common. In Macon, and throughout the South, segregation was total. Separate bathrooms, schools, entrances, and water fountains. The bus I took to go downtown had a sign in front that read: "White people seat from front. Colored people seat from rear."

Though Dr. Mudd's place in the assassination of the President was never clarified, he came from a family of slave-owners and was known to have hated Lincoln. Though our Dad never evinced any racism we were witness to, he performed his medical duties independent of the surrounding politics or social circumstances, at least so far as we knew.

We were children, of course, but not unlike his Jewish family's tacit complicity in the status quo racism of the South that Tony Kushner exposes in *Caroline or Change*, our family's responses to the pervasive racism in the South, likewise the subject of the Kathryn Stockett novel and film, *The Help*, were hardly at the forefront of social activism, which scarcely existed in those years in rural environments in any case. In fact, apart from my mother forbidding us ever to use the word "nigger" that everybody used at school and most everywhere else in Macon, except in Temple and *Schul*, I don't remember Mom or Dad ever really discussing the still festering racism of the South that otherwise felt like home to us, the only home we kids had ever known.

Such was the depth of that Stephen Foster and Ray Charles sense of home that when I learned we were to move to Chicago in 1958, when I was 11 and Steve was 17, I cried. We retained our home in Georgia for another 50 years. To this day, I still experience a heartfelt comfort in the South and in the presence of Southerners that can only be described as primal. As with my initial *Heimat* love of Wagner, no matter how far down the road I've traveled, my heart still sometimes longs for the old folks at home, even as my head knows I can never go home again.

Nor did our parents ever discuss the other behemoth in our living room, the Holocaust, which was unfolding during Steve's childhood. It wasn't until I was 12, in Chicago, that my mother first said something in my presence about Hitler having murdered millions of Jews. While it may have registered for the future, at that young age of youthful assimilationism, of trying to be as un-Jewish, as "cosmopolitan," as "American" and "normal" as I could get away with while having my *bar-mitzvah* and socializing in a predominantly white middle-class Jewish milieu, I had no questions or interest in hearing anything more about what had happened to those people, old people from history, old Jews in Europe, not real living modern people like us.

Such was this disconnect during those years of not uncommon levels of deeply internalized antisemitism that when I got to know our East German cousins, who survived the Holocaust as *kindertransport*ees—whose close friend was Szymon Goldberg, the first violinist of the Berlin Philharmonic who likewise fled Nazi Germany, never to return—it still didn't occur to us kids that their relatives were our relatives, and that they were not just "those people," but us.

Meanwhile, I don't remember anyone in our family, including our relatives in Chicago or anyone at Temple or *Schul* discussing or even mentioning the Holocaust during the years of our upbringing in Georgia. Periodically, though, my parents spoke Yiddish, which they both grew up with and which I did not understand, apart from a few words. Steve doubtless knew more. Could it be that some of their "crazy Jew talk," as my sister once referred to it and I myself tended to think of it, were times when they spoke of what happened in Europe or otherwise about antisemitism?

Around the time my clearly dismayed father caught me trying on a pleated lamp-shade as a kind of ballet skirt (I must have been 5), adolescent Steve was invited to join Dad and several of Dad's golfing buddies and their sons on a fishing trip off the Georgia coast. I remember my mother saying something about one of the best-known of the resorts being "restricted," the term that was used for No Jews Allowed. Dad was an outstanding golfer and I recall some issues around the best golf courses there and their policies of restriction, issues I recalled a short time later when we were among the first Jews to be invited to join the beautiful Idle Hour Golf and Country Club in Macon.

Although I had no real interest in fishing or golf (my big sports interest was swimming), I was jealous that Steve, as the older brother, got to go on that Sea Island jaunt and I didn't. Steve, meanwhile, had his jealousy of me as the younger brother displacing so much of his family's time, attention and affection. Although I never experienced any of the primal Cain-and-Abel physical violence that can erupt in circumstances of rivalry among siblings, of the older chick trying to push the younger one out of the nest, one incident stayed with me.

At age 5 or so, I acquired a little plastic change holder, a colorful toy version of the metal ones our bus drivers wore on their belts. It was either a gift from my uncle in Chicago who managed a convenience store or from the Macon toy store owned by the Kaufmans, one of the town's oldest Jewish families. (Marian Kaufman, the matriarch and a Weslyan graduate, compiled a history of the Jews of Macon.) Press the various levers and the change holder would dispense quarters, nickels, dimes and pennies. Steve was jealous and after first threatening to destroy it, in response to some real or imagined provocation but more likely out of sheer spite, he grabbed this favorite toy from me, threw it on the floor and stomped on it as hard as he could, repeatedly and breaking it into many little pieces. I remember crying.

Figure 51 - Our father, Dr. Max Mass, family photograph

Whatever the incidents and rivalries, Dad, a stern disciplinarian, didn't seem partial to any of his children. Later, I would learn that he was a closet journalist who eventually gave up his writing—except for medical publishing and writing children's stories in letters to nephews and nieces—to more fully embrace his calling of medicine. Beyond his gift for literary expression and illustration, he was a skilled visual artist who continued to paint and create even after losing fingers from the skin cancers that were a high risk of the radiologists of his era from the Cobalt 60 and other radioactive materials used in early efforts to treat cancer patients. A heavy smoker, Dad died from cancer of the pancreas at the young age of 63. Whether that cancer was likewise a consequence of radiation exposure we will never know.

Beyond polymathic creativity, there was another of Dad's traits that Steve and I shared. More than our similarly creative sister and notwithstanding our skills at getting on well with people, the Mass men harbored a notable distrust of humanity, a *Weltanschauung* of humankind as prone to relentless and endless aggression, marauding, plundering and pillaging, which is how Dad characterized history in one of the journal fragments he left behind. While my sister ardently believed in the promise of progressivism and socialism, Steve and I, like our Dad, were a lot more skeptical of humankind's potential to transcend its baser inclinations.

In his last years, Dad became my close friend, to the extent that he was the first relative, in fact the first adult, I came out to. Responding to my inquiry, Dad didn't recall any homosexual inclinations he had ever had as a young amateur boxer and wrestler, though he did express concern that in professional and social circles I'd be "found out." This was 1969, the year of the Stonewall uprising that sparked the modern Gay Liberation Movement in America, but still 4 years prior to the declassification of homosexuality as a mental disorder by the American Psychiatric Association.

In those days, laws against homosexuality were still universal and there were no civil liberties protections anywhere. Being openly gay was still limited to a handful of very brave activists, like my life partner Arnie Kantrowitz, who I wasn't to meet for another decade. Coming out as I did to my Dad was still highly unusual. A distinguished physician and mammography pioneer who specialized first in pathology and later in radiology, and after whom they named the Macon Hospital library—the Max Mass Library—Dr. Max Mass died 2 weeks before I was accepted to medical school.

By contrast, though I later came out to him without any discomfort, Steve was not one I would seek out very often to confide in. The problem was never any prejudice or judgment so much as an absence of any affection, friendship or bond. That there was no genuine or reliable relationship seemed perhaps attributable to his being 6 years older than me. While this failure of bonding might seem a source of enduring enmity, and notwithstanding the incident with the toy change holder, it never seemed personal. Even in those early years of my child's ignorance and vulnerability, Steve's self-absorption, remoteness, his avoidance of intimacy and his reclusiveness seemed impersonal and global.

Figure 52 - Helen Mitsios with her mother, Rasia Kliot, from *Waltzing With The Enemy* by Rasia Kliot and Helen Mitsios, Urim Publications/Penina Press

Though Mudd Club Steve seemed to know everybody, the only sustained relationship I ever knew him to have had was with an ex-girlfriend, the writer and anthology editor Helen Mitsios, whose collections of Japanese and Icelandic fiction have been praised, and who co-authored a bracing memoir, with her mother, *Waltzing With The Enemy*.

*Waltzing* is the story, in her own words, of the experience of Rasia Kliot (Helen's mother) of Holocaust survival, and of Helen's story of her own coming of age. The book is divided into two parts, Rasia's

Story and Helen's Story. Hiding her Jewishness was the great secret that her mother had kept, so tightly that not even Helen, who she raised as Catholic, never knew of it until she came of age.

Helen's loyalty to Steve sustained itself, even as he moved to Berlin and she went on to marry architect and landscape artist Tony Winters. Was Helen's enduring relationship with Steve best explained by attraction, codependence, genuine friendship, his connections and intersections with the world of writers and artists, or a deep empathy that withstood and transcended the not-thereness from which so many of those who knew Steve eventually detached?

As described by Helen in *Waltzing*,

> "Like my mother, [Steve] kept the fact that he was Jewish a secret. Like [her], he had a totally different private and public persona. He didn't trust people and assumed everyone was out to take advantage of him...[He] had little faith in human nature. However, in public, his persona was completely different. He was gregarious and an iconoclast, so stylishly oblivious with his beard and plaid flannel shirts that he became the very essence of hip."

Figure 53 - Waltzing with the Enemy (Amazon.com)

In the film, *Driving Miss Daisy*, Patti Lupone plays the 1950's daughter-in-law who, dressed in red-and-green plaids, overdoes Christmas as her way of blending in. Miss Daisy (Jessica Tandy) likewise defuses the surrounding antisemitism by being the genteel Southern white lady who, in the wake of the bombing of a local synagogue, must inevitably face her minority kinship with her black chauffeur (Morgan Freeman).

Miss Daisy reminded me of our own mother, Mignon Masha Segal Mass Thorpe (after Bill Thorpe of Chester, Pennsylvania, her second husband), who delighted in being called "[Mzzz Maze]," a pronunciation that made her feel more Southern. For the Mass family children, the drive to assimilate was to take alternate routes. For me, there was opera, Wagner and gay life. For my sister, progressive politics and environmentalism. And for brother Steve, the enterprise of entrepreneurial creativity around artists, writers, musicians and club life.

Recently, after all those years of estrangement, and as arranged by Helen, the three of us had a reunion. Looking remarkably youthful and healthy at 75, ever-observant Steve, on a visit from Berlin where he still has residence, had trenchant observations about Germany and Wagner today. It seems obvious to him that there is no longer any real controversy about the preeminent and surpassing esteem for Wagner in German history and culture.

Perhaps the most important and influential of contemporary Wagner lovers and defenders cited by Alex Ross is Chancellor Angela Merkel, whose annual trademark appearances at Bayreuth Festival opening nights is a bellwether of Wagner's current place in Germany. Even though his milieu was pop culture, he had majored in philosophy, with an emphasis on such German heavies as Marx, Engels, Hegel and Jaspers. Though never a Wagnerite himself, his awareness of Wagner in relation to Germany was informed, observant and sophisticated.

Yes, Germany and Bayreuth have done much to distance themselves from the past. So has the American South. But scratch the surface, as Donald Trump has done, and as the clock is ticking to do with Wagner, and the old prejudices, values and racial loyalties are right there. Though Mrs. Merkel has been scrupulous in distancing herself from overt xenophobes, racists and antisemites, and welcoming to immigrants, her championing of Wagner arouses concern in a time of far-right resurgences.

When I first became aware of her Wagnerism, I found it troubling. In my fantasies of change in postwar Germany, I somehow imagined that a figure like Merkel, even if she shared a nearly universal appreciation of Wagner as composer and artist, might, as Chancellor, want to keep her distance from the citadel of Hitler's Reich that was Bayreuth. But that, as it turns out, was wishful thinking.

Clearly, Helen Mitsios gleaned in Steve Mass some of the same deep wounds, secrets, and honed instincts of survival, specifically Jewish survival, that were hallmarks of her mother's story. But is her perception of Steve as a kind of survivor and indirect victim of the Holocaust fully revealing and explanatory? Or are the keys to a broader understanding likely to be found in other contexts and viewpoints, such as the Japanese sensibility Mitsios (who edited the *NYT* editor's choice anthology, *New Japanese Voices: The Best Contemporary Fiction from Japan),* has shown such affinity for? Indeed, the story of Steve Mass, which he is episodically endeavoring to write himself, may be more redolent of the legendary Japanese tale of *Roshomon*, (originally a medieval *Noh* play and eventually a Kurosawa film classic.)

As we finished our pleasant mid-afternoon get-together over coffee and pastry at Greenwich Village's Marlton Arms Hotel, Steve, Helen and I took our leaves cordially. Helen and I embraced. When I turned to embrace Steve, my open arms were met with a two-handed handshake that was at once warm and distancing. When he and I had dinner a few nights later at the Knickerbocker, with its large collection of Hirschfeld portraits of celebrities, neither of us initiated an embrace or handshake, despite apparent good will on both our parts. Steve had to cut the dinner short, rushing off, as he was always wont to do, this time to catch what he said was the last train to his suburban hosts. The following week I got an email from him that was signed "Warm Regards." It was not only the warmest but also the only written expression of well wishes I can recall ever having received from my brother.

# Art, Addiction, *Enfants Terribles* and *Monstres Sacrés*

***"Heroin, be the death of me Heroin,***
***it's my wife and it's my life... "***
**– Lou Reed, "Heroin"**

Figure 54 - "Queers in Love! Bi guy Lou Reed marries lesbionic performance artist Laurie Anderson today" by feastoffun.com, Creative Commons

***"Not pleasure alone lies close to my heart.***
***In the midst of joy I crave after pain."***
**– from Tannhäuser's Ode to Venus**

Figure 55 - Grace Bumbry as "Black Venus," Bayreuth, 1961, bibliolore, The RILM blog

In his song, "Heroin," Lou Reed admits surrendering to his addiction to opiates. In a film biography, "Born To Be Blue," musician Chet Baker chooses heroin over his family. In Mozart's opera, *Don Giovanni,* the antihero is unapologetically addicted to seducing women. In Wagner's *Tannhäuser,* by contrast, the protagonist seeks to escape his enslavement to erotic pleasure.

All addicts need healing, what we call recovery. But not all addicts want it and fewer still want it badly enough to pursue it and stick with it, even when it's a matter of life and death, as it inevitably tends to be. After years of fighting drugs and alcohol, Reed and Baker joined the multitudes of their confreres who died while still actively addicted to alcohol and drugs. Don Giovanni remains evermore defiant as his sex addiction accelerates. He dies unrepentant, as he is carted off to hell. Among these exemplars of addiction, despite several near-relapses, only Tannhäuser sustains his commitment to healing. All achieve posthumous redemption, Wagner's great theme, via art.

Wagner wasn't known to be alcoholic, drug addicted or sexually compulsive, but like Tannhäuser, he struggled with character defects and troubled inclinations that cast a dark shadow on his life and work. Tannhäuser dies in his quest for the grace he finally achieves, but Wagner's fate is more like Moses's. Wagner's descendants—his music dramas—are granted entry, albeit increasingly qualified and monitored, into the promised land of enduring artistic acclaim while the composer himself is detained at the pearly gates.

Figure 56 - Alison Bechdel at the Boston Book Festival by Chase Elliott Clark, 10/14/11, Wikimedia Commons

For his 75th Birthday I took my life partner Arnie Kantrowitz to see the musical *Fun Home*, based on Allison Bechdel's memoir of growing up lesbian with a closeted gay, alcoholic father. "Fun Home" is short for the funeral home where Bechdel's father worked and which serves as a metaphor for the moribund state of their family relationships.

I found myself keyed into the mystery that is at the play's center: why couldn't she and her father find a way to better communicate, be more real and genuine with each other, and be friends? That almost happened on some occasions, but inevitably the father would retreat into the closet and isolation, into drinking and otherwise effortful imitations of being the dad, breadwinner and standard-bearer. Allison, meanwhile, longed to understand her father's private life, feelings, beliefs and hopes, so many of which she was sure they shared. But it was never to be. What she was left with were fragments of memory, a few posthumous revelations, and lots of questions and unresolved feelings.

In *Fun Home*, the protagonist goes back in time to her first glimmerings of awareness of her father's gayness, his compulsive trysts with young hustlers, and his drinking. The extent of her father's drinking is more implicit than clarified in the play. Like his daughter, Mr. Bechdel is creative, with an interest in literature and theater.

Like Bechdel's father, and more than my other immediate family members, my brother Steve Mass always seemed to be not present, off in another world, preoccupied, evasive, and hiding secrets. On so many fronts it seemed we were kindred spirits. Even with his being 6 years older than me, why couldn't we bridge the communications gulf between us?

My field is addiction medicine and I myself am a person in recovery. Not surprisingly, I am primed to see people through this lens. Not unlike homosexuals and many artists throughout history, addicts are perforce alienated from society, which so unrelentingly misunderstands, stigmatizes, neglects, abuses and discourages them when they are most vulnerable and struggling. Yet they are admired and rewarded with outsized adulation when successful. How society treats addicts and artists is not unlike how the Romans treated gladiators. We aversively condition them, like dogs for dogfights, to kill and die for us. When they succeed, we venerate them as champions. Top gladiators have been described as the rock stars of their day. When they are less than champions, we abandon them, often contemptuously.

In the age of Trump, the public stigma upon and neglect of opiate addiction has turned evermore deadly. There simply is no other way to describe the tens of thousands of deaths of the opioid crisis that have been preventable but which the public, with its ignorance, prejudice and especially its politics, still widely abets. Beyond fitful, patchwork progress, it still recoils from understanding, compassion and life-saving actions such as needle exchanges, opiate maintenance, detox, rehab, overdose prevention and other treatment services. A more serious and sustained approach with genuine leadership would also help prevent attendant epidemic recurrences of HIV and Hep C infection such as those that rocked Mike Pence's Indiana. Alas, the promises of preventive medicine have no more currency than environmental protections for an administration hellbent on deregulation and cost-cutting at the expense of science, common sense and humanity.

It's difficult to overstate the problem of stigma addicts the world over still face. The death squads of Philippines dictator Rodrigo Duterte's death war on drugs seems of a piece with the empty rhetoric and gestures of the Trump administration. As social outsiders and often enough literally outlaws, however, addicts do tend to share traits that are not always wrongly regarded as antisocial or sociopathic, especially when they choose to reject treatment and recovery, as they so often do.

Stereotypically, addicts not yet stabilized in treatment and recovery are characteristically in situations of emergency. They are invariably absent or late for events, in some kind of trouble, often legal and financial, and defensive with excuses that don't add up. The cumulative impression you have with an active addict is that a real person simply isn't there. They're not dependable or reliable. Honest communication and genuine intimacy are always elusive. They're disingenuous and emotionally unavailable, except when a scarcely concealed need for money or refuge emerges from a guise of caring. This is why most of the significant others of addicts who aren't in recovery eventually fall by the wayside after years of codependence, enabling, and mollification. Though it's predictable that an addict will take family members and significant others hostage emotionally and financially, it's likewise characteristic for even the most codependent of enablers to eventually see the light and want out.

Psychoanalytic theory, which Freud and his followers developed and which dominated American psychiatric practice for decades, is now mostly history. Though psychoanalysts are still in practice and psychoanalytic constructs and methods are still respected and utilized, their older explanations for human behaviors have long since given way to behavioral and biological models.

Two examples of the death knell of older psychoanalytic theory are homosexuality and drug addiction. As psychoanalysts struggled to retain their theories of homosexuality as a developmental disorder of family relationships (e.g., the overbearing-mother-and-absent-father paradigm to explain male homosexuality), sexology was running rings around them with new studies (Kinsey, Masters and Johnson, Bell and Weinberg) that were far better-researched, far less obviously biased and far more sophisticated in perspective. In less than a generation, psychoanalytic explanations of homosexuality became completely discredited. This does not mean, however, that psychoanalysis no longer had anything of interest or value to say about homosexuality or to gay people.

The same is true of psychoanalytic theories of drug addiction. Today, if you are diagnosed as an alcoholic or drug addict, no mainstream physician or institution would send you to a psychoanalyst for initial or primary treatment. Rather, you would most likely be guided into various levels of addiction treatment—detoxification, rehabilitation and long-term recovery using 12-step programs based on the model of Alcoholics Anonymous.

Early psychoanalytic writings did, on the other hand, hit the nail on the head in their characterizations of the behaviors of drug addicts. These turn out to be the same behaviors psychoanalysts have observed in artists and gay people—behaviors that fall under the rubric of what they call "narcissism."

Figure 57 - Carl Jung, Wikimedia Commons

Narcissism is a key psychoanalytic concept that is used primarily to describe the psychopathology of self-absorption and concomitant retardation of emotional development. Simply put, narcissism can be understood to mean immaturity. In common parlance, narcissists are people who feel entitled the way children do and who lack a developed sense of responsibility in interpersonal relations. Because narcissism can also be described as an absence of empathy or spirituality, it's not surprising that the addiction recovery movement was indirectly spearheaded by Freud's more spirituality-oriented acolyte, Carl Jung, and further developed by Dr. Harry Tiebout, another psychiatrist of that period of the mid-1930's who envisioned spiritual development as key to behavioral change.

Figure 58 - Dr. Harry Tiebout, Alcoholics Anonymous, aa.org

The recovery landmarks that emerged—the "Big Book"of *Alcoholics Anonymous* and *12 Steps and 12 Traditions*—are remarkably consistent in expressing that addiction was, as manifest in attitude and behavior, a disorder of emotional and spiritual retardation and impairment. As these founders of the recovery movement noted in their literature (from *12 Steps and 12 Traditions*): "We...had to admit that we were childish, emotionally sensitive and grandiose."

A fascinating window on all this is provided by Bradley Jones, an openly gay psychoanalyst in New York who came to his profession via his publicly acknowledged experience with drug addiction (primarily cocaine). For Jones, the "God" and "Higher Power" concepts of recovery, developed from the Christian-identified principles of the Oxford Group, proved troubling. Though 12-Step recovery is explicit about not being allied with any denomination or sect but does conceptualize "God" to be "as we understood Him," Jones was more drawn to the paradigms of psychoanalysis. He sensed that the serious underlying psychodynamic issues in his interpersonal relations were less about "Higher Power" and "spirituality" than what Jones himself identifies as narcissism.

His journey took him not only from recovery to psychoanalysis but to actually becoming a psychoanalyst. As conveyed in his indeed fabulous one-man cabaret show, "Dr. Bradley's FABULOUS, Functional Narcissism," his self-realization took place primarily via "self-psychology," an offshoot of psychoanalysis developed by Heinz Kohut.

In his show, Jones, who was a member of the cast of *A Chorus Line* on Broadway, dances and sings his journey with perception, elan, and passion. For someone with such talents, and as the show reveals, it was challenging to learn how to relegate the self to become more right-sized, to becoming, as 12-step recovery puts it, "a person among persons." But how inspiring to see a person take what recovery can seem to relegate as a character defect, narcissism, and turn it into a principal engine of creativity, self-realization and celebration.

Figure 59 - "Dr. Bradley's Fabulous Functional Narcissism," starring Dr. Bradley Jones, theatrical poster

While it may seem that artists and addicts are the way they are because they are wounded from their upbringing, or because of the self-preoccupation that can seem bound up with their creativity, their behavior is often perceived as narcissistically troubled. Like addicts, many artists feel that they must have what they must have when they must have it, regardless of consequences. If an addict or artist must break the law to meet his or her needs, so be it. If she or he must dominate, exploit, endanger, neglect or abuse to meet needs, so be it.

When otherwise unremarkable adults behave this way in everyday life, they may be regarded as sociopathic. When they happen also to be admired artists, we call them *enfants terribles*, after the 1929 novel *Les Enfants Terribles*, by Jean Cocteau. If they are of even greater stature, say a Picasso or Wagner, we may call them *monstres sacrés,* after the 1940 play *Les Monstres Sacrés*, also by Cocteau, himself a heroin addict.

*Les Enfants Terribles* is about a twisted sibling relationship literally poisoned with opium addiction. For an artist and/or addict to be an *enfant terrible* or *monstre sacré* is like having an exemption, a free pass from the harsher expectations and judgments of society. As Donald Trump put it in terms of his fanatical base, "I could shoot somebody and not lose any voters." The same might be said of another great category of celebrities—artists. Figuratively, and sometimes literally, if their base is strong enough, they can get away with murder.

Figure 60 - Jean Cocteau, author of *Les Enfants Terribles* and *Les Monstres Sacrés*, Studio Harcourt, 1937, Wikimedia Commons, public domain

Among the exemplars of this aspect of artists is Picasso, who famously observed that when he was a fledgling artist he was taught to paint like an old man, but when he became an old man, he finally learned how to paint like a child. It's an insight about creativity that everyone can appreciate. But the flip side of this indulgence of the inner child, the price of being childlike in circumstances requiring maturity, tends to be glossed over or ignored.

The disconnection from reality and responsibility addicts seek is captured in many images and stories. *Tannhäuser* is a good one, but none is more trenchant than a key scene in Danny Boyle's film, *Trainspotting,* about heroin addicts and their lives. The camera begins a startlingly slow-motion scan of heavy drug usage, mostly of heroin, in a crash pad, capturing a panorama of addicts in advanced stages of intoxication. Eventually it settles on an unwitting participant, the baby of one of the addicts, now dead from hours of neglect. In the greater perspective of addiction so incomparably achieved by Boyle in *Trainspotting* and *Trainspotting 2*, as in the constructs of state-of-the-art addiction medicine, craving and seeking are seen to trump everyone and everything else.

Figure 61 - Trainspotting, directed by Danny Boyle, Miramx, 1996, theatrical release poster

Because of Jackson Pollock's stature as a great artist, and notwithstanding his vehicular manslaughter of a girl (and injury of a second passenger, his mistress) during a drunk-driving spree, the wreckage of his personal life and its alcoholic deaths are couched in a certain romance. The same is true of writer William S. Burroughs, a gay man and opiate addict who "accidentally" killed his wife in a drunken William-Tell-like game. Her death was declared "culpable homicide."

Gaugin is another of these easy-pass *monstres sacrés*, an artist whose decision to abandon his wife and children to pursue his art became legendary—culturally sanctioned, admired and envied. The list of "bad boy" artists is not simply big. It's more the rule than the exception. This is how important art is to the artist, artists believe and their admirers accede, whatever the consequences.

THE ARTIST AS DEBTOR
THE WORK OF ARTISTS IN THE AGE OF SPECULATIVE CAPITALISM

Figure 62 - artanddebt.org

Acceptance of Wagner can be seen in this context as a manifestation of our exoneration of ugly and reprehensible behaviors and prejudices—arrogance, theft, adultery, bullying, exploitation and malignant antisemitism—in the name of art. And however we may judge his work, Wagner's most infamous and ardent disciple, Hitler, was also an artist. Even Donald Trump's pathological narcissism seemed initially blunted by being sold as the "art" of the deal.

License to be a narcissist is a given in the world of artists and celebrities, just as it is with addicts. Gay people, so neglected and abused by the intractably arrogant, ignorant and vicious, were outraged when society expected us to change as well. Even though it was true that too many of our behaviors were self-destructive and endangering to public health, such as high-risk sex and drug use as the AIDS epidemic raged. Gay people, who share backgounds of neglect and abuse with artists and addicts, likewise share with artists and addicts great reservoirs of anger at the otherwise overbearing indifference, expectations and regulations of mainstream society. We've tended to hold society responsible for all our troubles and to regard it with a retaliatory, reciprocal contempt.

This drama of the individual versus society has been striking as well during the Covid-19 pandemic, but in this case, the resistance was primarily with religious and other far-right political extremists who balked at social distancing and mask guidelines, especially when they became mandates. Just as the unsafe sex many gay men balked at giving up in the wake of bathhouse and other sex venue closures posed a health hazard to society, so did religious and political gatherings pose risks to society amidst the pandemic of Covid-19. Hence the title of medical ethicist Ron Bayer's book, *Private Acts, Social Consequences*.

Artists, addicts, queers, transgender folk, punks; creative people, outsiders, and social misfits with issues and grievances. This is the world Steve Mass fit right into. He understood the psychology of artists, of those who feel misunderstood, struggling to find their place and have their say. He was one of them, though he wasn't gay, wasn't a more stereotypical social misfit and had no real artistic talent. He was not a visual artist or musician. Nor was he a writer, though at various points he flirted with the idea of becoming one.

Nor did he appear to have any great love of specific artists, musicians or writers. At home or otherwise with us, his biological family, Steve was not someone who went around singing the praises of music that had seduced him. Nor did he reflect worshipfully on great artists or wax ecstatic about books he had read by favored writers. He was never seduced by any specific writer, artist or musician the way I was with Wagner.

Rather, Steve's creative gift turned out to be something related but different—being entrepreneurial. In this, although he never sustained their levels of success, he can be compared to other cultural entrepreneurs—e.g., Leo Castelli, Henry Geldzahler; oh, and Wagner's agent, Angelo Neumann.

Though he dabbled in philosophy and cultural studies and commentary, Steve's skills were more in the area of identifying, nurturing, staging and marketing creative individuals, subcultures and energies. Easily at home with art and artists, Steve seemed more inspired by the business of art than by art per se.

Early on, he demonstrated a sophisticated appreciation of the art market. In casual conversation he'd talk more about the Rockefellers, the lives of the super rich and corporate CEO's, than about specific artists, writers and musicians. On the one hand, icons of financial and corporate success were the people we were all in rebellion against. On the other, with their material trappings of success, of wealth and power, they were the ones everyone had fantasies of being. When the Mudd Club became big, Steve took flight lessons. Like CEO's who experience sudden jackpot success, perhaps he'd soon have his own jet.

At Northwestern University where he studied philosophy, Steve has said he took inspiration from Melville Herskovits, founder of the university's African Studies program and whose *Myth of the Negro Past* was considered groundbreaking in advancing the cause of ethnic equality. Another influence at Northwestern, prominent Germanist Erich Heller, loomed larger.

Like Steve, Heller was a lifelong bachelor and also the son of a Jewish physician. He barely escaped Nazi Germany where he was imprisoned briefly by the Gestapo for his anti-Nazi writings. In recalling her uncles, Erich and his brother Paul (who endured much worse persecution by the Nazis), Caroline Heller wondered if Erich's escape might have been paid for with sexual favors.

When Steve was at Northwestern majoring in philosophy, Heller came to our home in Chicago to influence our parents to support Steve's taking leave of his studies to travel abroad. I've no certainty that Heller was gay and notwithstanding all the gay life in his orbit at the Mudd Club, I never had any sense that Steve was. Perhaps Heller was gay and hoped that something would emerge with Steve. And who knows, maybe something did happen at whatever level. It happened like that between Wagner and King Ludwig, where Ludwig's homosexual inclinations were subtly played upon by Wagner. Or perhaps Heller hoped Steve, as a Holocaust survivor (even if Steve never consciously thought of himself as such) might bring his youth, Jewish heritage and impressive intelligence to bear on the fallout of Hitler and Nazism.

Heller is said to have made only one trip back to Germany after the war, at which time he met with his old colleague Martin Heidegger, the acclaimed philosopher and Nazi collaborationist whose love affair with Hannah Arendt provides another window on the social masochism of even the best Jewish minds. Whatever reconciliation of viewpoints Heller had hoped for with Heidegger apparently did not happen.

Figure 63 - Erich Heller, National Portrait Gallery

What Steve's place was in all this remains a mystery. Though he would bring home monographs on such giants of philosophy as Hegel, Kant, Jaspers, Kierkegard, Engels, Kafka, Schopenhauer, and Marx and must have had significant knowledge of Wagner, I never had the sense that Steve cared very much about philosophy or German culture per se, any more than he cared about any other writer or artist or anybody else per se. To my knowledge, though he lived in Germany for decades, I don't think he speaks much German.

Rather, academic philosophy was a world where for whatever reason, personal and/or intellectual, Steve had entree and an opportunity to set out on his own path, to ease on down the road of his own life, wherever it might lead, that individual path being the kind of realization of subjective knowledge and experience, of self, that philosophers like Heller, Kierkegaard and Nietszche tried to explain and extol.

"Know thyself," Thomas Carlyle's great exhortation, was also the culmination of Wagner's philosophy of self-realization, albeit within racial awareness. From Siegfried's perception of the genetic otherness of his foster-parent, Mime, an intensely antisemitic caricature, to *Parsifal*, where the pure fool learns to recognize his calling through intuitive compassion for his own kind (his fellow whites and Germans), the individual's journey of self-actualization was thematic in Wagner.

Beyond some journal fragments, what Steve brought back from his travels abroad were several Dutch-masterly paintings, portraits and still-lifes that ended up on our family's walls. One hangs in my living room. My sense is that with these purchases, even if he had little sense of it at that time, Steve had begun his career, his calling, as a middleman of art, fashion, and culture.

Figure 64 - Unidentified portrait by unidentified artist, one of the first pieces of art collected by Steve Mass, photograph by Lawrence D. Mass

Even in his post-graduate stint with the University of Iowa Creative Writing Workshop Steve seemed to distinguish himself more as an entrepreneur than as a writer, dropping out of the program before completing it. I don't recall any real writing Steve ever did, there or elsewhere, before or since. Apart from the journal fragments he kept during his travels, mostly during the Mudd Club years, there was no writing anyone ever heard about and nothing he wrote was published or even rumored. If you google Steve Mass, there's nothing written by him.

During that stint in Iowa, however, Steve began his own publishing company, producing works of some artists of renown, like a collection by the poet Maryann Moore. Alas, the quality of the publishing was rudimentary. There were a lot of printing and editing errors and Steve quickly found himself beset with complaints and financial problems. Though his immersion in this milieu of creative writers and writing doubtless informed the highly original happenings of the Mudd Club, to my knowledge Steve never returned to writing or publishing. Now in his early 80's, he hopes to write a memoir of the Mudd Club, his own version of a history already written and published by Mudd Club doorman Richard Boch.

Couching the bursting creativity of the Mudd Club were other initiatives—a medical concierge and ambulance service, a stint in teaching ESL (English as a Second Language) at Touro College, collecting Haitian street art, and a restaurant in Soho. What they all had in common were two characteristics that would plague Steve and those in his circles throughout his life: financial crisis and what might be called vacancy of personhood—that is, a sense that there was no real, identifiable person behind the entrepreneurial facades.

Figure 65 - Burnt, directed by Steven Knight, The Weinstein Company, 2015, theatrical release poster

There's a film that came and went with little notice. It got mostly bad reviews, mostly deserved. It was called *Burnt* and starred Bradley Cooper. It's the story of an exceptionally gifted celebrity chef and drug addict who managed to destroy every opportunity he'd ever had and alienate all those who tried to love and help him.

In addiction recovery, people talk about "the wreckage of the past." Here, the wreckage was gross and everywhere. What happens in the film is that the Cooper character, still beloved and believed in by leading *restaurateurs* and ex-lovers, managers and foodies, finally agrees to enter recovery. Miraculously, his old love sees him through and with her inherited money is able to settle his considerable debts. A happy ending.

For much of his life, Steve, like the Bradley Cooper character and also like Wagner, was plagued by debt. He seemed always in financial crisis, as artists and drug addicts are wont to be, even those with outsized fame and success—e.g., Elvis Presley, Michael Jackson, Judy Garland, Jackson Pollock and so many others. Just as typically, arrogance and attitude betrayed insecurity. This similarity of the traits and circumstances and hurdles of his own life to those of addicts and artists seemed the basis of a genuine empathy on Steve's part. The hand-to-mouth, for-the-moment way of life, the willingness always to pay the price of crisis—of recklessness and irresponsibility—for their individuality, for meeting their needs, for being themselves, for their creativity— is the way Steve lived. Art and addiction. This was his milieu. Artists and addicts. These were his people.

Inevitably, however, there were those realities of business and finance. Like the culinary efforts of the Cooper character in *Burnt*, Steve's Soho restaurant, Bernard and Steve's, tanked under the weight of expenses and the exigencies of operations. Of course, in the intersecting worlds of art and addiction, those seeking payment of debts were cast as outsiders—squares, villains and buffoons.

Those who became patrons of famous artists were sometimes gratefully enshrined as such—e.g., Wagner's patron King Ludwig, Tchaikovsky's Madame von Meck, and people like Theo van Gogh, Peggy Guggenheim and Marylou Whitney. Just as often, however, patrons are also seen by artists, especially those who are struggling, as chumps. This mentality is well-captured in the film *Basquiat*, directed by Julian Schnabel and featuring David Bowie as Andy Warhol. One scene takes place in the Mudd Club (re-created for the film), where Basquiat was able to feel at home as a painter, musician and heroin addict. Another briefly features Steve Mass himself, nonspeaking and grimacing with lust for the bar lady, a snapshot that seemed to convey little of the reality of Steve's actual personal life.

It may be that my sense of Steve as one whose sex life was relegated to creative life is a distortion from being a family member. It's difficult to be real, to be sexual, to laugh without restraint, to really have fun, to be uninhibitedly creative, to be truly and comfortably yourself and alive with your own family. For childish but also for practical reasons you don't want them to know the real you. For family, you become this pretend person of exaggerated family expectations—of caring and responsibility, of personal sacrifice, of morality and ethics, of duty, of loyalty, but consequently also of reticence and disaffection. That pretend person is not someone anyone wants to be, but rather feels pressured to be.

Virtually every coming-of-age story is about breaking with one's family—for addicts, artists, gay people and most others. And it's as sobering for me to realize that I was part of that family system for Steve as he was for me. Steve did not want to be the desultory older brother of the sibling who entered a profession, earned a regular pay check, and succeeded financially and professionally on a sustained basis. Nor did he want to have to endure the endless codependence struggles that are embedded in virtually all family relationships. For Steve, with whom brotherhood was sometimes like living in a play by Eugene O'Neill, I was a participant in that drama. Like O'Neill, the master of family drama and its dynamics, and the many other writers who chronicle failed family relations, however, we were better at calling out, indicting, judging and leaving our families of origin than genuinely transcending them.

There was one big moment of exception to the recurrent financial crises with Steve: when the Mudd club hit its mark of being the premiere downtown new-wave alternative to the uptown citadel of old-guard glitz that was Studio 54. In the heart of an after-hours no man's land that otherwise had the appearance of a ghost town after the workday of nearby Wall Street, the club quickly became this huge success, and money was pouring in. Eventually, even Studio 54 icons Steve Rubell, Halston and Trump's mentor Roy Cohn showed up there.

Figure 66 - Roy Cohn with Joseph McCarthy, UPI, 1954, Wikipedia Commons, public domain

I don't recall Steve ever mentioning to me either of his principal collaborators and co-founders, new-wave art curator Diego Cortez and downtown punk scene figure Anya Phillips, but he did pay respectful tribute to Phillips in the most substantial interview with Steve from those years (*East Village Eye*, 11/83, by Leonard Abrams). Whatever the challenges of management—stealing by bartenders was a continuous problem—such was the club's success that Steve was able to buy the building that housed it at 77 White Street. Alas, a year or so later, dire financial trouble reemerged when Steve was investigated for alleged attempted bribery involving an IRS officer. It was a debacle from which neither the Mudd Club nor Steve's finances would recover. Steve lost the building that was subsequently bought by its earlier owner, artist Ross Bleckner. The club closed soon thereafter.

Apart from the financial trouble, the club had run its course after several years. Like many restaurants and plays, clubs tend to be short-lived. Downtown began to emerge from its deep sleep of decades, an awakening the Mudd Club had iconically inspired. Accompanying that awakening was the epidemic that would soon become known as AIDS, decimating the gay men, trans folk, artists and drug addicts that dominated the club's ranks.

Steve never suffered any other enduring legal sanction we knew of, but again he was broke or seemed to be. In *Burnt* the Bradley Cooper character is menaced by goons, loan shark types; at one point, he's beaten up. We never learned anything very specific about Steve's financial troubles. In the wake of the Mudd Club's demise, Steve was involved in new enterprises—the medical and ambulance business followed by the restaurant, both of which were short-lived, despite flickerings of possibility. A fellow physician and friend who worked for Steve had no complaints, and the food at Bernard and Steve's, when you finally got it, was distinctive and deserving of its good Zagat rating. A restaurant postcard captured the moment with a hulking Bernard in a white wedding dress, looking skeptical and disgruntled, as he clasped hands with Steve, the happy groom, clutching a bouquet of flowers.

The collapse of these enterprises in the wake of the demise of the Mudd Club in 1984 set the stage for Steve's relocation to Berlin, where artists could expect more support from the socialist government and where bohemia seemed once again ascendant; fertile ground for new shots at life, and club life.

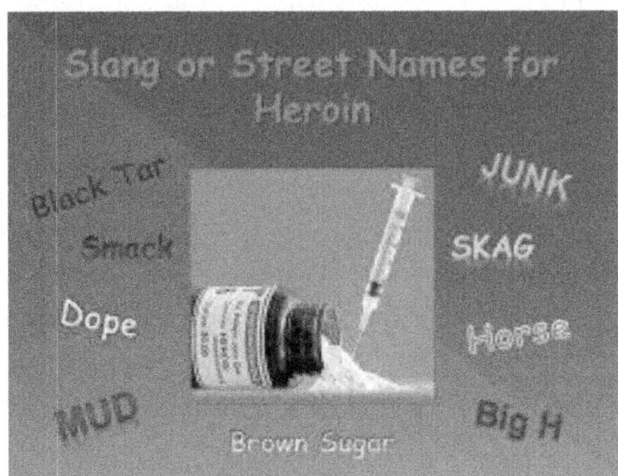


Figure 67 - Graphic of slang names for heroinm which include "Mud" and "Horse"

Dr. Samuel Mudd was pardoned by Andrew Johnson, the Southern racist who succeeded Lincoln and did his best to gut reconstruction. He was also the first American president to be impeached. To say that Johnson bears similarities to Donald Trump in being racist, reactionary, incompetent and beholden to his base would be an understatement. The connection of Steve Mass, who hails from the South, to this history of Johnson—who pardoned Mudd for conspiracy to murder Lincoln and for treating Lincoln's assassin, John Wilkes Booth—is an endless labyrinth. As earlier observed, Steve himself suggested there was nothing to be made of it, dismissing it as an impulse of the moment.

In being controversial and provocative, however, it proved to be a successful and characteristic public relations strategy. Not so unlike Donald Trump, and for that matter Larry Kramer, Steve became a master of using sarcasm, insult and rejection to attract attention, the winning ticket of being in the public eye. As Kramer, echoing others and prefiguring Trump, once observed, that they're talking about you is more important than what they're saying about you. This strategy of being controversial and provocative has served many other masters of public relations, most notably in our own time, Donald Trump; and among artists, Richard Wagner.

There is another association with the name "Mudd." "Mud" is common slang for heroin, referring to a brownish version called "Mexican Mud."

I was never much of a club person. I never went to Max's, Peppermint Lounge or Danceteria, though I did go to other, mostly gay dance emporia—12 West, Limelight (2 blocks from home) and the Saint, whose owner Bruce Mailman also owned the always busy St. Mark's Baths. The Saint featured a spectacular planetarium-illuminated dome and hosted the first of the big "black and white" parties which morphed internationally and are still touchstones of fast-lane gay life and travel. Proudly and publicly gay, Mailman also produced groundbreaking off-Broadway shows—Tom Eyen's *The Dirtiest Show in Town* and *The Neon Woman*, and Al Carmine's *The Faggot*. Alas, Mailman, the most successful of all the gay entrepreneurs, was among the early casualties in the tidal wave of celebrities engulfed by AIDS over the ensuing decade.

THE LARGEST BATH HOUSE IN THE COUNTRY
6 SAINT MARKS PLACE (8TH ST AND 3RD AVE.) NEW YORK. 212-473-7929.

Figure 68 - "Mysterious Rider" by Boris Vallejo, 1978, postcard of original public display poster, with permission

In those pre-civil-liberties days of the late 70's early 80's, openly gay business figures, in the absence of elected political officials, became de-facto political leaders. Thus Mailman found himself publicly embroiled in various gay political controversies such as those surrounding public health policy and bathhouse closures as the AIDS epidemic unfolded.

But it was Danceteria's Jim Fouratt who would survive and surpass all the other club entrepreneurs with his track record of consistent and often controversial activism on multiple, mostly leftist political fronts. Like others of the gay left, and also like less doctrinally leftist Larry Kramer, Fouratt expressed early and unpopular concern about the "privileged white men" dominating gay life. We were accused of giving priority to promiscuity at the expense of economic, racial, gender and transgender inequities. For all his skill and notoriety as one of the premiere party makers, in gay circles where sex culture remained central even as the epidemic raged he became surpassingly known as a party pooper. Not unlike Kramer and with Kramer in arousing gay mainstream ire, he could seem to be a malcontent with a personal agenda.

In his memoir, *The Rest of It*, Martin Duberman recalls the alarm that people of the left felt as the preoccupation of gay men with "sexual freedom" seemed to have such dire consequences for health and society. That Fourratt could seem so "self-aggrandizing" and "contentious" in debates on sexual license versus restraint is a measure of how polarized the community was at the outset of the epidemic, of how defensive we were against criticism that, as Larry Kramer put it, "fucking was the gay male community's highest priority."

Figure 69 - Jim Fouratt, Westview News

In the span of a few years AIDS would affect everyone, left and right, straight and gay, rich and poor, old and young. Even Republican President George W. Bush would eventually pitch in, albeit in partnership with homophobic evangelicals, offering impressive help with AIDS in Africa. It was amidst the political differences between the gay left and the gay mainstream that initial organizing in response to the epidemic took place, but not among the more idealistic leftists, nor from ranks of the new-wave downtown punk club scene. Rather, the initial organizing of the gay community in response to AIDS came from the "privileged gay white" Fire-Island party types, those hardest and most publicly hit by the epidemic. The result was Gay Men's Health Crisis, GMHC, which quickly became the first and is still, after nearly 40 years, the premiere AIDS information and service organization and one of the gay community's most revered and enduring institutions.

Dominated by mainstream gay men, many of whom may have been comparatively "privileged" for being white and middle class but all of whom had experienced in greater or lesser degree the homophobic bigotry that was universal in society at large, these early community responses to AIDS under the auspices of GMHC eventually gave way to ACT UP. Likewise co-founded by Larry Kramer, ACT UP quickly became notably more activist, confrontational and inclusive than GMHC, which saw its role as more educational and supportive than activist.

ACT UP was more explicitly committed to inclusion and representation for women, people of color and transgender people, and to the tactics of disruptive but nonviolent protest that were developed in the American Civil Rights movement. From the downtown club scene, the ranks of ACT UP swelled with culture, media people and artists, some of them emerging stars, like David Wojnarowicz and Keith Haring.

Figure 70 - Poster by Richard White for "Showers," early GMHC's fundraising event, at the Paradise Garage, 1982. GMHC Archives. Original public postcard of publicly displayed poster

I also went to a few of the other clubs, like Palladium and Flamingo, once each. At Flamingo that one time, there was Andy Warhol all lit up in fuchsia, like one of his silkscreens. I loved going to the Mudd Club, which was crackling with offbeat and illicit energies. Even when I was stoned on booze and grass, as I always was on late nights out, as Steve's brother I could go right up to the doorman, Richard Boch, and get immediate entrée ahead of a line of clubbies and greater or lesser celebrities past, present and future. Boch's memoir, *The Mudd Club*, is well written, engaging, and documents in gripping detail the club's heady atmosphere of art and celebrity, and the extent of drug use, including heroin, on the club's premises and by the club's denizens and custodians, especially himself but less specifically with regard to Steve.

In those years of my own bottoming out on alcohol, marijuana, cigarettes and occasional MDA, my music preferences were for opera, especially Wagner, and my venue preferences were for bathhouses. Prior to the emergence of the bear subculture that was a better fit for me, I gravitated to the leather bars with back rooms. Hence my relative disinterest in clubs, though, as Boch reveals, there was plenty of clandestine sex at the Mudd Club as well.

In this age of globalism and media we've all become cultural polymaths, interested in and participatory in disparate arts, literatures and cultures. We might belong primarily to one milieu but be open to exploring others. Though not a dance person, I've seen great *danseurs*, albeit mostly in opera. I still treasure my vivid memory of seeing the newly-defected Rudolf Nureyev in his American debut with the Chicago Lyric Opera in Borodin's *Prince Igor* in 1960. But I've rarely preferentially sought ought dancers, just as I rarely sought out punk, heavy metal, rock or even jazz or blues musicians. I once took the initiative to see Ray Charles, whose music I really did love, but the way non-opera people love Pavarotti. I did love Madonna and sang her to myself, but not Frank Zappa, Patti Smith or Lou Reed. I think the same was true of Steve. Though I have no recollection of his ever doing so, he might go to an opera, be interested in it and react intelligently to it, but it never was and never would be a preferred venue for him.

Though Steve may have seen me as this opera person who belonged more at places like Studio 54 or Regine's (neither of which I have ever been to), it was an adventure hanging out with him, especially at the Mudd Club. I got to see his apartment in Greenwich Village on 8th Street not far from the Marlton Arms Hotel where we had our reunion in 2015. The apartment was an utterly unkempt crash pad, clothes and papers strewn everywhere, Brian Eno incongruously sprawled out on a mattress with messy sheets on the floor. When my sister went to visit Steve in Berlin years later, she was not invited to his place, presumably in comparable disarray.

Another notable and regular presence in Steve's milieu was celebrity and counterculture biographer Victor Bockris, the author of *Punks, Poets, Provacateurs: New York City Bad Boys 1978-1982*, and books on Warhol, Burroughs. Lou Reed, Keith Richards and Patti

Smith. "Heroin was an enormously damaging force," Bockris said in an interview with photographer Marcia Resnick, another leading chronicler of the downtown scene of those years. "But the heroin honeymoon is where you do your greatest work. It lasts for about three years. You might do some great work, but then you're finished."

Other luminaries came and went, including Frank Zappa, composer of an ode to the Mudd Club, which the Anti-Defamation League decried, alleging antisemitism for his use of "Jewish Princess" epithetically ("I want a nasty little Jewish Princess") in his song of that title, an accusation Zappa vigorously rejected.

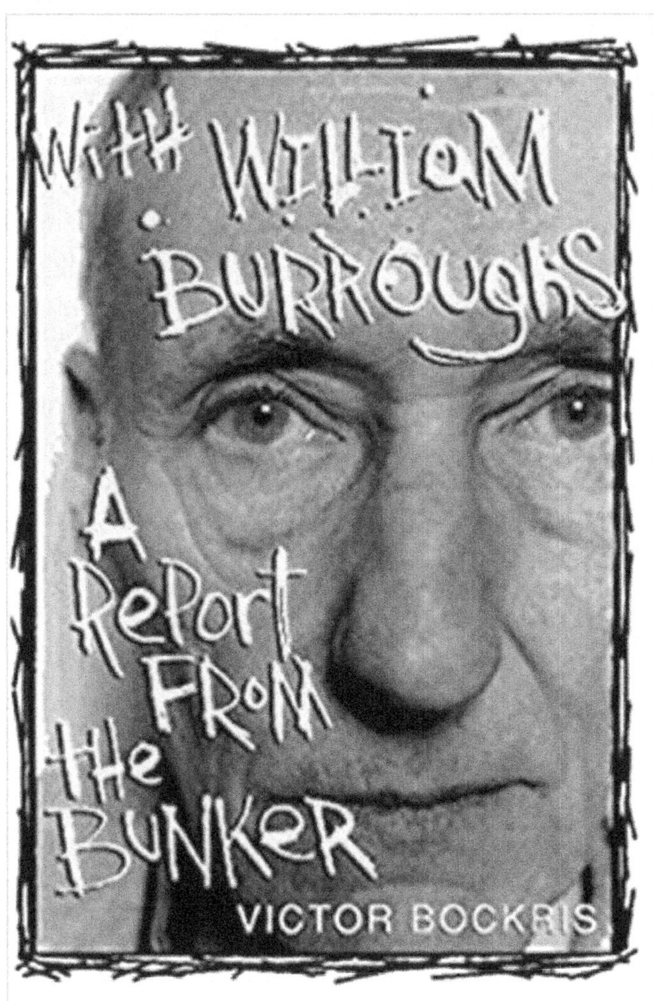


Figure 71 - *With William Burroughs: A Report From the Bunker* by Victor Bockris, Amazon.com

The club was a mecca for New Wave artists, musicians, writers, fashionistas, and the leading outsiders of the day, LGBTQ people.

In those years of the club's heyday, which coincided with the early AIDS epidemic, how we in the tiny, beleaguered gay and AIDS activist communities wished that Warhol and other club scene regulars we knew to be gay—.e.g., Robert Rauschenberg, Susan Sontag, Steven Sondheim, Elton John, Lily Tomlin—would come out and stand with us in protests and demonstrations. In the Whitney's impressive 2018 exhibit on Andy Warhol, the narrative deceptively states that Warhol was "openly gay." Although he never denied being gay and anyone who wasn't blind or deaf might well assume him to be gay, Warhol, like Rauschenberg, Jasper Johns and Larry Rivers, in fact was not publicly out as gay or even as "bisexual," an identity that could always serve purposes of cover.

How we wished those with the stature of Warhol and Rauschenberg would do what Ian McKellan, one of the first leading actors to do so 5 years later in 1988, did when it was still risky: be a visible participant and standard-bearer for gay liberation and AIDS activism.

Alas, putting themselves on the line like that is not something most of these folks were inclined to do. Rather, their reticence and closetedness betrayed their calculation that being known as gay within some cultural circles and at some venues was enough, enough for the gay community to claim and revere them and enough risk for them to take in being out. How lucky we gay community types were just to be able to claim such famous, accomplished, powerful and glamorous celebrities as Andy Warhol and Susan Sontag, right?

Meanwhile, their precious energies would not be sidetracked and their precious reputations as great artists would not be sullied by the not very aesthetic messiness of street politics. It was great and inspiring to see Keith Haring (not as famous in those days) in the front lines of ACT UP demonstrations, but where were the Warhols and Sontags? And where were Steve Rubell, not officially out but known to be gay, and for that matter Steve Mass, who wasn't gay but who was a de-facto leader of gay artists and outsiders? While AIDS may be lurking in the interstices of Warhol's art, and was everywhere at the Mudd Club, where were AIDS and gay liberation more specifically in all of that? The conclusion is inescapable that neither gay liberation nor AIDS were forefront concerns of Andy Warhol and

Susan Sontag, and most of their celebrity/artist confreres, including the likes of Steves Rubell and Mass.

Despite the legions of gay and trans folk at the Mudd Club, where we were given sanctuary and where so many of the theme parties were gay-oriented, I don't recall any special outreach to the LGBTQ community per se by Steve or at the club. I don't recall Steve ever being either homophobic or judgmental about LGBTQ people, but neither did he seem particularly interested in what was happening to us. I mean, in contrast to, say, Bruce Mailman and Jim Fouratt (but not unlike Steve Rubell), it's not like you'd see Steve at gay protests or otherwise taking the initiative to raise funds for gay causes, the way he did more recently with the 2015 Rummage sale benefit for the Bowery Women's Shelter. As with Sontag and Warhol, expectations of greater involvement in our plight seemed neither welcomed nor encouraged.

The celebrated downtown-scene photographer Nan Goldin was a Mudd Club regular. In the winter of 2018 she led an ACT-UP style, on-site protest of the Sackler family's prominent patronage of the Guggenheim Museum. Her group was called P.A.I.N. (Prescription Addiction Intervention Now). The Sacklers were owners of Purdue pharmaceuticals with its off-the-charts profiteering of the premiere opioid crisis drug, Oxycontin. Exposés had revealed a level of callousness and indifference to public suffering caused by the drug's manufacturers that recalls the mentality of slave profiteers.

It's beyond splendid that Goldin did this, and ACT UP, with its pioneering attention to the addicted populations affected by HIV and AIDS, is always to be hugely credited in any such efforts. It's because of ACT UP that we got the needle exchanges that Mike Pence initially refused to sanction in Indiana. Such willful ignorance and neglect fostered big outbreaks of HIV-AIDS in the Midwest many years after needle exchanges had been thoroughly established as the most successful of all harm reduction treatments; so successful that they all but eliminated HIV-AIDS among drug addicts in disease epicenters.

In the heyday of the Mudd Club, ACT UP was yet to be, and the civil disobedience that had characterized Stonewall (1969) and the Gay Liberation Movement had yet to erupt. Still, it seemed disappointing that no such civil-disobedience protest was discernible in club life. Biting satire, defiance of social mores and a notorious tolerance and coddling of drug use, rather than sober organizing and protest were the heart, soul and keepsakes of club memories.

In its silences around gay and AIDS activism, the situation in the clubs reminded me of my years at the University of California at Berkeley. There, too, I recoiled from leftist organizations and demonstrations because of their relegation of gay activist concerns. Even as they befriended and greatly benefitted from gay individuals in their ranks like Bayard Rustin, they seemed disinclined to get overtly involved in our struggles. But nor were gay activists promoting gay consciousness within those ranks. A real sense of this reality, of our invisibility, is inadvertently revealed by Mark Kitchell's 1990 documentary on *Berkeley in the Sixties*, which makes no mention of gay people or gay liberation.

Defending the Mudd Club against accusations of overt and excessive drug use and for not being more involved in LGBTQ struggles is Gabriel Rotello, a club regular and one of ACT UP's leading activists. Rotello was an editor of the gay newspaper *Outweek* and is best known for his prescient book on the AIDS epidemic, *Sexual Ecology*, which predicted the spread of the disease throughout the gay community. Rotello says he does not recall actually seeing people using drugs on the club's premises. Nor did he ever have a sense of anything but warmth and welcome for LGBTQ people there. If there wasn't more explicit outreach to or involvement in LGBTQ politics and affairs, that's not a beef Rotello recalls himself ever feeling.

Other Mudd club regulars left darker recollections and impressions—e.g., Vanity Fair's 1987 piece on "Club Culture" and a memoir by Brad Gooch. They complement Boch's *The Mudd Club* in chronicling the drug-besottedness that pervaded club life in the 1970's and 1980's. Andy Warhol, meanwhile, directed his artistic eye to the world of the clubs and club people, many of whose lives and deaths were being determined by drugs.

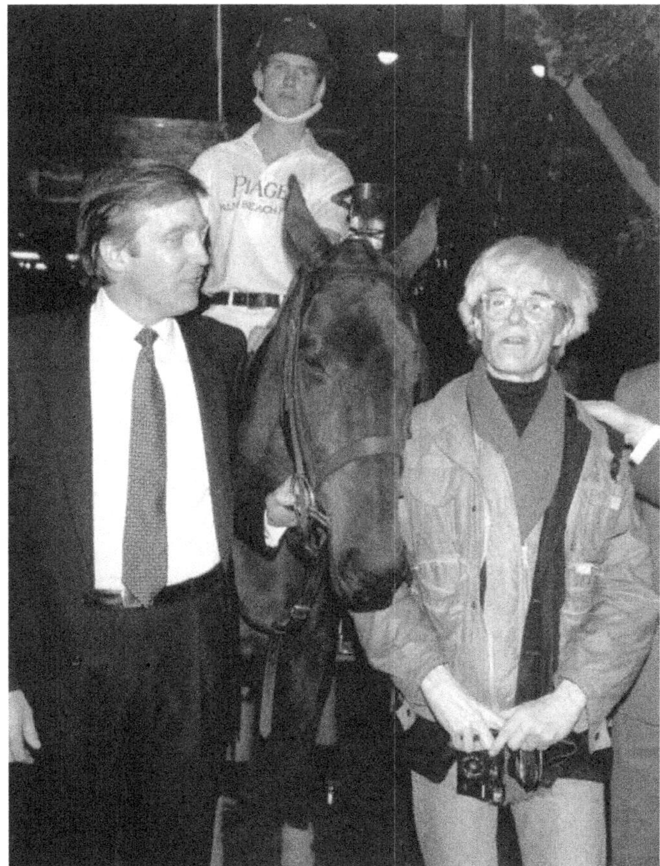

Figure 72 - Warhol with Trump and horse, 1983, photograph by Mario Suriani, AP

In the late 1990's I had a brief but intense love affair with an older man—a psychoanalyst, film scholar and *cineaste* who I'd met at the East Side Sauna bathhouse, and who became the inspiration for my short story, "Tiepolo's Dispassion." The East Side Club, one of the few city gay sex venues to remain open during the epidemic, catered to sex addicts like us. Its clientele was notable for its inclusion of bisexual and married men like him. For all I know, he still goes there. Doubtless he's still in the closet, still married, still blaming and emotionally abusing his wife for his dishonesty, meanwhile reaping the social and professional benefits of being in the closet with intolerant colleagues and his even more intolerant working-class Italian family.

One day the *cinéaste* took me to Film Anthology Archives to see Warhol's film *Horse*. Horses were a frequent subject of Warhol at various points in his career. Prior to my mentioning it, however, I don't think the *cinéaste* had any idea of connecting the dots that the horse, (like the white horse Bianca Jagger famously straddled at Studio 54) evoked one of the most common metaphors for heroin. *Horse* featured Warhol Factory girl, Mudd Club regular and heroin addict Edie Sedgwick who died from a heroin overdose.

Figure 73 - Unidentified Man with Hypodermic Needle, Andy Warhol, 1951, Andy Warhol from A to B and Back Again, The New Whitney, 2019

Though I only once observed Steve intoxicated, there was one occasion, a late-night emergency call from Helen Mitsios, when Steve appeared to have overdosed. On what? Cocaine, she suggested uncertainly. I helped arrange for an ambulance and don't recall what happened after that, except that he survived. There was no follow-up. Not that I was really seeking an explanation. Crises with vague causes and outcomes were so typical of Steve that our surpassing wish as family members was that the extent of our involvement, to bail him out with money or shelter, was kept to a minimum. When I met with

Helen in the late spring of 2016, I asked if she remembered the night she called me for Steve's drug emergency. No, she said, she did not. After so many years, was my senior memory or some unconscious bias deceiving me? As it turns out, my partner Arnie clearly remembers that night, the request for emergency help from Helen, and the ambulance call by me.

In the wake of Richard Boch's tell-(mostly)-all *The Mudd Club*, it's evermore clear that drugs were a predominant feature of the club scene. In Steve's case, I suspected heroin and would look at his arms for tracks, which I never saw. But many heroin addicts are snorters and others are so meticulous about avoiding telltale track marks that you would never suspect them to be skin-poppers or mainliners. As documented by Boch, the Mudd Club was known for its stars of heroin chic such as Burroughs, Reed and Basquiat. However truly a hub and sanctuary for art and subcultures, drug access and use figured prominently for many. As one denizen of the club from those years, now in recovery, put it recently, "Steve Mass was the Great Enabler."

Was Steve a periodic heroin snorter? You might have a stroke from cocaine abuse, but you wouldn't go into a coma as you might from a heroin, alcohol, pill (benzo) or multi-drug overdose. And because of the extreme stigma and Draconian legal consequences, if you're a heroin user, you do everything you can to make sure no one else, certainly not family members, knows about it, a situation best insured by minimizing contact. Such is the stigma of opioid use that many addicts have spouses, parents and children that don't know they're in opiate treatment.

Periodic heroin and/or other drug use would seem to explain a good deal of Steve's erratic behavior, his self-absorption, the frequent dropouts from family events and business, except that those behaviors were manifest even in childhood. They were especially noticeable with Steve's restaurant endeavor. Having had a number of lunches with Steve at Odeon, the trendy downtown French diner and bistro that was a short walk from the Mudd Club, I could sense Steve's flair for food, presentation, pricing and promotion. The location, atmosphere and cuisine of his new Soho bistro, Bernard and Steve's, were great, but Steve would just disappear for extended periods. Where was he? What happened? This is what I suspect in real measure led to the demise of the Mudd Club and the loss of 77 White Street. Even more than any deep-seated early childhood insecurity about being Jewish, it could also explain the strange distance Steve kept from everybody, the vacancy of personhood—of presence, of caring, of involvement, and the financial crises, though, again, much of this behavior seemed present going back to childhood.

Everybody had the same reactions to Steve, the same impressions—e.g., Helen Mitsios in her memoir, *Waltzing With The Enemy*. Even Richard Boch's considerable praise of Steve seems qualified by the taciturnity that existed between them. Were they *really* friends or more like bar buddies? How much of who Steve was or wasn't were projections and figments of Boch's imagination?

Following the string of enterprises that began with the demise of the Mudd Club, Steve announced that he was heading to Berlin. There were no details, no other information, except that he was opening a Berlin version of the Mudd Club. There seemed to be several versions and locations of the new club over time. The first of these is the one my sister saw when she visited Steve in Berlin and which she described as "lively." For someone with such a loyal following here in New York and so many admirers in art, music and club scenes, it's surprising that we've read and heard virtually nothing in the media of his experience there. When Steve returned to the US for my mother's memorial service in 2000, he acknowledged that one of the big draws of Berlin was its greater network of resources and supports for artists and foreigners residing there.

Another factor may have played a role in Steve's expatriation—his tendency to recoil from the celebrity culture he was so skilled at cultivating. Steve always seemed to intuit that while celebrity may have been a demarcater of success, it was also a death knell for creativity. I remember the dismay on his face when he described Sylvester Stallone showing up at the Mudd Club one night in a limo. Of course, ambivalence about art and fame is common enough among artists. Steve seemed to want fame as badly and was as good at achieving it as any other celebrity, but he also instinctively and simultaneously shunned it. Learning to achieve, accept, navigate and harness fame and success would prove to be a painstaking, preoccupying, deceptive and never-ending process.

It was my mother who wondered if Steve's departure to Berlin was about some level of financial or legal trouble he hadn't acknowledged. With his silence and reticence, maybe he's trying to protect us, she suggested. Even after she finally entered recovery for codependence, it was very difficult for her to appreciate that her behavior had been enabling. She kept bailing him out, giving him money and shelter without any change in his attitudes or behavior, without his life ever getting back on track, and with little in the way of gratitude. He would dismiss her grave maternal concerns and importuning as "hysterical" and "catastrophizing," characterizations with which I would all too often collude. But she did keep going to the codependence recovery meetings I introduced her to and eventually admitted that she was exhausted and disappointed by Steve and wanted him out of her home.

Finally, he left—his family, New Jersey, New York and the US, though he did return for our mother's memorial service and spoke of her in remembrance and tribute. Relationship issues persisted, however, with my sister and me, and with Helen Mitsios, who he seemed to treat as neglectfully and exploitatively as everyone else who tried to get close to him. Helen did move on, marrying another, and wrote a remarkable memoir of her mother's harrowing journey as a Holocaust survivor that dovetailed with her own coming of age. There, in her memoir, *Waltzing With The Enemy,* she affirms her friendship with Steve in a critical period of her life, when he introduced her to Jewish culture and club life, and advised her how to dress. To what extent they had been lovers is not spelled out. Also missing is that she continued to give him money and allow herself to be used as a go-between in requests for money from my sister and me. Not that she liked that role, though the relationship with her mother also revealed a level of codependence she seemed less than fully aware of.

Did Steve ever read her memoir? I asked her when she and I had coffee, just the two of us, in 2015. She seemed caught off guard and couldn't say yes. Tactfully, I didn't pressure her for a more certain answer. Apart from a genuine level of caring between her and Steve, with whom she admitted to having had very little sex, what was keeping them connected? Beyond questions of codependence, I noticed that Jay MacInerny, another Mudd Club regular, had blurbed one of her books. Like so many in Steve's orbit, Helen was serious about creativity, in her case writing. Hopefully, she will write another memoir of her club experiences and more about her relationship with Steve.

About 4 years ago, after a hiatus of many more years, Helen called me at work. She began talking about Steve and almost immediately I could sense that this was another money call. Sure enough, Steve was once again in some emergency situation and she had been enlisted to hit us up—my sister and me—for money. I've done a lot of work in recovery, including on my own codependence, which I was able to translate into action on my own behalf. In recovery, one learns of the addict as well as of the behavior of others more generally that "we didn't cause it, can't control it and can't cure it." We can't change people. But we can learn to shift the focus from trying to control others to living our own lives. Detachment, we call it.

The tricky part about detachment is to do it without resentment. This could quickly return us to the cycle of people-pleasing as a way of assuaging our guilt and shame at how much resentment we feel for failing to rescue the other person and for that person's indifference to our concerns and needs. In codependence recovery, one learns to say what we mean, mean what we say, but don't say it mean.

So when Helen made this call for money on Steve's behalf, I was able to maintain my boundary of not communicating with Steve about money, but without being angry or judgmental. The bottom line both my sister and I have set is simple. We wish Steve well, are proud of his intelligence, creativity and accomplishments, and are always open to meeting and communicating with him on an equal footing, but it can't have anything to do with money.

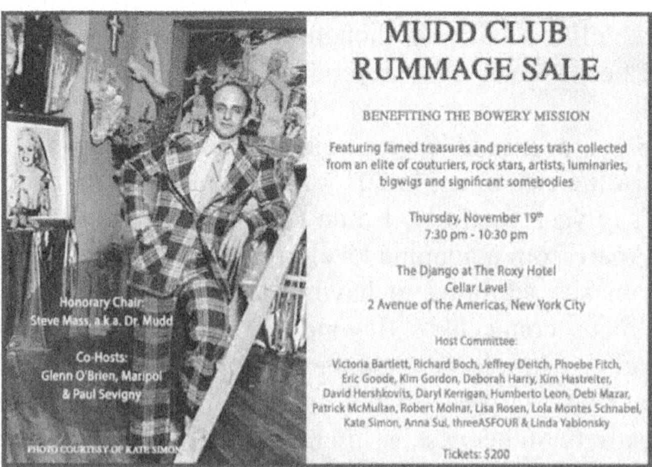


Figure 74 - Steve Mass, aka "Dr. Mudd," poster for the Mudd Club Rummage Sale Benefit for the Bowery Mission, 11/2015, created by Richard Boch, author of *The Mudd Club*, Rummage Sale flier photo courtesy of Kate Simon

When Steve returned to the US in 2015 for the Rummage Sale to benefit the Bowery Women's Shelter, we got another of those calls from Helen. Though he would be in New York for only a few days, Steve wanted to meet with us, to "set things right." As always with Steve, everything was happening at the last minute and everybody was put on the spot. I suggested a couple of possible time slots for getting together, but I warned Helen up front that if the meeting had anything to do with another request for money, my advice was to cancel it. A few days later, she emailed me to say that Steve was swamped with finalizing arrangements for the event and had to drop out of any plans to get together. I emailed her back to say that we understood and wished Steve well with the event and safe travels back to Berlin.

The behind-the-scenes motivations for the Rummage Sale, helping women who had come to New York to escape oppression—joblessness, homelessness, poverty, abuse, neglect, rejection, bigotry—were of a piece with the Mudd Club, offering sanctuary to floundering and wandering artists and musicians. The tribute to Steve as someone attuned to the dispossessed, to the misfits and refugees of corporate America, seemed deserved, whatever the qualifiers and incongruities.

But when you are in a personal relationship with an artist or other VIP, no matter how esteemed or otherwise successful or famous, it becomes crucial to distinguish their needs from yours and your boundaries from theirs. It was true of *enfants terribles* like Steve Mass, just as it was true of *monstres sacrés* like Jackson Pollock, Pablo Picasso and Richard Wagner.

Retrospective of the club scene in New York is a *New York Times* review of *On Drinking,* a posthumous collection of poems by the late Charles Bukowski that can serve as an epitaph for the writer's defiant celebration of his life as alcoholic and addict. The review by David Orr, "What Charles Bukowski's Glamorous Displays of Alcoholism Left Out," looks at Bukowski from the vantage point of sobriety and sanity, and of the expectation of our appreciation of the sacrifices of his life for self-expression, for art.

But "people think about drunken driving much differently in 2019 than they did in 1981" writes Orr. "*On Drinking* is a parade of small evasions and tall tales...Bukowski talks about plowing around hammered in a car, yet every episode carefully avoids any sense of the possible horrific consequences for other people...Addiction plunges people into a subterranean space that separates them not only from their friends and family, but from their ability to feel family as *family*, rather than as vehicles for the fulfillment of a craving."

# Codependence and Recovery

Figure 75 - "Steve Mass, the owner of the Mudd Club, 1978," photographic portrait with permission by William Coupon

I don't recall ever getting a birthday, graduation or any other gift from my brother, or vice versa. It's not something we did in our family. Both parents, especially my mother, came from levels of poverty where unnecessary expenses could mean not having food for the table.

My mother had the same psychology of deprivation as the mother of Hansel and Gretel. Mom's father was an alcoholic Hungarian-Jewish shoe cobbler and her mother was an ultra-religious Romanian Jew. Poverty menaced and haunted their daily lives. In the fairy tale of the Brothers Grimm, however, other villains lurk in the thornbush—witches, sorcerers. These horrifying tales of evil enchanters and enchantresses also inspired Wagner protegee Englebert Humperdinck, who helped Wagner prepare *Parsifal*. *Parsifal* also features witches and sorcerers from the depths and soul of German lore. And who were these phantoms? Jews, homosexuals, child-molesters, cannibals, serial killers. Take your pick

So deeply instilled was this mentality of poverty that my mother could destroy a family gathering if one of her children, even when adult, ordered a coffee not included in the price of the meal. She would be similarly upset about wasting money if we gave her a gift for Mother's Day. Birthday gifts to us tended to be thrift shop items, more notable for their cheapness than any thoughtfulness. Paradoxically, however, when it came to our needs—for schooling, travel and housing, our parents were often generous beyond their means.

The discomfort of unnecessary expense from such a background is understandable and arouses compassion. But relegating celebration altogether was neurotic and had unintended consequences. Beyond a rare informational or list-serve email, there was never any correspondence to communicate milestones among any of the siblings. While this situation fitfully and painstakingly changed with my sister, it persisted with Steve. We never exchanged cards or even well wishes. It seemed sad and awkward not to be able to acknowledge and celebrate Steve's 75th Birthday at the 2015 Mudd Club Rummage Sale benefit.

Actually, I can recall 3 offerings from Steve over the course of our lives. Though I don't recall comparable gestures from me, they may be forgotten, too painful to remember. Though it has been challenging to acknowledge, I played my own role in our dynamic.

The first of these items was a bongo drum when I was 10 or so. It was from South America, where precocious, late-teenage Steve did some kind of apprenticeship with the Diplomatic Corps. The instrument was large and made wonderful sounds. Despite having no more inclination for beating a drum than playing piano, I loved it.

The second item he brought to a dinner I co-hosted with Arnie at our home in New York in late 1981. The guests included our friend Rosa von Praunheim, the German gay activist and underground filmmaker who lives in Berlin (and who adopted the name "Rosa" in homage to the Polish-German-Jewish socialist hero and martyr Rosa Luxemburg), and writer Martin Duberman, another illustrious figure of the gay left who was a close friend and mentor in those years. What Steve brought was neither wrapped nor inscribed. It was one of those hardcover used books with faded covers and discolored page corners that lotus-positioned street peddlers sell on blankets.

The book was a memoir by television news commentator and personality Shana Alexander, who kept using the phrase "Jabberwocky time" in this chatty tome about her life in media and the arts. From the moment I got this oddity, I sensed that it was intended as camp. For Steve, people like Shana Alexander may have inhabited the same planet but had no more in common with him and fellow hipsters than the trans street tarts and druggies who star in Sean Baker's film *Tangerine* had with the family-traditionalist Armenian mother-in-law of one of their regular hookups.

This was one of those times when I couldn't help but wonder if Steve saw me as this uptown opera type, in sync with his and his club's legendary snobbery about anyone not certifiable as authentic downtown counter-cultural, though I have no recollection of him ever demeaning my interest in opera or my Wagnerism. On the basis of his own study of philosophy, so much of it German, he must have been intrigued by my preoccupation with Wagner. Meanwhile, that's not something we ever talked much about. Whether Steve ever consciously considered the issue of internalized antisemitism that shaded both our lives is not something I was ever consciously aware of.

Apart from people dressing up and down and appearing in often retro guises, satirically pretending to be other than who they were, nor was any such sensibility sentient at 77 White Street. But the Mudd Club did become a singular venue for the intersection of the worlds of serious music and cutting-edge culture. Though I don't recall Wagner or opera being sent up, put down or being otherwise discernible in any of the club's happenings, several events there were produced by Pulitzer-prize winning music critic Tim Page. They combined contemporary classical with rock and pop. I got to know Page a bit in those years via my own writing about music, which was mostly about homosexuality, music and the closet.

The third offering from Steve was one I continue to ponder. In the heyday of the Mudd Club I was experiencing my own descent into alcoholism, with which I finally hit my bottom as an alcoholic in late 1983. The Mudd Club closed not long after, two years into the first press reports, many of them my own, of the AIDS epidemic. Though I had already stopped drinking for some weeks—and for that matter eating, sleeping and having sex, I was hospitalized for major depression in the psych ward at St. Vincent's Hospital. St. V's, as we referred to it, is also the hospital where our mother died nearly 20 years later from metastatic cancer. It's now a luxury condo complex that faces an AIDS memorial park with a single, circular, quote from Whitman's *Leaves of Grass*.

The park's serenity and the power of Whitman's words obfuscate the reality that the hospital's ministry to the gay people of Greenwich Village, the charitable ideal of Mother Theresa notwithstanding, was often discernibly and distressingly homophobic, especially in the early period of the epidemic. This was in contrast to Beth Israel, widely known for a pioneering, embracing outreach to underserved communities, especially drug addicts and persons with AIDS. One reason Beth Israel became such a beacon of hope for the dispossessed and underserved is because of the vision of its most illustrious director, Dr. Robert Newman. Newman, who died in 2018, tirelessly championed the trailblazing efforts of Drs. Vincent Dole, Marie Nyswander and Mary Jean Creek in establishing Methadone Maintenance treatment, which quickly became the standard of treatment for opioid dependence. Thus did Beth Israel become one of the world's largest and most distinguished centers of addiction research and treatment services.

The AIDS memorial park obfuscates the harsher reality that the conversion of this precious community resource into luxury condos left Greenwich Village with no hospital. In fact, with the similar loss of Beth Israel years later, most of lower Manhattan is now without full-service hospitals. It seems a sad but telling coincidence that the loss of Dr. Newman, a voice of conscience and advocate of minority concern, coincides with the loss of such advocacy by the country's political leadership.

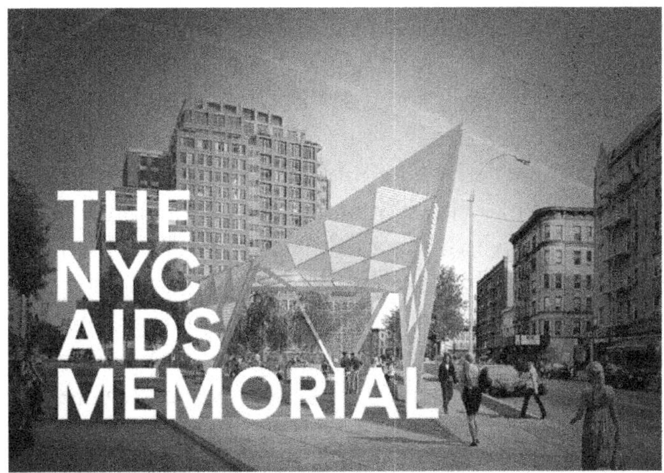


Figure 76 - The NYC AIDS Memorial, opposite the site of St. Vincent's Hospital, now a luxury condo complex, public domain

Larry Kramer wrote his version of my "nervous breakdown" and hospitalization at St. V's in his composite character of "Mickey Marcus" (named after an Israeli general) in *The Normal Heart*. My own experience of it was very different. I hadn't yet admitted that I was alcoholic, which took me years of detours in denialism. I'd begun attending recovery meetings, of flirting with recovery, but never taking the full leap to admit that I was alcoholic, powerless over this compulsion, and that my life had become unmanageable.

The main source of this breakdown for me, as I saw it, was the pain I felt in not being able to give myself more fully to my writing at this key moment of the unfolding of the AIDS epidemic, with its life-and-death importance to the gay community as well as to drug addicts. My writing about the epidemic soon to be known as AIDS was mostly for the gay press, all of it unpaid.

But I also understood at a deep visceral level that telling my own story as well as writing about AIDS, gay health, arts and culture, was of vital importance to me personally and in my emergence as a writer. Not unlike many of the writers as well as artists and musicians Steve gave sanctuary to at the Mudd Club, when I couldn't find ways of being my authentic creative self, of being the writer I most wanted to be, I became ever more prone to hedonistic and self-destructive behaviors, behaviors which can stoke the embers of creativity as they render them more dangerous for causing fires and burning out.

Those most vulnerable to the epidemic included virtually all of those who went to the Mudd Club. Talk about spoilers and party poopers. What I was reporting was not something any of us wanted to hear or discuss. I can't really indict Steve for an indifference that was common and which I myself could collude with. Not entirely unlike Trump with regard to the Covid pandemic, I didn't want to stoke panic. Steve, like most of those I knew, initially made little effort to deal with the rapidly and increasingly terrifying information. Meanwhile, so far as I was able to glean, few club people were reading my articles. Nor were they being distributed in club venues; nor was I pushing to place them there. Of those few who were reading my articles, fewer wanted to discuss it further. This widespread disinterest, indifference and distancing enabled my low self-esteem and codependence, exacerbated by an increasingly clinical depression, in a matrix of alcoholism, "recreational" marijuana use and 2+ packs-a-day cigarette smoking.

Adding to the mix was my own defensiveness of gay sexual life and liberation. If people didn't want to imagine the worst—that we were on the cusp of one of the greatest epidemics in recorded history, a cataclysm that would force us to rethink all our values and behaviors—I could be right there with them, at least in spirit. Even as a physician who should and did know better, I was their defender. I was one of them. Even as I continued to report on what became "the most important new public health problem in the United States" (the title of one of my early pieces),I remained a standard bearer for gay liberation and the greater sexual revolution. As such, I would find myself speaking out of both sides of my mouth, though the "sexual revolution" that I championed was not the 1960's America playground of Playboy magazine and Plato's Retreat, but the far more sweeping and edifying sea change conjured by Wilehelm Reich in his book, *The Sexual Revolution.* While its concepts of sexual liberation did contain precepts of sexual freedom and liberation and was tolerant of promiscuity and polyamery, it had mostly to do with a bigger picture of expanding sex education, sex research, women's and sexual minority rights, access to contraception, STD treatment, and health care.

Clearly, we were all in this together. More support for my efforts would have been welcome, but I didn't have the self-confidence to push for it more insistently. Meanwhile, it wasn't forthcoming from

Steve or my two closest friends—leading music critics Peter G. Davis and Richard Dyer. Nor from another of my closest friends in that period, historian Martin Duberman. What support there was felt more obligatory and delimited than genuine and helpful. Granted, I'm not and never would be a Martin Duberman and my writing even by my own estimation was too often turgid and tangential. OK. But an early primitive effort to put together a book proposal on the emerging epidemic entitled "Chronicles of The Violaceous Death" was sharply rejected by Marty's agent, Frances Golden, with no follow-up encouragement, neither from her nor Marty. Nor for that matter was there any encouragement to submit the proposal to her in the first place. While I often told brother Steve how impressed I was with what he had achieved with his club, just as I'd often told Marty of my admiration for his work, and my admiration and gratitude for Dick and Peter knew few bounds, there was no reciprocity of affirmation or encouragement of me or my work. A classic circumstance and setup for codependence.

The memories I have of Dick and Peter include many that were personal and based on friendship, but are more primarily of the many concerts, operas, cabarets, restaurants, trips, parties and haunts we attended together, usually with me as their guest. In Boston, I got to meet Dick's close friends—the poet Lloyd Schwartz, who eventually won a Pulitzer for music criticism that mostly appeared in the *Boston Phoenix*. Others in Dick's entourage were Lloyd's partner, the painter Ralph Hamilton, poet Frank Bidart, whose extended monologue about Callas (whose "portrait" Hamilton had painted, I tried to love but didn't), songwriter Tom Lehrer, Randy Fuller (of the Fuller Brush Company), who eventually produced a road-show *Ring* cycle and became Boston's leading opera patron, Michael Steinberg, the music critic and program annotator who was one of Dick's mentors, and Peter McNamara, the unhappy gay son of then Secretary of Defense Robert McNamara.

And many singers. There was mezzo Carolyn James, who became Dick's good friend; Mary Strebing, whose living-room piano rendering of Doretta's song from *La Rondine*, with its soaring tessitura, was as passionate as her bawdy tales of policemen with big night sticks; Mark Pearson, the fey, fastidious basso profundo and choral director; and David Arnold, the ebony-black bass-baritone whose struggles with race, career and being gay were poignantly shared by Dick and others who championed him.

Alas, tragedy struck with the suicide of one of our close friends, Joseph R Ruggieri, Jr, who suffered from severe depression, greatly exacerbated by the extreme homophobia of his father. Joe was a connoisseur of Chinese cuisine and had gotten to know Boston-Cambridge cooking celebrity Joyce Chen. Another Cambridge celebrity of cooking, who I'd see on the street, was Julia Child, perhaps history's most famous—and doubtless tallest—female chef. She shopped at Savenor's, an old unassuming neighborhood grocery where she could be seen negotiating with the butcher.

Another notable of Dick's Boston/Harvard/gay and music circle was the composer Daniel Pinkham of the Lynn, Mass family of Lydia Pinkham, who famously marketed alcohol-based home remedies for "female ailments." Several examples grace my collection of antique American medicine bottles, likewise mostly "special" or "home" remedies, alcohol-based and without any medical value. Quackery, that time-honored American tradition behind the ascendancy of history's greatest snake-oil salesman, Donald Trump. Pinkham taught at the Boston Conservatory, Boston University and Harvard.

There was the Boston premiere of crossover success, *Final Alice,* with the resplendent Barbara Hendricks in glittering white and sequins as soloist, with the beaming composer of the piece, David del Tredici, in the audience. Years later in New York, David would become my friend. Many of these composers were gay, David openly and controversially so, rattling the closets of those, including Dick and Peter, but also Ned Rorem, who embraced more respectable professional decorum. Not unlike Warhol and Sontag, it was OK with them if people knew or surmised they were gay, but being publicly, outspoken or confrontationally so, the way David del Tredici could seem so invested in doing—wearing dresses for performances and being otherwise "unnecessarily provocative"—was another matter.

Though they had little sense of it, Dick and Peter were mentors as well for my writing. In contrast to my characteristic turgidity and discursiveness, Dick's writing was as natural and conversational as it was professional. It's Dick who taught me, as a writer, that you could say things like "that that" and that that would be OK. From Dick and Peter I learned values I wanted to be as good as they at applying—objectivity at the expense of subjectivity, and reticence. That less is often more is a maxim most writers must learn, often and certainly in my case, the hard way.

That Dick and Peter were neither front-line activists for gay liberation nor out may have been regrettable, but their more modest efforts of not bothering with "beards" (female escorts who could help one pass as straight), were brave for their time and contributory to social and political change. Rather than tossing Molotov cocktails, they would drop "hairpins" (pre-gay liberation vernacular for hints of gayness). Dick, for example, occasionally wrote gay-ish book reviews for the *Globe*. (To my knowledge, neither Dick nor Peter ever wrote for the gay press or was ever interviewed therein.) One such review by Dick was of J.R. Ackerly's *My Father and Myself,* about the closet. I don't think Peter ever overtly denied who and what he was, even for the *New York Times* under his homophobic bosses Abe Rosenthal and Arthur Gelb, but mentions of gay figures as such or discussions of gay subject matter or implications were scrupulously careful, impersonal, and otherwise rare during the propulsively expanding early period of AIDS and gay liberation.

The role of music critics was also changing. In earlier decades, music critics exerted more influence. They more often wrote big "think pieces,"as Dick and Peter called them, essays with more substance than the pre-event puff pieces of today. Yet even the older, more fulsome music criticism would rarely challenge us to consider information previously off-limits as too personal or extrinsic to sacrosanct art and artistry.

As the role and power of music critics continued to erode, the only critic of renown to have a regular column, to express himself (female critics were few and far between) at greater length on issues of moment was Andrew Porter in the *New Yorker*. Alas, Porter was likewise closety, reticent and apolitical. Eventually, only Peter G. Davis had a regular column—in *New York*—and even that tenure was summarily halted when *New York* abruptly eliminated its regular music coverage.

Now there are only Alex Ross's intermittent pieces, again in the *New Yorker*. Ross is openly and sometimes thoughtfully gay, as is senior *New York Times* music critic Anthony Tommasini (who Dick was mentor to in Boston), but both alternate with other music and culture writers and their think pieces are increasingly thin and irregular. Both have written books. Tommasini is the author of a biography of Virgil Thomson and Ross is the author, most recently, of *Wagnerism*. Inexorably, however, the trajectory of music criticism has been downsized from substantial essays on big topics to perfunctory performance reviews and artist profiles.

The affirming perspective one can have of Dick and Peter is that which is so impressively achieved by Todd Haynes in his 2002 film, *Far From Heaven*. Here, as in Haynes's equally impressive film *Carol,* the protagonists are not soldiers leading charges. In fact, they're not even political. Rather, they are ordinary people who find the courage to take small, unheralded steps toward honesty, happiness and fulfillment in their own lives. Arguably, it's they, more than confrontational activists, who are carrying out the great sweep of social and political changes that became variously referred to as gay liberation and the sexual revolution.

Figure 77 - Maria Callas and Giuseppe di Stefano, Schiphol Airport, Holland, 1973, photograph by Anefo Onbekend, Wikimedia Commons, public domain dedication

For a fellow opera queen, Dick's and Peter's surpassing love for singers and opera was like the discovery of vast and unending hoards of treasure. My most cherished memory of this bounty was Maria Callas, who I so loved and admired, on her farewell tour in Boston. Would she show? It was down to the wire. Finally, she arrived, though without her partner—the legendary but also way-past-prime Italian tenor Giuseppe di Stefano, later revealed to have been Callas's ex-lover.

There she was, flashing that famous from-the-side smile for a throng of fans outside the stage door at Symphony Hall. (We were watching it all from across the street.) Though Callas's voice was broken beyond measure, there were more than enough magical moments to validate the esteem held for her by a formidable majority of music and opera lovers. From the highest ranks of her colleagues in music, opera and the arts, she was widely regarded to be the greatest operatic artist of our time. I will be forever grateful to Dick for giving me this gift of one of the peak experiences of my opera-going life.

Not quite in that league but not so far from it was Beverly Sills in her varied roles for Sarah Caldwell (Rosina in *Barber of Seville*, Giulietta in Bellini's *I Capuletti e I Montechhi*, Norma) in Boston. Caldwell was a forerunner of Peter Sellars, offering deconstructive, creative productions of standard and offbeat works. How much did she influence her Boston contemporary Sellars? Sills, we learned, sang what had to be one of the most "sizzling" (as Peter once described her best singing) of her recorded performances, the great final scene in *Maria Stuarda*, literally on fire with a cold and fever.

Another highlight was Mabel Mercer at Boston's Copley Plaza, a stone's throw from Dick's principal haunt, the Napoleon Club, a piano bar and one of the oldest gay bars in America. The Napoleon Club, which finally closed in 2013 and was said to have been visited by the likes of Judy Garland, Liberace and Elton John, was too frou-frou for me. In those years I preferred scruffier venues. Mercer had to have been in her 80's. Peter was with us that evening and, in his own Capote-esque gay voice and passive-aggressive demeanor—dispositionally, Peter was the Andy Warhol of music critics—drew comparisons between Mercer's singing and Eleanor Roosevelt speaking.

Dick and Peter, but especially Dick, were voice connoisseurs who could revel in being irreverent; they could wax as ecstatic for warblers of low and offbeat talent as for the greatest. It's Peter who introduced me to Olive Middleton and Florence Foster Jenkins, and later to Ira Siff and La Gran Scena Opera. As for Dick, there wasn't a moment of Nadine Connor's career that he didn't cherish. Likewise Dorothy Kirsten. And so many local singers, like Debbie O'Brien, a former runner-up for Miss America. We went to hear her sing with the Boston Pops on the Esplanade conducted by legendary Arthur Fiedler. She was the featured soloist that evening for Mozart's *Exultate Jubilate.* At the climactic moment of her high note in the cantata's conclusion, a gust of wind blew her dress up, like Marilyn Monroe's in *The Seven Year Itch*. What fun we had!

Such delectable moments also brought into relief another aspect of Dick's character. He was American and a New Englander in the truest and best sense. Dick was not religious but his family belonged to a Christian-American sect with an honorable heritage of liberal openness and outreach. Dick personified values Americans used to cherish. He was the most unself-pitying and loyal person I'd ever met. Even though his wit and criticism could be lacerating, Dick seemed incapable of being gratuitously mean or petty. In this he was like Oscar Wilde, who he otherwise could seem to resemble physically as his portliness, like my own, became more pronounced.

Personal accountability and integrity were givens for Dick. If you have a problem, deal with it. Don't blame, exploit, demean or betray others for your own shortcomings or advancement. When I went on and on about my dilemma in being a physician, activist and writer in the years prior to my first pieces for the gay press, Dick's observation was typically tough-love honest. "I love these people who keep asking, what am I going to do for the rest of my life?," he said with pitiless impatience. "Suddenly you're 65 and you've done it!"

At one point, Dick's friend and protégé David Denby was enlisted to get Dick to replace Alan Rich as music critic of *New York* Magazine. Dick was likewise being sought to become senior music critic of the *New York Times* (replacing Peter). When Dick declined both offers, the positions were filled at the *New York Times* by Dick's protege at the *Boston Globe*, Anthony Tommasini, and at *New York*, by Peter G. Davis (via my introduction of Davis to Denby). After decades as a senior music critic at the *Times*, Peter's position there was eliminated. Some thought Dick was crazy to pass up such spectacular opportunities. But Dick was too loyal to Boston and in his friendships to just drop everyone and everything there and to upstage Peter this way. Career success was one thing. Personal advancement at the cost of one's highest values and loyalties was another.

In his appreciation for singers, Dick was linked with our mutual friend Andrew Karzas in Chicago, whose old records collection was world-renowned and whose WFMT radio show was a feast for connoisseurs. These included his later colleague at WFMT, Andrew Patner, the openly gay music critic who died in 2015 and to whom Ross's *Wagnerism* is dedicated.

Karzas traveled to attend every performance of his most beloved singer, Licia Albanese, to the bitter end of *Traviatas* and *Bohemes* in her 80's in places like Sarasota. He was also devoted to May Higgens, the surviving companion of legendary British Diva Dame Eva Turner. Dick and I never went that distance with Andrew for Licia, but he and I did trek to Providence to hear what may have been Anna Moffo's last *Traviata*, Moffo was visibly nervous; the voice was still there but the singing was smaller. Providence was home of another of our favorite lesser divas—Marguerite Ruffino, who founded the largely Italian opera company there and whose voice could be impressive. Of her stage presence and skills, Dick observed, "every so often she'd remember to add an interpretive touch." When the book is written on gay sensibility and opera, Dick's would be a shining exemplar.

At the summit or nadir (however you choose to think of it) of our cabaret slumming and at the prodding of their friend, gadfly Henry Edwards, we all showed up to hear Francis Fay in what seemed like somebody's attic in the Times Square area. Fay pretended that she was plucked by surprise from our table to perform.

Figure 78 - Richard Dyer, The Boston Globe, Sendai International Music Competition

Dick and Peter were fabulous figures of sensibility, lore, wit, wisdom, accomplishment, and generosity of spirit. Alas, when it came to the battlefronts of gay activism, which increasingly inspired, challenged and dominated my work, they evinced minimal interest or engagement. From neither Dick nor Peter did I get genuinely supportive feedback about my work. It was not forthcoming for my activism, which could seem to strike them as, well, distasteful, nor for my efforts to report on the disease that was already decimating the worlds of music and opera, art and culture..

It was understandable that they were preoccupied with themselves and their career responsibilities, but it was telling that they were so disconnected from and unsupportive of disease and political crisis developments and efforts to deal with them, however chaotic and scary. When I was with them, the scruffy gay activist I had become felt increasingly disaffected and lonely. My place as a proper opera queen, escort and mascot were being compromised and I was the only one failing to see it.

Although they weren't happy about discrimination in the arts and society and certainly not homophobia, they were like most career homosexuals of their ilk—openly gay in social circles but still closeted professionally and with their readerships in times when being publicly gay could still pose real career risks. As I saw it, the biggest problem with their closetedness and reticence about homosexuality was the damage it did to their integrity as writers and critics whose priorities otherwise were ostensibly to tell the truth. It's not that they were telling overt lies or that they didn't care. It was what wasn't being said, what was omitted or obscured that contributed to misunderstanding and discrimination. As AIDS and activism advanced, their reticence became entrenched, especially around my support for outing, which must have seemed personal and threatening. Alas, in their unwillingness to buck the status quo, they revealed themselves to be counted among its custodians.

In contact that became increasingly rare, and when directly confronted about it by me, Dick acknowledged my memoir, *Confessions of a Jewish Wagnerite,* but I don't think he or Peter actually read or took seriously anything I wrote. Beyond my roles of escort and mascot, they had little genuine in-depth interest in the real me or my writing or the issues I kept talking and writing about. It didn't seem in reaction to me personally so much as that they couldn't be bothered with anything so marginal as the gay press and messy as gay politics.

It was a less extreme version of the Roy Cohn double-think and cognitive dissonance captured by Tony Kushner in *Angels in America.* Because gay people have no real power, Cohn believed, he couldn't and shouldn't be identified as gay. Like the majority of their contemporary gay colleagues, their negotiable worth, so far as they could measure it, had little to do with being gay. Professionally, being openly gay was still felt to be a liability and risk. It must have been the same with music and arts critics who were gay and Jewish in Nazi Germany. That's the way it was well into the AIDS period even with our most illustrious gay, bisexual and lesbian *culturati,* such as Warhol and Sontag. Their closetedness kept reenforcing the rules of the game. In broader public venues, their minority identities were studiously relegated by them and their standard-bearer protectors (editors, other writers) to the margins, where they remained mostly hidden. While they may not have liked such cultural constraints, they characteristically elected the safer options of the closet—reticence and silence. That such actions wouldn't be noticed or counted was a miscalculation.

Figure 79 - Peter G. Davis (right) with Riccardo Muti, New York Times and New York Magazine music critic, Remembering Peter G. Davis by Lawrence D. Mass on medium.com

I remember a penultimate telephone conversation with Dick, who had developed a friendship with Astrid Varnay. She was the great Wagnerian soprano whose Kundry I saw at Bayreuth with Hans Hotter as Gurnemanz, and whose Letitia Begbig in the Met's *Mahagonny* was a highlight of our operagoing years. Following the publication of my *Confessions*, amidst discussions of Varnay and others, I remember trying to further explain my transformation around Wagner. I wanted to elicit a greater awareness if not sympathy for what I'd experienced. Yet my memoir was indeed an indictment of the closetedness of the world of music criticism and journalism he, Dick, Dale Harris, John Ardoin, Andrew Porter, Martin Bernheimer and virtually all other gay music critics represented. In the case of Wagner and antisemitism, I wanted them to appreciate that their reticence was of a piece with their being in the closet as gay. I no longer recall what was said so much as what wasn't said. In what was to be among the last of our exchanges voice-to-voice (face to face was never again to be), Dick exhaled deeply and a long silence followed, a silence that spoke volumes.

What that silence was saying is that, yes, they (Dick and Peter) recognized a personally and socially codependent (masochistic was the word we used in those days) component to my Wagnerism, with my 5 pictures of Wagner on my living room wall and my "pilgrimage" to Bayreuth. This silence also revealed how tacitly aware the music world was (and continues to be) of the seriousness of these issues.

Silence and taciturnity. The music world would feign objectivity around what they secretly knew and felt versus what they would say publicly. Their defense of Wagner was standard for our post-war generation—that some of Wagner's close associates were Jews, that the antisemitism isn't explicit in the music or libretti, that Hitler misunderstood and misused Wagner, that Jews continue to be among the most devoted of Wagnerites. But deep down even then they all knew better. Just as the closet was still the easier, softer way, so it was with regard to the reality and toxicity of Wagner's antisemitism.

I don't recall ever thinking that anything Dick or Peter ever said or did was antisemitic. Of course in those days I was still in a lot of denial, As for things Jewish, on the contrary, Dick and Peter seemed if anything to be semitophilic. Many of their best friends were Jews. Dick was very close with poet Lloyd Schwartz and Michael Steinberg, the former music critic of the *Boston Globe* who Dick succeeded there. And Peter was very close with the leading artist agent Cynthia Robbins of Edgar Vincent Associates and her partner Steve Rubin, who became head of Doubleday in the years when Jacqueline Onassis worked there. In the time I knew him, Peter had two lovers, both of them Jewish. Eventually, he settled into a life partnership with the second of these.

Cynthia represented Beverly Sills, who Peter was so often at odds with. There was an angry late-night call to Peter from Sills herself; she was said to have used epithets in denunciations of his criticism. Of her later administrative efforts (and triumphs), Peter sustained his reputation as a tough critic—once dismissing her style of management and donor outreach as like trying to run a delicatessen. In drawing what could seem persistent criticism from Peter, Sills could seem like another regular target of Peter's disappointment, composer Phillip Glass.

With none of this, however, did I ever have a sense of any element of antisemitism, but which was not something I was inclined to look for or acknowledge in any case. Though Peter's criticism could seem ungenerous, there were legitimate issues with Sills as there are with Glass and for that matter another target of his criticism, Leontyne Price, the latter for not being more adventurous with repertory.

I did, however, occasionally wonder about some things. Why did Peter keep a single framed Wagner-autographed postcard above his bed? And why was Dick so *un*enamoured of Bernstein's "The Unanswered Question," the composer's series of talks on music and culture at Harvard? I no longer recall what Dick wrote, but privately he seemed to feel that the talks were neither centered nor revelatory. Rather, to Dick they came across more as posturing and scattered theorizing.

Nothing heretical or biased there. I myself wasn't the greatest fan of Bernstein in those years. I recoiled from *Mass*, which still divides critics and which struck me as pretentious on initial hearing and even when I saw it again decades later. Apart from *West Side Story, Candide, A Quiet Place* and some television appearances, I sensed Lenny's "extravagant" persona in much of his work and tended to find the whole cult of "Lenny," to be, well, of questionable taste. So why would I have an inchoate uneasiness years later when Dick had that same sense about "Lenny" and his lectures, which I myself never bothered to listen to or read? In the peak years of my Wagnerism, if, when and where something subtly or indirectly antisemitic might be afoot, it's not only unlikely that I would have recognized it as such. More likely, I would have agreed with and endorsed it.

In one of Peter's last pieces for the *New York Times*, he covered the Bard Festival offerings Leon Botstein assembled in 2009 on "Wagner and His World." As noted by Peter, the season turned the tables on expectations in being more about those who influenced Wagner (Meyerbeer and Mendelssohn) than on Wagner's influence on others. The piece was Peter at his best—scrupulously professional, observant and dispassionate. You got all the information, some of it impressively insightful and detailed, but without any real sense of how Peter himself felt. Except for odd moments such as the *Siegfried* performance we attended together (as recounted in *Confessions of a Jewish Wagnerite*), I still have little sense of Peter's personal feelings about Wagner.

What I'm left with are fragmentary memories—images, moments, comments. There was that autographed postcard of Wagner situated protectively on the wall above Peter's bed, and recollection of Peter's dispassionate awareness that the Nibelungs in the Bayreuth Centennial *Ring* cycle directed by Chéreau were depicted as Jews. As questions about Wagner and Wagnerism began to formulate, I pondered Wagner appreciation in different contexts and cultures. On reading about a planned production of *Lohengrin in Russia*, I wondered why Russians, with their acute sensitivity to what happened in World War 2, would want to do Wagner unless it featured a postmodern approach, a political underpinning that commented on their experience. How do Russians, who fought Germany and the Nazis so bravely and at such horrific cost, feel about Wagner? Peter, who could become impatient with such nontextualist probings, answered sarcastically: "Maybe they think the music is pretty."

For critics of Peter's generation, social and political context and subtext were regarded more with suspicion than open-mindedness. While they could acknowledge and even cautiously praise experimentation and imagination, they did so from their base, their ethos that looked with skepticism at anything extrinsic to the artwork and its appreciation. The resulting silence and taciturnity, however, could also seem myopic and collusive in obfuscating the importance of minority perspectives as well as those of sexuality and politics in the lives and times and works of composers. In too many cases, these perspectives were illuminating and central to greater understanding and appreciation.

So *is* Wagner appreciation in Russia distinctive? Had he been more open-minded and less defensive, Peter, who is not mentioned in Ross's *Wagnerism*, (nor are Dick Dyer, Andrew Porter or me) might have been surprised by how much Ross uncovered about this subject in his book's chapter "Ring of Power: Revolution and Russia."

In 2015 Boris Mezdrich, the director of a postmodern production of *Tannhäuser* in Siberia was sacked by the Russian Culture Minister after being accused of offending the religious sensibilities of Russian Orthodox Christians. Protestors carried pro-Putin banners. So, yes, however pretty Wagner's music, the greater subject of Wagner in Russia turns out to be another window on the past, present and future of Wagnerism.

The question of how Russians might tend to regard Wagner did not seem of critical interest to Peter. Though he might make note of a theme that was clearly key to a director's vision, it's not likely Peter would have had any more inclination to explore social or political subtexts extraneous to the confines of the work itself than questions regarding the homosexuality of Tchaikovsky. Like his colleague Dale Harris, Peter would be more likely to accept without qualification or protest the status quo of Tchaikovsky as a *Russian* composer, with all else of negligible pertinence. Indictments like mine of the silence of the Metropolitan Opera and its Russian stars Anna Netrebko and Valery Gergiev regarding the oppression of LGBTQ people in Russia under Putin would be considered way too personal, political, extraneous. Alas, what Peter and Dick ended up mostly doing were performance reviews, and evermore bloodless ones at that.

But what of my own role in all this? A sense of grievance linked to a failure to relate to others is a classic feature of codependence. The codependent person fails to adequately express his needs to those he needs to express them to. Certainly, I was codependent in those years with Dick and Peter, as I was with my brother, my sister and most everybody else, including artists like Ned Rorem who I thought were good friends but who were not. Most notably, of course, was my codependence evident in my devotion to Wagner. Did those 5 pictures of Wagner on my living room wall mitigate the realities of who Wagner really was? Did it influence the appreciation of Wagner—my own and that of others—for the better?

No matter how determined my denial and rationalizations, I could finally see that I had failed to get commensurate validation from these sources. Inevitably, those with whom I felt closest turned out not to be there, neither for me personally nor for the community, social and political concerns I took for granted that we shared. When I finally did face the reality of the demise of my friendships with Dick and Peter and better understood the extent of my own codependent role in that failure, the indictment remained that they weren't there as writers and tellers of some of the most difficult and challenging truths of our lives and times. When confronted with the opening up of new frontiers on homosexuality, Wagner's antisemitism and AIDS, they weren't there.

If not for them, however, how would I ever have gotten here? In this question and its answer is one of the promises of recovery: we will not regret the past, nor wish to shut the door on it.

So there I was on the flight deck at St V's in the Spring of '83, now with my own money problems. I had been working furiously on my unpaid writing, mostly on the unfolding of the AIDS epidemic but also with pieces on culture, on opera and gay health, barely managing to stay afloat with part-time work in Methadone Maintenance. With my hospitalization, however, I was no longer working and was unable to pay my rent, which contributed to my depression.

I didn't want to see my mother. I couldn't deal with that. But my brother showed up. Not only did he show up, he agreed to write me a check for what I needed to cover immediate expenses, which was about $2000. Though he scarcely looked at me and never called back or returned to visit, I vaguely recall him saying something reassuring, that whatever I was going through I would get through it and be OK.

And there was more. Regarding what I saw as the bottom line of my depression—my inability to find a way to earn a living with my writing—he said something encouraging about how you don't really have to do anything you don't want to do; that you can find a way to do what makes you happy. Not only was it a unique instance of Steve showing up and seeming to care, I believe it contributed to my situation not worsening. I was on the verge of getting shock treatments for depression. Steve's visit was a reprieve. Was this the Steve Mass who ministered to the down and out, the outsiders and the misfits?

Several years later, I returned the favor by saying yes to a request for money from Steve, for the same amount, $2000. Though I repaid him promptly for his loan to me, it wasn't surprising that he never repaid my loan to him. Eventually we deducted it, along with money he owed my sister, from his portion of my mother's estate, divided among her three children, when she died in the year 2000.

A visit during that hospitalization from my sister Ellen ("Helen" in *Confessions of a Jewish Wagnerite*) went less well. As recounted in *Confessions*, she made the mistake of giving me the manuscript of a book her son had been working on in his progressive school in Cambridge, Mass. His teacher was none other than gay writer and activist Eric Rofes. It was called *The Kids' Book of Death and Dying*. It was a source of progressive pride that her son was working on such a challenging project with a gay teacher and mentor. Her pride was well placed and shared by me. However, just seeing that book's title exacerbated the tensions in my lifelong relationship with my siblings, on top of my clinical depression. Did it not occur to her that someone hospitalized with a major suicidal depression might be uncomfortable with being given a book about death and dying, especially from within a family rife with interpersonal dysfunction?

With my paranoia easily triggered, I couldn't help but wonder if some deeper level of sibling rivalry and resentment were operating subconsciously. When we were children I remember Ellen and I playing jump-rope in our living room in Macon, Georgia, in the house on our street, The Prado, where we were born and raised. I was the jumper and she held one end of the rope. The other end was tied to our chandelier, which promptly crashed, leaving my arm gashed and with a scar that is still there. I have no memory of the stitches that must have been involved. I told Arnie and the hospital staff on the psych ward at St. V's that under no circumstances was Ellen to be allowed to re-visit or call me.

Detach with love or with an ax, as we say in codependence recovery. And some years later, with Ellen as my principal qualifier (the main person in relationship with whom one decides to enter recovery), I commenced in earnest the hard, daily, never-ending work of codependence recovery. Eventually Ellen and I reconnected and resumed our often effortful but sometimes very gratifying and loving relationship.

At my urging and like our mother, Ellen herself dabbled with codependence recovery (she's been to a handful of meetings over the years), as has her son. Over the ensuing decades, however, she remained resolute in her refusal to discuss what happened at St. V's. Whenever she might sense criticism, accusation, blame or judgment, or where she might feel confronted about an absence of critical self-reflection and acknowledgment of mistakes or regarding how others had been affected by her, she would withdraw emotionally.

That same unwillingness re-emerged years later when Ellen casually recalled another childhood incident. She and a friend had stolen and hidden my bicycle, for which I, not knowing better, had to take the blame from our parents. I had no memory of this incident. When I tried to press her for more details about such early sibling dynamics, however, her refusal to further discuss it was characteristically intractable.

On the one hand, I can appreciate that she was careful to avoid disadvantageous subjects and discussions that opened the door to criticism, especially ones where she, as a woman, might encounter the abuses of sexism that were commonplace among men. But why not at least try to be honest about such rivalries, get them out in discussion, try to clear the air, and move on?

Eventually, I began to appreciate that some of Ellen's patterns may be more imprinted and reflexive, more psychiatric than logical, thoughtful or willful, perhaps a kind of PTSD from having been ridiculed or threatened by others such as our father or her brothers in childhood.

A recent recurrence of this reaction was impressive. Ellen was visiting us in New York in 2018 and had arranged to meet me at the New Whitney Museum to see the Grant Wood exhibit (in which Wood's closeted homosexuality comes to life). Though Ellen's punctuality and accountability have improved notably over time, on this occasion she failed to show up. I called her and she was still at her hotel, surprised by my reminding her that we had agreed to meet in front of the museum at 10 am. As we get older, we become more forgetful, a senior human error that's common enough. She quickly got herself together and arrived at the museum a short time later. As in the past, however, there was neither acknowledgment of any mistake, nor any apology. When I confronted her about how her failure to acknowledge what had happened was baffling and hurtful to me, she became silent, but in a way that seemed more clinical than having anything to do with me personally. She looked away and said nothing in response to my questions. What at first seemed bizarre and maddening began to be better appreciated as regressive, the embarrassed withdrawal into silence of a threatened child, In confronting her, had I transferentially become the menacing, punitive father, brother or other men of childhood fears and abusive experience?

Being an intelligent and sensitive young girl in a patriarchal family and parochial social milieu might seem to explain the impenetrability of Ellen's defenses. But not all women from comparable backgrounds are comparably affected. Yes, our Dad came from Jewish patriarchal systems that expected women to defer to men. And yes he had been corporeally punitive with us in the vein of the ambient Bible-Belt ethic of not sparing the rod to not spoil the child.

One such occasion, when Ellen was a little girl, I still vividly recall. What was most memorable was her unwillingness to yield even in the smallest measure to Dad's anger and frustration at what he perceived to be her stubbornness. She would not verbally respond to Dad's increasingly exasperated demands for her to answer him. It was that same silence I'd encountered with Ellen at the Whitney. "I hate you, I hate you!" she finally shrieked, in tears after unyielding silence in response to being repeatedly slapped by Dad for her belligerence.

Not letting Ellen have her way proved increasingly difficult for our parents, as it has proved for many others who have interacted with her. When she turned 16 and demanded an MG sports car that would render her status the equivalent of wealthier friends, our parents, who could ill afford such an expense, reluctantly acceded.

Years later, when my mother was in her last days at St. V's, Ellen and I both had precious time for closure. We both had made real progress in our relations with our mother. In my case, Mom blessed me on her death bed by affirming that between us there were no unresolved issues, that where we had come in our journey of reconciliation was "perfect." Following Mom's death and on reflection years later, by contrast, Ellen felt that her closure with Mom was incomplete. I couldn't help but ponder how much this feeling of incompleteness was because of absent self-reflection, unacknowledged conflicts, unasked questions, and unexpressed regrets and apologies.

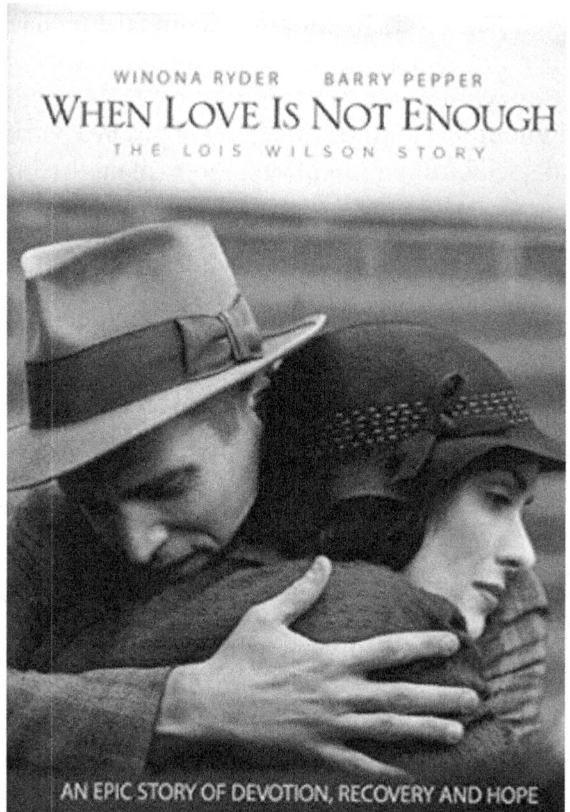


Figure 80 - Bill Pepper as Bill Wilson, co-founder of Alcoholics Anonymous, with Winona Ryder as his wife Lois, who co-founded Alanon, Hallmark Hall of Fame premiere 2010, Wikipedia

People who are codependent tend to harbor inchoate anger at those with whom they are codependent because those people seem indifferent to needs that were never adequately expressed or because they were incapable of better responding to those needs or expectations. In my life, nowhere has this been more the case than with my sister, with whom I've managed, however effortfully, to sustain a more functional bond with than my brother.

Central to the dilemma and drama of codependence is that each party feels the other has failed to be there appropriately and coequally. "The human condition," one might observe. There is of course truth to the observation that what is clinically characterized as "codependence" are just issues of the dominance and inequality, of love, which are universal phenomena in relationships. Just as it's true that what we call addiction can also be seen in wider context as a comparably universal human quest for pleasure and escape. At what point do these phenomena become "clinical"? While there are definitions, there are no incontrovertible answers. What's codependence or addiction for some may be rationalized as being just the human condition for others. Those of us who self-identify as codependent and/or addictive know that we crossed a line from functional to dysfunctional, even if that line can seem arbitrary. Those of us who end up in recovery for codependence and/or addiction tend to have an intuitive understanding that we belong there.

For my sister, there was acute and chronic sensitivity to sexism in patriarchal family relations. Favoring of male offspring was a notable issue in our Dad's family, where his sisters were expected to defer their educations and careers in favor of their brothers, as well as in society in general. These issues were as difficult for her and us to conceptualize and articulate growing up as were my feelings of being bullied by my two older siblings as well as my Dad.

Too much of this inchoate anger of codependence got displaced onto Ellen's son, Max, whose paternity was never clarified. It has been acknowledged by Ellen and Max that Max's biological father was Middle Eastern, beyond which information only Ellen knows for sure. Max was conceived in Israel, when Ellen's husband Larry was doing graduate work via a scholarship from Brandeis in Israel and France.

Max, now in midlife, has always been bright, decent, enterprising and athletic. He ran in many marathons and set up his own creative business of online newsletters, personal training, sales and services to runners of all ages. Most people have little idea of the difficulties of independent business life, one of the biggest pitfalls of which is isolation. Eventually, Max found himself increasingly isolated and prone to "recreational drug use," primarily with alcohol and marijuana. Max also began smoking cigarettes, which was shocking for someone so fit and health-conscious.

Ellen, divorced when Max was a child and a committed socialist, believed that there's "no such thing as bad students, only bad teachers." She wanted me to step in as an interim father figure for Max. The need for a role model and mentor for Max was genuine, honorable, acute and chronic. I was ideally situated to help, especially later, given my professional as well as personal experience with addiction and depression.

But it also seemed another instance of being called upon for others who had always seemed to relegate my needs in favor or their own. However legitimate, her needs and wishes for her son could seem more redolent of the leftist politics so many of her generation had so strongly embraced than a reasonable development of genuine, nurtured, earned and trustworthy family relationships. In her case, as with many leftists, dominance and demand kept emerging in an atmospheric context of theoretics, entitlement and expectations.

At her most extreme, Ellen wasn't that far afield from the socialist and communist dictatorships she was ardently supportive of in her views of how people should be in society, and therefore in relationship to her. Yet I did show up, and so well and over so long a period that even Ellen acknowledged my efforts and thanked me appropriately, even as she retained her skepticism of my often critical, reluctant and delimited involvement as a kind of recovery evangelism rather than what she believed should have been the more unquestioning and unqualified availability and generosity expected of me as her brother and, well, comrade.

Moments of thanks notwithstanding, the crossing of boundaries kept recurring. Communications devolved into performance evaluations, not so unlike those of corporate America, which she excelled at serving to others but consistently and aggressively disallowed for herself. Not surprisingly, Ellen's earlier tenure as a schoolteacher ended peremptorily in confrontations with staff and administration. Here was a socialist who had a lot of trouble being, as we say in recovery, and as is an imperative of socialism, a worker among workers and a person among persons.

I sensed this exceptionalism in Ellen's relationship with her ex-husband, Larry Lockwood, who must have felt pressured to continue in his role as Max's father, even after the divorce and Ellen's acknowledgment of the long-suspected truth that he was not Max's biological father. Though Larry's bond with Max was not necessarily any less valid emotionally than if their relationship were biological, Larry went on to marry another and raise his own children.

To what extent could Max or Ellen expect him to continue as a father, or expect me to be a substitute? Though the answers to such questions could be challenging, expectation and entitlement continued for Larry Lockwood as for family members like me, with little discernible compassion for his own life and circumstances and little sense of their own role, of their own expectation and entitlement, in Larry's disaffection. The situation with Larry seemed of a piece with other of Ellen's relationships in its deployment of a kind of emotional hostage-taking. People who might otherwise make the choice to disengage from their relationship with Ellen, especially blood relatives and childhood friends, could find themselves reluctant to do so as a matter of conscience. Short of being unkind, the easier softer way for most of us was to be tolerant, forbearing, caring, sensitive and creative within legitimate efforts to maintain our own boundaries.

The crossing, however, of my often deferentially unexpressed boundaries with Ellen was unyielding and conversations not infrequently terminated in anger. If I people-pleased enough with Ellen and Max (taking his cues from his mother), I might get rewarded with thanks, a dollop of affection, and acknowledgment of milestones with the occasional sign-off of "Love" instead of "Regards," "Best," or "Peace." Meanwhile, such was the incessant barrage of unsolicited and unwelcome emails from her that I had to devise creative, codependence recovery-based strategies for dealing with them.

As I eventually came to see it a lot better, Ellen's pride in being leftist, feminist, progressive, independent, in having a social conscience and being a single mother, was not displaced and not to be disparaged. It can't have been easy to navigate the turbulent seas of sexism, which she did with notable courage and fortitude. Nor is it easy to be leftist in relentlessly middle-brow, exclusionary, materialist, Judeo-Christian America. Consistently sensitive to issues of racism and class, against the grain of the mainstream of Columbus-celebrating America, Ellen authored a book called *Population Target* about the targeting of indigenous, third-world populations—who were offered tokens such as free radios to get them to use birth control—by corporations seeking to profiteer from their lands and resources. Her book was a remarkable and pioneering achievement about levels of corporate, often mass-murderous malevolence that no longer surprise us.

Figure 81 - Ellen Mass with Larry Mass at the Alewife Preserve, Cambridge, Mass, 2018, personal photographs of Lawrence D. Mass

What were the origins of her strength of character and social consciousness? As Jewish and a woman, and like Steve (Jewish) and me (Jewish and gay), Ellen had her share of being the outsider. But for Ellen another big childhood challenge influenced the shape of things to come.

Ellen was literally crippled by a serious spinal scoliosis from congenital polio, unrecognized until her adolescence. The scoliosis was originally thought by our parents to be a willful indifference to the discipline of maintaining good posture. With vintage gay humor, gay men of a certain age still threaten to send real or perceived miscreants to "charm school," but for young women of Ellen's time and place, such threats were more real and dreaded than funny. Over several years the scoliosis was repaired in two heroic surgeries by one of the world's top specialists in California. One of the procedures necessitated a heavy and encumbering body cast that had to be worn for nearly a year. Whatever the fallout in her relations with others, to come through such an ordeal as well as Ellen did—to have endured this huge physical hardship alongside our parents' and society's sexist expectations, mostly without complaining or ceding personal integrity and independence—required measures of grit Ellen sustained throughout her life. Consolidating her strengths were traits that were also those of the best of America and New England. Like Dick Dyer she was relentlessly unself-pitying and true to herself.

Crowning her achievements, Ellen has worked with singular leadership and dedication to nurture the Alewife Preserve, an environmental conservation endeavor in Cambridge. For decades she worked tirelessly and independently, enlisting young people to serve and learn about the environment and land preservation and to contribute mural art in the wake of ever-worsening corporate encroachment.

As summarized by Madelyn Holmes, a feminist historian whose books include *American Women Conservationists* and who became Ellen's friend, Ellen's work with Alewife has been notable for its enterprise and commitment to environmental restoration. As cited in Holmes's book and quoting from *The Cambridge Chronicle*, "whether scrambling down a bank overgrown with invasive plant species to confirm a beaver sighting or leading a group of schoolchildren on a nature walk...Mass has come to embody the very spirit of the place."

This trajectory (as portrayed in Robert Redford's 2012 film, *The Company You Keep*) from political activism to environmentalism was followed by most members of the Weathermen Underground Organization of the late 1960's, which developed out of SDS (Students for a Democratic Society). Terrorism may never be justified, but what alternatives were there to confront the intolerably racist, sexist, inequitable and murderous society that America was in those years, that America to which Trumpery so rapaciously returned us?

Figure 82 - Mural Art, Friends of Alewife, Cambridge, Mass, Environmental Conservationist and Alewife Projects Coordinator Ellen Mass with unidentified volunteer

Environmentalist activism is certainly laudable, but more global rallying around the targeted, dispossessed and threatened could raise questions. In my own journey of self-awareness as Jewish, it seemed as if Ellen were always pressing pro-Palestinian views. There were Seders at our mother's home with *Haggadahs* (the Jewish texts for the Passover Seder) Ellen supplied that reworked the story of Jewish enslavement and exile from Egypt to be about the Palestinian experience. In and of itself, such repositioning could be appreciated as thoughtful, reasonable and sympathetic—like the Jews of Egypt, Palestinians in Israel were dispossessed—but a lot less so in its relegation of the Jewish meaning and experience of the holiday.

Though our mother could seem cowed by Ellen's propagandism, some of her engagement with Ellen's leftism was genuinely feminist, willing and enlightened. With Ellen's help, Mom was able to better appreciate how much her own considerable native intelligence was relegated by her family, its patriarchal religion and society.

What troubled my mother and me was not Ellen's championing of the Palestinians, which seemed justified, so much as her lack of greater awareness of and sensitivity to antisemitism, especially the casually genocidal antisemitism avowed by Islamic extremists, including many Palestinians explicitly committed to Israel's destruction. As his grandmother, my mother loved Max unconditionally and thereby came to accept his paternity, about which she may have known more truth than I, but my mother had an innate and much stronger experiential sense of her own Jewishness and antisemitism, and was instinctively and reflexively a lot more concerned about antisemitism, terrorism and the security of Israel.

Several years ago, during an Xmas visit in New York, Ellen gave Max a *keffiyeh*, the Arab headdress, which seemed to elicit no interest from him in response. From what he's seen of religion, ethnicity and factionalism, he wants as little to do with any of that as possible. Admirably, in multi-cultural Cambridge where he resumed residence after nearly two decades in Washington D.C., he was raised not to place much stock in religious or denominational specificity. In Max's liberal milieu it makes sense that he would feel compassion for the plight of Palestinians. And it makes sense for him to explore his paternal background. But giving him a *keffiyeh*, with no comparable affirmation of Jewish heritage (no *yarmulke* or *kippah*), seemed an awkward, troubled and even hostile effort at balance. It also begs the question that needs to be asked of all pro-Palestinian leftists, especially the many who are Jewish: Do we really want to encourage respect for and tolerance of Islamism without more explicitly condemning extremist Islam, and without a comparable respect for and tolerance of other religions? Whatever the realities and ubiquities of Islamophobia, does it make more sense to embrace Islamism than any other denominationalism, even when it's coupled with notable poverty and disenfranchisement?

In later years, Ellen has shown a keener appreciation of Jewish culture and traditions and has eased away from leftist orthodoxy, in the heyday of which she would steadfastly refuse to criticize or even acknowledge the problems of socialist governments and countries, most of which were police state dictatorships under authoritarian control —e.g., China, Russia or Cuba. Many of these countries were as anti-gay as their Western counterparts. Because gay people were not always singled out as such for discrimination but were regarded, rather, as ordinary citizens, it could seem we were seeking special consideration and treatment in a setting of white, privileged capitalism, not unlike the way Jews and others seemed to cling to the sectarianism and subcultural identification that socialism was ostensibly all about transcending.

In the mid-1980's our mother and Max were "delegated," as I derided it at the time, by Ellen to accompany her on a trip to Russia. There, they visited some memorial sites where mass executions of Jews had taken place, including the area from which our grandparents had emigrated. Moscow now has a center of Russian Jewish history and culture. At the time of their trip, however, victims of massacres in Russia were identified only as "Soviet citizens." No questions or concerns about the elimination of Jewish history were being sanctioned in Russia, and none were voiced by Ellen or her son on their return. My mother, who just wanted the family to all get along and be stable and happy, voiced no opinion on any of this. Nor was my own questioning of this experience clear or persistent.

Prior to that time, Ellen had dismissed as "sentimental" our relatives' support of the movement to free Soviet Jewry that saw a million Soviet Jews emigrate to Israel, even as she evinced that socialist sense of entitlement and expectation with those same relatives. As she saw it, they needed to be more inclusive and universal than tribal and concentric in their relations with us and with society at large. Meanwhile, her requests for greater welcoming of Max and herself were often experienced by these relatives as "demands." Perceived expectations from others were contrastingly ill-received by Ellen. As one hears in recovery, expectations are premeditated resentments. At their worst, such demands could seem in the vein of what we think of as communist or socialist "reeducation" or "reprogramming," where people are simply informed of expectations and disciplined for conformity. Meanwhile, none of Ellen's expectations of fealty from Jewish relatives seemed ever to evince any real feeling for being Jewish or concern about antisemitism.

I do recall a singular instance of reaction to repeatedly expressed concerns by me that she seemed lacking in an ability to identify and empathize with being Jewish: "There's more than one way to be Jewish." There it was, finally! An unequivocal acceptance that whatever else she is, however surpassingly a citizen of the world, she's also Jewish. Past such rare moments of circumspection and personal acknowledgment, however, there were few second thoughts and no apologies for the authoritarian turn taken by most of the movements she had been so supportive of.

As summarized by Bret Stephens in "Mugabe and Other Leftist Heroes" in the *New York Times* (11/17/17) the Robert Mugabes, Fidel Castros, Mao Tse Tungs, Yassir Arafats and Russian autocrats "never lacked for admirers on the left. The result has been decades of moral embarrassment for the left, though it's rarely acknowledged and only occasionally examined. Being progressive, as the conservative saying goes, means never having to say you are sorry."

*"What do you want with these special Jewish pains? I feel as close to the wretched victims of the rubber plantations of Putamayo and the blacks of Africa...I have no special place in my heart for the ghetto: I am at home in the entire world, where there are clouds and birds and human tears."*

- Rosa Luxemburg, Polish-German-Jewish hero and martyr of socialism, executed 1919.

Figure 83 - Rosa Luxemburg, sculpture by Rolf Biebl, Berlin, Creative Commons

Like many Jews of the left, Ellen may have been in denial about the persistence of antisemitism and the challenge of Jewish self-identification, even if socialism among Jews can also be appreciated as an effort to contain antisemitism. Indeed, there are many ways to be Jewish, among the proudest of which are secular humanism, socialism and environmentalism. Ellen joins a proud and distinguished legacy of historical Jewish champions of social justice, from Jesus to Marx, from Rosa Luxemburg and Emma Goldman to Tony Kushner, Sarah Schulman and Bernie Sanders. In the ever-darkening age of Trump, their light shines ever-more brightly. Ellen likewise belongs to that pantheon of strong Jewish women, some of whom are best-known as defenders of Jews and Judaism—from Biblical Judith and Esther to Golda Meir and Phyllis Chesler.

My Manhattan neighbors Daniel and Judith Walkowitz are distinguished professors of history who have contributed notably to progressive literatures and perspectives. Daniel's most recent book is called *The Remembered and Forgotten Jewish World.* Here, as he uncovers and reclaims his own Jewish family history, he documents the vital role played by the Jewish socialist world in workers' rights initiatives. Leftists who in earlier decades might have eschewed their Jewishness are now reclaiming it. In her travels to Russia with our mother and her son, a proper reckoning with our own family's Jewish past was once again evaded, notwithstanding Ellen's sleuthing of some aspects of Dad's *shtetl* background. It's work that neither Ellen, Steve nor I have done very much of.

For Ellen, pride of heritage was of progressivism. For Steve it was art, culture and counterculture. And for me it was opera. Following the assimilative living of so much of our lives in evasion of the specifics and realities of our backgrounds, each of us seems finally more aware of the broader mosaic we are motes within. Too late for all that precious archival work Ellen seemed belatedly inclined towards and Max is inquisitive about but which the Masses were all too otherwise engaged to pursue.

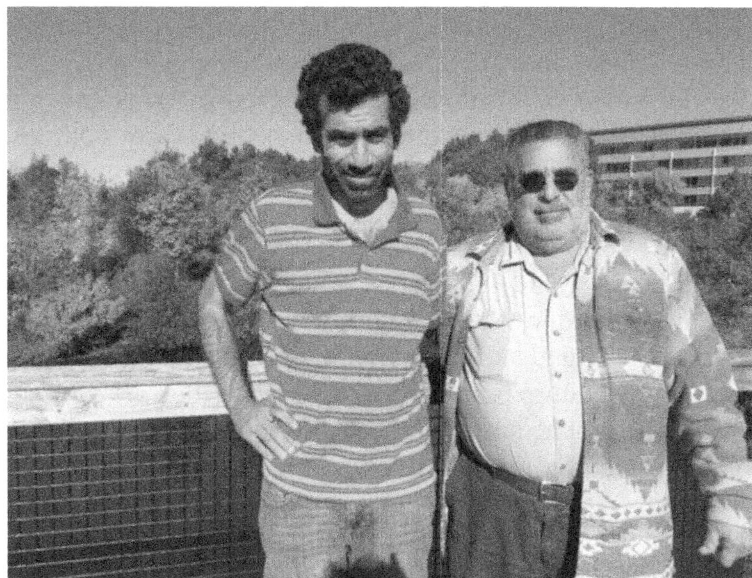

Figure 84 - Nephew Max Lockwood with Uncle Larry at the Alewife Preserve, from the personal photograph collection of Lawrence D. Mass

Strong Jewish women and strong Jewish mothers. The saga with Ellen and Max peaked 30 years later with Max having a midlife crisis comparable to my major depressive episode, but stopping short of hospitalization and eschewing medication; all of which aroused in me a level of paternal concern partly codependent, but also more heartfelt than any of us imagined possible.

Sister Blue Buffalo. A pinnacle of Ellen's life as a single woman, mother, sister and progressive was a voyage of discovery of her own planning in the mid-1990's. It was a bold itinerary that necessitated sleeping in her van in naturalist areas and enclaves ignored by tourists. It was an American odyssey as true and brave as they come.

Years in the making, she headed solo to points south and west in her gear-stocked, dark blue Toyota mini-van. Visiting sparsely populated, little-known and neglected areas such as the Florida panhandle, Indian reservations, and the slums of Appalachia, and including some 45 national parks and environs, she took notes and photographs and made sketches of environments of poverty, of the underserved and dispossessed. In the vein of such American originals as Ansel Adams, Georgia O'Keefe and Alfred Stieglitz, these impressions and images, in black and white as well as color, captured the beauty, dignity and spirit of heartland America, as well as her own wayfarer's journey and voice, with authenticity and grace.

We celebrated my 75th Birthday at Salam restaurant, with its delectable Syrian cuisine, where we'd celebrated my 50th and her 60th Birthdays, and which has been my special favorite New York restaurant since before owners Joan and Bassam's now grown children were born. Hosted by Arnie, it was a happy evening, attended by Max, Ellen's friend the writer Madelyn Holmes, my friend the writer Jaime Manrique, Attila en route back to Florida from his family visit in Hungary, and our new friend, Aleksander Douglas, whose devotion to gay culture is so animated and inspiring.

Ellen's gift could not have been more loving or cherishable, a photo album pictorial of past family gatherings in New York. With love and art, Ellen had fashioned it all into a forever keepsake. Following on the heels of our last family gathering, when we finally—after years of effort—got tickets to *Hamiltion*, we headed out to the Imax premiere of *In The Heights*.

Following my release from the hospital, alcoholism recovery became my primary journey but would take another year to commence in earnest. My hospitalization for MDD (Major Depressive Disorder) was my bottom, as we say in recovery, a truly life-threatening development in the progression of addiction. Steve's visit had seemed a reprieve, a gesture of genuine caring and hope, but so singular as such in terms of our relationship as brothers that I couldn't help but wonder to what extent he had been pressured to do so by my mother, who at that time was giving him shelter and financial support. Would he have shown up at all if she hadn't mandated him to do so? Were his few words of support heartfelt? Were they more wishful thinking than what actually happened? Because of its singularity before and after, it became ever harder to believe that absent my mother's prodding, the one visit to the hospital would ever have happened.

So there you have them, the three instances of receiving something personal from Steve: the bongo drum, the sidewalk-blanket peddler's used book by Shana Alexander, and the $2000 check hospital visit. The majority of other occasions with Steve had to do with his residing with my mother and her requirement that he attend holiday dinners and do the driving. Once he departed for Germany, and apart for my mother's memorial service, I had no direct contact with him for 15 years. His only efforts to communicate with us—my sister, her son

Max and myself—were several emergency requests for money via Helen Mitsios. Such dissociation and exploitation burned so badly for my sister as well as me that when he phoned on Xmas day from Berlin years later, we declined to take the call, concerned that it would quickly become yet another request for money, shelter or both.

"What is a moment of compassion?" is a question asked in codependence recovery. The answer: "A moment of compassion is a codependence slip." The slippery slope for someone codependent is relapse via compassion into thinking the perpetrator can or will change because of the codependent's love and sacrifice. In codependence recovery we talk about the "4 m's," characteristics of codependence: mothering, manipulation, management and martyrdom. In the vulnerability of moments of compassion, the boundaries are once again loosened, then tread upon, repeating the cycle of people-pleasing, anger at the failure of the people-pleasing to elicit change, and then guilt that there's so much anger instead of what our overwrought conscience insists should be compassion.

I could see the strong identification of Steve with the world of artists and musicians. This was his milieu and family, however dysfunctional. I had compassion for how his Jewish upbringing and minority otherness influenced the solitary person he became. I could see and admire his fellowship with outsiders, especially artists. At the inception of the Mudd Club, Steve was their custodian, even if he was also using them in his career as a spin doctor and wheeler-dealer.

But Steve and I have not managed to sustain a genuine, functional relationship. A natural, comfortable primary bond never developed. The work to nurture such a bond was not done. Because of that, I cannot let down my guard around boundaries. I can't let my appreciation for Steve's talents and achievements lead to codependently abandoning my own integrity and well-being. I can't let compassion for Steve as an *enfant terrible* and wandering Jew open the floodgates of enabling. It's one thing to understand and admire Jackson Pollock and his art. It was another to go joy riding with him. It's one thing to have an appreciation of Picasso. It was another to be in a relationship with him. It's one thing to have an appreciation of Wagner's music. It's another to sustain that appreciation in the face of a sober awareness that he was one of history's most consequential antisemites.

Figure 85 - Desecrated Gravesite of Hermann Levi, Partenkirchen, photograph by Ebab, 2018, Creative Commons

Following that call from Helen Mitsios for an ambulance for Steve, I did try to speak to him about recovery. Why not just try some meetings, I suggested during the first year of my own recovery. "Stephen Saban [a well-known chronicler and arbiter of New York night life] goes there," he said. In other words, he couldn't go to recovery meetings because gossips would find out truths they could and would then exploit. Sadly, I didn't have the presence to say to him what was said to me when I expressed similar concerns: "If Elizabeth Taylor can do recovery so can you."

Most recovery programs are based on the practice of 12 steps that begin with admission of unmanageability and powerlessness, move on to the work of self-inventory, making amends and being of service. Resentments are examined, realities are accepted, and one attempts to be accountable for one's own role in what has happened. We make our best efforts to forgive, live, let live and otherwise move forward with honesty, open-mindedness and willingness (the HOW of recovery).

This work inevitably involves family members and I have made efforts to speak to each member of my immediate family and make amends for regrettable past behaviors as best I could.

Figure 86 - Mass family gathering, Westerly, Rhode Island, 1999: from left, brother Steve Mass, stepdad Bill Thorpe, Larry Mass (me), mother Mignon Thorpe, partner Arnie Kantrowitz, nephew Max Lockwood and sister Ellen Mass, from the personal photographs of Lawrence D. Mass

With Steve, this attempted amends work took place at our last greater family gathering, in Westerly, Rhode Island, the year before my mother developed rapidly metastasizing and fatal cancer. Sadly, the R.I. event turned out to be a family dysfunctional disaster. My sister evinced a primitive sibling-rival jealousy of me and my partner Arnie which she never acknowledged and refused to talk about subsequently. What triggered the jealousy moment and subsequent cascade of reactivities was my mother's giving Arnie, who loves rocks, a rock she found for him on the beach. Ellen was acutely resentful that attention she felt should have been paid to her was being paid to another. It's a childlike behavior she evinced in myriad situations, always with the bottom line scenario of others relating well, which she narcissistically interpreted as unjustly excluding or relegating her.

Taking Steve aside at that gathering, I admitted that I had judged him for choices he'd made that seemed heedless of the concerns, feelings and needs of myself and others. I could admit that I hadn't always given him adequate credit for his own creative vision and work and for the hardships he faced in trying to survive financially and professionally.

Alas, I did something amends work should never do. I sought to explain (and thereby indirectly to "justify") some of the discomfort between us, in this case on the basis of childhood trauma. I mentioned that early childhood memory of his breaking my favorite toy, that plastic coin dispenser. I wasn't asking him to apologize, but I did feel the need to mention this imprinted memory of hurt. I was totally unprepared for his reaction. In fact, it was the angriest I'd seen Steve since his enraged German roommate Helmut at Northwestern tried to kick down the door to their shared dormitory room for reasons I was never privy to. Visibly enraged at my bringing up the coin-dispenser incident, which apparently he remembered, Steve remonstrated with startling vehemence: "And you know what? If I had it do over again today, I would!!!"

Steve's reaction of resentment and spite seemed deeply troubled, more like a child or an addict not in recovery. Yet the failure to make amends was also my fault for sullying accountability with a "justification." As we learn in recovery, "justified" anger and resentment are major pitfalls. In this age of Trump, reckoning with justified anger is something many of us must face continuously.

Even when amends work is done perfectly, without discussion of the other person's role, there is no guarantee that the recipient will respond well, be forgiving or change, especially if that person has never himself been in recovery. The principal beneficiary of the effort to make amends is the amends maker. Making a genuine, serious effort to come to terms with one's past is indeed liberating. However failed circumstantially, this effort with Steve has freed me of bitterness and resentment. It also facilitated limited future communications and well wishes between us. Enduringly, it has given me the serenity of acceptance of what I can't change.

∇

On the psych ward, when I came so close to getting shock treatment for my depression, I had to come to grips with the realities of my life. Lower your expectations, I was told. Either I could live for my all-important creativity, my writing, hand to mouth or face the difficult challenges of compromise.

This meant recovery and a greater commitment to my profession of medicine, relegating my writing to the back burner when necessary.

With the help of therapy and later recovery, I made the excruciatingly difficult choice of prioritizing earning a living rather than being dependent on others. Through my own experience as a writer I'd seen that such dependency often comes with contempt for "straight" living and a smug certainty that any resistance to alternative lifestyle choices comes from a place of envy. It's not a mindset I wanted for myself, or to be the object of.

This reaction formation of self-contempt, of thinking that anybody who would like and welcome you must be a sucker and loser, is what we see so floridly in Donald Trump. It's also what's so funny about Groucho Marx's legendary quip that he wouldn't want to be a member of any country club that would admit him. For clubbers like Steve Mass, the showman persona Steve Mass wouldn't want to be a member of a club that would welcome the real, flawed, insecure human being underneath the disguise. For someone emerging from depression and alcoholism and trying to seek the higher ground of recovery, I was going against stereotypes of the artist's way.

In view of this difficult choice I myself had to make, I experience ambivalence in my relationships with artists and writers, especially those who place creative freedom far above personal responsibility to the extent that they become unselfconsciously parasitical and insufferably self-important. I can still be generous with those writers and artists who are friends and my heart can still go out to them for their struggles. If I sense that place of entitlement, self-importance, exploitation and disrespect, however, I recoil.

Figure 87 - A scene from Meyerbeer's "*Les Hugenots*," an epochal depiction of one of the most notorious chapters in the exhaustive history of European religious intolerance and genocide; Act 5, scene 2, 1836, Charles Alexandre Debacq, public domain

This is my sense of who Wagner was, an egomaniacal and contemptuous exploiter with pathologically narcissistic levels of self-importance and entitlement. He viciously turned on his Jewish patron, Meyerbeer, who he maligned and bullied with all the bloat, might and gross prejudice of a Donald Trump. And he was famously exploitive of his most ardent admirer and benefactor, King Ludwig. Most would now agree that Ludwig's legendary sponsorship of Wagner was far from regrettable. Despite nearly bankrupting Bavaria, their progeny is a legacy of art widely regarded as incomparable. But what of Wagner's manipulations of Ludwig, whose philosemitism led to confrontations with Wagner over Ludwig's insistence that Hermann Levi conduct the premiere of *Parsifal*? And what of the many Jewish Wagnerites whose regard and devotion Wagner so ruthlessly exploited as he assassinated the aggregate character of the Jewish people and schemed our demise?

I can now see how profoundly I've experienced the alienation of my affection for Wagner—who I counted as my first great love but who was consumed with genocidal hatred of my people—not of *those* people but of *my* people. Rejection and alienation likewise played out in my codependent relationships with family members and other writers and artists, especially those *enfants terribles* who opted for lives of "freedom" from the strictures of society at the expense of the drudgery of personal accountability. In light of which I can no longer wait, unselfconsciously and devoutly, in the cues of those all too ready to relinquish dignity and integrity in homage to Wagner and other *monstres sacrés* of Art with a capital A.

Yes, I still appreciate art and artists, including Wagner, but that appreciation has become far more cautious, qualified and monitored than when I was so floridly codependent and addicted to alcohol, marijuana, cigarettes, opera, music and Art with a capital A. While *enfants terribles* and *monstres sacrés* may remain standard bearers of art, they can no longer count on more loyalty from me than I have been able to count on from them. Eye for an eye justice? Aversive conditioning? Perhaps, but what it feels like to me is sanity, sobriety and recovery.

Figure 88 - Eduard Hanslick and Richard Wagner, silhouette by Otto Böhler (1847-1913), public domain

Though I never want to feel so self-righteous in "Art recovery" (Art worshipers Anonymous?) that I find myself a censor, I can no longer genuflect before even the most sacrosanct of art, and certainly one poisoned for me at its core and casting itself the "the artwork of the future." If that makes me more like Eduard Hanslick, the legendarily pedantic Viennese music critic who as a leading critic of Wagner became the inspiration for Wagner's vicious, antisemitic caricature Beckmesser in *Die Meistersinger*, and less like Richard and

Cosima Wagner's *Haus* Jew Hermann Levi, a devout Wagnerite who was a pallbearer at Wagner's funeral, so be it.

I resist the pressure to join in the obligatory, universal affirmation of the sanctity and transcendent importance of Art. I refuse to acquiesce to "A*rt Über Alles.*" I know full well that this puts me outside the mainstreams of Art appreciation and renders me more like the parents of the girl killed by Jackson Pollock than appreciative of the talent of the artist himself and his paintings; more like the slaves who built the monuments and plantations than afficionados of the architectural achievements themselves; more like those martyred in amphitheaters than those who surpassingly appreciate the ingenuity and power of Roman antiquities; and more like those rare few who still decline to hear Wagner in Israel than Wagnerites everywhere. So be it.

# Wagnerism and the Future

Figure 89 - An anti-Semitic caricature in Barrie Kosky's production of *Die Meistersinger* at Bayreuth, orig 2017, foto dpa, Jüische Allegmeine

In 2017 Barrie Kosky, the acclaimed theater and opera director who has described himself as a "gay Jewish kangaroo," became the first Jewish director in the history of the Bayreuth Festival. His production of *Die Meistersinger* seemed to reflect a new level of consciousness of co-directors Katharina Wagner and Eva Pasquier Wagner of Bayreuth as having been the premiere shrine of Nazism. As for his complex relationship to Wagner, Kosky's grandmother, most of whose family was murdered by the Nazis, told Kosky that in order to understand Germany and its culture, he needed to speak German and know Wagner. Overflowing with deconstructions, numerous allusions to Wagner himself, to antisemitism and Nazism, Kosky's production is set in the war-crimes trial courtroom at Nuremberg. The "unofficial capital" of the Holy Roman Empire, Nuremberg was the backdrop of this, Hitler's favorite opera, and the home of Nazism's biggest and most iconic rallies, as captured in the films of Leni Riefenstahl.

In 1298 thousands of Jews were slaughtered in the *Rindfleisch* massacres throughout Germany after accusations of desecration of the host (a slander in the vein of Kundry's sin of laughing at Christ's Crucifixion agony in *Parsifal*). Behind this largest pogrom since the First Crusade was the desire to combine the northern and southern parts of the city. A market was built on the site of the old Jewish quarter. Nuremberg was later the seat of the 1935 Nuremberg Laws, which denied citizenship to those not of "German or kindred blood." With nearby Bayreuth as principal shrine, no locale is more central to the symbolism of Nazism than Nuremberg.

Figure 90 - Alex Ross, Amazon.com

No comment on the Kosky production was initially forthcoming from Alex Ross in his *New Yorker* column. At the time of the production's premiere and notwithstanding reviews and commentary from other critics, including those of the *New York Times*, he did issue a piece on Wagner, and on a subject related to race and antisemitism in Wagner—that of themes of incest in the composer's works.

Instead of highlighting the obsession with "the purification of the German race" in Wagner, however, Ross wanted to show this issue in a different light—that of the ubiquitousness of incest as a subject of art and literature. In other words, placed in broader context, Wagner's preoccupation can be appreciated as less atypical and less revelatory of an obsession with racist and antisemitic themes. In this survey, "Wagner, Incest and *Game of Thrones,*" he compares the *Ring* cycle with artworks since *Oedipus* in which incest has been thematic and has continuously fascinated audiences. Though eye-opening, Ross's comparison of the *Ring* with *Game of Thrones* unwittingly echoes questions about the quality of Wagner's art. Does it stand as firmly alongside Sophocles, Bach, Beethoven, Mozart and Shakespeare as we've always believed it to? Or is it more in league with works like Tolkien's *Lord of the Rings* and *Game of Thrones*?

Ross had already made clear his distaste for more overt discussion of Wagner and Nazism. At the same time, however, he could seem comfortable with the innuendo of productions that do what Wagner did —comment indirectly on Jewish character and history, such as the new production of *La Clemenza di Tito* that opened the 2017 Salzburg Festival. As directed by Peter Sellars, Roman Emperor Titus, who as Ross points out is known for having led the brutal Roman wars against the Jews, is played by African-American tenor Russell Thomas. Sellars is not one to overlook such tensions, Ross observed in "Panoply of Power," his *New Yorker* commentary on this production. In a program note, Sellars had compared Tito to Nelson Mandela which, as Ross puts it, "makes his moral vision even stronger through his casting." So we're not to read Jewishness into Wagner's characters when Wagner hasn't made their Jewishness explicit, but we should be attuned to such associations in the work of others?

In the *NYT* Zachary Woolfe delivered detailed and thoughtful coverage of the premiere of the Kosky *Meistersinger* but barely mentioned the Sellars *Tito*. Ross's affirming reportage on a revival of the Kosky *Meistersinger* in a subsequent season sat uncomfortably alongside Ross's otherwise thematic "Nazi rut" argument.

Ross, meanwhile, is not the only critic to be fitfully perturbed about the ongoing focus on Wagner's antisemitism. Former *New York Times* music critic John Rockwell is another. He appears to have admired the Kosky *Meistersinger* as thoughtful and well done, in contrast to what he described as Katherina Wagner's "grotesquely anti-anti-Semitic *Meistersinger*" in 2007-8. He recently prefaced his remarks in *Journal of the Music Critics Association of North America* with echoes of Ross: "Yes, Wagner railed against the Jews...and Hitler loved Wagner...but enough is enough." Like virtually all the music critics of the former era, Rockwell, who prides himself on being a critic of protean sensibilities and tastes, was never one to storm the barricades of silence surrounding Wagner's antisemitism. In this he was one of the tone setters of the decorum of taciturnity around Wagner that is now showing its unairbrushed face.

Figure 91 - John Rockwell on the panel "Voicing Transgression," Pop Conference 2015, photograph by Joe Mabel, Creative Commons

In my days at UC Berkeley in the late 1960's, after the free speech movement, when Wieland Wagner brought *Salome* starring his mistress Anja Silja to the San Francisco Opera in their American debuts, I became acquainted with Rockwell. Like me, he was a devout Wagnerite. I recall our shared admiration for the leading Wagner tenor of the day, Wolfgang Windgassen. We marveled at his theatrical *Otello* in German that was more declaimed and shouted than sung. It was the "Bayreuth bark," a manner of singing encouraged by Cosima Wagner and exemplified by Max Lorenz,"Hitler's Siegfried," (who, unbeknownst to us in those years, was homosexual and whose wife was Jewish). In those days of the late 1960's, tapes of performances like a Windgassen *Otello*, unlikely ever to be recorded, were prizes that made select rounds.

I remember my first *Meistersinger* recording, its first studio recording, on Decca-London, with Paul Schöffler, Hilde Güden, Gunther Treptow, conducted by Bayreuth stalwart Hans Knappertsbusch. I recall showing the album, with its old-fashioned cover, to brother Steve, but don't recall any reaction or comment. That was more than 60 years ago. Today, I no longer take special pleasure in Wagner and no longer go to revivals or new productions with any regularity. But I have made it a point to re-experience each of Wagner's operas via supertitles (despite their generally flat translations) and HD cinema close-ups and commentary. *Meistersinger* in the Met's 2014 revival was the most recent of these.

Never say never, but now in my 70's, I doubt I will ever see *Die Meistersinger* again, not even the Kosky production which sounds so illuminating, like the Chéreau *Ring.* As I recently put it to an acquaintance, a Jewish Wagnerite whose love for Wagner can be winning, the opera is one of the longest ever written and is a comedy by a composer not known—nor his people—for their humor. (Wagner's second opera, *Das Liebesverbot,* based on Shakespeare's *Measure for Measure*, was an early attempt at comedy. It was not successful and never entered the repertory.)

The premiere of *Meistersinger* took place 50 years prior to the metastasization of Nazism. Wagner nemesis Eduard Hanslick, whose pedagogy inspired Wagner's satire but whose misgivings could seem more global than punctilious, had no way of describing the opera's finale as the closest thing to a Nazi rally anyone would ever see on the stages of high culture. But in the spirit of Hanslick, it's hard not to look at *Meistersinger* critically. I honestly can't help feeling that the greater truth about *Meistersinger* is that for all its glorious music, it is truly overblown—a six hour evening of alleged romantic comedy that isn't in the least measure or moment genuinely funny. Though it does have light-heartedness, romance and jubilation, is there a truly funny moment in the entire work? Is laughter common in *Meistersinger,* or for that matter, and even if it's grossly pejorative to ask, in Germany at all, even the sadistic antisemitic laughter so importuned by the composer at many turns? The work feels so bloated and, well, pedantic that it becomes reflective of the very pedagogy it is otherwise so long-windedly at pains to ridicule. I know it would constitute the most extreme heresy, but has anyone ever tried editing the work down, say, by a third or even by half, however challenging such an effort to "de-fat" a great Wagner *Gesamtkunstwerk* might seem at the outset? Short versions of Wagner's works for children have been presented at Bayreuth. Should such adaptations be considered for wider distribution?

When I was a young man and my opera snobbism was at its peak, I did shun a lot of what I regarded as common popular entertainment, priding myself on being a lot more discriminating. *Hello Dolly* was one such boundary for me. Home for me was not raucous Jewish humor and *hazarai,* but the enchanted realms of Richard Wagner. Two years after the world premiere of *Hello Dolly* in 1964, I would make my "pilgrimage," as I referred to it, to Bayreuth.

Figure 92 - *Hello Dolly* revivial starring Bette Midler, Schubert Theater, Broadway, 2017, photo Raph_PH, Creative Commons

*Hello Dolly* was *way* too *declassé,* too "coarse" (code for too Jewish), and for that matter also too "queeny," for my refined Wagnerite sensibilities. Which is not to say that my internalization of antisemitism was always so marked. Though more analytical than spontaneous and never an afficionado of comedy, I loved Woody Allen and many of the great Jewish comedians and artists I would see on television over the decades. I would allow for talent outside of the mainstream—whether it be operetta (which Hitler also loved), musical comedy, off-off Broadway or at the Mudd Club, but I drew the line with schmaltz like *Hello Dolly* and the *schtick* of more annoying stereotypes, like Jerry Lewis. Now I'm haunted by all those legendary *Dollys* my snobbery kept me from seeing—Carol Channing, Mary Martin, Ethyl Merman, Pearl Bailey, many of them cherishable gay icons, to say nothing of Dolly's creator, Jerry Herman. And now, at the time of Jerry Lewis's death at 92, I want to see *The Nutty Professor* and the *The Day The Clown Cried*, a Holocaust film that was mired, like the last film of Orson Welles, in legal purgatory.

Figure 93 - Jerry Lewis, 1926-2017. Lewis co-wrote, directed and starred in the 1972 unreleased American film, *The Day the Clown Cried*, about a circus clown imprisoned in a Nazi concentration camp. Still from BBC News, 2016.

In 1960 we took our first field trip from junior high school in Chicago to New York City, and were given the choice to see one Broadway show. I remember choosing Richard Burton as Hamlet over Barbra Streisand in *Funny Girl.* My incipient Jewish Wagnerite self was choosing serious theater over coarse *schtick.* It's not that I couldn't appreciate popular entertainment; rather, I relegated it. My first musicals were Rogers and Hammerstein films, which I did love, and my first live viewing of a musical was *West Side Story,* the thrill of which is still with me. Sure, I loved the best of Jewish culture, like Mahler and Leonard Bernstein, even as I shared veiled misgivings about a level of "vulgarity" (another code word for Jewish) in Lenny's splashy public persona, and even in Mahler, where the Eighth Symphony's chorus of a thousand and the cowbells of the Sixth Symphony could seem...extravagant.

As it turns out, it was Lenny, and not the music critics whose coded misgivings I absorbed and which abetted my internalized antisemitism, who was immediately interested in the new epidemic that hadn't yet been identified or named as AIDS in 1981. Lenny was deeply concerned, less about any risk to himself, which he scarcely asked me about when we met one-on-one in 1981, than about the greater impact of the epidemic. His humanity and humanitarianism were genuine.

My growing love for Mahler was a later development that tacitly accompanied the growth of my Jewish consciousness, even though

Mahler himself was a classic Jewish Wagnerite in evincing notable internalized antisemitism. Unlike Meyerbeer and Lenny, and though comparably successful, he was a convert to Christianity and self-abnegating as Jewish. Notwithstanding our efforts to assimilate, whether converted or not, or Wagnerites or not, all Jews—Wagner's Jews as well as his Jewish or half-Jewish colleagues and critics—ended up summarily reviled by Wagner for being Jewish.

Mahler may have been ambitious and successful and may have had his own Jewish consciousness under the circumstances of antisemitic Germany and Europe, but his conversion to Christianity, while not uncommon among Jews for career and social advancement, stands in contrast to Meyerbeer and of course Lenny. Because of his Jewishness and notwithstanding the ongoing presence at Bayreuth of Hermann Levi, Mahler, even though he had become a Christian convert, was not invited to appear at Bayreuth by viciously antisemitic Cosima. Cosima nonetheless continued to seek his counsel, which he gave. If she was sadistically antisemitic, he was masochistically self-effacing as a Jew. Their circumstance is well-captured, however grossly satirized, in Ken Russell's film *Mahler*.

But *Hello Dolly*?! Never. Never, that is, until Arnie and I celebrated our 35th anniversary by seeing the 2017 revival with Bette Midler. Jerry Herman is no artistic equivalent of Wagner. But, hey, he's not just chopped liver either (such "yinglish" feels as foreign and awkward to me as it must read in context here). But do believe me when I say that I had a much better time at *Hello Dolly* and laughed and cheered a lot more than at the Met's last *Meistersinger.* Despite the splendid singing of Michael Volle and the fine conducting of James Levine, it felt like nothing so much as an endurance test. So stressed out was I by the opera's length and ponderousness— being already inured to the xenophobia and antisemitism—that I considered walking out before the big finale. I staggered out of the theater at 12:45 am, exhausted and half-asleep.

Walking out on a performance is something I rarely did. The only other time I can recall doing so was at a concert version of Wagner's early opera *Rienzi*, likewise considered a failure and only very rarely performed. There were rumors that it might come to the Met, directed by Katherina Wagner and conducted by Daniel Barenboim and Christian Thielemann. *Rienzi* is the most bombastic opera I have ever experienced; it's as if it were composed by Donald Trump. When I shared this impression and the vignette of walking out on *Rienzi* to Gottfried Wagner, he noted that in *Rienzi* Wagner was trying to imitate Meyerbeer.

Figure 94 - Giacomo Meyerbeer (1791-1864), photo by Gaspard-Félix Tournachon, 1860, Wikimedia Commons, public domain

It's easy to appreciate the influence of Meyerbeer on Wagner. It's everywhere in his work: the great sprawl and length, the grandeur, the marshaling of unprecedented resources of staging, and the musical themes that became Wagner's signature system of *leitmotifs*. But the bombast is uniquely Wagner's. So is the racism, bile and spleen, and the bullying. The theft and disparagement of Meyerbeer, whose only offense was to be Jewish, successful and to have served nobly as a patron and inspiration to Wagner, were truly monstrous. It may well be that Wagner was trying to imitate Meyerbeer in the creation of *Rienzi,* but what resulted was more in the vein of Wagner's disciple, Adolf Hitler, who was inspired by the opera. For our own time, a postmodern staging of *Rienzi* could showcase the ascendancy of Donald Trump.

Meyerbeer's concern about bombast and the vulnerability of religious minorities resonates throughout *Les Hugenots*. This masterpiece is rarely performed, not because of the usual excuses given—that it's too expensive to mount and too difficult to cast—but because of the ongoing poisonousness of Wagner's antisemitism in the world of opera. Its last performance at the Metropolitan Opera, where one might otherwise reasonably expect to see periodic revivals of so great a work, was in 1915. Meanwhile, with a university workshop budget, New York's Bard College under the direction of Leon Botstein mounted an impressive full-scale production of the politically ferocious opera in 2009. In today's overflowing caldron of religious and ethnic hatreds, Meyerbeer, shouted and shoved down by the bully pulpit of Richard Wagner, still exhorts us with a voice that is prophetic, plaintive, terrifying and unceasingly engaging.

Even Alex Ross is perplexed that a work of such power and import is such a rarity, though he stops short of exploring the absence of *Les Hugenots* from the Met and elsewhere. He also doesn't ponder the work's relationship to Wagner—an impressionable 23 at the time of the opera's premiere in 1836. But in his review of Botstein's audacious, astonishing achievement ("Intolerance," *The New Yorker,* 8/24/'09), Ross is right there in awareness and appreciation.

> "The irony is that while Wagner inspires endless political debate, this opera—a dramatization of the massacre of French Protestants by Catholic forces in 1572—carries more of a message than anything Wagner wrote. It is a passionate denunciation of religious extremism, and the bloody final scenes raise the rafters while shaking the soul. Meyerbeer deserves to hold the stage again."

Figure 95 - Bronze Equestrian Statue of Confederate Leader Robert E. Lee, Lee Park, downtown Charlottesville, Virginia, commissioned in 1917 and dedicated in 1924; the statue was the site of Unite The Right rally and riots, 8/2017; the statue was removed 7/10/21;

Georgia, the road leads back to you. As I write this now, in August of 2017, we remain deeply embroiled in the nightmare of Charlottesville. There, white supremacists, neo-Nazis and the Klan gathered to carry symbols of hatred and the venom of racism, antisemitism and homophobia to an extent without precedent in recent times. Ostensibly, these extremists were protesting the planned removal of a statue of Robert E. Lee, who led the Confederacy. The movement to relocate such symbols of racism and hatred—mostly statues and confederate flags—from the public sphere keeps gathering momentum.

Such efforts also invite legitimate debate. In his predictably noxious defense of white nationalists Trump could seem to be trying to articulate that not everyone with questions and concerns is an extremist. There is in fact truth in that. My close friend Joel from Elberton, Georgia, wonders how this will play out in his hometown, where there are a number of such statues and symbols. Joel, whose family does include those who served in the Confederacy, is a committed liberal who has fought for civil rights. Like many Southerners who deplore racism but feel connected to their heritage, and others concerned about censorship, he feels he can't help but ask, at what point have we crossed the line into obfuscating, even censoring history. Donald Trump's equating of the alt-right with the "alt-left" is obviously deeply troubled. Even so, *are* statues of Washington and Jefferson, both of whom had slaves, likewise tainted? Will they eventually be targeted? Where are the boundaries? (Tangentially, am I the only one who notes the striking resemblance between the Washington monument and a hooded Klansman?)

Figure 96 - 1911 Statue of Richard Wagner in Cleveland's Edgewater Park, a location some have begun to protest; Cleveland Statue Guide, cleveland.com

Will busts and statues of Wagner become controversial? Will people start removing them? Part of me might be pleased by that, just as part of me might be pleased if the allies had bombed the *Festspielhaus* in Bayreuth. But the more sane and sober part knows that it is not a credible or sober path. Uneasily, Joel and I agreed that neither history nor works of art should be destroyed, erased, rewritten or censored and that the most offensive of these—symbols of the confederacy, of Nazism—should be relocated to museums or places where they can be more suitably viewed with context. This solution is notable in eastern Europe capitals such as Sofia, Bulgaria and Budapest, Hungary, where art parks warehouse but do little to maintain ageing, decrepit statues of Stalin, Lenin, Marx and other communist leaders, who now preach and declaim only to each other and to all of whom these countries thereby seem to be saying a mockingly respectful Good Riddance.

And what then of the Breker bust of Wagner that still dominates the environs of Bayreuth? Where controversial works can't be relocated or aren't, demarcaters of historical context should be prominent and plentiful, especially for the more offensive symbols.

Ahead of any art park solutions such as those of eastern Europe, what Bayreuth and Wahnfried need, like southern plantations and confederate statues, is not obfuscation but qualification. As for Wagner and his music dramas, the answer is along the same trajectory, a process already underway. Hopefully, it will progress with respect for differing viewpoints. But just as it is troubled to call for the banning or censorship of Wagner and his operas, it is likewise troubled to call for a moratorium on discussion of Wagner's antisemitism and its influence on Hitler and Nazism.

Erasure, obfuscation and muting are not the answers. A friend, taking his lead from an article by *New York Times* music critic Anthony Tommasini, wondered what he should do now with his James Levine recordings. We still listen to and attend Wagner, I told him, so why shouldn't one continue to listen to Jimmy's recordings? Wagner is now seen by a growing number of observers as a virtual perpetrator of the Holocaust, but no one is suggesting that Wagner be excised from history, banned or censored. Though I no longer display them, I still possess several of the 5 pictures of Wagner that once dominated my living room wall. I have many books and recordings of Wagner still on my shelves, albeit long overdue for reorganization.

Of note among these artifacts is a pair of porcelain medallions, scenes from *Lohengrin*, that are of high quality. Still safeguarding that special place of awe they initially inspired, I could never just discard them. Though I no longer want to display them, I am seeking to place them in a more suitable home.

Figure 97 - Lohengrin's *Ankunft* and Lohengrin's *Abschied*, glazed terra-cotta medallions from a flea market, origins unknown, photographs by Lawrence D. Mass

Down the street from where we lived in Macon was the neglected property of the German-American family with that sign in their driveway: "No Dogs or Jews Allowed." Though I'd heard about the family's gun collection from my brother, I don't recall ever crossing paths with any of them. Steve's classmates included their son. So far as I ever knew, he and Steve got along well.

Meanwhile, I played on the property with the other boys. There was no discussion about it with Steve or our parents, and none of the other boys ever said anything. Or if they did, I've forgotten.

What was most notable about my decision to ignore the sign at such a tender age was not its bravery but its instinct for survival. We were children. These boys were my friends, we were all playing together and they weren't saying anything about the sign or my being Jewish. The antisemitism they learned from their parents would emerge later.

Since no one was saying anything, I figured I was one of them rather than being a dog or a Jew, or that anything was wrong. From such circumstances—prior to my later encounters with overt antisemitism—it seemed resolving to think of myself more as just one of the boys, and from there as Southern, as American, as cosmopolitan, as a citizen of the world, as whatever other categories of identity might seem surpassingly inclusive. Assimilation. That such prejudice might be targeting me rather some generic, even abstract designation of others for danger, oppression and persecution, and because it wasn't being directly experienced when playing with the other boys, it was easier to be in denial about it.

It's with just such denial that I became a Wagnerite. Just as I was an American, a cosmopolite and citizen of the world, never just a "Jew" or even "Jewish Wagnerite," I was an opera lover and

Wagnerite. Just as I played with those boys in the abandoned pool of the "No-Dogs-or-Jews" house, so I experienced *Die Meistersinger*, the *Ring* cycle and *Parsifal,* in the security of all those Wagner qualifiers (some of Wagner's close associates were Jews, etc.) and the inclusiveness of fellow opera lovers and Wagnerites. Yes, there was Hitler, Nazism and Wagner's antisemitism, but I was American and in good company with those Germans who outspokenly resisted Nazism—Lotte Lehman, Fridelind Wagner, Frida Leider and history's greatest Hans Sachs, Friedrich Schorr (who was Jewish), and even if, as it would turn out, none of these heroes ever really expressed concerns about antisemitism in Wagner's life and works. Perhaps they shared my denialism about it. If they were aware of and troubled by it, it's apparently not something they or anyone else of their generation sought to discuss.

As a Wagnerite I felt secure, the way Joseph Horowitz does, that I wasn't one of *those* Jews, the kind Wagner hated, the dirty, envious, money-grubbing kind he ranted about. Today, I understand that explaining to antisemities that "I'm not one of *those* people" isn't likely to save me. As I've finally come to understand, the "No Dogs or Jews Allowed" of Wagner's operas meant and means me as well. While I could get away with trespassing and playing there, my assimilationist denialism wouldn't prove to be as protective as I'd imagined.

Today, existentially, I'm less in denial and more consciously inclined to make less dystonic, less cognitively dissonant choices. It's simple, really. Whether it be Wagner, my own siblings or others, when I sense that I'm not genuinely valued or that I'm resented or rejected, I no longer choose to keep trying to force myself to be valued or accepted. Affection and regard that are not forthcoming cannot be willed. With greater attenuation to reality and more realistic choices, today I seek the serenity to accept the people I cannot change as they are, to change those I can, and I pray for wisdom to know the difference. With the help of forgiveness and detachment, who and what *can* change mostly turns out to be me. Wagner's not going to change. Nor is Steve Mass. But I can change where I go to look for oranges from the hardware store to the greengrocer.

Figure 98 - Katz's Delicatessen, Lower East Side, New York City, Wikimedia Commons

*Dinner with Arnie's brother Barry Kantrowitz at Katz's Deli on the Lower East Side.*

Arnie was back in the hospital with pneumonia and cellulitis. He is prone to both as complications of diabetes and from immune suppressant medications for the kidney transplant he underwent for diabetic ESKD (end-stage kidney disease) in 2012. This was Arnie's 48th hospitalization in our 35 years together. Arnie's father died from complications of diabetes and his brother Barry has it too. Amazingly, considering my girth, Jewish genes, age and the presence of diabetes in at least one close relative, I don't. In Katz's I looked around at all the overweight Jews like Arnie, Barry and me. One might almost call it a Jewish disease except that it's widely prevalent in the general population, especially as obesity, the major risk factor for type 2 diabetes (the more common, "adult onset" type), becomes evermore quotidian.

## Wagner's Brothers, Envy and Greed

When Barry, who voted for Trump, suggested we go to Katz's, I reflexively cringed, the way I used to cringe at the thought of *Hello Dolly*. Even in the worst days of my internalized antisemitism I liked pastrami on rye, but making that something to celebrate always felt dystonic to my acculturated self. Our waiter turned out to be stereotypically pushy to the extent that even Barry, a Jewish extrovert himself, was incensed. "Get me out of here," my inner Wagnerite kept nudging, like our black cat Tallulah when she wants food or petting.

I recall a greeting card I purchased at a news and convenience store in the nearby NYU area run by Arabs. It played on *Cats*, the musical, showing a black cat with big yellow eyes, the slits of which were dollar signs. At first it seemed cute and even amusing, even though it was conveying the boilerplate global and transhistorical stereotype of Jews as rich and "money-grubbing." My purchasing it must have been a psychological effort to defuse it by embracing it; not so unlike the way I kept embracing Wagner with evermore outsized passion and rationalizations in the face of what I already knew of the seriousness and depth of his antisemitism.

Parked next to the deli was Barry's Maserati. He also has a Mercedes. Extricating Barry, whose materialism trumps many humane concerns but whose humanity is discernible in many aspects of his family life, from this trope of prejudice—of Jews as stereotypically materialist—was a never-ending challenge for me, as it has been as well for Arnie.

Notwithstanding the considerable differences of opinion on matters social and political that have challenged them over time, it's difficult not to ponder and compare the brotherly love Arnie and Barry have sustained with that which failed to develop between Steve and me. Wagner explores family relationships and their dynamics at length and dramatically so in the case of the sibling rivalry of two sets of brothers—the chief Nibelung villains Alberich and Mime and the giants Fasolt and Fafner, all of whom we are introduced to in *Das Rheingold*, the opening work of Wagner's tetralogy.

The scheming, devaluing, exploitive and malevolent relationship between Alberich and Mime stands alongside that of the covetous and murderous Fasolt and Fafner, the first to fall prey to Alberich's curse of renouncing love for power. Arrogance and corruption are not limited to the Nibelungs in the *Ring* cycle, where "arrogance of power" is a principal *Leitmotif,* but the Nibelungs do carry the onus of culpability for all the ills that subsequently befall heaven and earth. In Wagner's *Weltanshauung*, virtually all the trouble that ensues emerges from their constitutional inferiority and their consequent envy and hatred of others.

This lust for power, with its supreme symbol of the *Rheingold*, is the affliction and devil's bargain with which the Nibelungs proceed to infect everyone and everything else. On the surface, there can appear to be an equilibrium, an equipoise of corruption among all the players in Wagner's music dramas. But that complexity inevitably if paradoxically serves to validate rather than undermine the images of Jewish envy, vindictiveness and villainy that later served Nazi psychology.

However opposing their political viewpoints, the mutually loving and caring relationship Arnie and Barry have nurtured seems a rebuke to Wagner. At the same time, the failure of Steve and me to establish such a bond can seem to reify Wagner's antisemitic stereotypes of the Nibelungs—the Jews—as loveless. In the mind of Wagner and in the bigger picture he has rendered, the pursuit of power of the Nibelungs—the Jews—inflicts on the greater worlds of the gods and humanity the curse of their own soullessness.

Envy in the eye of the beholder. Though I count Wagner as my first great love, my first real love affair was with an older, wealthy priest, John-Claude Cavendish ("Andy Bullen" in my *Confessions of a Jewish Wagnerite*). Though I fell deeply in love with John and always thought of him as the first of the great loves of my life, after Wagner, the inequalities between us resulted in considerable friction and unhappiness. I was 20 and he was 40. He was an upper-class WASP and I was a professional-class Jew with *shtetl* origins. He was wealthy and I was a student. Though he owned property in California and elsewhere and traveled widely, he was a country priest based in Kentucky and I was an undergrad at UC Berkeley. He was Republican and I was a 60's liberal. In those days there were no civil liberties for gay people and most of us were not out to our families, at work or even to ourselves. This was true for both of us. The "marriage"—the monogamous bond for life—with Andy I at age 20 initially and so deeply wished for in a world where civil liberties for gay people were still nonexistent, was far from any realistic possibility of fulfillment.

In response to my recurrent, often inchoate complaining about these realities that kept intruding on our globetrotting idyll of romantic love, John, a mentor and sage, suggested that some of my unhappiness and resentment that our affair could not be more equitable or committed was more a manifestation of my own immaturity than society's prejudices and proscriptions. Specifically, what he sensed in my complaining and wanted to warn me about was the problem of envy and greed. Though we were both drinkers who popped Miltowns (meprobamate, the then popular tranquilizer later replaced by benzodiazepines like Xanax), which he introduced me to, Andy's accusation wasn't retaliatory, intoxicated or mean-spirited so much as part of the often heavy-duty dialogue between us about matters psychological, philosophical, spiritual, social and political, as well as about the realities of our lives, individually and together.

Andy, a pastoral psychologist as well as an Episcopalian priest, was attempting to give me paternal, spiritual and therapeutic as well as professional guidance. He felt that with my empathic nature, gift for analytic thinking and great interest in psychiatry, I should aim for a career in psychiatry. In the course of these exchanges, he introduced me to his own gurus, Carl Jung and William James, both of whom would prove important to me vis a vis their roles in spearheading the recovery movement. Andy gave me a copy of James's still widely read and admired *The Varieties of Religious Experience.*

In sync with our discourse and knowledgeable about Freud and the Freudians that were still in vogue in the psychiatry of those years of the late 1960's, Andy also gave me a book by psychoanalyst Melanie Klein, *Envy and Greed*, which sees these character traits arising in early maternal deprivations, especially the withholding of breast-feeding.

Eventually, John conceded that a major barrier between us was class. Though born of wedlock, he was of noble lineage, a scion of the Earl of Cavendish. To a remarkable degree for someone of his station, he had included me, a Jew, in his social and professional life. I never sensed overt or even the casual antisemitism of his social milieu, though in those years of my own internalization of antisemitism I was more likely to collude with than recognize and recoil from its more subtle manifestations.

It wasn't until many years later that I would more deeply contemplate the taint of envy within constructs of antisemitism. Once you appreciate at a visceral level Wagner's *Leitmotiv*ic framework ("Nibelung's hate") for envy as the chief instigator of Alberich's curse and all that befalls, you can never go back to the Wagner apologist rationalizations of Wagner as an equal-opportunity diagnostician and indicter of corruption. Envy may be in the eye of the beholder, but nowhere so conspicuously and malignantly as among the Jews as they are conceptualized and portrayed in the music dramas of Richard Wagner, especially in the *Ring* cycle, *Die Meistersinger* and *Parsifal.*

This issue of envy in the eye of Wagner and others would reverberate many years later in my friendship with the Colombian writer Jaime Manrique. The plot of *Calle Cervantes*, Jaime's biographical novel of Miguel de Cervantes, the great Spanish writer and author of *Don Quixote*, is driven by a fictional character also named Miguel, a Salieri-like figure conceived as deeply envious of Cervantes. The novel is rich in history and drama. Because of my own life experience, however, especially with Wagner and as well with John Cavendish and others, I had developed my own experiential sense of envy as too easily explanatory, derogatory and defamatory, and as a facile and inevitably over-used artistic and literary trope.

This reading of envy into the motivations of others, especially critics or competitors, infuses Wagner's antisemitism, Nazi psychology and the ravings of Donald Trump, who castigates all critics and rivals, even deceased war heroes, as envious and therefore as "losers and suckers." Indeed, as Alex Ross recaps in an erudite and engaging summary in *The New Yorker* of how far we've advanced in our understanding of who Salieri really was in artistic circles and in his relationships, including with Mozart, we can no longer exploit one of our culture's premiere mythologies of art and envy as others have—e.g., Pushkin's *Mozart and Salieri* and *Amadeus,* the film of Peter Shaffer and Milos Forman. Salieri was not the stereotype of envy artists and writers have made of him and that we've all been led to believe he was.

In *Calle Cervantes*, Miguel has ambitions for writing but not much talent. The story line is that his personal wealth and station are pitted against Cervantes's superiority of spirit and artistic talent. As the novel plays out, Cervantes overcomes many hardships, including imprisonment and enslavement, to succeed as a writer and lover where Miguel fails. By the time of the novel's conclusion the street on which aristocratic Miguel had lived and which was named after him is changed to *Calle Cervantes.*

Throughout my reading of *Cervantes Street* Jaime's portrait plucked this chord of envy in terms of my relationship not only with others but also with Jaime himself. While I was more stable financially and professionally and seemed to fare better with love and romance, especially in the earlier years of our friendship, Jaime seemed further along in having a more traditionally successful career as a writer. In addition to bridging Anglo and Hispanic languages, cultures and literatures, Jaime primarily writes historical fiction. As readers of this narrative will have little trouble appreciating, my trajectory as a writer has gone in the opposite direction of a growing consciousness of and greater regard for truths that art and fiction can ramify but also blur. Virtually all of my writing has been nonfiction.

Reading *Calle Cervantes* while working on my Wagner pieces, I could not help but wonder whether Jaime saw me as Miguel-like, ill-at-ease with and envious of his friend's success. I doubt that I was a prototype for Miguel. In fact, it would not surprise me to learn that such a thought never entered Jaime's consciousness. But was it there implicitly? Even if it were entirely my own projection, did my self-reflection in this portrait carry deeper truth I needed to contemplate?

The most important and enduring relationship of Jaime's life was with an artist and publisher, Bill Sullivan, who was also a friend of mine. Bill was a gifted painter, mostly of tropical landscapes of brilliant luminosity, reflecting his adventures with Jaime in South America. Eventually, Bill found a distinguished place for himself among the latter day ranks of the Hudson Valley painters whose legacy he has festooned with his boldly colored visions.

Bill's artistic calling was conjoined with a pioneering but financially disastrous stint as a publisher of emerging gay literature, motivated in real measure to promote Jaime's early writing. In the process Bill lost all his money, his home and just about everything else, including his health, his sanity, and finally his life. As Bill's fortunes deteriorated, everyone had moments of losing patience with his endless problems, too many of which could seem of his own making, such as when he resumed smoking after a major heart attack, and when he wrecked the new car Jaime had so generously and lovingly bought for him.

Both Bill and Jaime were often financially challenged and without health insurance. Their circumstances were to some degree societal, political and unfair, and I was happy to help them on the many occasions they called on me as a physician and friend to do so. Bill had a series of heart attacks, which resulted years later in his death. And Jaime, with whom I was a lot closer, had problems with his knee, back and recurrent depression. Though they periodically expressed their thanks for my acting as their on-call physician, including house calls and writing and calling in prescriptions, and even though they weren't my patients and I was therefore putting myself at some risk legally, the thanks I got often seemed perfunctory and sometimes left me feeling exploited.

As we all know proverbially, giving should be unconditional. And in any case, what did I want or expect? Jamie and I grew closer as friends and shared supportive and productive dialogue about writing, culture, politics, love, romance, addiction, codependence and recovery. That was more than enough. And I had many occasions to tell Bill as well as Jaime how much I admired their work. I never wavered in my fondness for both of them, and my friendship with Jaime has deepened with time.

One day many years later when times were much better for Jaime, he took me to lunch, which made a bigger impression on me than he would have noticed or imagined. I had often paid for our lunches and dinners together, but this was the first time (and not the last) that he had ever treated me to a meal. I did not mention this perception, of course, but I remembered often thinking how good it would have made me feel if, during that period when they leaned on me so heavily, they had made me a dinner, even if they couldn't afford to take me out. Alternatively, in Bill's case, I hoped he might give me a drawing or painting, as he'd done with others. I think I was disappointed when I realized that, instead, he hoped I'd purchase something from him. With all my avowed admiration of his work and my being a doctor, perhaps I'd become a patron. In any case, no such moment of satisfaction seemed to happen, and I remember wondering, with my codependence sensitivity about such things, if Jaime and Bill harbored that sense of entitlement, that sense that as artists they are above the rules for expressions and exchanges of gratitude that otherwise serve to keep human relations in good balance.

Were they evincing that attitude I sensed in my brother and that was otherwise not uncommon among artists, struggling and otherwise, that any disgruntlement from mainstream types—from the "little people," as Leona Helmsley and Edmund White have referred to us ordinary mortals —were from our own envy? Was this a case where the unmet expectations of the little people—for loan repayment, punctuality, thanks, and reciprocity of caring—were more about our wannabe place among real and recognized artists and others of rank than from reasonable expectations of civility, courtesy and responsibility, especially in a context of ostensibly close friendship?

Putting down people for being losers, for the envy, spite and resentment that are seen to be the consequences of their own manifest inferiority, is the essence of Wagner's thinking about the Jews. Wagner, like Donald Trump and buffeted by comparable bully-pulpit success, willfully and sadistically misinterpreted and belittled the criticism and dismay of Jews and others who took issue with the composer's entitlement, savage hectoring, and murderous prejudice.

It bears continuous repeating that the entire *Ring* cycle is built on the premise that Alberich, because of his genetic ugliness and inferiority, is consumed with envy for his more divinely (genetically) endowed and entitled betters. In broader context, it's the same superficial construct that has been endlessly used to stigmatize and explain the envious and "unmanly" motivations and actions of "homosexuals" towards "authentic" masculinity; to understand the "penis envy" of women; and to racially demean Blacks, Hispanics and other minorities.

Of course, envy can be a powerful and worthy subject, as in Shakespeare's *Othello*. As with Jewish prototypes in Wagner, the absence of specificity of Iago's "motiveless malignancy" in *Othello* endows his character with dramatic tension. In *Othello*, however, we have little certainty of the real cause of what can seem to be Iago's intense envy. That it might be primarily racist is a possibility but not a conclusive or persuasive one. Wagner's portraits of Alberich, Mime, Beckmesser and Klingsor, by contrast, are very clearly about their envy of their genetic betters—of those who are more naturally and beneficently endowed with superior traits. Though they are never specified as Jews by Wagner, their envy is clearly all about their constitutional inferiority, failure and rejection as Jews. For the Jews of Wagner's universe, their malignancy is anything but motiveless.

Tension with Jaime also arose around the legendary film critic Pauline Kael, who became his close friend, and a photograph of whom is on his living room wall. Jaime was a member of her inner circle and loyally defended her from the attacks of her critics. Yes, she could write well and insightfully, but was her cult status otherwise entirely deserved? Or was it based too often on her skillful ability to purposefully provoke and goad her detractors into denunciatory fits and screeds, inevitably enhancing her own celebrity as a bad-ass iconoclast?

In the gay community and especially among gay activists, and despite the many gay men in her entourage, including her biographer Brian Kellow, Kael was widely regarded as homophobic, mostly on the basis of her reticence about homosexuality. Activists complained that she never lifted a finger for gay perspectives or concerns when the gay community was desperately beleaguered and under fire. This reticence sat uncomfortably alongside an aspect of her private life not widely known at the time. She was married to a gay-bisexual man, James Broughton, an avant-garde filmmaker, poet and member of the early gay activist movement, Radical Faeries, with whom she had a daughter, Gina, with whom Jaime was also and has remained close. Early in their marriage, Broughton left Kael to lead his preferentially gay life and make his experimental films, which Kael never acknowledged in her *New Yorker* writing, though apparently she did recognize his talent and personally encouraged him to become more mainstream in his career ambitions.

Where in all this for Pauline Kael was *The Celluloid Closet,* Vito Russo's groundbreaking study of homosexuality and film? Whatever the details of her amorous disappointments with gay men, for Kael the theoretical place of homosexuality in film was similar to that of other minority designations in being irrelevant.

However her personal life was playing out, whatever the skeletons in her own closet of being Jewish and married to and then separated from a preferentially gay man and experimental filmmaker, Kael was a chief promulgator of the ageing but entrenched aesthetics of insisting that everything of significance be contained within the work of art. It's the same value system that enabled the reticence and silence of the music critics, so many of them gay and closeted, around issues of homosexuality, and as well their silence and taciturnity around Wagner's antisemitism. Whatever Wagner's known antisemitism, if it's not clearly and specifically in the works, you couldn't talk about it. In Kael's case, coincidentally and conveniently, this standard of silence delegitimized questions about her private life, for others and as well apparently as for herself.

Kael's writing about film was prototypical of the arts criticism of her day in her belief that a given art work should never require social, political or historical context for understanding and appreciation. For

Kael the question was simple: was it a good film or wasn't it? Period. Within her own self-assurance from this vantage point, she could be gloatingly, arbitrarily and intoxicatedly intolerant of anything "extraneous."

The film *Making Love* featured the first openly gay love affair and the first male-to-male kiss on the mouth since *Sunday Bloody Sunday*, pathbreaking in depicting gay life and romance a decade earlier. It offered a rare and affirming image of gay humanity when the vulnerable gay community was under particularly brutal siege politically. For Kael, however, the fact that it was a minor, mediocre film artistically made such extraneous political considerations unworthy even of mention.

Much worse and confounding in its arbitrariness was her relentless championing of an utterly mediocre (by the measure of, without exception, every other critic and a largely and consistently indifferent public) filmmaker, Brian De Palma. De Palma's bloody film, *Dressed to Kill*, relied heavily on transphobia for its appeal at a time when transgender persons were being murdered, as they are today in the age of Trump, in greatly outsized numbers and in no small measure because of the insensitivity and indifference of its cultural agents—like De Palma and Kael.

Her comments on Jews could seem likewise revealing and goading, especially those suggesting that some actors seemed purposely to exaggerate their Jewishness. These concerns came to a head with Kael's review of Claude Lanzmann's epic *Shoah*, the most detailed and thereby most important documentary to date on the Nazi mass murders of millions of Jews. Kael found the film itself to be "logy and exhausting." Of director Lanzmann, she observed that he "could probably find anti-Semitism anywhere."

Despite some valid criticism of the arduously lengthy film's weaknesses, what she was doing was indicting a specific tree with a defiant unwillingness to acknowledge the forest. It's exactly what she did in the face of criticism of insensitivity around issues of homosexuality, racism and sexism. In this case, at least she made an effort to explain herself, but it only made the situation worse: "I ask the forbearance of readers for a dissenting view of a film that is widely regarded as a masterpiece." As captured by Richard Brody in his *New Yorker* commentary on *Shoah* at 25:

> Pauline Kael's misunderstandings of "Shoah" are so grotesque as to seem willful. The wild subjectivity of her approach to the film—her writing about the feelings of her backside rather than the feelings of the people in the film or of its maker—suggests, overall, the basic problem with her criticism. She used movies as a pretext to give voice to her assumptions and her prejudices…

The problem with Kael's criticism wasn't its pointing out of the flaws or deficiencies of its unschooled director. It was the narcissism of assuming that the shortcomings are of greater interest than the subject matter itself, and the childlike immaturity, complete absence of humility, of personal identification and feeling, and the grandstanding of prioritizing and showcasing her nitpickings about technique and structure.

How would Jaime, who has written eloquently of the genocides of millions of indigenous peoples in the Americas, feel if Kael had written a comparably condescending screed about a technically crude documentary on that subject? As Jaime admitted with discernible discomfort, Kael, whose parents were Orthodox Jews, likely harbored varying degrees of internalized antisemitism. She was above all a *provocateur*, he conceded, which somehow served more successfully for him as an excuse for her callousness than it did for the rest of us.

I have no problem affirming my love for Jaime, my regard for his work, and my compassion for the challenges and choices of his being in a personal and doubtless also codependent relationship with a difficult but gifted and admired figure like Kael. After all, was his love for and loyalty to Kael really so different from mine for and to Larry Kramer? With Kael as with Kramer, Jaime and I both have work to do in understanding and acknowledging the impact of these *monstres sacrés* on the sensitivities of others. Jaime has said he hopes to write about his friendship with Kael. I think that would be a wise and good thing for all. And I do need to write more about the pitfalls of my 50-year friendship with Kramer. In both cases, we've developed a lot of rationalizations and excuses for people who have greatly inspired and nurtured us but who left havoc in their wake. Hopefully we will do that work of inventory. Meanwhile, my gratitude for my friendship with Jaime is surpassing and I count it among my life's blessings.

At Katz's Deli, Barry and I talked about Arnie and his strength of character. For what seemed the first time, I began to appreciate the real person that Barry is beneath his Jewish "demonstrativeness" and "extrovertedness." Like that captured in the title of the Larry David comedy series, Curb Your Enthusiasm, such "Jewishness" always made me uneasy, the way assimilated Blacks feel in the presence of "street" Blacks. In the wake of an unwanted and unanticipated divorce, how was Barry managing to be so resilient? "I guess I have some of what Arnie has," he posited. It's what Jews often call moxie. Yes, I agreed. We left the deli and next to the Maserati we embraced.

Hugging other men was always a challenge for Barry, who has struggled to overcome his homophobia. When their father Morris died, Arnie wanted to bring his closest friend, Vito Russo—the great gay and AIDS activist and author of widely acclaimed minority film studies standard *The Celluloid Closet* who was our closest extended family member—to accompany him to the funeral. But Barry, who knew Vito had AIDS, forbad Arnie to do so. "This isn't about your cause!" he said at the time.

Barry has come a long way since then. After more than 40 years, he finally read Arnie's autobiography *Under The Rainbow*. I wondered if it were the only book he's ever read cover to cover. The embrace with me beside the Maserati still seemed awkward. His body stiffened and his head turned away. But then, as I started to leave, Barry took the initiative to re-embrace me, this time warmly. "Thanks for being family," he said. Yes, I realized. For better or for worse, that's what we are.

A piece in the *New Yorker* by Alex Ross on Willa Cather. Cather was an important American writer in the period of World War 1. She won a Pulitzer Prize for her novel *One of Ours*. She wrote of frontier life and the American Great Plains. She wrote a story called "A Wagner Matinee," was a friend of the Wagner soprano Olive Fremstad and figures as an exemplar of Wagnerism in *Wagner Nights*, Joseph Horowitz's chronicle of Wagnerism in America at the turn of the century. [She is also celebrated as such and at length in Ross's *Wagnerism*.] Cather's lesbianism tends to be overlooked, relegated or denied the way Walt Whitman's homosexuality continues to be overlooked, relegated or denied by heterosexuals more generally, but as well by social constructionists, some feminists and others because "gay" and "lesbian" are alleged to be modern concepts and inadequate demarcaters of evermore complexly, variously identified and conjoined phenomena of sex and gender in different times and places.

Writing in the *Washington Post* ("Just Plain AntiSemitism," 1/12/90), Doris Grumbach ranks Cather with 6 other leading American writers who were notable for their antisemitism: H.L. Mencken, Ernest Hemingway, Ezra Pound, T.S. Eliot, F. Scott Fitzgerald and Edith Wharton. Incidentally, Whitman was apparently aware of Wagner and outlived the composer. The great American poet was legendary for his love of Italian opera, especially bel canto. *Leaves of Grass* is full of allusions to it. His apparent lack of interest in Wagner, in view of the explosion of Wagnerism that overlapped with his life, as chronicled by Horowitz and touched on by Ross, seems worthy of exploration beyond Ross's conjecture in *Wagnerism* that the absence of references to Wagner in Whitman's writing was simply a casualty of timing and coincidence.

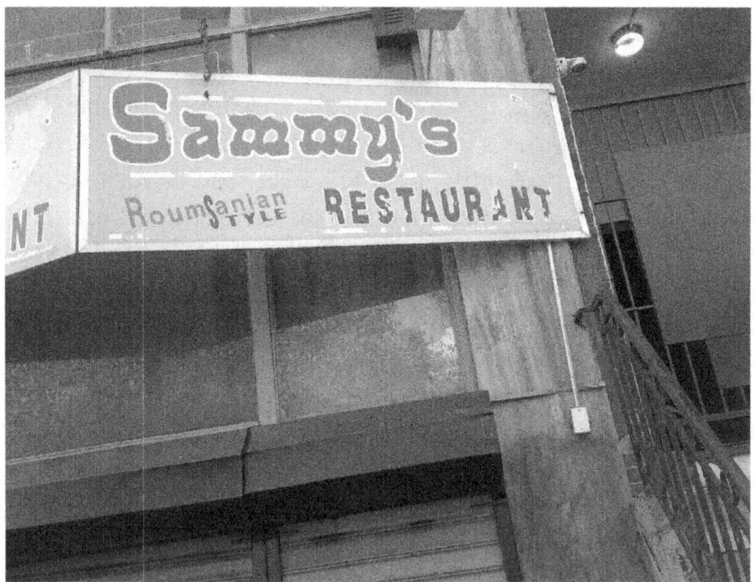


Figure 99 - Sammy's Roumanian Style Restaurant, legendary remnant of New York's City's Lower East Side Jewish community and Cuisine, photograph by Jm3, Creative Commons

*Rosh Hashonah* dinner several months later at Sammy's Rumanian Steak House with Arnie and Barry. Literal schmaltz in a syrup pitcher on the table, egg creams made from on high—the waiter standing on the table pouring the chocolate syrup into a cup on the table below. Rumanian steak, like the ones they now serve at most

Greek diners. Stuffed cabbage, chicken liver with grebenis, matzah ball soup, kosher dill pickles, brisket, mashed potatoes, potato latkes, salad, challah, ruggelach, a fabulous master of ceremonies who sang, kibitzed and guided everyone to outbursts of singing, dancing, clapping, vulgarity, laughter and good cheer. Not so unlike Sammy's, I am a remnant of the long history of Jewish assimilation, and of another of its chapters, that of Jewish Wagnerites.

If we could only see ourselves we'd see gestures, behaviors, patterns that others see more readily. One of my patterns, while universal, is notable for someone who struggles with codependence. When someone evades a glance or doesn't return a smile or greeting, I take that more personally and with greater insecurity than might be warranted. Sometimes avoidance betrays ill will. But too often it's not real and has nothing to do with me. How many times have I been staring straight ahead, and missed a friend or acquaintance directly in view? And how often did that have nothing to do with the other person?

For someone struggling with codependence, these situations can be more challenging than for others who would just shrug them off. For someone with codependence, the discomfort of such moments may be so acute that the codependent will feel compelled to redress and correct it, often with outsized urgency. So, say, the acquaintance doesn't say hello or smile or otherwise acknowledge my presence. Rather than just letting it go, I might try to find a way to purposely cross that person's path or confront him in a way that forces him to return my greeting. The discomfort I experience in my perception of his not engaging with me is like that of a child being rejected or abandoned, or an addict being denied immediate gratification. When amplified in intimate as well as in more casual relationships, you have the greater panorama of codependence. Apply that to the case of Wagner for a codependent Jew and you end up with five pictures of Wagner on his living room wall.

So there I was at a recovery meeting. Across the room was someone I'll call "Len" who I've known from these meetings for years, but who still seems to recoil from interaction with me. He will never initiate a smile or hello and seems to purposefully evade doing so. At one point I confronted him about it. "Hey Len!" When the response seemed inaudible, I confronted him again: "Aren't you going to say hello?!" When the response still seemed inadequate, I confronted him still further. "Is there some problem between us?" I demanded. "I'm shy," he finally said after a brief silence and evading eye contact. Was his claimed generic "shyness" credible or was it a reaction to me years ago when, during his droning share at a meeting, my demeanor may have betrayed my boredom and impatience? Or was his perceived recoil more about my ethnic appearance and pushiness (he was WASP)?

In the past, such perceived *froideur* would be so uncomfortable for me that the temptation to try to correct him would be irresistible. It was like an addict's need for a fix. But the last time I saw Len something different happened. Rather than indulging my reflex consternation, I reminded myself of the codependence recovery wisdom, that "what other people think of me is none of my business." Let him be.

Let it be. That's what I'm still learning to do with the others in my life with whom I'm codependent, including Wagner. Beyond my awareness and acceptance of the reality of Wagner's antisemitism, what Wagner thinks of me is none of my business. There's no point in trying to make him someone he wasn't and never can be.

Lunch with Hilan Warshaw at Café Le Monde. Recently divorced, documentary filmmaker Warshaw, creator of *Wagner's Jews*, is completing his film *Lyric Suite* about Alban Berg and his mistress, and is working on a new documentary about refugees and the experience of Jews trying to emigrate to America on the ill-fated MS St. Louis from Nazi-occupied Europe. He still hopes to proceed with his screenplay about Hermann Levi. I had an idea for another project I was sure he has himself considered: a Wagner's Jews II. In fact, he has thought about doing a sequel, a "Jews' Wagner." The idea would be to chronicle the evolution of Jewish Wagnerism via interviews from Wagner's time to the present (Though *Wagner's Jews* features commentary from contemporary observers, the Jews under discussion in that film are the Jews in Wagner's circles.)

Warshaw recently taught a course on how film intersects with works of history, literature, art and music. Though he didn't include Ken Russell's films this time, he is considering doing so in the future. While praising the filmmaker's genius, and as he had done in earlier conversations with me about Russell, Warshaw criticized the extravagance of his caricatures of music luminaries, especially

Wagner, Cosima, Mahler and others. It's a view I have encountered as well among most music critics and music lovers.

My view has been very different. Yes, Russell's music films can seem over the top to the point of absurdity. But that's what the best satire usually is and that's what Russell has shown himself to have a real gift for. He's the Sasha Baron Cohen of music and opera. Meanwhile, Russell's satire was deadly serious, like Cohen's, in the truths it was revealing, truths that were otherwise being obfuscated by mainstream critics and their readers. On antisemitism in Wagner (in his films *The Music Lovers, Lisztomania, Mahler* and *Salome's Last Dance*), Russell has been brave, brilliant and singular.

Warshaw mustered his own boldness to warn me of the problem he sees with my work. Yes, it's insightful and timely and of value. But not unlike Russell, it's going too far, he felt, in its sweeping indictment of Wagner appreciation.

To wit, he shared an observation he recalled me making: that I (Larry Mass) have yet to meet a Jewish Wagnerite who does not reveal a significant degree of internalized antisemitism. Was this true, Warshaw asked me, of Theodore Herzl, the founder of Israel, who loved Wagner's *Tannhäuser*? Was it true of Leonard Bernstein?

First, a correction. What I actually said is that I've yet to meet a Jew (not just Jewish Wagnerite), no matter how seriously Jewish, no matter how knowledgeable about antisemitism, who does not relatively quickly reveal some significant manifestation of internalized antisemitism. But that observation needs to be put in the context of the internalization of prejudice that is notable in all minorities. It can be gleaned in the hair-straightening of blacks, muscle building and combat-boots of gay men, and the over-celebration of Christmas, nose jobs and Wagnerism among Jews.

Warshaw's observation challenges me to reconsider. Are there not Jewish music lovers—e.g., Herzl, or Leonard Bernstein, alongside some we've already discussed, such as James Levine and Daniel Barenboim, whose love and appreciation of Wagner does not invite such scrutiny and questions?

As recounted elsewhere in these writings, I got to know Bernstein briefly but personally in the early period of AIDS. In 1981, the year of the first press reports of AIDS by me in the *New York Native*, I was introduced to him by his boyfriend at the time, Tom Steele, my close friend and editor at *Christopher Street* and the *Native*. Lenny had asked Tom to arrange for us to meet. He wanted to hear more about the new epidemic that was worsening but still so sparsely covered in the mainstream press and media. Though diagnostic certainty would remain elusive until HIV was identified as the cause of AIDS in 1983, it seemed to be the condition underlying the serious progressive illness of Lenny's previous boyfriend, Tommy Cothran, who died from complications of, as I recall, AIDS-related CNS toxoplasmosis. In the small world of gay men, I had known Tommy when I was at Berkeley. A believer in meaningful coincidences (what Jung called synchronicities), Lenny seemed a little spooked that the messenger informing him of this new, at some level communicable and uniformly fatal disease already involving loved ones, had the same name as his home town, Lawrence, Mass.

In the precious minutes we had together alone at his home in the Dakota, it was clear that chain-smoking Lenny, now 70, was not only concerned about the two Tommys he loved and his vulnerability to the new disease, but even more for his communities of gay men and the arts. Out of these encounters Lenny agreed to conduct the first big benefit for the organization we were putting together that became Gay Men's Health Crisis (GMHC), the Ringling Brothers Circus at Madison Square Garden in 1983.

One of several visits to his home followed a bravura performance with Michael Tilson Thomas, the two of them playing Stravinsky's Rite of Spring for Two Pianos, every moment of which was breathtaking. Back at the Dakota after the performance, there was a fabulous party with lots of friends, wine and sumptuous food.

One of these friends was George Perle, whose unceasing devotion to Berg climaxed with the discovery of the missing third act of *Lulu.* With Perle right next to him, Thomas banged out an impromptu ragtime version of Lulu's Song he called "The Lulu Rag." Perle looked more appalled than amused. Lenny, meanwhile, sang and danced the *Porgy and Bess* number, "I ain't got no shame, doin what I likes to do." Magic doesn't get any more magical.

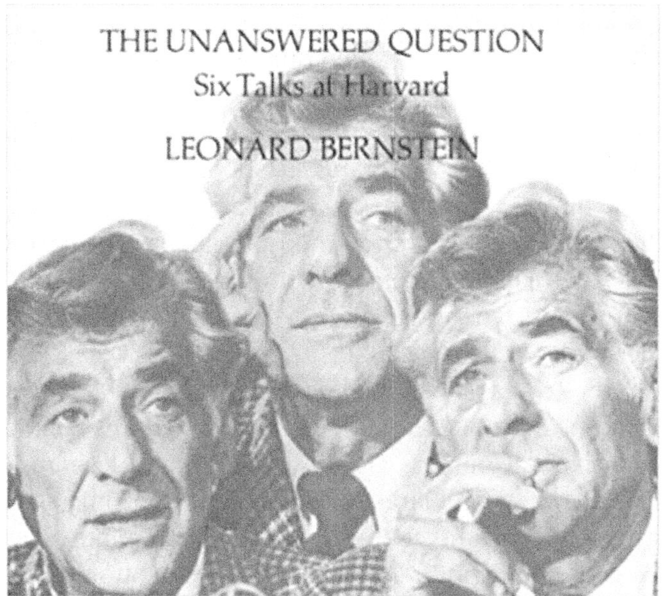


Figure 100 - Leonard Bernstein, The Unanswered Question, Amazon.com

A footnote re Perle and *Lulu*. Perle, Berg's biographer and a distinguished composer in his own right, is among those who deserve credit for the restoration of *Lulu* and the current version completed by Frederic Cerha and which premiered in Paris under Pierre Boulez in 1979. The completion of *Lulu* was an epochal event for the worlds of music and opera, but as well for me as a gay man. One of my great concerns as a writer and activist was opening up of the closet doors of music and opera. Via a series of interviews, book reviews and essays, I'd hoped and intended to put together a book on homosexuality and music with the title of *Musical Closets*. In this, *Lulu*, with its explicit lesbianism, was a sentinel development.

An early version of this collection had the working title *Homosexuality and Music: An Introduction to Gay and Lesbians Persons, Themes and Issues in Music and Opera*. Summarizing my experience in prying open these closet doors was an expansive essay, *Musical Closets: A Personal and Selective Documentary History of Outing and Coming Out in the Music World.* The essay was originally commissioned and then abandoned with cold feet at the eleventh hour by *Gay and Lesbian Review* editor Richard Schneider (at that time the quarterly was known as *The Harvard Gay and Lesbian Review*. A few years later, Harvard University demanded Schneider remove the name

Harvard, with which the publication had no actual affiliation). This essay, updated to include my falling out with Schneider over the piece, was later published by Michael Bronski in his anthology, *Taking Liberties: Gay Men's Essays on Politics, Culture and Sex* (Maquerade Books, First Richard Kasak Edition, 1996, pages 387-440).

As the first explicitly homosexual character to enter the international operatic repertoire, Lulu's lover, the Countess Geschwitz, has a landmark place. Ned Rorem alleged that I tried to smear George Perle in suggesting that he was hostile to giving any prominence to the issue of lesbianism in *Lulu*. Is it possible that in my enthusiasm for *Lulu* as a benchmark of my subject I was excessive in my expectations of how to regard and understand this character?

Not only is the Countess Geschwitz explicitly lesbian but also a figure of nobility who declares her intention to become a lawyer and work for women's rights before she is slain, minutes after Lulu herself, by Jack the Ripper. Pledging eternal devotion to Lulu as she dies, she is given the opera's final words. Had I expected Perle to make her lesbianism loom as large for him and the mainstream as it did for me and for LGBTQ history and the gay civil rights struggle? Whatever my thinking, certainly I hoped for more context and commentary from him.

"More shall be revealed," says my close friend Joel. Apparently, this is true not only for lesbianism in *Lulu*, but as well for Berg and questions of antisemitism in the opera's depiction of bankers and Berg's accommodations to Nazism, a perspective Warshaw had been trying to evaluate. It may be that my sense of Berg's depiction of the Countess as heroic could be wishful thinking on my part about an opera showcasing grotesqueries. It's true that Lulu's and the Countess's lesbianism would be regarded by many as epitomizing their degeneracy rather than their nobility or heroism. And certainly the inferences to the slimy "*Jungfrau*" stocks and bankers conjures antisemitic tropes. But reconceptualizing the opera as more of an indictment of Lulu and her milieu seems completely out of sync with the profound humanitarianism of Berg's other operatic masterpiece, *Wozzeck*. However they decompensate under social pressures, we glean the transcendent humanity, nobility and heroism of Wozzeck and even Marie, just as we appreciate those qualities in Lulu and the Countess.

Re-enter Dr. Jack ("Gene Thoreau" in *Confessions*) He is the close childhood friend who introduced me to opera, Callas, Wagner, Richard Strauss and, along with my father, medicine. Like the music critics and my brother, during the AIDS crisis when I was bottoming out on alcohol and marijuana, Gene—Dr. Jack Bulmash—wasn't there. As recollected in *Confessions,* my 40 year relationship with him had many twists and turns. While Jack spent the first twenty years disappointed we weren't lovers, I spent the next twenty disappointed we failed to sustain what had seemed our lifelong, very close, deep and abiding friendship. In recovery, I can't continue to blame people who weren't there, some of whom, like Dr. Jack, withdrew during those peak years of my alcoholism.

In recovery we talk about the problem for alcoholics and addicts of "self-righteous anger" and "'justified' resentment." In my own case, as my partner Arnie has pointed out, there is a matrix of undifferentiated anger always looking for targets. A big source of such anger for me was the closet and what became known as outing—revealing the homosexuality otherwise being kept secret by and for public figures who were harming us by their active or passive participation in anti-gay politics, often as a way of obfuscating their own homosexuality. With good and successful people, their staying in the closet, and the enabling of that by the media, was hiding truth from the public that would be of benefit to the politically-besieged gay community as a whole by positive association. Among public figures, there were desperately few who were openly gay.

Another pattern touched by outing is of mainstream gays shunning gay activism because it wasn't in the interests of their profession or class. If you're rich, that becomes a much bigger priority for many or most than minority identity, especially when that identity is in many ways a social and professional liability. In the 1980's feelings about all this were very strong and finally erupted in fiery public debates about outing. I was on the side of outing those whose closetedness clearly contributed to gay oppression, especially if they were public figures. Roy Cohn is a good example. Ed Koch was another.

During these years my activist anger had yet to be tempered with recovery. Arnie, a leading gay activist of the early post-Stonewall period, was always more cautionary about outing. As was Vito Russo.

As a writer, I felt that the issue was simple and clear. If you are a serious writer, your highest priority is to tell the truth, not to obfuscate.

Nothing is more important than the truth, I would declaim. If an artist or actor or composer or singer were gay, how can you not tell such important truth?

With his characteristic and teacherly calm, patience and wisdom, Arnie observed that in fact there is something more important than truth. He then shared an exchange he had with one of his students, a young woman. "All bright-eyed and bushy-tailed," as the priest John Cavendish used to say, she asked Arnie, her professor and mentor, what he thought of her new dress. He looked at her and decided to tell her the truth, that it was awful, that it didn't flatter her, that the colors were wrong, that it was a mess. Crestfallen, she meekly confessed she had made it herself. In that moment, he realized that there was clearly something more important than truth: kindness.

I came to see that a lot of my outing anger was troubled. As in all revolutionary movements, there is danger in revolutionary zeal, however ostensibly justified, which can become as unchecked as the hegemony it would smash. Yet even in the wake of the Reign of Terror, it's difficult to regret the French Revolution. Decent and innocent people are often victimized when the barricades are stormed. My anger at Dr. Jack for not being more activist or supportive of our gay and AIDS activism did not seem to have any devastating consequences for him, but I can appreciate that it was hurtful and may have put him in harm's way. I'm glad I made a sincere effort to make amends to him in the wake of the portrait of "Dr. Jock" in my *Confessions*.

"Enemy of the people" ("Nemico della patria") is one of the blockbuster arias of Italian opera. Here, in *Andrea Chenier*, Girodano's great verismo opera about the French Revolution, the baritone Gerard, a revolutionary, admits to his growing disillusionment with the tribunals. He has become a cog in the wheels of the Reign of Terror. Today, we recognize this phrase along with "fake news" as a signature mantra of Donald Trump, who seems hell-bent on fomenting a far-right reign of terror. Now these insurgencies seem to be happening throughout the world at the rate of approximately every ten minutes. Trump uses stock fascist postures and dog-whistle phrases, with the originality, finesse, and subtlety of Mar al Lago's gilded décor. It's doubtful that Trump shares any of Gerard's moments of conscience or misgivings.

In recovery people say there are no coincidences. In the activist fervor for outing, for AIDS and gay liberation, former friends were seen as turncoat enemies. With the din of Trump's tantrums and tirades in the background. Gerard's aria was selected by what I call my unconscious jukebox. Without any conscious stimulus, I suddenly find myself singing or humming refrains from works that comment on my consciousness, circumstances, relationships, current events and conscience.

After a falling out of more than 30 years, Dr. Jack and I reconnected over a 3-hour brunch at a favorite spot—the restaurant Robert overlooking Central Park. Jack, his husband Michael, Arnie and me. I'm not sure whether Jack ever finally came out in his tough Chicago outland work for VA hospitals and administrations, but he eventually married Michael, his life-partner of more than 40 years. Now retired and living well, they are grateful for the benefits of activism for their lives and marriage. They have become hearteningly mindful and articulate about the current populist dangers. Unlike the debacle of the amends work with my brother, who Jack recalls as "arrogant" and "nasty," I was able to do a well-received ninth step that was long overdue. I acknowledged my regret for any pain or harm from self-righteous anger, and "justified" resentment, and properly thanked him for the gift and bounty of our professional, creative and personal lives and the friendship that nurtured them.

As previously observed, it's Dr. Jack who introduced me to Wagner and who became my closest friend and fellow Jewish Wagnerite. From the beginning he was aware of Wagner's antisemitism and the close connections of the Wagner family and Bayreuth to Hitler and Nazism. Like all Jewish and non-Jewish Wagnerites of our time, we simply separated the man from his art. Great art, bad man. Simple enough. And in any case what were we to do about art that we ourselves felt to be so great and that was so widely and surpassingly revered? As our Wagnerism grew we would discuss big subjects like Wagner and antisemitism and the stodginess of opera in our time. Though far from being front-line activists for modernity with its predominance of atonality, we couldn't help but notice how like a museum or even mausoleum the art form had become. "What opera needs," Dr. Jack memorably observed, "is another Richard Wagner." Neither of us batted an eyelash at this truth. Not since Wagner has anyone so shaken the rafters of music, art and culture.

Dr. Jack and I continued our Wagnerism journey together, learning about leading singers, conductors, directors and composers of the Nazi era and what they did and didn't do in response to Hitler and Nazism. We collected virtually the entire series of German recordings under the label of *Lebendige Vergangenheit*, live and studio recordings of Helge Roswaenge, Frida Leider, Friedrich Schorr, Alexander Kipnis, Tiana Lemnitz, Erna Berger, Elisabeth Rethberg, Max Lorenz, Lauritz Melchior, Lotte Lehmann and other-label recordings of such artists as stratospheric coloratura Erna Sack and Joseph Schmidt, the incomparable lyric tenor who died trying to flee Nazism.

Though a recording of Wagner's immolation scene conducted by Lenny with Eileen Farrell, who was appearing with the Chicago Lyric Opera, inspired our admiration, I don't think we ever talked much about the conductor. As there was no other Wagner or Strauss to speak of that he conducted in those years, and our interest in Mahler had yet to develop, he didn't seem as interesting to us. As for his being Jewish and conducting the occasional Wagner piece in concert, we just assumed he was like us, comfortable enough separating the man from his music. Bernstein is a subject Dr. Jack and I still haven't returned to.

So did Lenny reveal the internalization of antisemitism I've alleged of all Jews, especially Jewish Wagnerites? I must admit that it's not something I've ever had much sense of, except in his rare but extravagant praise of Wagner's gifts as a composer, which seem more revealing of Lenny's extravagant humanity than of any psychopathology around his Jewishness. Where I see antisemitism in relation to Lenny is more in the appreciations and criticisms of others of Lenny's "extravagant" persona. In his inability to curb his enthusiasm, it's implied, is he not too....over the top? So, yes, there are people like Bernstein and Herzl and Korngold and Bloch, people whose Jewishness was deeply felt and who genuinely revered Wagner's musical gifts, who would seem to contradict my generalization, but who doubtless absorbed and betrayed degrees of internalized antisemitism in their relationships to Wagner and the world at large.

Again, however in broader context, my observation about what can seem a nearly universal internalization of antisemitism by Jews shouldn't seem so controversial. It's the internalization of prejudice found in anyone of minority status—women, LGBT people, Blacks, Asians, and Hispanics. Through my own experience, I've been helped to see how being a Jewish Wagnerite is like being a black or gay Republican. Sure, gay and black Republicans, Hispanics, women and Jews for Trump, are out there and not all of them are insane, stupid or pathologically self-hating. But a black or gay Republican, or a woman, Hispanic or Jew for Trump, his pro-Israeli stances notwithstanding, calls for a better understanding of where they're coming from. I mean, in plain language, can you really be black, female or Jewish, knowing what we know about the history of racism, sexism, slavery, antisemitism, fascism and Donald Trump and not be in that place of psychopathology we call cognitive dissonance?

The same is true of Jewish Wagnerites. I want to understand where Jewish Wagnerites like Joseph Horowitz, James Levine and Daniel Barenboim are coming from the same way one wants to better understand the mentality of black Republicans like Clarence Thomas, Ben Carson and Omarosa Manigault. While I might abjure tainting Leonard Bernstein with a label of mental illness for finding *Tristan* beautiful, I will retain my discernment about those who are less circumspect in the extent of their involvements with more questionable figures and ideologies.

Lenny was not averse to hearing or playing Wagner's music or acknowledging its greatness, and could even wax ecstatic about it. "I hate Wagner but I hate him on my knees," he said. And there's that excellent recording of the Immolation Scene with Eileen Farrell and the New York Philharmonic. And there are notable excerpts from *Die Walküre* and a virtually complete *Tristan* (each act recorded separately) but a full-length performance of a Wagner opera never happened.

Bernstein was in discussions with Wolfgang Wagner to conduct *Tristan* at Bayreuth. Bernstein was interested in recording it and wanted to enlist Ingmar Bergman to direct it. This would have marked a departure from the previous division of directorial responsibilities between Wieland and Wolfgang Wagner, with Wieland directing most productions. It's unclear whether the brothers supported this initiative to bring Bergman to Bayreuth. In any case it's a collaboration that never happened, ostensibly because of scheduling difficulties. Yet it's difficult not to glean from Lenny's intersections with Wagner a hesitancy that may have been more intuitive than articulate.

As a conductor, composer, pianist, lecturer and persona, Lenny was spread pretty thin, a frequent criticism. As a result, he dabbled with many genres and composers, not just Wagner. Still, it seems unlikely that Lenny's involvement with Wagner would have grown much beyond where it got left. James Levine and Daniel Barenboim conducted at Bayreuth, but Lenny never did.

Lenny could seem to understand instinctively that the Wagner situation was deeply troubled even without knowledge of the full extent of the Wagner family's Nazi collaborations. It was one thing for Lenny to conduct Beethoven, Richard Strauss and even Wagner in Vienna to enormous acclaim, but it was another to conduct Wagner at Bayreuth.

8/25/2018 marked the 100th anniversary of Lenny's birth in Lawrence, Mass, an occasion to savor Lenny's impact and celebrate his legacy. Testimonials and retrospectives abounded. But none got it so right in conveying Lenny's appeal and impact as a personal appreciation by Alex Ross in the *New Yorker*. Everything of interest and importance is at least touched on here. Ross generously acknowledged Lenny's impressive legacy and the absence of anyone comparable or remotely qualified to succeed him as a leading figure of musical culture. The one notable omission to "everything of importance," however, is the subject of the book Ross had been writing for the last decade: Richard Wagner and Wagnerism.

Like his *New Yorker* piece on Bernstein's legacy, Ross's *Wagnerism* contains no discussion of Lenny in relationship to Wagner. There are however, two references to Lenny in the book, both of them cryptic. The first alludes to Bernstein and Wagner's gravesite:

> When Leonard Bernstein stopped at the site he joked that the slab was big enough that you could dance on it. Bernstein was undoubtedly thinking not only of Wagner but also of Adolf Hitler who, on his first visit, in 1923, stood at the grave a long time, alone.

The second reference occurs late in *Wagnerism* when Ross is talking about musical trends in the post-war period:

> Classical music maintained a high profile in American culture with Leonard Bernstein explicating Beethoven on television and opera singers making the rounds of talk shows.

A cloud remains around Leonard Bernstein and Wagner, one that Ross steers clear of.

It's said that Lenny regarded *Tristan* as the one repertory standard Wagner opera that's completely free of antisemitism. I myself have seen it that way, and felt reassured in that impression by Marc Weiner. Coincidentally, at Weiner's urging, I watched excerpts from a musically impressive performance of the opera from the 1993 Bayreuth Festival, featuring Waltraud Meier and Siegfried Jerusalem, conducted by Daniel Barenboim and directed by Heiner Müller in a framework of Kabuki gestures and conventions. The version I was watching had French supertitles. There, in Act 1, in Isolde's narrative and curse, I was startled to discover a reference to "*race degeneré*." I crossed it by Marc, who dismissed it as an idiosyncratic turn of phrase, a moment of anger directed at Brangäne, But he noted that I was not the first to comment on it (Thomas Grey had apparently expounded on it at length) and seemed open to reconsidering it in the context of Wagner's antisemitism.

The other writer I know of who raised questions about *Tristan* and antisemitism is Paul Lawrence Rose, whose *Wagner: Race and Revolution*, suggests that Melot's betrayal has antisemitic implications. In his critique of this book for the *German Quarterly*, Ross colleague and mentor Hans Rudolf Vaget is likewise dismissive, revealing the same defensiveness and accusations of emotionalism that characterize his *German Quarterly* critique and exchange with Marc Weiner regarding Weiner's *Richard Wagner and the Anti-Semitic Imagination.*

A new, feminist-deconstructed production of *Lohengrin* at Bayreuth directed by Yuval Sharon, an American whose parents are Israeli, beckons me to expound. How much of Bayreuth's enthusiasm is about the production's success, or about identity politics? Is Bayreuth's appreciation a measure of Wagner apologism, of how far Wagnerites have come in regret for the past, or is it more about using Jews who pardon Wagner as a defense around ongoing accusations of antisemitism in Wagner? In other words, is the use of Sharon, Barrie

Kosky, James Levine, Daniel Barenboim and other Jews by Bayreuth like Trump's use of Ben Carson, Herman Cain and Kanye West? With blacks prominently supporting him, how can Trump be said to be racist? With so many Jews at Bayreuth, how can Wagner at Bayreuth be said to be antisemitic?

As flagged by Adam J. Sacks, a scholar of Jewish-German musical culture and an editor of this collection, Sharon was televised with Bayreuth's music director (principal conductor) Christian Thielemann (who has been accused of right-wing sympathies), placing a stone on Wagner's grave. I witnessed the moment in a short video clip and have wondered about it since. Is this something that Thielemann does ritually with all his directors or others at Bayreuth? Is it something Leonard Bernstein was asked to do? Is it something others at Bayreuth—Jews and non-Jews—do ritually or otherwise? Or was it a photo-op? An interview with Sharon from *Deutsche Welle* wasn't very clarifying. When asked about his feelings about being Jewish and the reactions to his Bayreuth engagement by his Israeli parents, his responses were politically correct but perfunctory; there was no probity. That he placed a stone on Wagner's grave doesn't come up in the interview.

A call to me from Dr. Melissa Freeman, one of the longest-serving physicians in the history of Beth Israel Medical Center and the profession and practice of medicine in New York or anywhere else. Now in her mid-90's and still participating part-time in practices of internal and addiction medicine, Dr. Freeman is black and her generations of experience with minority and underserved communities is notable and distinguished. I'm proud to have her as my mentor, colleague and friend.

Dr. Freeman is also a passionate Wagnerite. Years ago, we had a long talk about Wagner that became unpleasant. When I explained my viewpoint of surpassing concern about Wagner's antisemitism, it didn't seem to register. Since then, and because senior memories can have gaps, when the subject of Wagner would come up between us, I was never sure if she recalled my feelings or our sparring, or whether she ever read my *Confessions*, which I had told her about. Did I plan to see any of the 3 scheduled *Ring* cycles at the Met for the coming season? She asked this as if my perspectives on Wagner and movement away from Wagnerism had never been expressed.

Prior to codependence recovery, I would have wanted to confront her. This time I didn't. I didn't even say something uncontroversial about the widely shared disappointment with the Robert LePage production. Instead, I acknowledged the buzz about the Brünhilde of Chrsitine Goerke, who has the big, thrilling voice to do the part justice. "And Eric Owens," Melissa added, mistakenly under the impression that Owens, one of our best Wagner singers and who is black, would be singing Wotan.

While I didn't want to see the *Ring* cycle again, in this production or probably any other, I would be curious to read any discourse in the press regarding the casting of Owens as Wotan. It's not likely there would be anything explicit about having a black singer portray Wotan. When Owens sang Wotan in Chicago's post-modern *Die Walküre* in 2017, there was no such discussion; nor from Owens himself in interviews about his singing this part. Silence and reticence are proofs of the success of assimilation, right? Yet the presumption that all issues of race are now resolved seems premature and simplistic. One of the great concerns of Wagnerism and the future is that even when silent or seemingly surmounted by multi-racial casting or directorial deconstructions, race consciousness may still be tacit and more influential than any of us would be comfortable acknowledging or discussing.

*My Parsifal Conductor*, by Allan Leicht, billed as a comedy, at New York's Fireside YMCA theater. The play is rich with historical tidbits and conjures an unequivocal picture of the centrality of antisemitism for Richard and Cosima Wagner and their household at Wahnfried. It also posits a self-awareness on Wagner's part that antisemitism is his muse and key to his creativity. Though lacking in brilliance and even coherence, the play is persuasive in conveying the greater reality of the relationship between Jews and Wagner.

Notwithstanding Wagner's exploitive involvements with Jews at multiple levels of patronage and commerce (e.g., Meyerbeer and Angelo Neumann), it's Jews, going back to and epitomized by Levi, who have taken the initiative to insinuate ourselves with Wagner and Wagnerism rather than the other way around. So, yes, the relationship between Wagner and the Jews went both ways. They needed and exploited each other. As epitomized by the relationship between Wagner and Levi, however, the dynamics were not those of mutual regard. Rather, they were more characteristically pathological: master and slave, abuser and abused, sadist and masochist, codependent and enabler.

Coincidentally, Levi's remains have been transferred to the Jewish cemetery in Munich from Garmisch-Partenkirchen, where his grave was defiled by Nazis and has been neglected ever since by this town where he died. "A shabby end," observed Norman Lebrecht on Slipped Disc, "for a dignified man who coped with Wagner's antisemitism in his lifetime and his legacy ever after."

Melanie Yolles accompanied me to the play and found it stimulating after "abstaining" from Wagner over the summer. In apparent denial about the grave having been antisemitically defiled, she had a more equivocal reaction to this news and the failure of any redress by locals. "I wonder how many graves of notable/forgotten conductors are well tended, especially if they have no family living nearby." On reflection the next day, she offered to contribute to the site's rehabilitation should any such effort get underway. Hilan Warshaw, who documented these desecrations in his film, *Wagner's Jews*, noted that Levi's gravesite was being used as a garbage dump. "In the meantime, Richard Strauss (who moved to Garmisch as a young conductor largely to be close by to Levi) is lavishly memorialized."

Stimulated by a Wagner Society announcement of a discussion with the playwright that was passed on to me by Melanie, I had my own afterthought about the play, shaped by the findings of Marc Weiner's *Richard Wagner and the Anti-Semitic Imagination*. The world of the Wagner Societies, with their ever-present Jewish members, is different from that of mainstream German Wagnerites, steeped in antisemitic folklore and common prejudice. My intuition is that the latter accept Wagner's antisemitism as a given, even if it's not openly discussed. Intuitively as well as historically, they understand this foundational premise of Wagner, just as they understand the Jewish inferences of the *Ring* cycle, *Parsifal* and *Meistersinger*. They might well understand that as a Jew, Levi was foisted onto Wagner by politics and economics rather than being his conductor of choice. Therefore, one wouldn't expect the same respect for Levi that other Wagnerites, especially Jewish ones, might feel. In *My* Parsifal *Conductor* the maids are shown to be crudely antisemitic; not surprising considering their surroundings. In sum, perhaps many non-

Jewish Wagnerites feel about Levi the way Richard and Cosima Wagner did.

On my first trip to New York City when Dr. Jack and I were 14, and as mentioned, I was given the choice to see either Barbra Streisand in *Funny Girl* or Richard Burton in *Hamlet*. I chose the latter. Shakespeare was already important to me and my newly adopted Wagnerite snobbery about low "*Kultur,*" so I chose the Burton *Hamlet*.

On that same trek, I made another choice for higher culture. The play was Chekov's *Ivanov* with Vivien Leigh and John Gielgud. The title character, a debt-ridden landowner marries Anna, a disinherited "Jewess," as he refers to her in a moment of pique. Anna, who renounced her wealthy family and converted to Russian Orthodox Christianity to marry him, is dying of consumption. It registered at subterranean levels that the play raised serious questions about money, class, Jews and antisemitism. My reason for selecting it over the likes of *Hello Dolly* was more about seeing these great serious actors than the play itself. In fact, in my attitude towards *Hello Dolly*, I shared Ivanov's snidely antisemitic snobbery, salvaged by it being directed at the great Vivien Leigh. Beyond the glamour of her star power and the greatness of her achievements as an actress, that I shared her character's psychology of codependence and her legacy of unsuccessful assimilation never occurred to me.

Fortelling where we're likely headed with Donald Trump is the fate of Margherita Grassini Sarfatti, Mussolini's Jewish mistress. An Italian journalist and art critic, she was a propaganda advisor to the National Fascist party, which allowed Jews to be members. Like Jewish Republicans for Trump in America today, she wasn't the only prominent Jew to join with the fascists of Italy before the outbreak of war. Many of them ended up dead, though Sarfatti emigrated to South America in 1938 and returned to Italy after the war. In 1925, she wrote a biography, *The Life of Mussolini*.

The prototype here is Queen Esther in the story of Purim. This key Jewish fable is one of marrying into power as a means of self-protection for oneself and one's people. Esther became Queen of Persia, of what today is Iran. Haman, advisor to the King, was the prototype of genocidally antisemitic former President Ahmadinejad and the still all-powerful mullah Ayatollah Khameni. What I'm curious to know more about is what became of the Jews following

Queen Esther's marriage and the vanquishing of Haman. In the short term, the Jews were saved. But what happened subsequently? Over the long term, most Jews left Iran under duress after the Islamic revolution which deposed the Shah in 1979. Will the Kushner-Trump marriage initiate the same cycle? Especially in his simultaneous unleashing and coddling of extreme displays of white nationalism and antisemitism, how long is this strategy likely to forestall the fate it's supposed to be preventing?

There's a new and unprecedented exhibit at Monticello about Sally Hemmings, a slave of Thomas Jefferson who bore him 6 children. What Hemmings did with Jefferson is what Queen Esther did with the Persians, what Hannah Arendt did with Martin Heidegger, what Margherita Sarfatti did with Benito Mussolini, and what Hermann Levi and many other Jews, including me, did with Richard Wagner. Without greater self-awareness, we pursued questionable and extreme routes of acceptance, authenticity, assimilation and survival. We were lambs appealing to wolves to protect us.

I decided to attend that panel discussion of *My* Parsifal *Conductor* led by Hilan Warshaw. About 15 people from that evening's performance stayed, including actors, the director, and the playwright. Several questions revolved around the shared reaction that though the play was intended to be a comedy, it wasn't very funny. Others probed how the actors felt playing such virulent antisemites.

Alas, very little of what was said placed the play's subject of Wagner and the Jews in perspective. Warshaw, who has written eloquently about Levi's inner conflictedness around his Jewishness and Wagner's antisemitism, has considered doing a film about him. Yet he did not press his misgivings about the play's rendering of Levi as secure in his Jewishness. In fact, terms and concepts like codependence and social masochism were absent from this discussion. The playwright seemed weary rather than funny in conveying his inner conflictedness. Another self-described Jewish Wagnerite, he shared with other Jews his oil-and-water mix of feelings about Wagner: an admiration of the artist and love of his music embittered with repulsion and hurt by his prejudice. Neither the play nor the panel pointed the way to reconciliation or a way forward to the future.

The last question for the panelists was mine. "Do you think Jewish Wagnerism has been good for the Jews"? I asked. Much like that of the play, my humor missed its mark. The responses were otherwise mixed but sometimes animated. The actor who played Nietzsche had the most upbeat reaction: the answer is yes if the play stimulates discussion.

In the audience for the panel, as it turns out, was a Wagner Society regular, my old sparring partner Professor Alberich! Hastily, with our original good will, we renewed acquaintance. He gave me his card and we spoke of reconnecting. I wrote him subsequently and we had several exchanges. In the course of which he gave his own answer to my question of whether or not Jewish Wagnerites are "good for the Jews."

> "Absolutely not...Witness the compulsive and really pathetic attempt of nineteenth century German Jews to win acceptance from their gentile acquaintances - everything from baptism to the absurdities of the Reform movement that really tried to turn Judaism into Lutheranism. Luther rejected them, as did the German people, and as did the National Socialists, and all for the same reason: They could see that it was a fraud. The Jews would forever be labelled as "aliens" by the "true" Germans, even those like Cosima with a French mother and a Hungarian father. Talk about fuzzy boundaries and hypocrisy."

Lost in the bigger picture of Wagner and the Jews is the reality that the attempt of Jews to integrate with Wagnerism garnered circumstantial coexistence but virtually no genuine reciprocity. Jewish Wagnerites may have seen themselves as a vanguard of high culture, but no such recognition was ever forthcoming from Wagner or the custodians of culture Wagner most aimed to reach. On the contrary, what emerged from Wagner regarding Jews was the opposite and taken to extremes.

By participating in Wagnerism at all levels and lands, Jews achieved the appearance of integration and only what seemed to be acceptance. What Wagnerism achieved in turn was a softening of the taint of antisemitism, a taint potentially so severe as to unsettle the entire world of Western art. In an all-out clash on this front of Wagner and the Jews, Wagner might well prevail, but the damage to Wagnerism and culture would be incalculable. Alas, any truce between these polarities is not only tentative, but false. There is no happy ending, nor can there be to the saga of Richard Wagner and the Jews. For all their codependent engagement with Wagner, the Jews got Hitler as a return on their investment while Wagner got a provisional and endlessly effortful blind eye from the worlds of culture, an EZ-Pass to the future that will have to be continually renewed.

There can be no "das ende" to this situation. I have no illusions, nor should anyone else. I summarized my feelings for Melanie in our ongoing dialogue:

> No one, certainly not me, wants to ban Wagner's operas. What I do think might happen over time is that Jews ourselves, more enlightened about Wagner, his operas and history than earlier generations, will choose to interact with Wagner with greater circumspection and reserve. In the bigger picture, what might be achievable is less enshrinement and more depedestalization of the composer, with an acceptance that Wagner is no more likely to recede altogether than Martin Luther.

I should qualify this generalization with a repeated acknowledgement that there are those, episodically including me, who do in fact support a ban on Wagner in the special circumstance of Israel because I understand, respect and support the rights of those war veterans and Holocaust survivors who associate Wagner with Hitler and who want the ban to remain in place as a symbol of remembrance and resistance. I support their position much as I supported the Jewish protestors of *Klinghoffer*, some of whom wanted that opera banned from presentation. While I could not join their ranks because of their calls for censorship, I secretly cheered for them from the opposite side of the street because they represented something far rarer and more important—brave and outspoken Jewish protest of antisemitism.

Periodically this controversy reemerges as it did with regard to Gottfried Wagner and his support of Israel's ban on Wagner. In an editorial in the *Jerusalem Post* in 2001 by E. Randol Schoenberg, grandson of composer Arnold Schoenberg, he calls the ban wrong-headed and inappropriate and frames Gottfried as misguided. This viewpoint reflects the older thinking that easily distinguishes the art from the man. Wagner may have been a terrible antisemite but his music is glorious and remains a gold standard of Western musical culture. Among the many who embraced such a facile distinction was the great composer Arnold Schoenberg, an exile from Nazism who continued to count himself an admirer of Wagner, even as he came to embrace Zionism.

Toscanini, also an ardent Wagnerite at the same time early and ardently supported Israel and the Israel Philharmonic. What would or did Toscanini have to say about Israel's ban on Wagner? Even heroic figures like Toscanini were of a generation that did not appreciate the extent to which antisemitism infuses not only the life and times of Richard Wagner but the art works themselves. Yes, Toscanini refused to conduct at Bayreuth but not because of Wagner's antisemitism. It was because of the takeover of the festival by Nazis and the banning and persecution of Jewish artists.

"I was distressed to learn that Gottfried Wagner, who had done so much to expose his family's entanglement with Hitler, has written in support of the Wagner ban in Israel," E. R. Schoenberg wrote in the *JP* editorial. "In this thoughtless gesture he is behaving no differently than his antisemitic ancestors, who also might not have wished Wagner to be performed by Jews…" The editorial concludes that "Jews have nothing to fear from Wagner…Don't tell Jews what they should and should not listen to."

Gottfried was expressing respect for the sensitivities of Jews and Israelis, of survivors of the Holocaust, for which he counts his family as perpetrators. Gottfried is certainly not in favor of censorship. Nor am I. Neither of us is mounting campaigns to prevent opera companies from staging Wagner.

I do appreciate the point made by Leon Botstein that allowing Wagner in Israel would facilitate education and enlightenment, for musicians as well as audiences. But I also believe that the Israeli ban on Wagner has been a remarkably powerful if all too rare symbol of Jewish resistance to antisemitism—a clear, blunt and courageous response to the incalculable damage to Jews wrought by Wagner. Thus, I cannot regret my support of the ban on Wagner in Israel. At the same time I could support future changes in that policy, if such changes emerge from a consensus along with a commitment to placing Wagner in context, as was done with *Mein Kampf* in Germany. [See also "Wagner Intoxication," my interview with Gottfried Wagner.]

A visit to New York City by the Hungarian State Opera under the regime of populist autocrat Viktor Orban. For a regime and country that oozes state-sponsored antisemitism in its Orwellian demonization of Hungarian-Jewish George Soros, and which frequently brandishes rampant homophobia, the visit was puzzling. Unlike President Trump, who has never evinced an iota of interest in the arts and culture, Orban, like Putin, has made the celebration of his native culture a showcase of his regime. Though Putin has yet to pull the historical trump card of antisemitism, he has been the ringleader of an international onslaught of homophobia.

The visit itself left me with multiple conflicts. First, it was a singular opportunity to see and hear an historically significant opera company doing rare works. Among the offerings were Goldmark's *Queen of Sheba*, a Jewish-themed work by a Hungarian-German-Jewish composer that had its premiere in 1875. I was also drawn to the visit by the easily obtained and inexpensive tickets, and the opportunity to take in a major Hungarian event in view of my relationship with Attila. This man whom I married has a few Hungarian friends in Florida but had not been able to visit his parents and homeland because of immigration barriers.

The personal conflict of attending a populist-promoted and promotional event loomed large for me. Having expressed myself passionately about the importance of political activism in the arts, here I was, ready to relegate that activism. It made me very uncomfortable that I was not engaged in active protest or boycotting this event, if not in public demonstration(s) than at least in the choice not to attend.

But attend I did, and the absence of protest was as notable outside as inside. Not one placard. No lone voices or wolves outside the theater or in the audience on any of my three nights at the opera. In fact, the only discord I took note of anywhere was a sentence or two in Anthony Tomassini's *NYT* piece on the company's visit. The *NYT* had earlier posted a story on the Orban regime's cancelling—as "gay propaganda"—the musical *Billy Elliot*.

As for the gay opera *demimondaine*, it was like entering a time warp. On the way to the Men's Room there was Bruce-Michael

Gelbert still dressed in full leather regalia, noting as I passed him that he wasn't surprised to see me at "a Jewish opera." Not to him nor to veteran opera goers John Yohalem, Daniel Goldman or even to *Gay City News* opera reviewer Eli Jacobson, did I bother to ask "What are we all doing here? Shouldn't we be boycotting this or otherwise protesting?" Whatever misgivings I may be expressing now, my not asking them these questions was a measure of my own resignation to the status quo.

*Maestro*, an historical documentary-musical theater piece about Arturo Toscanini and his outspoken, lifelong resistance to fascism. Selections, from Toscanini's letters to a lover, pianist Ada Mainardi, were reenacted by the actor Ron Noble against the backdrop of biographical and historical events. Chamber musicians performed a range of compositions by composers who were significant in the life and times of the great conductor. There was Mario Castelnuovo-Tedesco, who was Jewish, hounded by the Nazis and sought support from Toscanini, and whose *Quintetto* for piano and strings was given a rare performance by onstage musicians, as well as *Berceuse* by Aldo Finizi, another all-but-forgotten Toscanini-associated, Jewish composer under Nazism.

The onstage concert selections featured other rarities: Verdi's otherwise unknown, all-instrumental string quartet, alongside pieces by Guido Alberto Fano and Giuseppe Martucci, and pieces by two other composers who were important to Toscanini: Wagner and Gershwin. It's revealing that for all of Toscanini's brave resistance to Nazism, his philosemitism and refusal to conduct at Bayreuth, even in this play one has no sense of what he thought about the antisemitism in Wagner's life and work. As noted, other such ardent and courageous anti-fascists as leading Wagnerians Lotte Lehman, Lauritz Melchior and Fridelind Wagner as well as Toscanini seemed comfortable and even complacent in separating the composer from his art, as later counterparts like Daniel Barenboim and virtually all Wagnerites have continued to do.

After seeing the play, Gottfried Wagner put me in touch with Harvey Sachs, the musicologist and author of *Toscanini, Musician of Conscience*, whose partner, pianist Eve Wolf, was the creator of *Maestro* as part of a series on other historical figures and works such as Tchaikovsky, Mary Shelley and van Gogh. Sachs' biography is the gold standard for appreciation of the legendary maestro in relation to

Hitler and Nazism, but on the basis of my correspondence with him—we've yet to meet—not even Sachs has an answer to the conundrum of why Toscanini never took issue, at least that we knew of, with Wagner's antisemitism. So absolute, apparently, was this distinction between Wagner the antisemite and his art, that it never figured into decisions about where, when and what to conduct. The troubles that emerged between Toscanini and Bayreuth, Germany, Italy, Europe and antisemitism were about Nazism and fascism, but ignoring Wagner's role as a leading instigator of it all.

*Maestro* summons us to appreciate a level of heroism glaringly missing from the worlds of classical music and opera today. Toscanini was denounced and beaten bloody by fascists, had his passport revoked by Mussolini, and emigrated from the Europe that had so revered him. He called out Furtwängler, Richard Strauss and his own mistress (Mainardi) for being collaborationist. There is no Toscanini equivalent today, neither musically, ethically nor morally. Figures like Leonard Bernstein and Daniel Barenboim come to mind, but for outspoken clarity of moral conscience, raw courage, and personal sacrifice, Toscanini was all too singular. Those who do not learn the lessons of the past are condemned to repeat them, we say, and nowhere is this yet again proving to be more true than among artists and audiences, who are generically and continually revealing themselves to be just as timid and reticent as their forbears. As Toscanini might have put it, Shame on all of us!

Two editors have been helpful in bringing together this collection. The first, Richard Howe, is a musician and scholar of classical music who has recently completed translations and editing for books on Bach and the LaSalle Quartet. He has also worked for many years on an in-depth history of the city planning of Manhattan. Richard and I were mutual friends of Bill Hoffman and we've all been through various mills of life together.

The other editor is Adam J. Sacks, PhD in History, who has done groundbreaking work on Mahler, Bernstein and the Doctors Chorus in Berlin between the wars and regarding the little-known effort to bring Bach into the synagogues. Adam has worked with Gottfried Wagner and was recommended to me by Gottfried.

As my partner Arnie Kantrowitz observes, I tend to be a pessimist. Like my father, a great admirer of the dark humor of H.L. Mencken (cited by Doris Grumbach for his antisemitism), I can be cynical. I follow in my dad's footsteps of seeing history as an endless cycle of warfare, of despoliation, plunder, pillaging, marauding and victimization. Both Richard and Adam are more sanguine than me about Wagner and the future. Neither is naive nor in denial about the seriousness of Wagner's antisemitism, but both are more humble about unknowable and unforeseeable developments. They are likewise more open than me to the possibilities of the inchoate and inexpressible. In this they are most certainly admirable. I do want to embrace a humility that allows for the future to follow its own course, beyond my understanding and intuition. As I write this, the unconscious jukebox selects an unsubtle and possibly sarcastic accompaniment: recently deceased Doris Day singing "Que sera, sera, whatever will be will be, the future's not ours to see, Que sera, sera," from the 1956 Alfred Hitchcock film, *The Man Who Knew Too Much*. Like the Doris Day character, I'm part of a plot, the sprawl and advancement of which I may have only the faintest inkling. Or none at all.

"Never Look Away" is one of history's—and life's—more important lessons. Not coincidentally, it is also the title of a remarkable 2018 film from Germany by Florian Henckel von Donnersmarck, who directed the Academy award winning film (for Best Foreign Film in 2006)), *The Lives of Others*. Both films are about life and death under totalitarianism, from the Nazi period through the cold war era in Germany. *Never Look Away* tells the apparently true story of one of Germany's most discussed painters, Gerhard Richter, who struggled mightily for self-expression against the forces of fascism, conscience and personal demons. In real life, as in the film, the notoriously reticent and cryptic Richter has had little to say regarding his experience and subject matter.

The film's biographical story revolves around the Nazi persecution and "extermination" of the mentally ill. (I always find it disturbing when this term is used without quotes, as it so often is, to describe Nazi mass murder.) Richter's aunt was schizophrenic. After being forcibly incarcerated, she was sterilized and eventually "exterminated" by the Nazis. The chief perpetrator is a high-ranking Nazi physician, eventually identified in the film as the real-life Carl Seeband, who manages not only to evade war crimes prosecution but is able to manipulate his way into the higher ranks of medicine, gynecology and medical research and policy under the East Germans during the ensuing cold war period.

In a further twist, the Nazi gynecologist turns out to be the father of the artist's girlfriend. The girl becomes pregnant and her father, still practicing the Nazi eugenics that was so inspired by the American eugenics movement, deems the artist genetically inferior. Falsifying a claim that she has a congenital gynecological deformity in order to maintain his allegiance to the eugenics ideology of Nazism, he performs an abortion on his own daughter, murdering what would have been her and Richter's child.

"The Nazi gynecologist" is also what I've called "Hans Kahlzwerg," the antihero of my chapter, "Rachel Teufelsdreck Carves Her Name in the Cathedral of Ulm" in my *Confessions of a Jewish Wagnerite*. In real life, "Hans Kahltzwerg" was based on Dr. Ralph M. Wynn, head of the Department of Obstetrics and Gynecology at the University of Illinois School of Medicine in the early 1970's. There he spearheaded ground-breaking and widely acclaimed research in placentology and uterine physiology. He became a leading figure in American Obstetrics, notable for his editing of and contributions to leading textbooks and many publications. He was a likewise skilled and admired teacher.

Not unlike the Nazi gynecologist of *Never Look Away*, Wynn could be politically correct and seem genuinely empathic, as in a filmed interview with an infertile black patient made for the medical students. But on closer scrutiny there were darker issues. Not unlike the Nazi gynecologist of *Never Look Away*, Wynn's marital and family relations were peculiar. Married, bisexual and closeted, his wife was subservient and childless for presumed infertility. Neither I nor Dr. Jack, both of us triangularly involved with him, intimately as well as professionally, ever got very far in trying to solve the riddle of the childlessness of the Wynns. If his wife were infertile, as was alleged by Wynn, why not adopt? We thought it was endlessly amusing that Wynn's sardonic explanation was that he hated children. But we also thought it strange that he would do a gynecological procedure on his own wife, the nature of which was unclear.

In *Never Look Away*, the Nazi turned Stasi gynecologist performs an abortion on his own daughter in his forsworn, surpassing and ongoing fealty to eugenics. To what extent was Ralph Wynn subservient to these principles? That's a question that became so pressing in the wake of his increasingly manifest racism and antisemitism that even with all our youthful (we were 20), denial, naivete and fecklessness, we began to acknowledge it to each other. As related in my *Confessions*, there was more and worse. We realized we had to extricate ourselves from his malevolent influence, and we did. Though I would occasionally see him at a distance at the Met Opera, we lost track of him.

A number of Wynn's colleagues were Jewish and he seemed to get on well enough with them, even if there were some exceptions, such as Jewish Dr. Panigel in France, who Wynn kept describing, ostensibly with that sardonic humor, as "dirty." In private as well as in public, Wynn often made appropriate, even sensitive observations about Jews, women and sometimes even about racially-designated others. Via our privileged access to such a high ranking academic and scholar as well as at a personal level of joking, having fun and our shared passion for opera, Dr. Jack and I felt confidence in appreciating him to be not only a person of genius and entrée to medicine, but as well our good friend.

At first, we were in such denial that we appreciated as self-satirical, as self-consciously over the top, what we might otherwise have more quickly and easily identified as his prejudices. Over time, however, in circumstances where there seemed little or no risk for him, as with us, his racism, antisemitism and sexism became evermore outspoken, to the extent of his using explicitly racist and sexist slurs and epithets.

During that time of my Wagnerism at its peak, Wynn would play the devil's advocate about Wagner, tempering my pathologically outsized Wagnerism by alerting me to this excess of alliteration or that grotesquerie of double entendre. "*Heraus aus der scheide zu mir,*" sings Siegmund as he pulls the sword from the vagina/tree. That nugget conveys a sense of how sharply brilliant Wynn could be and why our friendship with him could seem so precious. Other nuggets were more ominous, as when his hatred for his wife's cat would erupt. With his strictly obedient wife ordered to remain in her room during our visits with him, her cat was left to roam the house. What he hated most about cats, he said, was their tendency to pursue those who liked them least.

That Wagner was a fierce antisemite was known and a given, not something Wynn seemed in denial or defensive about. And "Dr.

Wynn"—as I called him, rather than Ralph, even in bed—was an American who seemed clear and affirming of America's place in WW 2. As in *Never Look Away*, however, lurking underneath that surface of what otherwise appeared to be mainstream political correctness, professionalism and geniality of demeanor, were toxic viewpoints that would eventually emerge like dead bodies.

With Hans Kahltzwerg, as with the Nazi gynecologist of *Never Look Away*, if Nazism failed to achieve full Aryanization, that didn't mean that those visions and objectives were or should be abandoned in the wake of defeats of World War 2. Nor did it matter within which ideology such totalitarianism would be sanctioned. It just meant that they needed to be reconfigured for new times and places, with renewed commitment and perseverance. Does anyone still believe there is any real difference between the autocracies of far-left communist nations like North Korea and those of the far right like Nazism? It would be fascinating now to know what Wynn's opinions were regarding the Chinese limitations on how many children families could have. Meanwhile, Wynn's support of abortion as a legal option had an ideological underpinning few would ever have suspected.

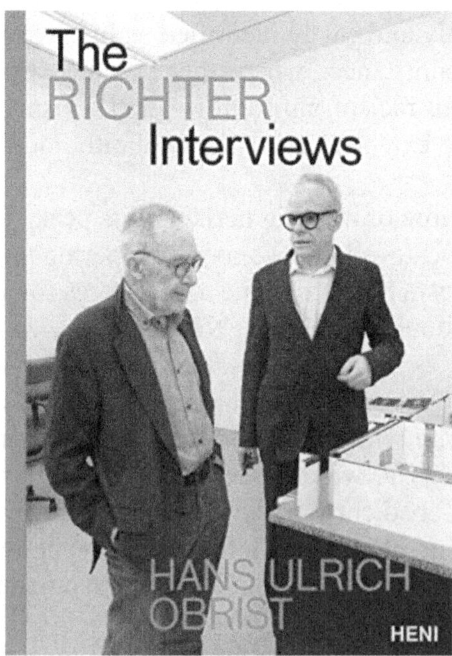


Figure 101 - The Richter Interviews, Hans Ulrich Obrist, Amazon.com

In *Never Look Away*, the protagonist, "Kurt Barnert" (based on Richter and played by Tom Schilling) is struggling to find ways to express what was throbbingly and incessantly at the threshold of his consciousness. He sought the artistic means to express the most traumatic and determining experiences of his own life, especially the persecution and murder of his aunt, and thereby to reflect on his surroundings and life events. With neither comparable artistic skills nor success, I have felt impelled to try to put together a narrative that can seem like Richter's blurred faces. No other recent work conveys so strongly as this film the challenges and imperative of telling one's own story, especially one intertwined with repressed trauma. Richter hadn't found a way to identify the perpetrators of what happened to him and his family under fascism. Comparably, I've struggled to give voice to my own experience with antisemitism, racism, Nazism and their perpetrators and apologists.

The belief in self-realization via artistic expression is not always laudable. It's sobering to keep in mind that such was also the struggle of Wagner. His muse was antisemitism, the artistic expression of which may have culminated in some of history's greatest art, but also in one of history's most extreme movements of minority prejudice and violence. The same whore, art, that served Wagner has served Gerhard Richter and me.

This imperative of telling one's own story is perhaps the most common cause of art. I've come as close as I can to telling that story, to carving my initials onto the walls of musical cultural posterity. On the surface of that metaphorical wall, as in the Cathedral of Ulm literally, my carving of "R.T. Loves H.K" ("Rachel Teufelsdreck Loves Hans Kahltzwerg") that is the *denouement* of my "love affair" with the Nazi gynecologist in *Confessions of a Jewish Wagnerite*, may seem indistinguishable from thousands of similar carvings and scribblings. But like them, it partakes of greater and never-ending narratives.

It's futile to keep trying to change Wagner or Wagnerites, just as it's futile to keep trying to change my brother, sister, Donald Trump or any other persons, or to try to permanently vanquish antisemitism, racism, sexism and fascism. What I can do is what I've tried to do—fight the worthy fight and offer a modicum of input to the discourse on Wagner, Jews and culture; and in doing so to tell my own story. What I've learned is not to push beyond reasonable measure to win arguments and settle scores so much as to reconfigure my expectations.

I began my journey like Hermann Levi, Klingsor and Parsifal, doing everything I could to belong in the realms of Richard Wagner and the knights of the Grail, of *Heilige Kunst*. I strove to be an authentic Wagnerite, to demonstrate my loyalty to Wagner and the poisoned realms within which I had become so enchanted. I rationalized Wagner's antisemitism. Unconscious strategies of adaptation and reconciliation under a spell of opiated arts promised transcendence, acceptance and assimilation. This sacrifice of my soul turned out to be nonreciprocal and worthless. It was a pact with the devil, a sale of shadow and soul for the promise of rewards that never were to be.

This journey has taken me far, but steering clear of that place of envy, hate, and bitterness that Wagner personified in Klingsor. Rather, this journey has taken me to an acceptance of the irreconcilability of my love for Wagner with his hatred for me; to a place where I no longer seek what is never to be; to that place where I no longer seek to be who I am not and to make others who they are not; to a place where I no longer seek to be loved or appreciated for who I am not or who I could or should be, or to love others for who they could or should be or who I might wish them to be but who they are not; from a place of forced and false "self-transcendence" to a place of genuine self-possession; from an artificial self to an authentic self; from a place I've come to realize I can never call home, that is actually a place of self-destruction, to a place I can legitimately and honestly, if not always safely, call home. Whatever its byways and moments of looking away and back, the direction of my own journey to the future is now forward.

Figure 102 - Bust of Richard Wagner (above), Hitler's favorite composer, Bayreuth Festival Park, by Arno Breker, 1939, Wikimedia Commons

Figure 103 - Bust of Adolf Hitler (above), by Arno Breker, Hitler's favorite artist, 1938, Wikipedia, Wikimedia Commons

# Wagner's Body: Pandemic Wagnerology with Marc A. Weiner, Author of Richard Wagner and the Anti-Semitic Imagination

– *Medium*, 5/31/2020

Figure 104 - Marc A. Weiner, Professor Emeritus, Germanic Studies, Indiana University Bloomington

books by Marc A. Weiner:

*Arthur Schnitzler and the Crisis of Musical Culture*
*Undertones of Insurrection*
*Richard Wagner and the Anti-Semitic Imagination*
—book cover illustrations from Amazon.com

## Homosexuality, Music and Undertones of Insurrection

On completing a draft of my book, *On The Future of Wagnerism,* I reached out to two figures of renown in musicology for feedback and in efforts to secure advance endorsements.

The first was Richard Taruskin, the eminent author and scholar and beacon of conscience and ethics in music. Taruskin had written affirmingly of my work in the past ("Thank God for Larry Mass!," he commented in response to my *Huffington Post* piece, "Beckmesser, Kissinger and the *Klinghoffer* Controversy"). "The appearance of this perceptive, courageous book will hearten those who believe that high art, and discourse about it, will either reconnect with human concerns or wither away," read his blurb for my *Confessions of a Jewish Wagnerite.*

The second of these esteemed figures was Germanist Marc A. Weiner, author of *Richard Wagner and the Anti-Semitic Imagination,* a book published a quarter century ago that remains on the cutting edge of Wagner discourses. Having met during the period of his book's publication, we've remained collegial and friendly.

In neither case was the feedback very affirming. Richard felt my work had "coarsened" over time, marred by what seemed to him *ad hominem* attacks, such as my commentary on Joseph Horowitz, whom I've characterized as a Wagner apologist and codependent. Also discernible was a widely shared fatigue about the ongoing pursuit of Wagner for his antisemitism; a sense that the world now understands and enjoins the reality of Wagner's antisemitism to nearing the limits of what can be reasonably expected. Here was a champion of moral consciousness with regard to antisemitism in music who could also be a bellwether of mainstream sensitivities and reactivities. Richard was of course right in essence and broad perspective, and I remain profoundly grateful for the time he took to consider my efforts and for his insights. My limited interaction with him has been among my work's greatest rewards.

Marc likewise demurred, discomfited, as in some of our past exchanges, at my intimation that Wagnerism among Jews is inevitably to some degree psychopathological. But in this case, he clarified, the issue for him was that my book's narratives on Wagner, AIDS, addiction, my family and being gay seemed too disconnected from one another. Though these are misgivings I myself can share, I've found no way to eliminate or relegate any of these major components of the narrative of my life, work and viewpoints.

In the course of our exchanges about the manuscript, differences emerged in sharper focus.

With Richard, as he invited me to address him, there was another issue in the background. Over time he has progressively updated me on state-of-the-art thinking about Tchaikovsky ("Chaik"). Though I had been admittedly out of the loop of these discourses, I tried to articulate my stirrings of discomfort around what can seem a kind of abandonment of our earlier sense of the composer as a gay man who doubtless suffered as such in times and places of pervasive ignorance, suppression and oppression of homosexuality.

Yes, I'd had an essentialist orientation, hoping in fact to put together a collection of my pieces on homosexuality and music. That book never happened, in part because the subject did indeed prove too sprawling and my essentialist framework too delimiting. One of the questions at its heart was whether it's legitimate to call Tchaikovsky "a gay composer." "Tchaikovsky was a Russian composer," music critic Dale Harris had riposted to this challenge decades ago. Most would agree with him, including Robert Hilferty, the deceased gay and ACT UP activist, savvy music writer and film documentarian (*Stop The Church, Milton Babbitt: Portrait of a Serial Composer*).

Though we now know much more about the real gay life and times of Tchaikovsky and a lot more about his final days, thanks to a landmark study of the composer by Alexander Poznansky — *Tchaikovsky: Quest For the Inner Man*, vetted by Richard and others, rewriting the old "homosexual tragedy" image of Tchaikovsky can seem to veer in the opposite direction of appreciating the composer as an everyman at the expense of a more balanced appreciation of his being gay. Rather than being like his contemporary Oscar Wilde in bearing the deepest scars for being gay, Tchaikovsky was perhaps more like Walt Whitman, I suggested — someone whose gayness was discernibly more affirmed and affirming than we've granted in the life he actually lived and the art he created, notwithstanding his unquestionably darker outlook on life, love and himself, and who nonetheless struggled, like most gay people in recorded history, with opprobrium, secrecy, mendacity and social and legal risk.

What can still feel uncomfortable to me has to do with the new normal for important historical figures who we now know to have been gay. After protracted and ongoing struggles to bring and keep figures like Whitman and Tchaikovsky out of the closet, the mainstream public has made its position clear, often with academic collusion. It will now allow for the updated information but not "dwell" there. In this, it can feel redolent of the public's acknowledgment of Wagner's antisemitism.

While fair enough in theory, what this usually means in reality is that beyond acknowledgment, that figure's homosexuality is still largely ignored, not so unlike the way mainstream appreciations of Wagner continue to ignore Wagner's acknowledged antisemitism. Just as Tchaikovsky remains for the mainstream public in Russia, here, and everywhere else a Russian composer, period, Whitman remains, here in America and everywhere else, an American poet, period. Whoever or whatever else they were or however their gayness may have influenced their lives and work is still relatively easily relegated. In the absence of a major scandal such as that which engulfed Oscar Wilde, this important if admittedly not all-defining dimension of a leading artist's life, times and work will continue to be circumnavigated by mainstreams.

Clearly, it can be a fine point. We gay people used to say that one day being gay will be no more notable than being left-handed or brunette. Careful what you wish for, right? Meanwhile, that middle ground where all important considerations are in equipoise doesn't feel in place yet. With Tchaikovsky, for example, when gay protests over Putin's anti-gay onslaught took place at the Metropolitan Opera on the eve of its 2013 season opening-night production of *Eugene Onegin*, there was virtually no discussion — neither backstage during the Met intermission feature broadcast or otherwise in the news coverage of the protests — of Tchaikovsky having been a gay man who, today as in the past, might be menaced as such. These concerns, expressed in an essay for *Huffington Post* (https://www.huffpost.com/entry/boo-to-the-metropolitan-opera_b_4116080), are among the opening contents of *On The Future of Wagnerism.*

Richard neither rejects nor belittles legitimate concerns about homophobia in Russia nor antisemitism anywhere, subjects on which he's a world-class authority. Nor does he in any measure generically devalue minority perspectives. Quite the contrary. As with Wagner's antisemitism, however, he seemed to feel that newer historical narratives had already said much of what there was to say for now. In the wake of Poznansky's book, we can't go back to the older, ill-informed, romanticized perspective of imagining that Tchaikovsky's life and work were always subtextually about his being gay and suffering as such, any more than we can continue to assume that our postwar knowledge of Wagner's antisemitsm, Hitler and Nazism makes for easy cause-and-effect generalizations. As a leading academic, scholar and musicological sage, Richard is understandably wary of essentializing anyone or anything, even at the risk of challenging minority assumptions that can veer into becoming prerogatives.

It's through Richard Taruskin's exposures of antisemitism in the lives, milieus and works of Russian composers that many of us have a broader sense of the depth and sweep of antisemitism throughout the history of western music. It's a panorama that does provide a context and counterweight to what can seem the special case of Wagner. When musicologists and critics point out that antisemitism was pervasive in the worlds of many composers, as they still do reflexively in discussions of Wagner, it's now easier to appreciate that they aren't just being apologists. What they are saying is in fact so true that Jewish naïfs like me keep finding ourselves veering from one composer to another, including Tchaikovsky, in the wake of the latest revelations of antisemitism in their letters, lives and imaginations. In my defenses of Tchaikovsky as a gay man, I have found myself in that same place of "apologism." While Wagner's antisemitism retains its status as more serious and consequential than that of the others, it is, as Richard Taruskin has helped us appreciate, evermore challenging to see the case of Wagner as unique.

∇

Though Marc and I have been in agreement about the depth and pervasiveness of antisemitism in Wagner's works and though we've remained friendly over the years, we have always been at an impasse over differences in how we've personally regarded and processed what I refer to as our "adult knowledge" of Wagner. Whereas Marc, like the mentor we shared, Robert Gutman, author of *Wagner: The Man, His Mind, and His Music,* has chosen to make peace with his own love of Wagner's art, I've moved in the opposite direction in what I call my detoxification from Wagner.

Having done the very difficult and challenging work of exposing Wagner's antisemitism in all its enormity, Marc has paid his Wagner dues and has done so probably more pointedly and effectively than any other scholar or writer. Sitting awkwardly alongside this Olympian achievement, it can seem to an apostate Wagnerite like me, Marc does not deny his abiding admiration and enjoyment of Wagner, something that became hard-wired in him at an impressionable age. By contrast, and though I fell deeply in love with Wagner in my youth, and though I can still appreciate and even enjoy Wagner, Wagnerism is no longer *Heimat* for me, unless you would argue, as you might, that my doing all this work of telling of my experience and feelings is my own *metier* of ongoing attachment to the composer and his art.

In the sometimes harsh light of self-reflection, in fact, it's possible to see both Marc and myself as jilted lovers, aggrieved spouses, or battered wives, one of whom (Marc) is refusing to recognize Wagner's demand for divorce, and the other (me), drawing that process out. Within us both in this analogy, the flame of hope still burns that like Fricka, we will somehow prevail in setting things right.

*"As I've said, throughout all of this,"* Marc acknowledged, *"I never wavered in my love of Wagner's music dramas, my growing conviction of the extent of the degree to which his antisemitism informs them notwithstanding. I can understand intellectually that someone may feel it's too uncomfortable to indulge in the enjoyment of a work that so clearly evinces the traces of its creator's nefarious antipathies and hatred. I choose to live with that contradiction, simply because I find the works so enthralling, endlessly fascinating and moving, and so worthy of indulging in their undeniable beauty and ingenious singularity."*

While I do think our differences are in real measure irreconcilable, I'm ever-less inclined towards the finalities of divorce than leaving the future open to possibility and chance, which it seems to me is how the future unfolds in any event.

Today, when I see Wagner operas, it's primarily for the alternative experience of seeing them in the cinema, with its often bland supertitle translations, scanning its audience (at 74, I'm still among the youngest there), and surrendering to the superficiality of the intermission features which, so far as I can tell, have yet to betray a single moment of controversy. I've now seen 9 of the10 standard repertory Wagner operas in televised or cinematic renderings and was set to see the last of these — Wagner's first repertory success, *The Flying Dutchman,* in this past season's new production — when the Covid-19 pandemic public-space closings set in. Yes, I was looking forward to seeing and hearing the vocally-endowed Bryn Terfel in the title role but had planned to attend, even after learning of his cancellation, for this alternative experience of Wagner at the cinema and confessedly as well to once again see and hear a beloved favorite opera.

Whatever my explanations or rationalizations for my own ongoing involvement with Wagner, I must continue to revisit the likelihood that critical studies of Wagner, such as that by Marc and including tomes like mine, are manifestations of Wagnerism — ours and the world's. I think Wagner and Bayreuth would agree. However heated these controversies around antisemitism have been and can become, they have served the composer, and with him Bayreuth and the Wagner family, impressively for 170 years (since the publication in 1850 of Wagner's infamous screed, *Judaism in Music*). Put another way, would our books and countless others have been written in the absence of Wagner's antisemitism? Would the works themselves have been created?

For Marc, it felt neither dystonic nor otherwise troubled for him to revisit Bayreuth. While I wouldn't rule out for myself the possibility of a trip back there or anywhere else in Germany, it's something that would feel more dystonic to me now. Being greeted by the Nazi-era Arno Breker bust of Wagner that still serves to welcome "pilgrims" to the Festival is not something I want to expose myself to again. When Marc was there in 2019, he saw the exhibit on Wagner and the Jews that Gottfried Wagner had dismissed as "a whitewash." Marc seemed pleased with the progress the exhibit seemed to him to represent and comforted by the role "we" may have played in growing consciousness and accountability.

In exchanges that began in early March of 2020 with wishes for safety during the advancing pandemic of Covid-19 (I had sent around Bill Gates's 2016 Ted Talk on Pandemic Preparedness to everybody I knew) and which moved into various aspects of what I'm calling Wagnerology, Marc and I found ourselves in a free-ranging discourse on the ways and byways of Wagnerism and pondering future directions.

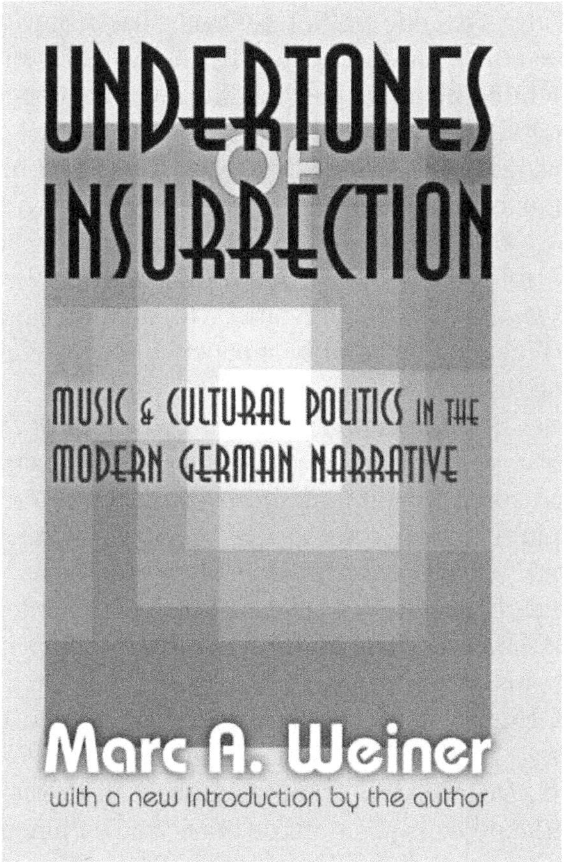


Figure 105 - Undertones of Insurrection: Music and Cultural Politics in the Modern German Narrative (Amazon.com)

Recognized and criticized by some leading Wagner scholars and critics (e.g., Thomas Grey, Joseph Horowitz), *Richard Wagner and the Anti-Semitic Imagination* continues to be evaded in Wagner and opera circles. In what was probably the most widely read commentary on Marc and his book, "The Specter of Hitler in Wagner" in the *New York Times* by Joseph Horowitz, Marc is given short shrift as someone who perceives antisemitism in every nook and cranny. One would have little idea from this critique that Marc is a Germanist of high rank and esteem. Until his retirement last year, Professor Emeritus Weiner led one of the country's leading departments of Germanic Studies at Indiana University at Bloomington, a premiere musical education institution. Nor would you have any idea that he is the author of other scholarly texts that complement his extensive research on Wagner.

Instead of being given due credit for what he has achieved, Wagnerite critics can seem in a conspiracy to deny him what by any reasonable measure should be his distinguished, however challenging, place in today's discourses on Wagner.

My exchanges with Marc took place by email between early Spring and into the Summer of 2020. They proceeded with my reading of his book, *Undertones of Insurrection* (abbreviated here as *Undertones*), followed by a rereading of *Richard Wagner and The Anti-Semitic Imagination* (abbreviated *RW*) and his paper in defense of Gottfried Wagner, and an offbeat paper he did on Wagner's music called "Primal Sounds."

*Undertones of Insurrection: Musical and Cultural Politics in the Modern German Narrative* was originally published in 1993, preceding and complementing *Richard Wagner and the Anti-Semitic Imagination* in 1995. It looks at key works of writers who wrote notably about musical-cultural sensibility from the *fin-de-siecle* period to the early post-WW2 years. The principal writers and works discussed are Thomas Mann and his novella *Death in Venice*, Franz Werfel and his novel, *Verdi*, Herman Hesse and his novel, *Steppenwolf*, Hugo von Hofmannsthal and his libretto for *Die Frau Ohne Schatten*, Arthur Schnitzler and his novella, *Rhapsody*, and Mann's novel, *Dr. Faustus*. Throughout these discussions, reference is made to influential disquisitions on music and culture dominated by the leading German traditionalist composer Hans Pfitzner.

What Marc deconstructs are the controversies and crises of culture that were percolating beneath the surfaces of these works, which their audiences and readerships would have sensed. In approach it's parallel to the achievement of his *RW*, which is more directly about what audiences would have perceived in Wagner and his music dramas. Erudite and of real value in conveying *zeitgeist*, *Undertones* evinces a problem Thomas Grey observes in his challenging critique of *RW* in the *Cambridge Opera Journal*: the relative absence of actually demonstrating with harder evidence audience and readership appreciation of these undertones. As in *RW*, the reader is left with little tangible certainty that audiences gleaned what Marc assumes they did or most likely did or may have.

In *RW*, this problem is emerges more clearly. Here it is being claimed that audiences of the day would most likely have recognized Wagner's myriad, pervasive antisemitic codings and dog whistles from their own deep-seated, widely shared and commonplace touchstones of this prejudice. Marc is persuasive in making a case for this and for the taciturnity enshrouding it — no need to more literally spell out what we all know and recognize — in *Undertones* as well as in *RW*.

Critics, meanwhile, have seized on this as absence of proof — the gold standard of Wagnerism defenses— of Wagner's antisemitism and antisemitic intent. Just as nowhere does Wagner, who had Jews in his entourage, spell out that Alberich, Mime, the Nibelungs, Beckmesser, Kundry, Klingsor and Hagen are Jews, neither in his music dramas, nor even in his many antisemitic writings, likewise nowhere is there direct proof that Wagner's audiences were reacting and interacting with these works from their own common-knowledge base and feelings of prejudice. Apart from Mahler's oft-cited recognition of himself in Mime in a letter he wrote to Nathalie Bauer-Lechner, quoted by Marc in *RW*, there seems little in the way of reviews, news items and letters saying clearly that this was obviously all about the Jews and that everybody knew it.

Adding fuel to this fire of Wagner's intentions around antisemitism are other phenomena that can smoke efforts to have more certain perspective and which aren't subjects Marc addresses. The *Nibelungenlied* is a mythological narrative believed to have been written around 1200 and known to have been a source of Wagner's *Ring* cycle. Easy as it now seems to read the *Nibelungs* as Jews in Wagner's works, it cannot be discounted that these Germanic and Norse sagas were not making such connections, so far as we know, even though antisemitism was pervasive as well in medieval Europe.

Another confounder can be the vastly popular *Lord of the Rings* by British philologist J.R.R. Tolkien. Despite the coincidence of Wagner's *Ring* cycle having preceded his work and Tolkien's awareness of it, there seems a consensus that Tolkien's creation was little influenced by Wagner, and Tolkien's saga itself has no imputation of his villains as Jews. On the contrary, Tolkien was an RAF hero whose political and social views could not have been more different from Wagner's.

*Undertones* commences with a discussion of *Death in Venice*, published on the eve of the Great War in 1912. Mann's novella is seen as revealing many of the tensions in art and music that were reflective of greater political and cultural ferment within Germany and its encroaching European neighbors. Bringing these issues to a low boil were the proclamations of Pfitzner on the sanctity of German music and culture, epitomized by the subject and reception of his opera, *Palestrina*, which had its premiere in Munich in 1917. As Marc deconstructs it, the hubbub within intellectual circles from Mann, Busoni, Mahler, Hesse, Schnitzler and others was an aura surrounding Mann's tale of Gustav von Aschenbach, a light beckoning the moths of counter-cultural dissent.

While Marc does capture that multi-faceted moment of cultural change in his analyses of the writers and writings of time and place, it was fascinating to me to contrast this portrait with my own experience of Mann and his novella. In my struggles to come out as gay, *Death in Venice* was a touchstone, as it was for many gay men. However sad Aschenbach's demise along the older narratives of homosexual tragedy, and however reverberant for what was happening in German literary and musical life, here was an "overt" story an "overt" homosexual (as it used to be said — e.g., by leading homophobic psychoanalyst Charles Socarides, author of *The Overt Homosexual*) at a time when such overtness of this subject matter was still overtly taboo.

Where Marc found himself awash in the *zeitgeist* of the fictional composite Aschenbach as a leading German writer modeled partly on Mahler (who wasn't gay), gay men then and ever since have read the novella as a Rosetta stone of closeted gay life and taboos of desire — Mann's as well as our own. The exchange on this with Marc was rich. Just as Marc's work helped me appreciate Mann's place in the cultural controversies of the day, especially as a kind of riposte to Pfitzner, Marc was able to better appreciate the gay perspective, culminating in his delight on my sending him an essay, "The Real Tadzio of Thomas Mann" by Gilbert Adair, on the real-life Polish family of the boy that Tadzio, Aschenbach's love interest, was based on.

Leading music critics may have implicitly dismissed Marc's work as marginal rather than as more serious and challenging scholarship. But that hasn't stopped them from utilizing this work to inform their own. A case in point is an exchange that took place between Marc and *New Yorker* music critic Alex Ross regarding the question of whether German audiences of the day would have recognized Mann's allusions to the implied criticism of Pfitzner in *Dr. Faustus*, or Schnitzler's covert references to Mahler via his character Georg von

Wergenthin's antisemitic reflections in Schnitzler's play, *The Road Into the Open*.

Especially with regard to Schnitzler, Marc is reasonably certain that he, Marc, is the first to have made note of these undercurrents. In each of these cases, Marc had done the path-breaking work of discovery which Ross, to Marc's surprise and dismay, failed to credit him with in his writing in the *New Yorker*. Not only did Ross reference this material, according to Marc, but he quoted from it *verbatim*. When Marc registered his disappointment, Ross explained that reference to Marc was omitted editorially in the interest of keeping Ross's discussion from seeming too academic. Meanwhile, and though reference to Marc's work on Schnitzler is acknowledged in Ross's *Wagnerism*, Ross has not otherwise mentioned Marc or his *RW*.

Nor, for that matter and not surprisingly, has he mentioned my work. I know he has seen my *Confessions* because I personally handed him a copy following a talk he did on "The Wagner Vortex" in 2012. When I gave him the book he recoiled, saying he'd already seen it, thank you. But it's inscribed to you, I persisted. As I have with other Wagnerites not known to be Jewish, I inscribed it as follows: "For Alex Ross, Honorary Jewish Wagnerite."

Though he has likewise not mentioned me or my work in his pieces, I did have the experience of meeting one on one with Joe Horowitz, an exchange that was honest and challenging, even if we found ourselves on opposing ends of the spectrum of opinion about Wagner and antisemitism. With Ross, and as well with Horowitz and other Wagnerites, I feel like Larry Kramer, the loudmouth who is speaking his mind without much regard for decorum. I'm the elephant in the living room everyone wishes and pretends weren't there.

A case of inflated self-importance on my part, perhaps, but I can't help but think that the custodians of discourse on Wagner might be more interested in the personal experience and reflections of a Jewish Wagnerite, especially one solely identified in the literature as such. Unless, of course, they simply do not want to hear any more whining — or frankly anything more at all — on the subject of Wagner, Jews and antisemitism.

Despite the more incendiary findings of Marc's research and the implicit conclusions of his *RW*, our exchanges make clear that Marc is neither grudging nor pugilistic. Although he admitted that he felt what Ross did was "unfair," he retains his admiration of Ross for being an intelligent and fine writer, which no one could deny. Even after acknowledging disappointment about what happened, Marc delighted in Ross's essay, "Othello's Daughter," a link to which I sent him. A passionate Wagnerite, Marc reveled in this offbeat history of Wagner and Bayreuth and their planned casting of a person of color as one of the Valkyries in the world premiere of *Die Walküre*. Marc also appreciated Ross's contexting of W.E.B. Du Bois's 1903 work, *The Souls of Black Folks*, which references Wagner and *Lohengrin*.

As Horowitz shows in his book *Wagner Nights*, Wagner's vast influence could be felt in unexpected quarters, such as the early American women's movement and, as Ross shows, as well among persons of color seeking to create their own iconographies of art and society. When I told Marc of my take on Ross's piece — of it being an exemplar of "the exception to the rule" in being one of several needles in the haystack of Wagner's otherwise epochal racism and antisemitism, as captured most notably by Marc himself, he wrote me back:

*"Thank you very much for sending me this piece, which I found both informative and fascinating. I had heard of Du Bois's employment of* Lohengrin *in his* The Souls of Black Folk *from an article that my dissertation director, the Germanist Russell Berman, published when I was still the editor of* The German Quarterly *in the mid 1990s, but I had never even heard of Luranah Aldridge. Both she and her father Ira sound rather extraordinary, and I was simply astonished to learn of both Richard Wagner's and Cosima's praise of them — and I didn't even know that Cosima spoke (and allegedly could even write a rather stilted) English. So thank you very much for sending this to me. It demonstrates once again how fastidious, devoted, and thorough Alex Ross is in his research (not that he always documents it!), and as well, of course, how beautifully he writes."*

***Richard Wagner, The Body and Antisemitism***

***What Marc's critics want to say is that the whole business of finding antisemitism in Wagner is more overkill and misreading than intrinsic and illuminating. To such thinking, it's likely Marc's work***

***will continue to seem onerous. But in the wake of this work, it will be one thing to note similarities between Wagner's and other stock villains, but evermore challenging not to see them as Jews.***

Figure 106 - Richard Wagner and the Anti-Semitic Imagination

*"Again and again, Wagner's verbal and musical histrionics incorporate and exploit the icon of the Jew's damaged and different body. Beckmesser's lack of stability is a less explicit reference to the motivic tradition of the lame Jew than that found in the slithering, limping and clumsy Nibelungs, but it is equally evocative of the image lurking in the back of the cultural imagination in nineteenth-century Germany and was thus appropriate for Wagner's construction of a character so imbued with anti-Semitic stereotypes...Every Jewish stereotype in Wagner's works, as in his culture, is defined by his or her damaged body and by features deemed idiosyncratically different and inferior to those of the German...Germany's racial future, Wagner hoped, was on sure footing, and the image of that stability is grounded in a host of iconic traditions in his culture that identified*

*evil and difference in the bodies of those who could not march with the German.*"

— **from the conclusion of Chapter 4, "Feet: Club Foot, Heroic Foot,**" of *Richard Wagner and the Anti-Semitic Imagination*

*Richard Wagner and the Anti-Semitic Imagination* does not have a subtitle, but it could have adapted the title of its Introduction for that purpose: "Wagner and the Body." In fact, Marc's original working title of the book was "*Wagner's Body,*" which he changed to its published title at the editorial suggestion of University of Nebraska Press. The book was originally enlisted by Sander L. Gilman, the eminent American cultural and literary historian and prolific author known for his contributions to Jewish studies and the history of medicine. Gilman was likewise supportive of my *Confessions,* giving it an enthusiastic advance blurb.

What follows the Intro of *RW* is a veritable encyclopedia of corporeal imagery in Wagner, and the invariable relationships of that imagery to Wagner's racism and antisemitism, as Wagner expressed it most notably in his essays: "Opera and Drama," "Judaism in Music," "Art and Revolution," "The Artwork of the Future" and "Know Thyself."

Figure 107 - Richard Wagner and Judaism, caricature, from Floh, Vienna, 1879, from Richard Wagner and the Anti-Semitic Imagination by Marc A. Weiner

The book also features telling illustrations, although some of the most interesting of these are of Wagner himself. As expressed in this Introduction and as parodied in numerous satirical cartoons, one of which is featured on the book's cover, Wagner worried about the possibility of his being part Jewish. He had physical features, such as shortness of stature (5 feet, 5 inches) and a large head and nose that seemed more stereotypically Jewish than an Aryan ideal.

This is long-familiar material that *RW* takes note of but does not push. But the possibility of Wagner's own Jewishness has figured in some psychological interpretations of Wagner's antisemitism. In psychoanalytic theory, one of the defense mechanisms is introjection, which implies internalization of a dominating or sadistic role model. Via introjection, the victim becomes the perpetrator. However speculative, that Wagner introjected German antisemitism at least in part as a defense against appearing less than ideally German himself remains intriguing as a clue to Wagner's persona and imagination.

The book then proceeds with its chapters. "The Eyes of the *Volk*," which surveys Wagner's vocabulary of physical appearance and perception; "Voices," about vocal register and auditory traits, and which includes subheadings on "Mussorgsky's Nibelungs," "The Invention of the Heldentenor" and "The Voice of the Effeminate Jew"; "Smells," with subheadings "Smells in Wagner's Music," "Smells in Wagner's Sources" and "The Odor of the Orient"; "Feet: Clubfoot, Heroic Foot," with its discussion of "The Devil and the Jew"; and "Icons of Degeneration" on onanism and masturbation.

At some points, Marc's copious textual and musical examples and analyses, obviously on the mark for the bigger picture, can seem effortful or incomplete. The *Heldenteno*r, he observes, is a nearly baritonal timbre that contrasts as such with the characteristically high tessitura of villains and of the more traditional Italian and French tenor roles. Even those, like Alberich and Klingsor, but especially Beckmesser, who are basses or baritones, are often scored to sing unnaturally high for their range.

As he virtuosically demonstrates the ubiquity of this strategy of Wagner's for distinguishing villainy, Marc can seem less sure-footed in attributing Wagner's creation of the *Heldentenor* as intentionally or even primarily within this framework of higher versus lower tessitura. What he does not explore is the designation of "*Helden-*" as also being about the weight and size of the voice and its ability to cut through

Wagner's unprecedentedly formidable orchestral fabric, whether that voice is a tenor, bass, baritone, soprano or contralto.

Though the roles of Siegmund, Tannhäuser, Lohengrin, Walther, Tristan, Parsfial and Siegfried may lay more "naturally" and comfortably lower than the big tenor parts of the Italian and French repertoire, some of Wagner's *Heldentenor* music is indeed high, and in the case of Tannhäuser, Walther and Siegfried, punishingly so. Though it's here that Marc finds himself most vulnerable to the criticism of reading strategies and meanings into Wagner that are less than certain or consistent, he prevails in being nonetheless insightful. The *Heldentenor* is indeed a creation of Wagner and in its portrayal of manliness and Germanness is in notable contrast to the annoyingly shrill, whiney *oy-veying* of villains like Mime or the more stereotypically high-flying French and Italian tenor parts.

Although his subject of antisemitism in Wagner's texts and music has been the most controversial in all of Wagnerology, in his reluctance to engage in skirmishes around heated emotional and political perspectives and discourse, Marc stands in contrast to his colleague, Paul Lawrence Rose, author of *Wagner: Race and Revolution*. Marc is a dyed-in-the-wool academic who is personally humble and unflappably professional and scholarly. He hopes his work will be taken seriously but is not motivated to besmirch reputations or discredit individuals, no matter how critical their reactions or differing their viewpoints.

This steadfast refusal to speak ill of others extends to Richard and Cosima Wagner. Yes, he must agree that they were extreme racists and antisemites and that this was most regrettable. Yes, they were sometimes the "monsters" (my word, not Marc's) of our worst accusations of them as such, notwithstanding Joseph Horowitz's sarcastic abjuring of this word for Wagner in his *WSJ* review of Simon Callow's satirical book, *Being Wagner*. But notwithstanding his own revelations, Marc has never lost his ability to appreciate the humanity Horowitz is so notably keyed into that's discernible not only in Wagner himself, but as well in Cosima.

A case in point was a reference he came across from Cosima Wagner's *Diaries* recounting the first time RW played the music of Wotan's Farewell. How he wished he could have been a fly on the wall to witness the expression on her face at that moment of first hearing this incomparably moving music, Marc mused. "Therein lies the difference between you and me," I snapped: "I can't imagine anyone I would less want to be in the presence of than Cosima Wagner!" No matter how many times or how many ploys you use to try to get Marc to reconcile his "adult knowledge" of Wagner's racism and antisemitism with his personal Wagnerism, he will not take the bait.

Like most of us in this discourse, Marc has a history of involvement with music, opera and Wagner. They include opera apprenticeships at the Bavarian State Opera, with stints of communal living and working with Wagner artists —e.g, James King. He has warm memories of many important German singers, like Theo Adam and Dietrich Fischer-Dieskau. He saw the latter in offbeat works, as the fabled king in Arlbert Reimann's *Lear* as well as in Hugo Wolf's *Der Corregidor*. He has great storehouses of Wagner and opera lore and an ability to appreciate the myriad nuances of differing interpretations of the same passages and songs. Did I know that Fischer-Dieskau owned a controlling percentage of shares in Deutsche Grammophon? I shared my own indelible memory of this incomparable artist's presence, live as Mandryka in *Arabella* in Munich, and posthumously, as captured in a Classic Arts Showcase video of *Die Schöne Müllerin*.

When I tried to discuss Fischer-Dieskau's commentary in a documentary on Max Lorenz, however, Marc's reticence reemerged. In the film, Fischer-Dieskau, a former *Hitlerjugend*, states his own — and Germany's — familiar position, paraphrased by me here, on the *Nazizeit*: We didn't know all that was happening and weren't endorsing of the extremes of Hitler, Nazism and antisemitism. Rather, we were German citizens and soldiers in the service of our country. In showing up and performing our duties as such, we were acting honorably. With Fischer-Dieskau, there turns out to have been another consideration. His younger brother, mentally retarded, was euthanized by the Nazis. Marc hadn't known this fact that was featured in a sympathetic *NYT* obituary by Daniel Lewis in 2012 on the legendary German baritone, and we were both touched to learn of it.

Marc did not share my opinion that, musically, Beckmesser, however formidably negative an antisemitic stereotpye, was a hopeless and irredeemable challenge. On the contrary, he felt that casting Hermann Prey did indeed lend the role a rare poignancy. I had to agree with him that Fischer-Dieskau might have done something notable with this part had he ever assayed it.

In the bigger picture of my exchanges with Marc, his characteristic reluctance to renounce or condemn was a recurrent *leitmotif*. Such was this penchant on Marc's part that one day I spelled it out. I know I'm asking you some questions, I said, you would rather not answer. In some cases it's because you don't have the answers. In others it's because you've not found it constructive to engage further. That's OK, I said, in the interest of not losing our otherwise productive connection. As people say to each other in addiction recovery, take what you like and leave the rest. Which is what Marc did, and often.

For example, in discussions of Bayreuth. Did it make him uncomfortable that the Wagner bust by the Nazi sculptor Breker — who did busts of other Wagner family members, including Cosima, Winifred and Wieland, as well as Hitler and other Nazi leaders — still welcomes visitors to the *Festspielhaus*? Our shared mentor Robert Gutman was invited to do a master class there. Was Marc ever invited to participate in any programmed events at Bayreuth? In that exhibit on Wagner, Bayreuth and the Jews that Marc affirmed and that was dismissed by Gottfried Wagner as a whitewash, was there any mention of Flossenbürg, the concentration camp near Bayreuth that Wieland Wagner was named by Hitler to be titular head of?

When it came to the running of Bayreuth today, Marc seemed to share some level of disappointment in Katharina Wagner, daughter of Wieland's brother Wolfgang, who became notorious for the over-the-topness of some of her productions, like a *Meistersinger* that lambasted the Nurnbergers of the final scene as a bunch of drunken Nazi louts. A better choice for directorship of the festival, Marc felt, would have been Nike Wagner, Wieland Wagner's daughter, whom he'd met, who showed some interest in Marc's work and who is otherwise known to be bright, accomplished and capable. Do you know if Nike has ever publicly discussed her father's directorship of Flossenburg, wherein 30,000 inmates were murdered, I asked?

With each of these inquiries, the reticence continued and per our tacit understanding, I backed off when the answer was vague or not there at all, though I would sometimes later return to these subjects. With regard to Bayreuth, for example, Marc noted that although his book was translated into German, a printing that had sold out, it was not in the book-gift store there at the Bayreuth Festival, where he has otherwise not been invited to lecture or participate on panels or consulted regarding exhibits.

Nor has he been welcomed by Wagner Societies. His only such foray was in Chicago, when his book was first published. He said the audience simply "did not buy" his findings of the depth, extent and intention of antisemitism in Wagner's texts and music. Like me, and like Gottfried Wagner, but in contrast to Hilan Warshaw (creator of the film documentary, *Wagner's Jews*), Marc was not approached to speak at the Wagner Society of New York. Though he has lectured widely among peers — scholars of German and musical culture — and on panels, his work remains controversial, unique in the literature on Wagner in challenging the old bottom-line boundary of antisemitism not being clearly discernible in Wagner's texts and music and therefore questionably present. In this, it's possible to see Marc's *RW* as one of the most important books ever written on Wagner.

That those Chicago Wagner Society Wagnerites "just didn't buy it" would certainly have rung true for me in the heyday of my own Wagnerism. We Wagnerites, non-Jews as well as Jews, were characteristically defensive on the issue of anyone going too far in trying to despoil our beloved Wagner around the taint of antisemitism or anything else. In our protective willingness to relegate the obvious, we were like Trumpers in defense of Trump.

But our criticism could be challenging. However true it may ring now that Wagner's villains are Jews, Wagner's tropes and stereotypes are also archetypes that have been exploited universally — throughout the history of art, literature, opera, theater and film — to convey evil and turpitude. Villains of every stripe have always evinced the traits Wagner imbues them with. For example, the "feminization of the Jew" Marc describes is what we in the gay community have always recognized as "faggification of the enemy." Gay villains are exactly like Jewish ones in being stereotyped as effete and unmanly, with high voices, stutters and stammers, and being otherwise depraved, immoral, criminal, weak, cowardly, sinful and evil.

So are critics of your work onto something, I asked Marc, in suggesting that you've cited "Jewishness" more than is warranted in what can otherwise be seen as Wagner's stock villains and situations? Is that what the Chicago Wagnerites who "just didn't buy it" were conveying?

*"I most certainly understand your point, and I don't at all disagree with you,"* Marc replied. *"I was simply trying to catalogue the degree to which the images Wagner imbued into his villains already had overtones of racism in various cultural iconographic traditions, especially in the Church since the Middle Ages, and in other beliefs that were widespread in Wagner's time, such as the belief that Jews smelled bad and walked poorly. But of course those are also stock features of a host of negative characters throughout the history of art, drama, music, and literature as well. So I hope that I'm not reading something into Wagner's works so much as reconstructing, through a kind of cultural archaeology, an horizon of expectations that may have obtained in Wagner's time."*

Clearly, Marc is vulnerable on this point. But in ignoring, rejecting or relegating Marc's findings of anti-Semitic acuity in Wagner's imagery, texts, characters and circumstances, Wagnerites want to go back to pretending that these things aren't there anymore significantly or differently than they are in other narratives. What Marc's critics want to say is that the whole business of finding antisemitism in Wagner is more overkill and misreading than intrinsic and illuminating. To such thinking, it's likely Marc's work will continue to seem onerous. But in the wake of this work, it will be one thing to note similarities between Wagner's and other stock villains, but evermore challenging not to see them as Jews.

Marc's reticence about Bayreuth and its politics past and present is mixed with precious insights — for example, with regard to Wieland Wagner. Wieland was one of opera's most gifted and celebrated directors. Known for his trademark minimalism and iconic images that captured panoramas of atmosphere and perspective, his artistic visions held the attention of the world of opera from the first postwar resumption of the Festival in 1951 until his death in 1966. One of those icons dominates the set of Act 2 of Wieland's production of *Die Meistersinger* at Bayreuth in 1956. For a non-German like me, the large circular blowup of elderberry blossoms appeared to be an effective evocation of springtime and its rites of love and creativity, a good overarching symbol of what seemed to me in those naive Wagnerite years to be the opera's principal themes.

Figure 108 - from Act 2 of Wieland Wagner's production of Die Meistersinger at Bayreuth, 1956

But in an example typical of Marc's work, the elderberry closeup is revealed to signify a lot more. Known to have its fullest flowering around the time of the opera, on the occasion of St. John's Day, in common German lore the aromatic elderberry bush is also known to ward off witches and other evil spirits. In Marc's *RW*, the context of this discussion is of the motivic use of smells and fragrances by Wagner. Within this discussion are other iconographic bodily images and functions which include a number of references to the conflation of Jews and blacks in German racist lore and demonology and specifically in Wagner. Wotan's reference to "black Alberich" has more context than garden-variety non-German internationalist Wagnerites like me would ever have appreciated.

Meanwhile, the importance of smells in Wagner — of aromas, fragrances and stenches, and in view of Wagner's insistence on every facet of an artwork being given its own premiere value, leads Marc to speculate that in a more modern age, Wagner might enthusiastically have availed himself of cutting-edge stagecraft and cinematic technologies to introduce smells into productions of his music dramas (remember smell-o-vision?) for key scenes like the perfumed gardens of *Parsifal* and the elderberry blooms in *Meistersinger*. While such a supposition might seem the height of blasphemy to the traditionalists who booed Wieland's *Meistersinger* and *Parsfial* for taking too many liberties with Wagner's explicit stage directions, it otherwise rings true for Wagner the colossus of the theory, practice and future of art, and for Marc's discernment of Wagner's meanings.

*"The spirits of the elder (who resemble the magical dwarves found under the tree because they love its scent) move out of German legends and into the idiosyncratic, personal and anti-Semitic motivic vocabulary of* Die Meistersinger*...one of the most anti-Semitic dramas ever to have appeared on stage."*

When I tried to probe further about Wieland Wagner, Marc was evasive. I asked if the casting of Grace Bumbry as "*Die Schwarze Venus*," which 60's generation Wagnerites like me had wishfully assured ourselves was primarily about breaking racial casting barriers at Bayreuth, Marc did not reply. Neither Richard Wagner's nor Wieland Wagner's designation but rather a catchy newspaper callout, "*Die Schwarze Venus*" was apparently a rabbit hole Marc did not see as promising to explore. And in fact, when I myself saw this production of *Tannhäuser* at Bayreuth in 1966, the year of Wieland's death from lung cancer, Venus was sung by his mistress, soprano Anja Silja, who also sang one of the *Blumenmädchen* in that season's *Parsifal*. Meanwhile, the thought lingers, all the more so now in view of Marc's findings, that casting Bumbry in this part was reverberant of the folkloric associations conflating blacks with Jews, and race with sorcery.

Marc's textual and musical analyses can seem arcane in their baring of subtexts we today would have little conscious awareness of. In his last chapter, "Icon's of Degneration," Marc devotes considerable attention to deconstructing the character of Hagen, the half-Nibelung (half-Jew), as afflicted with a sickness of sexuality that was a preoccupation of the day, onanism, and its relationship in popular belief to the various aspects of racial degeneracy Hagen would have been seen to embody. As it turns out, there was quite a literature and discourse on masturbation, not only as a manifestation of degenerate psychology, spirit and race, especially of Jews, but as well of its cumulative threat of undercutting civilization itself. Wagner believed that Nietzsche suffered from some version of this ailment and also questioned its presence in others. And in himself?, it made me wonder. It wouldn't be the only time Wagner may have been spying and telling on himself to depict degeneracy and evil.

Trying to explain *basso profondo* Hagen's power of musical presence and personality finds Marc once again scrambling for qualifiers, exceptions to what could seem his rules regarding tessitura as a demarcater of racial degeneracy. It's the same irresolute place where Eva Rieger is left in her study, *Wagner's Women.* After showing us how predictably undemocratic Wagner can be in his musical characterizations of heroism and power in women vs men, she is at a loss to explain or even to qualify the power of a figure like Kundry.

Although I can honestly say that I never really thought much about the specifics of Hagen's sexuality, it's in the character of Hagen that I've always sensed Wagner speaking to his audience under the trance of his art. As with Alberich speaking poison to Hagen in *Die Götterdämmerung*, the antisemitic poison being imparted to an awakening Germany is happening not explicitly, but osmotically via a state of hypnosis. Under the mesmerism of Wagner, we are all Hagens.

A window on Marc's work on Wagner and the body is a paper he did for *The Opera Quarterly* in 2008 called "Primal Sounds," analyzing what has been long and widely recognized as the uniquely "drug-like," "intoxicating" nature of Wagner's music. We may be transported, healed and ennobled by Mozart, Beethoven, Brahms or any other composer, but only of Wagner do we speak so often and strongly in terms such as "mesmerizing" and "hypnotic," in the vernacular of altered states of consciousness.

Loss of consciousness and transcendence of corporeal reality are recurrent themes in Wagner. Beyond the disembodied voice of Alberich dream-speaking to Hagen one need think only of the love-death music and language of *Tristan* or of Gurnemanz's "Here, time becomes space" in *Parsifal* to recognize this discussion as pertinent and worthy.

Marc is intrigued by the work of the German philosopher Peter Sloterdijk, who theorizes that our pleasurable experience of sound and music can be traced back to our lives pre-birth when we were lulled by the most primordial of all sounds, the pulsations of our mother's womb. It's this prenatal level of physiological connectedness and pleasure Marc suspects Wagner somehow taps into, a viewpoint that doesn't strain credulity to me as a physician who tends to appreciate so much of who and how we are as physiological.

Meanwhile, for all our Wagnerite talk, including Marc's, of Wagner's music as "drug-like," "hypnotic," "intoxicating" and "addictive," descriptives we can all agree on, I seem to be the only one who wants to explore this issue further in the paradigms of addiction. As a physician who specializes in addiction medicine and as a person in recovery, I tend to see many things through lenses of addiction, and certainly what Nietzsche called "the case of Wagner." So pertinent is this context, as I've come to appreciate it, that my book, *On The Future of Wagnerism*, has a secondary subtitle: "Art, Addiction, Codependence and Recovery."

However interesting, his discussion of the singular power of Wagner's music is also exposing of pitfalls of Marc's analytical thinking. In "Primal Sounds" he postulates that the *Ring* cycle is all about origination and dissolution. As with his explorations of antisemitism in the imagery of the body in Wagner, he cites numerous examples of musical, textual and motivic expressions of birth, death, rebirth and regeneration in Wagner's works. But so strong is a sense of schema in this, as Marc initially expresses it, that it gives the reader who is acquainted with Marc's other work pause. Wasn't he saying in his earlier *RW* that the *Ring* cycle was primarily if mostly subtextually about Germany's perceived racial struggles with the Jews? Are these differing analytical constructs complementary or coincidental? Or is it just Marc's style to pick out patterns and give them each a prominence that hasn't been previously articulated as such, regardless of any considerations of rank in importance?

Does such dexterity of perspective give credence, as Marc certainly does elsewhere, to the multiplicity of approaches, meanings and interpretations of Wagner's art, and to regard them as being in an equipoise of importance? If the answer to that question is unquestionably yes, then it might seem, subtly and tacitly as such, to undermine his other work. But that's not something Marc would have a problem with. One person sees the *Ring* as primarily about race, another as primarily about cycles of birth and dissolution. In Marc's case, both people become one, a little like the way time becomes space in *Parsifal*. To which Marc, and perhaps even Wagner with him, might reply with the immortal words of Walt Whitman: "Do I contradict myself? Very well, then I contradict myself. I am vast. I contain multitudes."

One more note re Marc's analytical skills. In another paper, "Lingering Discourses: Critics, Jews and the Case of Gottfried Wagner" from the 2007 anthology *Richard Wagner for the New Millenium*, Marc surgically observes how the disparagement of Gottfried and his viewpoints is often done with constructs of antisemitism. Here, Gottfried is analyzed as being demeaned and rejected in the ways Jews have been and still are.

V

Marc is younger than me, but we are both children of the same ilk and era of post-war reassessment of Wagner, a period that began with a guarded acknowledgment of Wagner's antisemitism and the collusion of Bayreuth with Hitler and Nazism. Still far from full disclosure, this limited, mostly tacit acknowledgment enabled Wagnerites like Marc and me to love Wagner without the fear and anxiety that would come with our ever-broadening adult knowledge of the seriousness and irresolution of these issues.

For me, initiation into the glories of Wagner took place in the 1960's via the opera, *Tristan und Isolde*, via the new London Records Georg Solti recording with Birgit Nilsson, in tandem with a new Solti *Ring* cycle, commencing with a sound-effects spectacular *Das Rheingold*, both in still new state-of-the-art stereo. For Marc, following an introduction via recordings, it was an actual performance of *Tristan* at the Met with Nilsson and Jess Thomas in 1971. And a performance of *Tristan* at Covent Garden became the romantic evening that led to his marrying his blond German date, Antje, a young colleague in German studies who shared his enthusiasm for Wagner.

Marc's recollections of growing up Jewish included antisemitic bullying at school. As with me, his identification was increasingly with the world of cosmopolitan culture, where issues of ethnicity were less forefront and in which Wagner and German culture could still be held in high esteem, notwithstanding what happened during the war.

It was his mother who first instilled in Marc a love of Wagner's music that became hard-wired, as it did for so many of us. His *RW* is inscribed to her: "For Bobbie West Weiner, whose love for Wagner has been a most precious affinity." Marc acknowledges that his love-at-first-hearing of Wagner set the stage for his life's work in Germanic studies.

As for the Jews of Europe and their fate, we would both find our niches of orientation in intellectual and cultural discourses rather than in more traditional venues of community with other Jews. Marc may not have deeply internalized antisemitism in some of the ways I discovered I had done, but neither for him was his ethnicity per se much of a source of identification or pride, except indirectly, as with figures like Arthur Schnitzler, with whom Marc shares characterological cosmopolitanism, courage and charisma.

For me there was a turning point in coming to grips with my own Jewish ethnicity and the reality that, like it or not, evade it or not, I was one with those people against whom antisemitism was and is directed. That life-altering moment was my falling in love with another Jew, writer and gay activist Arnie Kantrowitz, with whom I've shared a life partnership of approaching four decades. Falling in love with Arnie was like Siegfried tasting the blood of the dragon and thereby enabled of a greater discernment of nature. Henceforth, I was to have a depth of understanding and compassion for Jewish people that had previously eluded me.

During the time he spent in Europe and Germany, did Marc ever visit a concentration camp? Theresienstadt (*Terezin*), perhaps, with its history of interned artists and musicians, where Viktor Ullmann's opera *Der Kaiser von Atlantis* was composed and staged, and where Richard Strauss attempted to intercede on behalf of the mother of his Jewish daughter-in-law, Alice? No, Marc said. He'd always avoided the camps. Not even Dachau in the environs of Munich, where he spent a summer apprenticing at the Bavarian State Opera?

Challenging the perceived wisdom of such ritualized experience, he observed that he "always knew that it would just be a far too horrible experience to make it worthwhile, as though somehow empathizing with those who suffered in the camps itself had any moral value greater than one that one had to have anyway from simply knowing about their existence." A better way of remembering and mourning, he suggested, would be to read Paul Celan's short, devastating poem, *Todesfuge*, which deals with life and death in the camps. He found it beautiful and cathartic and has taught it to his students. This is the poem, he noted, that led Theodore Adorno to change his notorious opinion that "to write poetry after Auschwitz would be barbaric!"

I did visit both Dachau and Theresienstadt. But I have balked at seeing some Holocaust documentaries, like the most monumental of them, *Shoah*, by Claude Lanzmann. At the time of its release, I just didn't feel I could handle it. Marc, meanwhile, did see it and found it "quite moving." In fact, Marc, who also taught a course on film, met with Lanzmann when the filmmaker brought *Shoah* to the Indiana campus. Did he, Lanzmann, regret that he didn't have the resources Hollywood directors had for their blockbusters?, Marc asked him. No, Lanzmann told him. With so much greater a preoccupation with technique and technology, the film would doubtless have been weaker in impact. (Lanzmann has been criticized for making such a long — 7+hours — and ambitious film with limited resources and directorial skills; Pauline Kael infamously found it tedious and ill-fashioned. Was there comparable criticism for Hans-Juergen Syberberg's 9 hour *Hitler: Ein Film aus Deutschland?*)

V

Like many Jews of our post-Holocaust generations, including me, liberal, intellectual Marc Weiner has found his own brave *metier* for expressing himself in relation to his cultures and their shared past. Don't judge, wisdom has it. It's a lesson Marc has taken to heart in his tolerant and forgiving attitudes toward Germany, its art and artists, and as well to critics of his work. Especially as one ages, wisdom counsels not to judge too harshly those who made what can seem questionable choices.

Inevitably and surpassingly, time will always reclaim its mantle as the great leveler. History, meanwhile, continues to pick its heroes largely from among those who made choices against the grain of what might have seemed more prudent in time and place. Notwithstanding the difficulties of their circumstances, the great heroes of World War 2 musical culture are not the Dietrich Fischer-Dieskaus, Max Lorenzes or Richard Strausses, but the ones who more boldly confronted and rejected what was happening and who did so at greater personal risk: the Lotte Lehmanns, Lauritz Melchiors, Arturo Toscaninis and Friedelind Wagners.

All of those figures of lesser and greater heroism, it's worth noting, were Wagnerites. When the world next finds itself on the brink around issues of race, authoritarianism and genocide, when people must once again make individual and collective choices of life and death, where will today's Wagnerites fall in the spectrum of heroism, and how will the future regard us? Will it be possible, in retrospect, to judge today's cultural preferences, our Wagnerism among them, in the light of future political fallout?

# *Wagnerism* in the Shadow of Black Lives Matter: Alex Ross's Testimonial to the Life, Times and Art of Richard Wagner

***Wagnerism:* Art and Politics in the Shadow of Music**
**by Alex Ross, Farrar, Straus and Giroux, 766 pages, 2020**

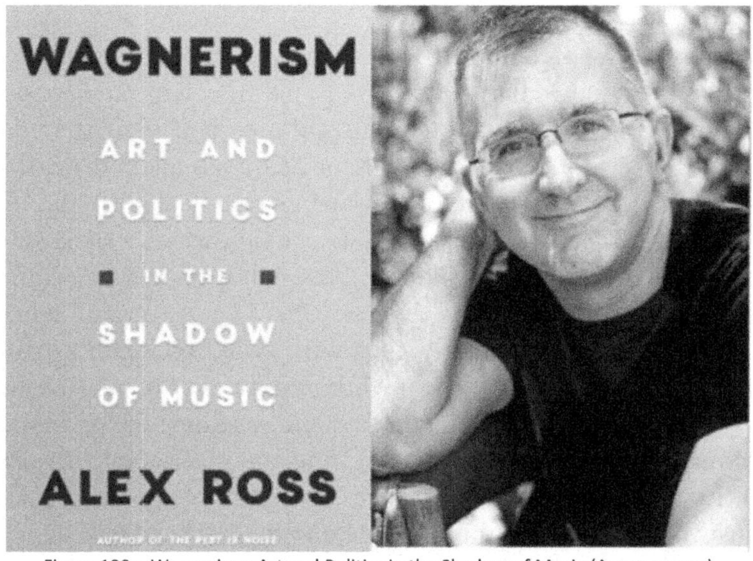

Figure 109 – Wagnerism: Art and Politics in the Shadow of Music (Amazon.com)

*For every window on Wagner we think we've already peered through, Ross has found more lenses and prisms through which to re-view them. At his best, Ross gives dimension to individuals, artworks and events, and captures their intersections with one another and the wider world of the past. But for all its evocation of the life and times of Wagner and the "artwork of the future" — Wagner's and that of his many disciples, there's little that looks to a salutary future for Wagnerism.*

Alex Ross's *Wagnerism* is erudite, expansive and elegiac. Extensively annotated, compellingly laid out and compulsively readable, it's brimming with juxtapositions and gems of detail and insight. Its greatest success is in demonstrating with endless examples what we already know — how widespread and powerful Wagner's appeal has been to so many individuals and factions of culture, politics, history, religion, race, ethnicity, gender and sexuality.

As everyone also knows, Wagner's art is dogged by questions of its entanglement with the character and prejudices of Wagner the man and his place in the advent of Hitler and Nazism. However otherwise gifted and influential as an artist, the documentation and affirmation of which are the principal motivation and achievement of *Wagnerism*, Wagner was also a colossus of grandiloquence and mean spiritedness. Legendarily bigoted, spiteful, vindictive and heinously antisemitic, he was redolent of Donald Trump in being mendacious, appropriating, and a divisive, sadistic, bullying, tyrannizing, predatory, scapegoating German and white supremacist. Whatever else he was, he was also, to quote Alex Ross — in turn quoting Auden, who also called Wagner "perhaps the greatest genius who ever lived" — "an absolute shit."

In view of the virtually universal recognition of Wagner's greatness as a composer even among his detractors, it comes as no surprise that Ross, whose own Wagnerism is hardly a secret, is easily successful in re-establishing Wagner's art as the most protean, in terms of its allure and impact, in the history of musical culture. At the same time Ross is skilled at demonstrating the balance of complex forces at work in Wagner's imprint on individual lives, times and, with infectious enthusiasm, his milieus. Though the book is close to 800 pages, Ross retains his gift for rendering complexity with acuity and economy.

Ross is adroit, for example, in sketching in a few sentences how Tannhäuser's journey could be so viscerally appealing to Theodore Herzl, the founder and visionary of Zionism, and as well to W.E.B. Du Bois in his pursuit of a heroic new African spirit. He's comparably adept in parsing how, beyond questions of antisemitism and homophobia, an exemplar of self-hatred like Otto Weininger could engage so much interest. The relationship between Wagner and Nietzsche seems more accessible here than when we kept trying to put the pieces together ourselves.

Setting the stage by opening with the closing event, the composer's death in Venice in 1883, *Wagnerism* commences with "Rheingold," a look-back reminiscent of the Hollywood heyday movies Ross later explores as having been so inspirited by Wagner. A whirlwind tour of Wagner's creative life ensues with the *Ring* cycle components as touchstones and in counterpoint to Wagner's vacillating relationship with Nietzsche.

Along the way of what's only the first 64 pages, we are helped to gauge Wagner's artistic maturation within the *Ring* itself and in the two great operas, *Tristan* and *Meistersinger,* that were composed amidst the mammoth 26 year project of the cycle. Onward to the events leading to the establishment of the Bayreuth Festival in 1876 and the groundwork for *Parsifal* and its early controversies.

A later chapter, "Grail Temple," begins with a survey of the "Esoteric, Decadent and Satanic Wagner" that encircles the Wagner of *Parsifal* that Nietzsche found so objectionable. Past pages on the philosophical murk of so much *Parsifal* literature, art and commentary, however, we still don't have the summary perspective of key issues and controversies Ross can be so good at. That may be more because of Wagner's cunning than Ross's inadequacy. As Wolfgang Wagner put it in a backstage aside in Tony Palmer's film of and about the opera, does anyone really understand *Parsifal*?

Meanwhile, however, neither he nor Ross wants to underscore that in its portrait of Kundry, however otherwise enigmatic and compelling her character and notwithstanding such phenomena of Jewish Wagnerism as Thomaschefsky's Yiddish rendering of the opera in Brooklyn in 1904*, Parsifal* showcases and perpetrates the most incendiary of antisemitic slanders: that of the Wandering Jew who laughed at Christ's Crucifixion agony. Because of its stature as supreme composer Richard Wagner's last and most musically advanced work, and because of obligatory reverence for it by multiple parameters as *Heilige Kunst*, and notwithstanding references to the Wandering Jew in other artworks and literatures, *Parsfial* becomes the most potent and portentous weapon of antisemitic propaganda in the history of art.

Stripped of its high art trappings, what Wagner does to the Jews in *Parsifal* is what Trump and QAnon have done to Hillary Clinton and the Democrats, without the "compassion" but with comparable malevolence.

Antisemitism is present in the work of many composers, from Bach to John Adams (Kissinger in *Nixon in China* is as much an antisemitic caricature as Beckmesser in *Meistersinger*, neither of them specifically designated by their composers as Jews), but in its depictions of the black arts seduction evils of Kundry and her self-castratingly envious master, Klingsor, the antisemitism of *Parsifal* is truly in a league of its own. It's right up there with, and firmly in medieval German *Volk* traditions of, rendering Jews as witches and Satanic demons with horns, hooves, tails and forked tongues.

In his review of the Met's revival of *Parsifal* for his *New Yorker* column, Ross seemed deeply moved by director Francois Girard's compassionate portrayal of Kundry — so compassionate that she doesn't clearly die at the end as she's directed to do by Wagner. And it's she in this production, rather than Parsifal, who raises the Grail cup as the opera concludes. Just as Wagner, having done the damage of laying out the libel against her, against the Jews, is then inclined towards crocodile-tears forgiveness, so is Ross inclined towards what are ostensibly the opera's transcendent themes of compassion and forgiveness. As Wagner apologists are wont to do, Wagner's more humanistic meanings and intentions are intuited and projected onto the opera as well as the composer. Even if they are genuinely there, however, the old libel of Jews as mockers of Christ, like the Passover blood libel, is preserved and consecrated as never before and nowhere else in the highest ranks of art.

Somehow mitigating the odium of the Wandering Jew for Wagnerites is its presence as a theme throughout Wagner's own life and work, going back to his first major operatic success, *The Flying Dutchman,* based on a tale by Jewish Heinrich Heine. Confounding as well, it can seem, is the character of Wotan as the Wanderer in *Siegfried.* Here, Wagner's stand-in has become so diminished in his dealings with the Nibelungs — the Jews — and the resulting devolution of all that he has virtually become a Wandering Jew himself.

And the source of Wagner's venomous preoccupation with the Jews? Here, as in other passages in *Wagnerism*, Ross shows his gift for staring Wagner's antisemitism in the face and saying what needs to be said, albeit with Ross somehow emerging from these skirmishes with his Wagnerism undiminished:

*"Political sentiments and professional jealousies fail to explain the fervency of Wagner's hatred...It welled up from deep in his psyche. As he admitted to Liszt: 'This rancor is as necessary to my nature as gall is to the blood.'"*

***Stripped of its high art trappings, what Wagner does to the Jews in* Parsifal *is what Trump and QAnon have done to Hillary Clinton and the Democrats, with greater "compassion" but comparable malevolence.***

In the throes of antisemitic obsession, Wagner can be seen in another paradigm of human behavior, one also touched on by Ross— that of intoxication, compulsivity and addiction. More on that anon.

The story of Nietzsche pro and contra Wagner is deftly interwoven throughout Ross's narrative. For what may have seemed a more clear-cut break around polarities between the two figures, Ross notes of the outcome that "Wagner and Nietzsche darkly complete each other in the Nazi mind," though it's Nietzsche who gets the last word in *Wagnerism*: "One day my name will be linked to something monstrous — to a crisis like none there has ever been on earth." To a monstrous crisis, yes, and to the *monstre sacré*, Wagner, who enkindled it.

Reflecting our own attraction and ambivalence, Nietzsche is an ideal companion to accompany us on Ross's junket. Inspired by the Patrice Chéreau centennial production of the *Ring* at Bayreuth, Ross writes of the conclusion of this towering creative achievement that the Wagner-Nietzsche relationship nurtured: "the most monumental artwork of the nineteenth century is merely a prelude to future creation. The audience must write the rest."

The book then moves into a narrative of Wagnerism as it bewitched, invaded, wrought havoc and flourished in various milieus — French, British, German, Jewish, Feminist, Black, Gay, Lesbian, American, Russian, Marxist, Socialist, Boleshevik, Nazi, Modernist, Poetic, Occult, Symbolist, Theosophist, Psychoanalytic, Futurist, Dadaist, Fabian, Romantic, Weimarian and other stopovers on its Wanderer's road to where it has ended up — Hollywood. Much of this material, updated for this collection, appeared over the years in Ross's *New Yorker* column.

Ross inventories a wide range of notable artworks in relation to Wagnerism. From the novels of Charles Dickens and George Eliot to those of Garbiele D'Annunzio, Thomas Mann, Heinrich Mann, Hermann Hesse, Franz Werfel, Robert Musil, Joseph Conrad, James Joyce, D.H. Lawrence, E. M. Forster, Virginia and Leonard Woolf, Marcel Proust and Upton Sinclair to the poems of Sidney Lanier and T.S. Eliot; from the *danse moderne* of Isadora Duncan to the *Ballets Russes* of Sergei Diaghalev; from the drawings and paintings of virtually all of the leading French Impressionists and post-Impressionists to expressionist Wassily Kandinsky and mixed-materials German painter and sculptor Anselm Kiefer; from the skyscrapers of Louis B. Sullivan to the fantastical edifices of Antoni Gaudi. In many instances, works, especially novels, plays and poems such as those of Joyce, Woolf and Eliot, are summarized and interpreted from standpoints of Wagnerism. The panorama can be breathtaking. In the encyclopedic inclusiveness of its many inventories, which as such can eventually seem formulaic, it can also be stultifying.

The first major stop on the Grand Tour of Wagnerism, "The Tristan Chord," recreates Wagner's experience in Paris and with the French. As most everywhere else, Wagner's impact was momentous, inspiring individuals, artworks, movements, tracts and upheaval. Yet for all the stars in the French firmament of *Wagnerisme*, the French cult of Wagner— Baudelaire, Mallarme, Verlaine, Cezanne, Gaugin, Von Gogh, Renoir, Monet, Delacroix, Zola, Gautier, Sand, Maeterlinck, Proust, Bizet, Saint-Saëns,— what struck me was Ross's observation that "[Wagner's] reputation depended in large measure on his revolutionary pamphlets" (with their miasma of revolutionary antisemitism) and his conjoined observation that Wagner "had many fans on the left."

Tony Kushner's effusive blurb for *Wagnerism* reads like a capstone to this enduring reality. Ross quotes Wagner's contention that "only when the demon [money] that keeps people raging in the madness of party conflict can no longer find a time and place among us will there be — no more Jews." In this are the similarities between Wagner and Karl Marx in the latter's tract,"On the Jewish Question," that can so resonate with partisans of the Left, not a few of them Jewish.

Likewise arresting from that period and milieu of the French is another clue to his art from Wagner himself: "The mark of a great poet is to let the public grasp in silence what is left unsaid." As Ross later observes, the absence of characters specifically designated as Jews in Wagner "enabled liberal Wagnerites to create a kind of firewall between the composer's despicable views and the ostensibly humane content of his works."

While Ross can be unflinching in denoting antisemitism, widespread in France as elsewhere in Europe and beyond, that attributed to Degas and Renoir is not explored in context. There's mention of Degas's hooked-nose Jew at the Bourse, and Renoir's portrait of a fleshy Wagner is one of *Wagnerism*'s sparsely identified illustrations, many of them so small and grainy in black-and-white you have to squint for clarity. Mention also should be made of *Wagnerism*'s flat chartreuse-yellow cover with no design. Certainly, there will be enough readership for this important book, whatever the caveats, to justify better presentations of it.

Early in his chapter, "Swan Night," on Victorian Britain and Gilded Age America, Ross quotes at length from an otherwise unremarkable entry in the *Nebraska State Journal* in 1894 on a wedding that took place in Lincoln to the organ accompaniment of "the triumphant tenderness of Wagner" (The Bridal Chamber music — "Here Comes The Bride" — from *Lohengrin*). Its author was "a precocious University of Nebraska student named Willa Cather."

There's no discussion at this juncture of what some have imputed to be Cather's antisemitism, racism and views that could be considered reactionary, which Ross does touch on later in an extended consideration of Cather, her work and background ("Brunhilde's Rock: Willa Cather and the Singer Novel," is an entire chapter devoted to her).

In being more open to exploration of racism and antisemitism in American Wagnerism and elsewhere, Ross at first can seem in contrast to Joseph Horowitz, whose history of Wagnerism in turn-of-the-century America, *Wagner Nights*, Ross acknowledges as authoritative. For Wagner apologists, however, *Wagnerism* will cinch Horowitz's implicit case that Wagnerism in America at the turn of the century had little or nothing to do with racism and antisemitism. As with Horowitz, this transcendence of Wagnerism beyond the confines of still incendiary issues of race and antisemitism is the thrust, heart and soul of what Ross most wants to tell us about Wagnerism's place in our lives and times, past and present.

Subsequent chapters delineate manifold phenomena of Wagnerism. The pre-Raphaelites and art-nouveau decadents were mesmerized, Ross observes and as we know from the drawings of Aubrey Beardsley and others, by the eroticism of the Venusberg and *Tristan*. But "most of all, Wagner captured the Victorian imagination because of his proximity to the Master of Britain — the tales of King Arthur, the Knights of the Round Table, and the Holy Grail."

Of keen interest is the material on British novelist George Eliot, a musician herself and admirer and social consort of Wagner, as possibly the first to use the phrase, "the propaganda of Wagnerism" in her unsigned 1855 essay, "Liszt, Wagner and Weimar." Despite her later essay on "The Modern Hep! Hep! Hep!," evincing alarm about the escalation of antisemitism, and notwithstanding the expositions on Jewishness of her "proto-Zionist" novel, *Daniel Deronda* (published in 1876, the year of the *Ring* cycle premiere), Ross notes that Eliot may not have seen Wagner's essay "Jewishness in Music," likewise unsigned at that time (in its initial printing of 1850), and may not have appreciated the extent of Wagner's own antisemitism.

Fast forward to the concluding chapter on Hollywood, which unfolds feverishly and is so top-heavy with names and references as to seem more a catalogue or appendix than a *denouement*. At first it seems ironic, even funny and a kind of justice that Wagner should end up being so appropriated by Hollywood, with its predominance of Jewish refugee and emigre composers, film producers, directors and actors. But bemusement fades as one realizes that what Ross is leading up to is his sense that Hollywood's exploitation of Wagner for its blockbuster films is not only a kind of propaganda, as America descends ever further into racism and fascism, but as well a playing out of Wagner's vision. As Ross concludes in his adaptation of this material for his recent *New Yorker* piece, "Wagner in Hollywood":

*"The urge to sacralize culture, to transform secular pursuits into secular religion and redemptive politics, did not die out with the degeneration of Wagnerian Romanticism into Nazi kitsch."*

What can be gleaned between the lines here is the Shavian, socialist view of Wagner that Ross looks at in other contexts and that was the basis of that legendary Bayreuth Festival Centennial *Ring* cycle production. Staged as a parable of the Industrial Revolution and modeled on *The Perfect Wagnerite* of George Bernard Shaw, Chéreau's Nibelungs were overtly depicted as Jews. Connecting the dots, what Ross is insinuating, however paraconsciously and elliptically, is that the answer to questions of the future and its dangers, to the question asked by Friedelind Wagner in her introductory comments to the telecast of the Chéreau *Ring* — "Who knows when another Alberich will come along to set the entire cycle in motion again?" — may be glimpsed in Hollywood and the hegemonics it increasingly betrays.

"It would be a mistake to say that Shaw and his fellow leftists found the 'true' Wagner," Ross concludes in his chapter, 'Ring of Power: Russia and Revolution.' "But it would be a mistake to say they misunderstood him."

For all of *Wagnerism*'s evocation of the life and times of the "Sorcerer of Bayreuth," an appellation attributed to Nietzsche, and of Wagner's "artwork of the future," however, and even with its malleability within infinite avenues of political interpretation, a more certain and salutary direction for Wagnerism in the future is neither conceptualized nor invoked by Ross.

The socialist perspective of Wagner showcased by Chéreau is inescapably betrayed by its double vision. On the one hand Jews are seen as victims of racism and antisemitism. On the other they are indicted for being premiere perpetrators of the capitalist greed that leads to their own undoing and that of everyone and everything else. In its double-think it can echo the double talk of Donald Trump, today's supreme practitioner of hypocritical blame-the-victim stratagems and oratory. Trump rages against "socialism" as he plots and schemes in collusion with leading socialist autocrat Vladimir Putin for police state dictatorship power, just as Wagner raged against the very materialism he himself coveted, demanded and wallowed in. In both cases, left and right elide via their common ground of authoritarianism, racism, antisemitism and scapegoating. Antisemitism — "The Socialism of Fools," Seymour Martin Lipset called it, echoing the German Social Democrats of the Wagner era, in his blistering critique of antisemitism on the Left in the *New York Times* in 1971.

Concluding his section "Wagner in America," Ross observes that with polarities of viewpoint on gender and race predominant,

"Wagner's work and ideas provided fodder for both sides of a battle over American identity that is ongoing."

In "American Siegfrieds" Ross looks at the contributions of poet and musician Sidney Lanier and his ode to Wagner. His assessment of the limits of Lanier's efforts to try to develop a narrative to tell the stories of Native Americans (*The Song of Hiawatha)* is perspicacious:

*"The idea of a national mythology based on the legacies of conquered, murdered and enslaved peoples was not one for which Wagner provided a precedent."*

Though Ross notes upfront in *Wagnerism* that Lanier, the most famous son of my hometown of Macon, Georgia, fought for the Confederacy, it's not denoted in context that some institutions named after him have since changed their names because of that legacy. Ross does not designate any overlap of Wagnerism and racism in Lanier, as he does with Lanier's contemporary, Owen Wister, likewise a poet, author and composer. Wister is best known for *The Virginian*, a cowboy novel that was the basis of Hollywood films.

As Ross has written elsewhere and as is otherwise well-established, American racism was extreme and variously conjoined with antisemitism (e.g., Henry Ford). It had many manifestations beyond slavery, many theorists and leading practitioners, and was antecedent and contributory to Nazism. Yet, any linking of that reality to its presence in Wagnerism in America can draw reflexive blanks from those inclined to Wagner apologism. In Ross's narrative, as in Joseph Horowitz's *Wagner Nights*, one can sense that firewall for liberals Ross described between the composer's despicable views and his ostensibly more benevolent influence.

***To what extent does the audience appreciate that it is being invited to legitimately participate, albeit tacitly and under the mantle of high art, in levels of racism and antisemitism that are otherwise proscribed?***

In *Parsifal*, Gurnemanz explains to the young knight that in the realm of the Grail, time and space become one. In the real world, or rather in escaping from it, there's another place where time and space meld. That place is one I've come to recognize from my personal background and work in addiction, and from my own experience of Wagnerism. It's the realm of what Gottfried Wagner calls "Wagner intoxication." As it progressed (in the vocabulary of addiction "progression" is used to denote the advance from intoxication to addiction*)* in my own life and milieu, and though it's something more intuited than scientifically quantifiable, Wagnerism can seem fueled by this process; as can Ross and his book.

That Wagnerism can exude the exhilaration and intemperance of drug addiction is not a new idea; nor that Wagnerism can be cultish, a descriptive Ross himself isn't shy about using. Notwithstanding that they don't discriminate on the basis of identity, both phenomena — addiction and cultism — are notable for their insularity. This phraseology of Wagnerism in metaphors of drugs, intoxication and addiction, like those of sorcery and enchantment, is familiar to Wagnerites.

"Lisztomania" is a term coined by Heinrich Heine, the Jewish writer Wagner admired and whose original tale of *The Flying Dutchman* Wagner reconfigured for his own opera, to denote the frenzy of fandom surrounding Franz Liszt, the composer who would become Wagner's father-in-law. Wagnerism can seem similar in suggesting intensities of feelings that can be irrational, transitory and more in the nature of altered states of consciousness. While it might appear open-minded and inclusive, the cult of Wagnerism, like other cults (e.g., Trumpism) can be notably intolerant of dissent and disloyalty. However sober in narrative and however of value and interest its history, Ross's exhaustive compendium is testimonial to Wagnerism, rendering *Wagnerism* itself exemplary of the cultism it so extensively documents.

Wagnerism, which Ross makes little effort to define — yes, it's that vast, we intuitively concede — is something you can sense the first time you notice the enraptured, absolute quiet of a Wagner audience or the outsizedness of Wagner ovations, even for mediocre performances. Mainstream opera enthusiasm can become rowdy with cheers and boos, but the thunderous force of a Wagner ovation can seem of another species. In contrast to the standard repertoire works that showcase singers, Wagner himself is more discernibly the font of this most passionate enthusiasm of operatic experience.

Past the peak of progression of my own Wagnerism, this roar of Wagnerian ovation began to resound with greater menace. It seemed less secure, less the *Heimat* it had seemed to me in the throes of Wagnerism oblivion and denial. As I became evermore lost in the perfumed gardens of Klingsor and Kundry, I began to realize with gathering discomfort that I no longer felt I knew what that roar of the crowd was really all about. Was it truly, solely and simply in response to Wagner's musical and theatrical genius?

Further along in my own process of self-detoxification from Wagner, I realized I will never again be able to experience that roar as divorced from the darker energies wafting within and about Wagner and Wagnerism. The question that always lurked there had finally broken through: To what extent does the audience appreciate that it is being invited to legitimately participate, albeit tacitly under the mantle of high art, in levels of racism and antisemitism that are otherwise proscribed?

In his section, "Democratic Vistas," Ross looks at Mark Twain, a cockeyed Wagnerite who wrote of his 10-day trek to Bayreuth, and of his experience of Wagnerism:

*"Sometimes I feel like the one sane person in a community of the mad; Sometimes I feel like the one blind man where others see; the one groping savage in the college of the learned; and always, during service, I feel like a heretic in heaven."*

If you knew nothing else about this passage, you might be persuaded that it's the description of a first visit to an opium den.

Rounding up his survey of Wagnerism in America, Ross looks at America's greatest poet. It has always been a bit of a mystery that opera-loving Walt Whitman, whose heyday overlapped with the early Wagnerism movement in America, had little to say about Wagner, a casualty more of timing, Ross deduces, than of taste. To this Ross adds the resonant perspective that for some, Whitman's free verse and freethinking were the counterpart of Wagner's art of the future.

Though notable for its many windows and prisms, Ross's surveying of Wagnerism in America, with its formidable inventory of Wagnerism in Hollywood films and including many snapshots of gay, lesbian and Jewish Wagnerism, has important omissions. One of the bigger and more baffling of these, since it so impressively makes Ross's case for Wagner's impact on gay and Jewish sensibility and creativity, is *The Twilight of the Golds*, the play by Jonathan Tolins about Wagner, Jews, gayness, genetics and the future that ran on Broadway and was subsequently made into an award-winning film.

In his ambition to capture every nuance of the history and experience of Wagnerism Ross may not be scrupulously comprehensive, but he mostly seems bold, clear-eyed and comprehensive rather than intoxicated or evasive. Yet, for all its intelligence and careful covering of bases, key issues can feel sketchily explored, and the insularity of Wagnerism can seem to keep intruding, like the chalky faces in the offbeat film of encroaching death, *Carnival of Souls*. While the overarching specter of racism is touched on by Ross in multiple particulars and from different vantage points, including those of black artists, the result can be a slipperyness of perspective of Wagner's place in what eventuated in Germany, engulfing the wider world.

Luranah Aldridge was a mixed-race American soprano who was enlisted by the Wagners to sing one of the Valkyries in the world premiere of the *Ring* cycle at Bayreuth. Instead of placing her in a clearer context of racism in Wagner, in America and for Germany, which Ross does evoke elsewhere — e.g., in relation to Du Bois and his visit to Bayreuth in Ross's discussion of "Black Wagner" — we're presented with confounding glimpses of the Wagners' graciousness and friendliness to Aldridge against the grain of what we know to be their *Weltanschauung* regarding race.

As with Angelo Neumann, Wagner's Jewish international agent, and even with the more challenging case of Wagner's *Parsifal* conductor, observantly Jewish household guest and Wagner pallbearer Hermann Levi, the son of a rabbi, when it came to their own ambitions, the Wagners' principles could be relegated and prejudices muted. It's left to us to decide if these exceptions to the rule mitigate stereotypes of the Wagners around race and antisemitism to the extent that they seem to have done for Ross. Alternatively, perhaps what Ross is trying to elucidate is that while Wagner was clearly and profoundly antisemitic, the racism with which his antisemitism was entangled was notably less extreme and personally invested.

Ross's takes on racism and antisemitism can otherwise seem like generic white liberal takes on these matters. While such efforts to make things right and put them in perspective appear laudable in motivation and presentation, we have that sense of something missing. In the case of racism, what the usual cast of today's white liberal spokespersons has to say may be insightful and caring, but as Black Lives Matter is helping us better appreciate, what has been missing are the multitudinous, previously ignored voices of everyday black experience and sensibility. Their stories — especially of the likes of

George Floyd, Breonna Taylor and many others who have been so notably victimized— are finally being told and heard as never before.

Just as gay people of my generation grew tired of hearing ourselves described by heterosexuals and tired of seeing ourselves portrayed onstage and onscreen by heterosexuals, just as women have grown tired of hearing themselves spoken for by men, just as Hispanics and Asians have grown tired of seeing and hearing themselves portrayed and characterized by Caucasians, and just as blacks have reached their limits in terms of having their lives accounted for by whites, I can't be the only Jew to have grown weary of having my reactions to Wagner paraphrased and spoken for but otherwise ignored by others, notwithstanding their learning, ostensible compassion and good intentions.

Beyond the notable achievements of *Wagnerism*, distinguished by intellectual dexterity, a literary gift for engaging readers and a careful willingness to articulate how serious and odious Wagner's antisemitism can be, a question lingers, the very question that Ross cites as lingering at the conclusion of the *Ring* cycle. Where do we go from here?

I don't think anyone has the answer to that. But why not look for it, even in what might seem unlikely or suspect places? Not so exclusively in the art, memoirs and artifacts of the famous, infamous and offbeat that are the more predictable bedrock of scholarship as in *Wagnerism*, nor even at the historical and political developments that have so exhaustively inspired deconstructive postmodern stagings and cinematic appropriations of Wagner, but from the more mundane worlds of music and opera surrounding us.

Just as Black Lives Matter challenges even the most liberal and tolerant among us to see a greater landscape of black life and experience, so the ongoing scholarly ferment in Wagner circles around antisemitism should be more open to a greater canvassing of Jewish experience with a more forefront participation by self-identified Jews in that discourse. For all the discussion of Jews, antisemitism, Wagner and Wagnerism by Ross and many others among the *dramatis personae* in *Wagnerism,* however, such testimony *per se* is rarely if ever solicited or demarcated as such. Nor is its absence noted.

Testimony like that of my *Confessions of a Jewish Wagnerite* remains all too foreign in these realms — rare, suspect, unwelcome and ignored. It makes me feel like Twain at Bayreuth or that civilian in the opium den. In any context, of course, if you're a wheel but not willing to be squeaky, you're not likely to get oiled.

Not so unlike the slaves who voluntarily stayed with and fought for their Southern masters during the Civil War in *Gone With The Wind,* Jewish Wagnerites can seem generically and notably out of touch with our feelings about antisemitism and as well our ethnicity. As William M. Hoffman (*Ghosts of Versailles*) has put it, the post-Holocaust generation of Jews is numb.

Those of us who are liberal and urbane almost uniformly, wishfully think of ourselves as culturally cosmopolitan and well assimilated in our Wagnerism, the very hiding places Wagner, with Nazism in hot pursuit, so ruthlessly, relentlessly, obsessively and sadistically routed and indicted in his artworks, essays and other writings.

In Wagner's time and yet again in our own, we Jews have been all too susceptible to internalizing this prejudice, to introjecting mainstream viewpoints and judgments. Where conflict is recognized it tends to be denied, universalized, relegated, rationalized and dichotomized (bad man/great art). Not much more than in Wagner's time, and most paradigmatically in the case of Wagner himself, have the keepers of the flame of Western culture had much interest in or tolerance for "whiney" Jews, any more than for "uppity" blacks, or for "shrill" white or "angry" black women.

While it's now evermore widely accepted that *Die Meistersinger* and its caricature villain Beckmesser, along with other of Wagner's characters and situations, are infused with Wagner's antisemitism, few Wagnerites will admit that these stereotypes have or ever did have much currency in the mainstreams of Wagner appreciation. The most skillful of Wagner's defenders, like Ross, now acknowledge the composer's antisemitism warts and all, but still emphasize the ambiguities and absence of antisemitic specificity in the works themselves.

Pause for a moment to recall Ross's quoting of Wagner on the importance of not spelling everything out. Juxtaposition of that with Wagner's palpable rage over "mimetic" Jewish efforts to assimilate in their lives and art exposes a bigger picture of the ongoing dangers of Wagner's antisemitism. It's in this sense that my observation can reverberate:

***Those of us [Jews] who are liberal and urbane almost uniformly, wishfully think of ourselves as culturally cosmopolitan and well assimilated in our Wagnerism, the very hiding places Wagner, with Nazism in hot pursuit, so ruthlessly, relentlessly, obsessively and sadistically routed and indicted in his artworks, essays and other writings.***

Among the most articulate and influential of these spokespersons of Wagner's nonspecificity is Hans Rudolf Vaget, whose guidance is generously acknowledged by Ross in *Wagnerism*. Though they would bristle at being so labeled, a beneath-the-surface defensiveness of both Ross and Vaget can invite us to see them in a wider context of the Wagner apologism that few admit to but which seems key to the sustenance of Wagnerism.

Like Vaget, Ross is often at pains to establish the complexity of what might seem more monolithic considerations. "Once we get away from the concept of...some sort of supernatural master-disciple relationship," Ross notes in paraphrasing Vaget, "we can form a balanced, if still unsettling, picture of the Wagner-Hitler problem."

Actually, it's Vaget's contention, quoted by Ross and bolstered by Wagner's statements on the importance of taciturnity as opposed to literality in art, that "Wagner aspired to broad, even universal acceptance and therefore took pains to keep any overt indication of his very particular anti-Jewish obsession out of his operatic work."

The problem with Wagner apologism, a term that can be used accusatorily and that isn't explored in *Wagnerism*, is not that it seeks to exonerate Wagner but that it can betray its own ostensible openness to interpretations of Wagner. When Ross later dismisses Nazi readings of Wagner for their superficiality, romanticization and gutting of Wagner's complexity, it can seem tacit that he's also apologizing for Wagnerism's most shameful and tragic depths and mistakes.

I'm reminded how I myself, with secret shame for my Jewishness when I was growing up in Macon, Georgia in the 1950's, might say things like, Yes, I'm Jewish, BUT I'm not religious. Yes, there are troubling issues in Wagner BUT...Yes, some Nazis apparently played Wagner in the camps, BUT, Ross notes, few camp survivors attest to much presence of Wagner's music during their internment. Beyond this endless balancing act, and when all is said and done, that Nazis read what they did into Wagner seems no more or less legitimate than the ways in which many other Wagnerite factions have interpreted and appropriated the composer. The Wagnerism of Hitler and Nazism, in other words and it bears repeating, was no less legitimate or more unreasonable a reading of what's actually or intuitively there in Wagner than any other avenue of interpretation.

Antisemitism, racism, nationalism — all of these were major strains in Wagner, emphasized by some and relegated by others. In its varied, fragmentary, prismatic, qualified and irresolute assessments of the interrelationships of Hitler, Nazism and Wagnerism, "Yes, BUT…" is in fact a *leitmotif* of *Wagnerism.* But in this Ross is hardly alone. In fact, he's in good company. The Wagnerite Ross stands in greatest admiration of — Thomas Mann — was comparably conflicted and found himself variously in stances of affirmation, condemnation, defensiveness and apologism. Despite pages on Mann and his magnum opus, *Dr. Faustus*, however, clarity on Wagner remains elusive for Ross. Mann never had it. Nor does *Wagnerism.*

Most observers, including Ross, now concede that the stratagem of emphasizing Wagner's nonspecifity fails with *Die Meistersinger*, where Vaget can remain on defense. Closer to home, we Jews are inevitably troubled in our relationship with Wagner and do betray a bumbling Beckmesserian insecurity about our place in reaction and relation to Wagner. In our embrace of Wagnerism, we seem all too often like black Republicans in relation to Trump, too easily in betrayal of some of our deepest sensitivities and self-respect. Like Alberich and Mime, we're more likely to be at odds with each other than to confront the prejudices of greater nemeses.

To find a Jew who recognizes and articulates how much conflict can be involved in Wagner appreciation, who is not psychopathologically in denial and is willing to express themselves about this and find even a marginal platform for doing so remains rare. So rare, in fact, that I remain a singular example.

Yes, of course, there have been admissions of conflict and discomfort from Jews historically and today. There were even Jewish protests during Wagner's time, as noted in *Wagnerism*, though not in our own time, as not noted in *Wagnerism*. But as with blacks in pre-BLM America, testimony of the depth and extent of this turmoil has remained subservient to broader perspectives and platforms of accommodation and inclusion.

Jews are and always have been a conspicuous coterie of Wagnerism and Ross does marvel at the varieties of Jewish experience in these realms— e.g., Mahler, Schnitzler, Adorno, Hanslick, the refugee emigres to Hollywood and many others, and as well in various milieus such as in Israel, and in France, where the term Wagnerism (*Wagnerisme*) appears to have originated.

There's the legendary Tomaschevsky Brooklyn Yiddish Theater *Parsifal* in the lineage of conductor Michael Tilson Thomas. There's Karl Tausig, the Polish-Jewish pianist who became Wagner's disciple and friend. There's Wagner's romance with part-Jewish Judith Gautier. There's gay and Jewish Weininger, whose life, work and suicide Ross explores with fresh detail and perspective. There's Levi, who Ross sees as more independent than codependent. There's "Wagner's Jew" Josef Rubenstein, and Angelo Neumann. There's likewise commentary on Schnitzler's book *The Road* [*or Path*] *Into The Open*, about Jews and antisemitism in *fin-de-siecle* Vienna, this time referencing the pioneering work of Germanist Marc Weiner, who has notably engaged with Ross's mentor Vaget in debates about Wagner's antisemitism at Harvard and in the *German Quarterly*.

In the richness of its explorations of Wagner's antisemitism and that which was ambient in Wagner's time and milieu, Weiner's *Richard Wagner and the Anti-Semitic Imagination* is a benchmark and bellwether of Wagner studies. (See my commentary on Weiner, "Pandemic Wagnerology," on medium.com). Notwithstanding Weiner's own Wagnerism, however, his membership in the Wagnerism Club is still in dispute. Beyond referential acknowledgment, his work is not sentient in *Wagnerism* or otherwise among Wagnerites.

Returning to the challenge of making the case for a greater probing of the conflictedness of Jewish Wagnerites, let me recount my own moment of direct experience with Ross. What follows is excerpted from "Pandemic Wagnerology":

*"Nor, for that matter and not surprisingly, has [Ross] mentioned my work. I know he has seen my* Confessions *because I personally handed him a copy following a talk he did on "The Wagner Vortex" in 2012. When I gave him the book he recoiled, saying he'd already seen it, thank you. But it's inscribed to you, I persisted. As I have with other Wagnerites not known to be Jewish, I inscribed it as follows: 'For Alex Ross, Honorary Jewish Wagnerite.'"*

I include this anecdote repeated from my "Pandemic Wagnerology" not to be self-serving or disingenuous but as cautionary. While it may seem a reasonable response from an ardent Wagnerite like Ross to someone who considers himself an apostate in a process of detoxification from Wagner and Wagnerism like me, the status quo of non-Jewish Wagnerites remaining the custodians of Jewish sensibility and opinion about Wagner, even when they appear to be in happy partnership with us, should be more open to input. As with the Wagner Societies, once it's judged that one's Wagnerism credentials are inauthentic or otherwise lacking, the predictable result is ostracism.

Wagnerism discourse as we've known it should have no more right to being an exclusionary club than orchestras should continue to have an easy pass on excluding women or other arts institutions to relegate people of color. While Jews rank among its members, the Wagner Society of New York, the site of Ross's *Wagnerism* launch and where Vaget recently did an engaging presentation on the Jewish context of *Der Fliegende Holländer,* has kept its distance from the likes of Gottfried Wagner, Marc Weiner and me.

When Leonard Bernstein welcomed the Black Panthers into his living room, the scoffing of skeptics was unanimous. A repeat of such a moment is something you're not likely to find anytime soon in the living rooms of WSNY. Nor, alas, can we look to Ross and his book for a more probing inquiry into the origins, history and place of Wagner Societies in Wagner appreciation and promotion.

There's a psychology and strategy at work in *Wagnerism.* By being honest about the seriousness of Wagner's antisemitism and at the same time placing Jews and antisemitism in much broader, diluting contexts of complexity, other constituencies and concerns, the intention and hope is conveyed, albeit tacitly, that the monster will be thereby defanged. Now that we know this devil, we're safer and on more sure footing than when he was the devil we didn't know or admit to knowing as such.

It would be as if in our telling the truth about their racist hegemonics while appreciating them in broader contexts of regional and historical narratives, the confederate statues that have dominated central locations in Southern and other American cities can be left in their current places with qualifying plaques and the resulting expectation that their toxicity will be thereby defused.

Likewise with Nazi sculptor Arno Breker's bust of Wagner, which glowers like a security guard in greeting visitors to Bayreuth. It seems implicit that if we add plaques, extra program notes and mount occasional exhibits, we can continue to indulge with impunity the cultism that venerated a romanticized Southern world made possible by slavery, and the antisemitic art that so incomparably influenced and continues to dominate musical culture and that enabled the greatest recorded atrocity of genocide in the history of civilization.

Figure 110 - Bust of Richard Wagner by Arno Breker, Bayreuth Festival Park, Wikimedia Commons, public domain

***Arno Breker, leading artist of the Nazis, created three Richard Wagner busts which continue to welcome visitors to Bayreuth. Other Breker Wagner family busts in Bayreuth's Festival Park and environs include those of fiercely antisemitic Cosima Wagner and***

***Hitler confidante and collaborator Winifred Wagner. Breker is also known for his busts of Hitler, Goering, Goebbels and Speer.***

Though Ross does refer to the "soulless statues in the style of Arno Breker," of statues of Wagner in America he notes that the best known of these, in Baltimore and Cleveland, "still stand, despite occasional calls for them to be removed." When it comes to the tests of time, at least for the foreseeable future, *Wagnerism* too will likely stand its ground.

Ross's principal motivation seems to be to do whatever is necessary, including getting even more serious about the most difficult truth, not only to chronicle but to honor and preserve Wagnerism, the biggest obstacle to which in our time continues to be the ongoing fallout from Hitler and Nazism. The alternative — a quantum depedestalization of Wagner with its possible outcome of a relegation of Wagner in the repertory— remains unthinkable to Ross and fellow Wagnerites.

In this Parsifalian quest to make things right and with impressive sleight of hand, Ross manages to shift the onus for the association between Wagnerism and Nazism onto Houston Stewart Chamberlain, a leading racist and antisemitic theorist who married into the Wagner family. While it's plausible that Wagner himself might have had real problems with Hitler and Nazism, and Ross is always measured and qualified even in supposition, it does seem wishful thinking and less than fully persuasive to thus exculpate Wagner. Chamberlain did not write *Parsifal*.

Ross is determined that Wagner himself, however appropriately scolded or judged, will not be held primarily and certainly not enduringly or surpassingly responsible for Hitler and Nazism, however impressive ever-gathering circumstantial evidence might seem. And even if Wagner should be thus indicted, that can't be expected to supersede something as all-encompassing and all-important as Wagner appreciation. It can't be expected to unseat something as mighty, as vastly inspiring, as life-giving and enhancing, as sustained and sustaining as the opiate of Wagnerism.

It's like indicting religion, "the opiate of the masses," or the Church for the Inquisition and genocides of millions of indigenous peoples in the Americas. Whatever the criticism, however serious, however true, religion and the Church will prevail, however dogged and shadowed by politics and history. And likewise Wagnerism, in the future trajectory of which Alex Ross's testimonial will be a cornerstone.

Like the Wanderer standing against Siegfried, Wagnerites have what seems infallible authority. While the Confederate statues in contention with Black Lives Matter include figures of renown and daring, there is no equivalent among them, not remotely, of the sovereign genius of Richard Wagner, of what Thomas Mann called "the greatest talent in the entire history of art." Surely, such a superman must prove exempt from the rules of engagement for mortals.

Like no other work on Wagner or musical culture, *Wagnerism* makes the case for Wagnerism's legacy of influence on art and as well on stirrings and movements of minority and sectarian consciousness. Inevitably, as Wagner himself can seem to have foretold, his artwork of the future would wander from its path of being revolutionary and invincible to losing its footing along the shadowy byways of the future that became history. As the Buddhism that kept beckoning to Wagner doubtless helped him foresee, nothing of this world is forever.

∇

Epilogue. A close friend, Joel— a gay, liberal fellow Georgian whose grandfather fought in the Confederacy — and I were discussing the fate of Confederate statues. What should be done? Our first thought was that they should be consigned to arts parks, like those where statues of Marx, Lenin, Stalin and other Communist figureheads have been left to weather and leer at one another in former Soviet bloc countries. Alternatively, how can we mitigate the toxicity of these taxpayer funded (to the tune nationally of $40 million) relics of slavery and emblems of racism without getting into the unsavory business of interfering with artistic freedom? Joel's suggestion was that rather than remove them, we should consider placing statues of American Civil Rights leaders in meaningful juxtaposition to them. Opposite that of Robert E. Lee, for example, consider placing a statue of Frederick Douglass, Martin Luther King, Jr., Nelson Mandela, John Lewis or Barak Obama.

Meanwhile, there's a new statue, the first in 60 years for Central Park in New York City. The Women's Rights Pioneer Monument, as it's called, honors Susan B. Anthony, Sojourner Truth and Elizabeth Cady Stanton. They are the first women to be so honored, to break the "bronze ceiling" of what was heretofore a club for men only in Central Park, as most everywhere else.

In Germany today there are no legal public statues of Nazi figureheads. The issue of related figures, like Wagner, appears to have thus far skirted major protest. In my exchanges with Marc Weiner about the Breker busts, it's clear that neither of us has the heart or stomach to be involved in anti-art initiatives, notwithstanding the deep empathy we share for Black Lives Matter and other activism around minority concerns, including those of Holocaust survivors.

Meanwhile, I recall a postcard from Germany during WW2 that showed Hitler in apposition to Einstein. Putting aside tough questions of the public subsidization of such vestiges of Nazism as the Breker works, in a hypothetical future reconfiguring of public art for Bayreuth, which historical figures might occupy appositional places for Wagner?

In his penultimate chapter, "Siegfried's Death,"about the Nazi period and the war years, Ross notes that in recent seasons Breker's Wagner bust at Bayreuth has been "hemmed in" by an exhibit called "Silenced Voices" — a series of panels of Jewish musicians who served at Bayreuth into the Nazi period and perished during the war, a number of them at death camps like Theresienstadt. Were any sent to Flossenburg in the environs of Bayreuth, where Wieland Wagner was appointed titular head by Hitler and where 30,000 inmates were murdered?

Possibilities for figures that could give dimension and context to Wagner do come to mind: Giacomo Meyerbeer, Felix Mendelssohn Bartholdy, Hermann Levi, Friedelind Wagner, Arturo Toscanini, Lauritz Melchior, Friederich Schorr, Lotte Lehmann, Bruno Walter, to name a few.

And Gottfried Wagner? Farfetched as it might seem to pose such a comparison, are Gottfried, the most outspoken Wagner family member on the issue of his family's complicity in Nazism, and his aunt Friedelind Wagner, the only outspokenly anti-Nazi Wagner family member who risked her life and legacy to leave Germany during the war, less worthy of being rendered in bronze in the environs of Bayreuth than Winifred Wagner?

Though Winifred is known to have helped some Jewish artists escape persecution, Ross notes that her record of loyalty to Hitler and the Festival was "unwavering." Have we been tacitly granting surpassing credit to never-repentant Nazi collaborator Winifred Wagner for maintaining and guiding the festival through the period of her intimate friendship with and enthusiastic support for Hitler and Nazism, and beyond from the sidelines via the leadership of the Festival she designated for her sons, likewise never explicitly publicly repentant Nazi collaborators Wieland and Wolfgang Wagner?

In his chapter, "Venusberg: Feminist and Gay Wagner," Ross observes that "moral crusades in art seldom succeed in felling their targets, and Wagner is no exception." A corollary is that just as the BLM-led felling of Confederate statues cannot rewrite the legacy of racism and slavery, appositioning Breker's busts and statues with others cannot reconfigure the legacy of antisemitism and the Holocaust.

However daunting the prospects and challenges of change, a process of reconfiguration, if not yet the particulars, would begin to take shape as we become willing to step forward, in transition from the *ancien regime* of Wagnerism. In the shadow of Black Lives Matter and other movements of minority and sectarian consciousness and activism — including those seeking greater accountability for, and some of them inspired by, Wagnerism — the future will chart its own course.

# Wagner Intoxication: Listening to Gottfried Wagner

### "The Truth Nobody Wants to Hear"

Figure 111 - From Left: Michael Shapiro, Gottfried Wagner, John Corigliano, William M. Hoffman, Lawrence D. Mass, 1995, at the home of Michael Shapiro, Chappaqua, New York, personal photograph collection of Lawrence D. Mass

For Gottfried Wagner, my work on Wagner, art and addiction struck an immediate chord of recognition. I was trying to describe what Gottfried has long referred to as "Wagner intoxication." In fact, he thought this would make a good title for my book. The subtitle he suggested was taken from the title of his Foreword to my *Confessions of a Jewish Wagnerite*: "Redemption from Wagner the redeemer: some introductory thoughts on Wagner's anti-semitism." The meaning of this phrase, "redemption from the redeemer," taken from Nietzsche, is discussed in the interview with Gottfried that follows these reflections.

Like me, Gottfried sees the world of Wagner appreciation as deeply affected by a cultish devotion that from its inception was cradling history's most irrational and extremist mass-psychological movement. Like other intoxications, full-blown Wagnerism involves levels of denial and rationalization that have few if any counterpart in the appreciations of other art and artists, and none at all in intensity, consequence and persistence. Just as there is no Mozartism, Verdiism and Brahmsism (notwithstanding personality cultism around Liszt, Mahler and others), no other art demands such denial of its content and import. To be sure, there is antisemitism, just as there is racism, sexism and homophobia, in the lives of other artists and artworks, but none comparable to that which marks the life and art of Richard Wagner.

My connection with Gottfried was immediate and strong. In the late 1980's, as I was completing my memoir, *Confessions of a Jewish Wagnerite*, for which he would write a Foreword, Gottfried was visiting New York. He was to meet with colleagues and speak publicly regarding the enthusiastic collusion of the Wagner family and Bayreuth with Hitler and Nazism, and how Wagner himself and his music dramas contributed significantly to the *perpetration* of the Holocaust.

I use that word perpetration purposely here without quotes. Gottfried had been working with Dr. Abraham Peck, Director of Holocaust, Genocide and Human Rights Studies at the University of Maine, on a post-*Shoah* dialogue series. Dr. Peck is the author/editor of fourteen scholarly volumes, including *The Holocaust and History* (1998) and *Our Zero Hour: Germans and Jews After 1945: Family History, Holocaust and New Beginnings*, published in German and co-authored with Gottfried Wagner (2006).

It has often been observed that Gottfried is "truly a Wagner," not only physically but also in strength of personality and in his commitment to principles. It's a designation about which Gottfried is understandably wary but which he can also appreciate as salutary. As the sole indictor of the Wagner family as Holocaust perpetrators, he clearly is not a prevaricator. Unlike so many of us, he isn't stuck between that rock of Wagner's greatness and that hard place of the enormity of evil wrought in the wake of Wagner's antisemitism.

My own personal journey is instructive. Though I always knew of the extent of Wagner's antisemitism and its consequences, I was never able to get beyond what seemed his insurmountable greatness as a composer and incomparable influence on music, theater, art and culture. At the deepest level of personal experience I myself had fallen in love with Wagner's operas and my own powerful sense of his preeminence in opera seemed viscerally as well as intellectually and culturally impossible to challenge. Gottfried was the first leading figure, and still the only one of my experience, to be able to transcend this dilemma and thereby articulate a clear and unequivocal judgement and indictment of Wagner and the Wagner family.

But how did Gottfried develop from the intoxication of growing up in Bayreuth to becoming an outspoken anti-Wagnerite? Both prior to and since my first encounters with Gottfried, even the most critical and articulate of observers who recognized and analyzed Wagner's antisemitism—like Robert Gutman, author of *Richard Wagner: The Man, His Mind, his Music*, and Marc Weiner, author of *Wagner and The Anti-Semitic Imagination*—remained Wagnerites, and Jewish ones at that. Whatever the challenges, whatever the intellectual acrobatics, they remained self-confident in their ability to separate the man from his art. While I got to know both Gutman and Weiner as Wagnerites as well as critics, I felt less secure and more conflicted about the separation of Wagner from his art than they seemed to.

One critic of Gottfried Wagner has described him as "having a severe personality disorder" and being "a crybaby." Critics have pilloried his memoir, *Twilight of the Wagners*, as "an embarrassing rant" and its author as "a whiner who blames everyone else (loudly and viciously) for his failures and who wrenches his arm patting himself on the back for his few, really rather undistinguished successes." (These sabotaging quotes are from Amazon customer reviews.)

Such responses only endeared me to Gottfried and bolstered my admiration for his courage in the face of the isolation and hardship of his mission. In going so against the grain of common opinion and expressing himself in terms that alienated more than they attracted, Gottfried reminded me of another great and outspoken activist hero of our lives and times: Larry Kramer.

In fact, the only criticism that ever really challenged my appreciation of Gottfried Wagner was the insinuation that he had no discernible love for Wagner's work.

This brought me back to a singular memory of my opera-going experience, a dinner *a deux* with composer John Corigliano, who became a friend via his collaborations with my close friend William M. Hoffman, his co-creator of the opera *Ghosts of Versailles,* I understood that John did not count himself a Wagnerite. A master of musical styles, John has a unique understanding of the art of music. Though he has been accused by some of being more of an imitator skilled at pastiche, it's difficult to imagine another figure of contemporary music with a greater sense of the varieties of musical experience.

I remember our conversation over that dinner at *Josephina*, opposite Lincoln Center. "I know you to be one of the great composers of our time and to have an incomparable knowledge of musical genres," I said. "Among composers, especially modernists, there have been plenty who have regarded themselves as being anti-Wagner. Even Arnold Schoenberg, the godfather of atonality, however, appreciated Wagner's greatness and contributions. You, on the other hand, seem unwilling to be counted as within these ranks. How can that be?" John's response was simple, honest and heartfelt. He said he'd always been aware of the ferocity of the composer's antisemitic agenda and that no appreciation of this or that skill or effect, achievement or popularity could surmount that reality for him.

How, then, would he and Bill Hoffman proceed with their next collaboration, an original opera about Wagner, Wagner appreciation, opera and history called *Liebestod*? With Gottfried Wagner designated as *dramaturg*, the satirical work was intended to skewer the opera world for its Wagnerism and parochialism and to seriously look at issues through the only lens that might work for a broad public – humor. It would be a kind of *Ghosts of Versailles* of Wagnerism, a tantalizing prospect for everybody. Whatever John's discomfort or misgivings about Wagner, his musical conception would have to be built on a basic appreciation of Wagner's music and with that its greatness, wouldn't it?

Although there were sketches and outlines, how this would all have turned out we will never know. A proposal to do the opera was pitched directly to SFO general director Pamela Rosenberg by John and Bill for a new American opera. What I understood from Bill is that Rosenberg swiftly and rather contemptuously rejected the proposal, giving the commission instead to John Adams for what became *Dr. Atomic*. To Rosenberg, apparently, the idea of a serious satire about Wagner seemed preposterous. It was as if they'd proposed a serious satire of the Catholic Church to the Catholic hierarchy to be staged at St Peter's.

It's John Corigliano's response to Wagner that seemed to me to most closely resemble Gottfried Wagner's. While Gottfried does not explicitly deny the mantle of greatness upon his great grandfather, neither will he indulge it. Over the years I've many times asked Gottfried if he ever had the same great love of Wagner that I did. Always his answers have been evasive. If you push John Corigliano on this, certainly he would agree that Wagner's achievements were estimable and his success impressive. Certainly, Gottfried would do the same. But both are very careful not to allow an acknowledgment of any such greatness to alter or supersede their understanding of the motivation, import and consequences of Wagner's art.

True to himself, his vision and his mission, Gottfried completed another book that has yet to be translated into English. Following the publication of his autobiographical *Twilight of the Wagners* in 1997, *Thou Shalt Have No Other Gods Before Me* takes on the fallout of Wagner and what we are calling Wagner intoxication. There, in the Introduction and as translated by Adam J. Sacks, Gottfried expresses himself with raw sensibility and no uncertain terms.

> *Anyone who examines the musical wizard Richard Wagner finds himself/herself first and foremost confronted with the emotional impact of his music. He submerges the listener in a veritable roller coaster of emotion and triggers thereby extreme admiration as well as extreme aversion. But what lies hidden behind this musical ravishment? In my opinion, Wagner's worldview that shaped his life, his writings and his opera, is irreconcilable with the foundations of any humanistic ethic. His views were defined by his racism, misogyny, nihilism and megalomania. These pillars of Wagner's outlook on the world are the subject matter of the book at hand. I have undertaken to strip back the layers of the hagiographic quagmire constructed first by the composer, thinker and politician Richard Wagner. His authoritarian, anti-democratic, racist and sexist legacy is anachronistic, inhuman and anti-European; it is a radioactive, poisonous cesspool from the past, which calls out for a responsible decontamination."*

Figure 112 - Gottfried Wagner, Lpgeffen, 2013, Creative Commons

Unlike most others, Gottfried does not prevaricate around the challenge posed by Wagner. He hasn't allowed the intoxicating music and arts of Wagner to obscure its darker meanings and consequences. In his determination to stay the course, he has been like Parsifal, always mindful of the stakes involved in his mission. Gottfried has not allowed his viewpoint to be corrupted, neither by Wagner's art nor the family business of Bayreuth—"Wagner, Inc"— which he judges and indicts with clarity, perspective, surefootedness and passion. In thus positioning himself, he has been ostracized and vilified by his family and Wagnerites worldwide. As I came to see it over time, the price he has paid for this has been his life. Because of its tentacles in the wider world of opera, Wagner, Inc has done its passive-aggressive and pervasive best to marginalize Gottfried as opera's premiere *persona non grata,* a confirmation of his viewpoints Gottfried wears as a badge of pride.

There have been many writers in Gottfried's orbit. In my correspondence with him, some names were recurrent, including Theodore Adorno, Ralph Giordano, Hartmut Zelinsky, Paul Lawrence Rose and Harvey Sachs. At the time I met Gottfried he was working with Yehuda Nir, a Polish-Jewish concentration camp survivor and psychoanalyst living in New York. Nir had published a notably well-written and engaging memoir called *The Lost Childhood,* unique in its observations of daily camp life, its youth and explicit details of sexuality among the inmates. Meanwhile, Nir continued his innovative therapeutic work treating the PTSD of concentration camp survivors, which included participation on some of the cross-cultural panels with Gottfried and Abraham Peck. It was from this setting of post-Holocaust dialogue and testimony that Gottfried commenced his partnership with Nir on the development of *The Lost Childhood* into an opera.

The opera by composer Janice Hamer and librettist Mary Azrael, with Gottfried listed as director, developed under the auspices of American Opera Projects, Inc. in 2007. In 2019, the opera was staged by Opera UCLA in Los Angeles. Gottfried couldn't be present for the event in person because of visa problems, but he was able to attend remotely via Skype sessions, including for post-performance discussions. Meanwhile, however, there was controversy in the background. While the opera was welcomed and successful, Gottfried felt discouraged by an earlier visit to L.A. during a time of protest surrounding the staging by the L.A. Opera of Wagner's *Ring* cycle. As he makes clear in my conversation with him here, his viewpoints of Wagner were almost universally reviled in L.A, including by prominent Jews.

Most notable among these was E. Randol Schoenberg, grandson of composer Arnold Schoenberg, who noted that despite his grandfather's opposition to Wagner and his flight from Nazism, he did not feel that his grandfather, who loved and appreciated Wagner's achievements as a composer, could ever have supported any kind of censorship of Wagner, whether in Israel, L.A. or anywhere else. Gottfried was accused of a kind of reverse fascism as a German, and a Wagner at that, trying to impose a new censorship on art in his support of the ban on Wagner in Israel and his support for the protestors in L.A.

Alas, this experience was all too typical for Gottfried. Like Larry Kramer, Gottfried Wagner is a prophet who was initially rejected in his own land by his own people in his own time for reasons that could seem compelling. All but lost in these L.A. controversies were Gottfried's trenchant positions on Wagner intoxication and toxicity, Richard Wagner's pivotal role in the advent of Hitler and Nazism, and the dangers of Wagnerism for the future.

Despite his ostracism from the Wagner mainstream and virtually all of the Wagner family, Gottfried Wagner has continued his independent work on multiple fronts. Over the years, he has visited

Israel and has paid repeated visits to concentration camps, including Auschwitz and Theresienstadt. He has developed a biographical archive of his mother, Ellen Drexel, who was married to his father, Wolfgang Wagner, and a more extensive archive of his documents for the Central Library of Zurich. Gottfried has continued to lecture widely. He is the author of several books and numerous publications, including his biographical and autobiographical Wagner family history, *Twilight of the Wagners: The Unraveling of a Family Legacy*, and *He Who Does Not Howl With the Wolf*, a study of Wagner and his legacy.

The following biographical information is adapted and expanded from Gottfried Wagner's homepage: http://www.gottfriedhwagner.eu.

Gottfried H. Wagner was born in Bayreuth in 1947. He studied musicology, philosophy and German Philology in Germany and Austria. Awarded by the University of Vienna, his PhD dissertation on Kurt Weill and Bertolt Brecht was later published as a book in Germany, Italy and Japan.

Dr. Wagner has written extensively on the German and European culture and politics of the 19th and 20th century in connection with Jewish culture and history. His studies and interviews have been published in 16 languages. He writes, lectures and works internationally in a range of artistic and cultural settings and utilizing multimedia venues. He has received awards for his cultural and academic activities as well as for his humanitarian involvements.

In 1992 he co-founded with Dr. Abraham Peck "The Post-Holocaust Dialogue Group." His autobiography, *Twilight of the Wagners: The Unraveling of a Family's Legacy* (USA: Picador, 1999) was first published in Germany in 1997. It created worldwide interest and has been translated into 6 languages.

He is co-author with Abraham Peck of the book (in German), *Our Zero Hour – Germans and Jews after 1945: Family History , the Holocaust and a New Beginning,* with an Introduction by Raph Giordano (2006). This book was later published in the U.S. as "*Unwanted legacies – Sharing the burden of post-genocide generations*" (2014), an edition Gottfried has taken issue with.

Since 1983 he has lived in Italy.

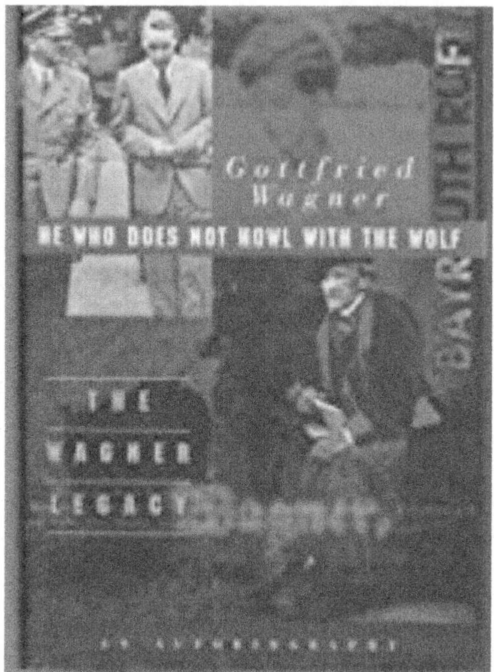


Figure 113 - *He Who Does Not Howl With The Wolf: The Wagner Legacy* by Gottfried Wagner, Amazon.com

## Interview with Gottfried Wagner

***"Dear Larry, we have this in common. We have decided no longer to take the drug of Wagner, and when you do that, you get hated." – Gottfried Wagner, May 9, 2019***

Like Gottfried, I have experienced shunning by mainstream operagoers and Wagnerites. Like Gottfried and inspired by him, I often feel like, and often am, a lone wolf. I have had a voluminous exchange with Gottfried going back many years which will be given to my collected papers at the New York Public Library. As Gottfried's English is more fluent than my German, most of this correspondence is in English.

What follows are the edited, annotated excerpts from Skype conversations, conducted in English, with Gottfried Wagner from his home in Cerro Maggiore, Italy, in early May, 2019, with some revisions in January 2021.

The interview was transcribed and edited by Dr. Adam J. Sacks, the esteemed colleague of Gottfried and myself who has assisted us both with the editing of articles and our current books. Dr. Sacks is a scholar of German and Jewish cultural history.

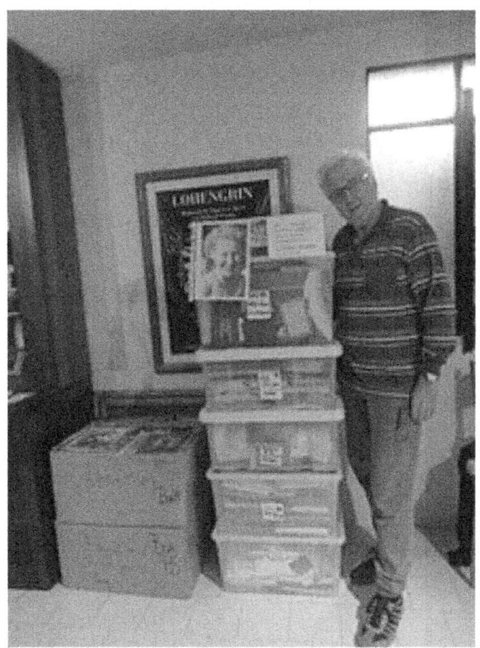


Figure 114 - Photograph courtesy of Gottfried H. Wagner, Wikimedia Commons

***Gottfried Wagner with the archive materials of his mother, Ellen Drexel, the first wife of Wolfgang Wagner (1919-2010), whose centennial was celebrated at Bayreuth in 2019. Following their divorce, Drexel became an outspoken witness to the Hitler period of the Wagner clan and Bayreuth.***

**"In the Case of Winifred Wagner, what we're now agreeing is that she believed what she was indoctrinated to believe, but which turns out to be what's really there in Wagner's meanings and intentions, in his writings and art."**
***- Gottfried Wagner***

***Introductory comment by Larry Mass***: It was my impression from Hans-Jürgen Syberberg's 5-hour documentary film interview with Winifred Wagner, who ran the Bayreuth Festival during the Nazi period, that she was intelligent as well as articulate. After seeing this record of the history of Bayreuth's collaborations with Hitler and Nazism, it's difficult to subscribe to the pretense that the Wagner family and Hitler had an unsophisticated understanding of Wagner and his operas. A key defense of Wagner apologism that also marks Alex Ross's *Wagnerism* is that Nazi appreciations of Wagner were ignorant, superficial, and insensitive to more nuanced and complex meanings. We can now appreciate with greater security and clarity that Winifred, the Wagner family, and many Germans and Wagnerites, did indeed understand the antisemitic foundation and meaning of much of the art of Richard Wagner.

Gottfried Wagner has been at pains to help us see and give proper weight to these antisemitic foundations. He does not feel, however, that Winifred revealed intelligence and awareness in her commitment to Wagner as much as her unquestioning subservience to antisemitism. This prejudice was virtually hard-wired from her upbringing in a milieu of leading antisemites such as Houston Stewart Chamberlain, and her fealty to Hitler. Notoriously, she had an intense and protracted intimacy with Hitler. As for the level of sophistication they shared about Wagner's art, Gottfried points out, one need only consider Hitler's sponsorship of the Nazi "Forbidden Art" purges and exhibitions.

**Gottfried Wagner**: I have a very clear opinion of what was going on in Hitler's work and his sense of Wagner and art. It's what Hannah Arendt talked about as the "*demaskation*" of pure mediocrity, of monstrous bystanders and the *Führer*. This is important when we come to mass manipulation, of what was *gleichgeschaltet*[1]. What was to be "German art" was decreed, and with that came the proscription of "non-Germanic" and "non-patriotic" art –"*Entartete Kunst,*" "*Entartete Musik.*"[2] Hannah Arendt and her book "*Eichmann in Jerusalem*" were criticized by many, also in some Jewish circles, for her concept of "the banality of evil." All of which, however, is pertinent to Winifred. When you analyze what she said, it's

[1] Literally: to tune in equally; figuratively: to coordinate. Nazi terminology for the system of totalitarian control of all institutions and organizations in Germany.

[2] Literally: degenerate art and degenerate music. Nazi terminology for art and music labeled Bolshevik. Generally all art and music made by Jews, leftists and almost all modernists fell in this category. One major exhibition of each occurred in Nazi Germany and much of the work was destroyed.

enormously banal, as Hitler was and indeed as so much of Wagner really was and is. Her viewpoints were not from a refined sensibility, but doubtless did accurately reflect what Wagner and his operas really were all about.

Hitler dominated the taste of Bayreuth, the stage direction, and it was accepted. That's who Winifred was and that's as deep and as far as her thinking about Wagner ever got.

She was filled with Nazi ideas and biases. When she talks about exile, and all the hatred that is connected with that for her, she talked about *demokraten*—not democrats, but *demokroten*—as in *Das Rheingold* where Alberich is changing not into a frog...but to something bigger and more loathsome…

**Larry Mass**: …a toad.

**Gottfried**: *demokroten* was the most derogatory term for democrats.

**Larry**: Meanwhile, most of the opera world has been acculturated to appreciate Wagner as the highest form of art. They don't really allow for Nazi viewpoints, which they dismiss as sentimentality and *kitsch*, not the *real* Wagner. But I think we're now in transition from seeing Wagner as the highest form of art to being something a lot closer to what Hitler and Winifred appreciated and what might now, and with a lot more credibility, be called Nazi art.

**Gottfried**: This idea of *Gesamtkunst*[3], where he brings everything—painting, literature, music—together and offers it as the most important vision for the world today and the future is today totally unsupportable. As for Hitler's appreciation of art, one need only look at his paintings. We must not forget that he was not accepted at the Vienna Academy of Fine Art because of his dilettantism. Had he been accepted, world history might have gone in a different direction.

**Larry:** All of us—and this includes the likes of Toscanini[4] and Friedelind Wagner[5]—thought of Wagner as the highest art and what happened with Hitler in the Nazi period as aberrant. [This viewpoint

---

[3] Literally: total work of art. Master term in Wagner's cultural program of fusing all of the arts as a form superior and more profound than the opera of his day.

[4] Italian conductor and most prominent Anti-Nazi in the musical world of the 20th Century.

[5] Anti-Nazi, confidant of Toscanini, this Wagner granddaughter who fled Nazi Germany and lived in New York during the war.

is tweaked but likewise promulgated in Alex Ross's *Wagnerism*], We objected to Hitler and the Nazis but a lot less to Wagner himself, and always with qualifiers. It has been a difficult and tortuous journey, but now we can finally say we know better. I think the days are finally coming to an end of pretending that Wagner and his music dramas are innocent of any actual role in the advent, trajectory and taint of Hitler and Nazism.

**Gottfried**: I think Harvey[6] Sachs went overboard in glorifying my aunt Friedelind Wagner. I said no, Harvey, there's a major difference between Friedelind and myself. Friedelind did not touch Wagner's profound antisemitism as a central point of his *Weltanschauung*[7] and as expressed in the works themselves. In this I'm radically different from Friedelind. I did try to talk to her about this, which she was open to doing. "Oh, you know, Gottfried, I really do have to reconsider," she told me. She was planning another book which, tragically, never happened. So, yes, I think we now know better.

In my paper for the officials of Bonn for the project of a Museum of Exile, I indirectly attack the millions in financial subsidies for Bayreuth. Why is Bayreuth, a premiere citadel and shrine of Nazism, receiving such copious government endowment in the absence of greater accountability?

**Larry:** As I indicate elsewhere in *On The Future of Wagnerism*, Eva Rieger, author of the latest biography of Friedelind, indirectly verifies what we're saying here about Friedelind—that she (Friedelind) never really expressed herself or apparently ever thought much about Wagner's antisemitism. But neither, likewise apparently, did Friedelind's close friend Toscanini [a reality likewise verified by his evasiveness on this matter in my correspondence with Harvey Sachs].

In email exchanges with me, Rieger initially seemed helpful in my efforts to open up this subject of what Friedelind did and did not recognize about Wagner's antisemitism. Nowhere in her book is there any indication that Friedelind, however aware and rejecting of

---

[6] Harvey Sachs, the author of many important music biographies, notably of Artur Rubinstein and Arturo Toscanini.

[7] German philosophical term indicating literally "a way to look out onto the world," appropriated by the Nazis to indicate having the right ideological viewpoint.

Nazism, understood that her grandfather was deeply antisemitic or that this prejudice tainted his work.

As I say, Rieger was helpful in teasing out this information, or lack thereof. But she became very defensive when I asked if she thought that Friedelind, who never married and whose father Siegfried was preferentially homosexual, might herself have been lesbian.

**Gottfried:** Of course it's most likely Friedelind was lesbian!

**Larry:** Tell that to Rieger. Such huge omissions from observation or even consideration. It's like the legions of writers who wrote about Walt Whitman and Henry James, always managing to skirt questions of sexuality and sexual orientation.

**Gottfried:** There is still need and room for a new biography of Friedelind, one less influenced by Rieger's friend, Nike Wagner, Wieland's daughter and a "new" Bayreuth apologist.

**Larry:** Back to Bayreuth and the question you raise of its funding and subsidies, which your father Wolfgang, "the unrepentant old Nazi," as I've called him, is credited with having done more than anyone else to secure. As you know, Angela Merkel is an ardent Wagnerite who regularly attends the festival and has even done an interview about Wagner that does what we all did prior to the current period—separate the man from the art. What is your feeling about her Wagnerism?

**Gottfried**: More than anything else, she is an opportunist. Her advisors, the German state, first West Germany, then the united, reunified, Germany, pay out millions to support the cultism of Wagner. Her support of Bayreuth and Kapellmeister Christian Thielemann is certainly questionable, leaving her politics questionable as well.

**Larry**: Are you saying you don't think her Wagnerism is genuine?

**Gottfried**: I think she is what her advisors whisper in her ear that she should be. In that sense, she reminds of my grandmother Winifred. When she explained to me the character of Alberich, she repeated what other people had said rather than an opinion that could be called distinctively her own.

**Larry**: Most of us Wagnerites, and this apparently includes Merkel [and now also Alex Ross] accepted the high-art perspective that the Nazis had no real understanding of Wagner. We keep being told how Nazi soldiers were forced to endure performances at Bayreuth they couldn't have cared less about. Just as Winifred was comfortable with Nazi perspectives of Wagner, so is Merkel comfortable with obfuscating postwar anti-Nazi perspectives. In neither case does notable intelligence or sensibility seem operant.

**Gottfried**: Clearly, I do not agree that most Nazis had no real appreciation of Wagner. Riefenstahl made her famous movie, *Triumph of the Will*, with Hitler flying into Nuremberg. In one scene we see the early morning awakening of the soldiers to the future Hitler harkens for Germany. The young Nazis are fourteen. In four years they will be ready to die for the *Führer*. In the background is music from *Die Meistersinger*. On the contrary, the Nazis and the German masses, including Winifred, knew very well what was behind Richard Wagner's *Weltanschauung*.

What we are saying is really the crux of the matter and must be the basis of any serious discussion of Wagnerism in the future. At the outset we must get rid of all these masks of ignorance of intentions and meanings.

Winifred knew all the antisemitic writings of Wagner and those of her in-law Houston Stewart Chamberlain. Then we come to Adolf Hitler and the extremist poison she absorbed in this malignantly antisemitic environment. Cosima was a terrible antisemite, and Winifred's adopted Danish family was likewise virulently antisemitic. The first vocal score of the *Ring* was prepared by militant antisemites. Winifred was brought up with the milk of antisemitism from infancy. In that mode of profound indoctrination from earliest childhood she did her duty, repeating reflexively what she was always told.

**Larry:** Do you think Cosima was like Winifred in being more indoctrinated than independent in her thinking?

**Gottfried**: The diaries of Cosima Wagner convey the real ideological context, the brainswashing, of Wagner appreciation. There's much discussion of whether she and Richard both had Jewish blood or not, which raises questions of self-hatred, of a pathological internalization of antisemitism. This poisoned atmosphere initially found province in Bayreuth with people who could be manipulated.

The Wagners did not go to the big cities to settle, like "Jewish Paris," as Wagner referred to it. Paris is where the French Grand Opera of Meyerbeer had reached its apogee. Nor did they go to Berlin, where Meyerbeer became the first to be leading director of music and opera of both Paris and Berlin, and where he was likewise admired as a modern marvel of being an opera director as well as a composer.

From *Robert Le Diable* Wagner copied *Rienzi*. In Dresden, Wagner made his entry onto the world stage with two operas, *Rienzi* and *Flying Dutchman*, with critical support from Meyerbeer.

**Larry**: Have you ever seen a staged version of *Les Huguenots?*

**Gottfried**: It's so rarely performed now. I have seen it once, but a long time ago in Frankfurt.

**Larry**: It's an astounding work. Wrenchingly historical and dramatic, and gloriously grand, it details the building up and finally the explosion of malignant religious hatred and mass murder. Virtually every critic who has seen and written about it in the recent period, including Alex Ross, has been thunderstruck by its power and agrees that it deserves an honored and regular place back in the standard repertory.

**Gottfried**: It's a scandal that the Jewish world especially in New York does not push for a Meyerbeer cycle instead of Wagner all the time.

**Larry**: I know we're in agreement that the only reason *Les Huguenots* is not where it should be in the standard repertoire is because of the enduring toxicity of Wagner's antisemitism.

**Gottfried**: For his Met Opera 30th anniversary concert, James Levine chose the overture to *Rienzi,* knowing the Hitler burden it carries of Hitler seeing himself as the savior of Germany, inspired by the music of *Rienzi*. When I tried to discuss this with him, he immediately withdrew. "Oh, I have no time!" he said, then quickly disappeared.

**Larry**: Levine was, like Barenboim, a favorite at Bayreuth and a champion of Wagner. But unlike Barenboim, he never showed any real willingness to discuss Wagner, Jewishness, Hitler, etc. Nor for that matter did he ever show any willingness to discuss homosexuality. For him, the separation of art from everything else was as absolute as you will ever see. Of course, now we see this bigger, more complicated picture of his reticence around his homosexuality. He was in the closet with all of it —his Judaism as well as his homosexuality.

**Gottfried**: As I saw it, such a top position as musical-artistic direction of the Metropolitan Opera carried enormous responsibility regarding cultural controversies as well as just the art.

**Larry**: While our awareness of his being gay and Jewish could imply support of or sympathy with this or that minority concern or initiative, his reticence was relentless. In this, the Metropolitan Opera has shown itself to be indistinguishable from most other arts institutions and artists. With rare but notable exceptions, as during World War 2, or with the opera *Klinghoffer*, they steer as clear of controversy as they can, even when they are conspicuous and troubled in doing so. The Metropolitan Opera and James Levine are like Richard Strauss. However simpatico we might surmise them to be, they remained aloof from most controversies to the extent of being passive collaborators.

**Gottfried**: A background story. As a scout for Levine, my sister Eva Wagner was sent all over the world with Levine's manager and private secretary, Sissy Strauss. They had a luxury apartment close to the Metropolitan Opera. I was invited to go to a party there when we presented *The Lost Childhood* (the opera by Janice Hamer, based on the book by Yehuda Nir). Knowing I wasn't really welcome, I said on entering, "Gottfried, the devil is here!" Sissy was embarrassed and tried to ease the ambient discomfort.

**Larry**: What comes to mind about the intransigence of Wagnerism is not so much the controversy around antisemitism as my experience in addiction. As you know, I'm interested in addiction in relation to Wagnerism.

Addiction is a term we often use casually in talking about our relationship to Wagner's music. If you go to a heroin addict and say we need to talk about drug addiction in your life, they may be willing to do that, but if you get to the point where you actually threaten to take away their drugs or access to them, then you are going to encounter very serious resistance. With the Wagner cult, when you threaten their drug of Wagner, you are getting into comparably dangerous territory. They don't want you messing with their drug. Like a prophet, so characteristically rejected and reviled in their own lands by their own people, you are the bearer of tidings they do not want to hear.

**Gottfried**: Dear Larry, we have this in common. We have decided no longer to take the drug of Wagner, and when you do that, you get hated.

**Larry**: Let's move on to the business of the denazification of artists in the aftermath of the war. Was it right that the Wagner family, especially Winifred and her two sons, Wieland and Wolfgang, managed to evade criminal prosecution?

**Gottfried**: No, of course not. What happened was a case of almost perfect manipulation and falsification by Winifred and her sons. Tietjen, the Mephisto of the German Opera world, did is part in the background. Winifred was first. We have the trial of July 2nd 1947, when she was in the second category of guilt. She talked very aggressively and without any humility: "I did my duty. I am not guilty."

**Larry**: That's what they all said, and still say, like Dietrich Fischer-Dieskau when interviewed in the documentary on Max Lorenz. As they saw and still see it, they were simply carrying out their duties as German citizens, soldiers and patriots.

**Gottfried**: Winifred's guilt is often qualified by claims that she helped Jews, but this was not because she was conflicted in her antisemitism and commitment to Hitler and Nazism. By her own admission, it was more about the efficient operations of the Festival. The antisemitic mistreatment of Jews at Bayreuth traces way back to the case of a Jewish patron who had been present at the first *Ring* cycle of 1876. Wagner and Cosima made humiliating comments to her: "We will save you. You will be like Kundry. We will give you redemption even as a Jew."

**Larry:** On this crucial subject of redemption that is the principal theme of *Parsifal*, what is your interpretation of what Wagner is saying?

**Gottfried**: With the financial fiasco of the first festival, Richard and Cosima had a mountain of debts. Cosima wrote in her diaries, "Now we need a very rich Jew to sweep away all our debts." Of course, Wagner's agent, Angelo Neumann, was Jewish. And indeed, Neumann helped to shape what became Wagner, Inc. The vicious and cynical antisemitic snipes in Cosima's diaries are so disgusting! And Wagner writes as well in the diaries, with his own "corrections." In the aftermath of the *Burgtheater* fire[8], where 35 Jews died, Richard writes that many more Jews should have perished. Here, already, is the first vision and mission of Auschwitz. Hartmut Zelinsky has studied the details connecting Cosima's diaries with those of Richard.[9]

---

[8] A famous fire of June 14th, 1881 during a performance of *Les Contes d'Hoffmann* in Vienna, 625 are said to have died.

[9] Contemporary German Wagner Researcher Harmut Zelinsky and his text *Wagner: Ein Deutsches Thema.*

**Larry**: So you don't think Wagner is saying the Jews are redeemed the way Kundry *appears* to be "redeemed" at the conclusion of *Parsfial*?

**Gottfried**: No, not at all. First, consider the problem between Kundry and Parsifal. Why can't they have sex? Beyond issues of plot, and good and evil, the surpassing reason is because an Aryan hero cannot have sex with a Jewish woman.

**Larry**: Ok, but then what is it that happens to Kundry at the end? She dies, but is she not redeemed?

**Gottfried**: Because she is Jewish, she cannot be redeemed and has to die. She dies so the man club of Aryan Grail knights can heal and prevail. The curse of her Jewish blood and the endless recurrence of her sins and crimes as Jewish and womanly, is finally ended with her death. Metaphorically, her death is that of the Jews. She cannot be redeemed. The best that can be hoped for the Jews is that in death, like Kundry, they may be forgiven.

**Larry**: It solves the problem of redemption by having her die.

**Gottfried**: Exactly. It's so dark at the very end: *Erlösung dem Erlöser* (redemption to the redeemer),[10] but the ending is clear. Parsifal is successful in resisting the temptation to have sex with the Jewish woman, in resisting her diabolically feminine and Jewish wiles. He remains pure but is no longer a fool. Rather than being wondrously ambiguous and spiritual, this is the worst and lowest of racist, antisemitic claptrap.

**Larry**: Of the many Wagnerites and others who have attended performances of *Parsifal*, how many of them do you think are aware that Kundry represents the Jews?

**Gottfried**: I think it's so clear, and from the moment she enters "wildly" enters on stage in Act 1, from "Arabia..."

**Larry**: Sophisticated, intoxicated Wagnerites play this coy game where they claim that because for example Beckmesser—like Kundry and Alberich— isn't explicitly stated by Wagner to be a Jew, imputations of antisemitism are therefore moot.

---

[10] A take off by Wagner of the Nietzsche saying: "I might believe in the Redeemer if his followers look more redeemed." Instead Wagner via *Parsifal* intends to redeem Christ himself, by purging him, and solving the greatest problem of Christianity in the "Aryan" imagination, the Jewish blood of Jesus.

Here's another question, do you think that there is a more poisonously antisemitic representation in all of art than Kundry? She is the character that laughed at Christ's agony. It's like the *Oberammergau*[11] passion play, but worse in sporting the mantle of high art and with a success and a level of influence that no other artwork has ever had.

**Gottfried**: In this way Wagner also indirectly condemns Jerusalem and Rome. Wagner writes very clearly that Rome is disgusting and "Judaified;" i.e., the Jesuits go there together with the Jews. We need Bayreuth to be the new center of Aryan spirituality. I grew up in the shadow of the headquarters of this most extreme and disgusting racist and antisemitic hokum.

**Larry**: Here in America I was the typical Jewish Wagnerite. I loved and revered the art and with it as well the artist, even though I knew early on that he was antisemitic. People claim to easily separate the man from the art, but how feasible is that? It wasn't until the last few years that I finally paid closer attention to what was actually going on in *Parsifal* and what this virtual passion play was really all about. Obfuscated by Wagner's layers of ambiguity and carefully evaded by our music critics was the whole business of Kundry as the Wandering Jew who laughed at Christ's agony. I knew that scholars and historians inveighed against Wagner for *Parsifal*, but I never allowed myself to actually see and digest that *Parsifal* conveys the most serious antisemitic slander ever perpetrated in a major work of art. That's not something our leading music critics want to take note of or ever have. They never speak of it directly and write circles around it.

**Gottfried**: Beckmesser[12] is also presented as a very brutal…

**Larry:** Beckmesser and the Nibelungs are brutal, hideous, toxic stereotypes. But because it's high art, it gets likewise rationalized and evaded, and inevitably with the ace card of "ambiguity." Trust not what's there in front of you but what is gleanable between the lines. In the West a lot of opera people don't know German so they don't

---

[11] A Passion Play performed since 1634 by all the inhabitants of the homonymous village. Though significant changes have been wrought since the Nazi era, the play was interpreted as an encapsulation of the worst elements of Christian anti-Judaism, e.g. deicide, supcercessionism, collective guilt, etc.

[12] The music critic character from Wagner's Die Meistersinger von Nürnberg, widely seen as an anti-Semitic caricature of the influential Viennese Jewish critic Edward Hanslick.

have a sophisticated knowledge and awareness of the very unsophisticated business of prejudice that are the heart and soul of these works. But certainly the Germans and Nazis did.

**Gottfried**: Yes, they did, and Kaiser Wilhelm did as well. And with them the lower social classes. That the Kaiser was falling on his knees before Richard Wagner is as political as having the leading antisemitic theorist and Wagner son-in-law Houston Stewart Chamberlain[13] as the advisor of the imperial family.

**Larry**: Lets go back to King Ludwig now. He worshipped Wagner as an artist but he was not antisemitic. Was he like Toscanini and Friedelind in not seeing these issues with Wagner? He fought with Wagner about Levi[14] and Ludwig prevailed in having him conduct the premiere of *Parsifal* at Bayreuth. There was a lot of back and forth between them about this. But did Ludwig not see the antisemitic stereotypes in the *Ring* cycle, *Meistersinger* and *Parsifal?* Or was he intoxicated into passivity on this the way Wagnerites everywhere have been ever since?

**Gottfried**: Yes, that's it. He was so under the drug of the music, of Wagner, that any such inklings were likely suppressed.

At the time of *Parsifal,* Ludwig was already seriously confused as a result of some degree of mental illness. He was already a therapeutic case. To what extent their relationship had sexual overtones remains open to debate.

**Larry**: Let's move on to your uncle, Wieland Wagner, Wolfgang's brother. How did they manage so to obfuscate his tenure at Flossenbürg[15]? We knew he was there, but nobody knew the full extent of what transpired there, nor did anybody ask probing questions. It was never discussed. His mistress Anja Silia[16] implies that he was very remorseful about what he had done. But did he ever himself address this publicly? Did he ever express any public remorse

---

[13] Houston Stewart Chamberlain (1855-1927) British born racialst, pan-German philosopher. Married into the Wagner family, wrote "The Foundations of the Nineteenth Century" and is seen as Hitler's "John the Baptist."

[14] Hermann Levi, noted German Jewish conductor. 1839-1900, most known for conducting the first performance of *Parsifal* at Bayreuth in 1882.

[15] A Nazi concentration camp (1938-1945) in Bavaria with slave laborers, around 30,000 people perished there.

[16] Anja Silia, German Soprano (1940-) had an affair with Wieland Wagner and later distanced herself from Bayreuth.

or regret about what happened or for that matter about Hitler and Nazism?

**Gottfried**: No, he never addressed this clearly, publicly. Behind the scenes, there was all kinds of skullduggery within the inner circle surrounding public discussion. Because of the delicate legal and reputational issues involved, there was an often tacit kind of blackmailing that went on among the Wagners and their circles. There was always the tacit threat of talking more explicitly about Flossenbürg.

Meanwhile, the strategy of the "new" Bayreuth after 1945 for dealing with its already widely-known enthusiastic collaborations with Hitler and Nazism had to be about more than silence. The answer? To be "friends" with Jewish musicians and Jewish Wagnerites, traditions of which go back to Wagner's creation of his music dramas. The other cornerstone of Wieland's remaking of Wagner was that instead of the symbolism of Nazism, he used Freudian and Jungian symbolism in the heyday of psychoanalysis, widely perceived to be have been a phenomenon of Jewish science, spirituality and sensibility. Thus did Wieland mask himself and Wagner's operas. It's "philosemitic antisemitism," as I have demasked it my website collage.

**Larry**: My sense of Jung was that he was, like Richard Strauss, a "soft" collaborator. I never got the sense that he was anything more than casually antisemitic. He didn't seem personally invested in it, notwithstanding all his work exploring and thereby validating the powers of mythology.

**Gottfried**: Having a Jewish daughter-in-law, Richard Strauss was perforce a "soft" collaborator. When he later awoke to the consequences of Nazism, he felt deeply ashamed. This became clear in my discussion with leading Strauss scholar, Dr. Stephen Kohler.

As for Jung, I think antisemitism is there, in his article on Wotan and in the implications of his theories of the "collective unconscious." Which brings us back to Wieland Wagner and his showcasing of Wagner with reference to Freud and Jung, shifting the dialogue from politics and history to psychology and psychoanalysis. The big German industrialist sponsors of Wagner and New Bayreuth, like Krupp, seemed to understand the need to back such abstraction in the immediate post-war period. It obscured not only the history and politics of Wagner and Bayreuth, but also the aesthetics: the

*Reichstagspartei*[17] scenery Wieland learned initially, under the protection of the *Führer*, who told Wieland to take the architecture and art of Nürnberg as his model. Wieland escaped to the French occupation zone because the Americans would have put him in prison. As we know, there are numerous photos and newsreels showing Hitler with Wieland and Wolfgang and likewise with Albert Speer.

**Larry**: They really were all war criminals.

**Gottfried**: Yes, they were. I suggested that in my own stage direction of *Lohengrin* for Dessau. Not surprisingly, it was hated. I recreated the box where Hitler was sitting in the Dessau opera house, which was built by Hitler. I made this box empty. I had wanted to put in a puppet of Hitler there but they did not allow me to do that.

**Larry:** Tell us more about this production. As I recall, a central concept was the whole business of not being able to question Lohengrin about where he comes from and otherwise about his past. What resonance for the Wagners, Bayreuth and Nazism!

**Gottfried**: In the middle of my production was a metaphor of the ideological training of Gottfried, the murdered Prince of Brabant around whom the plot revolves. In the picture of the set design we see the pillars of a church with its roots pulled up. What's being demonstrated is that when you cut off the Jews, you eliminate the basis of Christianity. You cannot discuss Jesus without the rabbinic tradition. It gets so absurd. I also showed Ortrud as the evil Jewess who poisoned the Aryan Elsa. Heinrich Mann[18] wrote on this, of her connection to Kundry.

**Larry**: Is there likewise any intimation of Jewishness for Venus?

**Gottfried:** Yes, when you consider the role of seductiveness and the falsity of that seductiveness, Venus bears striking similarities to Kundry. Sensual pleasure derailing sacred duties and journeys.

**Larry**: The world was marveling when Wieland did his *Tannhäuser* with Grace Bumbry as *Die Scharze Venus*." Everyone thought, oh, it's so liberal, so thoughtful, so opened up to have the first black singer at Bayreuth. But if you think about it from the racist

[17] Nazi party rallies held in Nuremberg (the so-called "city of the movement") almost every year.

[18] Gottfried may be confusing here Heinrich with his brother Thomas, as Heinrich was an avowed anti-Wagnerian, whilst Thomas engaged in a lifelong personal struggle with his own deep seated Wagnerism.

viewpoint, what the opera is really all about comes into sharper focus: As in *Parsifal*, the result of these forays into miscegenation is a dangerous mixing of the races. Visually, the appearance of very darkly black Grace Bumbry must have been a real red flag to legions of Germans and Wagnerites who really do understand the white supremacist foundations of Wagner's life and art.

**Gottfried**: Grace Bumbry did once touch on this in discussion in her later years, on the "liberality" that hides what's really there. Backstage at that time, you would hear these racist comments about her. So, yes, the issue of having a black singer break a barrier of racism for performers at Bayreuth obscured the bigger issue of what such racial casting implied in sync with the deeper meaning and import of the opera.

**Larry**: So if I were a Nazi I would at first be upset to have a black person on the stage, but then, if I got involved in the opera and considered the staging, I would say to myself: Tannhäuser is indulging in sensuality and at the same time flirting with miscegenation. Look at where this is taking him! And look where it's taking us, the German *volk*, this extreme mixing of the races, of Germans with other races—blacks, Jews!

**Gottfried**: It's all there.

**Larry**: Do you think Wieland actually knew, consciously and deliberately, that he was playing with this?

**Gottfried**: Yes, but he had to hide his own Flossenbürg past. I was hurt that my cousins (Wieland's children) were so supportive of and conspiring with this hiding, this secret of their holy father, Wieland, of his having been the darling of "Uncle Wolf" and hiding Wieland's obsession for power. Of going with Hitler's Mercedes form Berlin on the highway built by Hitler for military purposes, from Munich to Bayreuth to Berlin. The Mercedes took Wieland from Berlin to Bayreuth where slave workers did his preparations.

My father Wolfgang was also favored by Hitler. I have written about it in my autobiography, which caused his break with me. From the moment he became the sole director of the Wagner Festival following Wieland's death in 1966, this hidden obsession for power became more and more evident.

With their "*Ring* of peace," under the mantle of Jungian archetypes and symbols, Wieland and and his conductor Karl Böhm covered themselves. Böhm replaced von Karajan, whose career developed in the *Führer* times and who subsequently made his own empire in Salzburg with the old Austrian Nazis. Braunau am Inn, where Hitler was born, was half an hour by car from Salzburg. I was in Braunau and had occasion to speak in front of the Hitler house. They asked me, Gottfried, "What can be done with the Hitler house? My suggestion was that they have directional signs from the house to all the concentration camps, noting the six million Jews who were murdered there." There was no response. Hungarian TV reported on my visit, documentation of which is on my website.

**Larry**: In the Max Lorenz documentary, Dietrich Fischer Dieskau at one point takes center stage to give the German viewpoint of the relationship between ordinary Germans to Hitler and Nazism. In essence, what he says is now familiar: We were honorable people, we were German citizens, we didn't know everything that was happening, we didn't necessarily approve of what was happening, and we obviously didn't hate Jews. (The documentary features supportive commentary from a colleague of those years, Jewish Hilde Zadek.) We were not bad people. We were citizens and soldiers fulfilling our duty. Again, there was this situation of no expressed remorse or regret. Rather, there was denial and justification.

**Gottfried**: The deformation of the brain within the Third Reich went on after the *Shoah*. The need was very strong for people to find some way of preserving something good from their participation in what happened. I've quoted Bruno Bettelheim, and also Primo Levi. On one side is the great delusion and danger of denial. On the other, there might be hope for Europe, a hope that can only come from a radical opening up of this box of Pandora of the truth.

There has never been in Germany and Europe an honest denazification. That was a burden for the generations after.

Figure 115 - Gottfried Wagner, 2006, with permission

**Larry**: Let me jump from here to something else. Tangential to this discussion of coming to grips with the reality of fascism and national socialism and our passive collusions in these developments is our circumstance, in this country and globally, of dealing with our current presidency [Donald Trump], which has so stoked the flames of white nationalism and also antisemitism, even as the President has been pro-Israel and has Jewish grandchildren. This is very difficult for people like you and I who are very concerned about antisemitism, and about Israel, about the future of Jews and the ever-hovering possibility of renewed attempts at genocide. What can you say about Trump and what's going on in America and globally under his auspices?

**Gottfried**: It's very clear to me, actually. I have a close friend, David Friedman, who is the director of solar energy in Israel. His work is in the Negev desert. He comes from a Jewish English background, with a left liberal education. When it comes to these questions, when militant groups are constantly aiming to destroy and blow up Israel and kill you and your people, then of course, you have to think *a priori* about your survival.

**Larry:** I totally agree, but are you comfortable with Donald Trump as the vector for Israel's survival?

**Gottfried**: Virtually everything he does is inflammatory and under his influence hatred is spiraling out of control. As Spinoza observed, hatred will only increase hatred. Only love can overcome.

But not in the sense of what Daniel Barenboim is doing, going into the Gaza strip to perform the central European music of Beethoven and Wagner. What he really needs to do is find a way to include and integrate Arabic music in concerts. Inclusion, integration and love are not Trump strategies.

**Larry**: On the surface, it's good that Trump has stood up for Israel and that he's been confrontational with Iran and Islamic militants and about Islamic antisemitism, which is often explicitly genocidal. But all this hatred has been unleashed in the process. A lot of those rallying around Trump are otherwise extremely antisemitic. I don't see what's achieved in switching from Islamic antisemitism, which can be as bad as it gets, to neo-Nazi antisemitism, which can be indistinguishable in character and danger.

**Gottfried**: Trump is a violent capitalist. He has vailed in all essential aspects of his politics. He has strongly damaged the international image of the USA. Inevitably, what really counts in this kind of politics are markets. Israel and Jews are strategic, and extremely important as such. I mean, even though his family includes Jews, does he really care about Jews any more than he really cares about evangelical Christians? Nonsense! It's all business. It has nothing to do with moral and spiritual issues.

January 20, 2021 is not the end of Trump and his troups. Biden began in a contrastingly very modest way in his role as the new President, but he immediately signed important contracts and reopened the door for America and its citizens to the rest of the world. How he will negotiate the delicate situation of Israel remains to be seen.

At one point I was doing some teaching in the Gaza Strip, in a multicultural religious group with a catholic priest who is Arabic. He was forbidden in his school to display any kind of symbol, no Star of David, no cross. I remember trying to say to these kids that we have to find a way to talk with each other. We have to learn from each other. If we don't do that, we will be at war. When I crossed the border from Israel, the Israeli soldier screening me asked, "what are you doing there with the Arabs? Are you cooperating with radical groups?" I became a suspect for my attitude and efforts.

Do you know the author, Arno Gruen? He wrote on these issues, on "the other in ourselves." He and Ralph Giordano are my favorite authors. I met him and we talked about these difficult issues. He had escaped as a Jewish boy from Berlin. I also met the nephew of Einstein, Lou, who did not get any help from his famous uncle. He had endured pogroms. His rabbi was killed in front of him in Ulm. He would not talk one word of German until he met me. Then, after sixty years, he looked at me and spoke German with a *Schwäbisch* dialect. We sat together with his wife who was Jewish and who explained that he resolutely ceased speaking German after having been so brutalized growing up in Germany.

Communication can be sparked by ineffable connections of spirit that can be gleaned in the eyes, by one's countenance, but appearances can be deceiving. I'm often told I have the Wagner mien, that I resemble my great grandfather Richard Wagner. But I am so radically different from my forbearer. Yehuda Nir would always say something about my Wagner blood and I would many times counter that my blood is also that of my mother, whose makeup was far less German and far less Nazi. I do not like the whole "blood" discussion at all!

Yehuda died in 2014 in New York. I wanted to fly over for his funeral, but could not because I was still dealing with the fallout of my own father's (Wolfgang Wagner's) death in 2010. But it was not for reasons of mourning my father that I had to remain. I was never in denial of my having been the only son of Wolfgang Wagner. I needed to see how Thielemann, Katharina and Eva were dealing with his passing and legacy. As it turned out, I was informed by the newspapers rather than by the family of my father's death. The newspapers wanted to know what I had to say and I hadn't yet even heard that he died!

**Larry:** How do you feel about the current joint stewardship of Bayreuth under Eva and Katharina?

**Gottfried**: They struggled with each other for power, not so unlike the way their father Wolfgang and uncle Wieland fought with each other for power. It could seem like the two sets of brothers and other family feuds in the *Ring* cycle. Then of course there were all kinds of power alliances, some of them with Jewishness in the background, and sometimes in the foreground with figures like Daniel Baremboim and Georg Solti. Eva was always very close to Solti, who did not like my father at all.

**Larry**: Why is that?

**Gottfried**: Solti, a notoriously demanding Wagner specialist, came to Bayreuth to conduct a new production of the *Ring* cycle directed by Peter Hall in 1983. In the face of his considerable demands, my father became very nasty. He did not say to him "Oh you Jew!" but antisemitism was in the atmosphere. I met Solti in Chicago during his tenure as conductor of the Chicago Symphony Orchestra. He gave me an endorsement for my work on Weil and Brecht. "What can we do with Gottfried!" he joked. "He cannot be corrupted by anybody!" Sir Georg Solti has always been very generous with me.

**Larry:** Solti was another Jewish Wagnerite who evaded in-depth discussion of Wagner's antisemitism. For decades into the postwar period, they all still did—e.g., Barenboim, Levine, Solti, even Bernstein. They all came to that same conclusion: great art, bad man, there's no reconciling of the two and they don't have to be reconciled. Case closed.

Have you maintained relations with Eva and Katharina?

**Gottfried**: Having been informed by the media rather than directly by them when our father died was unforgiveable. Half a year before, Eva sent me an SMS, "Father would like to see you." As I had nothing to hide, I had no problem and was ready to get on the next plane. I planned to look him in the eye and say, "Father you made your choices for which side of the street to be on—with Uncle Wolf and Nazism. These are not choices I could ever have made or that I was ever asked to forgive. You were your mother's darling, the unrepentant Nazi and apologist for Hitler. Likewise choices I could never endorse and was never asked to forgive. These decisions determined your life, and with them, our lives diverged irreconcilably.

On the eve of my departure for Frankfurt to see my father, who I hadn't seen since my first trip to Israel and in light of his refusal to talk about topics deemed taboo for New Bayreuth, my father's Doctor (Thierry) communicated to me—not directly but through my father's office: "Your father is not in a condition to receive you tomorrow." They prevented me from seeing my father when he was still alive. My father was not senile, but he did have some symptoms of dementia. I have all the emails my sister collected when she wrote me from the hospital. Among them were one quoting my father saying, "I'm sure Gottfried never ever wants to see me," followed by a reply from me: "Of course I'm coming."

Eva and Katharina didn't want me to see my father while he was still alive, and not just to prevent stress and hurt. There was business to be finalized between Thielemann and Katharina. They had already decided every detail of the funeral program. It was to include Mendelssohn! Shows what good philosemites they all were and are, right?

Then the urn with my father's ashes disappeared. He was cremated without my being informed. Legally, Katharina could bring the urn in her suitcase to her apartment in Berlin, put it on her pianoforte, and play music from *Tristan*. They alleged that that was my father's wish, which he had clearly expressed, that for his funeral at the family grave in Bayreuth, only Katharina, Eva, and that old Nazi Verena (their other sibling), should be present. The bad son Gottfried was not to be there. This was his wish. That's why I was not informed by the family when he died. When I asked my sister's lawyer, Brandner, in Bayreuth, about the fate of the urn with my father's ashes, I was blocked. "We will not answer your questions."

This kind of behavior coalesced with the commemoration of Wolfgang Wagner at Bayreuth in 2010. Here, slimy Christian Thielemann declared himself to be the musical son of Wolfgang Wagner. Thielemann was the darling of Wolfgang and Gudrun Wagner, always strongly under the influence of his career-pushing mother and his ghost writer Lemke-Matwey.

At this service my father's very servile doctor spoke at length. Wolfgang Wagner was presented as a brilliant man of vision. It was made clear that it was Wolfgang's intention that his daughters should run the festival and have jurisdiction over all the World War 2 documents between Winifred, the Wagner family and Hitler that have yet to be made public. Winifred was careful to conceal those documents from the American forces that occupied Bayreuth—from "those Jews," as she described them—who asked that they be handed over.

It's important to know that Richard Wagner left no last will and testament, in the wake of which there was chaos, and false documents, eventually including Cosima's last will. All legal procedures of the Bayreuth Festival from 1883, the year of Wagner's death, onwards, including the last will of Wagner's son Siegfried and the New Bayreuth Foundation in 1973, are based on legal fraud. This scandalous situation has been documented by Professor Heinz Holzhauer. I did not want to get mixed up in all this.

**Larry**: So let me ask you about the infamous *Meistersinger* production Katharina did in 2007 that was criticized as so over the top in being anti-antisemitic. Are you implying that it was not coming from her own genuine vision and concern—that it just a kind of political correctness display?

**Gottfried**: What was genuine is that she thought she was doing a kind of exorcism at the outset of her tenure as co-director. The logic here was that now that Gottfried had done so much around the question of antisemitism, made so much public disturbance about it, we have to take the reins on this issue forefront at Bayreuth, with our productions and with Jewish conductors and directors. We have to co-opt what Gottfried has done. The time was again right for another major exorcism of the deeply rooted antisemitism of the Bayreuth Festival, and for the international business of opera and Wagner, Inc.

**Larry:** But when you think of it, is not this exorcism always the underlying quest for post-Holocaust Wagnerites? They are like Tannhäuser seeking salvation and Parsifal seeking to heal the otherwise mortal wound to Germankind—pilgrimages to purge the evil and sin of Wagner's antisemitism.

**Gottfried**: I was assistant to Patrice Chéreau and Pierre Boulez for the Centennial *Ring* cycle at Bayreuth. Boulez is of course a very ambiguous figure in this issue of reconciling the past. Just as Wieland would not sanction any overt discussion of politics or history, Boulez would not talk about what happened in Paris during the Vichy period or any other aspect of the dark side of France's collaborations with Nazism.

Initially, Father wanted to do this centennial *Ring* cycle with Peter Stein, the famous German stage director of the *Schaubühne* in Berlin, but Stein hated my father. When I took him from the Berlin airport to Bayreuth, I made a point of showing him all the places of the *Reichsparteitaggelaende*. I wanted to gauge his reaction when I showed him the places where Hitler sat with the Wagner family as millions passed by. His reaction was palpable enragement about the Nazi history of Bayreuth. In this mood, Peter Stein and Wolfgang Wagner met and hated each other. Stein's stage direction would undoubtedly have been more ideologically radical.

But I have to defend Chéreau. I was first assistant to him. I was present when he was working on scenes with Mime, and I asked him if he had read the essay "Attempts on Wagner" by Adorno. Wolfgang was there and became very nervous. In short order, my father offered me a free-time salary in efforts to try to get rid of me. He wanted me out of Bayreuth altogether. And I said to him, "Father, you can offer me a million and I will not go." I was then demoted to working with the second cast of the *Ring* production; but the attacks became so intense and persistent that I just couldn't do it any longer.

I escaped to Ireland, passing through London, where I met with Charles Spencer, who was director of the new Philharmonic Chorus. He had lost his parents in Auschwitz-Birkenau. This was my first Jewish family. I remember pouring my heart out to him. Charles, "What I'm trying to do is impossible. I just cannot do this any longer." Somehow this opened his eyes.

I am always very proud when I can make out of Jewish Wagnerites realistic human beings. What I ask of Jewish Wagnerites is just to think about their circumstance. Don't get so far into self-alienation and self-abnegation that you deny where you come from and who you are. I have done this with different Jewish friends. "Oh, but the music is so wonderful" is always the rejoinder.

I spoke in Hempstead at the synagogue and was invited to speak by the Wagner Society of England. Following my presentation, the Society's President, Mr. Adler, himself of German-Jewish background, took over and said, in front of everybody, "Shame on you! It's good that people like you no longer hold sway in Germany!" He then ran out of the hall, banging the door behind him. It was an unforgettable and shocking moment, but also a telling one about the depth of disturbance of this issue for Jews. I somehow had the presence to salvage the moment with a quip: "Oh my goodness," I said. "Here's what can happen when you are Jewish and a Wagnerite!" The room then erupted in laughter.

**Larry**: One of the problems you and I encounter with Jewish Wagnerites is the accusation that in supporting Israel's largely symbolic ban on Wagner we are calling for and endorsing censorship. How can we get past this impasse of seeming contradiction around the special circumstances of Israel?

**Gottfried**: We do not want a second Holocaust in Israel. Let's start with that. There's an enormous responsibility for all Europeans for the state of Israel. They are all responsible for its security. They cannot keep doing the dirty, double-dealing business of selling armaments to forces that are openly committed to Israel's destruction and then sell anti-missiles to Israel. What kind of support is that? When I speak like this, of course, I'm at my most unpopular.

**Larry**: So Israel is an exceptional case. But beyond respecting the wishes of those few remaining Holocaust survivors in Israel who initially called for the ban on Wagner, when it comes to Wagner, what are we saying we want to the world to do or not do?

**Gottfried**: Wagner can teach us a lot about antisemitism and racism and this should be always documented. And it should always be forefront. This is central to my discussions and lectures in Israel, as documented in my archives and on my website.

6 million dead bodies must always be remembered. If the work of remembering is not done, the consequences will be a Europe that falls back into nationalism and antisemitism, and America that follows suit.

**Larry**: I find myself in both places. While I do not want to censor or ban Wagner in principle, I affirm and support Jewish protest of antisemitism on those all too rare occasions when it happens, whether it be regarding the words of a politician or the creations of an artist. I remember how heartened I was to hear of the protests around staging Wagner's *Ring* cycle in Los Angeles, and later for *Klinghoffer*. These were all too rare occasions of Jewish protest.

**Gottfried**: I think it was significant that at that gathering at the Hempstead synagogue, the one person who did stand in protest of the LA Opera *Ring* cycle was reviled and booed. I stood up to defend him, but we were alone in what we were doing and trying to communicate.

I was invited to speak by a liberal Jewish congregation that was otherwise celebrating the LA Opera *Ring* with parties. There I spoke bluntly about the seriousness of Wagner's antisemitism in a manner that was otherwise absent from discussions in the media and events. Alas, I was the only one doing this thankless work, which was ignored. I was silenced. What I had to say was not accepted, not engaged, not liked, not welcome. That was made repeatedly clear.

I also spoke at the American Jewish University in L.A. on Wagner's antisemitism. The Jewish community with close connections with the Schoenbergs did not talk to me at all. I did not exist for them. My friend David Klein who was very committed to open dialogue was quite shocked at how disrespectfully I was being treated. [L. Randol Schoenberg, grandson of composer Arnold Schoenberg, is probably best known as the real-life attorney who assisted Maria Altmann, played by Helen Mirren, in retrieving looted artwork from the Nazis in the film *Woman in Gold*. Despite his sterling credentials as outspokenly anti-Nazi, Schoenberg was supportive of the LA Opera *Ring* initiative and took public issue with Gottfried for the latter's endorsement of Israel's ban on Wagner.]

**Gottfried**: So here we are, you and I, two outsiders of Wagner discourses. We have some differences of knowledge and experience in some areas, but in our contra-Wagnerism, we are remarkably similar.

**Larry**: Indeed, there have been many Jews who have been outspoken around Wagner's antisemitism, but I don't know of even one other Jewish Wagnerite like myself who came to see how deeply troubled his Wagnerism was and who has moved away from his earlier self-designation and indeed away from Wagner and Wagnerism altogether. Similarly, there are many scholars who have noted the seriousness of Wagner's antisemitism, and its influence on Hitler and Nazism, but I know of no other, like yourself, who has gone so far as to designate Wagner and the Wagner family as Holocaust perpetrators.

So where has this brought us? In your case, you've gone from defacing Arno Breker's bust of Wagner outside Wahnfried [there are 5 Breker busts of Wagner in the City of Bayreuth] when you were a child to giving testimony to the Wagner family having been Holocaust perpetrators.

In my own case, well, I've come to understand and respect the deeply troubled psychology of Jewish Wagnerism and to honor my need for healing. Needless to add, there are no longer any pictures of Wagner on my living room walls!

**Gottfried**: Yours is a story that should be told on film, as I suggested to Petrus Vonderleft, who made a feature on me and my *Twilight of the Wagners*. Hallelujah, Larry, for your coming of age and wisdom on Wagner. I am always so gratified when I help a Jewish friend to have greater self-awareness and perspective. We feel so much better when we don't have to live with so much poison.

# Context: Medicine, Community and Culture

# Collected Writing 2012-2021

# Larry Kramer, Hannah Arendt, Vladimir Putin and the Life-and-Death Importance of Speaking Out

– *Huffington Post*, 8/20/2013

Figure 116 - Larry Kramer by David Shankbone, 2010, Creative Commons

When you watch Gay Cable News Network, co-hosted by Andy Humm and Ann Northrop, there is an introductory montage of LGBT figures, demonstrations and events. The soundtrack is likewise a montage in which little is distinguishable, save for one clear voice that says that we're escalating our voices in protest "because that's the only way we're going to be heard!" Yes, that's the voice of Larry Kramer from an ACT UP demonstration. That Larry's was the earliest, loudest, strongest and most effective of voices to be heard in the course of what became the global pandemic of AIDS is hardly news and not in dispute. But it's worth taking a moment to look back at this voice that has cut such a huge swath across populations, communities, continents, time spans, literature, theater, medicine and science.

I am among many who sometimes questioned the pitch of that voice, especially in the early years of AIDS. I was among those who argued for greater moderation on various fronts, to the extent that I supported, albeit reluctantly, the reconfiguration in the leadership of GMHC that resulted in Larry's departure from the GMHC Board. After leaving GMHC, Larry then went on to found another leading AIDS organization, AIDS Coalition to Unleash Power (ACT UP), which brandished a principal logo, "We Are Fighting For Our Lives," and the symbol "SILENCE = DEATH," with a pink triangle. As Larry split from GMHC and ACT UP exploded into a grassroots movement for health care access and accommodation that remains — in ambition, breadth and Nobel Prize level of achievement — without historical precedent, there was growing discussion about the rationale for this organization. Why were such outspokenness and confrontational tactics necessary?

Obviously because we were "fighting for our lives!" Straightforward, clear and persuasive, yes, but where were the political and historical context and philosophical framework of how to proceed? Beyond specific concerns of health research and services, were we just wildly flailing about in anger and rage? Was that enough? Or was there more to this? Of course, there was the civil rights movement, with its proud and vivid history of civil disobedience and nonviolent protest that resulted in social change. Clearly, that was a role model. But while allusions and analogies to that movement were commonplace among gay and AIDS activists, there was another chapter of history that was embraced primarily by Larry Kramer, and with him ACT UP, as more immediately pertinent to our experience: that of the Holocaust of World War II.

I've known Larry Kramer for 45 years and knew something of his mentors and heroes, one of whom was Hannah Arendt, the influential German-Jewish philosopher, intellectual and political theorist. As reprised in a recent film dramatization, *Hannah Arendt*, directed by Margarethe von Trotta, Arendt was, not so unlike Larry, a remarkable but very controversial figure. The controversy that erupted around her stemmed from two key assertions that she made in the epic tome she published in *The New Yorker* on the trial of Nazi war criminal Adolph Eichmann in Jerusalem, which she attended. The first assertion had to do with her now-famous phrase "the banality of evil." As captured by Arendt, Eichmann seemed to come across more as a just-following-orders bureaucrat than a figure of Satanic evil. As we now realize (given a recent re-exploration of the matter in a *New Yorker* feature, and in von Trotta's film), Arendt's perspective of Eichmann was simplified and distorted by her critics.

Arendt's other assertion caused even greater controversy: She suggested that the Jews of World War II should have done more to organize and protest than they did. Had they done so, she concluded, it might have made a difference in the outcome. Larry Kramer found himself frequently under attack by critics, including me, who wondered whether there weren't elements of internalized anti-Semitism in his Arendt-inspired assertions that gays must not go silently to our own slaughter the ways Jews did in World War II. At that time I was undergoing my own very personal journey of coming to terms with my own Jewishness, and with internalized, historical and resurgent anti-Semitism. And here was Larry, who seemed to have little awareness of anti-Semitism in his own life and times, and virtually no inclination to address what was becoming a tidal wave of resurgent anti-Semitism across the globe, embracing a certainty that the Jews had worsened and hastened their own fate by responding sheepishly to the Nazi onslaught. Not so unlike Arendt, Larry seemed to be making judgments of those whose fight he himself had evaded. All this became the stuff of my memoir, *Confessions of a Jewish Wagnerite: Being Gay and Jewish in America.*

There were other questions about the appropriateness of analogizing AIDS to the Holocaust. How otherwise was AIDS comparable to Nazi genocide? "Genocide" was a term used frequently by Larry. It seemed disrespectful of the Holocaust, co-opting the great tragic experience of the Jews under Nazism for a very great but very different realm of tragedy, a disease that had become a public health catastrophe. Larry went so far with this as to entitle a collection of his political essays *Reports From the holocaust* [the lower case h in the book's title was intentional]. Though AIDS was not a conscious, planned act of genocide on anyone's part, "genocide" became the predominant metaphor used by Larry and many in ACT UP. Were government homophobia, indifference and weakness really the equivalent of the Nazi genocide against Jews? Were Reagan and Koch really the equivalent of Hitler? Were gays falling victim to a plague really like the Jews or even the gays whom Nazis persecuted in the camps under the emblem of the pink triangle? Weren't we more like blacks struggling for our rights, for tolerance and equality, for parity of health care access and services, than a minority targeted for genocide by a maniacal dictator?

So how did all this play out? Well, the way it played out proved that in greater perspective, Larry was right. And by inference and example, so was Hannah Arendt. What Larry realized, the experience that fueled his insights and energies, was that if gays did not organize and fight back against enemy forces that were understood to be no less than genocidal, however indirectly, even if standing up and fighting back were at great risk to ourselves, we were inviting even worse calamity. By standing up, acting up, acting out, by screaming bloody murder, by using every tactic we could muster, including character assassination, we had a chance. That Larry proved so right regarding gay people and AIDS could not be clearer or more impressive. Not so coincidentally, as Arendt's views are reconsidered, there is growing respect for her perspective about the role that Jewish silence played in the deaths of 6 million Jews. The experience of Larry Kramer and ACT UP invites us to look back now at the Holocaust of World War II with special attention to what might have happened had Jewish protest been bolder, more commonplace and more impassioned.

In other words, if the Jews of the world had had a Larry Kramer to organize and lead them in World War II, might the Holocaust have turned out differently? Hindsight is always relatively easy, and in this case extremely controversial. But it is impossible now to look back at the achievements of Larry Kramer and answer anything but yes. What Larry Kramer, inspired so profoundly by Hannah Arendt, and ACT UP have demonstrated is that the importance of our voices — of speaking our minds and our truths, of speaking out, of organizing, of acting up and out — can mean the difference between life and death, not only for ourselves but for others, for populations and times we know and those scarcely imaginable.

Which brings us to the situation in Russia. The distinguished British actor and activist Stephen Fry has already posted a public statement suggesting that Putin's anti-gay laws are eerily redolent of the early anti-Jewish laws of Hitler and the Nazis. Is he right? If the examples of Larry Kramer and Hannah Arendt are any measure, you can bet your life he's right! Which means that now is the time to act up and act out, to do everything we can to stop the pretender to the throne of Stalin. Appeasement, being "good Jews," hoping for the best, showing our best face to the world by winning some events in the Olympics? These are not the answer.

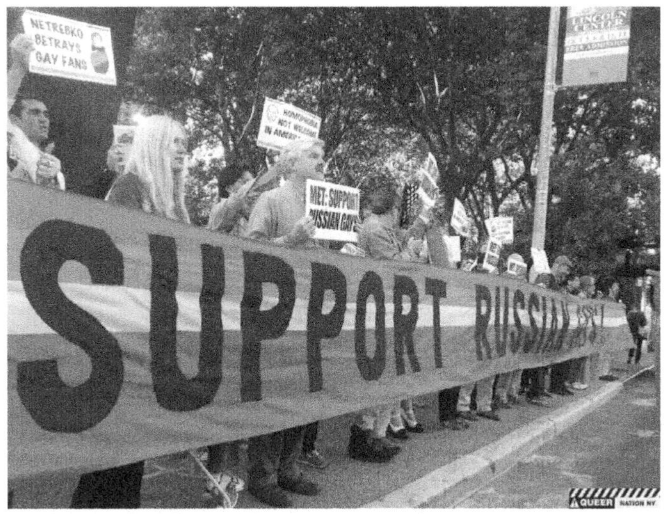


Figure 117 - source: queernationny.org

**Queer Nation protest at the Metropolitan Opera's opening night production of Tchaikovsky's *Eugene Onegin,* starring Russian superstar soprano Anna Netrebko and conducted by leading Russian conductor Valery Gergiev. What was being protested was the silence, and with that silence the passive collaboration, of the Met with Russia's anti-gay policies under autocrat Vladimir Putin. As reported by Michael Cooper in the *New York Times* (9/23/13, protest placards included "Anna, your silence is killing Russian gays! Valery, your silence is killing Russian gays!" Others were reported by Queer Nation: "We dedicate this GALA to Russia's Queers," "Homophobia Not Welcome in America," "Out of the opera and into the streets," "Netrebko Betrays Gay Fans,"**

# ‘Boo!’ to the Metropolitan Opera

– *Huffington Post*, 10/22/2013

We know who they were, the ones who spoke out and resisted, who put their careers on the line to protest what was happening in Germany: Arturo Toscanini, Lauritz Melchior and Lotte Lehmann, to name a few. We also know the ones who didn’t: Elizabeth Schwarzkopf, Herbert von Karajan, Wilhelm Furtwangler, Wieland and Wolfgang Wagner, to name a few. We also know those whose records were more equivocal: Richard Strauss and Kirsten Flagstad, to name a few. Although appreciation of artists who collaborated with the regime in varying degrees, actively or passively, has continued, just as appreciation of the works of Richard Wagner has continued notwithstanding his rabid anti-Semitism, the reputations of all these artists and composers are eternally tarnished and dogged. There is endless discussion and exhaustive intellectual acrobatics to separate their artistic achievements from their politics, prejudices and misdeeds, to exonerate and forgive them. The debates will never be resolved because they can’t be. As Lady Macbeth puts it, what’s done cannot be undone.

As already noted, the situation of human rights abuses of gays in Russia is not only very serious but seriously redolent of the early period of Nazi laws and persecutions of Jews. As with the situation in World War II, we look to our leading arts institutions and artists for help, for support. Let’s look at the Metropolitan Opera and what is and isn’t happening there. It’s now well-known that there was significant gay protest surrounding the Met’s opening-night production of *Eugene Onegin*, starring leading Russian soprano Anna Netrebko under leading Russian conductor Valery Gergiev. The Met was asked to dedicate the opening in protest of Putin’s anti-gay policies, which it politely declined to do, pleading decorum. If the Met were to officially sanction this protest, so the argument went, the floodgates would open for any and all other protests. (Sound familiar? If gays were allowed to be married, we were told, it would open the floodgates to incest, polygamy and bestiality. Gay marriage would set the stage for people to marry their pets.) The Met, it was affirmed, is an artistic, not a political, institution. If this were Nazi Germany, would the Met be making these same arguments? It's to the Met's considerable credit that, by and large, that did not happen during World War II. But how it would respond today is worth pondering, especially in light of its current reticence. Already we can begin to identify the Schwarzkopfs and von Karajans among us.

This protest of the Met was reasonably well-covered by openly gay music critic Anthony Tommasini in *The New York Times* (in the wake of an earlier article by Zachary Woolfe noting the controversies ahead of opening night), so notoriously lagging in its coverage of pressing human rights issues in the past, including the early Nazi persecutions of Jews and the early period of AIDS. At the first international conference on AIDS in Atlanta in 1985, I asked *New York Times* science writer Lawrence K. Altman why the *Times* wasn't covering AIDS more and better. His response? "We're not an advocacy journal." This time, for the Met's opening-night protest, the *New York Times* was there. But was that coverage, and the Met's response to this protest, adequate?

In my opinion, the answer to that is no. While it's a comparatively positive development that the whole controversy was not ignored altogether, as it would have been a generation ago, the Met said no to anything more than tepid, kid-gloves acknowledgment of the protest, making an antiseptic statement of neutrality. If you tried hard, you could interpret one or two of managing director Peter Gelb's phrases as veering toward thoughtful and sympathetic. But where was/is the statement by Gelb on behalf of the Metropolitan Opera of protest to his Russian artists, to the Russians themselves? Following opening night, the subject was dropped, both by the Met and *The New York Times*. (Here's a question for the Met broadcast intermission feature, Opera Quiz: How many of the Met's heavily gay staff participated in the demonstration outside the Met on opening night: many, few or none?)

Subsequently, I attended the cinema HD performance of the Met's coarse, unimaginative *Onegin* and was appalled to discover that the subject was not broached, not by reigning Wagner soprano Deborah Voigt, who conducted the intermission interviews, nor by any of those she spoke with, including Netrebko, Gergiev, and Gelb. The spectacle of knowing the reality of Tchaikovsky, who was hounded for his homosexuality—however active, ostensibly self-accepting and socially "tolerated"—and witnessing this cowardly silence was heartsickening, because I realized that in this silence and evasion was passive collaboration in what's happening in Russia now. Amidst the otherwise numbingly superficial commentary, no one mentioned that Tchaikovsky was gay, or that Russia is trying to eradicate that information, as it always has, by ignoring it. It's not so surprising when you consider how disconnected Voigt, Gergiev, Gelb and other Met Ring cycle participants have been from the controversies surrounding Wagner. Has Voigt ever uttered a thoughtful word on the composer whose works she's devoted her last 20 years to singing? Is her thinking about Wagner as rote and bland as her performances became?

The time has come for us gays to realize that we have been under a very big illusion, not only that we matter, but that we are really important within the world of opera. How wrong we were/are! This is a big subject, but my first inklings of all this emerged many years ago via my acquaintanceships with leading music critics, among them Richard Dyer, Peter G. Davis (both close friends in those years) and Martin Bernheimer, many of them closeted gay men who were too intimidated, self-hating and self-absorbed to come out in print or consider gay issues and perspectives. As Dale Harris entitled his *Opera News* rejoinder when I and others accused these critics of not dealing with Tchaikovsky's being gay, "Tchaikovsky was a Russian composer." The overwhelmingly pertinent observation to be made about Tchaikovsky, in other words, was that he and his music were Russian, not "gay." So insignificant was the gay perspective held to be as to continue to be unworthy of discussion or even mention. Harris died from complications of AIDS in 1996.

A similar awareness came to me via my appreciation of Maria Callas. Although gay people have been conspicuously involved with her, as fans, as chroniclers, as directors, the reality of Callas is that I don't think she ever expressed one public word about gay people, our lives, our struggles, just as I doubt she ever uttered a critical or regretful word about the Nazi occupation of Greece that cradled her early career. Did that bother the likes of her closest friends who were gay, like directors Franco Zeffirelli (an ultraconservative!), Luchino Visconti or Pier Paolo Passolini, or *Dallas Morning Star* critic John Ardoin? If so, they certainly never said so publicly. Rather, Callas was forgiven for everything because, as Ardoin wrote me, she was "a very self-absorbed artist." *Vissi d'arte. Art über alles.*

And what of the silence of the Met's biggest-of-all star, James Levine, regarding the Russian situation? Despite persistent rumors that he might be gay, Levine has never uttered one public word on the subject of gay people or, for that matter, anything else political, not in the past, not now. In any case, isn't it rather disconcerting that one of the most powerful figures in the history of American music has not found some way to say something about his most preeminent colleagues' support of the perpetrator of anti-gay policies, the policies themselves, or the safety of Met, American, Russian and other musicians and artists, to say nothing of music and opera lovers, ordinary citizens, in Russia? Is it really conscionable to remain silent when some of your biggest fans can now, under current Russian law, be fired, beaten to a pulp, jailed or killed if they intentionally or inadvertently say or do something "pro-gay"?

Again, where are the statements of dismay and protest from the Metropolitan Opera and its leaders about what's happening in Russia? From *Opera News*? Where are the statements from other musical and arts associations? From our critics? Apart from Tommasini's and Woolfe's coverage, critics predictably ignored this controversy, writing their usual superficial performance reviews, disagreeing with each other about this or that detail of acting, singing or staging, in what openly gay playwright William M. Hoffman, co-creator with openly gay composer John Corigliano of 1991's *Ghosts of Versailles*, has called "fairies' basketball." Hoffman, my close friend in those years, shared my interest and dismay in art and artists who were collaborators in Nazi Germany. He once suggested to me that *Capriccio*, Richard Strauss' last opera, should be split-staged with slow-motion scenes of Auschwitz on one side of the stage with the "action" of the opera on the other. (*Capriccio*, which had its premiere in 1942 in Munich, is possibly the wordiest opera ever penned; there's almost no action.)

Levine has been through a lot. He now conducts under considerable physical duress from a wheelchair. Is it fair to call him on his silence on Russia? Shouldn't he be allowed to just be the great conductor he is and otherwise left alone? To me, the answer to the question of whether Levine should not be judged for his ivory tower isolation as an artist is no, even if here in America, he is entirely within his rights to do so, and even if the histories of art, music and opera are dominated by artists who have made similar choices.

And what of Gergiev and Netrebko, both of whom claim reticence re Russian anti-gay policies in deference to their art? For starters, what is all this Russian presence at the Met all about, anyway? For years I think we've all felt intrigued and grateful to have such abundant post *-perestroika/glasnost* exposure to Russian art and artists, to have some of the great works in the operatic repertoire, a number of them rarely performed outside Russia, become more accessible, and in authentically Russian performances. Exchanges and alliances with such treasure-trove institutions as the Mariinsky Theater in St. Petersburg have been dreams come true. I've certainly treasured a number of Russian nights at the Met. But has it gone too far?

Anna Netrebko is a good singer who is musical and attractive and has a measure of stage presence. Alas, she has never been anything more than that. She's proficient and appealing, sufficiently so that it doesn't strain credibility that she's become a staple at the Met, even if nothing she's done places her in the same league as the greatest interpreters of the roles she's sung. The Met is a big business. It has to consider availability, casting and scheduling, and Netrebko has shown herself to be a valued professional. OK, but three Met opening nights and new productions in a row? Netrebko's superstar status at the Met is simply not supportable, unless there's some behind-the-scenes angle to it that we don't know. The same is true of Gergiev. He's a good conductor and a valued professional. But he's not in the ranks of the greatest conductors, not even the second-greatest that Levine belongs to. Would the Met suffer great loss without these resources? Behind the scenes, is this dominant Russian presence at the Met part of some strategy of *detente*? To what extent might the Met's budget and artistic planning be affected by more explicit dissociation from Putin and his policies? What would be the losses versus the gains, in other words, of a bolder level of confrontation between the Metropolitan Opera and its Russian partners? Whatever one's views of all this, I, for one, would greatly appreciate having updated information and perspective on the current state of relationships between the Metropolitan Opera and the Russian artists and institutions it has been so in bed with.

Whatever the complexity and value of those relationships (and coincidentally as we approach Halloween), a big "boo!" is in order for the Metropolitan Opera: to James Levine, Anna Netrebko, Valery Gergiev and Deborah Voigt, and of course the man they all answer to, Peter Gelb (son of Arthur Gelb, the managing editor of *The New York Times* in the 1970s, the heyday of its homophobic indifference to gay liberation events, issues and concerns), for their cowardly reticence and silence in these most pressing of times, for squandering precious opportunities to speak out, for putting their heilige kunst above the lives of opera's lifeblood: its gay people. Boo!

But let's end on a higher note: "Bravissima!" to Joyce DiDonato for being among the first musical/operatic superstars, along with Cher, to decline an invitation to appear in Russia, in protest of Russia's anti-gay laws. Postscript to Elton John: Are you still planning to appear in Russia, with the same logic that you performed at Rush Limbaugh's wedding (coincidentally earning $1 million for that gig), arguing that since you're known to be gay, your efforts can help gay people? If so, shame on you! It's not enough to just dress like Cher, Elton, even on the eve of Halloween. You would do a lot better to have her heart, courage and integrity, the very things missing from the Metropolitan Opera's opening night *Eugene Onegin* and its response to Putin's anti-gay onslaught in Russia.

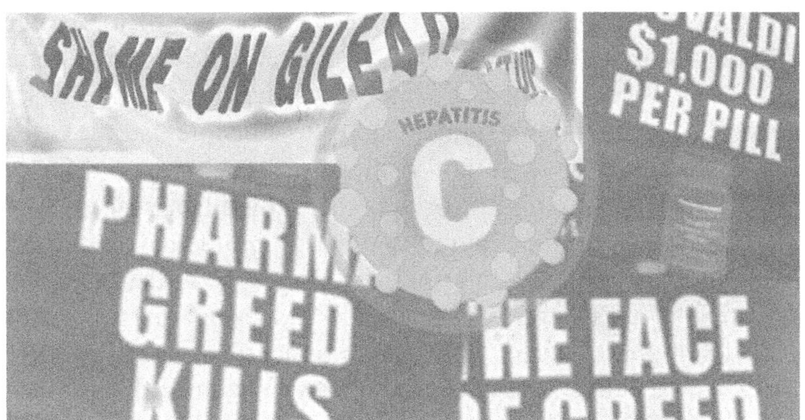

Figure 118 - Hepatitis C activism and advocacy 2014-2016, ACT UP / New York, https://actupny.com/history-of-victories-in-hep-c-movement

# Gay Men Should Be Tested for Hepatitis C

– *Huffington Post*, 10/30/13

Hepatitis C is the most common blood-borne infection in the U.S., and one of the most common worldwide. One in 50 Americans is infected. It accounts for more than 50 percent of all cases of end-stage liver disease and 50 percent of cases of liver cancer, and it is the reason for more than 50 percent of liver transplants. Yet it remains severely underdiagnosed. It's estimated that upwards of 75 percent of those infected remain untested and undiagnosed, as compared with 25 percent of those with HIV. More people now die from hepatitis C than from HIV.

Those of us who struggled through the early period of AIDS understand the meaning of "Silence = Death," the motto used by the AIDS activist organization ACT UP. So when hepatitis C began to emerge among MSM (men who have sex with men), the silence that ensued seemed eerily familiar. When I first started reporting on hepatitis C in gay men nearly a generation ago, the disease was already being called "the stealth epidemic," in part because of the typically long, silent progression of the disease in its chronic form, sometimes taking 20 to 30 years from acute infection to cirrhosis of the liver, but also because of the public silence about it. If people had the disease, they mostly didn't know it, and if they did have it and did know it, they didn't go public with it. Nor did those with the disease often seek treatment, which had the reputation of being prolonged, difficult and of mixed efficacy. Since the principal risk group for the disease was injection drug users, the public wasn't exactly clamoring to know more or be more involved. There was no mega-celebrity out there to help galvanize public interest and support who would admit to having hep C the way that Magic Johnson came out as having HIV. How much has changed in the intervening years?

Despite newer and often highly effective treatments that are essentially curative, not much has changed in terms of public awareness and indifference. Hepatitis C remains a stealth disease. Public health officials have long resisted the call to sound the alarm for hep C as an STI (sexually transmitted infection), citing the weak transmissibility of hep C sexually. For years, they didn't even urge that the partners of those who were hep C-positive be tested. Granted that HCV hasn't shown itself to be nearly as transmissible sexually as HIV, I expressed my concerns about what seemed to be excessive cautiousness around testing recommendations — in the gay press, in a cover-callout feature for *New York* magazine, as well as in a public health forum co-hosted by the CDC in Atlanta that also featured noted epidemiologist and journalist Laurie Garrett.1, 2 I argued that there needed to be greater awareness of and testing for hepatitis C as an STI, especially among MSM. As the call-out in *New York* put it, "Hepatitis C infections are spreading beyond high-risk groups, causing a few physicians to call for widespread testing. But the medical establishment is stalling. Sound familiar?"

Why was this so controversial? Why not just test everybody who might be at risk, even if that risk were "small"? The reason I was given by CDC epidemiologists and other public health officials was that urging everyone to get tested for hep C, even all MSM, could create unwarranted alarm and would be an unjustifiable expense in view of the relative minority of cases. Also, despite the increasing numbers of cases in gay men/MSM, those numbers remain "small," and it wasn't clear that other undisclosed risk factors such as injection drug use weren't responsible, since increased rates of sexual spread weren't being observed among heterosexuals.

So where do we stand with all this now? Amidst growing reports of new cases among clusters of gay men/MSM, especially in Europe, and growing numbers of cases in MSM generally, the latest review and recommendations from USPSTF (U.S. Preventive Services Task Force) from June 25, 2013, include the following:

> *The Task Force reviewed recent research studies on screening for and treatment of hepatitis C infection in adults. The final recommendation statement summarizes what the Task Force learned about the potential benefits and harms of screening: (1) Adults at high risk for hepatitis C infection should be screened for the infection. (2) Health care professionals should offer 1-time hepatitis C screening to adults born between 1945 and 1965.*

And who are they designating as being at "high risk"?

> *The most important risk factor for hepatitis C infection is the use of injection drugs. Other risk factors include having had a blood transfusion before 1992, having multiple sex partners, and getting a tattoo with an unsterilized needle.*

OK, so there, they've said it: "those having multiple sexual partners." But that recommendation is absent from their final, summary recommendations. There, they define those at "high risk" to be as follows:

> *People who use injection drugs now or have used them in the past. Having a blood transfusion before 1992 also puts a person at increased risk. Be screened only once. Some people with ongoing risk factors, such as injection drug users, need to be screened more than once.*

There's no mention in these final recommendations of those having "multiple sexual partners," which would include the majority of gay men/MSM, apparently because they are more "at risk" than at "high risk." OK, but then why not designate MSM as "at risk," even if that risk is believed to be low? Clearly, public health advisories re hepatitis C testing for MSM remain unclear.

So where does all this leave us? When it comes to hepatitis C screening, gay men must once again be proactive. If you are a sexually active gay man/MSM, if you've had sex with multiple partners over time, get tested for hepatitis C. If your doctor or health care provider declines to offer the testing based on perceived low risk and unclear public health services recommendations, seek testing from another health care provider.

***References:***

1. *Mass, Lawrence D., "C-Sick," New York, March 29, 1999.*
2. *"AIDS and Hepatitis C: Lessons from AIDS," from Emerging Illnesses and Society: Negotiating the Public Health Agenda,*

*edited by Randall M. Packard et al., Johns Hopkins University Press, 2004.*

# Dr. Joseph Sonnabend and the Battlefield of AIDS

*– Huffington Post*, 7/28/14

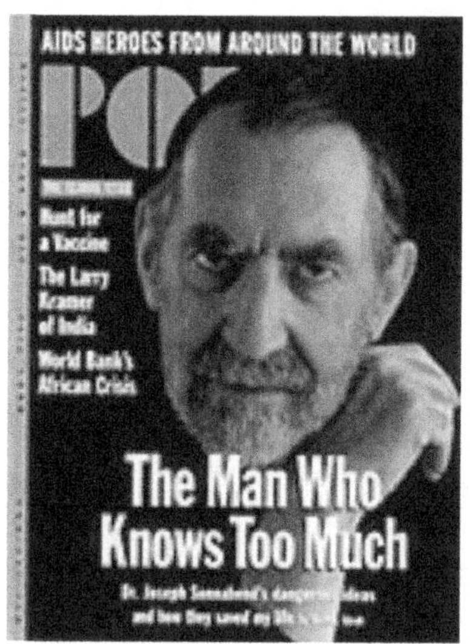


Figure 119 - Dr. Joseph Sonnabend, 2013, Poz.com

There's an edgy new film making the rounds of the gay film festivals. *Age of Consent* by Charles Lum and Todd Verow is about gay sex and its legislative battles in Britain. The story is told from the premises of the Hoist, one of London's few remaining leather bars. It has hot guys, hot sex and some commentary, including from British gay activist Peter Tatchell and South African and New York physician Joseph Sonnabend.

Sonnabend is known for his efforts on behalf of the gay community, preceding AIDS and throughout the epidemic — for GLBT health care outreach and advocacy, for research on STDs and treatments, for his co-authorship with Richard Berkowitz and Michael Callen of an early safer-sex guide, "How to Have Sex in an Epidemic," and for being a co-founder of the American Foundation for AIDS Research (AMFAR). In "Age of Consent," recalling that earliest period of the epidemic, Sonnabend observed that he, Berkowitz and Callen encountered hostility from elements of the gay community, including from Gay Men's Health Crisis (GMHC), and also alleging that I, Larry Mass, accused him of being a "mass murderer."

Larry Kramer leveled that accusation of "mass murderer" and "genocide" at everybody from Ed Koch to Anthony Fauci, but such big guns were rarely for lesser activists like me. Although I never made the accusation Sonnabend alleges in *Age of Consent,* however, the discord with GMHC that he was alluding to was real and worth looking back at.

Between 1981 and 1984 no one knew for sure what the cause of the epidemic was. Most likely it was a virus, almost certainly so by 1983, but the proof of HIV as the cause of AIDS wasn't fully established until early 1985. Meanwhile, doctors had to try to make the best suggestions we could, based on probabilities. On the surface, the safer sex guidelines developed by Sonnabend, Berkowitz and Callen in 1983 were unassailable. They called for condom use, and were upbeat and creative about incorporating s-m and other ways of being alternatively and safely sexual.

The problem is that their recommendations were bound up with a questionable theory of causation. Gay men were said to have had so much sex with so many partners, acquiring and transmitting so many STDs, that their immune systems were breaking down. Aggravating this breakdown, it was suggested, were cofactors such as poor nutrition, drug use, stress and depression.

On first hearing, this seemed a theory well worth considering, whatever challenges it might appear to pose to sexual freedoms and the progress of gay civil rights struggles. (At that time in New York, there were no civil liberties protections of any kind for GLBT people.) Promiscuity and STD rates were unquestionably out of control in cohorts of the gay community and chronic states of infection and infectiousness with Epstein Barr virus (EBV) and cytomegalovirus (CMV) were commonplace and known contributors to immune deficiency.

Even so, and even if they were only a minority of cases, there were some gay men who were getting sick who didn't seem to fit well into this paradigm. And what about the other major risk groups that were coming down with the new immune deficiency syndrome: Haitians, intravenous drug users and hemophiliacs? As conjectured by these theorists, the previously mentioned cofactors might be contributing in varying measures to comparable states of chronic infection in these groups, especially in environments of poverty.

Because of the vagueness of placing so much weight on "promiscuity" and other ill-defined "cofactors," because of the stretch involved in applying all this to the other risk groups, and because multi-factorialism has historically been invoked to explain disease phenomena in the absence of better explanations, it was clear from the outset to a number of us in medicine and science that this was not a bandwagon we could jump on.

Condom use and safer sex options seemed good recommendations, but not the outspoken theory that was attached to them. At that point prior to the identification of HIV as the primary agent in AIDS, and taking our guidance from CDC, and with the evermore vociferous doubt being cast by the multi-factorialists, we felt we still didn't have enough certainty about what we were seeing to make clear-cut recommendations even about condom use. In retrospect, we — CDC, GMHC and I — got that wrong. The promotion of condom use was definitely the right way to go, and Sonnabend, Callen and Berkowitz — in sync with Larry Kramer on moving a lot more aggressively forward on prevention regardless of certainty — deserve a lot of credit for promoting condom use as early and strongly as they did, whatever the theories.

Alas, the multifactorial theory of the cause of AIDS became increasingly defensive and intolerant of challenges well into the period of the establishment of HIV as the cause of AIDS. It would be different if this theory had been presented more clearly and consistently as one possibility among others, in the manner of good science and as Sonnabend, Callen and Berkowitz themselves did make fitful efforts to do — e.g., the full title of their monograph was: "How To Have Sex in an Epidemic: One Approach."

Notwithstanding that "one approach" qualifier, there didn't seem to be much actual tolerance for the probability, and later the certainty, that a single agent was primary. That was my impression and that of many colleagues. Throughout those early years, the single-agent hypothesis was bullyingly derided by Sonnabend — and with him, Callen and Berkowitz — as the "killer virus" theory. Over time, as a number of us in mainstream medicine perceived it, the rhetoric espoused by multi-factorialists grew evermore intransigent.

Historian Martin Duberman captures some of this atmosphere and dissonance in *Hold Tight Gently: Michael Callen, Essex Hemphill and the Battlefield of AIDS:*

"As panic mounted, so did internal squabbling. As usual in such circumstances, raging helplessness found its most available targets close at hand. Mike was far more sensitive to people, and more generous about their apprehensions and actions, than either Berkowitz or Sonnabend. Both of them, for example, disparaged Dr. Larry Mass. Berkowitz — and Sonnabend still more so — insisted that Mass, in Sonnabend's words, 'doesn't have the credentials to be writing in this area...It's a highly technical subject...He actually makes me angry.' When Mass told Sonnabend in one long discussion that 'there's so much epidemiological stuff for the single virus' theory, Sonnabend reported his own reaction as: 'Well, like what? And we waited and he had nothing to say. Just silence...his intellect [isn't] working...his intentions are good...he wants to help...he's not a bad man.' Mike told both Berkowitz and Sonnabend that they were being 'arrogant' and predicted that 'before it's all over [Mass will] be on our side.'" (from a series of mid-1982 to early 1983 transcripts of taped conversations, in various combinations)

Despite the good work each of these individuals did over time for safer sex, PWA empowerment and in support of research, that crossover to their theoretical viewpoint never happened. Once HIV was established as the cause of AIDS, a new designation emerged for those who remained unyielding on this issue of etiology: AIDS denialism. As many will remember, AIDS denialism was not a small, inconsequential movement. It became a cult phenomenon that overtook editors and writers of the gay press — most notably *New York Native* editor Charles Ortleb.

As time passed, as the diagnosis and treatment of HIV became increasingly standardized, and under mounting criticism from mainstream medicine and science, Sonnabend began to moderate his publicly expressed views. Finally, in the 1990s, he began to endorse HIV as the primary agent in AIDS and began to explicitly distance himself from AIDS denialism and denialists, albeit without ever acknowledging the extent to which he had initially overreached in his earlier certainty of his theory of multi-factorialism. Richard Berkowitz made a comparable retreat. In a film he made about his experience, *Sex Positive,* he acknowledged that he'd undergone successful treatment for HIV. Callen died from complications of AIDS in 93.

As Sonnabend began his slow, gradual, never complete withdrawal from his earlier insistence on the multifactorial cause of AIDS, others took up this theory, most notoriously Berkeley biologist Dr. Peter Duesberg. It's Duesberg's work, which Duesberg acknowledged was inspired by Sonnabend's theory, that became the basis for the infamous health care policies in South Africa that resulted in nearly a third of a million preventable deaths from the withholding of effective antiviral treatments.

Painstaking documentation of what happened in South Africa is the achievement of a remarkable 2 part (4 hour) 2006 documentary for PBS Frontline called *The Age of AIDS.* For additional perspective, see my *Gay and Lesbian Review* essay, "AIDS Denialism and African Genocide," written on the occasion of the 30th anniversary of AIDS. It's this essay, which notes the multi-factorialism origins of what became AIDS denialism, that must have seemed accusatory to Sonnabend, although there, as here, Sonnabend's distancing of himself from denialism and denialists is acknowledged.

It's to their credit that neither Larry Kramer nor ACT UP ever got pulled into endorsing AIDS denialism, though neither did they take on the challenge of confronting it, even as the catastrophe in South Africa unfolded. Meanwhile, the history of AIDS denialism remains one of the biggest, most serious and least documented chapters in the history of AIDS.

Never again, one would think with real confidence. If it achieved nothing else, certainly the South African holocaust of 330,000 unnecessary deaths would sound the death knell for AIDS denialism. But a recent experience proved cautionary. I was speaking with my doctor, whose primary care practice is made up mostly of gay men, a number of them in treatment for HIV. I asked him if he still sees AIDS patients who are denialists and refuse antiviral treatment for HIV. "Yes," he said, "though they are fewer and further between than a decade ago." The last death of such a patient in his practice, he said, was several years ago.

In advance of seeing him for an annual checkup, I was having routine blood work done by a bright, friendly lab technician who was the first to tell me that morning's devastating news: that the Malaysian Airlines flight that was shot down over Ukraine had a number of leading AIDS researchers on board. I explained that I was a physician in addiction medicine and had worked with AIDS patients, mostly intravenous drug users, as well as with the GLBT community. We commiserated about the crash victims, and then she asked me if I believed HIV was the cause of AIDS.

# Recasting History: Reflections on HBO's *The Normal Heart*

– *Huffington Post*, 8/20/14

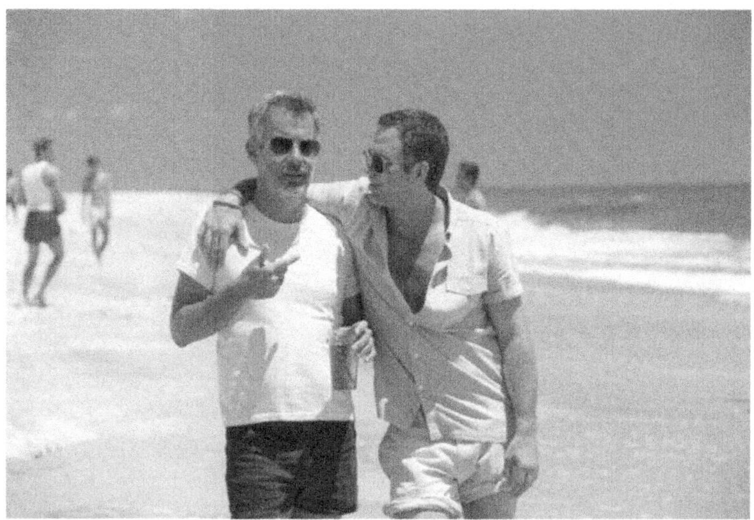

Figure 120 - Mark Ruffalo as Ned Weeks (right) and Joe Mantello as Mickey Marcus in HBO's *The Normal Heart*, HBO films

My reactions to the HBO film of *The Normal Heart* (*TNH*) are not much different from my reactions to the play. When it was revived on Broadway in 2012, I wrote a commentary, "*The Normal Heart*, A Generation Later," that is posted on the Gay Men's Health Crisis (GMHC) blog site. It takes a long, discursive look at the play, my relationships to it, and grapples with the most persistent of the concerns to emerge about it: that *TNH* is a dramatization rather than an authoritative history. At what point do we begin to question the great and powerful Larry Kramer on his saying of *TNH*: "this is our history"?

In anticipation of the film and at Larry's behest, I spent an afternoon with Joe Mantello, who in his various and frequent roles as writer, director and actor is perhaps the most prolific and protean figure in New York theater. Mantello played Ned in the Tony award-winning Broadway revival of *TNH* and plays Mickey, the character that is based partly on me, in the film. Up close and personal, Mantello is without pretense, sexy and engaging. In the course of our three-hour lunch at a Chelsea diner we covered every base. Joe had the same questions about the veracity of Felix (Ned's lover in the play) that everybody else has had. As most now know, Larry based this relationship that eventuated in a hospital bedside marriage in the play on an "affairette," as Larry has called the fleeting romances of gay men, with *NYT* fashionista John Duka.

Months later, in the lobby following the world premiere of the film at the Ziegfeld theater, Mantello sought me out and we embraced. Although Mickey is a composite figure and not me in important details (e.g., he's not a physician), there is truth and soul in the character that Mantello captured in his portrayal. I told him I thought he was great, that I loved him; and I recognized in that moment of disinhibition that I was also saying that I loved myself. It was a moment to look past all the qualifiers and just feel the love and pride of having been in the struggle, in celebration of all of us, but especially Larry, who did make it to the premiere but who had been in fragile health.

There were things I liked in the film that weren't in the play, beginning with the closeup of Ned's face as he comes upon an orgy in the meat rack on Fire Island. I also thought the hint of a dysfunctional romantic energy between Ned and Dr. Brookner was plausible and effective. Likewise Tommy's heartbreakingly modest and private gesture of pulling the file cards from his roladex of those who died and keeping them together with a rubber band in a separate drawer. And I was warmed by the gay bondedness captured in the disco fundraiser scene.

Like many others, I wasn't sure what to make of Ned's recounting of his single heterosexual foray and rendering Felix as having children from a former marriage. Were these additions there to make Larry, Ned and Felix more acceptable to straights and more appealing to the many gay men who prize bi-ness and straightness in their men? Doubtless an ick factor of gayness for gay men, and of gay sex for straights, is still out there. On reflection, though, these sexual details didn't strain credibility and did work dramatically. In bed after sex is a time when we're prone to drop pretense, to let our guard down and talk intimately and honestly about our lives. Who we are, who we were, and previous efforts at being straight are still deeply felt rites of passage in gay life. These are the kinds of subtle insights we wouldn't reflexively associate with the otherwise blastingly unsubtle Larry Kramer, but they are in fact foremost among his skills as a writer.

A kind of cognitive dissonance is the challenge with Mark Ruffalo, who on first impression seems so different from the real-life Larry Kramer that the reconciliation you want to make and are trying to make and finally do make seems more effortful than it should. I often felt that a strong interpreter of Ned on stage would have been Harvey Fierstein. So powerful was Fierstein's gay voice that it totally conquered New York's most vicious and often homophobic critic, John Simon. The original Ned Weeks, Brad Davis, was successful in conveying the intensity and character of Larry's anger, but Fierstein would have brought a gay verisimilitude as well as that sheer vocal authority that virtually none of the other Neds have had, though a number of them have been gay or bisexual. Of course, when *TNH* had its world premiere in 1985, no leading actor, including Davis (who was married) was out. When Larry and I passed him on the street a few years later, Tom Hulce, who next played Ned, berated Larry for outing him on a panel.

For the sake of AIDS and for the sake of Larry Kramer and all he has done, you want to go the distance of affirming the film and all that it stands for, and you want to do so as strongly as possible. Anything else at this point, let's face it, would also be politically incorrect. In any case, you do go that distance and you do mean it. Meanwhile, dreamboat Ruffalo managed to create genuine chemistry with Matt Bomer as Felix. I agree with *As Is* playwright William M. Hoffman that the love affair between Ned and Felix was sexier and more heartrending in the film than in the play. No wonder Larry was so pleased to hear about the explicit sex scenes in HBO's *Behind the Candelabra* (the Liberace story with Michael Douglas and Matt Damon). It meant they would be able to get away with doing that in *TNH*.

If the casting of Mark Ruffalo did manage to surmount old questions about straight actors playing gay roles, Julia Roberts also conquered misgivings. Although the role of Dr. Brookner seemed tailor-made for Roberts' penchant for conveying smoldering and explosive anger, Roberts' decision to underplay her big scene was as unexpected as it was inspired. It's as if she were trying to be true to Dr. Linda Laubenstein, the real-life figure Dr. Brookner was based on, who was a far less fiery activist in reality than Brookner is in the play. The real Linda Laubenstein would not have squandered her precious energies with a lot of screaming. It gave me new respect for Roberts' seriousness and integrity as an actor.

At a benefit that honored Elizabeth Taylor and Larry, I sat with Larry's brother, Arthur Kramer, and asked him if he would consider being a contributor to my Larry Kramer anthology. Flashing a Mona Lisa smile, he declined. Too bad because it's the confrontation between Ned and his brother Ben—played by the gifted actor Alfred Molina in the film—about what's "normal" that's at the heart of *TNH*. Alas, this most powerful of moments in the play gets diluted in the greater expansiveness of the film.

A dilution of tensions is likewise a consequence of the film's rendering of Bruce, played by Taylor Kitsch, the character based on GMHC's first president, Paul Popham. Paul's greater popularity and appeal relative to Larry's, which is hinted at in the play, gets lost in the film. In reality, Paul was the gentle daddy everyone gravitated to, in contrast to Larry's angry scold.

Tommy also suffers from sketchiness. As Larry would be the first to attest, Rodger Mcfarlane, another of Larry's affairettes—who became one of GMHC's first executive directors, Larry's closest friend and the character Tommy is based on—was as fabulous and likeable as he was enterprising, effective and heroic. Jim Parsons is wonderful but he doesn't get to do much. We will have to wait for the sequel to *TNH* that Larry is currently writing to better appreciate how truly gifted and irreplaceable Rodger was.

Related to Tommy is the issue of what might appear to be the film's one token lesbian and woman (apart from Dr. Brookner), the first such to volunteer for the fledgling group that became GMHC. I believe that character is based on the real-life figure of Dixie Beckham, a GLBT community psychotherapist and mutual friend of Rodger's and mine who also hails from the South (Rodger was from Alabama), in fact from my own home town of Macon, Georgia.

As for Mickey, a couple of comments beyond what's already been said. Larry has added a phrase indicating that Mickey is taking it personally that Larry was accusing everybody of being murderers. But beyond Larry's constant haranguing of virtually all of us in the gay community (and for that matter everybody else), individually and collectively, for not doing more and better, I didn't take such accusations any more personally than Larry took my indictment of our silence about the holocaust in South Africa from AIDS denialism. "We killed Vito." (This was Larry's opening statement at Vito Russo's memorial service.) "We" killed the South Africans.

The other aspect of Mickey that's worth noting in the film is his standing in the end with GMHC in its decision to separate itself from Larry's leadership. As is clear from my GMHC blog piece, although I had already resigned from the GMHC board, that rendering of me in sync with the GMHC board is fair. It was never the right thing for GMHC to be transformed into ACT UP, which is the direction Larry wanted to take us. Larry is not the only one to wish that GMHC, which he had variously denounced as "candy stripers" and "worse than Auschwitz," had been more committed to a stronger moral vision and much greater activism. That GMHC was and has remained far more modestly committed to giving people information, resources and services to help themselves continues to rankle those who had hoped and expected and fought for much bigger and more glorious levels of achievement and transformation.

What's missing from Ned's confrontation with GMHC is greater verisimilitude and detail. There's really only one moment in the play when you get an honest sense of the ferocity of Ned's anger. That's when Ned throws down the groceries he's bought for Felix, splattering the milk everywhere. "If you want to die, then die!!!," he screams at Felix. In the film, however, this dramatic high point seems more in the nature of a lovers' quarrel and a natural consequence of the stress they're under than a window on Ned and his rage.

This is also the way Ned's anger with Mayor Ed Koch, however justified, is depicted. You get virtually no sense in the film, and not that much more in the play, of how often and how far Ned's anger veered into bullying, blaming, vilification, character assassination and scapegoating. In real life, GMHC's pioneering service organizer and donor, prominent socialite Judy Peabody, was dismissed as "a hoity-toity rich bitch." Koch and Reagan were Hitler. Everybody, including Rodger Mcfarlane and Anthony Fauci, was a murderer. Everybody, including leading AIDS organizer and researcher Dr. Mathilde Krim, was a Nazi and committing genocide.

"Doctors are cowards," Kramer more recently told a young doctor during the Q and A following his on-stage interview with Tony Kushner at the New York State Historical Society's panel on its 2013 exhibition, "AIDS in New York: The First Five Years." She was working with the poor and earnestly seeking his advice. As Rodger Mcfarlane put it when interviewed by Michael Specter for the *New Yorker* profile on Kramer, "When it comes to being an asshole, Larry Kramer is without peer."

Notwithstanding the unquestionable veracity of that assessment, in the end it's unquestionably Larry's angry leadership that more than any other factor galvanized everybody. And it's unquestionably Larry Kramer who deserves a lion's share of credit for watershed breakthroughs in research, treatment and health care reforms.

If there is anything else missing from HBO's *TNH*, apart from the epidemic's impact on the other major risk groups—injection drug users, Haitians and hemophiliacs, AIDS in heterosexuals and women, especially in Africa and across the globe—it's any hint of the sequel to come, the truly epochal second half of the story of Larry Kramer and his founding and leadership of ACT UP, which went on to include many lesbians, heterosexuals, persons of color, and women. ACT UP addressed with breathtaking and unprecedented effectiveness key issues pertinent to all of these risk groups and cohorts and by extension to everybody else. Tempting as it must have been to extend the boundaries of *TNH* to suggest the later achievements and claim greater inclusiveness, you have to admire the commitment to the integrity of the play that prevailed.

We should be truly indebted to Larry Kramer, Ryan Murphy and HBO for bringing back the original AIDS, the horror plague, for all the world to see. It's a disease that even those who have HIV/AIDS today have little idea ever existed; a scourge that crucified most of its victims. It decimated our communities. The AIDS that *TNH* chronicles and memorializes was truly a holocaust. The horrors we lived through can scarcely be imagined, but the images brought back in this film do a remarkable job of doing just that. So even though the film is a dramatization, it conveys our history more effectively than any documentary I can think of, giving real credibility to Larry's claim that "this is our history."

Clearly, however, "history" is in a continuous process of being recast. As Ethel Rosenberg puts the certainty of millennial change to Roy Cohn in Tony Kushner's *Angels in America*, "History is about to crack wide open." Leading AIDS journalist David France, director of the acclaimed documentary *How To Survive a Plague*, is working on a new history of AIDS that should correct a lot of misinformation that's out there now. "Perhaps it will be the new version of *And The Band Played On*," I proposed. That would be exciting and enriching for everybody, but neither David nor I seemed to pick up on the unintended irony of this off-the-cuff suggestion when I made it in conversation with him. How often do we now return to Shilts' book with its Patient Zero or the HBO film of it with all its stars? My point is that so vast is the scale of AIDS that this landmark chronicle of the epidemic has already receded in history and time.

One of the amazing things about the PBS Frontline feature from 2006, *The Age of AIDS*, which focuses on AIDS in Africa, is the way it sweeps past the entire early period of AIDS. A film that was co-produced by gay people, it's not homophobic—the website for *The Age of AIDS* features a substantial interview with Larry Kramer—but such is the expansiveness of its perspective that the documentary itself scarcely mentions the gay community, Larry Kramer, GMHC or ACT UP.

As Larry and I agree in the big interview with him that closes my Larry Kramer anthology, *We Must Love One Another or Die*, knowing what we now know and keep learning about the past, especially about our sexual lives, it's hard to look at any history as authoritative, or imagine that any history ever could be.

"That's what [*The American People*, Kramer's forthcoming novel] is all about. So why do we think that anything we learn in science or disease or anything else is true?...Perhaps each of us," Kramer concludes, "has to create our own history of the world. One that we can live with. And learn how to accept that my history of the world is different from your history of the world. It might put a lot of colleges and professors out of business!"

HBO's *TNH* succeeds big time in giving us Larry Kramer's history of AIDS, which is a credible and moving recreation of AIDS as we've known it in the gay community. And it's right to lionize the experience of Larry Kramer, the epidemic's great hero, even if it's doing so at the behest and under the auspices of Kramer himself, and notwithstanding the film's softening of his persona and finessing of historical details. In this ever-enlarging and reconfiguring picture, however, and as I'm sure Larry would agree, the only thing certain about the history of AIDS is that it will continue to recast us all.

# Ebola, AIDS, and Plague Inc.

– *Huffington Post*, 10/16/14

Figure 121 - Thomas Frieden, CDC Director 2009-2017, delivers remarks at the HHS 2014 Budget Press Conference, April 10, 2013, HHSgov, Wikimedia Commons, public domain

**A new video game uses an epidemic model with a complex and realistic set of variables to simulate the spread and severity of a plague. Available as an app from iTunes, it has been dowloaded 25 million times. Now, with Ebola, *Plague Inc.*, as it is called, appears to have morphed from virtual into actual reality.**

"I will say that in the thirty years I've been working in public health, the only thing like this has been AIDS, and we have to work now so that this is not the world's next AIDS." After they showed Dr. Thomas Frieden, former NYC Dept of Health Commissioner (2002-2009) and now Director of CDC, making this statement on the evening news, my life partner Arnie and I just looked at each other. Clearly, the spread of Ebola is already a public health catastrophe. Meanwhile, too much of what we're still hearing from public health officials is weak reassurances and advice to stay calm.

It put into relief my own advisories to the gay community to try to stay calm and avoid panic in the earliest period of AIDS. Though panic is never a good thing, I was wrong then to be so cautious, and the health care officials who keep telling us to keep calm now are similarly wrong. With AIDS, only Larry Kramer somehow gleaned the true measure of what was happening, and the alarm he raised pulled out all the stops. CDC quickly called the emerging epidemic "the most important new public health problem in the U.S."

Simultaneously, however, CDC AIDS Task Force reps balked on issuing stronger advisories. In the absence of certainty of the cause of the epidemic, and to avoid political and civil liberties confrontations and panic, they retreated from more substantial leadership. Alas, too many of us in the gay community took our lead from CDC. The resulting excessive caution and inadequacy in issuing tougher guidelines based on probabilities, like the sluggishness of the *New York Times* in giving the epidemic priority coverage, is well-documented in Randy Shilts's *And The Band Played On* as well as in Kramer's own *The Normal Heart* and *Reports from the holocaust*.

So what's to be done for Ebloa? Airports have begun screening international passengers for fevers. That's like the advice we were giving early on for what was later identified as HIV and AIDS, to limit the number of different sexual partners and try to make sure those partners were healthy. Vastly inadequate. Consider the case of Ebola patient Thomas Eric Duncan, who traveled to the U.S. from Liberia to Texas and is now dead. He would not have been detected either in Africa or the U.S. because he was not exhibiting fever or any other signs of the virus when traveling here.

U.S. public health officials shy away from infringements of civil liberties and rightly so. I'm certainly glad they never did what Cuba did to contain HIV/AIDS — put gays into camps. Civil liberties concerns are extremely important, but they do not always supersede much bigger life-and-death concerns. When and where quarantine needs to be implemented for Ebola, it must not be evaded but must be transparent and to the greatest extent possible implemented with the participation, cooperation and support of the individuals and communities involved. We keep getting reassurances that if the procedures that are currently in place are stringently followed, containment will be secured. Yet that security appears evermore fragile and elusive. As UN Deputy Ebola Coordinator Anthony

Banbury admitted, "We need to [contain Ebola] within 60 days from 1 October. If we reach [this target], then we can turn this epidemic around ... We either stop Ebola now or we face an entirely unprecedented situation for which we do not have a plan."

Drug and vaccine trials are happening but not aggressively enough. As with AIDS, all experimental approaches in the pipeline need to be financed and expedited the way they were in the heyday of ACT UP's responses to the spread of AIDS. Crucially, medical activists need to find out what drugs and vaccines are in various stages of research and testing, and then put pressure on the FDA and drug companies to finance and speed their development.

AIDS activists sensed that gays were considered an expendable population, alongside drug addicts and (later) African nationals, and that the resulting indifference and silence from governments and society were tantamount to genocide. It isn't a big stretch to see that same history repeating itself when it comes to the black populations most affected by Ebola. The Ebola outbreak in West Africa is "unquestionably the most severe acute public health emergency in modern times," Dr. Margaret Chan, the director general of the World Health Organization, said. "When a deadly and dreaded virus hits the destitute and spirals out of control, the whole world is put at risk ... The rich get the best care. The poor are left to die."

For the moment, one can only hope that these statements of candor from Drs. Frieden, Chan and Banbury will set the stage for subsequent responses. While we may not need an "Ebola czar" per se, remember how hugely important Surgeon General C. Everett Koop's voice was as the AIDS crisis unfolded? At present, however, *the U.S. has no Surgeon General.* The president's candidate, Dr. Vivek Murthy, has been stalemated by Republicans not only because he was selected by Obama and was a supporter of Obamacare but because he supports gun control. So as we face a plague that could spread with the scale and devastation of AIDS, Congress is once again playing partisan and petty politics. The NRA's defense of its mass-murderous policies has now taken a quantum leap in its interference with the nation's health, from being accessory to the unnecessary deaths of thousands to potentially much greater numbers.

# *The American People*: Larry Kramer's Blistering Magnum Opus

– *Huffington Post*, 3/23/25

"Why do they hate us?"

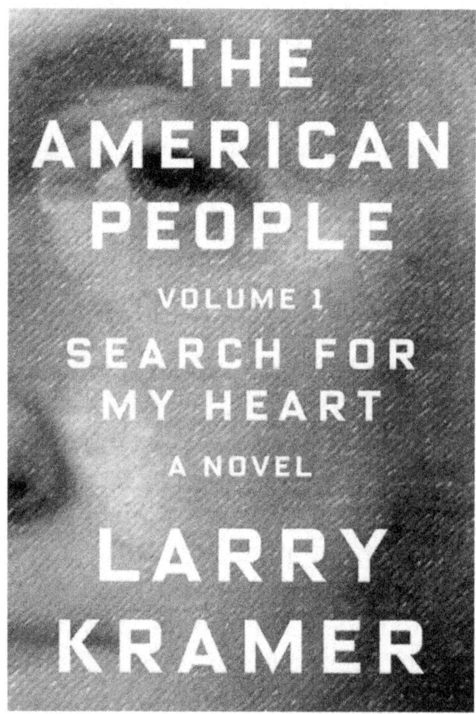


Figure 122 - book cover, amazon.com

"This is always history's greatest failure, its inability to believe what it sees, what, almost always, someone sees."

—Larry Kramer, *The American People*

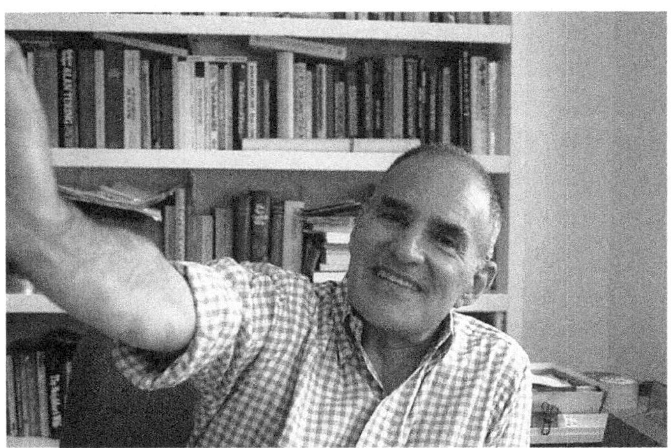

Figure 123 - Larry Kramer (6/25/35-5/27/20), photograph by Massimo Consoli, 1989, Wikimedia Commons

There's a paradox inherent in historical novels. Though they tend to inspire stronger and more personal feelings than historical chronicles, the safety net of fiction renders those feelings less directly true. We know that *Gone With The Wind* was more imagined than actual history. The same is true of *War and Peace*. We can see our own lives in these great historical novels to an extent that's harder to do with documentation-heavy histories. But when we want to know the specifics of what actually happened in Russia and our Civil War, we look to what are considered authoritative histories rather than historical novels.

Consider the works of Larry Kramer. Though his first novel *Faggots* viscerally captures the bigger picture of a sex-besotted gay community unraveling around its inability to integrate sex with love, fictionalization of the characters and situations, even those that suggest real-life figures, facilitates a level of detachment from the actual history of that community in time and place. The same is true of *The Normal Heart*, his dramatization of the early AIDS crisis, as well as his farce, *Just Say No*, about Ed Koch and the Reagans. By fictionalizing and conflating these histories and their protagonists, the bigger issues can be perceived in sharper relief, and developments and personas may more vividly and persuasively emerge. "Novels are the private lives of nations" and "Fiction is history, human history, or it is nothing." Kramer quotes first Balzac and then Conrad in the two pages of epigraphs that open *The American People*. But there's nonetheless a price to be paid for fictionalization and dramatization.

These works can no longer be claimed as authoritative history. This is the challenge that accompanies the literary and artistic achievements of Larry Kramer.

*The American People* is predictably commanding and passionate, its insights are stunning and endless, its narrative consistently compelling. But how much of the history it recreates is true? How much of it actually happened? Debates about fictionalization are among the greatest in all of literature and art, way too big a subject to try to resolve here. My suggestion is that we take *The American People* on its own terms — as we do *Faggots* and even *The Normal Heart* — as an extended evocation that reveals bigger truths than the historical details which in this or that instance and particular may be more a composite and fiction than accurate history. In the end, I have no problem with Larry Kramer's compositings, dramatizations and fictionalizations, even when they extend to my own experience, except when he asserts them to be "our history." Did Tolstoy proclaim "this is our history" for *War and Peace*? "It is not a novel, even less is it a poem, and still less a historical chronicle," said Tolstoy. Did Margaret Mitchell declare *Gone With the Wind* to be an accurate history of the American South and the Civil War? "No, not a single character was taken from real life," admitted Mitchell in an interview. Is it right for Kramer to keep affirming of *The Normal Heart* that "this is our history"? To what extent will he do likewise with *The American People*?

Conversely, is *The American People* the *War and Peace* or *Gone With The Wind* of LGBT history? *The American People* is so many disparate things that comparisons will inevitably fall short. It's a Swiftian journey through an America we never knew; a Voltairean satire of American life and ways; a literary offspring of Gore Vidal's *Lincoln* and *Myra Brenckenridge*; a pornographic American history through the eyes of a Henry Miller; a Robin Cook medical mystery. It's a Sinclairean expose of American industrial and corporate skulduggery, and otherwise breathtakingly testimonial to the art of muckraking. It's a treasure trove of historical findings, especially of the history of sex in America — of prostitution, communal living, of STD's, of medicine and infectious diseases, of sanitation and health care, of medical and historical institutions, research, opinion, publications, figureheads and testimony. It's an ultimate coming together (pun intended) of the personal with the political. And it's the grandest telling yet of Kramer's own story.

There is one critical difference between *The American People* and historical novels like *War and Peace* and *Gone With the Wind.* With Russian history and the history of the American Civil War, a lot of what actually happened has been documented and chronicled, however incompletely. By contrast, most of the LGBT history that is the great preoccupation of *The American People* has to be deciphered, decoded and imagined, albeit in light of the arsenal of rare historical materials Kramer has mined. This is the great journey that Kramer has undertaken and the full measure of its achievement is difficult to determine at this juncture. What Kramer has done is the equivalent of, say, American history being recollected from the viewpoint of a Native American, a black person, a Jew or a woman. With other minority identities, however, there are more and better recorded histories extant than anything we might call LGBT history, a tragic legacy that Kramer is at greatest pains to decry and redress.

There are several premises crucial to *The American People.* The first is to understand where "the plague" came from, to locate what is suspected to be the "underlying condition" ("UC"). The journey begins with Fred (as in Fred Lemish, the Kramer character in *Faggots*) and a cacophany of experts, historians, scientists, researchers, miscellaneous commentators and including a kind of virion (virus analogue), most of these serving as alter-egos. As the journey progresses through every realm of history, including Fred's own and that of his Jewish family and community in America's home town, Washington, D.C., elements accumulate that are or seem to be contributory to the spread of disease. As Fred and company venture forth, they exude Kramer's in-depth fascination with and sophisticated knowledge of the intersections of science, medicine, history and sociology with every conceivable circumstance of sophistry, chicanery, wickedness, depravity and atrocity. They venture back and back and ever-further back to when the virion seems first to have wended its way via monkeys devouring each other; and before that to when the virion was looking for a host. Before they know it, Fred *et al* find themselves not only discovering earlier outbreaks of diseases that may have been contributory to UC, but ineluctably reconstructing nothing less than a very unorthodox and most definitely unauthorized history of the American people.

Ultimately, from a slowly brewing matrix of early American ignorance, arrogance, indifference, hatred and the 7 deadly sins, UC is revealed to be bigger and more ramifying and subsuming than anything imagined by even the most fanatical multifactorialists (those who emphasize the importance of co-factors in disease outbreaks). It becomes slowly clear that whatever else UC will turn out to be in Volume 2, it is also nothing less than the great swath of humanity and history that is the American people. All of it, the American people past, present and future, the novel tacitly suggests, was necessary for the plague to take hold and spread in time and place. Conversely, it's implied, had the American people been even somewhat less selfish, arrogant , ridiculous, stupid, bigoted, thieving, lying, hypocritical, marauding, pillaging, plundering, dumb and dumber, hating, hateful, murderous, mass-murderous and evil, one of recorded history's worst global catastrophes, the plague (AIDS), might never have happened as it did. It's an unarticulated but spectacular premise that can be as difficult to swallow as it is to refute.

Just as you are witness to the burning of Atlanta and the sacking of Moscow and other battles in the otherwise personal, domestic and family dramas of *Gone With The Wind* and *War and Peace*, so you are witness through the personal accounts of Fred *et al* in *The American People* to officially designated landmark episodes of American history such as the Civil War and unofficially designated turning points such as the rise of the eugenics movement that helped spawn what became Nazism, episodes and events that have become otherwise so depersonalized by historians that we've lost our ability to appreciate them as three dimensional and its participants as flesh and blood; events and personages famous and infamous that have been desexed, otherwise whitewashed and often completely expunged from records and memory.

Kramer's narrative sardonically recounts so many examples and exemplars of egotism, of pomposity and religiosity, of religious cults and sects, of demented Jews and bigoted Catholics, of crazed Mormons and Baptists, of meanness, of stupidities and cruelties, of prejudices and oppression, of bullies and wusses, of fornicators and buggers, of people with plagues of various kinds, especially sexual, of blood and bloodletting and bleeding, of bloodbanking bunglings, of pus and sores and scabs, of bodily fluids, of odors and stinks, of waste management pollution and profiteering, of circumcision botchings, of the stigma of "illegitimacy," of incest (and plenty of it ), of hellish orphan life and orphanages, of the horrors of institutionalization, of eugenics, of involuntary euthanasia, of forced sterilizations and castrations by law, sanctioned and sometimes spearheaded by leading Americans including Teddy Roosevelt, John Harvey Kellogg, Henry Ford, Averill Harriman, John Foster Dulles and many others, of segregations, of massacres of slaves and Native Americans, of murders and murderers, of mass murders and mass murderers, of government backed edicts of hatred, of social diseases, of toxic home remedies, snake-oil cures and lifesavers, of the "real" history of poppers, of persecutions, of the violent suppression of sexual variance, of exterminations of admitted or suspected homosexuals, of concentration camps, of American collaborations with Nazis and Nazism, of the specifics of eugenical and Nazi medical experiments on children and those deemed genetically inferior, of starvations and cannibalism (and plenty of it ), of so much evil that incredulity can seem the only alternative to the otherwise continuous shock, horror, outrage and sense of genocidal tragedy. But it's just this incredulity on our part that Kramer most wishes to engage and conquer. *The American People* is evoking history, especially LGBT history but with it Jewish, Jewish-American and other American history, so that its reach and its import for our lives and times and for future lives and times can be more rightfully and confidently prioritized for research, appreciation and mourning. Beyond all the particulars, Kramer's greatest hope and expectation is simply that the vast expanse of LGBT history that has been relegated, denied and otherwise lost to us finally will be claimed.

Another of the premises of this undertaking is that there have always been LGBT people. Though we no longer hear as much about the never-resolved sexual orientation debates that dominated scholarly discourse on homosexuality in the period that followed the declassification of homosexuality as a mental disorder by the American Psychiatric Association in 1973-74, they fell under the broad rubric of "essentialism" vs "social constructionism." Social constructionists believe that gayness is a modern concept given outsized importance by great social forces, especially capitalism and colonialism. Essentialists are those like Larry Kramer who believe that LGBT people have always been recognizable and identifiable; that we have existed as such throughout history; that there have always been transgender folk, bisexuality and homoerotic desire that would be as recognizable in Native Americans and early Puritans as they are today; that gay men have always cruised each other, have always had cruising areas, have always had names and labels, depending on the society, era and location. Responding to allegations and arguments that historical letters and documents and histories do not support these contentions about LGBT life in other times and cultures, Kramer continually affirms his sense of the internal and external censoring that revolved around all aspects of sexual life but especially anything having to do with same-sex desire or relationships; and he quotes and references an amazing array of arcane archival as well as better known historical sources in support of his contentions.

Kramer's perspective is occasionally spelled out editorially, as in the following passages:

> *But [gay gathering places] were there. From the beginning of time, they were there. From the beginning of time, of people-in-groups, of people-in-crowds, there are such places. Why, oh why, has it been impossible for us to accept such an obvious fact? That there is so little record of them is a testament to what must have been a nonstop effort bordering on the superhuman to eradicate all traces of their existence on the part of city fathers, and of course historians, and sadly, no doubt on the part of [gay people] themselves. No town, or family or [gay person], wishes such information to be known...There is little we know that was not done then, determined though so many historians are to deny this. It is not much different today but for the numbers.*

Likewise editorially, Kramer's legendary exasperation, in this case with social constructionism and historians, is spelled out by one of the more potty-mouthed alter-egos: "History knows dipshit about ratshit...Modern history is a fairy tale told by idiots." In *The American People*, incidentally, the word shit doubtless breaks all records for appearances on a single page and in aggregate for any novel ever written.

That's Larry Kramer in his characteristic anger. "Let me say before I go any further that I forgive nobody," observes Samuel Beckett in the last of the 12 epigraphs Kramer has chosen to quote in introduction to *The American People.* As you might anticipate from familiarity with Kramer and his legendary capacity for outrage, and considering the scope of his endeavor, it's not surprising that there's enough rage in *The American People* to fuel a world war. And as it always has, Kramer's anger at various archvillains can betray a sadistic pleasure in their vilification, in assassinating their personas, in exacting revenge, even in scapegoating them. If only Reagan *et al* had spearheaded a public health effort comparable to today's containment of ebola, Kramer's narrative suggests, the plague could have been prevented. Kramer wants to make an even stronger case than in the heyday of ACT UP for Reagan ("Peter Reuster") being every bit as culpable, as evil, as Hitler.

*The American People* is especially notable in looking in depth at historical homophobia and anti-Semitism, individually and together throughout the greater period of WW2. Kramer of course has been outspoken about homophobia in our lives and times and it's thrilling to see him wax so ardently and intelligently about historical anti-Semitism and its entwinements with historical homophobia. If ever there were a supreme proponent of the ACT UP slogan Silence = Death, it's Larry Kramer. It therefore seems incongruous that Kramer has remained so silent about *contemporary* anti-Semitism. An unfair allegation, perhaps, in light of the forthcoming Volume 2 of *The American People*, which will cover the period from the 1950's on, but it's one that has come up before — e.g., with regard to the *New Yorker* profile on Larry from 2002, in which neither 9/11 nor anti-Semitism is mentioned, as well as in my Larry Kramer anthology. *The American People* does make reference to a homosexual in Truman's administration who commits suicide because of the gathering storm of Hoover's homophobia. "Jimmy" was against the establishment of Israel because he "foresaw that it would cause nothing but warfare in the Middle East forever." Even though it's the only such reference in the book, one can't help but wonder if Kramer thinks, like Jimmy, that the greater arc of today's anti-Semitism and Islamist extremism is because of Israel.

In *The American People* Kramer tells the story of several generations of Washington Jews, the Masturbovs, stand-ins for his own family, but with extraordinary twists. The sissy-hating, abusive father Philip turns out to be gay, working for an American firm that enables Hollywood to continue to do business with the Nazis. In the midst of an affair with a middle man in Germany, Philip travels back and forth there. Eventually, David, one of his twin sons, is detained by Nazi doctors, cohorts of Dr. Mengele, who is also represented as sometimes queer and otherwise sexual and whose fiendish experiments on children and especially twins are narrated in excruciating detail.

The good news: David returns to America alive. The bad news: this "liberation" is actually a transfer from Dr. Mengele's medical concentration camp unit in Germany to its partner camp in Idaho, where the same and worse medical experiments to cure homosexuality and effeminacy are carried out. Which turns out to be just two subunits of what is in fact a worldwide gulag — in Russia and Japan as well as everywhere else — of human guinea pigs designated for testing of the newest and biggest front of war: CBW or chemical biological warfare, aka germ warfare.

HBO's new documentary by Jean Carlomusto about Larry Kramer, to be broadcast during Gay Pride in June, is called *Larry Kramer in Love and Anger*. And indeed and never moreso than in *The American People*, bound up with all the anger at so much evil and injustice is Kramer's characteristic compassion, concern, caring and love, of all of humanity, actually, but especially of the weak, meek, defenseless and victimized, and especially of gay people.

Kramer analyzes a massacre of young men that took place in the environs of Jamestown during the earliest period of settlement and speculates that those who were murdered were gay. What must it have been like for gay people to have had no context for understanding themselves, to not know what to do with themselves or where or how or with whom to be, to have had no sense of place for themselves, to be living with the cognitive dissonance that what is deepest in their hearts and souls, or even just circumstantially relieving, is "wrong," "evil," "sick," condemned and forbidden by society? The gentleness and pathos with which Kramer imagines the hardships of these early LGBT pioneers who didn't have the resources to better realize that that's who and what they were, is overwhelming.

But soon matched by his recounting of the excesses and losses of the American Civil War. Kramer's passage (I'm not sure what else to call these chapterettes),"The Civil War" will invite comparison to the testimony of Walt Whitman, the most famous gay witness to this history and who Kramer quotes at length and in homage. *The American People* overflows with accounts of the grueling hardships of the lives of all young people but especially LGBT people — of the desperation of gay men and lesbians who needed to pass just to survive; of their mind-bogglingly courageous efforts to affirm themselves and their kind, often with the opposition of their own kind; of their inevitable murder by growing and peculiarly American brigades and lone warriors of hate. Search for my Heart," *The American People* is aptly subtitled and concludes, quoting Baudelaire: "Search for my heart no longer, the beasts have eaten it." But finding Kramer's abnormally big heart in *The American People* is as easy as being engaged by Kramer's volcanic anger and mighty voice. It's right there, front and center, in every word, each one lovingly and carefully selected, on every page. Whatever the disappointments and reckonings with history, with his own life, with the simple romantic love that he believed in so deeply as an innocent young gay man, with lovers, with gay life, with friends, with family, with America, there is one surpassing love and heart's home that has remained as unwaveringly faithful to Larry Kramer as he to it — his muse.

Following his leadership of ACT UP, Kramer moved on to establish a LGBT studies program, the Larry Kramer Initiative, at his alma mater Yale. Varyingly under the sway of stodgy traditionalists and social constructionists, the powers that be at Yale ("Yaddah" in *The American People*), seemed to be doing everything they could to undermine and relegate the LKI, which they believed, at best, belonged under the auspices of gender studies and/or that it wasn't an otherwise fully legitimate, justifiable enterprise. Clearly, *The American People* aims to upend the historians, scholars and custodians of traditions Kramer did battle with at Yale within wider spheres of academe. To say that Kramer believes that LGBT people have been deprived of our history with the collusion of academics, intellectuals and historians, gay as well as mainstream, would be the biggest understatement you could make about Larry Kramer and *The American People*. Not surprisingly, the muckraking Kramer has done about the origins and pillars of "Yaddah" and "New Godding" paints a very different picture than that which this otherwise most esteemed institution of American learning and American presidents would want the world to see. The Yale that is dissected in *The American People* is the alma matter of genteel homophobes like William F. Buckley and George W. Bush and was the home of the leading literary critic Newton Arvin, who committed suicide after being publicly indicted for "lewdness."

A launching pad for Kramer in writing his epic tome were Ronald Reagan's commonplace references to "the American people," which Kramer correctly appreciated as not including gay people. It is Kramer's agenda not only to make the case for LGBT American history but to make the case for it as something much greater than anything ever imagined by any of us. What Kramer envisions with *The American People* is nothing less than a complete rewriting of history as we've known it. By now, everyone has heard of the contention that Abraham Lincoln was gay. (For the record, there are comparable claims that Lincoln, who had significant and positive relationships with Jews, was part Jewish.) Kramer goes much much further, alleging that not only Lincoln but Washington, Alexander Hamilton, Presidents Jackson, Pierce, Buchanan and perhaps other presidents, as well as Lewis and Clarke, de Tocqueville, LaFayette, Burr, John Wilkes Booth, Samuel Clemens, George Custer, Oliver Wendell Holmes, visitors to America such as Sigmund Freud and his alleged lover Wilhelm Fliess, virtually every actor in Hollywood past and present, including one who became president, and so many others, were gay or did it with men at some point.

As part of its commemorations of Black History Month, the *New York Times* published an editorial about the extent and details of Washington's ownership of slaves, Why, in the harsh light of what we now realize about our founding father's willingness to exploit what he otherwise realized was the morally and ethically untenable institution of slavery, is it so inconceivable that this military man, in a passionless and childless marriage, might have been gay? The point of course is not that being gay has some kind of connection to or equivalency with endorsing slavery, but that Washington's relationships to slavery, like questions of his sexuality, are aspects of the life of Washington that people have relegated and don't seem to want to know much about. When recently asked if he were really so sure that Washington was gay, Kramer rejoindered: "Are you really so sure he wasn't?"

Not too surprisingly after the passages on Washington, Hamilton, Lincoln and Booth, Kramer seems eager to buy into the notion, on the basis of well-known circumstantial evidence, that Hitler was homosexual, notwithstanding that this exemplar of faggification of the enemy has never been made to stick. Even so, in light of its myriad examples of how aggressively homosexuality and any evidence of it was covered up, *The American People* is seductive in asking us to look yet again at the question of Hitler and homosexuality, just as it asks us to do with virtually every other known public figure of the past.

*The American People* is mesmerizing. Despite its Gargantuan length and sprawl, it is very readable, not only because Larry Kramer's writing is so accessible, so human, so personal, so caring, so heartfelt, so courageous and so resonant, but because of the way the book is constructed, as a series of mostly very short, readable segments. It's possible to sit down and read a vignette or chapterette for a few minutes. It doesn't demand that you read it for hours on end, though such a gifted writer is Larry Kramer that that's what you will inevitably want to do, especially since, as with most great novels, the momentum builds.

Volume 1 of *The American People* is 777 pages. Volume II is expected to be similarly voluminous. The two volumes together will probably be about the same length as *War and Peace.* In an introduction Kramer indicates plans to independently publish some 2000 additional pages beyond Volume 2. It seems almost preconceived that it cannot ever conclude as you might expect of a novel, drawing all the disparate strains together conclusively or even meaningfully. While there can't be any question that Kramer overshoots with so much fire — e.g., Lincoln's assassination is reinterpreted as a gay love triangle with Booth, gone south, that Clemens was gay and that his "Huck and Nigger Jim were lovers" — the greater truth Kramer so persistently makes the case for seems credible: that the histories of the American people that have come down to us, even from many contemporary historians, are so myopic, naive, reticent and constipated about the impact of sexuality and especially homosexuality and bisexuality in historical life and relationships and events, that nothing less than the entirety of this history needs to be reexamined and rewritten. For this reason alone, *The American People* is likely to find its place among the notable works of the Western canon.

How well does *The American People* work as a novel? The answer to that question must await volume 2, due out next year. Meanwhile, how well does what is there in volume 1 work, hold together? In his career as a writer, Kramer has sometimes misfired badly, or seemed to have, even by his own estimation — e.g., in the screenplay he did for the musical remake of the Hollywood classic, *Lost Horizon*, and with his play, *Just Say No*. But such are Kramer's powers of insight and his gifts for prophecy as well as his skills as a writer that even these works will have to be re-explored and mined for riches by future scholars, critics and historians. Like his activism, Kramer's writing has never been known for its tidiness or prettiness, for its surfaces or for decorum, although his writing is so confident and fluid that it seems to have, in league with the greatest writers, its own lilt, language and cadences as well as a signature blend of gay, Jewish and mordant humors. As a novel, it's likely that *The American People* will come under fire for a lot of violations of various rules of fine writing. Perhaps a better question than how well it all works and holds together might be does *The American People* help us to see and question our own lives and times and histories to an extent and with a success that can be claimed by few other writers? While it may be too soon to know exactly what places *The American People* will eventually find for itself, one thing's for sure. *The American People*, which one of our greatest leaders, champions, voices, thinkers, sages, prophets and writers has labored on for 40 years, is here to stay. Eloquent, powerful, epochal, defiant, relentlessly in your face and tough as shit on everyone and everything, this astounding novel is no more likely to accept the silent treatment or any other kind of rejection than Kramer himself ever would.

# Two Current Fronts of the American Health Care Wars: Hepatitis C and Cancer

by Lawrence D. Mass

– *Huffington Post*, 7/6/2015

**The Pharmaceutical Industry, Health Insurance and Recurrent Questions of Extortion, Murder and Evil**

*Asking patients to delay treatment for hepatitis C is like asking patients to delay treatment for diabetes or cancer.*

Figure 124 - Harvard Art Museum

**"Waiting for cirrhosis to happen to treat HCV is like waiting for cancer to metastasize or for diabetes to cause complications before treating it. In reality, all-cause mortality and per patient per year health care costs are tripled for patients with hepatitis C, whether they have cirrhosis or not."**

**— Dr. Douglas Dieterich, leading hepatitis C and liver diseases researcher and specialist at the Mount Sinai Hospital, New York City**

My friend John is a retired college professor who lives on a budget. He has hepatitis C, which he acquired from a blood transfusion before the development of blood testing and screening for hep C. He does have health insurance, but like most of those seeking treatment for this condition, he has been told that he must become demonstrably sicker to qualify for treatment coverage. Meanwhile, he must not drink any alcohol and remain vigilant for symptoms, especially fatigue. Since the progression of hepatitis C to cirrhosis of the liver and cancer of the liver can take decades, and John has already had this disease for decades, he is understandably concerned. In fact, he may die sooner from other causes, his untreated hepatitis C playing an indeterminate role. There is, however, an alternative for John. If he had the $100,000+ in cash to pay for the treatment now, he could be fully and safely cured in 8-12 weeks. John does not identify himself as a socialist, and he is willing to pay what he can for treatment, but the cost in this case is overwhelming.

Another friend, Alex, is a health care worker who contracted hep C sexually. He has had the identical experience as John in facing $100,000 pricing for insurance noncoverage in the absence of being demonstrably sicker. Recently, however, he had a stroke of luck. Through connections, persistence and good fortune, he managed to obtain one of a limited number of assistance vouchers from one of the drug companies that essentially entitles him to full coverage. Needless to say, he's elated. Otherwise an articulate critic of corporate for-profit medicine, he can't help but feel as if he just won the lottery.

Hepatitis C is a disease that leads to cirrhosis and cancer of the liver and death in large numbers of people. The World Health Organization (WHO) suggests that 350,000 to 500,000 people die each year of liver-related diseases from hepatitis C. In 1999, I wrote a feature on hep C for *New York* magazine called "C Sick" on what was then being called "the stealth epidemic," for which I interviewed Dr. Dieterich at length. Because the vast majority of those with the disease in this country had acquired this viral scourge via injection drug use, it was very difficult to arouse the greater public to any kind of action or even concern.

And there seemed little hope for developing more successful treatment because profits seemed more questionable for a disease, at least in this country, that is mostly limited to people with histories of drug use. Like the gay men with AIDS who were treated so abominably by Reagan era health care policies and systems, those with histories of injection drug use not only had the same experience with AIDS, they, and a growing number of gay men along with them, are experiencing comparable medical neglect and abuse around hep C.

So beneath the public radar was hep C, and for so long, that most of those who had it didn't know it. They were never tested and didn't know they should be. One of the biggest concerns motivating my investigation had to do with identifying hep C as an STD in gay men, who weren't even being encouraged to be tested. Fifteen years later, it is now finally acknowledged that hep C is seen as an STD in gay men, but sexually-active gay men still need to be informed and proactive enough to demand to be tested by their doctors, whose knowledge of hep C can still be surprisingly rudimentary.

Although it has taken many years longer than it should have to get there, testing for hep C is now more routine and there is more public discussion. Almost everybody has now seen advertisements for hepatitis C treatment on television. They're strange. They show well-groomed, middle class, middle-aged people who look hopeful and trusting, but the information accompanying these images is opaque. They say things like "there is treatment now," and they encourage those with the disease to "make further inquiries." As with virtually all other pharmaceutical advertisements, nothing is said about cost.

The latest of these advertisements makes it a lot more clear that, in one of the biggest and most important developments in the history of medicine, hepatitis C is now fully curable in the great majority of cases with only 8-12 weeks of treatment with medications that have few side effects. Not one of these advertisements, however, hints at the staggering price tag of $1,000 a pill.

Who can afford this? For pharma (the pharmaceutical industry) that's not the main question. The main question is how much will Medicare, Medicaid or other insurance pay for these drugs? In far too many cases, such as those in V.A. (Veterans Administration) systems, the answer is none.

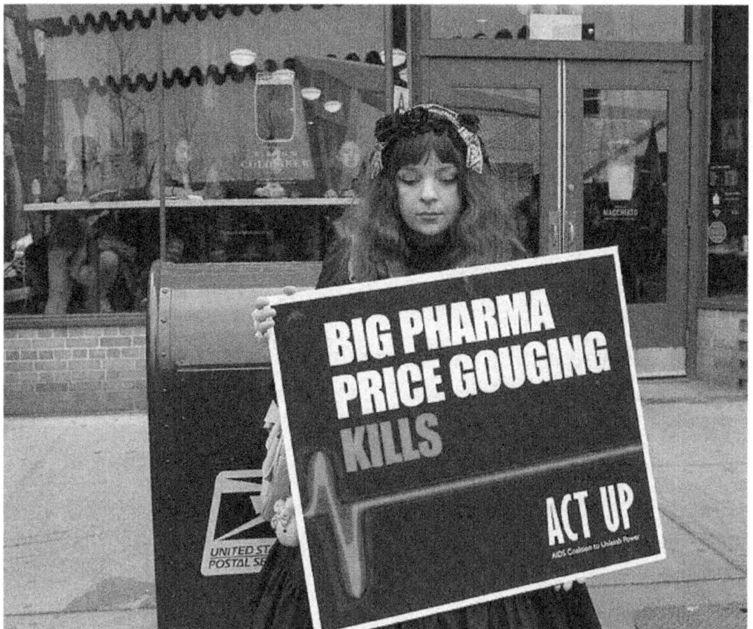

Figure 125 - ACT UP 30th Anniversary Gathering at the NYC AIDS Memorial, 3/30/17; ACT UP led protests of Gilead for price-gouging of life-saving medications for hepatitis C as well as for HIV; photograph by Elvert Barnes (Elvert Barnes Protest Photography), Wikimedia Commons

The overview is this. Many people who can't afford these medications, which in this country means the majority of cases, are not out of the running to receive them, and some insurance will pay for them, but in most of those cases, treatment is being delayed until there is serious disease progression — to fibrosis and early stages of cirrhosis, even though such delays place these patients at greater risk for cancer of the liver and other conditions. Once progression is demonstrated to be well underway, some insurance companies will then pay the costs for the new hep C treatments. While those costs are high, they are a lot less than what a liver transplant would cost them, which is the only other treatment option for end-stage cirrhosis and liver failure. In other words, the insurance companies are not paying for these treatments out of the generosity of their hearts so much as because they will likely have to pay a lot more if the disease progresses to liver failure and cirrhosis.

In my field of addiction medicine, and as anticipated, hepatitis C has eclipsed AIDS as the leading cause of treatable illness and preventable death. More than 90 percent of the nation's 300,000+ patients on Methadone Maintenance treatment for opioid dependence are hep C positive. Many of them have Medicaid. While some of those with advanced disease are now being treated, the majority have lesser disease and, like my friends John and Alex, are not yet considered eligible for treatment, though they do have the option of initiating lengthy appeals of insurance coverage denials and may hold out some hope for obtaining assistance vouchers from the drug companies. Meanwhile, as Dieterich put it, telling patients they must put off treatment for hep C is like telling diabetes or cancer patients to hold off on treatment until the diabetes or cancer is more advanced.

And there is another consideration regarding the treatment of hep C patients with histories of injection drug use. The earlier they are treated, the less likely they are to spread hep C to others via relapse.

If not for insurance and cost issues, those who, like John, Alex and those in treatment for opioid dependence, have the most to benefit from it now can't get it unless they are willing to pay for it. Most people have no way to pay such fees, but some do and others can go into debt. Cumulatively, the numbers of those who can get the money however they can are apparently enough to have swayed pharma to further leverage its collective soul by engaging in such devious financial schemes.

Remember Nixon's "war on cancer"? Well, some of the life-saving cancer-treatments that were then just pipe dreams are now reality. The problem is that most of those who need these newest and most effective drugs to save their lives are having to give up all their assets in order to afford them, to the extent of declaring bankruptcy.

As spelled out by leading cancer specialists in an expose on *60 Minutes* (originally broadcast 10/5/14 and updated 6/21/15), cancer costs are now among the biggest causes of personal bankruptcy. The general price for treatment is $100,000 a year. So out of control and damaging is this issue that financial toxicity and bankruptcy must now be regarded as major and probable side effects of cancer treatment. People's fears and anxieties are being exploited. Middle class patients aren't eligible for financial assistance. Pathetically, people are taking half the recommended doses of the newest and most effective treatments as a way of getting, at least hopefully, some treatment benefit. How many have died because they couldn't afford treatment?

In 2013, the *New York Times* published an article, "Doctors Denounce Cancer Drug Prices of $100,000 a Year." The cancer specialists interviewed here and on *60 Minutes* were unanimous in their denunciation of capricious drug pricing, which one of those on the *60 Minutes* feature described as dictated by "corporate *chutzpah*." In response to such criticism, pharma gives a standard defense: The high fees are necessary to cover the costs of research. In this case, because of the widely-seen *NYT* criticism, pharma agreed to reduce by 50 percent the prices of the drugs specifically under indictment by the cancer docs.

While it's true that we mustn't lose sight of the fact that the pharmaceutical companies are producing new miracle cures and treatments that otherwise might not have come about, and that the costs of research are considerable, in the bigger picture, pharma is nonetheless and indeed making a killing (pun intended) on these medications. As reported in the *New York Times*, as a result of its sales of Sovaldi, the new miracle cure for hep C, Gilead took in record profits of $10.3 billion in 2014, making it a close runner up to the world's best-selling pharmaceutical, Humira, the wonder-drug for rheumatoid arthritis, the costs of which can run more than $20,000 a year. Ever wonder why we're seeing so many advertisements for medications on television? As with any other products, getting the information out there to target populations is unquestionably the best way to boost sales. In other words, the plethora of advertisements for medications is a lot less about improving public health than it is about making bucks.

As criticism mounts, and not so coincidentally as windfall profits already have been made, the prices of the hepatitis C medications are beginning to come down. Alas, any optimism that might be attached to such limited and tentative success is like making incursions on one or two villages overtaken by ISIS and hoping democracy will replace Islamic extremism throughout the land. As characterized by one leading specialist interviewed in the *60 Minutes* episode, pharma has rendered drug-pricing "unreasonable, unsustainable and immoral." The same drugs in Canada and Europe cost 50 to 80 percent less.

Meanwhile, our Republican Congress will almost certainly veto any efforts by Obama to regulate the price of drugs.

Is pharma complicit in extortion and murder when unreasonable pricing and policies lead to casualties? Leading AIDS activist Larry Kramer certainly thought so, and he is legendary for denouncing as "murderers" and "Nazis" everybody who was not on the front lines of testing new drugs and getting them into patients with HIV/AIDS. Kramer was additionally clear about a subject he returned to again and again: "evil," which he defined as including sins of omission and silence as well as those more overtly deliberate.

As a result of the war on AIDS led by Kramer, people with HIV and AIDS got treatment despite seemingly implacable early resistance from pharma and its collaborators. In the case of AIDS, pharma lost, at least initially. Clearly, however, questionable research priorities, price-gouging and insurance coverage denials continue to erupt for new treatments for many other illnesses and conditions.

When the ultimate antiviral for HIV is finally developed, the one that can cure AIDS with the success that antivirals are currently able to cure hepatitis C, will there be more all-out battles over pricing and access? Alternatively, will pharma, as Larry Kramer currently believes, deprioritize developing that cure around issues of profit? Does NIAID (National Institute of Allergy and Infectious Disease) Director Anthony Fauci really have the power to more decisively lead the final push for curative treatment, as Larry Kramer suggested when he received the first Larry Kramer AIDS Activism Award (4/23/15) of GMHC (Gay Men's Health Crisis)?

Notwithstanding a second Supreme Court decision in support of Obamacare, it's clear that health care in the U.S. remains in a state of crisis. Millions of people still don't have health insurance, and pressures remain great to repeal reforms that have extended even bare-bones insurance benefits to the uninsured and underserved. "Big Pharma," as it's ever-more widely designated, remains unregulated. Notwithstanding the occasional gesture of assistance to the financially challenged with lottery-like vouchers and participating in some fair pricing coalition negotiations, pharma, insurance companies, lobbies and politicians, especially Republicans — those who stand to gain financially — have done everything in their power to prevent the implementation of anything remotely approximating equitable and humane health care for those who can't afford costs that have no controls and that have become so exorbitant that they can only be called extortion, comparable to loan-sharking and usury.

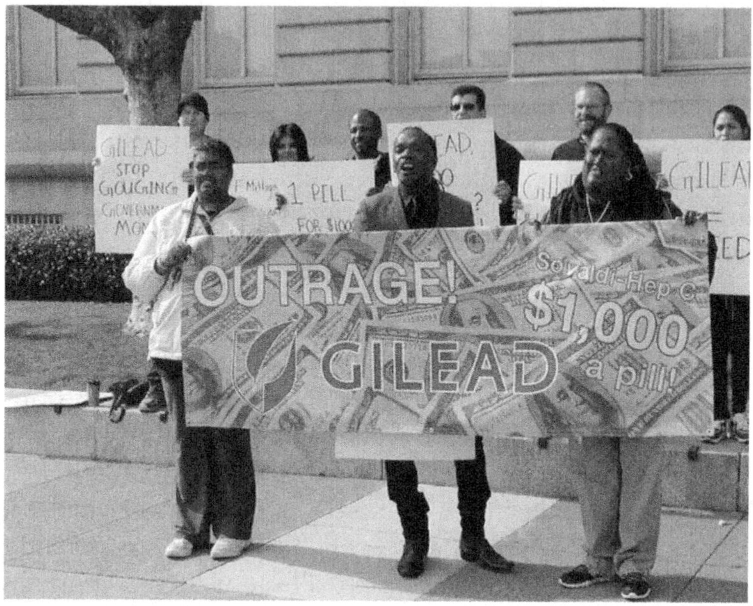


Figure 126 - "Gilead and the billion-dollar odyssey." Dark Money, The Conversation, 7/13/2017, Nick St.Charles, Wikimedia Commons

It's no longer shocking to hear stories about people who die of treatable cancer and other conditions because they had no health insurance or, if they did, because they couldn't pay the uncovered costs. By 2009, it was estimated that 45,000 preventable health care deaths were occurring annually. The ACA has doubtless reduced that number, but by how much, and can ACA coverage continue to endure the relentless incursions of for-profit interests? At what point do the rest of us do what Kramer and the AIDS activist organization he founded and led, ACT UP (AIDS Coalition to Unleash Power), did and are still doing: point fingers, name names, carry placards, stage boycotts, encourage divestment, and alert the media to planned demonstrations?

With ACT UP, demonstrations, protests, boycotts and civil disobedience established a track record of success for confronting unfairness and complacency in health care, especially with AIDS but beyond HIV/AIDS to hep C and other fronts. But ACT UP no longer has the resources, prime-time media attention and constituency support to have as much impact. To more effectively reign in pharma for access and costs of treatments such as those for HIV, hep C and cancer, representatives of the different affected constituencies — from those with histories of drug addiction and those in drug addiction treatment, from the poor who have no health insurance to middle-class patients whose insurance coverages are limited — would have to come together on a larger, broader and more determined scale than we have to date.

Like the new curative treatments for hepatitis C, ACT UP was another of the most important developments in the history of medicine. For the level of its achievement in unprecedented grass-health care activism, and the saving of hundreds of thousands of lives by facilitating the rapid development and distribution of unprecedentedly successful antiviral therapies for HIV/AIDS, ACT UP deserves the Nobel Prize. But don't count on that to happen anytime soon.

Sadly, such activism is still urgently needed, not only for AIDS, hepatitis C and cancer, but for the entire American health care system. For that to happen, the individuals and groups that would need to come together in much greater numbers and organize a lot more effectively turn out to be nothing less than the great aggregate of humanity, the history of which is the title subject of Larry Kramer's magnum opus: the American people. (*The American People, Volume 1: Search For My Heart*, was published by Farrar, Strauss, Giroux, April 1, 2015)

# Remembering Vito, 25 Years Later: Vito Russo, the Visual Arts and AIDS

– *Huffington Post*, 8/21/2015

**Vito Russo, the legendary gay and AIDS activist whose achievements have already earned him a biography and several film documentaries, is best known as the author of The Celluloid Closet and as a co-founder of GLAAD (Gay and Lesbian Alliance Against Defamation)**

Figure 127 - from left, Larry Mass, Arnie Kantrowitz and Vito Russo; photograph from the personal collection of Lawrence D. Mass

For the last three years, New York City has been host to The "Last Address" Tribute Walk. The event is coordinated by Alex Fiahlo, programs manager of Visual AIDS, an organization that "utilizes art to fight AIDS by provoking dialogue, supporting HIV+ artists, and preserving a legacy, because AIDS is not over."

Commencing with a screening of Ira Sachs's short, moving film, Last Walk, which lingers quietly and respectfully outside the last addresses of a number of artists and writers who died of AIDS-related illnesses and conditions, Fiahlo then conducts a walking tour to a selection of those addresses, where there are readings of remembrance and tribute by colleagues, friends or loved ones of these artists. Among those whose homes were visited in the film are Keith Haring, Hibiscus, David Wojnarowicz, Felix Gonzalez-Torres, Harold Brodkey, Robert Mapplethorpe, Reinaldo Arenas, Charles Ludlum, Assotto Saint, Jack Smith, Ethyl Eichelberger and Vito Russo. http://www.visualaids.org/blog/detail/alex-fialho-writes-about-his-last-address-tribute-walk

This will be the first year that Vito's home will be included in the walking tour and I was honored to be asked to speak about Vito outside his home, where I spent so many evenings, from the earliest period of having met him and of the epidemic in 1980-81 until his death in 1990. For the tour, I plan to read several passages from the wonderful biography of Vito, *Celluloid Activist*, by Michael Schiavi, as well as from the foreword to the revised Stonewall classics edition of *Under the Rainbow* by my life partner, Arnie Kantrowitz.

In the space I have here, and as we approach the 25th anniversary of Vito's death from AIDS, I would like to personally remember Vito, whose friendship was one of the gifts of my life. What warm memories I have. As Arnie's closest friend, Vito became family. Together with their other closest friend, NYC gay civil rights pioneer Jim Owles, I had married into an extended family of giants of the gay liberation movement.

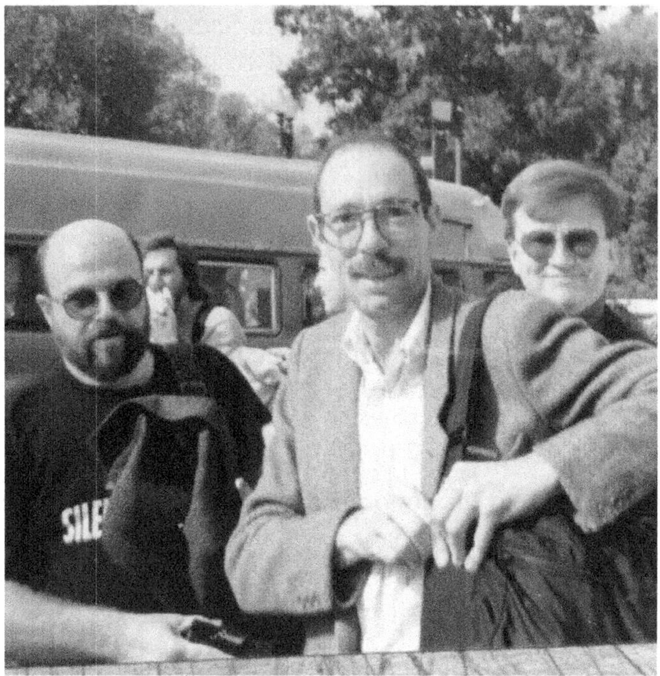

Figure 128 - Arnie, Vito and Jim Owles, photograph from the personal collection of Lawrence D. Mass

Even though Vito was someone we saw and talked to and about continuously, such were his aura and energies—his "sparkle and charisma," as Arnie captured it—that just to be in his presence, at his home, ours or anywhere else, always felt like a special event. Whether showing us snippets of new films with gay characters, actors, themes or issues, old clips of Bette Davis (Arnie's favorite actress) and Miriam Hopkins in *Old Acquaintance*, or regaling us with his favorite line from his favorite film, *Caged*, about women in prison: "Ok, you tramps, pile out. It's the end of the line!", Vito was always vibrantly present, always on, always a star, the brightest in our lives.

Incidentally, we inherited Vito's *Caged* poster which greets you now as you enter our apartment, on apposing walls of which are two other Vito posters, one from *Common Threads: Stories From The Quilt,* the 1989 academy-award winning documentary featuring Vito, and another from a New York City Gay Men's Chorus Night at the Movies that Vito hosted. It was always great to see the pictures of his favorite star, Judy Garland, that festooned Vito's apartment and the film clips of her he probably watched more often than Arnie saw his favorite film, *Gone With The Wind*. (How we all would laugh at the thought of "Scarlet Kantrowitz"!) Garland was, after all, the greatest singing actress in the history of film as well as the premiere gay icon whose death, as legend has it, sparked Stonewall. We loved her too, but it's Vito we remember most from all those Judy moments we shared with him.

Whether we were playing Yahtzee, Risk or poker, dishing the latest dish about this or that closet case or star (so often one and the same), celebrating our birthdays together, ganging up on "the Kantrowitz," as Vito called him, for always somehow being "the good one"; whether we were catching pearls of wisdom, fact and insight from his encyclopedic knowledge of film or catching him munching on the Mallomars he kept refrigerated and with which he always could be counted on to spoil his appetite for dinner; whether savoring the impressive Italian pasta sauce he made from scratch, ignoring the burping and flatulence that increasingly plagued him as AIDS advanced, or massaging his legs for the pain from the large KS lesions that covered his body, being with Vito was always a family connection, and always a gift.

Figure 129 - Vito and me at the joint 40th Birthday party Arnie hosted for us at our home, photograph from the personal collection of Lawrence D. Mass

So many treasurable moments. The first that comes to mind was also the last, in the sense that it happened just after Vito died, in fact as Arnie, Jim Owles and I were on our way to his memorial service at Cooper Union in New York. Featured speakers included Mayor David Dinkins, who had visited Vito in the hospital, and Larry Kramer, who famously began his comments with "We killed Vito." Alas, the soundtrack of the service was lost because of a recording error.

Our taxi driver, apparently bitter about his life, chose our ride to displace his anger." Life is terrible," he inveighed. "No money, no women, no friends!" "But that's just not true," I shot back. "We're on our way to a memorial service for our beloved friend, who also had no money, but who had more friends, so many of them women, than anyone I've ever known." What I'd said was impressively true. Vito was always broke, yet always managed to keep earning his way, never exploiting his staggering array of friends, many of them well-heeled and virtually all of them bending over backwards to help and love him in every way we could, even as we failed to rally in time the much greater forces needed to save him. I can't recall anyone who disliked or who was seriously alienated from Vito, apart from some misanthropes from the next generation of Zine queers, who criticized him for being too mainstream.

One of those well-heeled friends was the leading New York socialite, charity doyenne and GMHC buddy pioneer and patron Judy Peabody. They immediately struck up a genuine friendship, calling each other at all hours, laughing and chatting intimately about everyone and everything. Judy was just one of the many stars in Vito's orbit. Bette Midler, Peter Allen, Elizabeth Taylor, Lily Tomlin, Ian McKellen, Harvey Fierstein...the list is endless. The thing about Vito and these friendships is that they were all genuine. It's hard to imagine anyone better at making and keeping friends. When Mayor Dinkins visited Vito, Vito confided to him personally, as he would to any good friend, urging him to be true to himself and choose principles over politics and popularity.

Figure 130 - Vito with Marcia Johnson, photograph from the personal collection of Lawrence D. Mass

However glamorous and beloved a star Vito was in our firmament, his life's work was as serious and revolutionary as it was urgent. Before meeting him, I was keyed into his writing, especially *The Celluloid Closet*, which addressed a key perpetrator of what would eventually be called gay genocide by his increasingly close friend and comrade-in-arms Larry Kramer: the relentless representation of LGBT people in films and media as killers and psychopaths, as evil, sick, demented. *The Celluloid Closet* was the first book to catalogue what Vito called the "Necrology" of LGBT people in film. At that time I was writing my own first pieces in the gay press, one of which was called "Why is Hollywood Dressing Gays to Kill?" for the *New York Native,* for which I also wrote what became the first press report and weeks later the first feature article on AIDS in 1981. The previous year I had covered the trial of the serial killer John Wayne Gacy in Chicago for *Christopher Street* magazine. Individually and together, these developments seemed to have the potential, in the wake of the Dan White trial for the assassination of Harvey Milk in San Francisco, of igniting an unprecedented backlash.

If there is anything that unites the struggles against AIDS with those of homophobia in the arts, it's the issue that is captured by the ACT UP logo, Silence = Death. Just as Vito fought so bravely and lovingly to open the closet doors of cinema, so did he struggle mightily to open the eyes and hearts of the world to AIDS. Yet here is where another of Vito's qualities was revealed—the unconditionality of his love. Although he could be fiercely angry, disappointed, critical and activist, and a true leader as such, he was inevitably forgiving, and without lingering personal bitterness; and he continued to love us all, including closeted stars and celebrities who just couldn't for whatever reasons of circumspection and career bring themselves to come out publicly but whose confidences and friendships he simply would not betray, even when under considerable pressure to do so.

Likewise those within his own and extended gay families who fell short of expectations of who and what we could be and do, especially as AIDS raged on. In a moment that brought me to tears, just before one of his last public appearances, also at Cooper Union, I found myself once again inarticulate in trying to express to Vito how much we all loved him, how much he meant to us, how grateful we were for all he had done, how sorry we were that we hadn't fought harder and achieved more, better and faster. As Larry Kramer has often observed, the epidemic might have been quashed sooner and a lot more lives saved, including Vito's, had everybody's efforts been redoubled. I felt totally inarticulate and failed in my effort to communicate all this, but as our eyes met, he said, "I love ya, Lar."

Vito was especially inspiring to me in my own work on opening the closet doors of the worlds of music and opera. I'd hoped eventually to put together a collection of my essays, interviews and reviews, the working title of which was "Musical Closets," a worthy project that was never completed. Alas, there still is no overview work, no *Celluloid Closet,* on homosexuality in music and opera, though there are now, thanks in no small measure to Vito's pioneering efforts, a number of books on homosexuality and the fine arts.

*The Celluloid Closet* quickly became a classic that remains a premiere reference for LGBT experience and treatment in the arts, a standard that paved the way for subsequent studies and documentaries, and with which all other such work will continue to be compared. As adapted for film by Rob Epstein and Jeffrey Friedman, *The Celluloid Closet* was nominated for numerous awards, and GLAAD susbequently named an annual Vito Russo Award to recognize openly LGBT achievement in fighting homophobia in film and the media.

Figure 131 - Vito with his agent and close friend, Jed Mattes, who was at Vito's hospital bedside when he died from complications of AIDS November 7, 1990; photograph from the personal collection of Lawrence D. Mass

Alas, there is little of the fabulously engaging star, leader and persona that was Vito Russo himself in the 1995 film of *The Celluloid Closet*, but we are fortunate that Vito's appearances on film did not end there. There is ample footage of him in *Common Threads*, and also in Jeffrey Schwarz's 2012 documentary of Vito's life and work, *Vito*. As is now the case with Larry Kramer following the release of Jean Carlomusto's documentary for HBO, *Larry Kramer in Love and Anger*, there is now enough of the real Vito Russo preserved on accessible documentary film to give a genuine sense of who that person was, what he was like, why he was so important, and why he was so beloved.

As witnessed by Arnie and myself from behind Vito and Larry Kramer, and as recounted by Michael Schiavi in *Celluloid Activist*, the Gay Pride parade, Vito's last in 1990, passed Larry's apartment on 5th Avenue just above 8th Street. On Larry's balcony, Larry and Vito locked arms, acknowledging the roars that kept erupting from the passing throngs below. "Look Vito," Larry said. "These are our children."

Figure 132 - Vito with Larry Kramer, photograph from the personal collection of Lawrence D. Mass

RIP Vito. When you passed from our lives, the brightest of its light—sunlight and starlight—went with you. You may not have lived to see the AIDS treatment that eluded you by only a few years, nor did you live to see the "end of AIDS," as we are buzzing about it now. But your spirit and legacies of activism will live on, as will the love and gratitude of all those who knew you, all those whose lives your activism was key to saving and ennobling, including those younger and countless who did not have the gift of knowing you personally, "our children."

**photos from the personal collection of Lawrence D. Mass references from The Celluloid Activist by Michael Schiavi and the obituary on Vito Russo by Arnie Kantrowitz, Outweek, 11/21/90**

# Commentary on David France's History of AIDS

**Personal Reflections on AIDS Journalism, Denialism and Selectivity**

– *Huffington Post*, 3/15/17

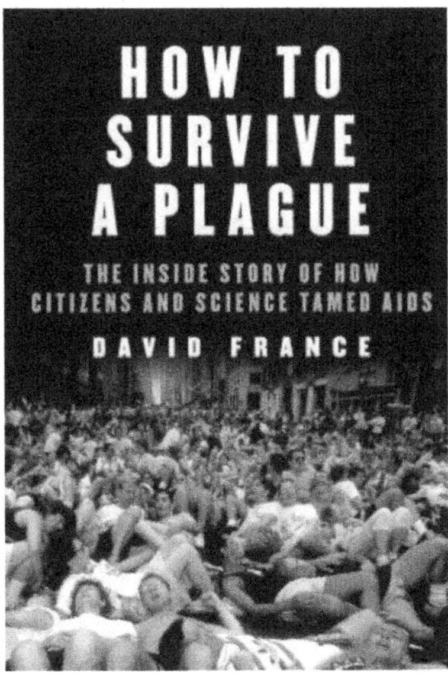


Figure 133 - Amazon.com

**In a book largely concerned about preventable deaths from AIDS, the greatest episode in the history of preventable deaths from AIDS goes unmentioned.**

Over the decades David France has written many thoughtful, informative, timely and engaging pieces on gay issues, lives and times. Most of this body of work has been on HIV/AIDS and the gay community, mostly for the mainstream press. Some of these articles were cutting edge, like one on questions of accelerated ageing in AIDS. Some could be simultaneously panoramic and meandering, like one on the widespread breakdown of condom use. And some could seem lurid—e.g., an overly-detailed *expose* of the drug-fueled decline of Dr. Gabriel Torres, who had been a beacon of leadership and hope in LGBT health and hospital services.

France is also the author of previous books. *The Confession*, about suddenly-out former New Jersey governor James McGreevey, and *Sins of Our Fathers*, about pedophile priests. Both were high profile and of value for gay perspectives, though both subjects were otherwise widely covered in the press.

France was never publicly confrontational or controversial in ways that earned him the kind of renown garnered by frontline AIDS and gay activists, as he himself acknowledges in his new book. By volume, mainstream placement and acclaim, however, this body of work eventually established France as our leading HIV/AIDS journalist, the successor to Randy Shilts.

Now, following a path similar to Shilts, France has written his big work, a companion to his documentary film of the same title, but covering the greater span of the epidemic from the earliest period of its unfolding here in the US in the gay community through the heyday of ACT UP and its epochal role in the development of unprecedentedly successful antiviral treatments. So successful that AIDS was transformed almost overnight from a disease that was nearly always fatal within 2 years to a disease that is chronic and manageable.

Redolent of Shilts in approach, it's a comparably commendable feat. *Plague*'s narrative drama and momentum, clarity on complicated medical and scientific aspects of HIV/AIDS, and many historical details and insights, interwoven with France's own personal story, make it a compelling and edifying read.

When he wrote *Plague*, France could not have foreseen the Trump *blitzkrieg*, but as we enter a period so reactionary that it threatens to turn back the clock on every front of social progress and concern, France's recounting of this history can feel as brave and trenchant as the activist responses he chronicles. As the fascist takeover of our country progresses, that same sense of courage under fire will likely attend his forthcoming documentary on legendary transgender figures Sylvia Rivera and Marcia P. Johnson.

At the end of *Plague*, France compares the suicide of leading AIDS activist Spencer Cox in the post-treatment period with that of Holocaust survivor Primo Levi. Though the camps had been liberated, Levi was still their prisoner psychologically. "Spencer Cox had never left the camps," France concludes." Maybe none of us did." In the wake of the Trump ascendancy, that analogy takes on a chilling reverberation.

Though still too few and far between, there have been numerous works—books, plays, films—about AIDS. In addition to Tony Kushner's beloved *Angels in America*, with its historical figure of Trump's mentor, Roy Cohn, the most publicized and widely known of these have been docu-dramatizations of AIDS in the gay community: Randy Shilts's *And The Band Played On*, Larry Kramer's *The Normal Heart*, and now France's *How To Survive a Plague*, each of which can seem composed to anticipate its future on film. (Though France's documentary film, *How To Survive a Plague*, preceded the book, the book's expanded history of AIDS would seem to invite a new film treatment, a television special or series, which in fact is currently being planned for the *National Geographic* network.)

While *Plague* extends beyond the other works to cover the period of treatment breakthroughs and a detailed history of ACT UP, what we still don't have is a more comprehensive AIDS history, reference and resource work that gives dispassionate measure to the full range of players and developments, globally as well as here in the US. For all its genuine achievement, *Plague* barely touches on other worlds greatly impacted by AIDS—addicts, people of color, women, hemophiliacs, Haitians, and AIDS in Africa, Asia and elsewhere. Of course, such is the scope of one of greatest epidemics in recorded history that compiling a truly comprehensive reference work would be unimaginably daunting. But as I'm sure France would agree, and we with him after reading *Plague*, no challenge is impossible.

Nor does *Plague* acknowledge much of the work of other AIDS chroniclers. Beyond its fleshing out of the real Gaetan Dugas, *Band*'s notorious "Patient Zero," so sensationally and unjustly stigmatized (and the entire gay community with him), even Shilts is relegated to just a few mentions. Though impressively annotated, *Plague* is less in league with more academic histories than with the works of Shilts and Kramer, and more recent examples of this more literary genre of almost-history—e.g., Roland Emmerich's *Stonewall* and Dustin Lance Black's television docuseries *When We Rise*.

Neither journalists nor writers in general nor even historians are required to make comprehensiveness and inclusivity their top priorities. Nor are they required to forgo embellishment or dramatization, however questionable such practices can seem. This has never been more true than today, with its penchant for docudramas and its extremes of fake news. Writers easily claim license to edit details in the interest of bigger truth, to composite, to be personal, selective and imaginative in telling stories. So long as the public does not have greater expectations or demands, works of proximate history will be accepted as indubitable history.

This is the case with France's *Plague*, just as it was the case with the comparably annotated *And The Band Played On* and the unannotated, more overtly semi-fictional *The Normal Heart*. There have been close to 200 books on polio and doubtless as many or more on syphilis and cancer. None is definitive. None is comprehensive. None could ever tell the whole story of phenomena that history keeps revising. Just as the 2006 PBS Frontline documentary *The Age of AIDS* focuses on AIDS in Africa and its catastrophic 330,000 preventable deaths from AIDS denialism, while scarcely acknowledging the unfolding of the epidemic in the US or in the gay community, each chronicle of AIDS will have its own timeliness, gaps and slants.

As it did in *The Normal Heart*, docu-dramatization proves an effective medium for showcasing some of *Plague*'s key perspectives, like that on Larry Kramer. Just as we are witness to Donald Trump endlessly repeating temperament-driven confrontations with virtually everybody on every front, *Plague* teases out how Kramer found himself in the same personality-centered conflicts with ACT UP that led to his ruptures with GMHC. Alongside the consensus affirmation of Kramer as the premiere galvanizer of AIDS activism, it's a sentinel insight. France is also incisive in gleaning that I was the only one of GMHC's co-founders to attend the world premiere of *The Normal Heart* and in appreciating the extent to which I was simultaneously critical *and* affirming of Kramer.

A comparably successful melding of perspectives around other figures proves more elusive. In sync with France's narrative theme of valorizing those who thought and acted outside the box, in contrast to more mainstream medical activists like myself, the case *Plague* makes for *New York Native* editor Charles Ortleb, community physician Dr. Joseph Sonnabend and his patients, activists Richard Berkowitz and Michael Callen, like its sketches of many of the heros of ACT UP, is often moving and winning.

Just as Ortleb, whose seriousness and intelligence could be inspiring, made sounding the alarm on the epidemic his top priority, Sonnabend, Berkowitz and Callen were pioneers who contributed early and notably to community awareness, especially around condom use and safer sex, as well as advocating for research and care, and criticizing the unconscionable bureaucratic delays in making treatments available that were already known to work for opportunistic infections—e.g., aerosol pentamidine for PCP. As with Kramer and Shilts, no theme is more crucial to *Plague*'s narrative than the endless failures of moral compass, the unwillingness of citizens, health care providers and scientists at all levels to care enough to do what could be done with already available resources.

Figure 134 - Joy Tomchin (left) and David France at the 73rd annual Peabody Awards, 2014, Creative Commons

What's missing, however, is a more credible measure of how controversial Ortleb, Sonnabend, Callen and Berkowitz also were as exponents of what later became known as AIDS denialism, a phenomenon that goes unmentioned as such in France's book. So smoothly is the scale and seriousness of this secondary epidemic of theoretical intransigence—of disparaging the idea that a single "killer virus" could be the primary agent in HIV/AIDS—evaded in *Plague* that you wouldn't necessarily take note of it, at least not initially.

The impression *Plague* conveys is that whatever controversies these figures may have stirred were not so unreasonable, given the circumstances. If they sometimes placed too much emphasis on their multi-factorialist viewpoint of the causes and dynamics of the epidemic, they were nonetheless brave and laudable for trying to think and act outside the box. Fair enough. But there's no connecting of the dots in *Plague* that Sonnabend's multi-factorialsm became the springboard of a fanaticism that later grew malignantly among adherents, including Ortleb and denialism guru Dr. Peter Duesberg (unmentioned in *Plague*), whom Ortleb introduced to the public in the *Native* and who claimed inspiration from Sonnabend.1

In its initial semblance of challenging medical and scientific orthodoxies and stasis, this characteristically overbearing resistance to the probability that AIDS was being caused by a primary agent, most likely a virus, seemed more annonying than disturbing. But instead of receding as epidemiological certainty grew and as HIV came be identified as primary in AIDS, adherents of denialism not only grew in number but in cultish theoretical entrenchment.

Then, in the early 2000's, came the biggest single catastrophe of preventable deaths in the history of AIDS. A third of a million South Africans died unnecessarily because AIDS denialism had advanced to the highest levels of government and life-saving treatments were made unavailable. If what Kramer was observing in the mass carnage of unnecessary deaths from AIDS here in America could be, as he called it, "genocide by neglect," what happened in South Africa could be called "genocide by sloth." (See "HIV Denialism and African Genocide" by Lawrence D. Mass, M.D., *Gay and Lesbian Review*, Volume 18, issue 3, Thirty Years of HIV, Part II.)

Even as he acknowledges Ortleb's paranoid breakdown and the consequent demise of the *Native*, France stops short of adequately conveying this bigger picture of denialism, of why these figures became so controversial and alienated so many in medical and scientific circles.

In the late 1990's Sonnabend finally acknowledged on his blog that HIV is the primary agent in AIDS and explicitly distanced himself from the cult of AIDS denialism. And in *Sex Positive*, the 2008 documentary film about him, Richard Berkowitz acknowledged that he'd received life-saving treatment for HIV. To my knowledge, Ortleb never admitted error and I'm not sure where this issue rested with Michael Callen at the time of his death in '93. *Plague* doesn't say. In fact, none of this is in *Plague*, towards the end of which France tacitly exonerates Sonnabend's multi-factorialism as still applicable, giving the example of Kaposi's Sarcoma (KS).

It was clear from the earliest period of the epidemic that the underlying condition of all persons with the new syndrome of immune deficiency—which appropriately became known as acquired immune deficiency syndrome (AIDS)—was immune deficiency, probably viral in origin, and setting the stage for a host of secondary opportunistic infections and other diseases, including KS. That other factors or cofactors—multiple factors—were involved in the great spread of AIDS diseases and differing manifestations in individuals was always a given. The problem was never multi-factorialism *per se*. The problem was the irrational hostility among multi-factorialists towards the early and ever-growing probability that a single virus could be the primary agent and principal cause of the underlying condition of immune deficiency in AIDS.

Sonnabend, Callen, Berkowtiz and Ortleb cannot be blamed for what happened in South Africa. Nor should their achievements not be appreciated. Nor should France be faulted for not giving a detailed history of AIDS denialism or AIDS in Africa or other locales in a book that is largely about the now legendary activist travails and triumphs of ACT UP. And obviously France, who painstakingly details the scientific understanding of HIV and who did write one piece about leading denialist Christine Maggiore, does not himself endorse denialism. But to relegate this controversy to nonexistence in a book that is also largely about the progenitors of denialism—*Plague*'s index entry on Sonnabend is the largest on any individual, with Berkowitz and Callen close seconds—does raise questions. And in a book whose theme of preventable deaths from AIDS is recurrent and often predominant, not to mention what happened in South Africa can seem a case of truth, selective truth but not the whole truth.

Viewed in this context, *Plague*'s elimination of my own role as the first writer to cover the epidemic in the press also seems questionable. Since most of that writing was for the *Native,* where

France began his apprenticeship as an AIDS and gay community journalist during that same time frame, and since there's a lot of discussion of the *Native* in *Plague*, such selective historicizing can seem obfuscating and strained. As France recalls it, the *Native*'s coverage during that earliest period was widely acknowledged to be authoritative and to have included numerous MD's and PhD's. Apart from a letter to the editor by Dr. Sonnabend and an appeal for research funding from Dr. Alvin Friedman-Kien, however, I can't recall any other MD's or PhD's who wrote articles for the *Native* in those first two years of 1981-82.

Meanwhile, you'd never know from *Plague* that the *Native* published the first news report on AIDS. (See "Today in Gay History, May 18, 1981: Dr. Lawrence Mass Becomes the First Person to Report About AIDS," http://back2stonewall.com/2014/05/today-gay-history-18-1981-dr-lawrence-mass-person-report-aids.html)
Likewise unmentioned in *Plague* is that this report preceded by several weeks another first for the *Native*, the first feature article on the epidemic, my "Cancer in the Gay Community" (among the opening displays of the Newseum) and 23 articles subsequently by me on AIDS and gay health. Nor is there any acknowledgment of this work as the first regular coverage of gay health issues in the gay press by an MD. That France was within his rights to be selective is difficult to contest. But to eliminate even passing summary reference to these developments can seem inconsistent with *Plague*'s commitment to documenting significant moments in the early history of AIDS, the *New York Native*, and the gay community.

If France had any qualms about such choices at least he's in stellar company. Larry Kramer did something similar in his composite of me as "Mickey Marcus" in *The Normal Heart*. There I became this generic community sexual-freedom activist whose only specificity is that he ends up in the psych ward at St. Vincent's Hospital. Likewise Randy Shilts, who was the first to inform me of something I hadn't previously realized when we got together at the first international AIDS conference in Atlanta in 1985: that my May 1981 press report was indeed the first press report.

"No one will ever be able to take that away from you," Randy kept insisting, even though I hadn't questioned him. But that's exactly what he himself did in *Band.* Inevitably, perhaps, it wasn't in Shilts's interest to acknowledge that during the first two years of the epidemic, when he was bottoming out on alcohol and not covering the epidemic, another gay journalist was. That I was hesitant about indicting gay promiscuity (I often placed that unscientific, pejorative word in quotes) and irresponsibility as the cause of it all probably didn't help, neither with Shilts nor with Kramer, Sonnabend, Berkowitz, or Callen. And in my reluctance to join the Sonnabend-Berkowitz-Callen multi-factorialism juggernaut, likewise David France.

Because of this expressed discomfort, personally and in my articles, with the outsized indictment of gay promiscuity and the theoretical intransigence of the multi-factorialists, there was always a tension between David France and me. Were there other factors—some inchoate failure of gay chemistry between us or rivalries as journalists? Though we were never close, we've become friendlier in recent years, especially around my appreciation for his documentary film of *Plague*, which makes no reference to the pre-ACT UP period of AIDS or to Sonnabend, Berkowitz or Callen.

As *Plague*, suggests, France felt close not only to Sonnabend, Berkowitz and Callen, but also to journalist James D'Eramo, who came on board at the *Native* following the period of my coverage of the epidemic from '81 to '83. It's true, as France recounts, that D'Eramo had a notable moment in confronting HIV co-discoverer Robert Gallo about the applicability of Koch's postulates to the virus that would soon become known as HIV. But much of D'Eramo's subsequent writing seemed less about scientific scrupulosity and convictions than as a shill for Ortleb's obsessive coverage of African Swine Fever Virus and a slew of subsequent, evermore paranoid pseudo-scientific denialist theories of the epidemic, what leading AIDS cultural observer Douglas Crimp (unmentioned in *Plague*) called Ortleb's "crackpot theories of the week"—e.g., "Chronic Fatigue Immune Dysfunction Syndrome." Like D'Eramo, France himself often seemed a relatively passive accomplice to much of Ortleb's craziness, remaining with the *Native*, together with intrepid editor Patrick Merla, long after the rest of us had abandoned ship.

In addition to D'Eramo, France also credits Joe Nicholson as a valued mentor and colleague. In those early years, Nicholson was one of the first openly gay journalists in the mainstream press, in this case the otherwise notoriously homophobic *New York Post.* Mentored by Nicholson, France got his first mainstream-press assignments with the *Post* during the period when the Gay and Lesbian Alliance Against

Defamation (GLAAD) held its first demonstration in 1985—against the *New York Post*. As France himself recalls in *Plague*, he was at that demonstration not as a protester, but as a *Post* reporter.

Whatever the misgivings, I will continue to praise and recommend *Plague*, as I will *Band* and *The Normal Heart*, for the singular, precious resources they currently and nonetheless are. At present, Sarah Schulman's ACT UP Oral History Project and the wonderful film she produced with Jim Hubbard on the history of ACT UP, *United in Anger*, and France's *Plague* documentary and book are the only chronicles of the epidemic that cover the history of ACT UP, whose Nobel-Prize level of achievement is a supreme endowment to posterity. Surpassing respect and gratitude are most certainly in order.

At this moment of pervasive anxiety and dread among minorities and the disenfranchised, the marginal and the meek, as well as throughout medical and scientific communities, *Plague* shows how the courage and resourcefulness of individuals can triumph over seemingly insurmountable personal, political, social, medical and scientific odds. As new Goliaths loom, *Plague* inspires us, like no other book out there now, to get out our slingshots. A true and heart-stopping story of survival, *Plague* shows how thinking and acting outside the box, whatever the mistakes, whatever the costs, can lead to the conquest of seemingly implacable foes and the realization of seemingly impossible dreams.

"Never Again" is a response to the Holocaust that Primo Levi's recounting of Nazi brutality and atrocities helped inspire. As France suggests, it can also serve as a metaphor for the gay community's experience of AIDS. But if history is not to be repeated, the mistakes and costs of AIDS denialism, together with the many other consequences of neglect, indifference, prejudice, intransigence and fanaticism that pervade the history of AIDS, must not be forgotten. Those who do not remember the past are condemned to repeat it, we say. What time has shown us, however, is that even when those lessons are remembered, the past will be repeated, so long as the perpetrators aren't held accountable.

# ‘Get That Monster Out of The White House!’ Larry Kramer Electrifies Gatherings in New York and Florida

***Larry Kramer himself is now upping the ante***

– *Huffington Post*, 4/3/2017

Figure 135 - David France (left) and Larry Kramer (right) at GMHC’s 35th Anniversary Gala, gmhc.org

Much has been written about the early breakup of Larry Kramer and GMHC, most notably by Kramer himself in his celebrated play and film, *The Normal Heart*, but also by me in my Larry Kramer anthology, *We Must Love One Another or Die*, and more recently by David France in his history of AIDS, *How To Survive A Plague*. The crux of the play is that the greater activism Kramer was pushing for was rejected by GMHC’s other co-founders in favor of thinking and acting inside the box. The apposing view is that Kramer wanted GMHC to become a lot more like the organization he then went on to found, ACT UP, a transformation that felt too drastic for the fledgling information, education and service organization that GMHC was in those early pre-gay-civil-rights years. *Should* GMHC have become more like ACT UP?

While the answer to that has seemed to be that we were all better off for having both organizations, Larry Kramer himself is now upping the ante. Two years ago, working with current GMHC CEO Kelsey Louie, Kramer re-emerged as a major presence at GMHC, after years of estrangement and disparagement of the organization in the wake of his earlier ouster-resignation. That night, May 24, 2015, to an enthusiastic and prolonged ovation, Kramer became the first recipient of the new Larry Kramer Activism Award. Although frail and with limited vocal strength, Kramer not only accepted the award with a rousing speech, but stayed for the full 5 hour length of the event.

The evening crackled with new energies, likewise on display the following year when Mary Fisher received the Larry Kramer Activism Award for her brave speech at the 1992 Republican National Convention, where she came out as a person with AIDS and exhorted the Republican leadership to begin dealing with AIDS more forthrightly, robustly and humanely.

This year, as GMHC marked its 35th anniversary, these energies were even more palpable. Kramer was a tough critic of GMHC's move to its current location, just north of the High Line, when the area was an even worse nightmare of construction obstacles, and much harder to get to and navigate. But all that seemed to fade in the excitement of being in the epicenter of what is now indisputably Manhattan's hottest neighborhood. The High Line is an explosion of cultural and real estate development that seems to boast every big name in art, design, fashion, architecture, culture and real estate, except one: Donald Trump.

Louie began the proceedings by affirming GMHC's proud history as a leading provider of supportive services, which are now expanding to include substance abuse treatment, mental health resources and housing. Paying tribute to Larry Kramer, he then noted that in the current governmental and humanitarian crisis looming under the Trump presidency, which has proposed massive cuts in AIDS funding, GMHC will need to become much more activist. At this juncture of the Trump onslaught, no one could disagree with him.

Larry Kramer is legendary for not mincing words. He never did. He still doesn't. At 82, and with some physical and vocal weakness, he is still exactly the same passionate, galvanizing firebrand he always was. Since that GMHC 33rd anniversary gala, there have been several notable appearances by Kramer, including a recent historic visit to South Florida as well as the 35th Anniversary Gala. In both situations, sell-out crowds hung on every word. On both occasions, the atmosphere was electric. What everybody was responding to so strongly was not only Larry Kramer, the great gay and AIDS activist hero, but Kramer in his role as visionary and leader as we once again face a terrifying, potentially overwhelming life-and-death crisis—i.e., the Trump presidency.

Alas, though a part-time South Floridian myself, I was not at the Fort Lauderdale-Wilton Manors events, but I heard about them from multiple sources. The stretch of coast between Palm Beach and Miami Beach is called South Florida and boasts one of the largest gay communities in the world. Halfway between Trump's Palm Beach compound Mar-A-Lago and the South Beach stretch of Miami Beach is Sunny Isles Beach, where more properties boast the Trump logo than any other trademark. Many of the residences here, mostly condos, have been bought up by wealthy Russian investors; hence the eponym for that area, "Little Moscow." Apart from bigger questions of the relationships between Russia and Team Trump, aren't these buyers worried about the beachfront erosion from global warming that is already causing frequent and ever-worsening flooding? I don't think you're any more likely to find that detail in Trump property brochures than you are likely to find Trump promoting initiatives for climate control. AA

During his recent visit to Florida, and on the eve of ACT UP's 30th anniversary, Kramer paid tribute to the landmark World AIDS Museum and Education Center that was established in Wilton Manors in 2011. In the course of several events, he signed copies of Volume 1 of his magnum opus, *The American People,* was interviewed by *Vanity Fair'*s Kevin Sessums, author of *Mississippi Sissy,* and showcased by the Gay Men's Chorus. Holding up ACT UP's new t-shirt that reads: **"I Can't Believe I Still Have to Protest This Fucking Shit**", he reminded us that **"We have to be seen and shove it in their fucking faces!"**

Not surprisingly, activism was the GMHC 35th anniversary Gala's keynote and theme. After Louie presented the first award to corporate and financial leader, Barclay's CEO Jes Staley, his brother Peter Staley was given this year's Larry Kramer Activism award, presented both by Kramer and David France, whose book on the history of AIDS I've recently commented on (http://www.huffingtonpost.com/entry/58c92b90e4b0009b23bd948e ). Staley is the celebrated ACT UP activist showcased by France, first in his 2012 documentary film, *How To Survive a Plague*, and now in the book with that same title. Notwithstanding some bruising observations about Kramer's role in ACT UP reprising personality-centered confrontations with GMHC, France's great respect for Kramer's surpassing role as the august figure of AIDS activism was palpable, just as I trust my own is, even after comparing (in my commentary on *Plague*) Kramer's penchant for confrontation with that of Donald Trump!

Staley's self-taught knowledge of pharma, business acumen, gay pride and street activist savvy—inspired by and occasionally in some conflict with the strategies of his acknowledged "activist father" Kramer—has resulted in the saved lives of countless millions. As France noted, the superlatives may have been exhausted, but the wonder and gratitude just keep growing. Staley graciously accepted the award, but with characteristic generosity, insisting it be on behalf of all those in ACT UP and activism, and with special appreciation for younger activists.

President Bill Clinton was to have received an award for his tireless, not forgotten efforts on behalf of AIDS globally. On short notice, he left to attend the funeral of Sinn Fein leader Martin McGuinniss with whom he'd worked closely to broker peace in Northern Ireland. In his place, daughter Chelsea Clinton spoke from the heart (no notes) about her family's commitment to the LGBT and AIDS communities. Honestly confronting her father's early, much-resented endorsement of DOMA (the anti-gay Defense of Marriage Act), she noted how he subsequently committed himself not only to acknowledging what a mistake that was (in an Op Ed piece he wrote for the *Washington Post*), but committing himself to a wide range of initiatives in support of LGBT rights, the gay community, and AIDS globally. I'd no idea she was such a confident and effective public speaker.

Concluding the evening was the Larry Kramer of legend—of hope and courage in the face of crisis. He had written an open letter to President Bill Clinton that he had planned to read before the gathering, which was to have included Clinton. Kramer called on Clinton and former Presidents Carter and Obama to join any other past presidents willing to take a much stronger public stand in new efforts to **"GET THAT MONSTER OUT OF THE WHITE HOUSE!"** This was vintage Kramer, asking more than what might seem reasonable from people who are otherwise friends and allies in circumstances that might seem questionable. Putting people on the spot. Making demands. Denouncing enemies in the strongest terms. Demanding activism from all of us, **NOW!**

As the evening's special guest star Billy Porter, fresh from his triumph in *Kinky Boots* and on the eve of a new blues album, put it, "We're galvanized again!"

# Remembering William M. Hoffman

– *Huffington Post*, 5/3/2017

Figure 136 - William M. Hoffman (April 12, 1939 - April 29, 2017) with composer Ricky Ian Gordon (left) at the premiere of their opera, *Morning Star*, Hoffman's last major theatrical work. Morning Star had its world premiere at the Cincinnati Opera 6/30/2015, City

William Moses Hoffman was an important and beloved figure in at least 3 communities: artistic, gay and Jewish. In each, he left an indelible mark.

Hoffman was a luminary of Greenwich Village's Caffe Cino. The legendary "birthplace of off-off Broadway," as it has been called, launched the careers of a host of playwrights, including Sam Shepard, Lanford Wilson, Joe Orton and Robert Patrick. Culling this experience, Hoffman edited a pioneering anthology, *Gay Plays: The First Collection.*

As a playwright, Hoffman is best known as the author of *As Is*. In 1985 it became the first Broadway play about AIDS, following Robert Chesley's off-off Broadway *Stray Dog Story* and preceding the premiere of Larry Kramer's *The Normal Heart*. *As Is* was a hit and is widely credited with an early and humanizing influence on public awareness of AIDS and its impact on our lives and times.

Following its run on Broadway, *As Is* became a film starring Colleen Dewhurst as the AIDS hospice worker. My eyes still swell with tears when I recall the *coup de theatre* that concludes the play. Despite harsh condemnation of homosexuality by the church, here was a nun whose compassion for humanity leads her to share the most deeply personal ritual of her charge, a gay man dying of AIDS. Reflecting on their last exchange, she lifts up her hands to reveal her nails, polished red. It was one of those moments that would mark Hoffman as a master of theater, and our hearts.

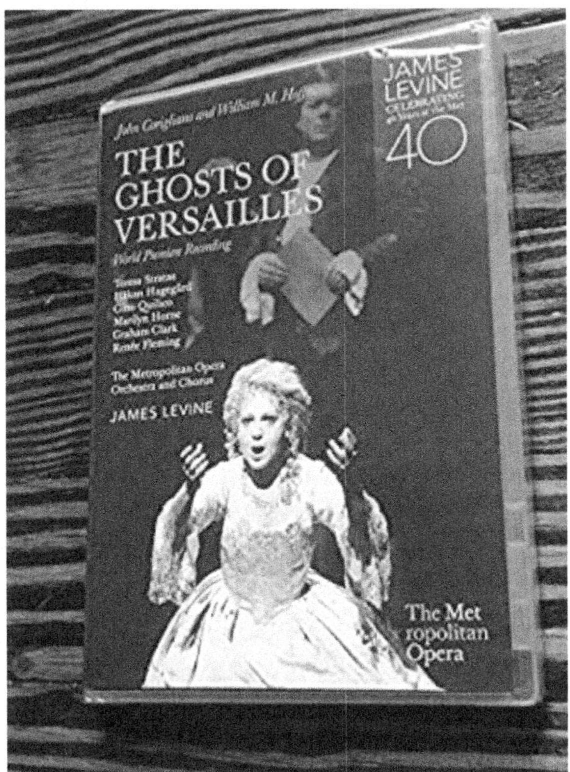


Figure 137 - *The Ghosts of Versailles*, World Premiere Recording, amazon.com

Perhaps the pinnacle of Hoffman's achievement was *The Ghosts of Versailles*, the opera he co-created with his lifelong friend and collaborator, composer John Corigliano. One of the most prestigious events in American operatic history, this very grand opera was a world premiere commission by the Metropolitan Opera to mark the 100th anniversary of the company.

At the start of what became a stellar career, Renee Fleming, who is currently retiring from opera, played the co-starring role of Countess Almaviva. The opera recaps, comments on, and develops the stories of some of opera's most famous and beloved characters—that jack of all arts and trades (and hearts) Figaro and those paragons (and parodies) of nobility, the Almavivas. They are the protagonists of two of the most famous and beloved operas, Mozart's *The Marriage of Figaro* and Rossini's *The Barber of Seville*.

*Ghosts* is also the story of their creator, Beaumarchais, and the fabled Marie Antoinette, with the ghost of whom the ghost of Beaumarchais is in love. The at once historical and magical tale is deftly constructed around Beaumarchais's lesser-known sequel to these plays, *La Mere Coupable*. "*The Guilty Mother*" takes place in the throes of the French Revolution, which the earlier plays are on the cusp of. So long as there will be opera, it's a certainty that *Ghosts of Versailles* will find an enduring place for itself alongside *Barber of Seville* and *Marriage of Figaro*. A *Figaro* cycle, like the *Ring* cycle, is an ideal trilogy project for future directors and opera companies.

For a life of contributions as rich and varied as Hoffman's, this summary will perforce omit much. But mention should be made here of the work Bill did on restoring the reputation and place of the librettist. To this end, he founded a Society, Prima La Parola e Poi La Music (First The Word and Then The Music). Hoffman felt that just as Da Ponte is recognized and celebrated as the co-creator of Mozart's operas and von Hofmannsthal of Strauss's operas, so should his own contribution be fully recognized, a co-equality likewise championed by composer Corigliano. It was an uphill battle Bill that would rarely win in traditional operatic venues.

Bill went on to write and revise other plays, many of them with gay themes, one of which, *Cornbury: The Queen's Governor*, was about Edward Hyde, the mythic first governor of New York who was known to have cross-dressed. Panoramically, Bill recreates the early New York of the Dutch, Queen Anne and Indian wars. The political insights are as copious as the humor. At various points, he hoped to make the play into a musical, which tweaked the interest of Hal Prince.

There were many other projects, greater and lesser, that Bill worked on. The biggest and most recent of these was *Morning Star*, a musical-dramatic co-creation with Ricky Ian Gordon about the infamous Triangle Factory fire in New York in 1911, in which so many garment workers, most of them young Jewish and Italian immigrant women, perished. The story revolves around a Latvian Jewish family. *Morning Star* was a co-production of the Chicago Lyric Opera and the Goodman Theater which had its world premiere in Cincinnati in 2015.

In the interstices of this work is another issue that hugely preoccupied Bill and which colors everything he wrote: his Jewishness. In the many revisions and stagings of his play, *Riga* (his parents were Latvian Jews who escaped the Holocaust but most of their relatives were murdered by the occupying Nazis), he agonized about anti-Semitism, past, present and future. Sharing these concerns, and in this time frame of the mid to late 1980s, I wrote and published my own story of coming to grips with anti-Semitism—historical, social and internalized. This memoir, *Confessions of a Jewish Wagnerite,* inspired Bill's growing interest in Wagner and became the basis of many years of fevered dialogue between us.

An offspring of all this was a proposal for an opera with John Corigliano for the San Francisco Opera, a dark satirical work to be called *Liebestod.* Gottfried Wagner, great grandson of the composer who had written an introduction to my *Confessions* and who I had introduced to Bill and John, was to be the dramaturge. Alas, Pamela Rosenberg, who headed the SFO at that time (early 2000's), subsequently announced that the commission of a new opera by SFO would be awarded to the team of John Adams, Alice Goodman and Peter Sellars, The opera was *Dr. Atomic.*

In the midst of his work on these plays, Bill established a salon of artists and writers concerned about anti-Semitism. Regular attendees included soprano Regina Resnik, writer Phyllis Chesler, my partner Arnie Kantrowitz and me. Alas, Bill's prophetic concerns could find him venturing farther to the right politically than some of us were comfortable with. In this frame of mind, his prototype for Lord Cornbury would be more like Rudolph Giuliani or Caitlyn Jenner than Harvey Fierstein or Divine. Even so, whenever Bill and I spoke during his last year, he seemed in clear agreement that Trump was a dangerous demagogue and authoritarian who could no more to be trusted with the fate of Jews and Israel than with any other politics, issues or peoples.

In his later years, Bill relocated to Beacon, New York, not far from Lehman College, where he directed and taught theater and did a television series of conversations with leading arts figures. There he staged original plays he wrote for the students, like *The Stench of Art,* as well as lesser known works by others—e.g., *The Blue Monster: A fairy Play in 5 Acts* by Carlo Gozzi, the satirist whose *Turandot* inspired Puccini's opera. His students loved him. There, in Beacon and at Lehman, he lived and worked with his husband, Russ Taylor. My last visit with them was in January. Bill had been suffering from increasingly serious and frequent illnesses, many of them stemming from severe arthritis and the side-effects of medications.

In my own life, his influence and role as my close friend for more than a quarter century has been inestimable.

Because so much of what he had to show and tell us foretold of the future as it recreated the past, it's certain that the story of William M. "Hoffperson," as he sometimes referred to himself, awaits a sequel, a *Ghosts* of the life and times of William M. Hoffman.

Rest in peace, Person of hope. And may your ghost haunt us forever.

*adapted from an Obituary written for *Gay City News*

# Immigrant Voices of Hope and Resilience, and Our Relentless History of Vilification of the Other, from Wagner to Trump

– *Huffington Post*, 10/11/2017

**"Art, if it is to be reckoned with as one of the great values of life, must teach...tolerance." —Somerset Maugham**

Figure 138 - Steven Lebetkin, composer, with Amy Andersson, conductor and founder of Orchestra Moderne NYC

Ever precious and however threatened in the current political climate, freedom and tolerance were in the air for the Carnegie Hall debut of Orchestra Moderne NYC, a youthful, culturally diverse and enterprising group that aims, according to music director and conductor Amy Andersson, to "connect audiences with culturally relevant and meaningful music...to create musical experiences that celebrate humanity and connect to important social issues."

The program opened with a rousing Overture by Lolita Ritmanis and featured the world premiere of a skillful and soulful *Violin Concerto* by Steven Lebetkin, impressively played by Momo Wong. The second half opened with Copland's ever powerful *Fanfare for the Common Man*, and concluded with Peter Boyer's celebratory *Ellis Island: the Dream of America.* Individually and cumulatively, these pieces evoked the hopes, dreams and courage of American immigration experience.

Figure 139 - The Journey To America: From Repression to Freedom, Concert Program

The parents of Lolita Ritmanis emigrated to America in 1944 from war-torn Latvia. Because of the Soviet occupation that followed the war, they never fulfilled their dream of returning home, but their daughter did. Her Overture to Light was inspired by a building designed by a classmate of her father who became a renowned architect. The National Library of Latvia is also known as the "Castle of Light." It opened in 2014 and is considered a symbol of freedom. Ritmanis has worked extensively in television and film, garnering 10 Emmy award nominations and winning in 2002 for *Batman Beyond.*

Figure 140 - Lolita Ritmanis, composer, lolitaritmanis.com

Steven Lebetkin is descended from a line of Jewish musicians and composers who immigrated to America during the Third Reich, including Karol Rathaus, who was a student of Franz Schreker. Indeed, in Lebetkin's shimmering *Jugendstil* textures, you can hear the distant sounds of the Austrian-Jewish composer's opera, *Die Ferne Klang* (*The Distant Sound*). Rathaus was a Jewish composer from Poland who was a pioneer in film scoring in advance of Erich Korngold. Rathaus emigrated to New York in 1938 and founded the Queens College Music Department in 1939. "I am here today as a descendant of this tradition," affirms Lebetkin, "and to carry the torch of great musical composition technique that survived the repression of Nazi Germany to the freedom of America that still rings true today."

Figure 141 - Momo Wong, violin soloist

Finally and climactically, there was Boyer's *Ellis Island: The Dream of America.* This immensely successful work (170 live performances by 75 orchestras) had its premiere in 2002 and is slated to be shown on PBS in 2018. The work showcases 7 voices from the Ellis Island Oral History Project. In their own words, immigrants from Poland, Ireland, Hungary, Greece, Italy, Russia and Belgium, a number of them war refugees, one of them Jewish, tell us heartbreaking and inspiring stories of their ordeals, strength and hope. Each of the actors—Stacey Lightman, Myles Phillips, Rori Nogee, Daniel Kreizberg, Annie Meisel, Austin Ku, Carol Beaugard, and Karen Johal—brought presence, passion and pathos to their lines.

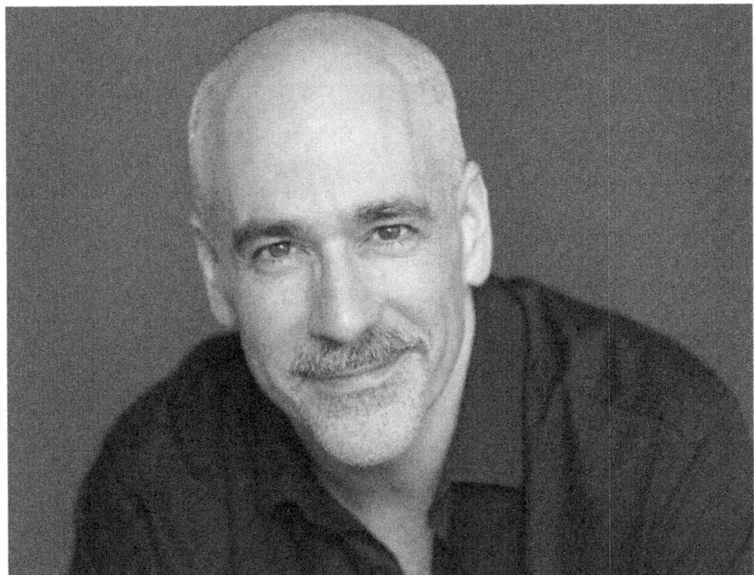

Figure 142 - Peter Boyer, composer of *Ellis Island: The Dream of America*, Wikipedia

The eclectic piece was accompanied by slides of Ellis Island scenes, mostly old black and white photos; all of which lead up to the inevitable concluding scrim, in full color, of Lady Liberty as one of the immigrants reads the immortal words by Emma Lazarus that are inscribed on the statue:

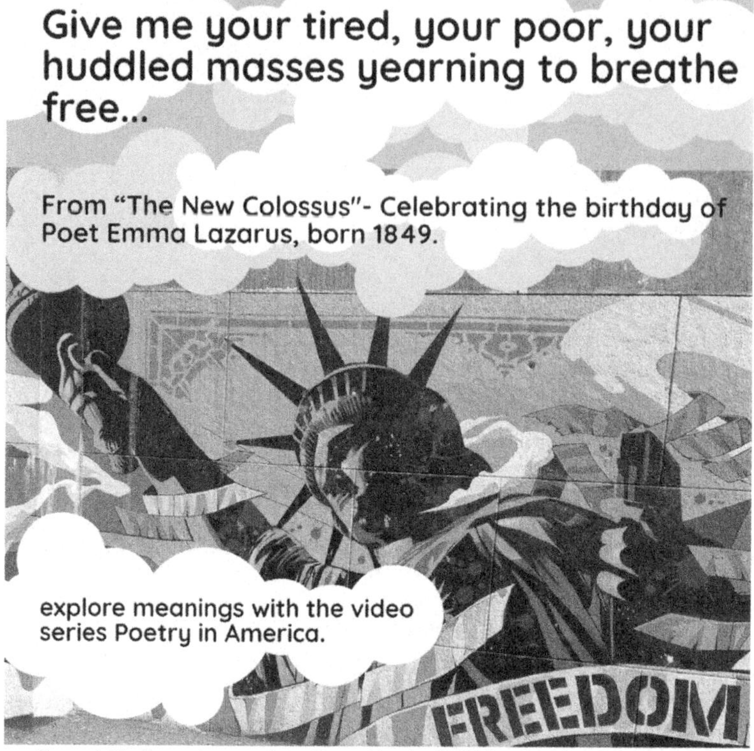

Give me your tired, your poor, your huddled masses yearning to breathe free...
From "The New Colossus"- Celebrating the birthday of Poet Emma Lazarus, born 1849.
explore meanings with the video series Poetry in America.
FREEDOM


Figure 143 - Emma Lazarus Avon Promotion by EWULibraries, Creative Commons

Still so moving. Because of the "interesting times" we live in, however, the evening also evoked the darker history of immigration in America. When was the last time you were at Ellis Island? It's worth a revisit now, for all the heartwarming history of hopeful humanity, of course, but also to view its museum showcasing of all the different peoples that were vilified as they immigrated in numbers to America. There is not an ethnic or religious group you can think of that escapes this breathtakingly long and comprehensive list: Irish, Italians, Germans, Scandinavians, Africans, Chinese, Japanese, Vietnamese, Muslims, Blacks, Catholics, Protestants, Jews, Hindus, and on. The only notable omission I could find was of gay people, who until very recently were regarded as "psychopathic personalities" and refused entry or subject to deportation as such. For the common man of immigration experience, vilification of the other has been their constant nemesis, their fraternity-hazing initiation into America. "Land of the free and home of the brave," yes, but also of the ignorant and bigoted; the land that also enslaved, restricted, segregated and bullied at every turn; a history that is repeating itself, more boldly, ignorantly and shamelessly, yet again today.

This history of vilification of the other is by no means limited to immigrants to America. It's everywhere else and transhistorical. One need only look at the histories of World War 1 and 2 and the present-day refugee crises in Europe, throughout the Middle East and everywhere else to appreciate the scope of this challenge to what should be universal values of humanitarianism.

All of which reverberated for me in Carnegie Hall, one of whose most featured composers has been Richard Wagner, musical history's greatest vilifier of the other. When it comes to prejudice, you have to search far and wide to find a more repellant voice of mean-spirited ignorance, bigotry and prejudice than Wagner. If you haven't ever done so, consider coupling that trek to the Ellis Island Museum with a reading of Wagner's infamous essay, "Judaism in Music." *

Here are two excerpts:

> *"Our eagerness to level up the rights of Jews was stimulated by a general idea rather than by any real sympathy...for we always felt instinctively repelled by any actual, operative contact with them."*

> *"The Jew speaks the language of the nation in whose midst he dwells from generation to generation, but always as an alien."*

Compare that with Donald Trump on Mexicans:

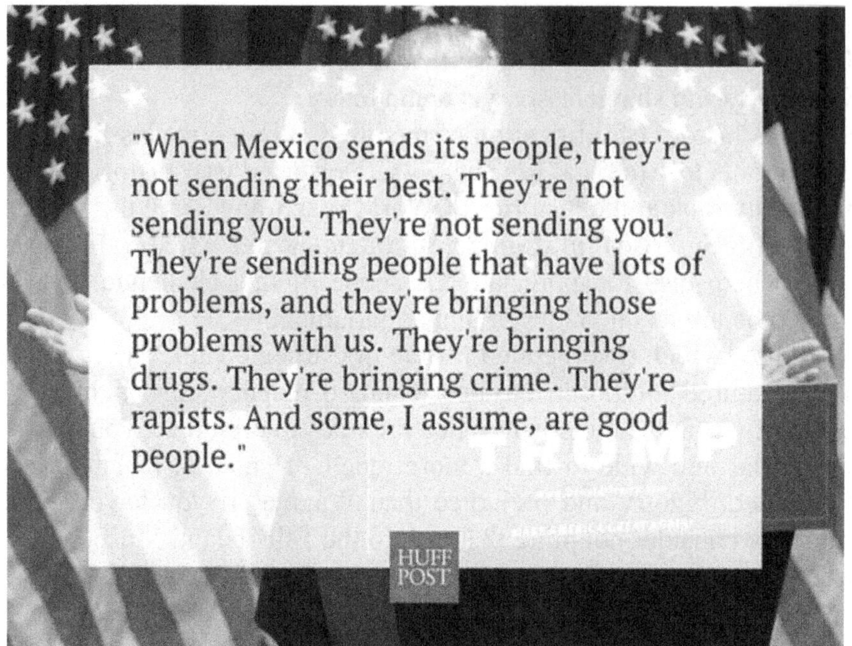

"When Mexico sends its people, they're not sending their best. They're not sending you. They're not sending you. They're sending people that have lots of problems, and they're bringing those problems with us. They're bringing drugs. They're bringing crime. They're rapists. And some, I assume, are good people."
TRUMP
HUFF POST


Figure 144 - Donald Trump on Mexicans, Huffington Post

As for the big takeaway from Wagner's opera *Die Meistersinger von Nurnberg*, in which vilification of the other is central to both plot and meaning (as it is likewise in other of Wagner's works), turns out it's the same as Trump's: Make our country great again!

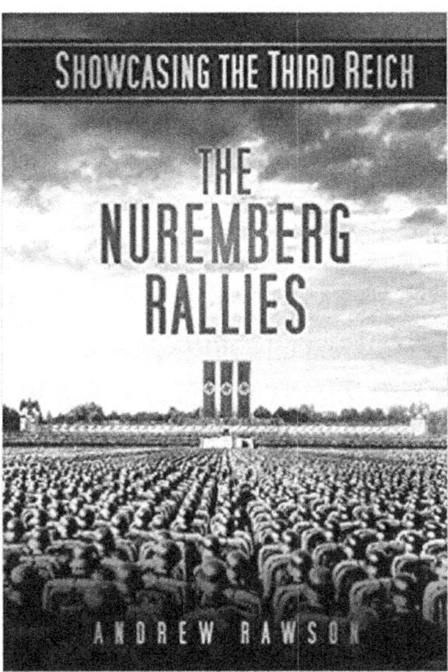


Figure 145 - book cover, amazon.com

The following admonition to the German Volk concludes Wagner's *Die Meistersinger von Nurnberg:*

> *Hans Sachs:*
> *Awaken! ...Beware! Evil tricks threaten us. if the German people and kingdom should one day decay, and foreign mists with foreign vanities they would plant in our German land, what is German and true none would know. Therefore I say to you: Honor your German Masters. Even if the Holy Roman Empire should dissolve in mist, for us there would yet remain Holy German Art!*

In an essay entitled "The Strangers in Their Midst" in a recent issue of the *New York Times Book Review*, two new books on current immigration crises are discussed by writer Pankaj Mishra. The first book, *The Strange Death of Europe* by Douglas Murray, posits that in its transformation into "Eurabia," Europe is committing suicide. The second, *The Crisis of Multiculturalism in Europe* by Rita Chin, suggests a far more complex picture of immigration patterns, past and current, and an affirmation of future possibilities. "As in the late 19th century," writes Mishra, author of *Age of Anger: A History of the*

*Present*, "demagogues displace the anxieties of powerless people onto a clearly identifiable social group: immigrants or refugees. The mechanism of scapegoating—catalyzing mass disaffection and providing it with a simple culprit—has gone into overdrive in Europe and America..."

*The Journey to America: From Repression to Freedom* is not over. That is, according to Orchestra Moderne Director Amy Andersson, this very successful event was actually a first part of what is currently envisioned to be an evolving creation. Part 2, she told us, will be about immigrants who did not come here through Ellis Island. Hopefully, the authoritarian incursions on freedom that have dogged immigrants historically and that menace us currently won't gain enough power to undercut or even censor such plans, as they did in Nazi Germany.

*Of interest to this discussion is a doctoral thesis, *Richard Wagner 1813-1883: Anti-Semitism and Immigration by Anton Douglas*.

# *Jews Queers Germans*: In Capturing the Past, Master Historian Martin Duberman Foretells the Future

– *Huffington Post*, 10/26/2017

***JEWS QUEERS GERMANS, a "novel/history" by MARTIN DUBERMAN***

Figure 146 - Martin Duberman, goodreads.com

*Jews Queers Germans* is an historical novel about a number of prominent figures of *fin-de-siecle* Europe whose lives intersect from the period preceding World War 1—"The Great War"—to World War 2. These protagonists are mostly German and mostly queer. Two are Jewish. The often subtle interplay of aspects of their lives is deftly captured by Duberman, who has never been more skilled, refined or economical in conveying situations of enormous complexity, especially the buildup to The Great War—an explosion of concurrences so labyrinthine as to defy even the best efforts, as here, at explanation and sequencing. But the bigger picture of the experience and fallout of that war is powerfully rendered. There is intimacy and timelessness in the details of how the war was conducted, of the terrible destruction and loss of life that resulted, of what it meant for Europe, the globe and humanity, and of how it set the stage for World War 2.

Beyond this estimable achievement, however, is the extent to which the book captures in temperament and ambience what we're going through now and where we seem inevitably headed. The resulting atmosphere of the churning of great and dread forces of history behind the scenes of personal relationships is reminiscent of many war fictionalizations (*War and Peace, Gone With the Wind*), but especially Austrian novelist Robert Musil's celebrated three-part, unfinished novel, *The Man Without Qualities*, a nerve-wracking chronicle of the confluence of people, places and things that eventuated in The Great War.

Duberman, a well-known figure of the left and an august figure of LGBT and historical communities and literatures, has said that when he wrote this novel he had little expectation that Trump would become president. Apparently, it was never his conscious intention for the book to be as disturbingly portentous as it turns out to be. How what turned out to be World Wars 1 and 2 went from being small partisan skirmishes to much greater and more violent confrontations with much greater consequences is rendered with such nonpartisan dispassion, insight and humanity that it's impossible for readers of any political stripe not to situate ourselves within it. It's books like these that make it impossible for us to look at the past, at other societal breakdowns, and think we are somehow different, that we will somehow prevail in ways that eluded these other times and places. That we are already repeating those storied "lessons of the past" we supposedly learned is inescapable. Even more than its treasures of LGBT, Jewish and European histories, it's this tacit sense of the inexorability of the worst of history repeating itself now that makes this novelization so compelling.

Figure 147 - Kaiser Wilhelm II, "the Donald Trump Kaiser," the last German emperor and King of Prussia, Wikipedia

*Jews Queers Germans* opens with introductions to its protagonists and a dazzling array of their contemporary luminaries in the arts and sciences—Maillol, von Hofmannsthal, Stefan Zweig, Richard Strauss, Max Reinhardt, Nijinsky, Diaghilev, Stravinsky, Bonnard, Rodin, Rilke, Einstein, Shaw, Chamberlain, Cosima and Siegfried Wagner, Colette, Rouart, Foerster-Nietzsche. Most of these figures are just mentioned, but with freshness and in the context of their social connections. You learn new things about each. Duberman may not be an opera person but if he were to see the Met's current production of *Der Rosenkavalier*, updated to the time of its premiere on eve of World War 1, he'd probably understand and appreciate the opera more than many who think of themselves as aficionados.

Past its many and precious cameos, the drama of *Jews Queers Germans* unfolds through the private lives and interactions of its leading players—Kaiser Wilhelm II, Count Philipp von Eulenburg, Walther Rathenau, Harry Kessler, Magnus Hirschfeld and Ernst Röhm.

Figure 148 - Count Philipp von Eulenburg, close friend and confidant of the Kaiser, Wikipedia

Count Philipp von Eulenburg was the closest friend and confidant of Kaiser Wilhelm II. As portrayed by Duberman, Wilhelm is a vulgar, self-important anti-Semite who became the principal pot-stirrer of the caldron of conflicts that became World War 1. Eulenburg had become less and less circumspect about being gay in a time and place where homosexuality had begun to be debated publicly but was still illegal and a source, as in Wilde's England, of extreme public opprobrium. When the taint of queerness threatens to smear the emperor and other leading figures, Eulenburg is summarily dropped and denounced by the Kaiser. The trial becomes a multi-phasic, protracted public scandal that tells us as much about calumny and "justice" today as then. The trial is also the counterpart to the book's later and most arresting confrontation—between Hirschfeld and Nazi SA leader Ernst Röhm.

Figure 149 - Walther Rathenau, Foreign Minister during the Weimar Republic, Wikipedia

Walther Rathenau, the Jewish industrialist who becomes armaments minister (not so unlike *nouveau riche* von Faninal in the Met's updated *Der Rosenkavalier*) and a largely unwitting socialist, is someone we would recognize from the annals of the closet, someone who might have made different and better choices had he been more in touch with his real feelings of same-sex attraction. It's not surprising that he's likewise not as cognizant of the ferocity of the anti-Semitism metastasizing around him as he should be. He might be compared today to any number of Jewish or gay Trumpers who believe that their proximity to the President will ultimately protect them from the malignant anti-Semitism and homophobia that, here in Trump's America, are once again ascendant.

Harry Graf Kessler
https://en.wikipedia.org/wiki/File:Harry_Graf_Kessler,_1917.jpg


Figure 150 - Harry Graf Kessler, German diplomat, writer and art patron

Harry Kessler, who enters a long friendship-flirtship with Rathenau, is a leading cultural critic and raconteur who left extensive diaries, a gold mine for a scholar like Duberman. Kessler doesn't have a precise counterpart today. Henry Geldzahler? Though not himself Jewish, he's more self-aware as gay than Rathenau, and he can likewise be more attuned to issues of anti-Semitism. The ease with which Kessler, otherwise so humane an aesthete, becomes a practitioner of war atrocities is chilling.

Figure 151 - Bust of Magnus Hirschfeld, Schwules Museum, Berlin, Wikipedia

The novel's star portrait is that of pioneering sexologist Magnus Hirschfeld. Though his story is told throughout, the big chapter on him is the heart and soul of the book. Duberman inventories his remarkable courage and character, and his protean involvement in the social, legal and medical developments and debates of his time. It also uncovers many specifics of his court testimonies, his other accomplishments as lecturer, man of letters and scientist, and priceless details of the legendary Institute for Sexual Science he founded and shepherded, and which was destroyed by the Nazis in the most infamous book-burning bonfire of the vanities since Savonarola. Hopefully, this portrait will be the basis of a theater and/or film adaptation.

Figure 152 - Ernst Röhm, head of Hitler's SA, the Nazi militia, Wikipedia

For those who keep wondering how it is that any self-aware, self-identified LGBT person could be supportive of highly reactionary elements—from the Republican fringes to the extremes of white supremacists—it's cautionary to review the history of Nazism, especially this very readable version by Duberman. It's well-known that Ernst Röhm, Hitler's closest associate, was openly gay. Yet homonationalists today seem in denial about how resoundingly such LGBT persons in the Nazi ranks were betrayed. Much as conservative Jews today believe that Trump, Bannon and evangelicals can be relied on for acceptance and support, LGBT conservatives today believe they will likewise be valued and protected by forces whose volatility and unpredictability they have helped to bolster and which metastasizes with each street clash, each Nazi-like rally of Trump and his base.

As is well-known, Röhm was assassinated in the infamous "Night of the Long Knives." Röhm and most of his army of SA troopers were killed on orders from Hitler. Duberman goes to lengths to show how for Hitler the issue was never homosexuality per se so much as the value that Trump likewise makes no bones about placing highest—loyalty. Röhm's longstanding closeness to Hitler was such that he was the only one of Hitler's henchmen to publicly address him by his first name. Such became Röhm's status and power, however, that he posed a threat to Hitler's hegemony.

The big confrontation that is in many ways the climax of the book takes place between Hirschfeld and Röhm. How much of this is fiction isn't clear. But what happens is that Röhm seeks the counsel of Hirschfeld—whom he otherwise reviles for being Jewish—to help him with a blackmail case. Hirschfeld became widely known for giving expert testimony in court cases involving homosexuality, and Röhm, who is totally out as gay, even with Paragraph 175 (penalizing homosexuality) firmly in place, wants to find a way to turn the tables on his blackmailer, a street tough. Röhm knows this is something only Hirschfeld, with his track record of success in such cases, could help him with.

The paradoxes are dizzying. We think of the stereotypes of conservative gays tending to be closeted, in contrast to those who are out. Röhm is often described as a roustabout who on any given night could be found in various leading gay sex venues. We think correctly of all the ways Nazis, who otherwise despised and persecuted Jews (and soon enough, gays), had no qualms about exploiting their usefulness in myriad circumstances. The paradox of Jewish Hirschfeld defending one of Nazism's most powerful figureheads is extraordinarily dramatic.

When all is said and done, what Duberman teases out is that regardless of knowledge or progress or tolerance, qualities that characterized the liberal Weimar republic that fell to the Nazis, just as they characterize our own era as it falls to the alt-right, forces of intolerance, of fascism, will always reconfigure themselves around vulnerabilities and scapegoats. What prevails in these situations is rarely about court law and justice or even politics. Rather, it's about the laws of the jungle.

# Phyllis Chesler, Sarah Schulman and Me: Strange Bedfellows in the Age of Trump

– *Huffington Post*, 10/30/2017

***Is Phyllis Chesler a "homonationalist"? Is Sarah Schulman a "Jew-washer"? Was it "fascistic" to out Kate Millett as lesbian?***

Figure 153 - Phyllis Chesler, dust jacket photo of *The New Anti-Semitism*, Gefen Publishing House Ltd, amazon.com

Phyllis Chesler is a feminist, psychologist and writer of renown. She's the author and editor of numerous books. She lectures widely and writes for an array of publications. For many years, like Chesler, my life partner Arnie Kantrowitz and I have watched with dismay the resurgence of anti-Semitism. On the right, even when conservative spokespersons are or may give the appearance of being philo-Semitic or are themselves Jewish (Team Trump), this most malignant and genocidal of prejudices is yet again ubiquitous and explosively dangerous. In the age of Trump, white supremacist anti-Semitism is once again overt and ascendant in America. On the left, where it has likewise always been present and where some of its best-known spokespersons (Karl Marx) likewise have been Jews, and where there is widespread complacency or worse about anti-Semitism, it feels more personally dismaying since Arnie and I pride ourselves on being liberal and progressive. In the relentlessly binary world of politics, Arnie and I often feel like misfits. We coequally value our minority identities of being gay and Jewish. We are mostly somewhat to the left of center. We don't identify as persons of the left or right. We voted for Hillary.

My introduction to Phyllis was via our mutual friend William M. Hoffman, the noted playwright (*As Is*) and librettist (*Ghosts of Versailles*) who died earlier this year. In the 1990's Bill spearheaded a salon that attempted to address resurgent anti-Semitism in the arts, media and society. Phyllis and I were regulars there. Though it would be another 20 years before I got to know Phyllis better, Bill and I had been very close since the early 1980's. Not only were we gay and Jewish and involved in opera and recovery, we were mutually keyed into phenomena of internalized anti-Semitism, especially among Jewish intellectuals, writers and artists. Bill's summary assessment of this behavior could seem very personal. "I hate liberals," he'd quip. The first time he said that to me, it felt like a slap in the face.

My window of adult knowledge, as I've called it, of my own and other Jews' internalization of anti-Semitism was primarily via my experience as a Jewish Wagnerite—as a self-effacing Jewish enthusiast of composer Richard Wagner, whose influence on Hitler and Nazism were such as to render Wagner a virtual perpetrator of the Holocaust. At the same time and in real measure because of my relationship with my socialist sister and many other persons of the left as well as of the center and right—I have a deeply personal and visceral sense of this issue.

Notwithstanding the risk of projecting my own experience onto others, what my coming of self-awareness as Jewish has suggested to me is that there probably isn't a single Jew anywhere, no matter how otherwise self-aware, brilliant, wise, brave or even observantly Jewish, who does not relatively quickly reveal a notable degree of internalized anti-Semitism.

Bill Hoffman, for instance, never visited Israel, seemed squeamish about marching in the Israel Day parade (he did so only once, and for only a few blocks), and grimaced with horror, incredulity and something like rage when I once suggested that he looked Jewish, all but demanding that I retract an observation he considered so obviously false. I've written at length about much of this in my memoir, *Confessions of a Jewish Wagnerite,* and currently in my *Huffington Post* blog series, "On The Future of Wagnerism."

Of all those in the recent period addressing this issue of anti-Semitism among people of the left—liberals, progressives, socialists, feminists and LGBT activists—Phyllis Chesler has been the most outspoken, incisive and courageous, especially in her criticism of the women's movement for giving priority to Palestinian liberation over what should be a far more forefront and activist commitment to combating sexism and homophobia in Islamic societies. Instead of women organizing protests of often brutally oppressive Islamic theocracies, laws, institutions and traditions— of female circumcision, of honor killings, of blatantly discriminatory laws—their activism has become most conspicuous around efforts like the BDS movement (Boycott, Divestment, Sanctions) against Israel. As this activism grows, it becomes evermore troubled with questions of anti-Semitism in relationship to anti-Zionism.

Why has BDS become such a rallying point for leftists, progressives, liberals and especially feminists? What's become of NOW and the ERA? Why aren't they more in the news? Time has passed and new organizations and initiatives have developed, including the massive Women's March on Washington D.C. earlier this year. Even so, it can't be denied that the women's movement no longer seems to carry the mantle of activism it once did. In her books such as *The Death of Feminism* and *The New Anti-Semitism*, and in screeds and lectures, Chesler's ability to conceptualize and articulate this issue can be stunning. And although her concerns about anti-Semitism are more centered on the dangers of Islamist extremism and terrorism rather than those now emanating from white supremacists, it's Chesler who asks with singular prescience if what happened in France, where large numbers of Jews began emigrating to Israel in the wake of anti-Semitic attacks, could start happening here.

Figure 154 - Sarah Schulman, reading at Politics and Prose, Washington, D.C., 2018, photograph by Slowking4, Wikimedia Commons

Sarah Schulman has been a prominent figure in the gay community for decades. She's an acclaimed author, filmmaker, essayist, speaker and professor of English. Her intelligence and courage are impressive and her contributions to AIDS activism have been legion and priceless. Her novel *Rat Bohemia* is the most compelling evocation I have read of the abandonment of LGBT persons by their families of origin and mainstream society. Her later book, *Ties That Bind*, adds dimension and gives voice to this issue to an extent that her work in this area has to be considered a benchmark of LGBT literatures. It's easy to appreciate how Sarah can empathize so deeply with another dispossessed group, LGBT Palestinians. Like and with Sarah herself, they struggle with rejection by their own families and Islamic homophobia as well as from Israeli occupation.

*Rat Bohemia* helped me to see the bigger picture of how I myself have been discriminated against, relegated by Jewish relatives and others, however subtly and however enabled by me. And in *Ties That Bind*, she's helped me both to accept and not accept what has happened and to better conceptualize what can't and can be done about it.

Sarah is a professor of English at the College of Staten Island (CSI, CUNY) where Phyllis is Professor Emerita of Psychology and where Arnie was professor of English and chairman of the English Department. We've known Sarah via our communites for many years. As with Phyllis, we're grateful for her activism around issues we care about. At a more personal level, I always liked and admired Sarah, even when I sensed we were sometimes in very different places. She was passionate about LGBT struggles and especially lesbian visibility when few others were, and we seemed to share the same feelings about outing, especially those whose closetedness was hurting us—either by their associations or absence thereof, or because of what they were or weren't saying, admitting or doing. I so wanted Sarah to be a contributor to my Larry Kramer anthology, *We Must Love One Another Or Die*, but at that particular juncture in time and her work with ACT UP, Larry had pissed her off so badly, as he had so many others, that she declined.

Again, one of the reasons I so liked Sarah is for her denunciation of the closet. In fact, in the Larry Kramer anthology, I noted that she had been outspoken about closetedness among lesbians of prominence, including Susan Sontag. When the book was published, however, I got a call from Sarah herself asking if I could somehow recall the books and remove the passage about Sontag. Sarah admitted that she was concerned about the damage this could cause her reputation in literary circles because of Sontag's influence. I was shocked by her request. Not only did I refuse, I wrote the whole incident up in a piece for *Gay City News*. Lest this seem like some kind of all-out indictment of Sarah on the issue of Sontag and outing or character, however, let me add that Larry Kramer was similarly loath to go after Sontag for reasons that were likewise inconsistent with his anger at comparable closet cases. Coincidentally, Sontag had already given Kramer an endorsement as "one of our most valuable trouble makers."

Apart from sending congratulations and expressing gratitude for her pioneering work with ACT UP (she is the creator and director of the ACT UP Oral History Project) on the occasion of the landmark documentary she produced with director Jim Hubbard, *United in Anger: A History of ACT UP,* I've had little direct contact with Sarah. In part this is because of her activism with Palestinians and her theoretics around so-called "pinkwashing." I too believe that the Palestinian issue is real and needs to be more equitably dealt with, though there is little evidence that a successful resolution of the Palestinian issue or any other Western effort would make even a dent in the global insurgency that is Islamic *jihad* and its extremism, sexism, homophobia, anti-Semitism and genocidal commitment to Israel's destruction. The problem for me with Sarah's efforts on behalf of Palestinians is that it would have a lot more credibility for me if there were a commensurately outspoken commitment on her part to denouncing Islamic homophobia, misogyny and anti-Semitism. In the absence of that, I can't help but conclude that what Chesler has to say about leftist critiques of Israel, the new anti-Semitism and the death of feminism can ring as true for Sarah as for others of the activist left.

For me, it's impossible not to look at the work of Sarah Schulman in light of what she's revealed to us about her upbringing, like that of *Klinghoffer* librettist Alice Walker, and not wonder about internalized anti-Semitism. That we may have been deeply hurt and want to get back at smugly or shamingly conservative or ostensibly tolerant but subtly homophobic Jewish parents and relatives is not the problem. The problem is when we have inadequate regard and compassion for who they are, and how and why they are as they are, and how, for better or worse, our fates our tied up with theirs in the context of anti-Semitism.

It's a problem when our drive for eye-for-an-eye justice for their rejection and relegation of us prevents us from having more self-awareness and humane concern for them and for ourselves in relationship to them. It's a problem when we don't feel the need to consider how our rebellions against them, however otherwise justifiable, are contributing to exceedingly dangerous, explicitly genocidal levels of anti-Semitism; for how they undermine the security and survival of Israel and with Israel, all Jewish people. As I see it, just as leftists demand tolerance and compassion for those who live under Islamic oppression and who are also victims of Islamophobia, so must they call for a commensurate tolerance and compassion for those for who are targets of anti-Semitism, notwithstanding the prejudices of Jewish orthodoxies.

Back to Chesler. Based on my own experience and impressions, and as requested by her, I gave Phyllis a strong endorsement for her book, *The New Anti-Semitism*, and spent several evenings with her and Bill Hoffman at her home in Manhattan. The first of these get-togethers went without a hitch. Phyllis can be self-important, discomfitingly blunt and overbearing, but she is an engaging figure and a gracious host. In the course of the second evening, however, a wrinkle emerged. Phyllis declined my offer to interview her for my *Huffington Post* blog. The reasons for that refusal were unclear. Was it because she didn't have time? Was I politically incorrect? What was the problem? She never offered an explanation, notwithstanding my standard offer to my interviewees of giving them editing approval of the final draft.

At subsequent gatherings, more wrinkles emerged. Susan, Phyllis's partner, made a snide comment for which she later apologized about how the only priority gay men seem to have is fucking. Because I know that feminists and lesbians sometimes have this perspective of gay men, and because I know it be virtually identical with Larry Kramer's critique of gay men, and finally because I myself can feel it to be stereotypically true, I let it pass. As gay people, we're all family and can speak our minds critically. That was the way I processed this moment. Incidentally, however, such a remark is not something Sarah Schulman would ever have said. She would never judge us that way. No wonder many gay men have such affection and regard for her. And therein may lie a key to Sarah's embracement of Palestinians without judging them for neglects and failures around what we think should be their other activisms.

With minorities, we can be critical of ourselves, but when that same criticism comes from outsiders we can feel defensive. Who are these people to be telling us who and what and how we should be? Did then still-closeted Susan Sontag have the right to judge gay men for our "vehement" sexuality? But Phyllis was one of us, right?

On our next visit with her, Phyllis asked us all to come into the television room. She had something to show us (Arnie was with Bill and me that night). It was a brief spot she did on the Mike Huckabee show ("Gov'ner Mike," as she referred to him). Although this was prior to the Kim Davis episode, it still should have set off alarms but somehow didn't at the time because of what I understood Phyllis to be doing and where I understood her to be coming from.

Bill Hoffman was the first to explain to me that Christian evangelicals were emerging as among the very few allies of Jews and Israel. Because of the seriousness of anti-Semitism, I could appreciate how this alliance was working and I could even feel circumstantially and momentarily tolerant of it, at least in terms of support for Jews and Israel. Of course, as a gay man there was no way I could endorse the seriously homophobic agendas of Christian evangelicals any more than I could have endorsed those of the Orthodox Jews who fought so bitterly to prevent us from getting our civil rights here in NYC.

Naively, I assumed that Chesler, in speaking on the Huckabee show about her book, *The New Anti-Semitism*, would also be conveying messages, even if only indirectly, that were pro-feminist and pro-LGBT. Appearing on the Mike Huckabee show is not something I could ever imagine doing myself. Nor would I expect to see other feminist or LGBT spokespersons there. Meanwhile, however, there is a large track record of politicos using oppositional media platforms to be heard and vice versa—e.g., Fox's Bill O'Reilly, whose guests periodically included Barak Obama, and Bill Maher, whose HBO show has repeatedly featured Maher's "friend," Ann Coulter. I myself have appeared on Al Jezeera (to discuss the unaffordability of hepatitis C treatments).

The last of the evenings with Phyllis was her milestone birthday party, a grand event attended by prominent figures like Alan Dershowitz. There was eloquent testimony from everybody, especially Phyllis. I gave her "a golden bowl for a golden soul." It was a wonderful evening, at the end of which Phyllis, after speaking personally about most everyone in attendance, looked around and asked, "Have I left anyone out?" "Yes," I suddenly found myself volunteering: "Susan." Until I suggested it, Chesler apparently was not going to acknowledge her partner Susan. Though she went on to praise Susan, it was not specifically said that Susan was her partner. Nor was there otherwise any explicit reference to anyone or anything else LGBT.

Is Phyllis in the closet? Bill Hoffman had implied that she goes in and out. I googled her. Her son pretty much outed her in an essay supporting gay marriage. But I couldn't find anything Phyllis herself had written acknowledging being lesbian, her partnership with Susan, or clear support for gay rights and concerns, though I sensed in her writings as well as personally that she does care about these issues. I appreciated the emails she sent me about Islamic homophobia and about Jewish and Israeli gay activists trying to confront leftist, mostly BDS-related anti-Semitism on campus. In one article she used the term "we" in generalizing about issues of concern to women and LGBT persons, not so unlike the way then still-closeted Sontag used that same "we" to talk about "The Way We Live Now" in *The New Yorker* in the heyday of AIDS.

Meanwhile, however, Chesler was writing for *Breitbart,* the *New York Post* and Fox News, was apparently supporting Trump, and declining to participate in the big Women's March earlier this year because it was honorarily co-chaired by Palestinian activist Linda Sarsour, a controversial figure whose activities and allegiances do indeed warrant scrutiny, especially in the context of any backdoor endorsements of anti-Israel or anti-Semitic initiatives. Yet it's also possible to see Sarsour's presence in the Women's March as participating in the activism Phyllis has criticized Muslim and other feminists for not doing. At the time of my own participation in this march, I had no knowledge of Sarsour's involvement and little awareness of who she was or what the controversies about her were. In any case, that awareness would not have kept me from being part of this historic event.

Whatever the issues about the closet, what Phyllis is saying is that a critic of Islamism like Ayaan Hirsi Ali, who is so bravely and eloquently outspoken in her indictments for biases and crimes of sexism in Islamic societies, is a conspicuously lone and reviled outsider in feminist and progressive circles. Linda Sarsour and Sarah Schulman, who should be in solidarity with Hirsi Ali, are nowhere to be seen on these fronts. On the contrary, what leftist critics like Schulman and Sarsour have to say about Hirsi Ali is pretty much limited to observations that she, Hirsi Ali, is appearing on venues like Fox News and is a member of a conservative think tank, the things I'm criticizing Chesler for. That Hirsi Ali is raising concerns of unassailable validity is neither acknowledged nor, apparently, respected. Indeed, it can be argued that Chesler and Hirsi Ali are associating with right wing media and enterprises because of the intransigence and hostility of their leftist critics.

On the other hand, is Chesler, however still in the closet, an example of Sarah Schulman's concept of "homonationalism"? As defined by Sarah, "that's when the only thing that kept people from a nationalist identity is homophobia, and once that homophobia is removed they embrace all these racist and religious supremacy categories. So right wing nationalists who are for the most part anti-Muslim and anti-Muslim immigration are now welcoming white gay people and some of them officially so." E.g., Milo Yiannapoulos. And Phyllis Chesler?

My efforts to discuss some of these identity politics issues with Phyllis left me unnerved. My biggest concern, as I wrote her, was that in flirting with Trump, *Breitbart*, Fox News, evangelicals and Republicans, she was undermining her own otherwise impressive critique of feminists and leftists. If you're critical of fascism, siding with an opposing fascism in retaliation is troubled, a pact with the devil, as I put it. It would be like embracing Stalin to oppose Hitler, a good analogy, especially for Phyllis since she does see the current struggle, and rightly so, as life-and-death in terms of the survival of Jews and Israel. Stalin was crucial to Hitler's defeat, yes, but remaining silent about and thereby exonerating such a brutal fascist would be a very different matter. If acute concern for Israel's survival is the main reason for Phyllis's current allegiances, she should find a way to say so, while also clearly acknowledging her displeasure and discomfort with rightist as well as leftist ideologues and agendas. It might not be easy but I do believe she could do so in a way that would help her better maintain the continuum, integrity and credibility of her work.

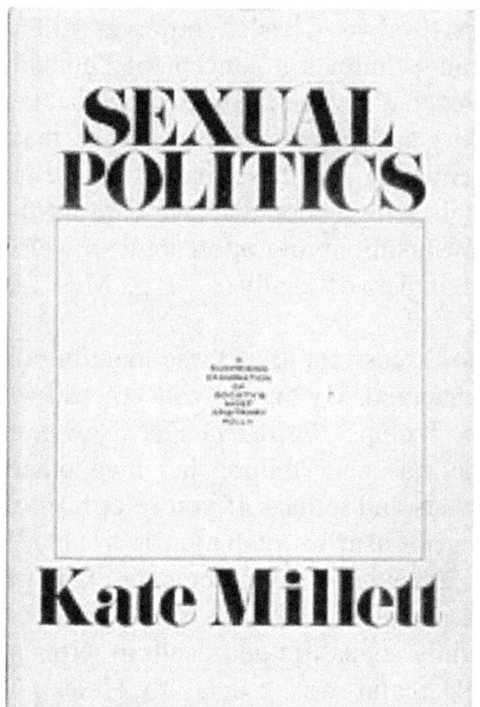


Figure 155 - Sexual Politics by Kate Millett, book cover, Wikipedia

Chesler denies being in lockstep with Trump but easily becomes insulted, most recently around my response to her comments in the *Washington Post* on the passing of the late pioneering feminist Kate Millett. As Chesler points out in the piece, when Millett was publicly confronted about whether she identified as lesbian, she (Millett) said "yes," but denounced her confronters and their tactics as "fascist." Years later, in a filmed interview with Sarah Schulman (Lesbian Central), Millett's thoughts on this issue were considerably less defensive. In my email exchanges with Phyllis, I tried to no avail to discuss the long-standing, challenging issue of the closet for bisexual people who are public figures. Like Sontag and Millett, Phyllis doesn't want to be pressured to accept an identity she feels to be inaccurate or incomplete, meanwhile conveniently distancing herself from and relegating the social and political problems of those she is in bed with. I couldn't help but raise this issue with Phyllis and ponder what Millett would have thought of a feminist who writes for *Breitbart* and is in essence stumping for Trump, in response to which there were several "How Dare You!"s. Diva time, as it can be as well when Sarah Schulman feels thwarted.

I guess where you end up in identity politics skirmishes is with that old bottom line of most strongly identifying with and clinging to whichever minority identity feels most threatened, and relegating the others. In some times and places, it's being a woman. In others it's being LGBT or a person of color, Palestinian or Jewish. I don't trust the politics of the left or right to rid me of anti-Semitic dangers. Nor do I trust either extreme to protect me as a gay man, our current fragile civil rights notwithstanding.

I never bought the concept of "pinkwashing" (defined by Wikipedia as "the promotion of the gay-friendliness of a corporate or political entity in an attempt to downplay or soften aspects of it considered negative"). On the contrary, while some in tourism and politics may be promoting gay rights in ways that seem to obscure Palestinian occupation and oppression, gay rights in Israel is mostly the hard-fought achievement of Israeli LGBT activists. Inevitably, calling out this issue to the extent that Sarah has can seem an example of what her critics have called "Jew-washing" (which Urban Dictionary defines as "claiming Jewish heritage for the sole purpose of gaining political leverage in a fight against Israel and the Jewish people"; i.e., I'm Jewish. Therefore I can't be anti-Semitic).

Yet to me, equally notable examples of Jew-washing are Jewish homonationalists who sanction anti-immigrant rhetoric and ally themselves with anti-immigrant, sexist, homophobic and Islamophobic forces, with no self-consciousness of themselves as members of minorities that have been and will continue to be comparably vulnerable to anti-minority vilification and scapegoating by those forces. "I'm not one of *those* people" can seem as reflective of Chesler as of Schulman. If Schulman can appear to have internalilzed anti-Semitism, Chesler can seem to have internalized homophobia.

On the other hand, haven't I myself done the equivalent of what I accuse Chesler and Schulman of—directly or indirectly supporting or tolerating leaders, countries, regimes and ideologies with questionable or worse human rights records and priorities? Haven't we all? I would be lying if I said I wasn't grateful for the Republicans and conservatives, including Netanyahu and even Trump, who forcefully called out and denounced the outrageous threats of genocide from Iran and others at the ineffectual and pervasively anti-Zionist and anti-Semitic United Nations and other public forums. Was my sometime support of bumbling but AIDS-benificent George Bush (who I didn't vote for; I've never voted for a Republican)—for calling out the "axis of evil" troika of Iran, North Korea and Cuba, and for initiating the Iraq war against the Hitlerian maniac Saddam Hussein—any different from Chesler's taciturnity towards Trump and the alt-right or Schulman's towards Islamist extremism?

Perhaps not, but here's where I feel we differ. I can state clearly that I have real concerns about Israel's treatment of Palestinians in the occupied territories, about the proliferation of settlements and the Islamophobia and zealotry of too many settlers. Arnie and I are both very troubled by the occupation and would like to see a just and lasting peace, ideally a 2-state solution. At the same time, what we still most want to see in the bigger picture of Islam vs the West and the plight of the Palestinians is an end to Islamist terrorism and its monolithic, explicitly genocidal commitment to the destruction of Israel, the one area where I found myself initially and fleetingly drawn to Trump.

But that was before Trump's pathological narcissism (see the psychiatric designations of "pathological narcissism" and "narcissistic personality disorder"), "pathological lying" (to use Bernie Sanders' phrase), ignorance, racism, sexism, xenophobia, kleptomania, scapegoating and mean-spiritedness more fully revealed themselves. In the long run, it seems clear to Arnie and me that the security of Israel and Jewish people, to say nothing of the rest of the world, will be dangerously undermined, not bolstered, by such an unstable megalomaniac as Donald Trump and Trumpism. If we had a dime for every time we've compared "that son of a bitch" (to use Trump's phrase) to Hitler, we'd be millionaires.

What I'm not seeing are comparable public statements from Chesler about the oppression and persecution of LGBT people, here and globally, except for denouncing Islamic homophobia and terrorist acts like the Pulse nightclub massacre by Islamic terrorists, something Trump has done as well. Nor am I seeing such statements from Schulman about Islamist anti-Semitism, homophobia and the oppression of women, though she did speak out about homophobia and AIDS in Cuba. Shouldn't anti-Semitism, honor killings of women and gays and female circumcision trouble her more? Does she think Israel's oppression of Palestinians justifies terroristic acts of mass murder and genocidal anti-Semitism, including hatred-and violence-indoctrinating children's school textbooks? Does she think because of her noble work with and on behalf of Palestinians that a sudden tsunami of anti-Semitism, such as has recurred so predictably and relentlessly throughout history, will spare her because she wasn't one of *those* people—Zionist extremists?

And does Chesler think she will likewise be spared the homophobic wrath of ignorant and bigoted evangelicals because she was once or twice in a heterosexual marriage and has progeny? Even if she doesn't see herself as gay and looks the other way on abortion? For all Fox News, *Breitbart*, the Huckabee show and the *New York Post* know, she's just one of *them*, a true conservative just-folks straight American.

My older leftist friends and acquaintances, like my sister, are still committed socialists. These are the ones who were passionately pro-Russia, pro-Castro, pro-Mao and against the war in Viet Nam. One of them, a 60's radical now nearly 80, asked me if I watched the recent Oliver Stone interviews with Putin. No, I didn't watch them (I abandoned them after 15 minutes) for the same reason I've not listened to Castro's perorations and no longer listen to Donald Trump's. These are authoritarians, demagogues, and were, are or would be police state dictators of police state dictatorships. I already know who they were and are, whatever the qualifiers. I can't bear Trump's unscripted harangues and rants and don't trust the scripted ones, even those that say some things I agree with, like calling out Iran as a terrorist state and Cuba as a police state dictatorship.

I guess the way I see myself as different from Chesler and Schulman is that I like to believe that where there is fascism, whether it's in Trump's America, Putin's Russia, Xi's China, el-Sisi's Egypt, and, yes, Netanyahu's Israel, among Islamic, Christian and Jewish fundamentalists and extremists, and other zealots, xenophobes, populists and nationalists, in Cuba, North Korea, Iran, Turkey, Hungary, Saudi Arabia, Israel, China, Russia, Cuba, the Philippines, Myanmar, Venezuela, Syria or anywhere else, I want to call it out and keep my distance from those regimes and their leaders and their apologists a lot more than I want to find ways to ignore or negotiate with them and thereby tacitly justify and endorse them. In other words, I would hope that I don't find myself passively or tacitly aligning myself with fascists and fascist regimes by not being more explicitly critical of them, by keeping silent about their more outrageous pronouncements and acts because of what may seem to be precipitating social circumstances (poverty, colonialism) or because they may be presently neutral or even favorable when it comes to other issues I care deeply about, like Israel's security or LGBT rights.

The core, the base, of nationalist movements is often made up initially of those who feel and who in fact are economically or otherwise disenfranchised. This was true of revolutions we think of as justified, like the American Revolution. But it was also true of the early Nazi movement and likewise true of much of the base that Trump panders to. Trump's base, like the Nazis (and some of whom are neo-Nazis), needs to be called out a lot more than it needs to be understood and appeased.

The reason so many Trumpers are indeed deplorable is not because of Hillary's failures and what *Breitbart* rabble rouser Steve Bannon calls "limousine liberals" or "the swamp" in Washington, or moderate Republicans. However disadvantaged Germany found itself after the first world war—"The Great War," a war of devastating aggression largely instigated and perpetrated by Germany—and however unsuccessful their efforts at assimilation and politics, the Jews and communists were not to blame for what World War 2. Hitler and Nazism were. The same analogy and square recognition of blame and responsibility are true as well of Trump and his followers.

Like any other regimes and figureheads of totalitarianism, these regimes, leaders, their thugs but also their more mainstream followers have crossed the lines of what's right and what's wrong, what's moral and what's immoral, what's evil and what's not, what's acceptable and what's not, what's despicable and what's not. They and not the greater society nor their scapegoats—the wealthy, the "elites," the Democrats, the Republicans, the "swamp," the "degenerates," the mainstream media, the liberals, the banks, Blacks, Hispanics, the Jews, immigrants, gays, lesbians and transexuals—are accountable for who and what they've said and done, for what they say and do, as well as for what they've failed to say and do.

The same is true for Islamist extremists. Just as there was no justification for Nazism, there is none for Islamic extremist or any other form of terrorism. Nor is there justification for passive tolerance of extremism and terrorism.

Here I must posthumously grant Bill Hoffman that there was no justification for the Reign of Terror that so dishonored The French Revolution. (His sympathies with the aristocracy and distrust of rabbles and mobs are the foundation of his opera, *The Ghosts of Versailles*, which has yet to be seen in France.) Terrorism, especially when it's committed on behalf of factions and ideologies, and especially when it's excused in the name of revolution, may seem inevitable and justifiable, especially in conditions of economic extremity and war. Surpassingly, however, the challenge of terrorism is not justification, mollification or appeasement. It's resistance, censure, judgment, prosecution, riddance and prevention.

Obviously, we can't transform overnight some cultures and traditions that have been marked by poverty, isolation, prejudice and totalitarianism, sometimes for centuries. And sometimes the enemy of my enemy may be my ally. That we have to work and negotiate with many deplorable people and quagmires, with each other and with where people are, may be a given. And, yes, the devil is in the details.

But let's be careful how far we go in embracing topical causes and communities dear to us at the expense of being silent about others we should and do care about and should be speaking out about, lest we lose track of who we are, where we come from, where we belong, where we can expect to find sanctuary in worsening times, and what we really believe. Lest we lose credibility for being equitable, fair-minded, balanced and rational. Lest we lose our integrity. Lest we lose our moral compass. Lest we lose our souls.

Being political bedfellows may give an appearance of propriety, but it can be a setup for dysfunction and insomnia.

Figure 156 - *The Rest of It* by Martin Duberman, Duke University Press, 2018, book cover photo, amazon.com

# The Passion of Martin Duberman: Searing Personal Testimony on Gay History, AIDS, Addiction, Recovery and More

– *Medium*, 2/14/18

**"All historical writing is interpretive" —Martin Duberman**

There have been few moments of American history more corroborating of leftist perspectives than the present. Throughout the land we are plunged back to the future of privileged white men, of the crassest elitism, racism, sexism, homophobia, harrassment and bullying. As the middle and working classes are raped of our "entitlements," "homonationalists," as Sarah Schulman calls them, are increasingly out of their closets of reactionary conservatism and fascism. The gay past that was Joseph McCarthy, J. Edgar Hoover, Roy Cohn and Ernst Röhm is now prelude to a future of far-right conservative support from the likes of finance mogul Peter Thiel and alt-right rabble rouser Milo Yiannopoulos.

Ergo, it has never been more timely to read leftist literature and consider leftist perspectives. In this context, anything from a historian as accomplished and challenging as Martin Duberman will be of moment and interest. Certainly, that's the case with his new collection, *The Rest of It: Hustlers, Cocaine, Depression and Then Some 1976*-1988, mostly personal reflections on events and issues in his own life and times, from the early period of the AIDS epidemic.

First, some disclosure. Marty and I were close friends during the years covered in the book, and my absence from these accounts is its own window on our overlapping interests and writing on many of the subjects under review here—e.g., AIDS, addiction, recovery, psychiatry, sex research and Christopher Lasch. Because of this friendship, and the personal nature of this collection, I've opted to use "Marty" rather than "Duberman" in the appreciation that follows.

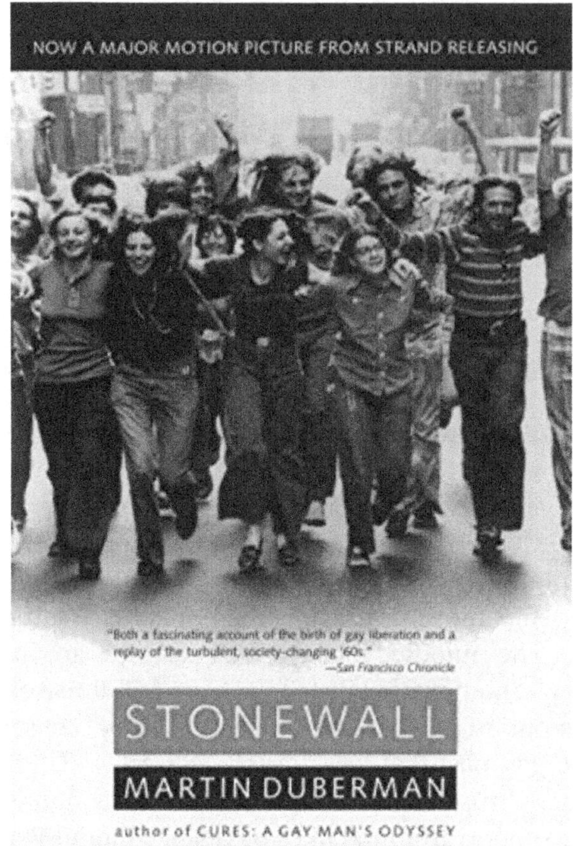


Figure 157 - *Stonewall* by Martin Duberman, paperback book cover photo, penguin-random house, 1993, amazon.com

All history, no matter how erudite or intentionally fair-minded, is selective. In his role as a distinguished historian and scholar, being accountable for selectivity and semi-fictionalization is important and comes naturally to Marty, and so disclaimers and qualifiers addressing this issue are always to be found in the introductions and commentaries of his many dramatizations and semi-fictionalizations as well as his more scrupulously documented scholarly accounts of historical figures and events. Even so, when all is said and done, Marty's historical dramas such as *Visions of Kerouac, Mother Earth, Stonewall* and other works, including his previous book, *Jews Queers Germans*, can be categorized with, rather than appreciated as somehow qualitatively apart from, such other notably selective and semi-fictional historical docu-dramatizations of our time as *And The Band Played On*, *The Normal Heart* and *How To Survive a Plague.*

Figure 158 - *Mother Earth: An Epic Drama of Emma Goldman's Life* by Martin Duberman, St. Martin's Press, 1991, amazon.com

Whatever the bottom-line "facts," history is inevitably and always a kind of Rashomon, a story that is told differently depending on the participant or observer, the "facts" being given different weights, colors, shades and prominence by each storyteller. The Rashomon analogy is mine, not Marty's, but it's one I know he would endorse, whatever the qualifiers. As Marty puts it in his essay in *Gay and Lesbian Review,* "Why Auden and Kallman Endured" (*GLR*, 1/18), "all historical writing is interpretive."

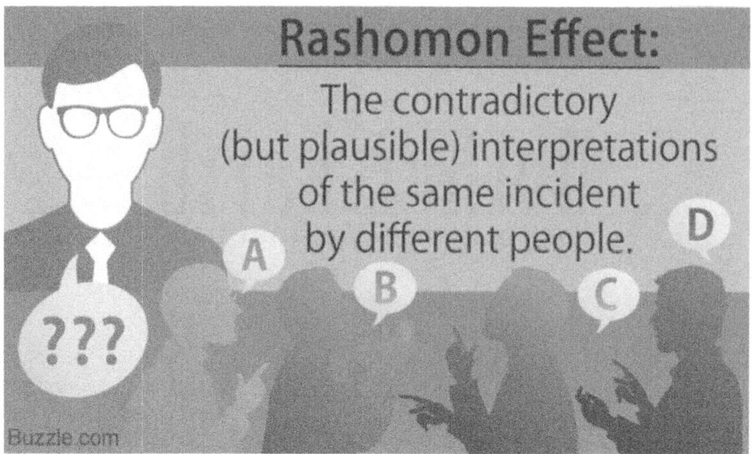


Figure 159 - Graphic image, public domain

In this age of fake news, it's heartening to know that there are writers like Marty, persons of conscience and ethics about their methods and sources. Even when he fictionalizes and dramatizes, he spells out his commitment to credibility and truth, as best he can capture it, and he maintains his scholarly approach with a fluent use of historical resources. For example, though there are no footnotes or indices in *The Rest of It* (likewise in *Jews Queers Germans* and other works) there are contextual references to sources, especially his own diary entries. The Rashomon analogy is pertinent for another reason. For all Marty's skills as a historian and scholar, he is likewise a master of storytelling. Always compelling, his writing can be as difficult to put down as his viewpoints can be to argue with.

It's not likely that anyone will ever catch Marty off-guard about these issues of selectivity, fictionalization and dramatization. Unflinchingly self-critical, there isn't any potential pitfall or vulnerability he himself hasn't weighed and articulated. But that he is consistently careful to acknowledge the possibility of bias in his writing shouldn't inhibit critical scrutiny and perspective. So in the interest of better capturing my subject along lines used by Marty himself, I'm going to proceed with commentary that will make reference to my own memories and subjective impressions alongside those that are less personal.

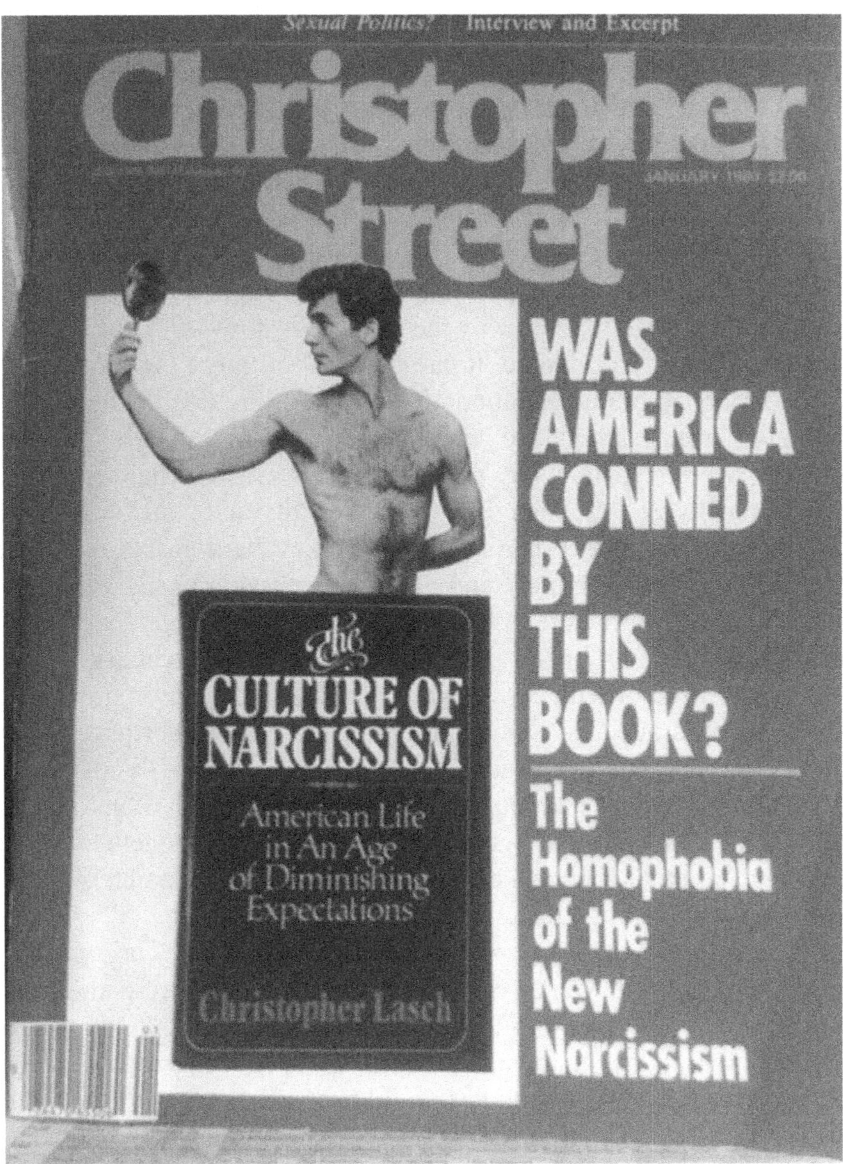

Figure 160 - "The Homophobia of The New Narcissism," cover story of *Christopher Street Magazine*, January, 1980, by Lawrence D. Mass

My essay, "The New Narcissism and Homosexuality: The Psychiatric Connection" was the first cover story of the 1980's of *Christopher Street* magazine. In *The Rest of It*, Marty's discussion of the author of that trendy book, Christopher Lasch, as a figure of the left, is very interesting and revealing, especially of how the heterosexist idealogues who dominated the intellectual discourse at that time kept relegating and stigmatizing homosexuality. From leftist points of view, and as Marty reprises it in his discussion of Lasch and Eugene Genovese, homosexuality was seen as self-centered ("narcissistic") and profligate at the expense of maturity and society.

Such judgment was consistent with my own experience when I came out in the late 1960's at the University of California at Berkeley. While the activism on campus tolerated gay people and accepted our support—not so unlike the way the right does now—the left not only wasn't there for gay people, it harbored, albeit more tacitly than the right, a lot of prejudice about us. In the film documentaries on Berkeley from that period and later (e.g., Mark Ktichell's film, *Berkeley in the Sixties*), gay people and concerns are neither visible nor acknowledged. Challenging gay invisibility and confronting anti-gay bigotry among the intelligentsia are key battlefronts on which Marty fought early, bravely and often. The passion of his arguments and efforts is everywhere in the testimony of *The Rest of Us*.

My own take on Lasch and his book was complementary to what Marty has to say here. As I wrote about it, "the new narcissism" discourse embraced by Lasch and his ilk reflected older psychiatric, mostly psychoanalytic jargon and theoretics, especially its newer designations of "pathological narcissism" and "narcissistic personality disorder" (designations I'm now guilty, together with a growing number of psychiatrists, of exploiting to characterize "the president who shall go unnamed").

These were the new ways that traditionally homophobic psychoanalytic psychiatry was finding to re-pathologize homosexuality following the landmark declassification of "homosexuality" as a mental disorder in 1973-74, a decision that remained as deeply unpopular in older, conservative psychiatric enclaves as Obama's presidency became among Republicans. Diagnosing social variance and political dissidence as psychiatric disorders is something the Soviets excelled at and became notorious for, as did American psychiatry, especially with its older official diagnostic categories of "homosexuality" and "ego-dystonic homosexuality," but more indirectly with its newer ones, like "pathological narcissism."

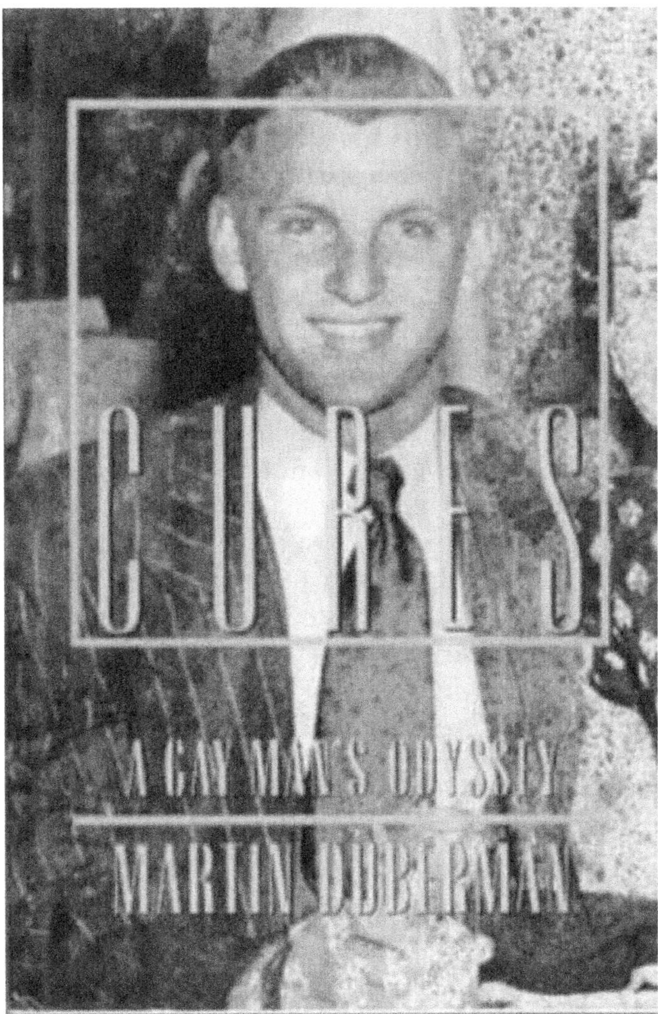


Figure 161 - *Cures: A Gay Man's Odyssey* by Martin Duberman, cover photo of original hardback, Dutton, 1991

Marty knew well of the work I had been doing as a watchdog for what was happening in psychiatry, and it's hard, at least for me, not to feel that his decision not to probe Lasch's seduction by these psychiatric concepts lessens his discussion in *The Rest of Us* of this turning point in American intellectual discourse. As Marty himself notes in in that *GLR* essay on Auden and Kallman, "Before meeting Kallman, Auden had considered his erotic life a failure, a narcissistic derangement as he saw it, limited and barren. His attitude reflected, of course, standard psychiatric assumptions of the day." In Marty's defense, *The Rest of It* makes no claims to being comprehensive. Rather, it recollects moments, situations, personalities and conflicts without a lot of context or exposition, often regarding matters he has discussed in other collections and memoirs.

Some additional notes about our friendship. It was never sexual. Rather, Marty was, like his nemesis Larry Kramer, a mentor and friend in the earliest period of my own writing and activism. I no longer remember how Marty and I met, but I had just written my first piece for the gay press on the homophobia I encountered in coming out during interviews for a residency in psychiatry at leading universities and medical centers in the Chicago area. That essay, "Trial By Ordeal," appeared in 1979 in *Gay Community News,* on the eve of my moving to New York from Boston, where I lived and did my medical training during most of the 1970's.

Thus began my own gay activist journalism, most of it centered on exposing "the shift in credibility of the best medical and scientific thinking about sexuality and homosexuality," as I put it, "from the temples of psychiatry to the laboratories of sex research." In New York I continued my writing, mostly for the gay press—the *New York Native*, *Christopher Street*, which Marty also wrote for, and the *Advocate*. Marty was one of the first people I got to know in the New York City whirl of gay life, activism and writing. We connected strongly on many issues of community and consciousness as well as at a more ineffable level of affection and regard. During this period I published many pieces about psychiatry and sex research, including interviews with key figures like Masters and Johnson, John Money, Thomas Szasz and Marty himself which later appeared in my two volume collection: *Dialogues of The Sexual Revolution*.

Regarding that takeover from psychiatry by sex researchers of the most credible thinking about sexuality and homosexuality, *The Rest of Us* makes telling reference to Marty's critique of the seminal Bell and Weinberg study, *Homosexualities: A Study of Diversity Among Men and Women*. Regarding the gratitude we all felt for this watershed development in the sciences establishing our "normality," Marty reveals here that he had tried to qualify his appreciation, to be more of a spoiler, in his *New York Times* review of the book.

*The "liberal" take on homosexuality had been exemplified by the Kinsey Institute's Alan Bell and Martin Weinberg in their book* Homosexualities...*In the excised section* [of Marty's review by the

*Times], I'd argued that although most gay people did share the prescribed values and aspirations of mainstream culture, a radical minority, lesbian feminists in particular, did not; that minority firmly rejected the liberal view that our national institutions were basically sound and that a little tinkering here and there around the edges would make them better still...The liberal Kinsey Institute, I argued, champions out of one side of its mouth the vigorous scrutiny of traditional assumptions about sex, but then blindly accepts a set of assumptions about human nature most in need of scrutiny—like the belief that a "maternal instinct" is innate, that recreational sex denotes immaturity or, conversely, that monogamy signifies adulthood.*

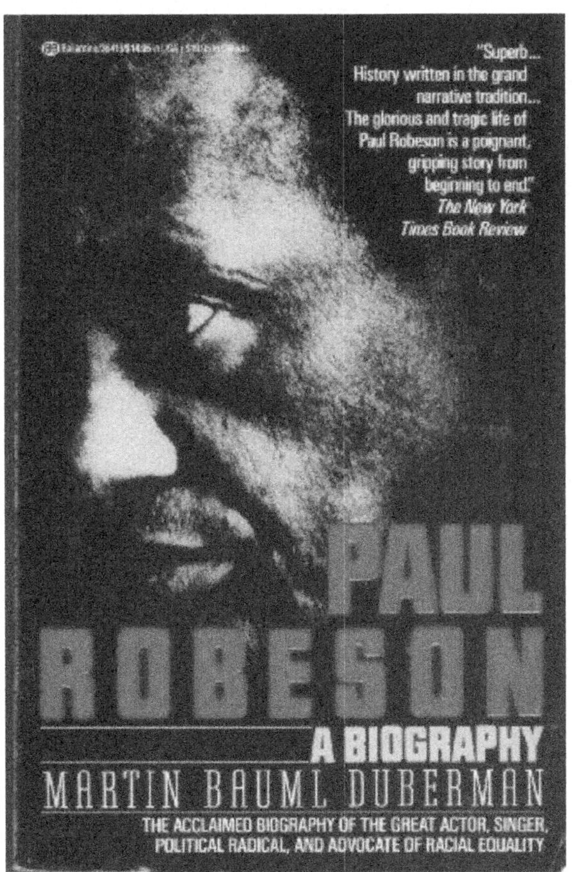


Figure 162 - *Paul Robeson: A Biography* by Martin Bauml Duberman, Knopf, 1989, book cover photo, public domain

There were many dinners and gatherings with Marty over years, some with our mutual friend Seymour Kleinberg. (author of *Alienated Affections,* not mentioned in *The Rest of It*). It was Marty who first explained to me how daunting it is to be a writer doing the kind of writing we were doing. Even his good friend Vivian Gornick, whose work appeared in the *New York Times* and who I got to know a bit through Marty, had to struggle to make ends meet. This insight and advice was something I recalled years later when, on a visit with Marty, I saw a pile of surplus copies of his books alongside the trash bins in front of his home in West Chelsea. He had been cleaning house. With rare exceptions, Marty observed, most writers don't make enough money to live on or gain much recognition or acclaim. It says a lot about Marty's character and integrity that having tasted commercial success (as he recalls in *The Rest of It*, he was given a $275,000 advance for *Robeson*, and that was 35 years ago!), his oeuvre has mostly consisted of more marginal works written more as personal imperative— for history, ideology and self-expression—at the sacrifice of more popular and financial success. In this and for me, Marty will always be a hero and role model. I had similar feelings about my other writer role model of that period, Larry Kramer. In retrospect, in both cases, I may have been somewhat naive about the roles personal ambition and hopes for commercial success were also playing in their efforts, however primarily inspired by their ideological commitments and passion.

Though I never met Marty's two closest friends from the preceding period, literary and arts critics Dick Poirier and Leo Bersani, the material on them seems consistent with what I recall Marty saying about them. I met others in Marty's circles, like Kate Stimson, founding editor of *Signs,* and was an early supporter of the Center for Lesbian and Gay Studies (CLAGS). A decade later, I would be a contributor to *Queering the Pitch: The New Gay and Lesbian Musicology*, co-edited by Stimpson's partner Elizabeth Wood, Philip Brett and Gary C. Thomas. Alas, the more controversial contribution that was submitted by me—"Musical Closets," about outing and coming out in the music world—was rejected with last-minute cold feet by both Wood and, earlier, Richard Schneider at *GLR*, but was included by Michael Bronski in his anthology, *Taking Liberties*. In its place the editors substituted my previously published interview with Ned Rorem.

I remember the many, ever-worsening scrapes with Paul Robeson, Jr. in the writing of *Robeson*, as recounted here, and Marty's heroic struggle to capture this great figure of culture, politics and world history. *The Rest of It* recaps many highlights of the vast research that was involved on *Robeson,* with riveting vignettes and details such as Robesons's affairs with actresses Peggy Ashcroft and Uta Hagen, and how their chemistry electrified the productions of *Othello* they co-starred in. But Marty is clear that the rumors of Robeson having been bisexual and having had affairs with Sergei Eiesenstein and Marc Blitzstein, rumors originally promulgated by Paul Robeson Jr, remain unsubstantiated.

Robeson's ordeals in undergoing ECT for bipolar depression are reviewed and updated with later psychiatric opinion. Marty's interpretation of Robeson's reticence (what critics have called "failure") to renounce Stalin and Stalinism is succinctly and persuasively re-articulated, bolstered by later findings and input, and the passages of time. Hopefully, *Robeson* will be the basis of a quality film. Likewise *Mother Earth* for anarchist Emma Goldman, a figure of social consciousness and activism especially dear to Marty; a love that was always discernible in his love for his Labrador Emma.

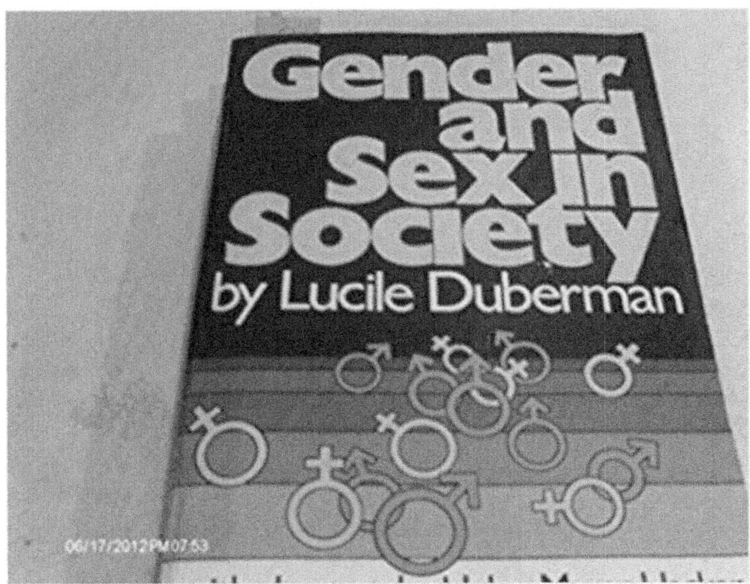


Figure 163 - *Gender and Sex in Society* by Lucile Duberman, 1975, amazon.com

Also via Marty, my life partner Arnie Kantrowitz and I became good friends with Marty's sister, Lucile, who had done intriguing work on the sociology of emotions. Arnie and I spent a summer with her and our cat Sid (Siddhartha) in Woodstock, as our drinking—hers and mine—escalated. Lucile's advice and encouragement about my writing I still revisit. If you write just one page a day, she said with her warm, distinctive voice and smile, at the end of a year you'll have a 365 page book. A day at a time. Little did we know then how important this precept would become in our lives. And deaths. Lucile died from complications of alcoholism in 2006 in New Orleans, where she had been living with her daughter.

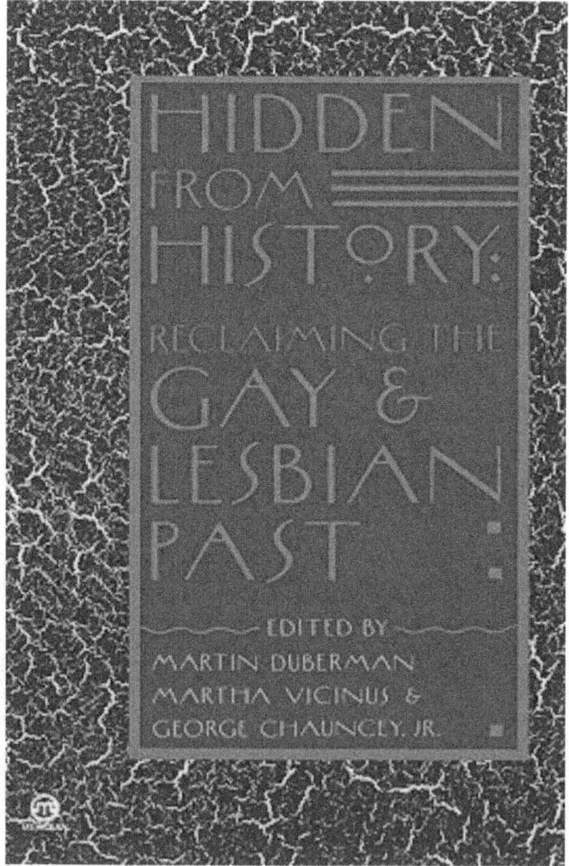


Figure 164 - *Hidden From History: Reclaiming the Gay & Lesbian Past*, edited by Martin Duberman, Martha Vicinus and George Chauncey Jr., Penguin-Random House, 1990

I also recall friendly (cough) skirmishes between Marty and George Chauncey over the co-authorship sequencing of names (over whose name should come first) of their seminal anthology, *Hidden From History.* Lost in this jockeying, it could seem, was the anthology's other co-author, Martha Vicinus.

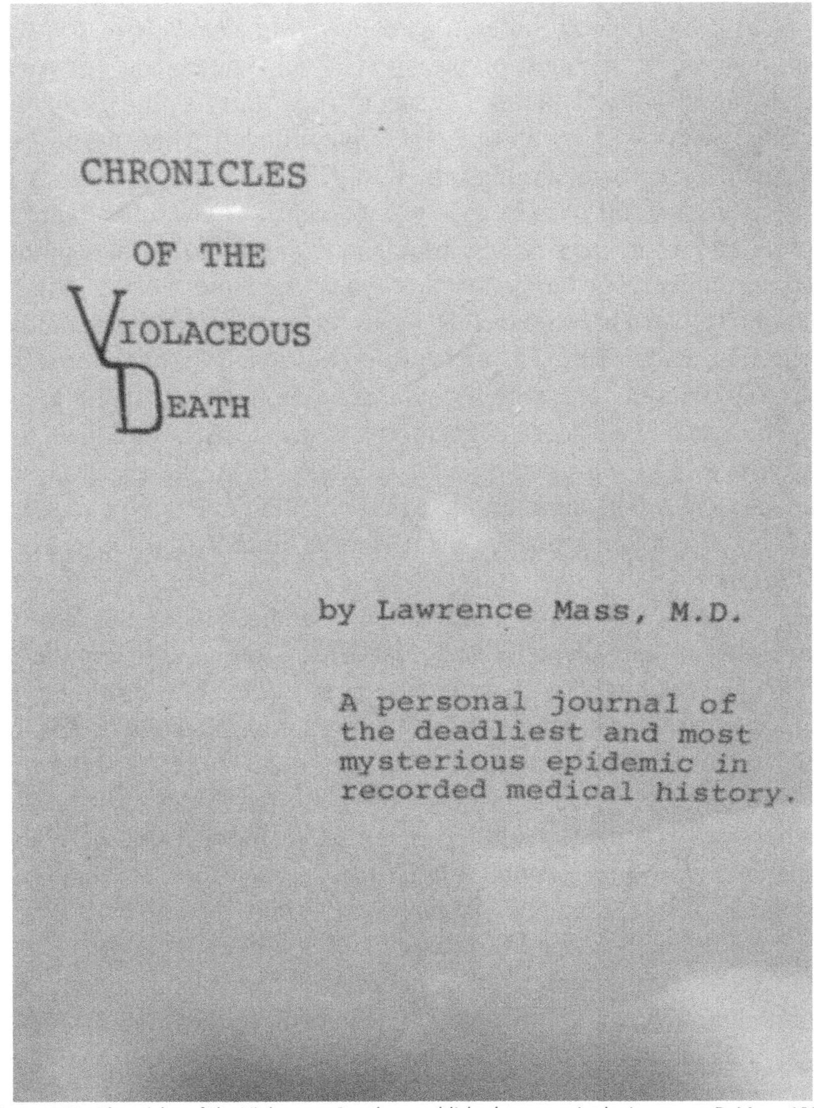
CHRONICLES OF THE VIOLACEOUS DEATH

by Lawrence Mass, M.D.

A personal journal of the deadliest and most mysterious epidemic in recorded medical history.

Figure 165 - *Chronicles of the Violaceous Death*, unpublished manuscript by Lawrence D. Mass, 1983, NYPL, LGBT collections (Lawrence D. Mass papers); written in the hedyday of my friendship with Marty and the unfolding of the AIDS epidemic.

I recall Marty's agent, Frances Golden who he writes about here with fondness and gratitude and who proved invaluable in helping Marty deal with Paul Robeson Jr. As the epidemic unfolded in 1981, I was ever-more desperate to find ways of getting my pieces together to better inform the public of what the Centers for Disease Control (CDC) had designated as "the most important new public health problem in the United States." As captured in *The Rest of It,* Marty was unhappy with much of the "privileged white male" discourse about "promiscuity" and the "sex panic" (not Marty's phrase) that was already metastasizing around the epidemic, At my urging and whatever his own misgivings, he asked Fran to have a look at my proposal for a book. What I gave her was a primitive collection of my reports and essays on AIDS, psychiatry, sex research and culture, pieces I culled together as an anthology with the working title of "Chronicles of The Violaceous Death" ("violaceous" was medical vernacular at that time for the purple skin plaques characteristic of Kaposi's Sarcoma and which could seem emblematic of the greater epidemic that was later to become known as AIDS). I had even sketched a logo: an upside-down Lambda on purple paper. Fran's response was swift, summary, and non-negotiable: No! Nor was there any encouragement from these quarters to further develop or direct this effort.

I remember Marty's cocaine and sedative-hypnotics (mostly Placidyl) use and dependence, his depression and insomnia, his ambivalence about admitting that he was an addict, his bottomings out and his experience in recovery, as surveyed in some detail in *The Rest of It.* In those years, the field of addiction medicine (I was among the first group of physicians to be certified by the American Board of Addiction Medicine in 1990) had not yet emerged, nor the SSRI's (Selective Serotonin Reuptake Inhibitors—Prozac and its analogues) and later anti-depressants. Addiction was still mostly overseen by psychiatrists with vestigial concepts and approaches. Today, people like Marty with complex of symptoms of depression, anxiety and withdrawal from addictive drugs would have been managed by addiction medicine and/or addiction psychiatry, now a subspecialty of psychiatry.

Criticism of 12-step recovery such as that expressed by Marty here is neither unprecedented nor uncommon, especially by those who reject it, which was initially but not ultimately the case with Marty. In the extent to which recovery insists on being apolitical and not involved in controversy, it can be as vexing to those who do their best to honor its precepts and remain in recovery as to those who choose to throw that baby out with the bathwater. The preamble of Alcoholics Anonymous states that "AA is not allied with any sect, denomination, politics, organization or institution, does not wish to engage in any controversy, neither endorses nor opposes any causes. Our primary purpose is to stay sober and help other alcoholics to achieve sobriety." Marty's impatience and frustration with such apoliticism—where conservatives and liberals are expected to interact in fellowship and service and relegate their judgments for their individual and collective well-being— could be anticipated and is in sync with what I remember of Marty's viewpoints from this time of entering recovery myself.

Following a denunciation in *The Rest of It* of a neighborhood meeting—in upscale West Chelsea, where Marty has lived all these years (currently the most expensive real estate in Manhattan)—for its predominance of privileged white males, it's to Marty's credit that he acknowledges going to other meetings where people of color and underserved communities were a lot more prevalent. Indeed, AA is not allied with any class, nor by any other measure, in terms of the diversity of its members. It cannot be designated as elitist, whatever the cliquishness, statements or peccadillos of individual members.

There are Trumpers in one of my still predominantly liberal home groups, as a result of which recovery can sometimes seem more challenging than ever. Like Marty, I want to question fundamental principles of recovery. I want to ask if Nazis and Jews should make nice together at meetings. Did they do so when AA was founded in 1935? The answer is a rather disturbing if qualified yes. When all is said and done and felt, I have no plans to lose my recovery over the politics of others, out of "the rooms," or in them. This was more or less Marty's journey as well.

Whatever his anticipated ambivalence about recovery, I was surprised that in writing of such candor, Marty does not mention a personal and medical decision that was not necessarily crucial to a discussion of the pros and cons of recovery but which was inarguably pertinent to his own experience and later distancing of himself from "the rooms" of recovery he does otherwise pay impressive tribute to. Following his heart attack and into his period of recovery, Marty was advised to consider having two drinks of red wine daily for its cardiotonic effects. Though alcohol was never Marty's preferred substance, and the alcohol was regarded as medicinal (and there is nothing bogus about the well-established facts of alcohol's cardiac healing effects), making the decision to go with the cardiology recommendation meant that continuing with recovery "in the rooms," which Marty does admit to having been helpful to him, would be challenging.

It's not clear from *The Rest of It* how long and to what extent Marty continued "in the rooms," but there can be no question of the enduring impact and importance of recovery for him. *The Rest of It* closes with the following testimonial:

*When I spoke at a Cocaine Anonymous meeting on my fourth anniversary of being "clean and sober," I talked about the comfort—not the supercharged excitement I'd earlier pursued—of my relationship with Eli. I choked up and had to stop for a few seconds. As I later wrote in my diary, "I've had little comfort (as opposed to acclaim) in my life—and feel so grateful to have it at last. I feel haunted with gratitude, surrounded by so much suffering in the world."*

I remember Marty's disinclination to travel, which yields some funny and endearing journal entries from a rare excursion to the countryside, in this case Maine. I remember his trigger impatience with some assistants and researchers, as recalled here, and at restaurants with waiters (not recalled here). I remember the realistic but repetitive designation of himself as a "privileged white male." I remember the sexual and romantic misadventures and dysfunction, the hustlers, the treks to Rounds, the upper east side gentlemen's hustler bar, and I remember how Arnie and I became unlikely role models, as a couple, for what would later become Marty's sustained partnership with Eli Zal. As recalled by Marty here, and as I likewise recall, he and Eli experienced real strains in their relationship early on. Comparably, Arnie and I had had our rough periods, yet we prevailed, and what they could see of what we had together Marty and Eli wanted as well for themselves.

Beyond recovery and his partnership with Eli, Marty's journey to greater balance and stability in his personal and creative lives is explored with sometimes breathtaking dexterity in *The Rest of Us*. For me, some of the book's richest passages are those describing the equipoise he comes to feel about all the different needs, impulses, persons and endeavors competing for his time and energies. Beyond challenges like drug addiction and sexual adventuring, he comes to see that he wasn't a freak, mental case or misfit, after all, even as psychiatry and society kept insisting otherwise. He comes to see and accept that writing, creativity, social consciousness and critical perspicacity were not his liabilities, not his illusions, not his defects and not his escapes so much as his essence and greatest passion, to be nurtured and cherished. Though he might be at once complimented by and aghast at the allusion, Marty is one of those who learned the hard way to proclaim, "I am what I am. I am my own special creation."

I also remember Marty's generous support of my memoir, *Confessions of a Jewish Wagnerite: Being Gay and Jewish in America,* which he blurbed and in fact introduced at a reading at A Different Light Books, owned and managed by my agent, Norman Laurila. I was reminded of this in *The Rest of It*, when Marty endearingly recalls his Orthodox Jewish room-mate at Payne-Whitney ("the loony bin"). Like most self-identified persons of the left, Marty was not deeply attuned to concerns of Jewish identity and anti-Semitism, especially as they were playing out in the Middle East, globally and in leftist discourses in those years. In view of which, and in light of the unremitting hostility of Orthodox Jews to gay civil liberties in New York, I was impressed with Marty's willingness to consider what I had to say as well as other viewpoints that may have felt less personal and compelling or even dystonic to him, while never relinquishing his ferocious commitment to social justice. Apart from his cognizance of the reality, enormity and threat of anti-Semitism in his historical novel *Jews Queers Germans*, and although he would occasionally put himself down for being a "Jewish prince," I don't recall him ever really discussing this aspect of his own background, either in casual conversation or in his writing. In not having ever acknowledged any personal experience of anti-Semitism (none that I recall), he was like Larry Kramer and many other Jews of liberal bent. If I ever knew anything about the Jewishness of his parents, his sister Lucile, Aunt Tedda or other relatives, I can't recall it now. Nor is it in *The Rest of It*.

There was, on the other hand, a telling email exchange between Marty and me following my review of *Jews Queers Germans* for *Huffpost.* Without specifying why, Marty said he identified with Walther Rathenau, the closetedly gay German-Jewish statesman who served as Foreign Minister during the Weimar Republic, as Germany raced towards Nazism. Rathenau was a philosopher of socialism who eased relations with Russia but who condemned Soviet methods. Inevitably, he incurred right-wing ire as a moderate liberal and Jew. I'm not sure what aspect of Rathenau's life and career Marty identified with most, but what keeps coming to mind for me is how Rathenau seemed relatively unaware of the enormity of anti-Semitism he was up against and that would eventuate in his assassination.

I think Marty and I both accepted the differences between us and our friendship seemed testimony to how those with differing viewpoints could still be good friends.

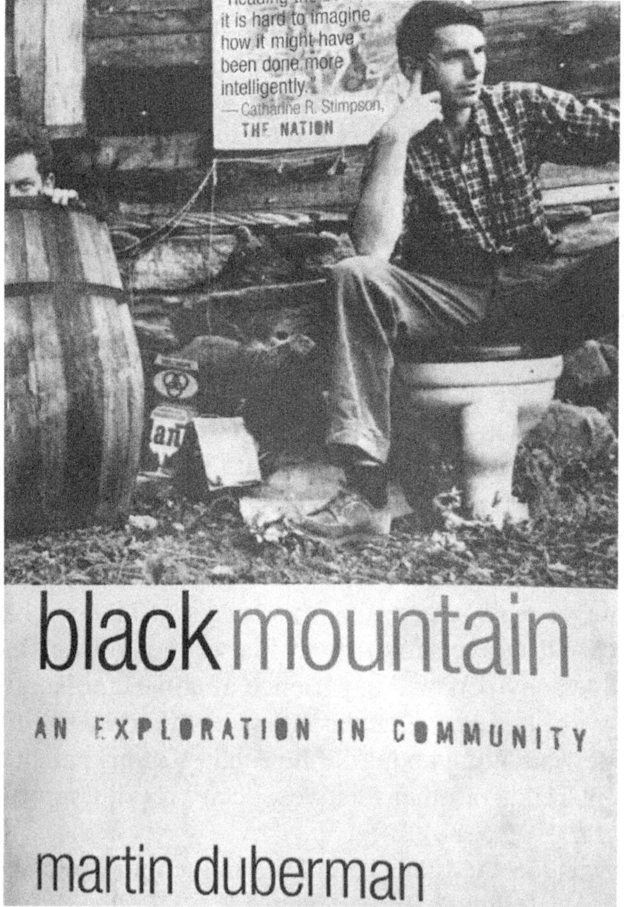


Figure 166 - *Black Mountain: An Exploration in Community* by Martin Duberman, Dutton, 1973, book cover photo, amazon.com

An additional note here re Marty's generosity. I recall another book event Marty hosted, this one at his home, for a friend of his who wasn't very well known in any circles and whose personal memoir had little social or literary interest and wasn't likely to have much reception or impact. It seemed reflective of Marty's deepest sense of commitment to helping those who are marginalized to have their say. I made note of this same aspect of Marty's character and service when I received a flier asking for support for a very marginalized group that Marty championed, so marginalized that it came and went in a matter of months: Queers for Economic Justice, which devoted its miniscule resources to acute problems of survival like homelessness. The tirelessness of such efforts of service on Marty's part, much of it heartbreaking and thankless, would be difficult to overstate.

Eventually, our friendship seemed to run its course. Nothing terrible happened, some minor misunderstandings that may have seemed like personal slights, but in the bigger picture, we were on seemingly different trajectories. If I appeared to be moving in the direction of more mainstream gay life with my Jewish identity and cultural issues and concerns about anti-Semitism and with my involvement in GMHC, Marty had taken the other fork in the road with CLAGS, which has done enormous good but which didn't seem especially welcoming to more mainstream LGBT persons like myself. In addition, Arnie and I grew increasingly uncomfortable with the anti-Israel rhetoric that we sensed to be veering into anti-Semitism on campus and otherwise from the left.

This inability to integrate at CLAGS was perhaps our own fault for not taking greater initiative to participate. If the left could seem boorish about "privileged gay white males"—a phrase or variant of which appears many times in the *The Rest of It*—and insensitive or worse on issues of Israel and anti-Semitism, we could be reflexively and commensurately defensive and critical of the left. I was never one to appear on panels. Arnie was better at that. Even so, and even if it's not an indictment, it felt subtly exclusionary that we were never invited to participate in anything at CLAGS, except to be supporters. The philosophy and vision of the epochal development of gay history and culture that is CLAGS and Marty's role in spearheading it, and highlights of the organization's early struggles and eventual triumphs, are summarized in *The Rest of It.*

Admittedly, I was and remain an odd duck. With my various interests in psychiatry, AIDS, hepatitis C, addiction, gay health, sexuality, the bear community, Jews, anti-Semitism, Wagner, music, opera, film and culture, I am someone who doesn't fit neatly in any camp. (Arnie, a CUNY professor of English and pioneer in gay studies, is a better fit for academic events and projects.) All OK. No hard feelings. Though we'd see each other and greet perfunctorily and sometimes awkwardly at movies in the neighborhood, we four (Marty and Eli, Arnie and I) dropped out of any regularity of communication for something like 20 years, from the mid-eighties to the recent period.

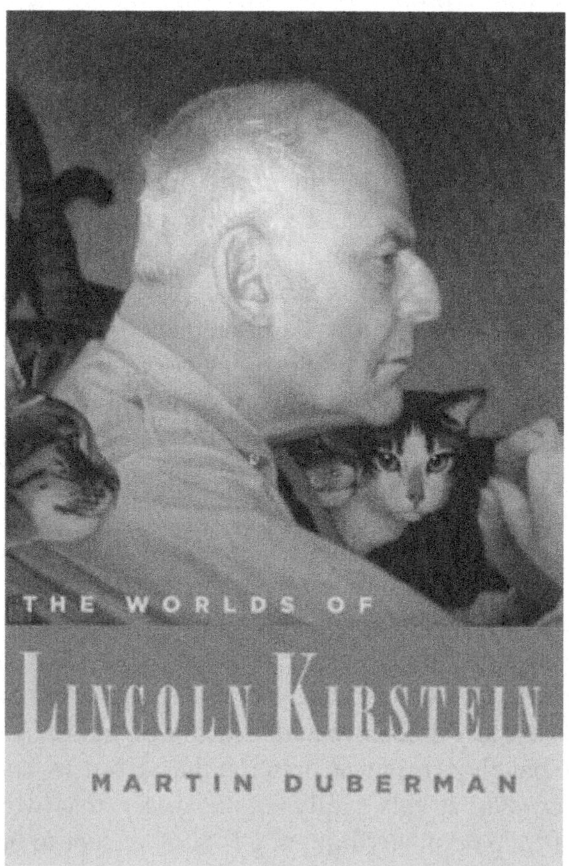


Figure 167 - *The Worlds of Lincoln Kirstein* by Martin Duberman, penguinrandomhouse.com, 2007

Some months ago, when I received a New York Public Library flier announcing Marty's reading from his new book, *Jews Queers Germans*, a subject right up my alley, Arnie and I decided to take the initiative in breaking the ice and attend the event. It was a wonderful evening and loving reunion. All our warmth of feeling and friendship returned, all of which repeated itself over a lovely dinner with Marty and Eli at their home some weeks later (at the time Marty did not know that I had read and was preparing a review of *Jews Queers Germans*). Joining us that evening was our old mutual friend Jonathan Ned Katz. It was wonderful to be back in Marty's and Eli's home, with its warm hues and arresting art and objects. Throughout his writing career, from *Black Mountain College* to *Lincoln Kirstein* to *Jews Queers Germans*, Marty has written about art and artists. Someday, I'd like to read his thoughts, if he ever wrote any down or has anything to say about them now, on the pieces he and Eli have collected over the years.

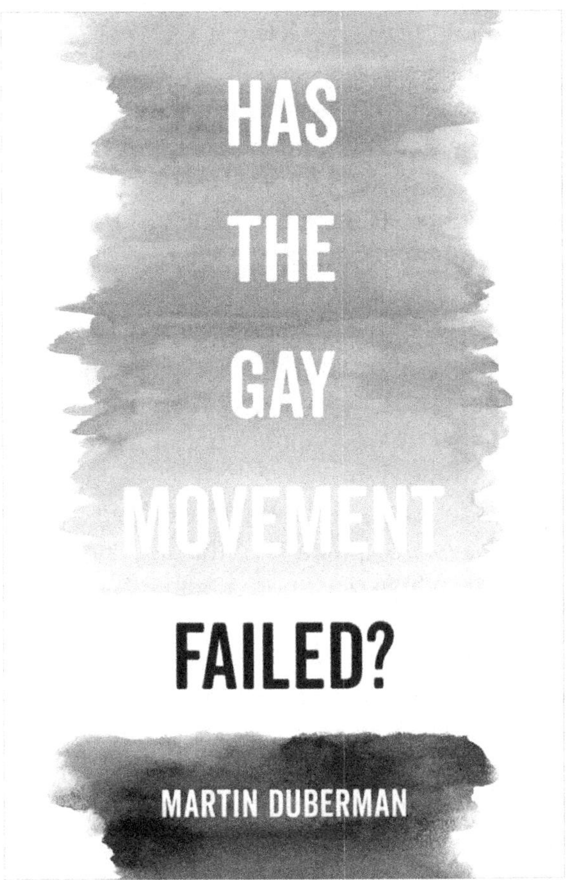


Figure 168 - *Has The Gay Movement Failed* by Martin Duberman, University of California Press, 2018, book cover photo amazon.com

For me, the most interesting passages in *The Rest of It* are the reflections on AIDS. It's honest and an accurate telling of his viewpoints as I recall them for Marty to clearly and repeatedly express his disappointment with the "privileged white male" centrism that seemed to characterize the trajectory of the greater gay and early AIDS movements. In the course of these discussions in *The Rest of It* there are interesting and worthwhile analyses of how a comparable dilution of energies and priorities into the mainstream overtook the civil rights and women's movements.

Yet there's also a quaintness to this discussion. For example, mere mention of the mainstream gay organization, the Human Rights Campaign Fund (HRCF), could elicit condescension and derision among leftists, as it does from Marty here in his recalling an expensive dinner at the Waldorf hosted by HRCF for Walter Mondale, whose support for our struggles was as lackluster as his speech. Meanwhile, acclaimed black actor Jeffrey Wright just gave what has to be among the most impassioned anti-Trump speeches of the current period at San Francisco's HRCF awards dinner.

On further reflection, is there not some failure of imagination and generosity of spirit in not recognizing that even "privileged gay white men" could be a vulnerable minority? Hopefully so, since anti-Semitism, historically and still among the most explosively virulent of prejudices, is likewise often rationalized around the scapegoating of Jews as an economically privileged elite, a phonemenon that can be as unmistakable in leftist economics rhetoric as in the more familiar racist vilifications of the right.

When it comes to left vs right, the truth about the early history of the unfolding of the AIDS epidemic in the gay community is not very flattering to the left, which was more notable for its absence than its participation. Paradoxically, in view of the strike against them for not ever having been involved in gay or other politics or activism, it was a ragtag of these "privileged white males" (a number of whom were Hispanic and black) who first responded to create the organization that became Gay Men's Health Crisis (GMHC). There is ample material in *The Rest of It* as well as in other chronicles of AIDS, including *Hold Tight Gently*, Marty's 2014 book on Michael Callen and Essex Hemphill, that explores this history of early responses and questions of perspective.

A note here regarding one of Marty's historical citations that seems obfuscating, however unintentionally so.

*"As early as 1981, a group of activists in San Francisco formed what later became known as the San Francisco AIDS Foundation, and soon after, New York City gave birth to GMHC, which rapidly became the largest organization in the country fighting AIDS."*

That there were already activists in both cities dealing with health issues is well-established. Likewise, one can generalize that gay activism in San Francisco was earlier, more progressive and successful than in New York. What seems misleading here is a sense that the San Francisco AIDS Foundation preceded GMHC and figured or even inspired its inception. As a co-founder of GMHC, I have no recollection of any such progression. Also, this description ignores the fact that GMHC also had its own forerunners, the first of which was the NYU Research Foundation for KSOI (Kaposi's Sarcoma and Opportunistic Infections), established months earlier, before the epidemic became officially known as AIDS. For the record, GMHC was incorporated in January 1982, the SFAF 3 months later, in April of 1982.

That many leftists were turned off by mainstream gay culture is understandable and, in retrospect, prophetic. Some of the most powerful material in *The Rest of It* is Marty's recalling how he felt about gay life back then, as most of us were living it.

*"I didn't feel at all confident about how 'left' the gay mainstream was...; discos, drugs and sex still maintained their primacy in urban, privileged, white male circles, preempting political activity...It felt increasingly true...that mainstream gay values were closely—and it seemed increasingly—indistinguishable from centrist, white middle class values."*

At this juncture, a few more words about my own background of coming out at UC Berkeley in the late 1960's. Though I was against the war in Viet Nam and generally on the same page with activists and protests in being against elitism, racism, sexism and homophobia, and though I participated in protests, I kept feeling left out and uncomfortable as gay in these milieus. As it turns out, my real coming out during those years at Berkeley took place in the bars and bathhouses of neighboring San Francisco with everyday working people, most of them personally and even conscientiously neither racist nor sexist, and some of whom were Hispanic and black, but who were not notably intellectual, political or activist. Rather, what they often seemed more notable for was sex, drugs, partying and being otherwise ordinary and detached from the political upheavals surrounding them, the very things the left has so relentlessly indicted mainstream gay men for. While the indictment may well have been justified, and I may have agreed with it then and later, it was these people, not the campus activists and leftists, who were the first to embrace me and make me feel real, comfortable, desired, happy and valued as a gay man.

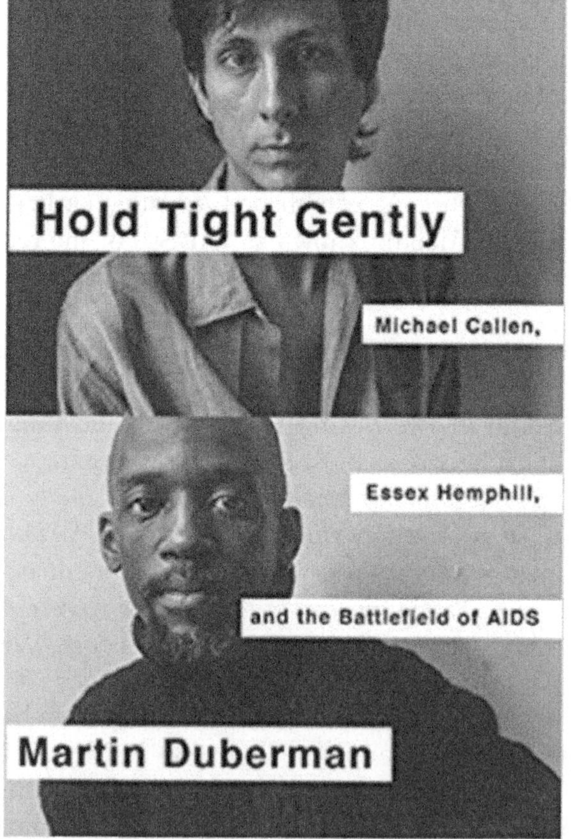


Figure 169 - *Hold Tight Gently* by Martin Duberman, The New Press, 2015

Of course, many leftists, especially women—Maxine Wolfe, Ann Northrop and Sarah Schulman, alongside others acknowledged by Marty, like Michael Callen—made huge contributions to AIDS and gay struggles in the heyday of ACT UP. Here too, however, Marty can seem to obsess on the extent to which activism was still dominated by mainstream figures and values. Consider the following passage about ACT UP's Treatment and Data Committee:

*...the prestigious and influential Treatment and Data Committee of ACT UP was primarily composed of entitled white men schooled from birth to believe that the world was their oyster; somewhere deep in the gut, they felt a kind of knee-jerk outrage that their presumptive destiny to lead comfortable, accomplished, untroubled lives had inexplicably run into a road block. Taught to overcome obstacles, they promptly devoted themselves to mastering the relevant science, and, remarkably, became peers of the scientific experts. The Committee's focus would remain on medical issues—who can criticize a determination to save one's own life?—refraining from involvement in 'peripheral' issues of social justice.*

At the conclusion of a later chapter, "The Salmagundi Controversy," a recap of that literary quarterly's hopelessly primitive but nonetheless pioneering effort to devote a whole issue to the topic of homosexuality, following devastating indictments of virtually all of the participants, Marty offers a more summary take on the aggregate phenomena of the gay and AIDS movements, as he had come to view them:

*Bland in deportment, narrow in social vision, the movement on the eve of the AIDS crisis was busily pledging allegiance to The American Way. It downgraded all talk of our "differentness," discarded any concern for the plight of the underprivileged (straight and gay), and energetically lobbied for the right to fully participate in a system that increasingly concentrated power and wealth in the hands of a few. Now and then, under extreme provocation—the Anita Bryant "Save Our Children" campaign or the California Briggs amendment to bar openly gay teachers—large numbers of angry protesters would take to the streets. (Yet even those were, at base, protestations of our ordinariness.) Those of us who—naively, perhaps—had believed the gay movement had the potential to become an instrument of transformational social change were shocked at the swiftness and ease with which it underwent a major face-lift and became a mere supplicant for equal "citizenship."*

*The AIDS crisis would reintroduce confrontational tactics, as well as demands for substantive change in standard health care procedures and the structure of medical research, but in the end ACT-*

*UP's imaginative lobbying only peripherally challenged existing social arrangements. The axis of privilege did not shift; the economic order did not reconstitute. Following the advent of protease inhibitors in 1996 and the shift in the focus of AIDS activism to a global dimension, the national gay movement featured, to the exclusion of almost all else, the assimilationist agenda of gay marriage and gays serving openly in the military...*

Having acknowledged these powerful feelings, which can seem more reactive, defensive, judgmental and resentful than his otherwise characteristic tolerance and compassion, what's remarkable and what can be surpassing is the soul-searching that ensues. At the conclusion of this section, "The Onset of AIDS," Marty writes, "Who was I to pass judgment?" After a cursory inventory of the actions he did take to help out with AIDS, albeit delayed and overshadowed by scholarly projects he was in the midst of (*Robeson*),

*"the nagging feeling remained," he observes, "that I wasn't doing enough to combat the AIDS crisis...something of an internal tug of war persisted...Perhaps if I'd felt more at risk personally, I would have reversed the ratio and invested more of myself in AIDS activism than in scholarship..."*

And less, one might add, in relegating and derogating those who did show up and help out. That said, one of the most winning things about Marty can be his willingness to consider and value opposing viewpoints without compromising his own. Thus it is that Marty initially battled heterosexism in rejecting older norms of monogamy as requirements for failed heterosexual standards of maturity, stability, health and happiness, even as he discovered that anonymous and casual multi-partner sex and sexual role-playing didn't work very well for him personally. Despite his own inner conflicts around casual and what would later be called "fast-lane" sex, and even in the face of the emerging epidemic of AIDS on top of a slew of other STD's, Marty was among the early and outspoken critics to bristle at old bugaboos of "promiscuity" and intolerance of sexual variance.

The same dialectic is apparent in his feeling about the greater history of AIDS and the gay community. Though he can't help but see how AIDS activism became this engine of mainstream gay values and priorities, he does acknowledge and praise the achievements of gay mainstream organizations like GMHC and the activism of ACT UP.

He himself became a GMHC buddy, though he was critical of Larry Kramer and *The Normal Heart*, which he felt:

"*'ruthlessly denigrates the good work of GMHC,' which for all its shortcomings had stepped into the breach when the heterosexual world (for the most part) turned its back, and had done heroic work in providing support for those suffering with AIDS...*"

Like me trying to warn everybody about sexual risk and, simultaneously, affirm the sexual revolution, Marty can seem to be speaking out of both sides of his mouth. Does he sometimes contradict himself? Very well, then, he sometimes contradicts himself. Not so unlike another sage of gay history and spirituality with whom he might be compared for compassion, valor, brilliance and vision, he is large and contains multitudes.

# Pearl in the Oyster: Is David Del Tredici the Robert Mapplethorpe of Classical Music?

***A new documentary captures the defiant gay soul of a leading "outsider" American composer***

– *Medium*, 5/27/2019

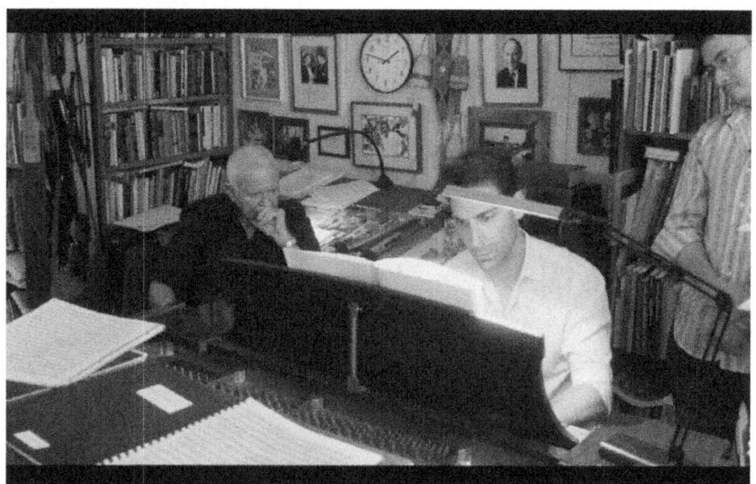

Figure 170 - Composer David Del Tredici with Filmmaker Daniel Beliavsky

Early in the course of my writing I embarked on a book project that was never completed. It was to be a collection of essays and interviews called *Musical Closets* on LGBT persons, issues and themes in music and opera. As part of that work (which included interviews with Lou Harrison, John Corigliano, David Diamond, Ned Rorem and others), but long after David Del Tredici (DDT) and I had already become friends, he and I worked on a conversation together that we eventually abandoned.

What David wanted to express and what he felt needed to be expressed about his life and work was somehow not emerging very well in our exchanges. That emergence is, however, achieved to a notable degree in a remarkable new documentary film by Daniel Beliavsky, *Secret Music.* Beliavsky, a filmmaker, pianist, composer and music theorist, is currently Chair of The Fine Art and Music Department of Yeshiva University. *Secret Music* took 7 years to create.

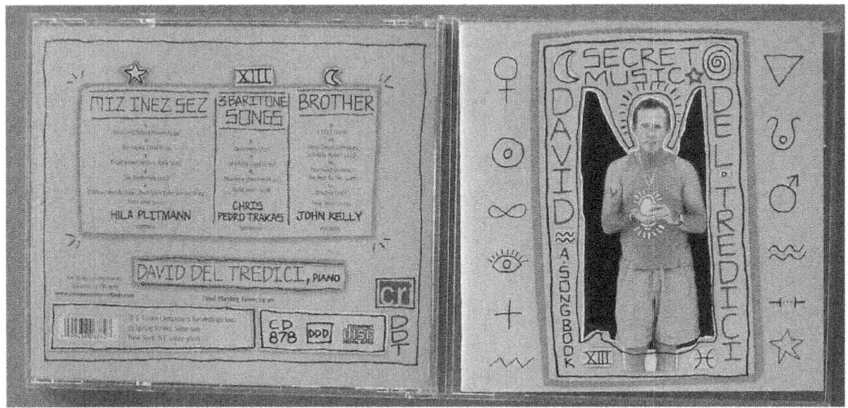

Figure 171 - Secret Music Songbook visual, Creative Commons

In that conversation with David, I was looking to ask questions that would shed a more analytical light on the gay erotics that seemed so insistently forefront in many of his compositions, especially the later ones. Was it because he was a product of earlier generations of gay men, when homophobic oppression was more global and menacing? As Beliavsky makes clear, such questions may be pertinent, but they are not the key to conjuring this genie.

Rather than ask why David and his music and subject matter are who and what they are—what *caused* all this?—Beliavsky starts from a place of appreciating the artist and his compositions on their own terms and seeks to experience and relate to them *a priori*. In thus identifying with the humanity and sensibility of David's art and music, the filmmaker captures what art is best at conveying: the universal in the individual.

With painstaking care, the film teases out and celebrates David's own very personal sense of the importance of his sexuality in his life and art, and in all its particulars, making no apologies or excuses and sparing the listener nothing. At first a bit awkwardly, but by turns evermore expressively, the filmmaker and an assortment of young, apparently mostly heterosexual singers and instrumentalists, passionately render lines that were mostly written for gay leathermen and gay s-m couples in David's own musical language and with effects that are possibly the most erotically explicit ever set to music. In "My Favorite Penis Poems" and other enactments of gay and s-m sex, there are such original "instrumental" ornaments as paddles, whips and chains accompanying cries and whimpers of pleasure and pain.

Figure 172 - David del Tredici with black leather jacket, daviddeltredici.com

***At first a bit awkwardly, but by turns evermore expressively, the filmmaker and an assortment of young, apparently mostly heterosexual singers and instrumentalists, passionately render lines that were mostly written for gay leathermen and gay s-m couples in David's own musical language and with effects that are possibly the most erotically explicit ever set to music.***

Under the guidance of the filmmaker, who is not gay, David and his soloists, one of them sporting *amour* handcuffs, bring all this to life with conviction and something more than *success d'estime*. David has endured years of subtle and not-so-subtle relegation from colleagues and critics and has too often faced less-than-sold-out performance spaces in pursuing his artistic calling. David may have become infamous for his dark humor and in-your-face subject matter, and exactly what he has achieved may continue to be debated, but what is certain and what is so inspiring in *Secret Music* is David's commitment to his muse.

He may have shown up at concerts—onstage and off—in drag or leather, often with a slave in tow and much to the consternation of colleagues, especially the more establishment and respectable gay ones. "One of our most flamboyant outsider composers" is how he was described by the *L.A. Times*. But in how true he has remained to himself and how fiercely he has persevered to express himself against the grain and against the odds, David Del Tredici is a heroic figure who deserves his distinguished place in musical and artistic halls of fame.

In the real-life world of academic music, of composing and teaching, of rank and status, David, a former Guggenheim and Woodrow Wilson fellow who taught at Harvard and other leading institutions, won a Pulitzer Prize in Music. Meanwhile, however, he has waged a war for nearly half a century to have gayness, s-m and leather, in all their colors, guises, vernaculars, outfits, fantasies, *accoutrements,* obsessions and compulsivities, enter the hallowed halls of a world that has yet to welcome women beyond the token few. It was in those decades of the heyday of David's career as well that blacks were still only beginning to break racial barriers.

The film is filled with gems, especially pearls. The reason there emerged such a predominance of gay composers in his day (e.g., Benjamin Britten, Aaron Copland, Leonard Bernstein, John Corigliano, Lou Harrison, Ned Rorem and many more), David suggests, is that they were all part of a generation of gay men who had struggled notably against homophobia. A fading of this plethora of gay composers, he feels, will be the price paid for the success of our present and future assimilation. It's like the pearl in the oyster, he mused. The pearl doesn't develop in the absence of an irritant. Take away homophobia and the setup is no longer in place for the production of so many gay pearls.

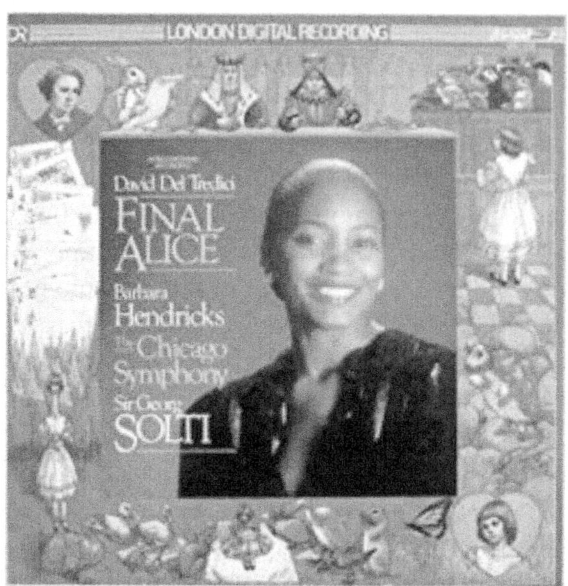


Figure 173 - Final Alice album cover, Grammy award-winning world premiere recording, starring Barbara Hendricks and conducted by Sir Georg Solti, amazon.com

Much of the mainstream public's knowledge of DDT is from his hugely successful crossover hit, *Final Alice,* based on Lewis Carroll's *Alice's Adventures in Wonderland* and its sequel, *Through the Looking Glass and What Alice Found There.* David wrote many *Alice* pieces, just as Mahler wrote many pieces based on the folk poems of *Das Knaben Wunderhorn*, but it's *Final Alice,* a great, sweepingly romantic and operatic concerto, if you will, for large orchestra and soprano that shattered success records for new works of classical music, won a grammy, and which saw David become anointed as the head of the "Neo-Romantic movement." For the sheer gorgeousness of its endless melodies, *Final Alice* is incomparable. One can see David in the character of Alice—and especially as portrayed by black soprano Barbara Hendricks— as an adolescent battling the overbearing forces of the "real" world of adults with its red queens, mad hatters and white rabbits, its rules and proscriptions, especially of desire. When David wrote the defiantly tonal *Final Alice,* it was in rebellion against the academic musical mainstream that had made atonality its party line, just as "flamboyant outsider" David, who has described himself as a "lapsed Catholic" (like another of his inspirations, James Joyce), was in rebellion against sexual repression.

In *Secret Music*, there's an emphasis on David's smaller and later works—e.g., Fantasy pieces, beautifully played by Beliavsky, the erotic works, and David's setting of Jaime Manrique's poem on the death and transfiguration of Matthew Shepard. There is engaging and affirming commentary from leading feminist musicologist Susan McClary, composer John Corigliano, singer Phyllis Bryn-Julson, conductor Leonard Slatkin and others.

When I described my elation about *Secret Music* on returning home from the screening to my life partner, veteran gay activist Arnie Kantrowitz, he commented on the resemblance of my descriptions to the saga of David's contemporary, photographer Robert Mapplethorpe. It's perhaps no coincidence that there's a new biopic of Mapplethorpe, who was like David in making s-m his principal artistic subject and whose darkly erotic sado-masochistic portraits are in counterpoint to the artist's menacingly beautiful renderings of flowers.

While AIDS lurks in the background of the life, times and work of both Mapplethorpe and Del Tredici, it never became the explicit subject matter of either artist in the heyday of their creativity. We need not further recap the controversy that stormed around Mapplethorpe, who later died of AIDS and who generously endowed AIDS research and care, except to note that when the exhibits of his work opened in several leading American cities, the powers that be did everything they could to close them down. In some cases they were successful. Remember Jesse Helms? That's why the need to show and to see *Secret Music* is urgent. Beliavsky says it has already been made clear to him by some producers and distributors that such is the level of his film's erotic content as it currently exists that it could not be presented in many public venues.

# Landscapes of the Soul: An Appreciation of Jaime Manrique

– *Medium*, 5/8/2019

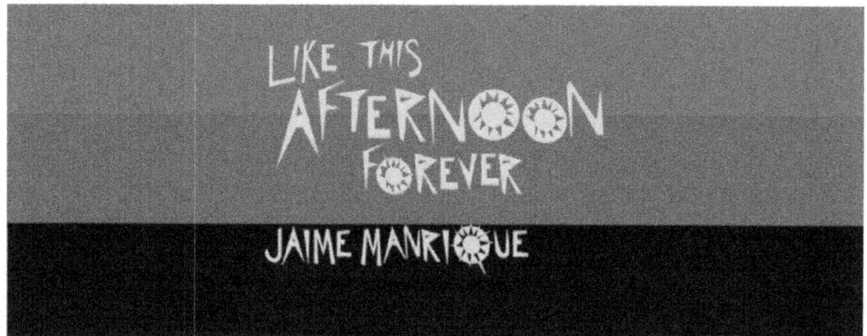


Figure 174 - book cover, amazon.com

**Like This Afternoon Forever is *an historical novel about Colombia and its indigenous peoples, its drug wars, the church, homosexuality and AIDS that captures the sweep of social conflict and change as it tells the stories of individuals, their lives and souls.***

Do you have any regrets? Most of the time it's hard to say you regret choices or actions or anything else because everything seems so bound up with everything else. Inevitably, the good is inextricably mixed up with what would otherwise be more clearly regrettable. Examples abound. Many alcoholics who have stopped drinking via recovery don't regret their affliction because they wouldn't otherwise have those priceless gifts of recovery—courage, wisdom and serenity.

In my own case, I can think of only one unqualified regret: that I never learned Spanish. The languages I did learn—French, Italian and German—were the principal languages of my first great love, opera. In the canon of Western opera, Spanish subjects and settings are commonplace—e.g., Mozart and Verdi, and there are rich traditions of Spanish operetta (*zarzuela)* andsong. However, though the opera houses of Spain, Mexico and South America have counted proudly in opera history and culture, as have many legendary Spanish opera singers—from Manuel Garcia to Placido Domingo and Montserrat

Caballe, Spanish composers of opera and operas composed in Spanish have been outside operatic mainstreams.

Where Spain and Spanish have turned out to be far more mainstream for me has had to do with the vibrant Spanish cultures with which I am increasingly surrounded in my life and work, coincidentally as I find myself evermore distanced from the world of opera that once loomed so much larger for me. If you were to remove Hispanic peoples from New York City and South Florida, my two homes, such is their presence that neither locale would be recognizable as such.

In my work in addiction medicine and AIDS, and especially with opioid use disorder amidst the present opioid crisis, a preponderance of my patients are Hispanic. Many of them don't speak English, a phenomenon that's even more pronounced in South Florida.

Figure 175 - Jaime Manrique, photograph by Isais Fanlo, Wikipedia

It's in this context of ever-burgeoning awareness of Hispanic cultures and their historical, ever-widening and otherwise incalculably great influence that I have been privileged to count as my close friend and colleague of 40 years leading Colombian novelist and poet Jaime Manrique. Protean and prolific, and with a family history of notable scribes dating back centuries, Jaime is a writer whose achievements are far too many to list. He has been called "the most distinguished gay Latino writer of his generation" by the *Washington Post*. He is the recipient of many honors and accolades, including, most recently in April 2019, the Bill Whitehead Lifetime Achievement Award.

For decades Jaime has been my friend in community as well as a colleague and mentor for my writing. In the recent period, we find ourselves endlessly upset and commiserating around the takeover of the world, here and nearly everywhere else, by what Jaime refers to summarily as "the caudillos." Trump, Maduro, Putin, Bolsonaro, Duterte, Orban, Salvini, Erdogan, Xi Jinping, Kim Jong Un, etc., all of them generic authoritarians.

I loved Jaime's first novel, *Latin Moon In Manhattan*, a collection of farcical tales of Manhattan, Latino and gay life that skewers the machismo that at once attracts and oppresses us. And it's through Jaime's *Eminent Maricones*that I became more intimately acquainted with such giants of international culture as Reinaldo Arenas, Manuel Puig and Garcia Lorca. Jaime's ability to render these great figures of our lives and times with flesh-and-blood dimension has been priceless, and has contributed notably to the pantheon of global gay history and culture.

Figure 176 - Twilight at Olana by Bill Sullivan, Hudson River Art, Hudson River Museum

It was during this period of *Latin Moon* that I became friends with Jaime and his partner, Bill Sullivan. Bill was a painter, mostly of landscapes. He and Jaime traveled together extensively in Latin America, where Bill captured shores, landscapes and sunsets of singular, often breathtaking color and luminosity. Eventually, Bill settled in Hudson New York where he became a regional painter of renown.

But Bill's pioneering talents and gifts extended as well to literature. Inspired by Jaime, he became an independent publisher of gay literature, most notably of Jaime's early work, during a time when outlets for gay writing were very few and far between.

As I was privileged to experience it with them, theirs was a tumultuous, artistically fruitful collaboration that was redolent of the relationship between Bill's beloved Frida Kahlo and her patron, lover and husband Diego Rivera. In both pairings, love turned out to be the catalyst for a continuous outpouring of serious and enduring art.

Bill adored Jaime and never wavered in his belief in Jaime's gifts, even as his own fortunes, commingled with illness, began to decline. Eventually, Bill died following a series of heart attacks. Although his life became painful and challenging, there was an always discernible, unshakable core of happiness with his own life's work as a painter and in his love for and belief in Jaime.

When Bill died at 68 in 2010 Jaime had just completed his novel, *Our Lives Are The Rivers*, about Manuela Saenz, the mistress of Simon Bolivar, and was at work on *Cervantes Street,* a biographical novel about the fabled author of *Don Quixote.* Each of these historical works took nearly a decade to research, create and publish.

Figure 177 - Books by Jaime Manrique in multiple languages, uncredited photograph, public domain

***Jaime Manrique is the author of novels and poetry collections that were written in English and Spanish and that have been translated into other languages, including Russian, Chinese and Hebrew.***

Along the way, there have been many notable poems, essays and collections by Jaime. One I had occasion to encounter again recently was his ode to Matthew Shepard, in which the victim of a vicious, lethal homophobic attack is left tied to a fence overnight to die from his wounds and exposure. As drying, crusted blood glues his eyes shut, he imagines the sunrise in all its splendor. This and other of Jaime's poems have been set to music by Pulitzer Prize-winning composer David Del Tredici. *Tarzan, My Body, Christopher Columbus*, follows Jaime's first poetry collection, *My Night With Garcia Lorca*, and includes an epic poem about Columbus, coinciding with the 500th anniversary of Columbus's arrival in the New World, and features an introduction by Reinaldo Arenas.

Figure 178 - photograph by Lawrence D. Mass

***Jaime Manrique with Isaias Fanlo, to whom* Like This Afternoon Forever *is dedicated, at the 2019 Publishing Triangle Awards, where Jaime was the recipient of the Bill Whitehead Award for Lifetime Achievement***

Jaime's new novel is called *Like This Afternoon Forever.* Based on a true story that created waves throughout Latin America, it's about two priests who grew up together and became lovers amidst the brutal, complicated 50 year civil war in Colombia between the government and anti-government rebels. In the course of their lives and relationship, Lucas and Ignacio must come to grips with challenges of faith, AIDS, drugs, war atrocities, and loss; and with the secret they uncover of the "false positives," mostly indigenous people whose only offense is to try to be treated humanely and who are murdered, then falsely dressed as armed, anti-government combat insurgents and rebels as a way of collecting bounties.

Like Jaime's other writing, the novel is fleet, clear, and so humbly and economically written as to seem effortless. In tone, it's as if a good, trusted friend or relative were telling you a story you could always follow and that is always somehow comforting, even as it draws you evermore deeply into realms of danger, suffering and tragedy.

Like *Our Lives Are The Rivers* and *Cervantes Street*—and like *Gone With The Wind* and *War and Peace—Like This Afternoon Forever* is an historical novel that conveys the sweep of social conflict and change across a great swath of the globe and recent history. Reverberating in the background of the novel are the news media sound bytes we in the West have heard over the years about the FARC (the Revolutionary Armed Forces of Columbia) and about the displacement, disappearances and slaughter of indigenous peoples, like those so desperately seeking refuge at our borders today. Likewise in the background are those vague, inadequate snips of information we would hear or read about liberation theology, alongside this or that war skirmish, rebellion or atrocity.

Jaime Manrique acts as our guide and shepherd by putting many of those disparate pieces together into a mosaic that not only conveys present day realities and looming disasters, but which brings the "manifest destiny" of European colonization with its bloody history of conquest, conversion, enslavement and the genocide of many millions of indigenous peoples, into a focus sharper than many of us had imagined possible for ourselves. Through Jaime Manrique, our world has become a lot larger and a lot more inclusive.

*Like This Afternoon Forever* is also a rich study of character and faith. Lucas and Ignacio have approached their missions from different backgrounds and temperaments. Together as soul mates, they travel otherwise apposing individual trajectories towards faith, always a deeply personal, inside job that no one else can do for them or, as they help us see, for ourselves.

Along the way are issues of the church, homosexuality and AIDS. Especially interesting is Ignacio who has the intellectual acuity, honesty and courage to admit that he cannot believe in God as most people do, or even at all, but comes, instead, to believe in the power of helping people. The faith he develops is not a belief in idols or images or rituals or institutions, but rather in the humility, power and happiness he experiences in helping others. Complex and thorny, these issues that play out in the lives of the two lovers reverberate globally. The personal is political, as we say.

Hopefully, the personal journeys of *Like This Afternoon Forever* will help lead to broader political changes that lessen prejudice against indigenous peoples, immigrants and gay people, and ignorance and intolerance around AIDS. If someone wants to know the realities of gay people and the church and AIDS, and not just in Latin America, they should read *Like This Afternoon Forever,* rather than the latest homophobic poison from former Cardinal Ratzinger, the former Pope Benedict. Hopefully, this book will be read by Pope Francis, who seems at least somewhat more open to a modern, compassionate understanding of gay people. *Like This Afternoon Forever* might help him find the same courage to stand for his principles against rising tides of murderous homophobia as he has shown for the desperately besieged indigenous peoples and immigrants of the world.

# Composer Michael Shapiro on Ethnicity, Judaism and Music

– *Medium* 12/10/19

Figure 179 - photograph from the personal collection of Lawrence D. Mass

***from left: Michael Shapiro, Gottfried Wagner, John Corigliano, William M. Hoffman at Lawrence D. Mass at the home of Michael Shapiro, Chappaqua, 1995. All were co-signatory to a Letter to the Editor published by the New York Times (November 22, 1998) critical of Joseph Horowitz's troubled NYT review of Marc Weiner's epochal Wagner and the Anti-Semitic Imagination.***

Like his American forbears George Gershwin and Aaron Copland, Michael Shapiro is a distinctively American composer whose works reverberate with the idioms, rhythms and colors of polyglot, melting-pot America. A glance at his website is like savoring a gumbo. So many ingredients. So much flavor.

He recently completed a large scale work entitled *Voices* for soprano soloist, chorus, and chamber ensemble based on Sephardic poetry of the *Shoah* which will be premiered in Spring 2020 in

Washington, D.C., with subsequent performances in Prague, Manhattan and Montclair, New Jersey.

His *Archangel* Concerto for piano and orchestra was recorded by Steven Beck with Michael Shapiro conducting the BBC National Orchestra of Wales. His *Roller Coaster,* premiered by Marin Alsop conducting the Cabrillo Festival of Contemporary Music Orchestra, and the entr'acte from his first opera *Perlimplinito, Opera Sweet, A Lace Paper Valentine,* have also been recorded, as have his song cycles.

He is currently working on a full-length musical theater work called *Getting In*, story by Greg Sego, as well as 24 piano pieces called *Passages* based on Torah and Haftorah portions, a revision of *The Headless Horseman* for the 200th anniversary of Washington Irving's *Legend of Sleepy Hollow*, and the Third Symphony.

His new work for band *Ol' Mississippi Sings the Blues* was performed by lead commissioner, the University of Memphis, Albert Nguyen, conductor, in Memphis and on tour in Tennessee, as well as at Kennesaw State University in Georgia.

This past year's performances of Michael Shapiro's music for the classic talkie film *Frankenstein* included its European premiere at the Bergen International Festival with a repeat performance by the Dallas Winds and the United States Navy Band in Dallas. His new operatic version *Frankenstein-The Movie Opera* will be premiered with the Los Angeles Opera in October, 2020.

Along the way, Shapiro's music has been played in dozens of venues nationally and internationally, with regional and chamber ensembles as well as major University and metropolitan symphony orchestras.

Regionally, he is best known as "Conductor Extraordinaire" of the Chappaqua Symphony.

Figure 180 - photograph from the composer's website, michaelshapiro.com

***Composer Michael Shapiro has given new life to* Frankenstein, *his operatic setting of which, based on the classic James Whale film, is set to premiere with the Los Angeles Opera in 2020***

My friendship with Michael Shapiro goes back more than 30 years, when I met him through Gottfried Wagner, great grandson of composer Richard Wagner. Gottfried is best-known as the black sheep of the Wagner family for their being what he considers to have been perpetrators of the Holocaust.

What follows is my interview with Michael, conducted over lunches and via correspondence in the summer of 2019.

**Larry**: A book project I had planned in the 1980's, before homosexuality came out of the closet in the music world, was "Homosexuality and Music: LGBT Persons, Themes and Issues in Music and Opera." It's a book I did a lot of work for but which was never completed for several reasons, one of which jumps out at me now: the subject is just too diverse, fluid and uncontainable. There are no characteristics that resonate across the great spectrum of LGBT composers the way nationality seems to for music. We are comfortable talking about French, German, Italian and Russian composers and musics but we shy away from talking about "gay music." Tchaikovsky may have been a composer who was gay, but if we wanted to describe him summarily, we'd say that he was a Russian composer or a romantic composer. In this same vein, we are comfortable talking about German composers—Bach, Gluck, Mozart, Brahms, Schubert (who may have been gay) and Wagner.

In fact, when it comes to this commonality of what is German or not, there was an epochal development: an essay "Judaism and Music" by Richard Wagner. Just as I wanted to find affirmative and affirming commonalities among LGBT composers and musics, Wagner wanted, like Donald Trump, to find and amplify any perceived racial or ethnic differences, in this case between Jewishness and German-ness, if you will, in music. So was Wagner right in his principle of drawing distinctions? *Are* we justified in talking about Jewishness and music? And by the same token, are we justified in talking about "Gayness in music"?

**Michael**: Of course Wagner wasn't right! Wagner's Jewish contemporaries Mendelssohn and Meyerbeer composed out of their life experiences and who they were (as did Wagner himself and as I do). I learned long ago that one cannot hide who one is when creating music. Who one is comes out in the notes. How deep your thought, how loving the message, how talented you are, how melodious, how learned.

I am a Jewish American born in Brooklyn, NY in 1951, exposed since to my family, my community (secular and religious), the popular and classical music of my time (and times before), to life's experiences. All of these come out in my compositions. The better the composer, the more these life experiences and the personality of the writer, are revealed.

**Larry**: OK, So *are* we justified in talking about Jewishness and music?

**Michael**: Yes, we are, but not in the way Wagner did in his infamous essay. There are certainly Jewish melodic strains or patterns in my music. Half of my music I would say is directly influenced by my background (my father Sam was a Klezmer clarinetist). This influence is sometimes buried in the phrases (such as in my Second Symphony or *Archangel* Concerto for Piano and Orchestra). Only more obvious in my pieces derived from traditional melodies such as my *Eliahu Hanavi* Variations for solo violoncello or my *Peace Variations* for solo violin.

**Larry**: And by the same token, are we justified in talking about "gayness" in music?

**Michael**: I am not sure what this means. Is Aaron Copland's unfussy orchestration the result of his being a gay Jewish boy from Brooklyn or more likely the influence of Boulanger and Stravinsky on clarity of musical thought? Is Tchaikovsky's golden orchestration a result of his closeted gay life or more likely, the result of composing in the elaborate and gilded culture of Czarist St. Petersburg?

**Larry***:* Clearly, like me and a majority of serious music lovers, Jewish and non-Jewish, you were smitten by Wagner's art. And also like me and others, but far fewer, you came to an understanding and acceptance of the seriousness of Wagner's anti-Semitism.

This seems likewise to have been the case with your close friend and colleague of decades, Gottfried Wagner. But Gottfried has been a lot more careful not to indulge memories or feelings of having been thus smitten. He's like Parsifal, determined at the risk of his own life never to allow arts of seduction to prevail. Have you ever known Gottfried to admit to having been seduced, like you and me, by the music and art of his great grandfather?

**Michael**: Gottfried has remarked to me that the only Wagner opera he likes is *Tristan*. It is a love story with no political or anti-Semitic overtones, no xenophobia; just a tragedy.

**Larry***:* If someone were to refer to you as a "Jewish Wagnerite" and ask if that were an accurate description, what would you say?

**Michael***:* I would object. As I have mentioned to you, I am a musician and am in awe of Wagner's great talents as an orchestrator and the creation of sounds like no one else has ever created. But I am repelled by his message of hate. There is nothing warm in Wagner's music. He is always passionate but it is ice cold.

Also, my Jewish background is not tied in any way to those Jews who pre-War took the pilgrimage to Bayreuth and prayed to the great god Richard.

**Larry***:* What is your sense of the world of Jewish Wagnerism and Jewish Wagnerites?

**Michael**: If such world contains a denial or ignorance of his abhorrent messages, then it is the practice of a kind of self-hate. Interestingly, Theodore Herzl had some of these traits. His appearance in top hat and tails in front of the Kaiser was almost Wagnerian.

**Larry**: Do you think Jewish Wagnerism has been good for the Jews?

**Michael**: I don't think so. It's hard, however, for a Jewish boy from Brooklyn in the 21st Century to put himself in the mind of Gustav Mahler in the early 1880s when his student friend Hugo Wolf and he met Wagner briefly in Vienna.

**Larry**: What I'm asking is something more global. Has all that devotion to Wagner by the Hermann Levis, Mahlers, Soltis, Levines, Bernsteins, Barenboims and countless other distinguished Jewish conductors and artists brought Jews and the worlds of music and culture to a more elevated place of understanding and transcendence?

**Michael:** Although there are examples or residue today of Jewish Wagnerism in some people, I think the *Shoah* knocked the concept on its proverbial t*uchis*.

Figure 181 - CD album cover, michaelshapiro.com

***Archangel Piano Concerto, Recording Project by composer Michael Shapiro with Steven Beck, pianist, and the BBC National Orchestra of Wales.***

**Larry:** Your latest piece is called *Archangel*. What a wonderful subject. Wikipedia notes that Archangel Michael is mentioned three times in the Book of Daniel, and that the idea that Michael was the advocate of the Jews became so prevalent that, in spite of the rabbinical prohibition against appealing to angels as intermediaries between God and his people, Michael came to occupy a certain place in the Jewish liturgy.

Archangels are apparently common as well to all the major and various minor religions. Beyond your being Michael, Jewish and gifted as a composer, what drew you to this subject?

**Michael**: I was first drawn to the idea of the Archangel when I was reacquainting myself with John Milton's *Paradise Lost*. His description of the casting out of Satan from Heaven and rising up with his demons against the forces of the Archangel Michael rang deeply. The epic story of the battle between good and evil rages on—in the arch of our lives, and beyond.

**Larry**: Are you, Michael Shapiro, one of our archangels? Are you an intermediary not only for Jews, but for the world?

**Michael**: I am drawn to the idea of righteous people (in Yiddish *tsaddikim*) fighting in their way against evil. My piano concerto is in two "parts" rather than movements. Part One depicts the war between the forces of good and evil (depicted in *Paradise Lost*, and Book Two portrays Adam and Eve (and the Serpent) in Eden and their being cast out into the world we all live in, a world of the rise of mechanized evil (the *Shoah* being the prime example), and the resistance against tyranny.

**Larry**: Your opera *Frankenstein* has a forthcoming premiere with the Los Angeles Opera. What can you tell us of your experience with this work and why it's still relevant today?

**Michael**: First, James Whale's great early talking film starring Colin Clive and Boris Karloff had no music. In 2002 I wrote the score which is played live simultaneously with the picture in movie theaters and concert halls. Its instrumental versions (chamber orchestra, full orchestra, and wind ensemble) have received over 50 performances worldwide including the European premiere at the Bergen International Festival in Norway, a recording by the City of Birmingham Symphony Orchestra in the UK, and about a dozen performances every year throughout the US and Canada.

The new operatic version uses the Latin *Requiem* Mass as its libretto. The *Requiem* Mass is about Resurrection. The Latin is magisterial and beautifully written. The film is also about, among other things, resurrection and the war between good and evil, as well as a doctor who plays at being G-d. The juxtaposition of the *Requiem* text with the film I believe will be potent.

**Larry**: Also, does it have relevance to our dialogue about Jews and music?

One of the movie's great themes is the depiction by James Whale of the Monster as "the other," not an unfamiliar theme for Jewish people (or Wagner's Wandering Jew, *The Flying Dutchman*).

**Larry***:* Does *Archangel* have comparable relevance?

**Michael**: It has the relevance I have programmed into the piece. The relevance that it is our responsibility to fight against darkness in any way we can. My piece is not only a depiction of this struggle, but I hope a warning.

# Colossus of Historical and Satirical Fiction: Volume 2 of *The American People*, Larry Kramer's Epic Novel of the AIDS Epidemic, Gay History and America

– *Medium* 1/3/20

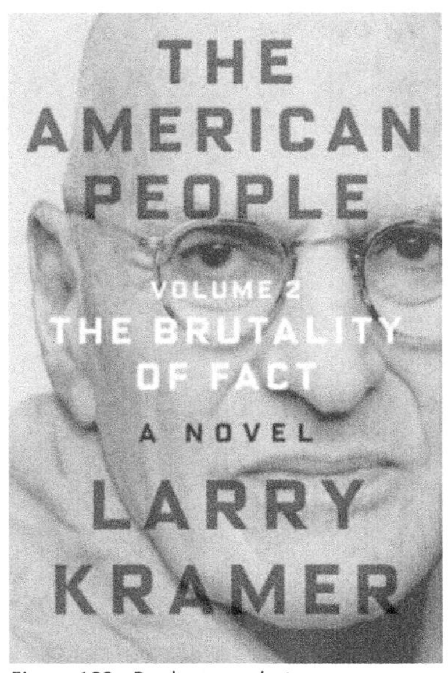


Figure 182 - Book cover photo, amazon.com

***The American People, Volume 2: The Brutality of Fact, a novel by Larry Kramer, Farrar, Straus and Giroux, 2020, 880 pages***

"If I couldn't write, I would die." — Larry Kramer

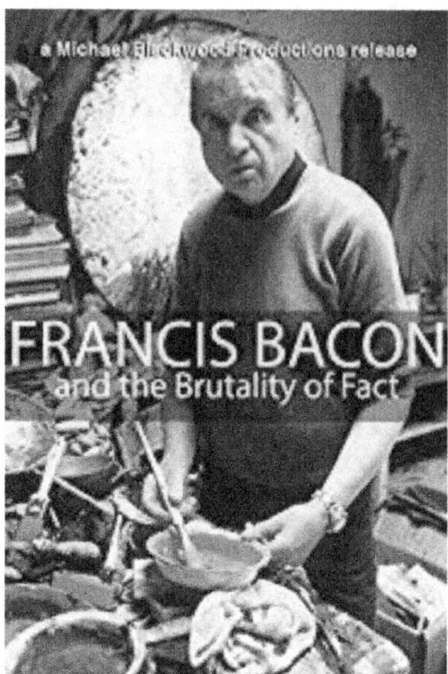


Figure 183 - film documentary, www.imdb.com

## *Francis Bacon and George Orwell*

The bodies depicted by the painter Francis Bacon tend to be horrifying. They emerge from darkness and appear to be disfigured, especially the face and mouth. When Larry Kramer was in London, he became acquainted with Bacon and spent time in his studio.

During the 1970's, in the aftermath of his screenplay for the academy-award nominated film *Women in Love* and amidst the early post-Stonewall explosion of gay liberation that fueled Larry's first novel *Faggots*, I had a handful of friends in New York, where I relocated from Boston in '79. Larry was central to this social life which included Alex Gotfryd, a distinguished photographer and the art director of Doubleday. Alex, it was known, had endured experimental surgery on his face as a child during his family's internment in Nazi concentration camps. Above the mantel in Alex's living room was a dark painting of a figure with an anamorphic face and mouth, an original work by Francis Bacon.

Larry recently said he has little recollection of Alex's background or his Bacon painting, but it occurred to me that a very dark portrait of the American people that oozes the horrors of torture, atrocity, totalitarianism and genocide would have been as natural a subject for Francis Bacon as it became for George Orwell and Larry Kramer.

Here is what Orwell famously said of humanity and the future:

**"If you want a vision of the future, imagine a boot stamping on a human face — forever!"**

And here is the epigraph that introduces the reader to Volume 2 of Larry Kramer's *The American People*:

**"The goal of every serious artist is to rework reality by artificial means to create a new vision of the world intensely more truthful than anything ever seen before."**
**— Francis Bacon, from *Francis Bacon and The Brutality of Fact*, 1987**

### *The Imperative of Writing*

The 2019 December Holiday issue of the *New York Times* Style Magazine is devoted to "Rewriting History through a Queer Lens." In a bravura piece by Jesse Green, the rapidly expanding canvases of gay art and culture are surveyed to show the many ways in which history is being reimagined and recreated and how the future of history is being thereby redirected. "The Future is Ours and So Is the Past," proclaims the cover. With great verve and enviable clarity, Green surveys the bevy of artists, playwrights and novelists in the vanguard of these developments, among whom is Larry Kramer. Of the first volume of *The American People*, Green observes: "It has the urgency (and chaotic despotism) of truth — if not always a particular truth, then at least a general one."

To have clarity about what Larry Kramer has achieved with his magnum opus, *The American People, Volumes 1 and 2,* we must begin with the imperative of writing in the author's life. A theme of my Larry Kramer anthology, *We Must Love One Another or Die: The Life and Legacies of Larry Kramer*, is the paramount importance of writing for Larry. That collection came together in the early 90's, still in the heyday of AIDS activism, and some of those I interviewed took issue with my contention that Kramer's writing was even more important — to him and to us — than his activism. Of course, both viewpoints are valid. While Kramer's writing and his plays are likely to surpass AIDS in interest and relevance, his activism will always be intrinsic to his legacy.

A window on this issue of the activism versus the art of Larry Kramer is how people have responded to Kramer over time. Whether it be the public call-to-arms Larry or literary-theatrical Larry, people are often initially put off by his tone and question his credibility. Not surprisingly, this is already the case with *The American People* (*TAP*). Most people I know, including many admirers of Kramer, haven't read it and don't plan to. Others put it on the shelf after initial efforts to peruse it.

Yes, Kramer is this great activist hero and writer, we all now reflexively concede, but the two-part novel is 2,000 pages (having been edited down by half), covers familiar territory, is filled with Kramer's trademark shit-and-fuck invective and once again declaims much that is semi-fictional and seems hyperbolic. Yes, Kramer turned out to be right about almost everything in the past, but this time, isn't it OK for us to indulge our old reflexes that Larry Kramer is the blaming, judging, unpleasant scourge we would always, at least initially, recoil from? And now that AIDS is treatable and gay rights have advanced, albeit in no small measure thanks to Kramer and even if it's all once again under great threat, do we really need another retelling of his story by him?

### *Moses vs Cassandra*

The answers to these questions are already obvious. If Kramer's track record of being prophetic, of turning out to be right, of capturing the essences of issues and feelings and trends, is so impressive, why are we once again hesitating to accord him the respect he has earned and give this greatest of his literary endeavors, decades in the making, the seriousness it deserves? Maybe it's because what he has to tell us is so dreaded. Maybe it's also because, as Kramer himself has observed, most recently in conversation with his biographer Bill Goldstein, he wanted to be Moses but ended up being Cassandra.

Petronius, Voltaire, Swift, Dickens, Orwell, Waugh. In trying to place Kramer in the context of other writers, it's helpful to recall how the early writings and speeches of Larry Kramer were initially received. Several early passages in Volume 2 capture reactions to *Faggots*. Though the work was ultimately acclaimed, it was initially greeted with outrage by most of the gay activist community it so relentlessly pilloried, including me.

In my *Confessions of a Jewish Wagnerite*, *Faggots* is described as follows: "It would be as if James Baldwin had written what was expected to be *the*major novel of emerging black consciousness in the early 1960's — a time when the overwhelming majority of portrayals of blacks was still mired in negative stereotypes — and all the characters turned out to be petty welfare chislers, pimps, alcoholics and heroin addicts who do nothing but victimize each other in a 'black' comedy entitled *Niggers*." In my memoir, I satirically refer to *Faggots* as "*The Sissy*" and *The Normal Heart* as "Here's What's Happened To The Community That Rejected *The Sissy* or I'll Show Ya Who The Sissy Is Ya Fuckin Faggots!"

So how did I go from there to later describing *Faggots*, on the dust jacket of its British re-release, as "the funniest and most dazzling evocation in all of gay literature"? That's what happens with the writings of Larry Cassandra Kramer over time. What initially seems arrogant, self-righteous, judgmental, vindictive, over the top and otherwise off-putting, becomes better appreciated as brave, truthful, soulful, deeply caring and visionary. Oh, and let's not forget funny!

### *The Reagans*

This challenge of Kramer's writing, of how it morphs over time, can be appreciated in my own experience of his excoriations of the Reagans. Starting with the premise that they were sexual, Kramer, in various personas as both Fred Lemish and Ned Weeks in *TAP*, ponders the mechanics of their sexuality. What did they do with each other, especially when they were younger? Did they prefer blowjobs, anal sex, three-ways? In Hollywood, did Reagan ("Peter Ruester" in *TAP*) never succumb to gay seductions? According to Kramer, there are plenty who attest he did. Did Nancy never sleep around? Did she not lust after others? Notoriously, according to Kramer, at least prior to Ronny. And what exactly did she like to do sexually and with whom? Can we agree she was into big cocks?

Is this not the worst kind of gossip and slander, even if it's also clearly satirical? Yet, as with the best of satire, the more Kramer asks these questions, and the more you ponder them, the more plausibly reflective of greater truths these caricatures become. Finally, even as we recognize them to be more in the vein of conspiracy theories and fake news, they resonate to strip the teflon emperor and his domineering wife of their political raiments to expose the Bacon-like bodies, faces and souls underneath.

Like too many others, I was somehow lulled into thinking that however awful, inexcusable and homophobic, some of what Reagan did, and especially what he failed to do, was more ignorant and bumbling than consciously, intentionally "Hitlerian" and "genocidal." In *TAP Vol 2* the Reagans are once again front and center, this time with big incorporated chunks of Kramer's failed farce, *Just Say No*, about them and their callousness. Chunks of *The Normal H*eart and earlier work on an unpublished novel, *The Masturbovs*, about Jewish Washington, are likewise interwoven into the fabric of *TAP*. Hitler was profoundly, intentionally, genocidally invested in anti-Semitism. Were the Reagans and Ed Koch comparably invested in genocide against gays?

In an early ACT UP demonstration, I carried a sign that read "We Need Experts, Not Bigots," rather than any of those showing Reagan as Hitler and sporting swastikas. But what Kramer had been declaiming from the outset is now in sharper focus. To remain silent about a major epidemic of a fatal disease with mass casualities in a stigmatized minority without civil liberties protections is indeed mass-murderous, Nazioid, Hitlerian and genocidal, just as what Western "civilization" has done to the indigenous peoples of the Americas, to slaves, to Jews in Europe and other vulnerable minorities was mass-murderous, Nazioid, Hitlerian and genocidal. This was Kramer's battle cry all along and is an encompassing theme of *The American People*.

### *Ron Jr.*

Yet I still reflexively wince at some of Kramer's allegations. In the case of the Reagans, for example, is Ron Reagan Jr. really queer and poz, as Kramer still so vehemently insists? This exposing of queerness in the family is a bulwark of Kramer's lampooning in *TAP* not only of the Reagans but of the Bushes and many other figures of prominence, especially politicians.

In my first year of medical school, my closest friend was a straight (no quotes) ballet and modern dancer in the mold of Ron Reagan Jr.

He had a girlfriend he slept with and eventually married. Like Kramer, I can be suspicious of sexual orientation claims by men who could seem otherwise by their externals. But I never had any doubts about Tom. In all honesty, I had the same sense about Ron Reagan Jr., who otherwise always seemed at ease with himself and admirable in his ability to own his considerable political differences from his parents, who apparently did worry that he might be a fairy when he was at Yale, when he chose to dance with the Joffrey Ballet. Today, Ron Reagan Jr. continues his public service as a commentator and program contributor to MSNBC. He's an outspoken liberal and "unabashed atheist" committed to the separation of church and state, and has been named to the Freedom From Religion Foundation's Honorary Board of Distinguished Achievers.

Again to be honest, the whole picture Kramer painted of Ron Reagan Jr, showcasing Kramer's skill at insightfully demeaning others, still strikes me as character assassination in the interest of serving his own scenarios and agendas, and doing so utilizing one of the oldest sexist and homophobic tropes — of interest in dance as the weapon of choice to faggify the enemy. It's the kind of weaponizing of difference the worst homophobes, our straight enemies, have always done. And it's the kind of muckraking only one other person in the current period has been known to do as characteristically: Donald Trump, who the *Washington Post* recently called out for his "trademark vindictiveness."

At one point in *TAP* 2, Kramer has a single sentence that reads like an add-on indicating his awareness of the fact that there are male dancers who aren't fags. Though he doesn't mention them, obvious front-runners include Fred Astaire, Gene Kelly, Bob Fosse and Michael Baryishnikov. This reminded me of my own run-in with Larry following the premiere of *The Normal Heart*. In the play Ned Weeks wonders why the raggle-taggle world of gay activists he has so stereotyped didn't fight for gay marriage. "But we did!" I yelled at Larry the day after the premiere. In a subsequent draft of the play, the Mickey Marcus character based on me earns an add on: "We did."

### *The Early Gay Movement*

In *TAP* Kramer meets the challenge of spelling out his indictment of the gay movement that preceded him and that he had seemed so homophobically loathe to join. After canvasing many of the terms like "gay" and "queer" used over time to designate us, he goes on to survey a summary history of early activist organizations. With intelligence, caring and humor, and with greater circumspection — doubtless facilitated by the universal respect he now commands — he hones in on the inadequacy of our earlier efforts to lay claim to ourselves. However touching and brave these initiatives, and however insurmountable the obstacles we faced, what was needed, he concludes, was greater vision. Here he compares lesbians and gay men, noting real differences in our priorities — especially around sex and sexual freedom. Instead of going on an angry tirade about how gay men had made promiscuity our highest priority and were fucking ourselves to death, he concludes with disarming compassion that we were "a movement founded on wanting too little and dreaming too small."

## *Rewriting History Through a Queer Lens*

Meanwhile, what Kramer achieved with his vilifications of the Reagans is what he achieved with his faggifying of George Washington, Hamilton, Burr and others. Whatever Larry really thinks about the sexuality of these figures, it seems not so much the certainty of their gayness or involvement in specific gay love affairs and triangles, any more than it's certain Ron Reagan Jr is gay and poz. It's that we can never go back to trusting the superficial images we've absorbed from history and the media. Nor can we go back to not seeing ourselves as part of the American or any other people. Within which perception is the genocidal extent to which gay history has been expunged from all the received annals of history, and which Kramer so heroically recreates and evokes with unflinching verismilitude, tirelessness and pathos. As Jesse Green's "Rewriting History Through a Queer Lens" helps us see, however mighty and singular Kramer's voice has been, it's no longer that lone cry in the dark, nor need it be ever again.

## *Edmund White and Sex Culture*

Not surprisingly, *TAP* is brimming with caricatures. Some of these, especially of the health care honchos whose failures are continuously indicted by Kramer as mass-murderous, are more seemingly over the top than others, but many are scrupulously detailed, even when the characters have fictitious names, as they mostly do.

One of the more scathing of these putdowns from the early years of the epidemic is of "Jervis Pail," a thinly disguised stand-in for "GCMP" (GMHC) co-founder and leading gay writer Edmund White. It's easy to read Kramer's satire here as a Trumpian counter-punch. Early on, White was an outspoken critic of Kramer. As such, White was expressing concerns about sex negativity and internalized homophobia we all shared about Larry and *Faggots*.

Where I parted company with Ed, however, and early on, was in my appreciation of Kramer's gifts as a writer, his concerns about the community's health and priorities, and with regard to the exclusionary literary clique White ruled, so aptly called "The Violet Quill." A lot of what this small, claustrophobic group of writers was producing, Ed most skillfully, was purplish prose. Yes, there was intelligence and refinement in the best of this work, especially Ed's, and there was bravery and value in its efforts to capture gay life and sensibility, especially by Ed and Andrew Holleran. Inevitably, however, especially as the epidemic unfolded and time moved on, for a growing number of us much of this school of writing increasingly betrayed a flaccidity of substance and soul.

Certainly, there was spirituality in our veneration of desire. But as it turned out, one could say the same for the greater sexual-revolution world of *Playboy* magazine and the *Playboy* mansion, both of which are objects of satirical scrutiny in *TAP* 2. Is there anyone today who would make the case that the spirituality of gay sex culture, even if gay men were a lot more menaced than straight men for being sexual outlaws, was of some higher metaphysical order than what went on at Plato's Retreat? And though Kramer fails to even try to see it, there was likewise spirituality in the all-leather, S-M funeral for "Leather Louie" described by one of Kramer's alter-egos in clinical detail in *TAP*. Yes, there was spirituality and humanity in our sex cultures. Yet so much of who and how we were as sexual beings in the 70's had to do with levels of sexual disinhibition that veered into hedonism and compulsivity. For too many of us, sex became increasingly disengaged from love, responsibility and commitment.

For gay men especially and gay people more generally, our sexuality was the force that bound us together and because of our long-standing pariah status in society at large and because we so cherished and craved it, we defended and romanticized it fiercely; we exaggerated its importance. It was also the fuel, together with what we called "recreational" drug use, of a lot of our creativity. It wasn't until decades later that we finally began to admit that the sex we had so uncritically over-valued was a failed substitute for what Kramer alone among us — outspokenly and courageously, if also judgmentally— had been trying to talk about all along as a community-level and ever-widening breach between sex and love.

Ed and I never developed a friendship, though we've had friends in common and would occasionally cross paths at the baths or in sex chat rooms. Whenever I tried to say hello in passing or wish him well (as when he had a stroke or at the opening of the New York Public Library exhibit Stonewall 50), I felt rebuffed. He never tried to initiate communication with me — or to respond to my few efforts to reach out to him — about the epidemic or GMHC in the nearly 40 years of their unfolding. His disaffection is perhaps understandable in view of my championing, though hardly uncritically, of his nemesis, Larry Kramer. Recalling White's own observation that people can hold contradictory opinions simultaneously, and even in the face of my earlier criticism of him in my Larry Kramer anthology, I naively hoped that he would say yes to my inviting him to be a contributor to that anthology.

Even if we had somehow bridged this communications gap in the greater interest of our communities, however, it's not likely that my reaction to the body of White's work could ever be much different. For me, the title of one of his books,*The Beautiful Room is Empty*, can seem more eloquent than intended. But Ed, who is poz and who lost lovers and friends to AIDS, has had his own stories to tell and has done so with distinction and acclaim. Preceding *The Beautiful Room is Empty* is *A Boy's Own Story*. Following it is *A Farewell Symphony*. Together they form a trilogy and are one of several gay *Ring* cycles, as I call them, with AIDS at their center. Others are Tony Kushner's two-part *Angels in America*; Larry Kramer's *The Normal Heart*, *The Destiny of Me* and a subsequent screenplay on the ACT UP period and aftermath that has yet to be adapted; Matthew Lopez's two-part *The Inheritance*; and Larry Kramer's two-volume *The American People*.

## *Yale and Gay Studies*

While Kramer's narrative was often directed at the gay community, what now fuels and infuses his work is a volcanic anger at the willful ignorance and prejudice of the broader public that even today cannot deal with the homosexuality of some of civilization's greatest exponents. Leonardo da Vinci, Michelangelo, Walt Whitman, Tchaikovsky. This year marks 500 years since the death of Leonardo. As we celebrate the achievements of one of history's greatest minds and artists, why hasn't there been a serious film that tells the truth about him or any of these other supremely gifted and revered figures? Throughout *TAP*, the history of homosexuality, even the acknowledgment of its existence, is shown through countless examples, great and small, to have been willfully ignored, suppressed and expurgated. As it traverses this lonely, baleful, tragic but also tragi-comic journey, *TAP*easily becomes the greatest work of mourning of these losses in all of literature.

All of which comes to a head in Kramer's recap of his experience with the Larry Kramer Initiative at Yale ("Yaddah" in *TAP*), which refused to acknowledge the legitimacy of gay studies, insisting on trying to bury it within "gender studies." It's easy to seize on Larry's adamancy that Lincoln and other figures were gay as one of the reasons. And it should probably have been called The Larry Kramer Initiative for Lesbian and Gay or LGBT Studies, like CLAGS (the Center for LGBT Studies initiated by Martin Duberman at The CUNY Graduate Center). But the takeaway is how right Larry turned out to be about the homophobia that still pervades academe.

That Yale could not see fit to sanction gay studies seems even more troubled now than it did at the time of all the confrontations. For me it brings to mind Hollywood's efforts to honor Tennesee Williams with a major film of his drama *Cat On a Hot Tin Roof* starring Elizabeth Taylor as Maggie and Paul Newman as her repressed gay husband Brick. The play is explicitly about everybody's "mendacity" about everything, especially Brick's homosexuality. Even here, however, the ending had to be rewritten a la Hollywood to be both straight and happy. Yet another moment of truth for Yaddah, for this otherwise so august and esteemed institution with its history, as Kramer revels in exposing, of slave-owners, Christian bigots and nasty, besotted presidents.

What Yale did with the Larry Kramer Initiative for Gay Studies is what Hollywood did with *Cat*. It chose mendacity over veracity. Because of Yale's cowardly decision and example, timely initiatives for gay studies have suffered their greatest setback. No wonder Kramer is so uncompromisingly hostile to social constructionists, with their determination to theorize gayness out of existence and history.

My life partner Arnie Kantrowitz was a pioneer of gay studies at the College of Staten Island CUNY, where he chaired the Department of English. When he retired, he explicitly warned CSI not to subsume gay studies within gender studies, where he could see it would get lost, which is exactly what happened.

### *Pharma and Slavery*

*TAP* is filled with insights about history and trends. And such are its gatherings of evidence and its evocations of personages and events that historians and scholars, especially of the gay community and AIDS, will need to keep mining these volumes. It's a rare pleasure to savor writing of such individuality and character, to share the intimacy of reading with a writer of such impressive knowledge and literary skills, someone whose written voice has its own distinctive eloquence, language, rhythms and humor, and who beckons us to join him in a forward march to a drumbeat of ever-gathering momentum to reclaim our lives, our communities, our history, our souls.

Just as Kramer's stripping the Reagans of pretenses is still revelatory and compelling, so are his other indictments, especially of pharma; it's another example of how appreciation of Kramer's perspective evolves over time. In the heyday of ACT UP, when life-saving treatments for HIV were finally being developed and made available, thanks overwhelmingly to Kramer and ACT UP, there could seem a dissonance between Kramer's denunciations of pharma as evil incarnate and its promise of transforming the epidemic, which is in fact what happened.

In David France's history of AIDS, *How To Survive a Plague*, the role of pharma is seen as more complex. France shows how negotiations, led by Peter Staley of ACT UP offshoot Treatment and Data Group (TAG), required levels of patience, strategy and savvy that were tough for Kramer. As he had with GMHC, Kramer wanted

ACT UP to do a lot more storming of the barricades rather than play games of compromise. The picture that emerges of Kramer in *Plague,* and inadvertently as well in *TAP,* is of someone who in ACT UP essentially repeated his history of falling out with GMHC over tactics.

But thanks to Kramer's hard lines on pharma, we are helped to see the bigger picture. Perhaps only slavery (my analogy, not Kramer's) can compare to the gargantuan profit-oriented malfeasance of this Bromdignagian industry over time. Consider first what might be called the affirmative, medical-model, American business take on the role of pharma in AIDS. In *The Inheritance* gay billionaire Henry Wilcox, who speaks for big money, praises the achievements of pharma, boasting that successful treatments for AIDS were developed in less than 20 years. Indeed, using the latest minimum side-effects antivirals preventively (PrEP), leading health officials now foresee the end of AIDS. Comparable affirmation could be imagined for slavery. Whatever the moral issues, slavery helped establish America's lead in world finance and trade, something even slaves themselves, a Wilcox might argue, would eventually benefit from.

There's a film, *Belle*, based on a complicated case of slave-ownership, in the course of which you're able to appreciate how much of the history of slavery was about business, finance, insurance and law. In much the same way that the debates about secession that led up to the American Civil War were mostly about states' versus national rights, trials involving slavery became all about technical issues of law. The moral issues were treated as secondary to non-existent. The only questions being asked were, what exactly was in the contract or law and was it violated, and if so, exactly how? Verdicts could be appealed, as they are today. Examples of this same indifference to moral issues of life and death and vulnerable communities abound in *TAP*, which, needless to add, does not share Wilcox's affirming view of pharma, even though it's pharma that will seize credit for gaining control of and eventually ending AIDS. Just as pharma will eventually claim credit for resolving the opioid crisis it created, fostered and has so mightily profited from.

In fact, the present catastrophe that is the opioid crisis renders Kramer's portrait of pharma a credibility that undermines *TAP*'s effectiveness as satire. There's nothing Kramer cartoonizes about the ruthlessness of pharma, historically and today, that isn't by now readily apparent to a much broader public than in the heyday of AIDS.

Even so, the clarity and power with which Kramer points out that pharma is and always has been overwhelmingly about financial profit at the expense of everything else, including lives, sometimes large numbers of them, sometimes *very* large numbers of them (in the millions)— as in the AIDS, hepatitis C and opioid epidemics and the history of the making, buying and selling of knowingly contaminated blood products — is Kramer at his soulful, x-ray vision, brutality-of-fact best. For anyone open to an all-out indictment of pharma, *TAP* is your book.

Emblematic of the experience of pharma in AIDS in *TAP* is the role of "ZAP" (AZT). In *TAP,* this earliest of effective AIDS medications that had such serious, often fatal, toxicity, is endlessly indicted as poison. As depicted in *TAP*, its promotion was all about money combined with the absence of motivation to find something less toxic and more effective; it's a viewpoint that has prevailed, even though the drug proved useful initially, later in combination with other drugs, and very effective in preventing maternal-fetal transmission of HIV. At every turn, the shining surfaces of pharmaceutical achievement are revealed to have a Baconesque underbelly.

### *Trump, Medicine, Health Care, Nazi Doctors and Mass Murder*

Can anyone who knows what's going on in America today with the skyrocketing cost of life-saving medications like insulin, asthma pumps, cancer treatments, the new treatments for hepatitis C and new generation antibiotics, among many or even most other medications, many of them now routinely advertised on television the way cars are, or who witnessed hedge-funder Martin Shkreli, "the most hated man in America" for his extortionist drug pricing, or who is witness to the ravages of the opioid crisis, have any doubt now about the validity of Kramer's war on pharma?

Again, the biggest problems with *TAP* for today's readers are that it is upended by reality and Kramer's own track record of proving right. The tension of uncertainty is gone. Today, the worst of Kramer's forebodings are front, center and in our faces. To assert that Reagan was Hitlerian could seem extreme. To assert that Trump ("Derek Dumster" in *TAP*) is Hitlerian a lot less so. The fascism with a friendly face — smiles and laughter— that Reagan perfected is no longer bothering with the friendly-funny-charm. In *TAP* 2, the press conferences of Reagan spokesperson Larry Speakes — which kept devolving into laughter at the sadistically homophobic expense of the gay men who were dying *en masse* from AIDS, which Reagan had yet to even mention— are quoted verbatim. Actual footage of that news conference is also a devastating highlight of Laurie Lynd's film documentary, *Patient Zero*. Today, those who are transgender are instantly deligitimized by a stroke of Trump's pen. Press conferences are dispatched with altogether.

While Kramer and ACT UP were presciently on target from day one about the Reagan administration, today's fascism is without pretense. It's right there, bludgeoning us incessantly, it's sadism overt. In fact, the unfriendly fascism of Donald Trump and at least a dozen other authoritarians like him dominating the world stage can make Larry Kramer's see-all, tell-all, spill-the-beans approach seem something you wouldn't think possible: quaint. Would it surprise you to learn, as you do throughout *TAP*, that there's an international gulag of concentration camps where undersirables and illegals, prominently including homosexuals, have been sent and continue to be sent for experimentation and liquidation? That new genocides of homosexuals and others are being planned as we speak?

**"In Trump's America, we doctors are silent and thereby complicit in mass-murder."— Larry Mass**

One of the most upsetting of Kramer's accusations was that we were all "murderers" — more by omission, by silence, than commission. Our failure to act, to more actively resist, to fight, to fight a lot harder, was relentlessly declaimed by Kramer. This is again the case with *TAP*, with its extended excerpts from *TNH*. It's Kramer's intention and success that his plays are in sync with the fabric of *TAP*. Only in *TAP* the outrage about lost lives is on a much grander scale, with amplification of all the bullshit that went on and on and on and on — for 4 years! — as those claiming to be the co-discoverers of HIV battled for the titles and profits of blood tests that were already available. Kramer was consistently vociferous in his assessment that these delays, together with those of health care professionals like those who led CDC and NIH and lesser functionaries in failing to issue stronger prevention guidelines, were tantamount to mass murder.

Mass murder is an accusation Larry Kramer leveled at all of us, even the likes of his and our beloved Rodger McFarlane, the early legendary AIDS activist. But who can look at what's going on now with immigrants, with Syria, with ongoing genocides like those in Myanmar, with the homeless, from gun violence, with Duterte's death squads in the Philippines, with victims of natural catastrophes like Hurricane Maria, with people dying from being unable to afford essential medications for diabetes and asthma, with the tens of thousands whose lives are being destroyed by the opioid epidemic and by increasingly out of control health care costs (tens of thousands die annually from their inability to pay for health care), and not see the truth in this calling to account of all of us?

Clearly, silence does equal death. I'm still working as a physician in a system that's neglecting large numbers of people who can't afford basic health care and life-saving medications. American physicians are not organized and with almost no exceptions are not standing up to these crimes against humanity. Are we therefore not unlike the majority of doctors of the medical profession who by their silence facilitated what was happening in Nazi Germany?

However self-righteous and judgmental these indictments may initially ring, Larry does include himself. In *TAP*, he estimates the many gay men he may himself have infected before there was certainty of the cause of AIDS and testing for HIV.

## *Jews, Jewishness and Anti-Semitism*

Another area where Kramer's viewpoint has gained authority is around Jewishness. One of the things that so struck me about Kramer and his writing in the heyday of our friendship and coming together around AIDS was a distancing of himself from his own Jewishness and from anti-Semitism. Kramer's big identity crisis and journey were around being gay. If there were issues around his being Jewish, they were far less traumatic and consequential, at least so far as Kramer seemed consciously aware. Kramer was never shamed and traumatized by his father and others for being Jewish the way he was for being gay. The minority identity crisis he experienced growing up was about being gay and being a sissy. While being gay was likewise a defining issue of my upbringing, the overt trauma I experienced growing up in the rural south was primarily about being Jewish.

Like Kramer, claiming my gay identity became my principal journey, until I discovered, after years of struggle to be self-acceptingly and openly gay, that I had hardly begun to scratch the surface of my Jewish identity and the realities of anti-Semitism, not only for history but for today. In myself I discovered reservoirs of internalized anti-Semitism. In fact, amidst the early unfolding of the AIDS epidemic, as described in my *Confessions*, an unprecedented experience of overt anti-Semitism on the eve of the AIDS epidemic became the touchstone of my own writing and activism.

In *TAP* Kramer is at pains to explore the connections between Nazism, racism and anti-Semitism in America, and to consider homophobia in the context of the fascist and eugenics movements in America and their counterparts and offspring in Germany and across the globe. These efforts and probings are among *TAP*'s richest rewards. Even with Kramer being an equal-opportunity satirist, however, when it comes to minorities and ethnicities, the special relish with which he skewers Jews and their pretensions can seem to betray a subtle disconnectedness, what he perhaps still sees as his own remove from anti-Semitism. Larry Kramer may be — to use the vernacular with which he is most comfortable — a "faggot" and he may be a "sissy," and he may also be a morbidly preocccupied or even "ugly old Jew," but at least he's not one of *those* people, one of those fanatical religious or mizer types — "kikes," a word Kramer does finally use, along with "niggers," "spics," "bitches" and of course "faggots," in this cockeyedly democratic narrative vernacular in which everyone is put down or sent up coequally, or seems to be.

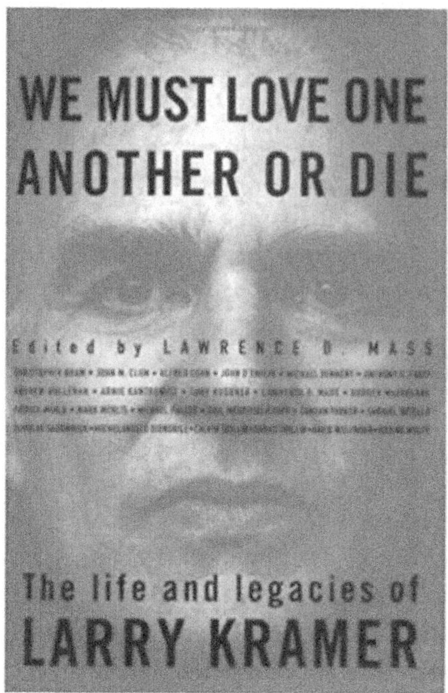


Figure 184 - book cover, amazon.com

On this issue of Jews and anti-Semitism I've given Larry a hard time. Like so many gay Jewish intellectuals, artists, progressives and leftists, Kramer can seem smug in his disconnectedness from Israel and its concerns about genocidal anti-Semitism, especially as clouded today by ever-worsening settlements controversies, by the BDS movement and Netanyahu's partnership with Trump. We gay people are the ones experiencing genocide now, Kramer endlessly proclaimed and what his *Reports from the holocaust,* with its intentionally lower-case h, intoned with what seemed little or relegated awareness of the recurrence of genocidal anti-Semitism, especially as we keep witnessing it today among Islamic extremists and white supremacists.

But the balance on this issue of Larry Kramer, Jews and anti-Semitism has shifted since the publication of my Larry Kramer anthology in the direction of giving Kramer's perspectives more credibility. What Kramer kept expressing was what Tony Kushner was showing us in his portrayal of Roy Cohn in *Angels in America* (Cohn also features in *TAP*) — that Jews can be just as crazy and fucked up and malicious and dangerous as everybody else, regardless of anti-Semitism or maybe because of it, just as gay people are all those things, notwithstanding our in many ways comparable history of genocidal prejudice. That we've sometimes played decisive roles in our own fate, as Jews, as gay people, is no longer contestable. Who can look at Trump's own *fuhrer*-obedient Kapo-in-Chief, Stephen Miller, currently coordinating the fate of oppressed, dispossessed, vulnerable peoples in America and globally, and think anything else?

### *Hollywood, From Bleak House to the White House*

Yes, Kramer's writing is still blistering. But the controversy that would always erupt around Kramer being more incendiary than credible is now much weaker. Now that Cassandra's prophesies have come true, Kramer is no longer Cassandra, even if we still initially and reflexively appreciate him as such. Whatever the facts— like who had sex with who, the mechanics of their sex, the exact details of Larry's alleged end-of-life reconciliations with the GMHC Board, which ACT UP or TAG members rejected him or didn't, who said or did or didn't say or do exactly what, when — they now seem so much less important, receding in interest alongside the brutal facts of the bigger picture. That Republicans can be like Nazis and include Nazis and white supremacists in their ranks and support is no longer as shocking at it seemed when Kramer first began suggesting this reality in the heyday of ACT UP, or even as recently as a year ago.

**"There is no other writer in America, or the world, who is responsible for saving so many lives with his writing." — Bill Goldstein**

Facts do still matter, of course, and always will. Hopefully. And now that Larry's greater credibility is incontrovertible, we want to know more of them, especially the bigger ones that remain hidden, including many uncovered in *TAP*. But why remains a good question. What will knowing knowing that America and the world have always been Nazioid tell us that we can't already see?

It has been said by Bill Goldstein that Kramer's writing may have saved more lives than any other writer. The appraisal that Kramer's literary voice has been so salutary seems accurate and deserved. But it's Kramer's insistent theme that so many more lives could have been saved had we all done a lot more, a lot better, a lot faster. OK, we can now concede, but will his example inspire new generations, not only of gay people, but of Jews, of women and of oppressed and menaced people everywhere, to stand up for ourselves, to take back the night of our own lives? Alas, it's in this sense that Kramer is most likely to remain Cassandra, his example marginalized and evaded until the worst is well underway.

As for the experience of *TAP*, while it may not be everyone's idea of "fine writing," it's writing at its finest. *As in Satyricon, Candide* and *Faggots,* we are guided through worlds of adventure and encounter at once strange and familiar, fictional and fantastical, commencing in wonder and retreating in disillusionment.

In *TAP*, an early such encounter takes place when Fred/Ned revisits his experience with the worst disaster of his career in film: *Lost Horizon* ("*Beyond The Mountains, Beyond the Stars"* in *TAP*). What started out as an adaptation of Dickens's *Bleak House* — about labyrinthine and endless legal battles *en famille* that reverberate to today's worlds of Donald Trump, Roy Cohn and Rudy Giuliani — ended up being about Shangri La! In the course of this greatest of Fred Lemish's misadventures, we are re-introduced to the film's producer, "Rust Legend" (based on Ross Hunter) who we met in *Faggots*. In *TAP*, Fred's entanglement with Hunter becomes a cockeyed introduction to the closeted worlds of Hollywood and inevitably of Rock Hudson and the Reagans.

This *Bleak House* background is a key to the crazy names that color *TAP*.

E.g., from *Bleak House*:

Mr. Tulkinghorn, Honoria, Lady Dedlock,
Conversation Kenge
Prince Turveydrop
Peepy Jellyby
Mrs. Snagsby
Mrs. Smallweed
Mrs. Guppy
Phil Squod
Watt Rouncewell
Mrs. Pardiggle
Arethusa Skimpole

from *TAP*:

Rust Legend
Purpura Ruester
Buster Punic
Mayor Kermit Goins
Drs. Oderstrasse and Maudilla Chanel-Bausch
Tolly Mcguire
Dr. Horace Vetch
Sister Grace Hooker
Bosco Dripper
Didier Lestrade
Adreena Schneeweiss

The Hollywood material peaks with Rust Legend in an extended monologue, explaining to naive young Freddy Lemish what's really going on with gays in the industry, as it's still unwittingly referred to. Among the allegations: Jack Warner was so rabidly homophobic he had James Dean killed for being a fag; that Jimmy Dean hated Jews as much as Warner hated homos; that mobsters like Meyer Lansky and Mickey Cohen got involved trying to save Warner; that Peter Ruester (Reagan) blabbed the names of commies and fairies at those UnAmerican Activities hearings; that George Cukor was fired from *Gone With The Wind* because Clark Gable didn't want a fairy director.

In *TAP*, Fred/Ned is joined by a gaggle of other personages, many of them alter egos or nemeses— scientists, doctors, researchers, nurses, lab techs, politicians, spies, preachers, tycoons, tricks, community activists, writers, artists and lovers, many of them already familiar from Volume 1, from earlier Kramer works, and many of them caricatures who are all doing what Fred/Ned sees as his principal and highest calling — to give testimony to what he sees, what he's been witness to. Like Candide, he wanders through this phantasmagorical world, pondering its oddities and suffering inevitable disillusionments, trying evermore against the odds to retain his soul. The biting satire that results of governments, religions, philosophies, individuals, events, locales and history conjures Voltaire in approach but with surpassing ambition.

In the midst of his romance-affairette-close friendship with Tommy Boatwright (Rodger McFarlane) from *The Normal Heart*, Fred falls in love with "David," who was abused and tortured, having been kidnapped in affiliated American and German concentration camp gulags when he was still too young to have any inkling of what was going on. As they make love, Fred can feel the ridges of the scars on David's back. Why this happened to him is a question both David and he would keep pondering. "Were all men like the ones I had to deal with in Mr. Hoover's whorehouse?...All I see are versions of the same thing. Over and Over. The inability of fellow humans to deal decently with others as a fellow human."

Along this journey, there are multiple stopovers and side trips, at historical phenomena like food handlers, toilet manufacturers, a history of shit; examples of the vast history (many of them imagined but based on historical indices) of the detention and punishments of homosexuals in concentration camps and prisons; histories of medicine, health care, hygiene and AIDS before it was identified as AIDS in Africa; histories of AIDS before it was identified as AIDS in Haiti in relation to Africa; a history of murderous and profiteering failures of sterilization and hygiene in blood products and treatments for hemophiliacs; a history of houses of prostitution and their relationships to leading political figures and crime.

### *Drug Addiction and Religion*

Though addiction figures notably in *TAP*'s foreshadowing of the opioid crisis as exemplary of pharma run amok, there's surprisingly little about drug addiction itself or addicts as a major AIDS risk population. Thanks largely to ACT UP's early championing of needle exchanges, HIV risk and spread from needle use and drug addiction (mostly heroin) was nearly eliminated in New York City and other major epicenters of AIDS. Yet here we are now, *post*-AIDS, experiencing huge setbacks in the prevention of AIDS and hepatitis C because of pharma greed and irresponsibility, on top of the ignorance and bigotry of morality politicians like Mike Pence who as governor of Indiana initially refused to sanction needle exchanges, even as the opioid crisis in his state exploded.

The greater history of the relationship between drugs, addiction, profiteering and malfeasance begs for the treatment of Dr. Larry

Kramer. (Yes, Kramer is now a real doctor, having been awarded an honorary degree by Yale!) Especially since a great majority of the drugs that were manufactured in this country for everything from "female troubles" to colds were bogus snake-oil products promoted by bogus snake-oil salesmen and the companies they worked for. Most were alcohol or morphine based, and knowledge of their addictive ("habit-forming") potential long preceded any warnings of such.

Alas, addiction isn't a paradigm that Kramer ever got very interested in exploring as such. Not so unlike Dr. Brookner's prescription for gay men to "just stop" having sex, his prescription for sexual compulsivity — and by extension for other forms of addiction — can seem not so unlike Nancy Reagan's approach of "Just say no." The treatments for addiction that injection drug users need beyond needle exchanges — from detoxes and rehabs to opioid maintenance treatment (e.g., Methadone, Suboxone), 12-Step programs and outpatient therapy — were not waters Kramer ever waded very far into.

While the murderous diatribes of religions and religionists are sometimes quoted verbatim in *TAP*, some of the more notable spiritualists in the history of AIDS are not mentioned — .e.g, Louise Hay. In the earliest period of the epidemic, when spirituality seemed an alternative to the unavailability of treatment, Hay was a real community presence. Faith-healing, her outreach seemed to me. But Hay, who continued to work successfully with persons with AIDS until her death in 2017, was more in the tradition of motivation therapy and self-help than peddling false hope, even when her book titles, like *You Can Heal Your Life,* might seem to suggest otherwise.

## *Women, Sexism and ACT UP*

Remember the (*Playboy*?) cartoons of Martians contemplating the significance of this or that earthling behavior, symbol or belief? That's the way Fred and his cohorts are in looking at phenomena like "*Sexology*"(based on *Playboy*), the sex periodical founded by "Mordy Masturbov" (How would Hugh Heffner like to be thought of by posterity as Jewish?) that went very far and very profitably in normalizing predatory male sexual behavior. The same sense of amazement overtakes encounters with anything and everything sexual, especially involving women — from the manufacture of brassieres to the horrors of back-room abortions and the realities and treacheries of prostitutes and prostitution, with their high rates of involvement in blackmail and murder, entangled with top government agencies like the FBI and officials like J. Edgar Hoover and their boys like Roy Cohn.

All of these mosaic pieces find their places in the three great puzzles that are the abiding preouccupation of *TAP:* the histories of the American people, gay people and the "underlying condition" (UC) — what became AIDS. Squeamishness, ignorance and bullying around the sexuality of women is everywhere apparent and assumes its inevitable place in the ignoring of women along with persons of color in the early period of the epidemic. This relegation of women by science and medicine is a notable study of *TAP*, alongside coruscating looks at our leading medical and scientific research institutes and their figureheads. Women have been marginalized and demeaned together with blacks, gays, Haitians, hemophiliacs, anuses, vaginas, STD's, the elderly, children and other categories of interest and relevance because of biases in science that reflected social mores and taboos, most of them masculinist or religionist, invariably both.

Women were so pejoratively excluded from consideration that CDC and other leading medical and research organizations initially refused to acknowledge that they were even at risk. A lot of pioneering work on addressing gender barriers and discrimination in health care access and research was done by ACT UP under the leadership of women. In *TAP* Kramer is clearly and rightly proud of Sarah Schulman, whose contributions to AIDS I've elsewhere described as "legion and priceless," Maxine Wolfe, whose star shines as brightly in *TAP* and otherwise as any activist in the firmament, and Ann Northrop, whose formidable presence is still so strongly felt via Gay Cable News.

Eventually, though not reprised in *TAP*, Mary Fisher, who was not affiliated with ACT UP, made a startling appearance at the Republican National Convention, coming out as a person — and woman — with AIDS. It was one of those moments, like Rock Hudson's acknowledgment of having AIDS, that greatly influenced broader public perceptions.

The sadistic relish and pride with which Fred/Ned and his *TAP* colleagues and friends expose the foolishness and failures around

AIDS and the pride with which *TAP* celebrates the triumphs of ACT UP and activism will come as no surprise. Yet the writing is endlessly fresh, even for people and events we think we already know. There isn't a sentence that seems rote, that doesn't breathe life and fire.

In *TAP,* as in *Satyricon, Candide and Animal Farm,* the brutal realities underneath various preposterous situations can require some teasing out, in *TAP* doubtless a lot more because of the relegation of gay history. Because of this paucity of verifiable gay history, however, everything in *TAP* must be mined for accuracy. Obviously the fictional names Kramer uses — .e.g., Drs. "Omicidio" and "Dodo" — weren't the real names of Anthony Fauci and Robert Gallo, but less obviously everyone else. In some cases, especially of heroic figures, Kramer uses real names — e.g., Maxine Wolfe, Sarah Schulman, Laurie Garrett, Michelangelo Signorile, Jim Eigo. With other figures, likewise heroic — e.g., Linda Laubenstein, Rodger McFarlane, Dr. Joseph Sonnabend, Ann Northrop, Spencer Cox, the names are fictionalized. Decisions about names often seem more situational or capricious than methodical. Many details may differ from reality, but often not by much.

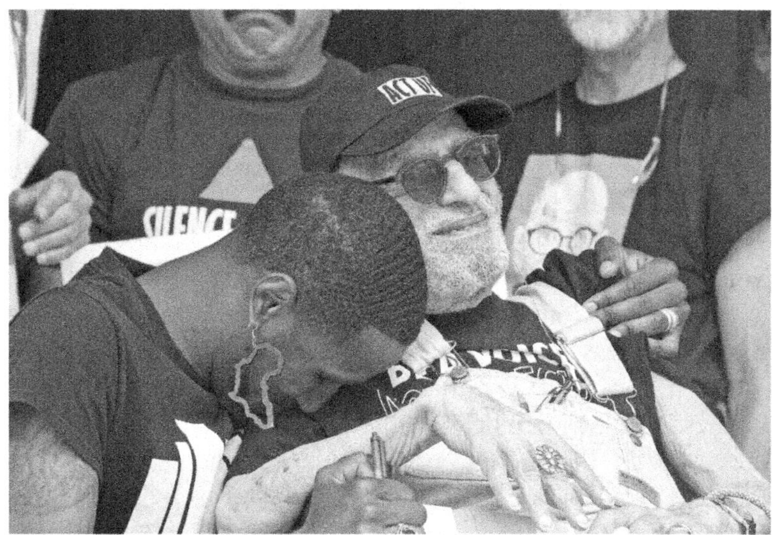

Figure 185 - Larry Kramer with activist Jason Walker on the rally stage in Central Park June 2019. The rally followed the Queer Liberation March. As captured by Andy Humm and Gay City News, and though Larry did make subsequent public appearances, this was Larry's

In *Animal Farm,* some of the characters — pigs and humans — are modeled specifically on historical figures. In some cases, characters are composites — e.g., one of the pigs, Snowball, combines elements of Trotsky and Lenin. The same is true of *TAP*. The character based on me, Mickey Marcus, is also a composite — of me and of Larry McDevitt, an early GMHC volunteer who worked for the city.

In contrast to what's said in *TAP*, I never slept with Larry. We were friends and the chemistry wasn't there. But there was a moment when I wished it had been. That conscious thought occurred to me as I took notice of the physical resemblance between Larry, so handsome in his prime in an ACT UP period photo, and sexy Mark Ruffalo, who plays Ned in the HBO film of *TNH.* It was a juxtaposition that took place with Ruffalo speaking live onscreen in a special tribute to Larry when GMHC bestowed its first Larry Kramer Activism Award to Kramer himself in 2015.

### *Barbra Streisand, Judy Peabody, Vito Russo, Mathilde Krim, Elizabeth Taylor*

Whatever the other facts of Barbra Streisand's years of inaction on Kramer's scripts for *TNH*, Kramer's sense was that "Adeena Schneeweiss" — spoofing the German background of Dr. Brookner in *TNH*, a role Streisand wanted to enlarge at the expense of Ned and the epidemic — was indeed the self-absorbed figure of legend, an assessment that feels in sync with Kramer's undressing of her as squeamish about appearing in a film that would feature explicit gay sex, even as he admits to being one of the gay boys who sings her in the shower. Darker suspicions linger. At some level, and notwithstanding her legions of gay fans and the gayness of her own son, did *TNH* strike her as representing phenomena she needed to maintain distance from culturally or politically?

Squeamishness about gay sex is also an accusation leveled at "Montserrat Krank" (Mathilde Krim) who worried that sexual explicitness would alienate wealthy donors and whose decision to partner up with Elizabeth Taylor made her medical director (Joe Sonnabend) so uneasy he distanced himself from their organization (AMFAR). Krank, who was not Jewish but who was married to a leading Hollywood producer, had always impressed Larry for her involvement in the Irgun, the Israeli guerilla-militia that served as a sometime model for Kramer's visions of gay insurgencies.

Fortunately, ACT UP was more scrupulous than Larry about the priority of maintaining boundaries of non-violence.

Krim is valorized in *TAP*, but comes under fire, like others, for not more directly importuning leading politicians she had social access to — e.g., the Reagans. But after dressing her down on several fronts regarding early decisions about outreach, *TAP* credits her, alone among early AIDS organization leaders, with stating clearly and emphatically that "this is a historic plague that need not have happened. It could and should have been prevented."

Meanwhile, squeamishness about gay sex was an accusation that was often leveled at Larry, who in *TAP* is disarmingly at ease acknowledging his own attractions, inclinations and adventures. So while he was himself still calling out gay men for being sex-besotted, he has no problem admitting the lust, mixed with bursting pride, he felt for the hordes of sexy gay men — the hottest in New York and around the world — who flocked to ACT UP. Of course, the bigger truth here, which can sometimes be hard to glean, is that Larry, for all his alleged moralizing, ostensible erotophobia and toughness on promiscuity, never actually excluded himself from this critique, just as he never excluded himself from the accusations of murder (second degree or felony or by neglect) he was constantly leveling at everyone else.

*TAP* features many portraitettes. There must be a hundred of them, usually lasting only a few paragraphs or pages, sometimes with brief reappearances. Among the most arresting of these is of "Perdita," based on Judy Peabody, the glamorous bejewelled society lady who pioneered the GMHC buddy system. At one point in that early period of his greatest anger and confrontations with GMHC, Kramer publicly called her out, among other people of rank and influence, for an imputed aloofness he saw as all too typical of GMHC's greater investment, as he would endlessly, bullyingly and shamingly characterize it, in "helping people die rather than live." That was Kramer at his most brutally truthful and confrontational.

In *TAP* he does thoughtfully and respectfully credit Judy Peabody's considerable achievements in developing GMHC's buddy system. At key moments in this description, however, he hones in on his failure to connect with her more personally as emblematic of the whole problem with all of us at GMHC and as well with himself in his failure to arouse the levels of anger and activism that were needed.

Yes, Judy Peabody was an angel of mercy, he concedes, but as such she came to be perceived by those dying of AIDS as "the angel of death." A visit from her meant it was the end and everybody knew it.

In some of his more patient and careful writing, Kramer goes on to explain that he tried to more personally confront some of these society people, specifically Perdita and a figure based on Joan Tisch, to urge them to intercede through their connections — access to Nancy Reagan — to influence the White House to act more decisively and humanely, to break its silence and inaction.

Even acknowledging how ferocious, insulting and off-putting his anger could be in frightening people off, which Kramer is honest about here, the fact that these alleged entreaties were not responded to lends credibility to his perspective that his falling out with GMHC had more to do with our failure to rise to the occasion of the much greater level of activism that was needed than with his problems as a communicator and trusted leader, or with GMHC being primarily an information and service organization. That "we" were all responsible for this failure stung deeply, as it did at the memorial service for Vito Russo, when Kramer began his testimony with "We killed Vito."

Judy Peabody was a heroic figure whose achievements will continue to be celebrated. And her genuine friendship with Vito Russo, which my Arnie, who was Vito's closest friend, and I were witness to gives at least indirect testimony to her support for greater activism. She and Vito spoke often and casually as friends, sometimes late at night. Mostly because of her friendship with Vito, I met her periodically. I always thanked her for her service, but was never able to get any further in genuinely, personally connecting with her. Though I wanted more, cool greetings in passing were my only exchanges with Judy Peabody.

Of course, genuine friendship is precious and must be nurtured. Vito had it with Judy, with Larry, with Arnie and me, and with virtually every one he ever met, even with his enemies or those designated as such, notwithstanding Larry's telling Michael Schiavi (author of the biography of Vito, *Celluloid Activist*): "[Vito] was furious at other gay people just like I was, no question. He was just more beloved than I am and was probably able to say it with an ability of not making other people as angry as I do."

I still well up when I remember Vito's final days, me sitting next to him on his hospital bed massaging his legs covered with KS and other lesions. When I tried to apologize for not being a more successful warrior on the front lines, he looked me in the eye through all his pain and said, "I love ya, Lar." Clearly, this ability to love and be loved came less easily for Larry, who everybody respected and revered and inevitably loved but whose judgment, censure and retaliation we were also afraid of.

Would Judy have tried to intercede with Nancy Reagan had Vito asked her? Would Vito, who always respected people's boundaries, have ever asked her in the first place? Who knows, but because of the genuineness and reliability of their friendship, Judy probably would have at least answered Vito.

Meanwhile, David France is on target in his history of AIDS in noting my dismay at never having been consulted by Larry, who I had thought of as my friend, regarding his depiction of me in *TNH*. All's fair in love, war and writing, I guess. Even so, and even if my tacitly siding with GMHC's leadership (I had already resigned from the Board in the wake of my hospitalization for a major depressive episode) in separating itself from Larry gave him the right to say whatever it is he felt he had to say, my own experience of the fraying of what had seemed our genuine and abiding friendship seems a window on these issues of friendship and trust. Judy had never had any relationship with Larry, and based on his constant fulminating against GMHC and everything it stood for, and explicitly including her ("a hoity toity rich bitch"), communicating with him was something she could not have been expected to trust.

It's to Larry's credit that he understood and articulated this difference between himself and Vito, who everybody so adored and respected but who nobody was afraid of. "I forgive no one," reads the final of 16 epigraphs that introduce Volume 1 of *TAP*; not his own father, and certainly not the Reagans or Koch or Anthony Fauci, but not a lot of the rest of us either. Even Elizabeth Taylor, who I witnessed at an AMFAR benefit giving Kramer a special award and who spoke without notes from her heart about all he'd done and about the urgency of AIDS and whose own contributions had been so brave and invaluable. I was sitting at Larry's table at the Governors Island event with Rodger McFarlane, Larry's brother Arthur and Kramer's old friend and fellow writer Calvin Trillin.

Yes, even E.T. is called out in *TAP*. Why didn't she, with all her star connections, do more? We all know how much E.T. did.

Following such moments of reminder of Kramer's relentlessness, of what "a difficult man," he could be, as the *New York Times* (the *New York Truth* in *TAP*) put it, it's heartening to read the passages in *TAP* that are filled with loving and grateful recognition of the many heros of ACT UP, like Maxine Wolfe and Jim Eigo, and even of some in government (before they were relieved of their duties) like pseudonymed C. Everett Koop, whose courage in speaking truth to power as a ranking government official was singular.

Other notable portraitettes include GMHC cofounder Nathan Fain and his harrowing final days back home in rural Texas, about which there has continued to be some dispute, as there continues to be regarding the AIDS deathbed exchanges between Larry and "Bruce Niles" (GMHC's first president Paul Popham). But there's no portraitette of our mutual friend Craig R,, who chose to die from AIDS at home, wearing the retro earrings and necklace I bought him at a thrift shop to help him fulfill his wish to spend his last days in drag as "Harriet Craig," the Joan Crawford 50's housewife camp classic and our affectionate nickname for him. Dearly departed "Craig*lach*." Among those closest to Craig was an ex-boyfriend, John, heir to one of the nation's richest dynasties. A Henry Wilcox type, he was concerned and caring about Craig but aligned with politics inimical to us.

### *Dr. Anthony Fauci and Rodger McFarlane*

Though "Dodo," based on HIV "co-discoverer" Robert Gallo, isn't far behind in Kramer's contest for Villain-in-Chief, the most expansive of these Baconesque portraitettes is of "Jerry Omicidio," based on Anthony Fauci, head of "NITS" in *TAP*. Throughout *TAP* Omicidio is called out for inaction and ineptitude. In view of his levels of at least titular responsibility, he is seen as a principal perpetrator of the holocaust of AIDS; he is seen as Ruester's accomplice in mass murder.

*TAP* is implacable in its indictments of do-nothing institutes, divisions and individuals. Fancy-titled head of this or that exalted-sounding department are continually revealed or declaimed to be just that, titular, bureaucratic and empty, accomplishing nothing — whether it be Fauci, Gallo, the NIH, CDC, GMHC or any other organization or person. The image of Omicidio as someone who wasted so much time and so many opportunities and resources for organizing, for leadership, is devastating and infuriating, even as questions of how fair this caricature is do keep intruding.

Towards the book's conclusion, when a sexual portrait of Jerry emerges, like those ascribed to the Reagans, it's success is questionable, the way the caricatures of Ron Jr. and Ed [Koch] were in *Just Say No*. Even with the failure of that play acknowledged by Kramer, he can't help expressing himself with these metaphors. Here, as *TAP* finally reaches for closure — which we know can never be real closure because the book had to be so edited down (there are 2000 more pages in Kramer's archives)— Jerry is revealed to be a repressed homosexual necrophiliac who gets off on ejaculating onto the corpses of the young gay men who perish under his lack of care.

These intimate details are related in a letter to Fred from Jerry's wife. Again, as with a painting by Francis Bacon, or an imagined episode with any of the Reagans or of Koch getting blowjobs under his desk from the ex-lover he's threatened to murder, what is clearly over-the-top caricature leaves you with questions you would never think to ask. In the case of Jerry, what was the psyche of this straight-laced man whose sexy wiry hairy Mediterranean body could be discerned at the edges of his shirt collars and cuffs? What *were* the Mayor's kinks? If we do succeed in imagining these publicly entrusted figures as sexual beings, what might that sexuality have encompassed, metaphorically as well as literally? And what might that suggest about the lives they led and didn't lead, even if we should know better that sexual fantasies, even the kinkiest, don't necessarily correlate with goodness or badness?

The most moving of the book's portraits is more tacit than explicit. Rodger McFarlane (Tommy) was Larry's best friend, ex-lover and one of the great heros of the AIDS epidemic. His death from suicide was felt by everyone as shocking, out of the blue, tragic and one of our great losses. No circumstances — e.g., back troubles, depression, debt, losing Kramer to David — are known that can account for it. Following Kramer's example of select, warm, measured, loving reminiscences of this unflaggingly humane and heroic character's charisma, courage, generosity of spirit and accomplishments, there are finally no words adequate to our grief, for the love we all felt for this wonderful man.

## *Dr. Joseph Sonnabend, Charles Ortleb and AIDS Denialism*

Another vivid portraitette that emerges in *TAP* is of "Rebby Isenfelder," based on Dr. Joseph Sonnabend, whose struggles to expedite treatment for opportunistic infections and co-founding of AMFAR and other organizations were pinnacles of early activist efforts. But in *TAP*, Rebby — and with him his patients and fellow activists Michael Callen and Richard Berkowitz — are also given a free pass on their role in what is still, even in *TAP*, the big unwritten chapter on AIDS, the chapter no one, including Kramer, wants to spend much time looking back at or talk about: HIV denialism, which was the source of the biggest mass casualty catastrophe in the history of the AIDS epidemic.

In the early 2000's, a third of a million people died in South Africa, all of them preventable deaths, when South African President Thabo Mbeki, an AIDS denialist, blocked access to treatments of proven efficacy. AIDS denialism can be most succinctly described as the belief that, as Sonnabend initially characterized it but in contrast to the early viewpoint attributed to Rebby in *TAP*, there was no single "killer virus" responsible for an epidemic that seemed far more likely — to Sonnabend initially if never to Kramer — to be due to immune overload from multiple infections, poor nutrition and drug use.

Kramer does acknowledge denialism, which ACT UP was notably successful in derailing within its own ranks, and does note his own later confrontations with Rebby and chief denialism enabler "Orvid Guptl," based on *New York Native* (*The New York Prick* in *TAP*) editor Chuck Ortleb. "He has blood on his hands," Larry said to me of the deterioration of the *Native*. The origins of the germ warfare theory that originally seemed so plausible to Ortleb and the rest of us have now been traced to Russian disinformation efforts. But the origins of denialism, however eventually disclaimed by Sonnabend, Callen and Berkowtiz, and the role it played in fueling fanaticism, cultism and the worst single swath of mass-casualties in the history of the epidemic are evaded in *TAP,* just as they are in David France's history of AIDS. Why seems a question worth asking.

In fairness to Larry, who even in a 2000 page book couldn't possibly acknowledge everybody who contributed or didn't and everything that happened or didn't, here is the statement that begins his page of Acknowledgments, placed to follow the book's conclusion:

**"This has been my history of the plague I lived through, a brutality few ever dreamed of. I do not pretend to have given an inclusive picture. There is no one who could give an all-embracing recital. I hope this book will encourage others to add their own experiences and histories so that the world will never forget."**

If my own commentary here has seemed expansive and discursive, I do believe it to be in the spirit of Kramer's invitation to all of us to add our own experiences and histories.

### *From Hamilton's "Black and White Law" to Crimes Against Humanity and War Crimes Tribunals*

Traversing the final passages of the epic saga and journey of *TAP,* the reader would anticipate the tying up of loose ends, statements of gravitas about what has happened and portentousness for the future. The payoff turns out to be much bigger.

In *TAP*, Fred/Ned is living out the rest of his post-liver-transpant and post- FUQU (ACT UP) days with David, his beloved, who is an attorney ("David" being a composite). The liver transplant was expedited by Jerry Omicidio! Between the lines of blaming TAG renegades in collusion with Montserrat Krank, GMPC and others, the demise of FUQU seems attributable to multiple factors, some of them ineffable. Whatever the variables, the Cassandrian fallout predicted in *TAP* now seems unassailable: there won't be enough FUQU left to protest when problems arise in the future. Though a reduced ACT UP is still out there and has intermittently continued to mount brave and effective protests — e.g., of the extortionist pricing of curative medications for hep C — it's easy to see that today's challenges could become as great as those faced by ACT UP in its heyday.

It's David who has those ridges of scars on his back, having been tortured as a child in Nazi concentration camps in hideous medical experiments to see how much pain could be endured and to test new drugs. These experiments, fiendish developments of pharma, would eventuate in drugs like the highly addictive amphetamine and opioid derivatives that were used by Hitler and his troops to sustain conscienceless violence, and to keep legions of contemporary gay men enslaved to conscienceless sex.

David, inspired by his journey with Fred, has been devoting most of his later-life time and energies to exploring the history of war crimes tribunals and archives. What he discovers is that these initiatives are altogether new. They didn't really get going until 2002. Like the United Nations, they are primitive, needy and faltering. The obstacles they face are overwhelming, but their having originated in the first place, it's suggested between the lines, could be as important for the future as the origins of democracy were in Greece (my analogy, not *TAP*'s), a development for all time. It's an epic statement of hope, even as the unofficial group of chapterettes that make up the conclusion of *TAP* begin with warnings about hope, which in Kramer's experience has usually been a euphemism for evasion of justified blame, responsibility and justice.

Hope for the future was not how to deal Nazi war criminals. According to *TAP*, "many" went unprosecuted. This is not the only time that what we thought of as Kramer's hyperbole turned out to be understatement. Just as the plague Kramer predicted eventually affected tens of millions more than even he imagined initially, it's not "many" but the overwhelming majority of Nazis who went unprosecuted. War crimes, or crimes against humanity, have only been designated as such in our time. They have only one precedent: the Nuremberg trials, which succeeded in prosecuting only a tiny fraction of Nazi war criminals.

Could those political and health care leaders who Kramer is unwavering in seeing as responsible for allowing the epidemic to become one of the greatest in recorded history (*TAP*'s conclusion includes a formal listing of the fictional names of those alleged to be principal miscreants), still be called to account for their crimes of neglect, their crimes against humanity, their war crimes? Even as *TAP* is otherwise so eloquent in giving testimony to the complexity of the origins of the AIDS epidemic (a subject amplified in *Patient Zero)*?

In tandem with David's explorations of war crimes trials is his discovery of Alexander Hamilton's "Black and White Act," which is alleged to be a consistently overlooked law still on the books that gives any individual or class the right to challenge inhumane social or political actions. It's this approach to intervening in the future of human rights catastrophes, like the allegedly preventable and containable epidemic of AIDS — as crimes of neglect, hate and genocide — that sees *TAP* conclude on high notes of love and hope. Yes, hope, which Kramer warned against. Not pie-in-the-sky hope, but hope with empowerment and justice. This is the blockbuster conclusion of *TAP*.

### *One of the Greatest Stories Ever Told*

In the end, alas, however powerfully these volumes render historical figures, events, atmospheres and meanings, they cannot be regarded as reliably accurate or comprehensive sources. This is the price Kramer must pay, like so many other writers of satirical and historical fiction — like Orwell in *Animal Farm* and Voltaire in *Candide*, like Tolstoy in *War and Peace* and Margaret Mitchell in *Gone With The Wind*, and writers of legend, like Virgil in *The Aeneid*. As with *Animal Farm* and the others, eventually who certain characters represent or are supposed to represent in *TAP* will be mapped out, if not directly by Kramer himself, who may already have done so, then by others. You'll be able to look it up online.

But the result is well worth the price. While Larry Kramer may have forfeited his place as an always credible historian, he has recreated the history of AIDS and gay people with incomparable art, truthfulness, detail, perspective, authority, imagination, vision and sweep. In doing so, he has drawn the attention of the world to three of history's biggest stories — those of gay people and the AIDS epidemic, and with them the American people. In each case he has been on the mark like no one else and with a voice compelling enough not only to capture but to re-create history and direct the future. Thanks to Kramer's lead and so long as history retains any credibility, it must henceforth include gay people together with the other of Lady Liberty's "wretched refuse of America's teeming shores." In neither the American Civil War nor in either World War were the casualties or the stakes higher than in the history of AIDS and the American People.

With Kramer at the peak of his powers, *The American People* can take its hard-earned, rightful and secure place among other classics of history, fiction, satire and legend. By any measure, it's one of the greatest stories ever told.

# Larry Kramer and Alcoholics Anonymous Turn Eighty-Five

## Larry Kramer, Compulsivity, Addiction and Recovery

– *Medium*, 7/3/2020

**There's a saying one hears in the rooms of 12-Step recovery: "There are no coincidences."**

On June 25, Larry Kramer, who died May 27, 2020, would have turned 85. On June 10, 1935, Alcoholics Anonymous was co-founded by Bill Wilson and Dr. Bob Smith in Akron, Ohio. June 10 is annually and internationally celebrated as AA Founders Day. If not for the pandemic, Detroit would be hosting AA's 85th International Convention this Independence Day weekend.

"Who looks outside dreams. Who looks inside awakes." — Carl Jung

Many things overlap and coincidences are common. Carl Jung, the psychoanalyst who broke with Freud to spearhead his own spirituality-oriented psychology, as well as the movement of recovery based on the 12 steps of Alcoholics Anonymous, believed that many coincidences also qualify as "synchronicities," the simultaneous occurrence of events which appear significantly related but have no discernible causal connection.

One of these "meaningful coincidences" is the June 2020 shared 85th birthday/anniversary of Larry Kramer and Alcoholics Anonymous. While there may be no other obvious link between Larry Kramer and Carl Jung, or with alcoholism, addiction and recovery, this intersection can serve as a touchstone for looking back at Larry Kramer in relation to phenomena of compulsivity, addiction and recovery.

In my five decades of knowing Larry, I had little sense of him being any kind of addict. He struggled episodically with cigarette smoking. And he was a "chocaholic." Last year on his birthday I brought him a chocolate cake so we could celebrate together (my 74th

Birthday was June 11), something we did in the old days. When he was hospitalized for his liver transplant in Pittsburgh, I sent him chocolate-covered Godiva cookies.

Many years ago, in opening one of Larry's desk drawers to retrieve something for him, I noticed a standard-fare gay sex videotape. I often saw Larry at the baths, but I never knew him to be compulsively involved with pornography. Larry was acrophobic and had a history of depression, but to my knowledge, he never suffered from a compulsivity or addiction so notable it got designated as such, except perhaps, by his own assessment, to writing. So absorbed and preoccupied was he as a writer that he would evade vacations and sometimes meals.

Larry was never in a detox, rehab or in a behavioral or self-help program for addiction or compulsivity, and it was a subject he otherwise never showed much interest in, at least from vantage points of psychiatry or addiction medicine. This was in contrast to the sharp medical expertise he developed and continually displayed for most anything having to do with AIDS and other phenomena of medicine and disease. I always found this surprising in terms of his remarkable literary acuity about gay fast-lane sex. However over-the-top, his descriptions of our behaviors in *Faggots* are also strikingly clinical in their specificity and accuracy, albeit rendered in Larry's own literary vernacular, without any of the jargon or reference points of medicine or psychology.

In the heyday of his plays, Larry didn't write much about the psychoanalytic psychotherapy he had been so immersed in prior to *Faggots*. Perhaps he had already intuited that the psychiatry of his era was as confused, biased and suspect about most other areas of psychology and behavior as it was about sexuality and homosexuality. Not surprising when you consider the severe homophobia of that era's predominantly psychoanalytic pathologization of homosexuality as a mental disorder, which wasn't officially withdrawn as such from the DSM (Diagnostic and Statistical Manual of Mental Disorders) of the American Psychiatric Association until 1973–4. This declassification, which took place several years prior to the publication of *Faggots* (1978), became a springboard of the Gay Liberation movement.

And not surprising when you consider Larry's tribute to the last of his psychiatrists, Norman J. Levy, an openly gay, life-partnered *mensch* who encouraged Larry's activism. Levy, from the more progressive psychoanalytic school of Karen Horney, was also my psychiatrist. Before me and before Larry he was my life partner Arnie Kantrowitz's shrink, and after me, Larry's beloved Rodger McFarlane's. "For Norman J. Levy, who succeeded where all others failed," reads Larry's dedication to *The Normal Heart*. As someone with an unparalleled track record for having his intuitions prove right, Larry would have been, yet again, spot on in his skepticism about psychiatry as having the best answers and solutions for compulsivity and addiction.

Perhaps as well because he could only devote so much of his time and interest to so many things, Larry never wrote much about addicts as one of the major AIDS risk groups and he had little to say about addiction as a treatable condition, though his sweeping indictments of pharma in *The American People* include its deliberate peddling of drugs it knew to be addictive. Also in his magnum opus is a character based on Spencer Cox, the ACT UP activist who struggled with addiction to amphetamines and eventually died from AIDS after discontinuing his HIV medications.

Among the crowning achievements of ACT UP were its pioneering efforts to establish needle exchanges for injection drug addicts, who were often co-infected with hepatitis C. So addiction does figure honorably in Larry's achievements. It's just that he himself had little to say about it.

Meanwhile, however, and again to my knowledge, 12-step recovery as a widely accepted option for self-help is not something Larry promoted or opined about as an option for the many within and on the periphery of ACT UP who might have benefited from it. Rather, his perceptions and advice were more general and along the lines of American practitioners of "the power of positive thinking," like Norman Vincent Peale or Louise Hay's "You Can Heal Your Life," though I don't recall his ever expressing himself about Hay as the AIDS community's own leading self-help guru.

In truth, one could intuit Larry's feelings about compulsivity and addiction as being not so unlike those he parodied in Nancy Reagan in his farce, *Just* Say *No*. "Just say no" was her notorious answer to the complex problems of drug addiction. That was what he felt gay men needed to do for the compulsive sex and drug use that placed us at risk for AIDS and other STD's. Get your act together was Larry's advice, rather than specifically urging people to seek professional help or to go to Alcoholics Anonymous, Sexual Compulsives Anonymous, Crystal Meth Anonymous or other recovery programs.

In one of our email exchanges in 2012, our erratic discourse on this came to a head. Larry berated me for being overweight. Why couldn't I just get on the stick of dieting and caring better for myself? Once again, I tried to raise the issues of compulsivity and addiction as they had manifested themselves in my life in multiple areas — food, sex, alcohol, cigarettes and marijuana. "Cross addiction" is common among compulsives and addicts, who are often differentiated from one another only by degree, and I worked recovery programs for those in my own life.

Was Larry sexually compulsive, like the rest of us in those heyday years of early gay liberation? To read *Faggots* is to share some of the most incisive depictions of sexual compulsivity anywhere. And as the name of the lead character, Fred Lemish, suggests, Kramer was presciently aware of the risks and dangers, for himself and the rest of us, that characteristically attend phenomena of addiction and compulsivity: self-absorption, disinhibition, hedonism, isolation, intoxication, irresponsibility for oneself and others, paranoia, harm to oneself and others, and death by suicide or from crime.

Apart from a vividly rendered overweight alcoholic in an early short story, and despite my repeated efforts to engage him on this subject, however, Larry had little more to say about compulsive behavior or substance abuse, or about any of their periodic scourges in the gay community — e.g., our recurrent, sometimes explosive epidemics of crystal meth abuse and dependence.

For me, this neglecting of context was as well a challenging aspect of his portrayal of me in his composite character of Mickey Marcus in *The Normal Heart*. Like me, Mickey ended up on the flight deck, the psych ward at St. Vincent's Hospital. But the significant role my incipient alcoholism played in that circumstance was neither rendered, nor, apparently, considered.

In Larry's orbit were many who struggled with compulsivity and addiction. But these are problems that Larry, not unlike Jung, saw as more spiritual — personal, communal, societal, political — than psychopathological. Jung believed that what alcoholics and addicts were seeking was spiritual recovery rather than medical or psychiatric treatment. No pills or psychotherapy were going to cure alcoholism, he felt, just as Larry intuited that no pills or psychotherapy were going to effectively treat gay self-hatred. These were maladies of the soul and society that needed spiritual solutions. Only awareness and action, self-discipline and service, honesty and willingness, changing oneself and one's world via caring, love and commitment, courage to change, and, yes, anger, from the inside out.

In this, as in most everything else, Larry was prescient and on target. In terms of what he saw and foretold of gay people and our liberation, of AIDS and its cure, of the American People and our sickness of values, of what we needed to do and "HOW" (Honest, Open-Minded, Willing), as they speak of it in recovery, Larry Kramer's prophetic vision might well be compared to Jung's.

A question Larry would often ask people, including me, was "Why aren't you more angry!?" My answer, after entering recovery in 1984, was always the same. When Larry acted up and out with anger, it always turned to gold. As a person in recovery, however, if I tried to do what Larry did the way he did it, I would more likely do more damage than good to myself and the causes we believed in and were fighting for.

While Larry's emphasis was on being in touch with and marshaling one's anger and shunning forgiveness, and recovery's emphasis is more about being wary of self-righteous anger and resentment and nurturing forgiveness, in both cases, cultural change is envisioned as an inside job from which the personal has the power to transform the political.

As their stars cross on what would have been Larry's 85th birthday and the adjoining 85th anniversary of Alcoholics Anonymous, we are comparably indebted to Carl Jung and Larry Kramer for the great spiritual movements of recovery they inspired.

# Before Larry, After Larry And Congressman John Lewis

## GMHC Founders Day Commentary

– *Medium*, 8/5/20

### *Before Larry*

August 11 marks a milestone. It's the first Founders Day commemoration since the passing of leading GMHC co-founder Larry Kramer.

It was nearly 40 years ago, in Larry's living room on that day in 1981, that six of us gathered to discuss our emerging health crisis. I was a physician working in addiction and a journalist writing about gay health and cultural issues for the gay press. Nathan Fain was a gay journalist writing about nightlife for the mainstream press. Paul Rapoport was a gay community organizer and philanthropist. Former Green Beret Paul Popham was prominent in gay social and professional circles. And Edmund White and Larry were acclaimed gay writers. Fain, Rapoport and Popham died from complications of AIDS. Larry was poz, as is Ed.

Indeed, a true crisis is what we were facing. At that time there were virtually no civil liberties protections for gay people. We could be and often were fired, evicted and ostracized by our employers, landlords, families, friends and coworkers for being gay. Even in progressive San Francisco, where a pioneering gay civil rights ordinance was passed in 1972, the atmosphere was bitter and riotous in the wake of the gay-hatred assassinations of Mayor George Moscone and Supervisor Harvey Milk, one of the first openly gay figures to be elected to public office. These terrible crimes were committed by Dan White, a failed politician who was acquitted on the basis of a gay-panic defense just months prior to the first press report, by me in the *New York Native*, of the epidemic that later became known as AIDS.

The risk of widespread public explosions of homophobic extremism seemed real enough as well in the wake of the 1980 Chicago trial of John Wayne Gacy, a serial killer of 22 young men, most of them gay, which I covered for the gay press. Gays taking over politics. Gay-related murders of young sons. Gays spreading a deadly new disease to the public. Our aggregate vulnerability on these fronts of sensationalization was terrifying.

As homophobic extremists like psychologist Paul Cameron continued to speak openly on television about final solutions for homosexuals, here we were trying to grapple with a new epidemic disease in gay men, on top of epidemic spikes of syphilis, gonorrhea, hepatitis and amoebiasis. In that earliest period of the first reported cases of this latest health crisis, we weren't even sure we were dealing with an STD.

From the beginning, Larry was pushing levels of public activism that were scary in terms of this atmosphere of homophobia and absence of civil liberties. Tell the truth and organize, yes, the other five of us agreed. But we also needed to tread cautiously, stick close to the facts and not carelessly add fuel to the fires of homophobia and hysteria.

After several of these meetings and early fundraising efforts, and with the help of Larry's brother Arthur, an attorney, we regathered at Larry's Washington Square apartment to officially establish a new organization, Gay Men's Health Crisis.

At the time, I was the lone holdout to the name, which I felt linked the disease with being gay in a way that wasn't scientific and could aggravate stigma. AIDS, as it had yet to be called, wasn't a "gay disease." It wasn't "gay cancer," or "Gay-Related-Immunodeficiency," as the epidemic was already being labeled. To my ears, calling the new epidemic "gay cancer" or "GRID" was like Trump calling COVID-19 "the China virus."

But I supported the group's decision in favor of "Gay Men's Health Crisis" and am glad I did. Although HIV/AIDS was a viral condition that doesn't discriminate on the basis of age, race, ethnicity, sex, gender, sexual orientation or geography, one of its earliest and biggest recognized outbreaks was in gay men and our initial efforts to confront it remains a distinguished chapter in our history.

As it turned out, this was a history not only of AIDS activism but of gay liberation and kindred minority struggles. It was also a milestone for medicine, science and America. Not so unlike the pride that still burnishes names like NAACP or YMCA, the name GMHC continues to reflect a proud legacy of humanitarian, community and minority efforts.

### *After Larry*

On May 27, 2020, just short of what would have been Larry Kramer's 85th birthday, the gay and AIDS communities lost their most powerful voice and advocate. While there were many brave and notable activists before and during Larry's time, none has come close to having such forceful influence. NIH director Anthony Fauci, a frequent target of Kramer's activist wrath who became his personal doctor and friend, has described the history of American medicine as "Before Larry and After Larry."

He wasn't exaggerating. At the time of ACT UP's storm-the-barricades pressuring of Fauci and the NIH to supercede leaden research protocols with revolutionary fast-track testing of experimental drugs, there had yet to be a successful treatment for any major fatal viral illness. What ACT UP, which Larry co-founded on leaving GMHC, achieved under his leadership was unprecedented in the history of medicine, science and grass-roots health care activism.

Larry was endlessly angry about injustice. Initially, we in the gay community were the targets of a lot of that anger. Anger that we couldn't get our act together. Anger that we were acting out instead of acting up. Eventually, that anger became focused on much bigger targets.

Larry's last work and magnum opus, his two volume, semi-fictional and satirical novel, *The American People*, is a volcanically angry, accusatory indictment of a country that was built on slavery and genocide. As the AIDS epidemic spread amidst public silence, Larry held "the American people" responsible for what he decried as our gay "holocaust" and "genocide." It's basis in homophobia — "Why do they hate us?" — he recognized as of a piece with the country's history of racism, sexism, colonialism, xenophobia and bigotry.

"Silence = Death," which became the logo of ACT UP, could be the subtitle of *The American People*. In its countless tales and images of our unacknowledged losses from AIDS, and of our being written out of history alongside indigenous peoples and other minorities, *The American People* is truly epochal in its declaiming and mourning of these losses and in its indictments of their perpetrators.

### *Larry Kramer and Congressman John Lewis*

With Larry's passing, we are officially launched on the treacherous seas of After Larry. The odds are once again stacked against us locally, globally and looming darkly into the future. Once again, we are David facing Goliath. But in large measure because of Larry Kramer, we need never again feel hopeless. As Larry showed us, anything is possible— like turning a rampaging, uniformly fatal global pandemic into a manageable chronic condition. So long as we believe, care, hope and are willing to stand up for ourselves, to fight injustice whenever and wherever it emerges, no matter how intimidating, we can prevail.

Larry was often described as being like one of the biblical or mythological prophets, rejected in his own time and land. "I wanted to be Moses but ended up being Cassandra," Larry himself observed. From his writing of *Faggots* to his gay and AIDS activism and the publication of *The American People*, Larry consistently demonstrated visionary foresight and courage of conviction. Even in the face of vociferous rejection, Larry's message was always clear. We cannot and must not remain silent. And we must not lose that quality of the American people and of all people that remains most cherishable — hope for a better and more just world. Hope for the right of *everyone* to pursue life, liberty and happiness.

The best way we can honor Larry Kramer today is to begin by nurturing that hope in our hearts for a future worth fighting for. As GMHC's public relations trailblazer Krishna Stone captured it on Larry's passing and the future of GMHC: "We will be with each other with Larry's spirit guiding us and yelling at us."

Although Larry was a leader and visionary like no other, much of the tough, nitty-gritty, heroic work of leadership has always been carried out by others. Through decades of angry criticism of GMHC by Larry, who dramatized his falling out with the organization in his play *The Normal Heart* and who finally returned to the fold as the recipient of GMHC's first Larry Kramer Activism Award in 2015, GMHC has not only prevailed, but has consolidated its reputation as the world's premiere HIV/AIDS information and service organization.

From ushering in Kramer's special place of honor in the organization, a feat no one but GMHC's CEO *Extraordinaire* Kelsey Louie could have conceived and engineered, to managing the organization and its many and varied client needs and services during our concurrent health crisis of pandemic COVID-19, Kelsey and the organization he has so proudly and successfully guided now carry that torch of hope.

As people in recovery say, there are no coincidences. With the recent passing of towering civil rights hero Congressman John Lewis, who was as well an ardent champion of gay civil rights and gay marriage, we can take pride and comfort from his legacy, and as it intersects with and reflects that of Larry Kramer and GMHC.

"Do not get lost in a sea of despair," Lewis exhorted us in 2018. "Be hopeful, be optimistic. Our struggle is not the struggle of a day, a week, a month, or a year, it is the struggle of a lifetime. Never, ever be afraid to make some noise and get in good trouble, necessary trouble."

# The Rudolph Giuliani Quiz

## WHY IS RUDY GIULIANI NO LONGER APPEARING IN DRAG IN PUBLIC?

– *Medium*, 11/27/19

Figure 186 - from youtube, public domain

MULTIPLE CHOICE AND TRUE-FALSE QUIZ

THE WINNER WILL RECEIVE 2 FREE TICKETS TO THE OPENING OF THE *RUDY GIULIANI IN DRAG* EXHIBIT AT THE NEW WHITNEY.

WHY HAS FORMER NYC MAYOR RUDY GIULIANI STOPPED APPEARING IN DRAG IN PUBLIC?

CHECK ONE OR MORE OF THE FOLLOWING:

A) ___BECAUSE HE CAN'T FIND GOWNS THAT FIT

B) ___BECAUSE IN TRUMP'S AMERICA HE NOW RUNS A MUCH GREATER RISK OF BEING ARRESTED, ASSAULTED

OR MURDERED FOR DRESSING UP, AND LAWYERS WILLING TO DEFEND HIM ARE IN SHORT SUPPLY

C) ___BECAUSE HIS PROSTATE CONDITION MAKES QUICK ACCESS TO BATHROOMS IMPERATIVE

D) ___BECAUSE THE PRESIDENT FAVORS YOUNGER WOMEN

E) ___ BECAUSE THE TRUMP ADMINISTRATION IS PLANNING TO REINSTATE THE OLD IMMIGRATION BAN ON HOMOSEXUALS AS "PSYCHOPATHIC PERSONALITIES" AND RUDY WOULD NO LONGER BE ABLE TO REENTER THE US FROM HIS FREQUENT TRIPS TO UKRAINE, WHERE HE COULD ALSO BE PROSECUTED AS A PROSELYTIZING HOMOSEXUAL WHEN UKRAINE, WITH TRUMP'S COLLUSION, IS FULLY TAKEN OVER BY RUSSIA

Figure 187 - realchange.org, public domain

WHY DOESN'T RUDY DEFEND TRANSGENDER RIGHTS?

A) ___BECAUSE GETTING UP IN DRAG HAS NOTHING TO DO WITH BEING GAY OR TRANSGENDER

B) ___BECAUSE RUDY IS NOT ONE OF *THOSE* PEOPLE!

C) ___BECAUSE RUDY IS A CERTIFIED HETEROSEXUAL

D) ___BECAUSE RUDY IS, AS A GAY POSTER SUGGESTED, THE IDEAL STAR FOR A REMAKE OF THE MOVIE *PSYCHO*

Figure 188 - Scene from Casa Valentina by Harvey Fierstein, Matthew Murphy, usatoday.com, public domain

RUDY NEVER SAW HARVEY FIERSTEIN'S PLAY, *CASA VALENTINA*, ABOUT I'M-NOT-ONE-OF-*THOSE*-PEOPLE! HOMOPHOBIA AND DISCRIMINATION AMONG STRAIGHT-IDENTIFIED TRANSVESTITES

TRUE ________

FALSE ________

LIKE CAITLYN JENNER, RUDY HAS WITHDRAWN HIS SUPPORT FOR TRUMP OVER THE TRANSGENDER ISSUE

TRUE________

FALSE________

WE CAN COUNT ON RUDY, LIKE TRUMP, TO CONTINUE HIS OCCASIONALLY EXPRESSED SUPPORT FOR GAY RIGHTS

TRUE________

FALSE________

WE CAN EXPECT RUDY, LIKE TRUMP, TO SPEAK OUT ABOUT AND AGAINST HARD-RIGHT HOMOPHOBIA AND OPPOSITION TO GAY RIGHTS

TRUE________

FALSE________

EVEN IF YOU DIDN'T WIN THE COMP TICKETS, DO SEE THE NEW WHITNEY EXHIBIT, OPENING SOON.

# Larry Kramer and Richard Wagner: Is There a Connection?

– *Medium*, 6/25/20

*A look back at the two great subjects of my writing on the occasion of what would have been Larry Kramer's 85th Birthday (DOB 6/25/35)*

Two great figures of their and our lives and times have preoccupied much of my writing: composer Richard Wagner and writer Larry Kramer.

Coincidence? Largely, or so it might seem. My infatuation with Wagner preceded my meeting Larry in 1969 by nearly a decade. And my naive, troubled Wagnerism, in its heyday during the early years of my lifelong friendship with Larry, well preceded the peaks of Larry's activism and writing in the 1980's.

Apart from his intimacy with his devoted patron, homosexual King Ludwig II of Bavaria, Wagner had little to do with gayness and Larry was not an opera person. I got him to go with me to the opera only once, to *Der Rosenkavalier,* with its "travesty" (trouser role for a woman) title character, at the Met. Notoriously lengthy, ponderous Wagner, however a phenomenon gay cultism, was never going to happen. To my knowledge, Larry's interface with Wagner was nonexistent. Apart from my being their unintended intermediary, there seems little commonality of ground between Richard Wagner and Larry Kramer.

But there is a connection, and it emerged in discussion with Larry Kramer's authorized biographer, Bill Goldstein, during his interview with Charles Kaiser at Hunter College 6/14/20, a zoom event in remembrance of Larry, who died 5/27/20.

Questions often arise about the relationship between Larry's writing and his activism. Which was more important — to Larry, to us? Still feeling his way on this central issue in appreciating Larry, Bill suggested that for Larry, art and activism were interwoven.

Though not controversial, that, of course, was likewise true for Wagner. With both Wagner and Kramer, the art they produced could be said to be subservient to their political agendas. In Wagner's case, what resulted politically was the greatest affirmation of Germanness, at the expense of the greatest contribution to antisemitism and genocide, in the history of art. In Kramer's case, what resulted was the greatest affirmation of gay people and the mourning of our historic genocide (literally but especially in our erasure from history), culminating in what Larry became famous for designating as our holocaust of AIDS, in the history of art. Which was more important to Wagner, to us— his art or his Germanism and antisemitism? Which was more important to Larry, to us — his art or his activist affirmation of gay people and our history? As with Wagnerism, will there be Kramerism?

With regard to Wagner, I posed this question to Marc A. Weiner, the noted Germanist and author of *Richard Wagner and the Anti-Semitic Imagination*.

"I've often felt that Wagner was, above all, a social theorist," he said, "but I wouldn't go so far as to claim that politics were more important to him than his music or his music dramas. For he was, above all, a musical genius, [even as] his musical creations always dovetailed in his mind with social issues."

Something similar can be said of Larry Kramer. Much of what he wrote was social, historical and political, but he was above all a writer. For Larry Kramer, literary and theatrical creations always dovetailed in his mind with social issues. Larry may not have been in the same league of artistic achievement and influence as Wagner, but as with Wagner, it was via Larry's artistic gifts that his influence was most widely appreciated and will most likely endure.

This crossing of the artistic and personal with the social and political is not uncommon in art. Less common is for an artist to try to extend his political art into the realm of religion, as Wagner did with his final opera, *Parsifal*, and as implied in one of his last and most passionate essays, "Religion and Art." To be a Wagnerite was intended by Wagner to mean that you subscribed with religious fervor to his political agendas of Germanism and its confrere antisemitism.

Larry Kramer was not attempting to have his gay chauvinism appreciated as religion. But Larry's agenda of rousing and galvanizing unprecedented masses of gay people to rise up and reclaim our history and stake our claim for the future was in some ways comparable to what Wagner did, and comparably ambitious.

Wagner's agenda was the reclaiming of Germany by Germans for Germans. Larry's was the reclaiming of gayness by gay people for gay people. With genocidal revolution hovering ominously in the background, Wagner wanted to rid Germany of its Jewish and other foreign pollutants. With social and political revolution hovering comparably in the background, Larry wanted to purge the American people of its homophobes, racists, sexists, antisemites, and fascists.

Whatever their differences or similarities, and however multi-layered my own attraction to and involvement with these great figures of art and society, no discussion of art and politics coming together could exclude two of its greatest exemplars and most notorious *monstres sacrés*: Richard Wagner and Larry Kramer.

# Remembering Dr. Joyce Wallace, Early AIDS Hero And Pioneer Of Health Care For Streetwalkers

– *Medium*, 10/30/20

Figure 189 - photo: Daniel Susott, *Village Voice*

*Wallace was a tireless advocate of health care for streetwalkers and the first to tell the gay community about the epidemic that would later become known as AIDS*

At 74, my memory can be spotty. But I have vivid recollections of Dr. Joyce Wallace. It was Joyce who was the first to tell me about a few cases of atypical pneumonia in New York City hospitals in 1981. Unofficially, her call was the first outreach to the gay community about the epidemic that would become known as AIDS.

Joyce was my friend and comrade in community medicine. She was an internist with an eye, ear and heart for outsiders. Worldwide, women probably are still the largest aggregate community of the underserved, alongside racial and other minorities — Blacks, Hispanics, Native Americans, LGBT persons, the poor. Here in New

York, it was women who had no community — addicts, prostitutes, the homeless — who became Joyce's calling.

"Streetwalkers," which became the preferred term for prostitutes, not only had no designated outreach or resources even in Ob-Gyn practices, but were universally illegal and stigmatized, except in a few progressive countries — e.g., Holland and Germany. Joyce saw early on that streetwalkers, especially in New York City and other urban centers, were a neglected coterie of persons highly vulnerable to STD's, including the emerging epidemic of HIV, and in desperate need of access to basic and specialized health care. In being on the margins of society and medicine, these women bore many similarities to the sexually active gay men at highest risk for AIDS.

It's through the early, primitive networks of health care in the gay community and addiction that I got to know Joyce. In 1979 I began writing articles for the gay press on a range of subjects, initially about how reactionary forces in psychiatry were trying to reclassify homosexuality in the wake of the still controversial decision by the American Psychiatric Association to declassify "homosexuality" as a mental disorder in 1973–74. It's a threat that's likely to resurface in the current conflagration of social services and consciousness of the Trump administration.

Writing in the *New York Native*, I found myself reporting ever-worsening spikes of STD's —syphilis, gonorrhea, amebiasis and hepatitis B — in gay men. Though there were a few notable gay community physicians and a few programs and clinics with outreach to gay men, such as Dr. Dan William and the Gay Men's Health Project, no physician or other writer had ever provided regular coverage of health issues in the gay press.

Via early community physician networks such as New York Physicians for Human Rights, work in addiction and my articles in the gay press, Joyce became my colleague and friend. One day in the late winter of 1981 I got a concerned call from her. Joyce was eccentric and discursive, traits that endeared her to me because they were my traits as well. That day she seemed notably agitated but also tight-lipped.

The gist of what she had to say was that there were gay men in New York City emergency rooms and intensive care units with an atypical pneumonia. Several had died. The underlying cause(s) had yet to be determined. She added that what she was telling me was strictly confidential. Apparently, she had been asked not to discuss these cases with anyone until more was known. The call with Joyce quickly terminated on this note of hush-hush.

Whatever the confidentiality demands from health care officials, what Joyce understood instinctively and immediately is that the community most affected by what had all the hallmarks of a new epidemic had not yet been informed of what was happening. It's a narrative that would consistently demarcate Joyce's commitment to the underserved. And it was a narrative that would play out big time with the media, the public and the gay community as AIDS spread to become one of the greatest pandemics in recorded history.

On the wings of Joyce's call but without identifying her I contacted the New York City Department of Health and gathered enough scattershot information to write what was the first published news report of the new epidemic (*New York Native*, 5/18/81).

As AIDS unfolded, Joyce was a singular presence in our physician networks, including the earliest of the AIDS task forces designated by the Centers for Disease Control (CDC) under director Jim Curran. Clearly streetwalkers, with their high rates of injection needle use and STD's, were at highest risk for acquiring and transmitting what would later be identified as HIV. It was Joyce's work as well that was among the earliest to counteract the false, pejorative (sexist and homophobic) narrative that heterosexual women were innately less susceptible to infection than gay men.

Joyce's outreach to streetwalkers was fraught with perils and setbacks at every stage. Chronically underfunded and shunned because of the outlaw status of her clients and the independence of her mission, she persisted against formidable odds. Eventually, her work was recognized and credited with a profile in *the New Yorker*, "Women on the Edge," an inspiring account of this remarkable hero of community medicine by Barbara Goldsmith in 1993.

A memory returns to me in efforts to say something personal in Joyce's honor. One evening I paid her a social visit at her home in Greenwich Village. There, about to leave, was her current boyfriend, who was very handsome. It was mysteriously in that moment of glimpsing the two of them together that I felt her sensuality and kindredness of spirit with those of us regarded as being on the fringes of sexual norms and mores. Like her and with her, we were all sentient and sexual beings, as worthy of dignity, respect and health care as any other coterie of human beings.

Far from being any kind of textualist in matters of humanity, gender, sexuality or medicine, Dr. Joyce Wallace would certainly be with those of us who would vote, if we could, to change the wording of the Declaration of Independence from "All men are created equal" to All people are created equal.

# Witness from the Persecution: How One Gay Soul Lived to Tell

– *Medium*, 11/12/20

***Banned from California*: - Jim Foshee - Persecution, Redemption, Liberation and the Gay Civil Rights Movement, by Robert C. Steele, Wentworth-Schwartz Publishing, 2020, 361 pages**

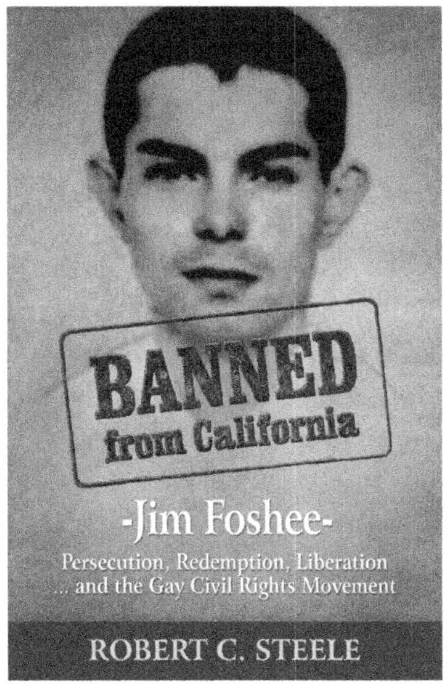


Figure 190 - book cover photo, amazon.com

Over the last half century there have been many notable exhibits on LGBT history and culture. A capstone of this legacy was "Stonewall 50" at the New York Public Library in 2019, commemorating and celebrating the 50th anniversary of the gay liberation movement sparked by the Stonewall Inn bar rebellion in Greenwich Village in 1969.

Typically, these exhibits are meticulously annotated and lovingly showcased. They tell of a history largely expurgated, ignored and otherwise denied us. They tell of the lives and times, the organizings and uprisings of generations past. We come away from these exhibits with a more informed sense of who and how we were and an enriched sense of the possibilities of who and how we are becoming.

But what of the devoted, tireless, mostly anonymous individuals whose painstaking work in collecting, cataloguing and preserving historical documents and artifacts made these exhibits possible? What do we know about them?

My papers and those of my life partner Arnie Kantrowitz are among the collections of NYPL So we have our own sense of these heroes, individuals with unique knowledge and skills, like Melanie Yolles, a specialist in rare books and manuscripts, and Jason Baumann, who directed and coordinated the Stonewall 50 exhibit.

A number of notable LGBT historians have mined collections and archives. Of my own acquaintance, several come to mind: John Boswell, Martin Duberman and Jonathan Ned Katz. Though Duberman's work is often also autobiographical, few of these histories explore the interface between gay archives and the actual lives of the archivists.

An exception is *Banned from California*, Robert C. Steele's biography of a previously little-known gay archivist and activist, Jim Foshee. Foshee (pronounced Fo-SHAY) survived considerable abuse and oppression as a gay man — including being literally tortured by the sadistic evangelical preacher who became his stepfather, and having to do hard labor in a Texas prison — to become a gay archivist and activist of distinction.

In the course of his travails through lands and times of unremitting ignorance and bigotry, from the 1950's to the early 2000's, Jim's life in the Western US — in Idaho, Texas, Arizona but especially in Colorado and California — unfolds with details that illuminate and expand a history of liberation too easily appreciated as a consequence of the Stonewall riots. *Banned*'s detailed history of gay community events and activism in Denver and Los Angeles gives dimension and breadth to this movement as emerging from a much broader confluence of individuals and events in localities across the country.

This history is not entirely new, of course. But for all that we already knew about such precursors as *ONE* magazine and the Mattachine Society, *Banned* tells us more. Especially notable is its painstaking detailing of the more complex role of gay bars and their relationships with the alcohol industry, local politicians and the local media in Denver. With its history of behind-the-scenes mafia and police corruption, the Stonewall Inn rebellion might be re-considered through the lens of what Steele documents as the complex interplay of bar ownership, advertising, operations and community relations. As *Banned* verifies, the devil — but also the divine — is often in the details.

*Banned* is handsomely assembled, has many vintage black-and-white pictures of locales and individuals and is written with economy and clarity. Not surprisingly and though easy and comfortable to read, it is meticulously annotated.

*Banned from California* is inspiring and edifying. When I attend a gay exhibit or visit a gay archives in the future, I will look for the names, if they're listed, of those who did the gathering and assembling and try to imagine them as three dimensional people, like Jim Foshee and others Steele brings to life in *Banned.* Instead of their usual anonymity or just listing their names in small print on the last page, future catalogues or brochures might add a sentence or two of biographical information about them and include their pictures, as is done for authors.

Steele is characteristically modest. His work is meant to be appreciated primarily as historical. It's hard to imagine that he'd be supportive of any revisionism for more personal recognition for archivists and researchers. But perhaps this book will spearhead a new and greater consciousness of doing for them what their work has done for us — giving recognition and thanks to largely unsung, pioneering heroes of their own and our lives, cultures and times. Where would we be and who would we be without them?

# The Supreme Court Decision on Civil Liberties and the Pandemic: Lessons from AIDS

## WORLD AIDS DAY REFLECTION

– *Medium*, 12/1/20

Imagine the headline: The Supreme Court Affirms the Right of Gay Men to Have Sex in High-Risk Venues.

On the basis of its recent decision about civil liberties in relation to gatherings for religious services, can we assume that the Supreme Court would have voted likewise in favor of not placing any restrictions on the gay sex venues, chiefly the bathhouses, that were comparably designated by health officers as high risk for the spread of HIV/AIDS?

When it came to gay sex in the early period of AIDS, there was protracted debate within the gay community as well as among mainstream observers about whether restrictions should be placed on gay sex venues. Eventually, bathhouses were closed in the highest risk areas.

In those times of the early 1980's when there were no civil liberties protections for gay people, voices of concern for civil liberties, including mine, rang out. If you give government offices the right to curtail private gatherings, how soon would that extend to private bedrooms?

Ironically, gay men who criticized the bathhouse closures were using some of the same arguments, and coming up with some of the same conclusions, as the Supreme Court in its recent decision on civil liberties and religious gatherings. In both cases, individual freedom and the right to assemble were held to prevail over social concerns.

The complexity and difficulty of the situation is summed up in the title of a book on the bathhouse controversy by medical ethicist Ron Bayer: *Private Acts, Social Consequences*.

As it turns out, these cases do not have a one-size-fits-all, one-time-fits-all solution. Many bathhouses have remained open, providing good venues for education and testing. Instead of being seen only as the problem, they became part of the solution.

The same could be done with religious gatherings. From within their own ranks, enterprising ways could be found to educate participants — to provide masks, testing, social distancing and other advisories. Instead of being only the problem, religious gatherings could become part of the solution.

# The Cassandra Of Revolutionary Feminism: Andrea Dworkin by Martin Duberman

## Commentary and an Interview with Martin Duberman

– *Medium*, 2/26/21

Figure 191 - book cover, amazon.com

**ANDREA DWORKIN: The Feminist as Revolutionary.**
by Martin Duberman, The New Press, 351 pages, 2020

**"Every truth passes through three stages before it is recognized. In the first stage it is ridiculed, in the second stage it is opposed, in the third stage it is regarded as self-evident."**
— Schopenhauer

*On The Future of Wagnerism*, the collection of my writing, devotes considerable attention to 3 writers notable for the extent to which they've gone against the grain of mainstream opinion and bucked the status quo — Larry Kramer, Gottfried Wagner and Martin Duberman.

Kramer needs no introduction as the firebrand who became the leading figure of the gay liberation and AIDS movements. Gottfried Wagner is the outspoken critic of Wagnerism and indictor of the Wagner family as Holocaust pepetrators. And Martin Duberman is the eminent gay and leftist historian, biographer, scholar, playwright and essayist who has been a consistent critic of the mainstreaming of cultural diversity.

They have all been role models for me, however not in sync I may have been with some of their viewpoints. Though not in the same league of achievement as any of these great figures, I've been inspired by them in the telling of my own story, to believe in the value of my experience and perceptions, however against the grain of mainstream opinion. When I feel most alone in that journey, I am often comforted by thinking of these exemplars of independence, perseverance and courage.

In the winter of 2021, as I prepared to post "Wagner Intoxication," my interview with Gottfried Wagner, I happened upon an episode of the television series "This is Life with Lisa Ling." It's subject was the illicit massage parlor industry. Not surprisingly, Ling probed deeper than her stated subject, exposing not only a bigger picture of sex trafficking among Asian and immigrant women but providing a window on the greater panorama of the oppression of women, especially the poor and dispossessed.

Coincidentally that same week, a *New York Times* opinion feature by Nicholas Kristof called "The Children of Pornhub" raised concerns about the internet mainstreaming of grossly exploitational, abusive and violent pornography, especially of women, minorities, the poor and children.

I had known about Marty's work on Andrea Dworkin, the research for which involved a number of trips to Boston, not the easiest gig for Marty, who has always eschewed travel and is now 90. I looked forward to reading it. Even knowing how trenchant and foresightful Marty's writing can be, however, I had underestimated how strongly Dworkin would resonate for today's world and for me personally.

Like Larry Kramer, Gottfried Wagner and Martin Duberman, Andrea Dworkin can still arouse strongly defensive reactions. Whatever their success with initiatives and publications, however esteemed they became, they are still seen as against the grain of mainstream viewpoints. As such, they can seem, as Gloria Steinem has described Dowrkin, more like Biblical prophets, suspect in their own lands and times.

Marty and I have been good friends for decades. As someone more linked to the mainstream gay world Marty could be so critical of, however, I carried stereotypical recollections of Andrea Dworkin as a kind of feminist Larry Kramer, a Cassandra who spoke important truth but who came across as troubled. Just as we more mainstream gays saw Larry as to an extent anti-sex and personally aggrieved in motivation, and as such a threat to the unqualified sexual freedom we clung to so tenaciously, so did we likewise view Dworkin as a threat not simply to the status quo of sexual liberation but to freedoms of speech and depiction. Especially in her attacks on pornography, she could seem, however indirectly and whatever the qualifiers, aligned with forces inevitably inimical to gay liberation.

How wrong were we? Quite wrong, as Duberman persuasively demonstrates in a biography that is sympathetic, balanced and sober.

As it turns out, the real Andrea, the complex human being with a commanding personality, expansive intellect and remarkable courage, was always there for us to appreciate. What has changed — subtly, progressively, and however fraught with relapse and regression — is the mainstream of thinking about women and sex. Past the extreme sexism and misogyny of the Trump presidency within the greater era of Rush Limbaugh with his disparagement of feminists as "feminazis," the MeToo movement became ascendant. American culture, albeit with still far too many exceptions, is no longer as monolithically susceptible to the old tropes of women as culpable and responsible for crimes against them and suspect for defending themselves— in marriage, in the workplace, in society.

In email exchanges, Marty generously agreed to respond to questions about his subject.

**Larry Mass**: Why this book now?

**Martin Duberman**: I have one general and one specific response. In general, as the gay movement has become more centrist, my interest in it has declined. I place more hope these days in radical feminism than in gay centrism. This happened almost behind my own back. It was only after I'd been digging out Naomi Weisstein's essays for a posthumous volume that I realized how much more her voice spoke to me than did HRC [Human Rights Campaign Fund] & friends.

The specific reason? I was reading one of Phyllis Chesler's books and came across what I thought was an outrageous diatribe against John Stoltenberg, who I'd known for many years. I called him to express my anger and support and in the middle of our conversation I suddenly asked — it really was a stroke of lightning — "Is anyone at work on a biography of Andrea?" John told me a movie was in the works, but not a biography. He also told me that her archives at Schlesinger were substantial and untouched, but he would open them up to me. I was hooked. I wanted to continue my exploration of feminism and the fact that I'd known Andrea heightened my interest.

**LM**: I remember Naomi Weisstein from the early 1980's, when I first met you. By that time she had become an invalid. Who was she to you and what became of the essays?

**MD:** I assembled and annotated Naomi's essays after her death in 2015. I included a long introduction as well. My publisher at the time, The New Press, turned down the manuscript. By then I'd given up having an agent and rather than go through the tedious process of finding a publisher, I self-published it as *Naomi Weisstein: Brain Scientist, Rock Band Leader, Feminist Rebel* (Off the Common Press: 2020). It runs 348 pages and got some wonderful blurbs, including from Gloria Steinem (though few reviews). Her scientific work was highly respected and two of her colleagues published a *festschrift* of her scientific papers after her death. As Steinem put it, "For years, I've been trying to explain that Naomi Weisstein was great at everything, from science and music to writing and friendship. If she hadn't existed, no one could have invented her." I'd love it if you could include something about her in your piece. She was bed-ridden for more than 30 years with chronic fatigue syndrome.

**LM**: Can you say something more about how you feel John Stoltenberg was maligned?

**MD**: I don't have the Chesler book at hand, but what I recall in general is that she accused John of having a long history of seducing and abandoning young men.

**LM**: In Dworkin your trademark skills as historian and storyteller are on prime display. As in your other biographies, you render complex individuals and circumstances with wisdom, heart and a lightness of touch that invites the reader to join you on a journey of uncertain destination. In the case of Andrea, is it a journey to the future?

**MD**: Indeed, Andrea's message to the future is strong and clear: "Get back up!" No-one that I know has ever been more consistently savaged by reviewers (and many others) than Andrea. Yet over and over, she picked herself up and went back to work.

**LM:** The subtitle of your book is "The Feminist as Revolutionary." In what ways was Andrea Dworkin revolutionary?

**MD:** Andrea was "revolutionary" (and not mainstream) because 1) she didn't believe in categories — in regard both to sexual orientation and gender. 2) she was an across-the-board radical — including being anti-capitalist.

**LM**: For mainstream gay men preoccupied with securing civil liberties protections, Andrea's initiatives against pornography for its exploitation and abuse of women could seem to be facilitating right-wing agendas of censorship and LGBT oppression. You navigate this complex and thorny issue with clarity and security, but did you have misgivings?

**MD**: Though often accused of allying with right-wing anti-pornographers, she disdained them as being merely puritanical. Besides, if A and B both detest C, that doesn't mean that A and B think alike or are joining forces; they also detest each other. Andrea refused to join forces with right-wingers. She was NOT puritanical. What she cared about was violence against women; she was against only the kind of pornography that fanned that violence — and there's plenty of evidence that some of it DOES.

Involved here are First Amendment issues — often misstated. The right of free speech has never been unencumbered. The amendment as interpreted by the Supreme Court restricts freedom of speech on various grounds-including libel and incitement to violence. The argument is between the First Amendment's right to freedom of speech and the Fourteenth Amendment's right to equal protection of the law. Andrea argued that the First Amendment has always favored those in power, while the less-used Fourteenth Amendment gives primary emphasis to the injuries done to women and to minorities.

**LM**: "The Children of Pornhub," the *NYT* feature by Nicholas Kristof, does not discuss Dworkin or the history of Women Against Pornography, but it does validate in excruciating and abundant detail issues of the exploitation and abuse of women in widely-available internet pornography. So did Andrea fail in her mission to curb pornography?

**MD**: Internet pornography is filled with material abusive of women. So, yes, Andrea lost. Even a scholar as respected as Whitney Strub (*Perversion for Profit*) vilely indulges in mocking Linda Lovelace, claiming (falsely) that she expressed regret when the shooting of *Deep Throat* ended! He also mistakenly characterizes Andrea and her sympathizers as calling on *the state* to suppress pornography — which they never did.

**LM**: Another thorny issue you touch on has to do with transgender rights and initiatives. Mount Sinai now has a Center for Transgender Medicine. Accusations of transphobia continue around J.K. Rowling. But first, last, front and center is the ongoing violence, topped by alarming spikes in murder, of transgender persons and blatant curtailment of their rights under Trump. In what ways can transgender folk, and we with them, look to Andrea Dworkin for inspiration?

**MD**: In Andrea's words, transgender people will find an unconditional defense of their right to name and be themselves.

**LM**: A book of Andrea's later years, *Scapegoat*, found her doing a comparative analysis of the experience of Jews and women. Not surprisingly, she found they had much in common. There was additional perspective on the oppression of women in Israel, and as well Palestinians under Israeli occupation. Her suggestion that there should be an Israel, a country of refuge, for persecuted women, is powerful and intriguing. Was there any further pursuit of this idea?

**MD**: To my knowledge nothing ever came of Andrea's idea of a nation state for women; there's scant evidence that she ever pursued it with any actual energy.

**LM**: Andrea's writing always drew heated criticism. Was that true of *Scapegoat* as well?

**MD**: I myself had never heard of *Scapegoat* until I did the biography. I much admire *Scapegoat,* but the book, from all I can tell, remains largely unknown. My guess is that its carefully reasoned, un-hysterical tone doesn't suit the stereotype of Andrea as a wild woman that her detractors insist upon.

**LM**: In her review of your *Andrea Dworkin* for *Dignity: A Journal of Exploitation and Violence*, Phyllis Chesler, author of *Women and Madness*, shares with you a discernibly deep affection and regard for

Dworkin, but takes issue with some details of your recounting of difficult exchanges between them.

**MD**: She doesn't "refute" my account of Andrea's interactions with her. My evidence is solid. Phyllis offers no real counter-evidence — she simply indulges in rhetoric, unsubstantiated.

**LM**: Many figures make brief appearances in *Andrea Dworkin*. Chelser is one, as is Alan Dershowitz, both of whom can be viewed as having drifted to the right during the Trump period. In both cases, I've tried, often with great difficulty, to appreciate that they see what they're doing as somehow ultimately in the greater interest of protecting basic principles of civil liberties.

**MD**: Seeing those two as "protecting basic principles of civil liberties" is a joke.

**LM**: What I mean is that I know Phyllis, and presumably Dershowitz as well, to be deeply concerned about resurgent antisemitism, as am I. Within that concern are difficult issues, especially for progressives, of freedom of religion.

In my own case, however, I found myself unable to join or condone their apparent strategy of defending, and thereby aligning themselves with, extremist right-wing forces — Trump, the Evangelicals, Orthodox Jews, most Republicans, right-wing media, as a way of standing against what they perceive to be, not incorrectly, as "The New Anti-Semitism" (the title of one of Chesler's recent books, for which I gave an affirming blurb), increasingly white supremacist extremist, but a lot of it Islamist and leftist as well. Dershowitz keeps pointing out that he voted for Hillary and Chesler denies being in lockstep with Trump. Meanwhile, however, there they are on Fox and Breitbart. (My experience with Chesler is discussed in my essay on *Huffington Post*: https://www.huffpost.com/entry/phyllis-chesler-sarah-schulman-and-me-wonder-women_b_59b7db53e4b0883782dec2e6). What's your take on this?

**MD**: Like Andrea, I don't doubt that there's been a resurgence of anti-Semitism. Neither of us, however, would seek an alliance with right-wing forces on the issue. Right-wingers have little or nothing to say about the legitimate grievances the Palestinian people have against Israel's oppressive policies. As a Jew I feel emotionally attached to Israel's democratic principles — but not when they themselves transgress against self-determination.

**LM**: And what of your own interactions with Andrea — did they follow a trajectory over time?

**MD**: I do detail and evaluate my own involvement with Andrea in the book. I relegated most of that material to the footnotes, to avoid calling undue attention to myself.

Yes, there was a trajectory over time. I distinctly remember during the early days of the Gay Academic Union (in the early 1970's) Andrea and several other women imploring the gay men to prioritize feminism — and how confused I initially felt, feeling then that feminism and gay liberation were related but separate issues. Yet I trusted those women more than I did many of the gay men (like Wayne Dynes or Jim Levin). Over time (I can't put a date on it) I fully embraced Andrea's contention that the *global* inequality of women is iniquitous and that their liberation should be at the top of the activist agenda.

**LM**: You share with Andrea a wry sense of humor. Did you or she ever write a work of comedy or satire?

**MD**: I hadn't thought of it before, but yes, Andrea and I did share a wry sense of humor. Most of mine went into my plays, especially *Payments*, which is about gay male hustling.

**LM**: Like Larry Kramer and Andrea Dworkin, you are both a writer and an activist. In Larry's case, people would argue about whether his legacy was primarily his writing or his activism. His legacy will be both, of course. The same, I'm sure, is true of Andrea. And of you. Any thoughts about your own experience of activism vs writing?

**MD**: I can't give you a clear-cut answer on "activist or writer?." In the past, whenever I was deeply involved in activism (anti-Vietnam; NGLTF; CLAGS, etc.) I was constantly kvetching about the lack of time I had to write; the same was true vice versa. Also, some of my activism — especially GAU and CLAGS-was involved in promoting gay scholarship (including writing). Except for marching in anti-war (and pro-gay) demonstrations, I was rarely a *street* activist. For 4–5 years I answered the phones for People With AIDS Coalition, but didn't picket the White House. I was arrested only once — during a sit-in on the U.S. Senate floor demanding an end to the war in Vietnam.

**LM:** For those of us looking to the future, or trying to, what better place to look than the next book project(s) of Martin Duberman. Can we ask what they are?

**MD**: My Young Adult biography of Paul Robeson will be published mid-March. I've also completed two other manuscripts: "Encounters on the Left" (my personal interactions with eleven radical activists over the years), and "At Ninety" (a long glance backwards). "Encounters" will probably be published in early Spring 2022 and "At Ninety" late in 2022.

∇

Martin Duberman is Distinguished Professor Emeritus at the CUNY Graduate Center, where he founded and for a decade directed the Center for Lesbian and Gay Studies (CLAGS). He is the author of many books, including biographies, memoirs, plays and essay collections. He has won a Bancroft Prize and been a finalist for the National Book Award and the Pulitzer Prize. He received the Lifetime Achievement Award from the American Historical Association and Honorary Doctorates from Amherst College and Columbia University.

# Remembering Peter G. Davis

*– Medium*, 3/5/21

Figure 192 - Music Critic Peter G. Davis (right) with Conductor Riccardo Muti, slippeddisc.com

How many sopranos have had their singing of *Dove Sono*, the Countess's great aria in *The Marriage of Figaro,* described by one of the world's most discriminating music critics as "note perfect"?

Only a few of my closest gay friends knew of my clandestine career as a Mozart soprano, the successor to Eleanor Steber (at the Continental Baths). My rendition of *Dove Sono* may have been more notable for its musicianship than tonal allure, but notable as well is that it was executed (cough) while descending the treacherously narrow staircase of Peter G. Davis's brownstone on Manhattan's upper west side near Lincoln Center.

A true confession from an enchanted time of coming of age, of opera in one of its heydays, of our lives as music lovers, opera people, as culture vultures, as New Yorkers, of ourselves as gay men coming to grips with our minority identity and sexuality on the cusp of the fledgling gay liberation movement. It was a time when being in the closet was still the norm, especially in the workplace and notably at the *New York Times,* where Peter was a senior music critic.

The tribute paid to Peter in the *Times* on his passing was generous, deserved and honoring of his legacy, especially for his commitment to the art of singing and opera. In the 1970s and well into the 1980s, however, the paper was still very conservative around the subject of homosexuality. This was the *NYT* that Larry Kramer went after for its relegation of the emerging AIDS epidemic in his play *The Normal Heart* in 1985.

That same year I attended the first international conference on AIDS in Atlanta, where I sought out *NYT* medical writer Lawrence K. Altman, himself a physician, to ask him why the *Times* was so lax in its coverage of our "gay men's health crisis." Even as it featured a cover story on a flu epidemic in Austria's Lippizaner stallions (harkening images of the aristocratic Hapsburg empire in the background of the Sulzberger family that founded and ran the *NYT*), it had yet to have comparably prominent coverage of what was from its inception a four-alarm global pandemic that involved other major risk groups. Altman's answer: "We're not an advocacy journal."

Although I don't recall him ever publicly lying about his being gay or taking "beards" to events, Peter did struggle to deal with the homophobia of his two bosses, culture and managing editor Arthur Gelb (Met Director Peter Gelb's father) and executive editor Abe Rosenthal. In terms of their oversight of what could and couldn't be discussed, Peter described the atmosphere at the *Times* as being "like the KGB."

Fortunately, the Rosenthal era (1977–88) is now passed. Apart from his having to deal, as we all did, with ambient homophobia, however, Peter was from an earlier generation when music criticism was characteristically more circumspect around social issues. Neither surprisingly nor atypically, Peter was less interested in advancing the frontiers of social change than in being consistent in his aesthetics and scrupulous about maintaining standards of quality.

If you were to confront Peter as I increasingly did about what seemed his relegation of social and political context in times when social and political concerns were otherwise gathering momentum — sometimes explosively, as with AIDS — he would retreat.

These aesthetics, standard for his time and ilk, were apparent in Peter's attitude towards trending approaches to opera. Yes, one can do deconstructive stagings, a trademark of the era that continues and that Peter acknowledged with qualified admiration — e.g., Peter Sellars, the Chéreau *Ring*. But what was crucial for Peter, the goalpost he never lost sight of, was clarity about the essential properties of a piece.

It was one thing to click into our time by staging *Marriage of Figaro* in Trump Tower. But it was another to muddy the human relationships that are the heart and soul of an opera that has earned its time-honored place as one of the great works of western civilization. The Trump Tower *Figaro* may have been on target in its reverberations for our time, but of any and all such efforts, Peter was consistent in his demand for accountability, for what worked and what didn't.

It's the same appreciation Peter applied to singers. Stylistic choices could be unusual and supportable as such, but questionable if they fought what gave the music its life. Peter was especially skilled in measuring the impact of such choices on the greater arc of a career. In assessing a later-years recital by Marilyn Horne, he weighed as if on a justice scale the tonal beauty and agility of her earlier voice against her later interpretive maturity. It was a matter of personal taste, he concluded, indicating his own preference for the latter.

Figure 193 - book cover, amazon.com

**Peter was an inspiration in the development of a community health initiative that never got off the ground but that remains worthy: a study of the health and health care of professional singers in the United States.**

Peter's heartfelt and thoughtful devotion to singers and singing inspired me in one of my own early public health efforts. Preceding my work on AIDS, gay health, addiction and other enclaves of community medicine (the gay leather and bear subcultures), was an effort I initiated to study the health and health care of professional singers in America. With the help of our mutual friend and colleague, voice connoisseur and opera polymath Conrad L. Osborne, a questionnaire was developed. Alas, in the wake of AIDS, the project was set aside.

It remains worthy. I wonder how often singers today, in the absence of being better informed, and in the absence of health care options better organized to meet their needs, end up being ill-served. A peak personal moment of this endeavor for me came when I met with beautiful Italian soprano Katia Ricciarelli, the Lina Cavalieri of her day, with her partner at that time, handsome divo Jose Carreras, to discuss her sore throat.

What Peter had to say to the public then still holds true. However distracted we might be by historical, social and political insights, whatever the tumult of history and politics and however applicable or trenchant they might seem in time and place, we must not lose our sense of what's essential to a work's integrity and appeal, and the original intentions of the composer. To this end, Peter often studied the scores of the works he reviewed.

While these standards and values may not seem particularly remarkable for music criticism of any period, they can seem unfashionable, even pedantic, in today's maelstroms of life, art and culture. Meanwhile, as an unwitting watchdog for cultural hegemony rather than cultural change, Peter wasn't notably attuned to life outside these boxes of aesthetics.

What subjects would he have pursued if he'd felt more at liberty and inspired to do so? Alas, apart from not going to great lengths to hide the fact the he was gay and having to deal with homophobia in the workplace and society at large, Peter was reticent and conforming around the challenges of social change. An internet search of music criticism for issues like sexism, misogyny, homophobia, racism, populism or antisemitism, all of which he shared concerns about, wouldn't yield many listings for Peter G. Davis.

Importuning him to try to be more in the stream if not the forefront of social change was largely for naught. Eventually, it became a wedge between us. News of the emerging epidemic was terrifying and you couldn't blame people for trying to eschew discussion of it. It was easier to evade the messenger and thereby the message.

Even so, his reticence seemed disappointing for a person of Peter's learning and character, and hurtful to me personally, especially in light of what I was doubtless overly invested in seeing as our mentor-mentee relationship. I don't think Peter ever read any of my pieces in the *New York Native* about what immediately became, as the CDC designated it from the outset, "the most important new public health problem in the United States."

For Peter, the gay press where these articles, mostly by me, were exclusively appearing, along with some of my early pieces on "musical closets" (homosexuality, the closet, music and opera), was just too marginal to seek out, or to set aside the time and consideration to actually read and discuss, even amidst the onslaught of AIDS. Consequently, there was no real encouragement from him for my work on these fronts, no sense that what I was trying to do might be of wider interest and value, whether it be activism and fundraising around AIDS and gay rights or opening the closet doors of the worlds of music and opera. Understandably for such a high-profile, professionally closeted figure at that time, such trendings may have been uncomfortable or even threatening personally. Surpassingly, as I sensed it then, they were simply outside the boxes and exigencies of his career interests, responsibilities and priorities.

Eventually, Peter did seem to develop respect for initiatives around gay health and activism, including those shepherded by me. After years of being out of contact, when I reached out to warn him, along with other of my gay friends, about the disturbingly higher rates of anal cancer (what Farrah Fawcett died of) in gay men and the importance of screening for it, something most gay men — and for that matter their doctors, even some who are gay— still know almost nothing about, he was appreciative.

The inhibiting atmosphere at the *Times* and his own shyness notwithstanding, why not write something modest, if discreetly and only to provide a bit more context, about your own gayness and about the gay themes and subtexts of composers like Britten, Tchaikovsky or some of the dozens of other LGBT figures in music and opera? These were questions I kept asking, to the extent of being pushy and having Peter react defensively. Alas, beyond perfunctory acknowledgement, these were subjects that would not engage him and lines he would not cross.

Eventually, he married his devoted partner of many years, Scott Parris. In coming of age and taking such a great life step, Peter had finally come into his own as an openly gay man. As a music critic, meanwhile, he remained tethered to the old aesthetics. Generations hence people may still want to listen to Britten or Tchaikovsky, but will anyone care if they were "gay," a nomenclature and understanding that may well have changed altogether by then? What will still be there, on the other hand, is their music.

In those days, critics commonly hid their own reticence and timidity within these aesthetics that eschewed anything "external" or "extraneous." If Tchaikovsky was gay, so the thinking and rationalizations went, that's not something that can be extrapolated with certainty from his music or otherwise appropriate for music criticism. If Wagner's antisemitism was serious, that's likewise not something unequivocally discernible or extrapolatable from his music and art and therefore not the province of objective music criticism.

This generation-gap dialectic is explored, and with it my relationships with Peter and others, in my memoir, *Confessions of a Jewish Wagnerite*, and its sequel, *On The Future of Wagnerism.*

As my interest in Wagner and antisemitism escalated, and I probed the reticence around it for its similarities to that which surrounded homosexuality, I remember asking Peter about Wagner in Russia. In response to my questioning why they would choose to do Wagner in patriotic Russia, where Wagner would be appreciated as a totem of the German aggression that resulted in the greatest war and loss of life in Russian history, Peter sarcastically suggested that maybe they were motivated to do an announced new production of *Lohengrin* there "because the music is pretty." (A generation later, following earlier reflections on Russians and Wagner by Richard Taruskin, and with reference to *Wagner and Russia* by Rosamund Bartlett, there would be more perspective on Russia, Wagner and Wagnerism in Alex Ross's *Wagnerism.*)

I was already well on my way to becoming a "noodge" of Wagnerism, as Taruskin now describes me. In those days I was clearly and likewise a noodge of gayness and music. Peter, meanwhile, became evermore entrenched in the status quos of his life experience, education and profession. He was not only not at the forefront of any kind of social consciousness or change, he could be impatient with those who were.

It was never entirely fair to indict these critics for not doing more around social issues. Although they continued to occasionally write more expansive "think" pieces, they were increasingly marginalized by their publications to doing performance reviews. Like Andrew Porter at the *New Yorker,* however, when Peter became music critic of *New York* Magazine, he had a regular column. Though also devoted primarily to the performance reviews that became droning as such, the opportunity was there nonetheless to say and do more. As with Andrew Porter's *New Yorker* column, however, reticence and "discretion" were too often discernible and overriding in what was discussed and what wasn't, a reticence that was no longer an editorial imperative.

This is in some contrast to Ross at the *New Yorker* today, and as well to Anthony Tommasini at the *Times.* Whatever the proscriptions of the older order that Peter and Andrew had to deal with, Ross, Tommasini and others seem more attuned to social and political change and controversy, and supported in that by their publications. Whatever my issues with Ross around Wagnerism, his openness to such discussion, however selective, can seem refreshing.

Peter reminded me of Claudius, the Roman emperor. Just as Claudius was afflicted with a stammer that made him seem vulnerable, so Peter's lispy soft-spokenness and passive demeanor could suggest weakness. But Peter was not weak. Like many artists, Peter had learned to fashion what might have been personal liabilities into strengths. In this, he was inspiring.

Peter was a role model, as a gay man making his way in the world with purpose, aplomb and grit, as a professional committed to principles of objectivity and fairness, and in the wisdom and spirituality of his appreciation of music and opera. In having this special friendship I was truly fortunate. Less so Peter, as the avuncular doyen of a gaggle of opinionated young opera queens, often demanding attention, and in my own case increasingly outspoken, undisciplined, sometimes inebriated and overbearing in challenging his authority.

The other de facto leader and figurehead of this extended family was Richard Dyer, music critic of the *Boston Globe.* Dick was our close mutual friend during the 1970's, my years of medical training in

Boston-Cambridge, and coincidentally the period of Beverly Sills's memorable collaborations with Boston opera wizard Sarah Caldwell.

Like Peter, Dick was passionate about singers and singing, and he was a precious and endless font of information, intelligence and lore about singers and opera. He nurtured chummy friendships with the likes of Marilyn Horne and Astrid Varnay, and generously appreciated lesser-light but surprisingly colorful (as he specialized in helping us see) figures like Nadine Connor and Dorothy Kirsten, beauty-pageant contestant "Debbie" (Deborah) O'Brien who sang with the Boston Pops, and cabaret luminary Greta Keller. Dick was an equal-opportunity fan. You needn't be the most famous or best to garner his devotion. An apostle of nostalgia, he was a largely unwitting standard bearer of gay sensibility.

It was Dick who invited me to accompany him on one of the most treasured experiences of my life, to see the greatest operatic artist of our lives and times, however past her prime (or anything close to it) — Maria Callas on her farewell tour in Boston. However vulnerable in the twilight of her great love affair with the world of opera, magic was still there. I really did think I'd died and gone to heaven. And it was Dick with whom I shared another unforgettable evening — the Boston Symphony premiere of *Final Alice* by David del Tredici, who would continue to figure in my life as a composer and friend.

Recently, Dick annotated a collection of the recordings of the beloved American Wagner soprano, Helen Traubel.

For the record, Dick and Peter dubbed me "Mavis," after Maeve, the legendary and ultimate diva of James McCourt's satirical novel of opera queenery, *Mawrdew Czgowchwz*. Climactically, the literally possessed "ultrano" transcends life and art with a *Liebestod* in ancient Gaelic.

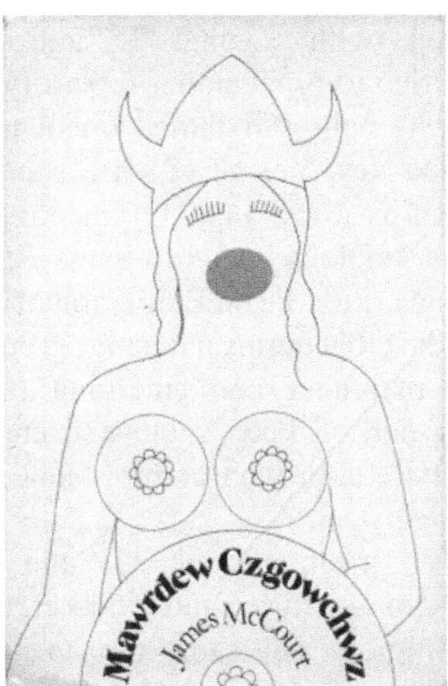


Figure 194 - The book that launched a thousand queens; book cover, amazon.com

Priceless memories of opera and gayness. Of our gay-vernacular pastime of dishing everyone and everything. Of *La Gran Scena* and a solo evening in his living room with Ira Siff, master opera comedien(ne) and scholar of singing whose unexpectedly personal and heartrending "Remember Me But Forget My Fate" (which I kept hearing — mistakenly? — as "Forget My Face") from Purcell's *Dido and Aeneas* concluded the offerings of otherwise side-splittingly funny opera parody. Of a late night trek to see cabaret diva Frances ("Caught in the Act") Faye with Peter's culture buddy and fellow camp enthusiast Henry Edwards. Of Olive Middleton and Florence Foster Jenkins, beloved doyennes of opera wit and satire. Of Dick taking Peter and me to Boston's Copley Plaza to hear legendary Mabel Mercer, then in her 80's, and Peter's observing, in his own Truman-Capote-esque croak of a voice, that her singing sounded like the elderly Eleanor Roosevelt speaking. A later night stopover at the Napoleon Club, America's oldest gay piano bar, even then a relic of *régimes anciens*. Of verismo icon Magda Olivero. Of Peter's sometimes heated disputes with megastar Sills, whose anger at some of Peter's more challenging criticism could turn homophobic, and of whose efforts to wield the business of opera Peter mused: "You can't run an opera company like a delicatessen!" Of Philip Glass, who Peter kept pushing to be more musically inventive. Of Leontyne Price, who he once contrasted with Leonie Rysanek in a tough-love encouragement of Price to broaden her repertory. Of many nights at the opera and concert halls. Of famed opera personality Matthew Epstein's star-studded New Years Eve soirees at the Ansonia. Of late night dinners at nearby Cafe Lux. Of meeting the incomparable Donald Gramm on a fabulous junket to Santa Fe, where we mingled with *L.A.Times* music critic Martin Bernheimer (who secretly offered me a Maalox under the table during a raucous group lunch), arts patron Robert Tobin and raconteur and emerging publishing eminence Stephen Rubin, partner of Peter's close friend and Sills's agent Cynthia Robbins. It's Rubin who commissioned Peter's book, *The American Opera Singer.*

Peter was never mean-spirited. On the contrary, however preoccupied, he was good-natured and kind-hearted. His wisdom and decency were uncommon. The same is true of Dick Dyer. For a profession whose practitioners could sometimes seem like ax murderers in rendering their verdicts, Peter and Dick, in the heyday of my intimate friendships with them, were gentlemen. They were persons of character, humanity, sensibility, wit, spirit and courage who I was privileged to get to know, and love.

# Opera Queens, Fandom, Wagnerism and Germany

– *Medium*, 5.22.21

**"Despite Germany's praiseworthy culture of remembrance, many Germans have a jarringly tenuous grasp of the extent of Nazi crimes or the population's involvement." — James Angelos**

Figure 195 - Rosa von Praunheim, askania award 2016, photo by Emilio Espardo, Wikimedia Commons

*Rosa von Praunheim's* **Opera Divas, Opera Queens** *looks at the world of opera in Germany through the lenses of gay men. Probing, empathic and entertaining, it's also reticent and nonjudgmental.*

What if one day it came true that being gay would be no more notable than being blonde or left-handed? In an idealized future, acceptance of human variance would be a given. Though it once seemed sensical to distinguish left-handed people as constitutionally different and indeed to demonize and medicalize them as such, it no longer does. Do blondes have more fun? Meanwhile, being an opera queen, as if it were a psychiatric condition, is all about being gay, right?

Imagine a book called "Gay Sensibility." It would likely have many scintillating examples of gay wit, fashion and taste held together by gossamer theoretics. But it would be doomed at its inception by its inability to be contained. We're sure enough of the existence and influence of gay sensibility to speak of it casually even as we realize it's a phantom. The more you try to get your hands on it, the more elusive it becomes.

The same is true of "Homosexuality." One could imagine any one of a number of big books with that title. They might have chapters on homosexuality in ancient Greece and Rome, among Native Americans, under Nazism and the modern Gay Liberation movement. But sex researchers Bell and Weinberg wisely titled their compendium *Homosexualities*, recognizing at the outset the fluidities and pluralities of their subject. The closer we look at categorizations, whether of race, ethnicity, nationality, gender, sexuality or behavior, the less certain they become.

Another recent example is "Wagnerism." Alex Ross's book of that title is an appreciation filled with names, lists, categories, anecdotes, references, shards of history and perspective. Though it shies away from attempting to define its subject, it's implicit that there is a matrix phenomenon, "Wagnerism," that interconnects the many individuals and artworks influenced by the composer. Such is the tacit agreement between author and reader on its existence that whether there is anything we can clearly designate as "Wagnerism" is not a question that even gets asked.

Add to these catch-phrases "the opera queen." Terrence Mcnally, who died last year from complications of Covid-19, wrote a play about it. *The Lisbon Traviata*, structured around a treasure hunt for an alleged pirated tape of a live Callas performance, was largely about an opera queen whose zeal to possess the tape is stereotypical, operatic and theatrical. That character was based on Terrence's real-life sparring partner, Mendy, a manic collector who became notorious as such, shadowing the playwright's own worship of Callas. Mcnally's better-known *Master Class* came later and is about the drama of Callas's personal life behind the scenes of her role as the ultimate diva. Late in his career came another if indirect love letter to Callas, *The Golden Ag*e, which pays devotional tribute to the *bel canto* composers who showcased her— Bellini, Rossini and Donizetti.

I was not among those fortunate few who got to attend the Master Classes Callas gave at Juilliard in 1971. Coincidentally, however, I couldn't help but notice how *non*-gay the Juilliard events seemed to be. For someone at the apex of the opera world whose star seemingly depended on gay people — "opera's lifeblood," as I've described us— there was this whole wider world of leading musicians and Callas afficionados that had nothing to do with gay people or gayness. The images conveyed about these sessions was in marked contrast to those of the 3-day-long lines of gay men who waited with sleeping bags outside the Met for standing room tickets to one of her last two appearances there as Tosca in 1965.

It's true that some of Callas's closest associates and friends were gay — film directors Luchino Visconti, Franco Zeffirelli and Pier Paolo Pasolini, and the music critic John Ardoin. That she was influenced by gay men is unquestionable. Like other divas — e.g., Judy Garland — of her time, however, she never directly addressed or spoke of gayness or her gay following as such. Whatever our roles behind the scenes as devout fans, colleagues, advisors and friends, we weren't nearly as important, singular or determinant as we imagined. Take gay men out of the bigger picture of Judy Garland and you still have Judy Garland, the greatest singing actress in the history of film. Take gay men out of the bigger picture of Maria Callas and you still have Maria Callas, one of the most esteemed musical artists of all time.

Enter the German "underground" filmmaker Rosa von Praunheim, who has gone from being participant witness to venerable custodian of gay subcultural life. Though not an opera queen himself, Rosa has always intermingled in gay opera circles. When I told him of my concerns about Wagner and Wagnerism 40 years ago, he seemed bemused. The seriousness and passion still surrounding this encrusted icon of German romanticism and nationalism struck him, the way so much in cultural life does, as curious and amusing. I remember the smile on his face as I declaimed fiercely of my unhappiness as a Jewish Wagnerite.

Decades later, Rosa tried to connect me with his colleague, Enrique Sanchez Lansch, who was working with Rosa on what I believe became the current film about gay people and opera. Lansch is the creator of *Das Reichsorchester*, an important documentary about the Berlin Philharmonic during the Nazi period. Alas, my citing of the absence of expressed remorse in that film's narrative (see my *Huffington Post* piece on "The Nazi Legacy, German Cinema and Questions of Judgment": https://www.huffpost.com/entry/3-gernanfilms_b_8301714) must have landed me in hot water because I never heard from Lansch or for that matter Rosa again.

Bemusement is discernible in most of Rosa's work. However critical or disturbing may be the revelations in what are mostly docudramatizations, they emerge between the lines of a kind of trademark queer *Gemütlichkeit.* Because of my knowledge of the greater body of his work as politically conscious and motivated, as liberal, as socialist ("Rosa" adopted that name from Rosa Luxemburg), in light of our friendship and networks of community, but perhaps also in light of my own denial and codependence, it never occurred to me that the narrative and artistic reticence I had ascribed to Lansch and *Reichsorchester* could seem comparably salient in some of Rosa's work.

In any event, I wish I could say that the current film clearly achieves its tacit mission of uncovering important truths about gay people and opera, especially in relation to Wagner. As might have been predicted from the experience of phenomena comparable to "the opera queen" such as "gay sensibility," "homosexuality" and "Wagnerism," however, there are no conclusive revelations here or elsewhere.

Rather, as with Wayne Koestenbaum's *The Queen's Throat*, there are affinities, intimations, fragments, metaphors, possibilities and *mise-en-scene.* Along the way of this adventure that has no clear trajectory or destination, meanwhile, there's a feast of opera esoterica, lore, attitudes and considerations. Many tantalizing questions are asked, but never answered with certainty or satisfaction.

Because opera is more in the marrow of European life, there is a breadth of repertoire touched on here that will be dazzling for American opera afficionados— e.g., delectable moments of Regine Crespin singing the haunting music of Gounod's little-known *Sappho,* operatic rarities by Haydn, snippets of forgotten operettas and musical comedies. What wouldn't any opera person give to see and hear more?

Exemplary of the film's directorial savvy is its penultimate interview with Wayne Koestenbaum. I don't know how much of the sophisticated questions and framing of these scenes reflects the input of the film's designated co-creator, Markus Tiarks, or the assistance of Rosa's longtime associates and friends Mike Shepard and Brandon Judell, but the greater arc of narrative intelligence, energy and bemusement are unmistakably Rosa.

The *Queen's Throat* sequence begins as we see Wayne coming and going to the accompaniment of *Traviata* excerpts sung by his beloved Anna Moffo, widely considered the finest Violetta of her day, even though her rivals were none other than Joan Sutherland, Montserrat Caballé, Beverly Sills and Maria Callas. When asked in the film to project his own deathbed wish for musical accompaniment, he confounds expectations in choosing Callas rather than Moffo singing Mimi's Farewell from *La Boheme*, with its tumescing declaration of all-encompassing love. As the excerpt plays, we observe Wayne listening intently, his hands clasped in spiritual communion. In the ether of this moment is Moffo, who would advance from her youthful presence as Musetta in that Callas La Scala recording to memorably portray Mimi. Likewise in the background is the dedicatee of *Opera Divas, Opera Queens*, Rosa's colleague and friend Werner Schroeter. With palpable reverence for the ineffable, Wayne's composure conjures images not only of Callas and Moffo, but of Schroeter's own adored diva, the German experimental film actress Magdalena Montezuma.

Let's go back to Mcnally's play, *The Lisbon Traviata,* which had its premiere in New York City in 1989, based on an earlier version from 1985, a time when gay people had yet to secure civil rights. So pleased were we to see ourselves onstage that we fully conspired with Terence to see the fanaticism being portrayed as characteristically queer. It never occurred to us to regard such phenomena of fandom as equal-opportunity employers, notably present as well in the wider world of mainstream culture. Could it really be that straight fans were more similar to than different from their gay counterparts?

Late in his career, handsome New York City Opera tenor Richard Leech notoriously took off his shirt during the love duet that closes the first act of *Madama Butterfly*, heightening as perhaps never before the scene's already incomparable eroticism. Leech was known for having a fan, Rosemary Dunne, who was so ardent that she became her own case of history and legend. "Opera Fan's Magnificent Obsession," the *New York Times* called it in 1997. What role sexuality played in this shadow relationship remains unclear in a way that underscores the subtitle phrase, "*the Mystery of Desire,*" of Koestenbaum'*s The Queen's Throat.*

It's a mystery that takes on additional resonance in Rosa's film with its recollections of Ljuba Welitsch, famous for her portrayal of

Strauss's Salome, based on Oscar Wilde's still shockingly over-the-top (and some would say "gay" in its extravagance) play. As she romances the severed head of John The Baptist in the final scene, she sings: "*Und das Geheimnes der Liebe is Grösser aus das Geheimnes der Todes*" (And the mystery of love is greater than the mystery of death.) Whatever the components of the chemistry between Leech and Dunne, gender and sexual orientation seem less pertinent than fandom and desire itself.

Between the lines here are phenemona of obsession and compulsivity, seemingly in relation to sexuality. We want to understand Dunne as a kind of stalker, meanwhile deconstructing the opera queen, like Salome, as a Frankenstein of desire.

Another exemplar of this gay-straight spectrum of appreciation is media impressaria Arianna Stassinopoulous. Her reverence for Callas resulted in the launching of her own international fame and career by authoring a book on the diva — *Maria Callas, The Woman Behind the Legend.* Here as well, beyond what might be presumed to be the background influence of gays in fashion and culture, was a manifestation of fandom that had little to do with gayness.

And what about Lois Kirschenbaum, immortalized in James McCourt's fantastical novel of opera queenery, *Mawrdew Czgowchwz?* Kirschenbaum was an eccentric and ever-present figure of opera who may have set records in attending performances and collecting autographs, programs and photographs. Apart from serving as a blank slate for gay imaginations, however, she was not known to be gay or otherwise to partake of gay culture.

So whether you call someone an opera queen, person, afficionado, fan or fanatic is arbitrary. Who are the *real* opera queens? Koestenbaum? Mcnally? Stassinopoulous? Kirschenbaum? Rosemary Dunne? King Ludwig II of Bavaria? Me?

In my own coming of age in gay opera circles in Chicago, that person was record collector Andrew Karzas, host of a long-running show, "From The Recording Horn," on WFMT radio. Andy was a devout lifelong fan of Toscanini soprano Licia Albanese and a caregiver to the surviving partner of famed Turandot and Wagner soprano Dame Eva Turner. Andy became known for attending every Licia performance, to the bitter end of *Traviata*s and *Bohemes* in small towns. His alcoholic partner, who bore a striking resemblance to

Friedelind Wagner, did not share Andy's passion for Licia or opera, but did have his own diva — Ayn Rand.

I never saw Licia live but our mutual friend Dick Dyer (*Boston Globe* music critic) and I ventured to Providence to hear what we were pretty sure would be Anna Moffo's last *Traviata.* And last it was, at least for us. Andy's imitation of Licia was uncannily accurate and hilarious in capturing her vocal inflections, especially her breathiness. In his devotion to what we might call the cause — of voice, of opera, of gay sensibility in relation to them— Andy was a cherishable figure of knowledge, character and wit. Alas, that this mission seemed to preclude a more contemporary gay consciousness proved an ever-widening divide between us.

Some of the gay men interviewed in *Opera Divas, Opera Queens* seem typical creatures of this fandom of earlier gay life. We are shown Willi Egli, a trained butcher turned Lufthansa flight attendant who began his secondary career of being an opera queen after being smitten by Charlotte Berthold as the witch in *Hansel und Gretel.* It's a part often portrayed by male character actor-singers in drag. Such is the film's skill in mixing musical excerpts with images that we experience Egli's infatuation with Berthold. It's backstage at one of those Zürich Opera performances that Egli, who struggled as so many of us did with self-acceptance around being gay, met and eventually wed "the tenor." Alas, the tenor could not deal with his own gayness and committed suicide, still in his early 40's. When the lights go out in the opera house, Egli observes, gay men, so many of them repressed, find a happiness elusive in reality.

Eventually, Egli moved on to his veneration of Joan Sutherland. We see him, deeply moved, placing a heart-shaped bouquet of roses on her grave stone in Montreux. Callas's grave site at *Pére Lachaise* cemetery in Paris, which I myself visited, is shown comparably strewn with flowers and candles. We hear a keepsake recorded message from Sutherland explaining why she can't meet with Willi before her departure back to Australia, soon after which she died. We see him caressing a needlepoint rose-design pillow he requested from her estate, one he recognized from dressing room visits.

Inheriting Sutherland's mantle for Willi — on the wings of an infatuation with the passing generation's Edita Gruberova, who we see in the final moments of her mad scene as the ageing queen in *Roberto Devereux* and later signing autographs— is Diana Damrau.

Willi makes ceviche dinners for the younger diva, an imperial Queen of the Night, and hands her rose bouquets during curtain calls. She "crashes" Willi's wedding incognito. "Opera for me is *Heimat*," he concludes.

Willi's story is one of several that propel the film's narrative. As in a novel, we meet protagonists who reappear at various points, sometimes accompanied by Rosa. They include filmmaker Axel Ranisch, excerpts of whose production of *The Love For Three Oranges* seem overflowingly colorful and exuberant but whose casual speculation that gay infatuation with opera may be about death seems similarly extravagant.

Tilman Krause, literary editor of *Die Welt*, whose beloved divas include Regine Crespin and Elizabeth Schwarzkopf, waxes, sometimes ecstatically, about the special appeal of opera and Wagner to gays. Schwarzkopf's *Hitlerjugend* past is not mentioned, nor is he asked about it by Rosa, whose own father was a Nazi. Being gay is a gift, Krause posits. We're more fortunate than heterosexuals in having so much more access to sex. That gays are in a special relationship with opera is never in doubt, but articulating exactly why and how proves elusive.

Dietmar Schwarz, *Intendant* of the *Deutsche Oper Berlin,* speaks comfortably but generally about the importance of gays for opera. Musicologist Kevin Clark is contrastingly specific. His book, *Glitter and Be Gay*, time-travels back to uncover the considerable role of gays and eroticism in opera history. Perusing the journals of Offenbach, he learned how sexually charged stagings of the day were and how extensive the backstage carryings on. Yet he too, can venture questionably far in gleaning a special eroticism of female voices for gay men.

With his husband, Jörn Weisbrodt, who proposed their collaboration, pop idol Rufus Wainright speaks of their opera, *Hadrian*, with its edginess around intergenerational sex. That subject is otherwise evaded in the film's nonexploration of operas with more clearly gay content, such as those of Benjamin Britten. There is no mention of the Countess Geschwitsch in Berg's *Lulu*, the first explicitly gay character to enter the international operatic repertoire. (As Alex Ross has pointed out in writing about how the subject of gays and opera has gone from opera queens to gay-themed operas, there is earlier gay content, but in little known works.)

Edda Moser recalls her experience with openly gay composer Hans Werner Henze, who wrote music for her. "Gays understand women better than straight men," she observes. She always felt "protected" by the gay men around her.

Hubert Wild, who sings male and female parts, is seen doing *Lazarus* by David Bowie as well as the opening of the *Liebestod.* His passion is compelling. Rosa couldn't turn his camera away. We are enthralled, even if neither Rosa's film nor we understand why. Wild speaks of the appeal of unhappy endings for gays. Yet the works of Handel, who he excels at rendering, often end well.

Engaging as well are scenes of a modern-dress *Der Rosenkavalier* with Sophie Koch, who is shown as Octavian in clear attraction to, and later in a closeup passionately kissing, Diana Damrau as Sophie. Koch is articulate about how the *travesti* parts in opera she has played (Octavian, The Composer in *Ariadne*) and that are commonplace in opera tweak conceptions of the place of gay people in opera.

"Gays know what's beautiful....They will often be there when great art and culture arise." "Opera and sex belong together...alas not for straights." "Wagner is a narcotic...many people get addicted." And so on. Such observations are predominant here — copious, wistful, sometimes passionate, sometimes compelling, but never incontrovertible. There isn't a one — in Rosa's film, in *The Queen's Throat,* my own writing or anywhere else — that is more substantive than personal impression and speculation.

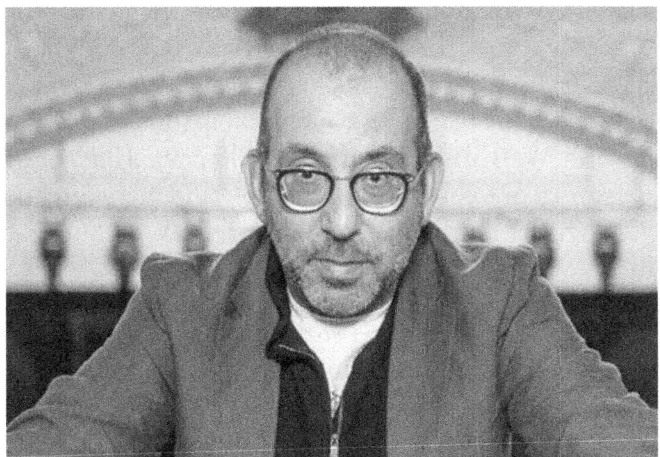

Figure 196 - Barrie Kosky, *Die Meistersinger* telecast, parterre box

Which brings us to what for me is the soul of Rosa's film, the interview material on Wagner, especially that with theater and opera wiz Barrie Kosky. Kosky directed Bayreuth's 2017 production of Wagner'*s Die Meistersinger von Nürnberg* and is the first Jewish director in the history of the Festival (Yuval Sharon, whose parents are Israeli, became the Festival's first American director in 2018). He is also the first non-Wagner to direct *Meistersinger* there. While such firsts might suggest transformation for Hitler-and-Nazism tainted Bayreuth, Jews have been notable players in Wagnerism and at Bayreuth throughout the history of both.

***Kosky is not German and his brilliant work does not satisfy the longing to hear Germans themselves express their feelings about Wagner's antisemitism, and about Bayreuth and the Wagner family in relation to Hitler and Nazism.***

Much of the surrounding commentary on Wagner by Krause and others in Rosa's film can seem typically ethereal — i.e., that gays are drawn to the grand and outsized in subject matter, characters, gestures, emotions and spirituality. Rosa cruises the "Green Hill" — Bayreuth and its environs — with soprano Nadine Secunde. In the background is discussion of Siegfried Wagner (SW), the composer's son, who ran Bayreuth until his death in 1930. Though he married Winifred, a young British girl of 17 who became intimately involved with Hitler during the ensuing Nazi period and with whom he had four children, he was always known to have been preferentially gay.

There is now a Siegfried Wagner exhibit at Bayreuth, but as the background narrative reveals (mostly Rosa in voice over), you will not find references to his gayness and participation in gay networks or his affair with a British boyfriend, Clement Harris, in official Bayreuth histories or exhibits. Nor will you find there directions to the "Siegfried Wagner Memorial Tearoom" or to SW as "the patron saint of gays."

The decision for SW to marry was at some level inevitable. In the wake of the Oscar Wilde trial in 1895, homosexuals of Siegfried's day and ilk had to be exceedingly careful lest they run afoul of the law as well as their families and the public. In the case of the Wagner family and its legacy, a lot was at stake. As it was for SW contemporaries such as Thomas Mann, likewise known to be preferentially homosexual. (As Adam J. Sacks has noted, there are no examples of Mann expressing opposite-sex attraction in his personal diaries.)

As for more explicit discussion of SW, the Wagner family and Bayreuth in relation to antisemitism, Hitler and Nazism, there's virtually none in Rosa's film. If you were to confront the film's German voices and opera people about this, I think they'd respond that judgment, dismay and regret are now givens; having been endlessly processed, it seems reasonable that they don't have to remain in the forefront of consideration or discussion.

The truth, however, is that only rarely have they been forefront in discussion and consideration; nor have they been put to rest. When it comes to Wagner and Germans today, closure on the past — as opposed to fully acknowledging and genuinely mourning the past—can seem to be an external pressure that belongs in the past. Do Germans or those designated as opera queens experience discomfort seeing the busts of Wagner and the Wagner family by Nazi sculptor Arno Breker that still dominate the environs of Bayreuth? As New York counterculture eminence Steve Mass, who resided in Berlin for decades, observed in response to my noting German Chancellor Angela Merkel's regular attendance at Bayreuth, full acceptance of the preeminent place of Wagner in culture is no longer questioned or qualified by most Germans.

As we might surmise from what we know of his *Meistersinger* production, set in a Nürnberg trials courtroom, Kosky can get very real and personal about Wagner's antisemitism and his own feelings. In doing so, he makes it challenging for critics like me to generalize that opera people, especially Wagnerites, often look the other way when it comes to the controversies of Wagner.

Kosky, who is Australian and who describes himself as "a gay Jewish kangaroo," is a figure of dizzying virtuosity and accomplishment. Bayreuth has had several "anti-antisemitic" productions of *Meistersinger*, inevitable in light of the work's antisemitic context and subtext and Bayreuth's determination to move forward in acknowledging these and other controversies in its endlessly deconstructive productions. Absent full disclosure of the history of Wagner, the Wagner family and Bayreuth in relation to Hitler and Nazism, however, it's a grappling that remains more obligatory and gestural than complete.

"A personal exorcism," Kosky describes his Bayreuth experience. His "very problematic and complicated relationship with Wagner," as he explains it, stems from his relationship with his grandmother who told him of her relationship with the composer. She understood first that she had to learn German because "it's the language of culture." And "you must learn Wagner because, after Mozart, he's the greatest composer." She took Kosky to his first Wagner operas. Her Budapest family was murdered in the Holocaust. "I have to say that I have a love-hate relationship with Wagner," Kosky admits with visible consternation.

Despite his success in Germany, Kosky is not German and his brilliant work does not satisfy the longing one feels to hear more explicitly from Germans themselves and from Wagnerites and opera people more generally about their feelings — specifically their consciousness of Wagner's antisemitism, and of Bayreuth and the Wagner family in relation to Hitler and Nazism.

Past many decades of intense discourse and scholarship around these controversies, aren't the film's bemused revelations accomplishing this credibly, adequately and appropriately, at least for this window on culture and moment and place in time? Though judgment of the *Nazizeit* may seem implicit, and though it may seem unreasonable, unfair and pushy to keep, well, pushing for greater expressiveness, and to keep singling out Germans for this, this sense of something missing lingered for me, accompanying identification and appreciation, as I completed the journey of *Opera Divas, Opera Queens*. It seemed in sync with my greater experience of being a gay opera person and Jewish Wagnerite, of having to keep my stronger feelings of ambivalence, anger, frustration and irresolution to myself.

The issue of taciturnity among Germans and throughout the opera world is enmeshed within that of aesthetics. Much of the greatest art, such as that of Wagner, is distinguished by degrees of ambiguity, of not spelling everything out. Understandably, neither Rosa nor any other serious artist wants to be pressured into an unaesthetic literalism by political correctness. At the same time, however, they want to be cautious about not being hounded by allegations of insensitivity.

In the case of Germany and Germans, ambiguity, even when under the mantle of art, can't help but brush up against ongoing cultural controversies. The fallout of this dilemma is captured by James Angelos in his VE Day (5/8/21) Commemoration in the *New York*

*Times, "Was Nazi Germany Defeated or Liberated? Germans Can't decide":*

"Despite Germany's praiseworthy culture of remembrance, many Germans have a jarringly tenuous grasp of the extent of Nazi crimes or the population's involvement...The danger is that many in Germany will end up conflating victims and perpetrators, and fail to fully grasp how the Nazis mobilized the masses. The point is not to saddle current and future generations with guilt, but to ensure that the unvarnished truth remains clear. No good lesson can be drawn from history without a full understanding that the guilty were all around, and that they fought to the end."

Apart from the Kosky material, there's little of such remembrance and reflection surrounding Wagner and Bayreuth in Rosa's film. Rather, it colludes in the narrative of what Gottfied Wagner calls "Wagner, Inc," that whatever controversy may persist around Wagner and Bayreuth, the showcasing of a Kosky is a kind proof of how far we've all advanced in dealing with acknowledging and thereby disarming and moving beyond it. Underneath a discernible impatience with more confrontation and judgment is the simple reality that when it comes to Wagner, the greater world of opera, epitomized by its opera queens, is on the same page as most Germans. We may be freer to be as critical and irreverent as we want now, but as Hermione Gingold put it in her cabaret act, don't mess with our drugs.

I haven't yet seen the Kosky *Meistersinger.* Despite my disaffection from the opera and from Wagner and Bayreuth at this juncture, from the excerpts I have seen in Rosa's film and what I've read and heard about the production, dovetailing with Kosky's commentary, I confess to feeling enticed to flirt with a relapse of my admittedly sometimes tenuous Wagnerism sobriety.

Key to Kosky's success would seem to be his greater vision of affirmation for German theater, opera and operetta. So many composers and artists were killed by the Nazis, he observes. The way to honor them is to bring out their joy and vitality, not to museum-ize them. Hitler didn't destroy you, Kosky is saying. Here you are again in all your glory. And fun. In the course of these passages, we see effervescent scenes from a new production of *Roxy and Her Miracle Team*, a "soccer operetta" by Paul Abraham. Can it be that with such an approach Kosky manages not only to cast light on *Meistersinger*'s suffocating atmosphere of antisemitism and German supremacy, but as well to unlock the good will, the *Gemütlichkeit* that Wagnerites appreciate as surpassing and universal in Wagner?

So if I can still react affirmingly to a figure like Kosky, and with him to Wagner, am I then like him, my writing a kind of exorcism? Yes, but exorcism is not a rite or ritual I feel inclined to keep repeating. Kosky is processing his ambivalence via his directing. I'm processing what I think is my position beyond such processing. I don't want to remain in thrall to Wagner, to opera, to fandom. Rather, I want to have a new level of appreciation —with abstinence, less vulnerable to intoxication and codependence, more sober and with greater detachment. I don't want to keep relapsing.

Am I deluding myself into thinking I can do this in a way that will ensure protection from vulnerability and pain? More than likely, and doubtless like Kosky, I will have to keep facing my qualifiers (as we say in the jargon of addiction and codependence recovery). I will have to remain mindful of my vulnerabilities in relation to Wagner — to artworks and other phenomena that have proven addictive and thereby toxic but which have also been wellsprings of desire, passion and creativity for me.

The greater goal for me, the prize I want to keep my eyes on, is to no longer be in this place of negotiating, like Kosky, a "love-hate relationship with Wagner." Rather, I feel ready to move on from it. I no longer want to drink, do drugs, act out sexually or with food, or have a love-hate relationship with Wagner.

Meanwhile, however deep and serious Kosky's misgivings about Wagner and his brilliance in exposing and indicting Wagner's antisemitism, one senses that he represents the limits of what Germans and the wider world of opera they continue to dominate will allow on the subject. Be the court jester, be as critical and irreverent as you like, goes the new normal; it's all ok, so long as you remain signatory to the sovereignty of Wagner's art and of German art and culture, coincidentally the explicit theme and exhortation of *Die Meistersinger von Nürnberg*.

The *Opernwelt* of Rosa's film is not asking for forgiveness or greater accountability from Bayreuth or the Wagner family or Germany around antisemitism and the *Nazizeit*. Nor is it asking for greater accountability around gayness. As in America, the opera queens of Rosa's film don't seem to be the gay people on the front lines of ACT UP demonstrations or activist protest of Putin's anti-gay policies in Russia. Rather, they seem sociopolitically middlebrow, tacitly satisfied with developments that have been to our advantage, like gay marriage and workplace acceptance. Deeper probing seems neither invited nor welcome. Rosa has come full circle, from a sensibility that's clearly outside the social and political status quo to one that's now more within it.

In the autumn of his career, Rosa continues to pay bemused, caring and insightful tribute to our gay forebears and contemporaries, in this case our idiosyncratic, resilient subculture of opera people. The idea that opera queens were merely a byproduct and manifestation of oppression is upended in this film's wide and forward gaze on a realm that against expectations and on its own terms continues to thrive.

Whether gay or straight, male or female, old or young, binary or not binary, if you're an opera queen or wonder if you are, *Opera Divas, Opera Queens* is wonderful and enlightening entertainment. If you're not an opera queen, or worry that you could be, or that you could be perceived to be, watch out for that old bugaboo of gay seduction. This could be the hit that turns you into one of *those* people.

# Epilogue: Journey of a Thousand Miles

– *Medium*, 5/27/21

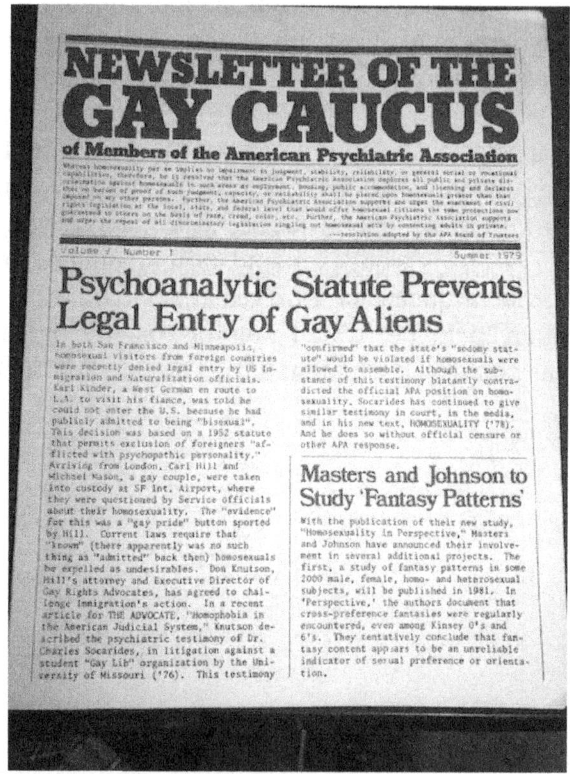

NEWSLETTER OF THE GAY CAUCUS of Members of the American Psychiatric Association

Whereas homosexuality per se implies no impairment in judgment, stability, reliability, or general social or vocational capabilities, therefore, be it resolved that the American Psychiatric Association deplores all public and private discrimination against homosexuals in such areas as employment, housing, public accommodation, and licensing and declares that no burden of proof of such judgment, capacity, or reliability shall be placed upon homosexuals greater than that imposed on any other persons. Further, the American Psychiatric Association supports and urges the enactment of civil rights legislation at the local, state, and federal level that would offer homosexual citizens the same protections now guaranteed to others on the basis of race, creed, color, etc. Further, the American Psychiatric Association supports and urges the repeal of all discriminatory legislation singling out homosexual acts by consenting adults in private.

---resolution adopted by the APA Board of Trustees

Volume [illegible] Number 1 Summer 1979

## Psychoanalytic Statute Prevents Legal Entry of Gay Aliens

In both San Francisco and Minneapolis, homosexual visitors from foreign countries were recently denied legal entry by US Immigration and Naturalization officials. Karl Kinder, a West German en route to L.A. to visit his fiance, was told he could not enter the U.S. because he had publicly admitted to being "bisexual". This decision was based on a 1952 statute that permits exclusion of foreigners "afflicted with psychopathic personality." Arriving from London, Carl Hill and Michael Mason, a gay couple, were taken into custody at SF Int. Airport, where they were questioned by Service officials about their homosexuality. The "evidence" for this was a "gay pride" button sported by Hill. Current laws require that "known" (there apparently was no such thing as "admitted" back then) homosexuals be expelled as undesirables. Don Knutson, Hill's attorney and Executive Director of Gay Rights Advocates, has agreed to challenge Immigration's action. In a recent article for THE ADVOCATE, "Homophobia in the American Judicial System," Knutson described the psychiatric testimony of Dr. Charles Socarides, in litigation against a student "Gay Lib" organization by the University of Missouri ('76). This testimony "confirmed" that the state's "sodomy statute" would be violated if homosexuals were allowed to assemble. Although the substance of this testimony blatantly contradicted the official APA position on homosexuality, Socarides has continued to give similar testimony in court, in the media, and in his new text, HOMOSEXUALITY ('78). And he does so without official censure or other APA response.

## Masters and Johnson to Study 'Fantasy Patterns'

With the publication of their new study, "Homosexuality in Perspective," Masters and Johnson have announced their involvement in several additional projects. The first, a study of fantasy patterns in some 2000 male, female, homo- and heterosexual subjects, will be published in 1981. In 'Perspective,' the authors document that cross-preference fantasies were regularly encountered, even among Kinsey 0's and 6's. They tentatively conclude that fantasy content appears to be an unreliable indicator of sexual preference or orientation.

Figure 197 - First Newsletter of the Gay Caucus of Members of the American Psychiatric Association, edited by Lawrence D. Mass, M.D., summer 1979, from the NYPL archives of Lawrence D. Mass

In the mid 1970's I began my journey of consciousness and activism as a watchdog for reactionary developments in psychiatry that threatened to reverse the 1973–74 declassification of homosexuality as a mental disorder by the American Psychiatric Association.

During my medical training and first work as a practicing anesthesiologist in the Boston area in the mid 1970's, I entered psychotherapy. Randomly selected Dr. Maxwell G. Potter was a Harvard-based, psychoanalytically trained and oriented psychiatrist who retained and perpetrated his profession's trademark homophobia beyond the period of the declassification.

That declassification may have won the day with gay activists and progressive psychiatrists, but it remained hugely unpopular in the mainstreams of psychiatry. Although Dr. Potter was so homophobic that one might imagine he could easily be sued for malpractice, think again. Even today, practitioners of conversion therapy, widely denounced as unethical and now illegal in a few states, have a free hand to do pretty much whatever they want. When was the last time you heard about *any* psychiatrist being successfully sued for malpractice?

Figure 198 - Dr. Richard Pillard, widely known as the first openly gay psychiatrist in America, was a specialist in genetics who went on to do landmark work on the heritability of sexual orientation, on homosexuality and science, and on "People of the Eye" — studies of deaf ethnicity and ancestry; Facebook

Although I did eventually confront Dr. Potter with the specter of malpractice and terminated "therapy" with him, the experience left me feeling deeply disheartened and adrift. Enter Dr. Richard Pillard, a distinguished Boston-area psychiatrist who became known for being the first openly gay psychiatrist in America. Channel surfing one afternoon, I chanced upon a forum that featured Dr. Pillard and enlightened discussion of homosexuality and the APA declassification, for which Pillard had notably given testimony.

In those days, affirmation of gayness was still not something one read, saw or heard much of in the media. On those rare television programs that featured affirming viewpoints, they were still always "balanced" with "experts" voicing the old "medical" — mostly psychiatric and mostly psychoanalytic — viewpoints of homosexuality as a disorder of society and mental health. But here, without such apposition, was this knight in a white suit speaking calmly and with authority about developments in psychiatry and their implications for gay people and society.

By the next day, I had left Dr. Potter and entered into individual therapy with Dr. Pillard. Without realizing it at the time, I had purchased a one-way ticket to a life of consciousness, activism and their principal outlet of expression for me — my writing.

The first big subsequent development for me was my determination to change the trajectory of my medical career from anesthesiology to psychiatry. At that juncture, what I most wanted to do was respond with my life and career to what I had experienced with Dr. Potter within its wider context of social and political homophobia. In those days, gay civil rights were still nonexistent. Developments like gay marriage, nondiscrimination in the workplace and by the military and immigration, and hate crimes legislation still seemed more like science fiction than imminent or even possible. With the guidance of Dr. Pillard, I decided to do a second residency in psychiatry.

I had a lover in those years in Chicago who I wanted to live with during my training. Hope and affirmation based on the APA declassification were beckoning me forward. But nothing had prepared for me what I would experience in applications for psychiatric residency programs in the Chicago area. Uniformly, the psychiatrists who interviewed me at Northwestern, the University of Chicago, and the University of Illinois medical schools were enraged at my openness about being gay. I was rejected by all of these departments. Without exception, everyone I interviewed with was a version of Dr. Potter.

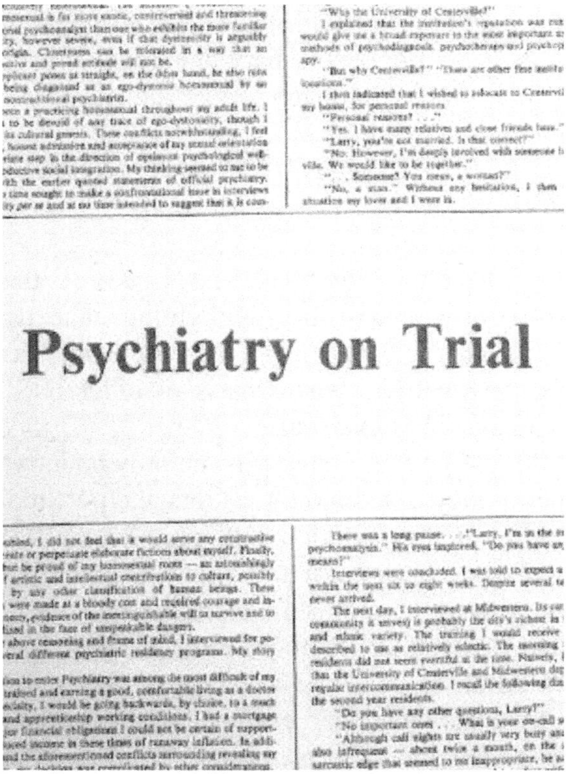

Psychiatry on Trial

Figure 199 - From "Psychiatry on Trial" by Lawrence D. Mass, Gay Community News, Boston, 8/11/1979; NYPL Archives of Lawrence D. Mass

So appalling and infuriating was this experience that I wrote it up in what became my first piece for the gay press and as a gay activist. Originally entitled "Trial By Ordeal," the editor changed that title to "Psychiatry On Trial." It was the centerpiece of the August 11, 1979 issue of Boston's *Gay Community News*.

With Dr. Pillard's encouragement, and in the wake of my bitter experience with Dr. Potter and the applications for psychiatry residency training, I joined the ranks of Dr. Pillard's fledgling group of openly gay psychiatrists. Originally called the "Gay Caucus of the American Psychiatric Association," the name had to be changed to "Gay Caucus of Members of the American Psychiatric Association," since it wasn't an official committee of the APA, as the APA was quick to point out.

Although not myself a psychiatrist, I joined these heroes as their newsletter editor, reconfiguring it from a message center to a venue for news stories and editorials. My first headline sparked controversy not only with the APA, but with the Gay Caucus as well, some of whose members were more cautionary than others; they did not want to jeopardize their limited but hard-earned status.

*"PSYCHOANALYTIC STATUTE PREVENTS LEGAL ENTRY OF GAY ALIENS"*

My banner headline for that first issue of the GCMAPA Newsletter was provocative in highlighting that psychoanalytic theory, with its characterization of homosexuality as a form of "psychopathic personality," was a basis of older INS immigration proscriptions against "homosexuals."

"Until 1990, the United States was the only country in the world with an explicit policy of excluding visitors and potential immigrants because of their sexual orientation. Although the word 'homosexual' has never appeared in U.S. immigration law, from 1952 to 1990 most U.S.courts interpreted the provision excluding persons 'afflicted with a psychopathic personality' to require the exclusion of any person identified as homosexual or who engaged in homosexual acts. Countless individuals have been excluded at the border, deported, or denied naturalization under this provision" (from "Sodomy and Public Morality Offenses Under U.S. Immigration Law:Penalizing Lesbian and Gay Identity" by Shannon Minter, The Cornell Study of Homosexuality and Immigration Law in the U.S., 1993).

How many LGBTQ persons were denied immigration status on the basis of such designations we will never know because crucial medical records of Ellis Island have been lost.

In that early period of my activism, I wrote essays and interviewed progressive psychiatrists and sex researchers in chronicling what I called "the shift in the credibility of medical and scientific opinion about homosexuality and sexuality from the temples of psychiatry to the laboratories of sex research."

Today, we don't hear much about people being denied legal entry on the basis of being gay, or even for having HIV. Hostility to immigrants, ever-present trans-historically, became far more global. The gruesome history of hostility to immigrants in America is captured in the common folk wisdom that "if it's hysterical, it's historical."

One of the pieces in *On The Future of Wagnerism* is called "Voices of Hope and Resilience, and Our Relentless Vilification of The Other, from Wagner to Trump." There I recount a visit I made to Ellis Island with its museum displays of America's history of immigration. They include one detailing the many immigrant groups that have experienced discrimination as immigrants. Every ethnic group you can think of is there — Irish, Italians, Jews, Blacks, Asians, Scandanvians, etc.

But there is one group that has experienced notable immigration discrimination that is not acknowledged in that Ellis Island exhibit: LGBTQ people. Has anyone at the museum been confronted with this, I wondered? That question would beckon to me during the endless, often ferocious immigration scandals of the Trump presidency, as I became personally involved in the plight of undocumented immigrants.

Coincidentally as we attempt to deal with yet another anti-gay onslaught from conservatives stoked by populist extremists and culminating in transphobic legislative edicts redolent of Nazi Germany, it occurred to me to be that person who inquires about this issue of omission in official history and exhibits of Ellis Island. In the wisdom of Theodore Roosevelt, and as echoed in the exhortations of ACT UP and recovery, I felt the call to "do what you can with what you have, where you are."

In his voice mail reply to my initial inquiry, Jerry Willis, Public Affairs officer of the Statue of Liberty and Ellis Island Foundation (within the National Park Service), sounded upbeat, noting that there were upcoming meetings where this issue would be timely for discussion. He referred me to Diana Pardue, Director of Museum Services and who has been praised for her leadership in working with the US National Committee of the International Counsel of Museums (ICOM).

Pardue put me in touch with Alan Kraut, Distinguished Professor of History at the American University in Washington, D.C., who will oversee a major updating of Ellis Island's programs and exhibits. Professor Kraut specializes in immigration and ethnic history and the history of medicine in the United States. He is currently writing a history of xenophobia and nativism in America. Kraut's research has been supported by the Rockefeller Foundation, National Endowment for the Humanities, the Smithsonian Institution, and the National

Institutes of Health. He is a past President of the Organization of American Historians and is the current President of the National Coalition for History. He is an elected fellow of the prestigious Society of American Historians. In 2017 he received the Lifetime Achievement Award from the Immigration and Ethnic History Society.

In a one-on-one zoom session with him 5/24/21, Professor Kraut made clear his commitment to update Ellis Island Museum information and exhibits to include LGBTQ experience. Not only were "homosexuals" discriminated against on the basis of designations such as "moral turpitude," he noted, but also as "LPC" — likely to become a public charge. Those designated LPC "were declared unlikely to be able to support themselves and would end up on the public dole or [dependent upon] private charity. Years later, in the 1930s, consular officials in Europe denied visas to Jews seeking to escape the Nazis using the same clause."

It's a concept that can still be gleaned in current policies, especially towards refugees of color. Our discussion seemed timely in advance of plans to redesign the museum and exhibits, an ambitious endeavor that won't actually commence for several more years.

Optimism seems warranted. In 1965, U.S. immigration laws were amended (The Immigration Reform Act became the Immigration and Nationality Act) to exclude homosexuals — "aliens afflicted with...sexual deviation" — from admission into the United States.

Under President Reagan, Congress added AIDS to the list of "dangerous, contagious diseases as a basis for excluding persons from the United States." Bans were implemented for people who were HIV-positive from entering the U.S. Only under strict circumstances could people apply for a waiver.

Since 1990, however, there have been more progressive developments involving not only persons identified as LGBTQ seeking asylum but as well those who are HIV positive.

My own quest for acknowledgement and reconciliation was for something more specific and seemingly modest, but also subtle and tricky: to include LGBTQ people not only in light of our experience of being denied immigration status on the grounds of pseudoscientific and pejorative medical and psychiatric theories and practices, but to have LGBTQ people designated in literatures and exhibits, like *and together with* the other groups, mostly ethnic and national, that have experienced immigration discrimination and anti-immigrant bigotry.

Would such inclusiveness arouse resentment, such as that we've seen over the years for LGBTQ participation in New York City's St. Patrick's Day Parade? That is, would some national and ethnic groups feel demeaned and sullied at having LGBTQ people included with them? Would it seem to them that they are being grouped inappropriately with degenerates or those formerly designated as such? How should it be presented and how should it be appreciated that homosexuals were, together with ethnic groups, discriminated against in the history of immigration in America? Would the more subtle colors of prejudice show through, even under the auspices of a new, more enlightened administration and reconfigured museum of immigration?

The story Larry Kramer tells in his massive two-volume satirical history, *The American People*, is of the suppression and loss of history, especially of gay people, but in tandem with other minorities. More than anything else, it is the story of how the despised and dispossessed have been expunged from history, and with that from memory and awareness. It wasn't until last year, in anticipation of the current centennial remembrance, that most of us learned of the Tulsa riot and massacre. Just so, Kramer intuits, recurrent atrocities collectively amounting to genocide have been perpetrated against gay people, their histories of "moral turpitude" expurgated as unsuitable even for documentation.

How the history of immigration will include LGBTQ experience and tell the story of anti-gay bigotry and exclusion continues to unfold.

Clearly, we will have our work cut out for us. Meanwhile, as they say, the journey of a 1000 miles begins with a single step.

# About the Author

Lawrence D. Mass, M.D., is a co-founder of Gay Men's Health Crisis and was the first to write about AIDS in the press. He is the author of *Homosexuality and Sexuality: Dialogues of the Sexual Revolution, Volume 1*, and *Homosexuality as Behavior and Identity: Dialogues of The Sexual Revolution, Volume 2*. He is the author/editor of an anthology, *We Must Love One Another Or Die: The Life and Legacies of Larry Kramer*, and the author a memoir, *Confessions of a Jewish Wagnerite: Being Gay and Jewish in America*. The sequel to that memoir is the current collection, *On the Future of Wagnerism* (*OTFOW*)

Mass has written widely on medicine, health and culture for mainstream and specialist publications.

A recently retired physician specializing in addiction medicine, Mass resides in New York City with his life partner, writer and gay activist Arnie Kantrowitz.

# Acknowledgments

I am indebted to Gottfried Wagner for his insight and compassion, for his incorruptible independence and brave noncomformity in matters of Wagnerism, and for his consistent inspiration and support.

I gratefully acknowledge the assistance of Adam J. Sacks, editor and creative consultant for this collection. His ability to appreciate multiple perspectives, especially those of addiction medicine as they pertain to aspects of culture and the arts, has been singular and invaluable.

With his rare knowledge of music, Richard Howe, a friend and polymath, was helpful to me in moving forward with the early pieces of *OTFOW*.

As a companion Jewish Wagnerite, as curator of the New York Public Library's Rare Books and Manuscripts Division and of our collected papers (those of Arnie Kantrowitz and myself), Melanie Yolles has been an invaluable resource and challenging sparring partner.

Others who have been helpful include Hilan Warshaw, Harvey Sachs, Eva Rieger, Robert C. Steele, Michael Philip Davis, Martin Duberman, Richard Taruskin, Marc A. Weiner, Michael Shapiro, Maryann Feola, Jason Godfrey, Aleksander Douglas, Brandon Judell, Felicia Bonaparte, Patrick Merla, Bill Goldstein, James Saslow, Richard Boch, Brian Kellow, David France, Dr. Douglas Dieterich, Henry White, Krishna Stone, Kelsey Louie, Joseph Neese, Joe Mantello, Larry Kramer, David Webster, Tony Pipolo, Rosa von Praunheim, William M. Hoffman and David Del Tredici.

Special thanks to Colombian writer Jaime Manrique, whose friendship, cross-cultural literary knowledge and wisdom have been inspiring and sustaining.

It's hard to imagine that I or my work would be here apart from my life partnership with Arnie Kantrowitz, a *mensch* and sage whose knowledge of English literature and language I've relied on consistently. It's Arnie who just reassured me that "sparring partner" implies that the adversaries are friendly.

I am grateful for the love and support of Attila Korodi, my handsome Hungarian mate; and to Joel Bradley, whose experience as an addiction professional and whose graciousness and generosity of spirit have been consistent and sustaining.

I wish to thank Dr. Jack Bulmash, who first introduced me—in our teens—to Wagner and opera, and who was a role model for my life's trajectory as a physician. In our 70th decade of friendship, we remain joined at the hip of intellectual curiosity and arts appreciation.

I am indebted to my family of iconoclastic role models: my father, Dr. Max Mass, a distinguished physician, artist and writer; my mother, Mignon Masha Segal Thorpe, a Jewish mother who became evermore socially conscious and activist, and who valued the arts; my brother Steve Mass, the downtown night-life arts and culture scene figure of interest; "Sister Blue Buffalo" Ellen Mass, an artist, writer, environmentalist and activist; and her son, my nephew Max Lockwood, whose social and political consciousness now carries the family torch. They have all challenged and inspired me to prize individuality and creativity over conformity and materialism.

"Only connect," E.M. Forster famously observed. For all the richness of people, relationships and influences in my life, the writing that is its soul is inevitably a solitary habitus. No one ever really fully understands, accepts and befriends you there. Not even you yourself. But it's there in solitude that you are finally at home, alone and comfortable with your most intimate and trusted companion.

# Index of Photos

# Appendix: Persons and Subjects

## Wagner Family Members

Wagner, Richard
Wagner, Cosima
Wagner, Siegfried
Wagner, Winifred
Wagner, Wieland
Wagner, Wolfgang
Wagner, Friedelind
Wagner, Verena
Wagner, Gottfried
Wagner, Eva Pasquier
Wagner, Katharina
Wagner, Nike

## The Wagner Operas

*Die Feen*
*Das Liebersverbot*
*Rienzi*
*Der Fliegende Holländer*
*Tannhäuser*
*Lohengrin*
*Der Ring Des Nibelungen:*
    *Das Rheingold*
    *Die Walküre*
    *Siegfried*
    *Die Götterdämmerung*
*Die Meistersinger von Nürnberg*
*Tristan und Isolde*
*Parsifal*

## Operas, Operettas and Musicals Referenced

*A Quiet Place*
*Andrea Chenier*
*Arabella*
*Billy Elliot*
*Candide*
*Capriccio*
*Caroline or Change*
*Der Kaiser Von Atlantis*
*Der Rosenkavalier*
*Dido and Aeneas*
*Die Ferne Klang*
*Die Frau Ohne Shatten*

*Die Zauberflöte*
*Don Giovanni*
*Dr. Atomic*
*The Barber of Seville*
*Frankenstein*
*Ghosts of Versailles*
*Hadrian*
*Hansel und Gretel*
*Hello Dolly*
*I Capuletti ed I Montecchi*
*I Pagliacci*
*King Lear*
*Kinky Boots*
*The Death of Klinghoffer*
*La Boheme*
*La Clemenza di Tito*
*La Traviata*
*Lazarus*
*Les Hugenots*
*Liebestod*
*Lulu*
*Madama Butterfly*
*Mahagonny*
*Marriage of Figaro*
*Moses in Egypt*
*Nixon in China*
*Orlando*
*Otello*
*Porgy and Bess*
*Prince Igor*
*Queen of Sheba*
*Roberto Devereux*
*Roxy and Her Miracle Team*
*Salome*
*Sappho*
*St. François d'Assise*
*The Faggot*
*The Love for Three Oranges*
*Theodora*
*West Side Story*
*Wozzeck*

## Wagner Characters Referenced

Alberich
Beckmesser
Brangäne
Brünhilde
Donner
Elisabeth
Elsa
Eva
Fafner
Fasolt
Fricka
Gutrune
Hans Sachs
Isolde
Klingsor
Kundry
Lohengrin
Mime
Ortrud
Parsifal
Siegfried
Telramund
The Wanderer
Tristan
Venus
Wotan

## Mass Family Members Referenced



## Names and Subjects*

*The following list is not comprehensive. Names and subjects can be searched in the eBook edition via the options menu.

## Bibliography (Books Referenced)

*12 Steps and 12 Traditions*, Alcoholics Anonymous World Services, Inc

*A Boy's Own Story* by Edmund White
*A Farewell Symphony* by Edmund White
*Age of Anger: A History of the Present* by Pankaj Mishra
*Alcoholics Anonymous* 4th Edition, The "Big Book," Alcoholics Anonymous
*Alice's Adventures in Wonderland* by Lewis Carroll
*The American Opera Singer* by Peter G. Davis
*The American People*, Volumes 1 and 2 by Larry Kramer
*American Women Conservationists* by Madelyn Holmes
*And the Band Played On* by Randy Shilts
*Andrea Dworkin* by Martin Duberman
*Arthur Schnitzler and the Crisis of Musical Culture* by Marc a. Weiner
*Banned from California* by Robert C. Steele
*The Beautiful Room Is Empty* by Edmund White
*Being Wagner* by Simon Callow
*Black Mountain* by Martin Duberman
*Bleak House* by Charles Dickens
*The Bridges at Toko Ri* by James Michener
*Calle Cervantes* (*Cervantes Street*) by Jaime Manrique
*Candide* by Voltaire
*Celluloid Activist* by Michael Schiavi
*The Celluloid Closet* by Vito Russo
*The Confession* by David France
*Confessions of a Jewish Wagnerite* by Lawrence D. Mass
*The Crisis of Multiculturalism in Europe* by Rita Chin
*Cures* by Martin Duberman
*Daniel Deronda* by George Eliot
*Death in Venice* by Thomas Mann
*The Death of Feminism* by Phyllis Chesler
*Diaries*, Cosima Wagner
*Dietrich & Riefenstahl* by Karin Wieland
*Dr. Faustus* by Thomas Mann
*Eichmann in Jerusalem* by Hannah Arendt
*Envy and Greed* by Melanie Klein
*Faggots* by Larry Kramer
*Friedelind Wagner* by Eva Rieger
*Gay Plays: The First Collection* by William M. Hoffman
*Gender and Sex in Society* by Lucile Duberman
*The Geography of Shame* by Maryann Feola

*Germans and Jews After 1945* by Abraham Peck and Gottfried Wagner
*Glitter and Be Gay* by Kevin Clark
*Gone with the Wind* by Margaret Mitchell
*Has the Gay Movement Failed?* by Martin Duberman
*He Who Does Not Howl with the Wolf* by Gottfried Wagner
*The Help* by Kathryn Stockett
*Heritage of Fire* by Friedelind Wagner
*Hidden from History* by Martin Duberman
*Hold Tight Gently* by Martin Duberman
*The Holocaust and History* by Abraham Peck
*Homosexualiti*es by Alan P. Bell and Martin S. Weinberg
*How to Have Sex in an Epidemic* by Michael Callen and Richard Berkowitz
*How to Survive a Plague* by David France
*Jews Queers Germans* by Martin Duberman
*The Jungle Boo*k by Rudyard Kipling
*The Kids' Book of Death and Dying*, edited by Eric Rofes
*Latin Moon in Manhattan* by Jaime Manrique
*Lazy Liza Lizard* by Marie Curtis Rains
*Leaves of Grass* by Walt Whitman
*The Life of Mussolini* by Margherita Grassini Sarfatti
*Like This Afternoon Forever* by Jaime Manrique
*Lincoln* by Gore Vidal
*Lincoln Kirstein* by Martin Duberman
*The Lost Childhood* by Yehuda Nir
*Lost Horizon* by James Hilton
*The Man without Qualities* by Robert Musil
*Maria Callas: Woman Behind the Legend* by Ariana Stassinopoulous
*Mawrdew Czgowchwc* by James Mccourt
*Measure for Measure* by William Shakespeare
*Merchant of Venice* by William Shakespeare
*Mississippi Sissy* by Kevin Sessums
*Mother Earth* by Martin Duberman
*Mozart and Salieri* by Alexander Pushkin
*The Mudd Club* by Richard Boch
*My Father and Myself* by J.r. Ackerly
*Myra Breckenridge* by Gore Vidal
*Myth of the Negro Past* by Melville J. Herskovits

*The New Anti-Semitism* by Phyllis Chesler
*New Japanese Voices,* edited by Helen Mitsios
*The Normal Heart* by Larry Kramer
*The Nuremberg Rallies* by Andrew Rawson
*On Drinking* by Charles Bukowski
*One of Ours* by Willa Cather
*Opera as Opera* by Conrad L. Osborne
*Othello* by William Shakespeare
*Orpheus Descending* by Tennessee Williams
*Our Lives Are the Rivers* by Jaime Manrique
*The Oxford History of Western Music* by Richard Taruskin
*Paul Robeson* by Martin Duberman
*The Perfect Wagnerite* by George Bernard Shaw
*Punks, Poets, Provacateurs* by Victor Bockris
*The Queen's Throat* by Wayne Koestenbaum
*Rat Bohemia* by Sarah Schulman
*The Remembered and Forgotten Jewish World* by Daniel Walkowitz
*Reports from the holocaust* by Larry Kramer
*The Rest of It* by Martin Duberman
*Rhapsody* by Arthur Schnitzler
*Richard Wagner for the New Millenium*, co-authored and edited by Matthew Bribitzer-Stull, Gottfried Wagner and Alex Lubet
*The Road Into the Open* by Arthur Schnitzler
*Sexual Ecology* by Gabriel Rotello
*Sexual Politics* by Kate Millett
*The Sexual Revolution* by Wilhelm Reich
*Sins of Our Fathers* by David France
*The Souls of Black Folks* by W.E.B. Du Bois
*Steppenwolf* by Herman Hesse
*Stonewall* by Martin Duberman
*The Strange Death of Europe* by Douglas Murray
*Taking Liberties*, edited by Michael Bronski
*Tchaikovsky: Quest for the Inner Man*, by Alexander Poznansky
*Thou Shalt Have No Other Gods Before Me* by Gottfried Wagner
*Through the Looking Glass and What Alice Found There* by Lewis Carroll
*Ties that Bind* by Sarah Schulman
*Todesfuge* by Paul Celan
*To Richard Wagner* by Sidney Lanier

*Toscanini: Musician of Conscience* by Harvey Sachs
*The Twilight of the Golds* by Jonathan Tolins
*Twilight of the Wagners* by Gottfried Wagner
*Under the Rainbow* by Arnie Kantrowitz
*Understanding Toscanini* by Joseph Horowitz
*Undertones of Insurrection* by Marc a. Weiner
*The Varieties of Religious Experience* by William James
*Verdi* by Franz Werfel
*Ricard Wagner and His World,* edited by Thomas S. Grey
*Wagner Nights* by Joseph Horowitz
*Wagner: Race and Revolution* by Paul Lawrence Rose
*Wagner: The Man, His Mind, and His Music* by Robert Gutman
*Wagnerism* by Alex Ross
*Waltzing with the Enemy* by Rasia Kliot and Helen Mitsios
*War and Peace* by Leo Tostoy
*We Must Love One Another or Die: The Life and Legacies of Larry Kramer,* edited by Lawrence D. Mass
*You Can Heal Your Life* by Louise Hay

## Filmography

(Films referenced with title and director)

*Age of AIDS*, PBS
*Age of Consent*, Charles Lum and Todd Verow
*Basquiat,* Julian Schnabel
*Behind the Candelabra*, Steven Soderbergh
*Belle*, Amma Asante
*Burnt,* John Wells
*Carol,* Todd Haynes
*Common Threads*, Rob Epstein and Jeffrey Friedman
*Cruising*, William Friedkin
*The Day the Clown Cried*, Jerry Lewis
*Dressed to Kill*, Brian De Palma
*Driving Miss Daisy*, Bruce Beresford
*Far from Heaven*, Todd Haynes
*The Girl Can't Help It*, Frank Tashlin
*Gone with the Wind*, Victor Fleming
*Hannah Arendt*, Margherete von Trotta
*Hitler: A Film from Germany,* Hans-jürgen Syberberg

*Hitler's Hollywood*: Rüdiger Suchsland
*How To Survive a Plague*, David France
*Judgment at Nuremberg*, Stanley Kramer
*Labyrinth of Lies*, Giulio Ricciarelli
*Larry Kramer in Love and Anger,* Jean Carlomusto
*Lisztomania*, Ken Russell
*The Lives of Others*, Florian Henckel Von Donnersmarck
*Lost Horizon*, Charles Jarrott
*Mahler*, Ken Russell
*The Man Who Knew Too Much,* Alfred Hitchcock
*Milton Babbitt: Portrait of a Serial Composer*, Robert Hilferty
*The Music Lovers*, Ken Russell
*The Neon Woman*, Tom Eyen and Ron Link
*Never Look Away*, Henckel Von Donnersmarck
*The Normal Heart*, Ryan Murphy
*Opera Divas, Opera Queens*, Rosa Von Praunheim
*Pete Kelly's Blues*, Jack Webb
*Reichsorchester,* Enrique Sánchez Lansch
*Salome's Last Dance,* Ken Russell
*The Seven Year Itch,* Billy Wilder
*Shoah,* Claude Lanzmann
*Stop the Church*, ACT UP, Robert Hilferty
*Tangerine*, Sean Baker
*The Company You Keep*, Robert Redford
*Tough Love (Härte)*, Rosa Von Praunheim
*Trainspotting 1 and 2,* Danny Boyle
*United in Anger: A History of ACT UP*, Jim Hubbard and Sarah Schulman
*The Wagner Family*, Tony Palmer
*Wagner's Jews*, Hilan Warshaw
*When Love Is Not Enough*, John Kent Harrison

Made in United States
Orlando, FL
29 November 2021